MONEY AND MACROECONOMICS

ECONOMISTS OF THE TWENTIETH CENTURY

General Editors: David Colander, *Christian A. Johnson Distinguished Professor of Economics, Middlebury College, Vermont, US* and Mark Blaug, *Professor Emeritus, University of London, Professor Emeritus, University of Buckingham and Visiting Professor, University of Exeter*

This innovative series comprises specially invited collections of articles and papers by economists whose work has made an important contribution to economics in the late twentieth century.

The proliferation of new journals and the ever-increasing number of new articles make it difficult for even the most assiduous economist to keep track of all the important recent advances. By focusing on those economists whose work is generally recognized to be at the forefront of the discipline, the series will be an essential reference point for the different specialisms included.

A list of published and future titles in this series is printed at the end of this volume.

Money and Macroeconomics

The Selected Essays of David Laidler

David Laidler
Professor of Economics, University of Western Ontario, Canada

ECONOMISTS OF THE TWENTIETH CENTURY

Edward Elgar
Cheltenham, UK • Lyme, US

Published by
Edward Elgar Publishing Limited
8 Lansdown Place
Cheltenham
Glos GL50 2HU
UK

Edward Elgar Publishing, Inc.
1 Pinnacle Hill Road
Lyme
NH 03768
US

A catalogue record for this book
is available from the British Library

Library of Congress Cataloging-in-Publication Data
Laidler, David E.W.
Money and macroeconomics: the selected essays of David Laidler/
David Laidler.
(Economists of the twentieth century series)
Includes bibliographical references.
1. Monetary policy. 2. Macroeconomics. 3. Chicago school of economics. I. Title. II. Series: Economists of the twentieth century.
HG230.3.L343 1997
339.5—dc21 97–14360
CIP

ISBN 1 85898 596 X

Printed and bound in Great Britain by Bookcraft (Bath) Ltd

Contents

Acknowledgements vii

Economics as a Way of Life – A Personal Memoir ix

1 'The Rate of Interest and the Demand for Money – Some Empirical Evidence', *Journal of Political Economy*, **LXXIV** (6), December 1966, 543–55 1

2 'The Results and Implications of Recent Empirical Work on the Aggregate Demand Function for Money in the United States' 15

3 'The Permanent-Income Concept in a Macro-economic Model', *Oxford Economic Papers*, **20** (1), March 1968, 11–23 35

4 'Money, Wealth and Time Preference in a Stationary Economy', *Canadian Journal of Economics*, **II** (4), November 1969, 526–35 49

5 'The Phillips Curve, Expectations and Incomes Policy', in H.G. Johnson and N.R. Nobay (eds), *The Current Inflation*, Macmillan, 1971, 75–98 60

6 'The Current Inflation – Explanations and Policies', *National Westminster Bank Quarterly Review*, November 1972, 6–21 85

7 'Monetarist Models of Inflation in Closed and Open Economies' 102

8 'Information, Money and the Macroeconomics of Inflation, *Swedish Journal of Economics*, March 1974, 26–41 115

9 'Monetarism: An Interpretation and an Assessment', *Economic Journal*, **91**, March 1981, 1–28 132

10 'A Small Macro-model of the Post-War United States', with Brian Bentley, *Manchester School*, December 1983, 317–40 161

11 'On the Demand for Money and the Real Balance Effect', in *Monetarist Perspectives*, Philip Allan, 1982, 39–65 186

12 'Did Macroeconomics Need the Rational Expectations Revolution?', University of Manitoba, 1983 215

13 'The "Buffer Stock" Notion in Monetary Economics', *Economic Journal*, 1984, 17–34 233

14 'Taking Money Seriously', *Canadian Journal of Economics*, **XXI** (4), November 1988, 687–713 252

15 'What Remains of the Case for Flexible Exchange Rates?', *Pakistan Development Review*, **XXVII** (4), Part I, Winter 1988, 425–50 280

16 'The Quantity Theory is Always and Everywhere Controversial – Why?', *Economic Record*, December 1991, 289–306 307

17 'Price Stability and the Monetary Order' in K. Shigehara (ed.), *Price Stabilization in the 1990s*, Macmillan, 1993, 331–56 326

18 'Monetarism – the Unfinished Business', *Cyprus Journal of Economics*, **5** (2), December 1992, 60–74 353

List of publications, 1966–95 369

Index 381

Acknowledgements

The publishers wish to thank the following who have kindly given permission for the use of copyright material.

Bank of Japan and Macmillan Press for article: 'Price Stability and the Monetary Order', in K. Shigehara (ed.), *Price Stabilization in the 1990s*, Macmillan, 1993, 331–56.

Blackwell Publishers for articles: 'Monetarism: An Interpretation and an Assessment', *Economic Journal*, **91**, March 1981, 1–28; 'The "Buffer Stock" Notion in Monetary Economics', *Economic Journal*, 1984, 17–34; 'Information, Money and the Macroeconomics of Inflation, *Swedish Journal of Economics*, March 1974, 26–41.

Canadian Journal of Economics for articles: 'Taking Money Seriously', **XXI** (4), November 1988, 687–713; 'Money, Wealth and Time Preference in a Stationary Economy', **II** (4), November 1969, 526–35.

Cyprus Journal of Economics for article: "Monetarism – the Unfinished Business', **5** (2), December 1992, 60–74.

Economic Record for article: 'The Quantity Theory is Always and Everywhere Controversial – Why?', December 1991, 289–306.

Institute for Social and Economic Research, University of Manitoba for article: 'Did Macroeconomics Need the Rational Expectations Revolution?', University of Manitoba, 1983.

The Manchester School for article: 'A Small Macro-model of the Post-War United States', with Brian Bentley, December 1983, 317–40.

Money, Macro, Finance Research Group and Macmillan Press for article: 'The Phillips Curve, Expectations and Incomes Policy', in H.G. Johnson and N.R. Nobay (eds), *The Current Inflation*, Macmillan, 1971, 75–98.

National Westminster Bank for article: 'The Current Inflation – Explanations and Policies', *National Westminster Bank Quarterly Review*, November 1972, 6–21.

Oxford University Press for article: 'The Permanent-Income Concept in a Macroeconomic Model', *Oxford Economic Papers*, **20** (1), March 1968, 11–23.

Pakistan Institute of Development Economics for article: 'What Remains of the Case for Flexible Exchange Rates?', *Pakistan Development Review*, **XXVII** (4), Part I, Winter 1988, 425–50.

University of Chicago Press for article: 'The Rate of Interest and the Demand for Money – Some Empirical Evidence', *Journal of Political Economy*, **LXXIV** (6), December 1966, 543–55.

Every effort has been made to trace all the copyright holders but if any have been inadvertently overlooked the publishers will be pleased to make the necessary arrangements at the first opportunity.

Economics as a way of life – a personal memoir

Life before economics

I was born on Tyneside in 1938. I was an only child. The Depression had caused my parents to delay the start of a family and the war deterred them from continuing with the enterprise. Those two catastrophes therefore very much formed me and they also dominate my early memories, the war directly, and the Depression at second hand through the overheard and only partly understood conversations of adults. The bombing we experienced in Whitley Bay was negligible in comparison to that visited on many of my contemporaries, but it came often enough and close enough to kill a few neighbours, children as well as adults, injure others, and damage our house more than once – with me inside it, because we had no garden in which a shelter could be dug and air-raids were therefore spent under a steel-topped kitchen table. I doubt that the war had much direct effect on my later attitude to economics, but it left me with an abiding belief that there is a large arbitrary element to life's outcomes. That is probably why I am irredeemably 'wet' when it comes to judging the merits of those redistributive arrangements that go under the label 'Welfare State'. The Depression was more directly influential in a completely conventional way: even at second hand, its memory prompted the usual questions: why? what could have been done? could it happen again? etc. etc.; and I have little patience for economics not motivated by socially important questions.

My father was self-employed, a fishmonger by day and a fish-fryer in the evening. Neither of my parents had more than a pre-First World War primary school education, and they were acutely insecure about their position in that appalling pecking order known as the British class structure. To be a self-employed shop-keeper put one in the lower-middle classes, but to be a fish-fryer, and on Tyneside at that, ensured that the emphasis was heavily on 'lower'. Education was the way-up of choice in such families. My father was a little too old for the army in 1939, and in any case he had been gassed in France in late 1917. Thus the shops were open during and immediately after the war, and the fish trade being rather profitable in those years, I was duly sent to a private day school, Tynemouth School, where, it was hoped, I would acquire not only the knowledge but also the accent and manners that might enable me to succeed – as an accountant, say, or even a solicitor.

From my early teens onwards, I worked with my father during school holidays, and sometimes on Saturdays too. The day started at 7:30 am with a buying trip to North Shields fishquay, and ended at about 11 pm after the last few stragglers from the pubs had bought their suppers and gone home. This too was meant to be part of my education, inculcating first-hand knowledge of what the future had in store if I did not pay attention to my studies. The experience certainly had that effect, but I am afraid that I never quite picked up the manners and accent that my parents had intended for me. After all, at the school they had chosen, boys were regularly reprimanded if they were seen eating fish and chips on the street. That, and more generally the repulsive snobbery it represented, strained my loyalty to the institution, and I quite self-consciously resisted much of the social influence that the place was supposed to exert.

Academically Tynemouth School was a curate's egg: the science side was mediocre, and I took only mathematics, and then only to GCE O level. On the other hand, History, English Literature and French, my three A level subjects, were superbly taught. History, and Economic History in particular, fascinated me. Although the syllabus for the latter stopped somewhere in the late nineteenth century, its relevance to my immediate surroundings – the coal industry, railways, engineering and all that – was both readily apparent and extremely appealing. Since the alternative was two years' military service, I had no difficulty in deciding to try for University although, much to my headmaster's anger, I refused to apply to Oxford or Cambridge. In the firm belief that Economics would be just like Economic History, I entered the London School of Economics (LSE) in 1956.

The LSE

I had been well enough taught at Tynemouth School to win a State Scholarship which provided a pretty good living in those days, even in London. Since that was a merit award, and not a grant, I can, and do, take pride in having been self-supporting through scholarships and work since the age of eighteen. After a miserable period boarding in suburban Kingsbury with distant family friends who had moved South to find work in the 1930s, I moved to Bayswater and began to take advantage of the city.

I had consumed music, but particularly opera, second hand at home, largely thanks to the BBC, and in the face of a certain amount of disapproval from my parents, who did not think that this was an interest that would be useful to a future accountant or solicitor (perhaps even an Urban District Councillor!). In London opera was there to be explored at first hand, and at very reasonable prices. A gallery seat at Covent Garden, for example, was 5 shillings (7/6 for Maria Callas I think), which was not much more than it cost to feed the gas-meter to heat a bed-sitter on a winter evening, and I spent a great deal of time there and at Sadlers Wells. I picked up a lifelong habit which it has cost me a small fortune, and a prodigious amount of time, to feed. How many extra papers might have been written had I spent fewer evenings in opera houses is hard to imagine but, given the length of this book's bibliography, it is quite clear that, on the margin, even more time given over to Mozart, Verdi, Janáček, Britten *et al.* would have been time well reallocated.

There was also politics. I had actually been a member of the Young Conservatives before university, but the summer and autumn of 1956, which coincided with my move to the LSE, saw the Suez Crisis. I joined the extreme left-wing Socialist (note, not Labour) Society, and took up the chorus of 'Eden must go!'. I still think I was on the right side there, but I am decidedly less sure now about my support for unilateral nuclear disarmament! My conversion to Socialism was not based on any hard analysis. It was mainly a matter of renouncing residual aspirations to the Urban District Council, but I took the Socialist Society seriously, serving as its secretary for a while. I attended meetings, listened and argued, and I read. I learned at least something of what Marxian Socialism was about, and if I eventually came to find the doctrine unconvincing, I was surely none the worse for knowing why.

By now the reader must be wondering if I had any time left to pursue the studies which had brought me to London in the first place. At that time, the first examinations LSE students encountered, Part I of the BSc (Econ.), occurred at the end of the second year. There was plenty of time to get into trouble in the interim, and I did, not least because, to my great confusion, Economics turned out to have very little to do with A level Economic History. But there was more to it. The plain fact is that it was much further, socially, culturally, and intellectually from Tyneside to London in 1956 than it is nowadays, and the transition left me bewildered. At the time, I thought of myself as making a big splash, but other observers, not least my later self, would find floundering around out of my depth a more accurate metaphor. My Part I results were unimpressive, and, as the LSE Careers Adviser cheerfully informed me at about this time, thinking that he was giving me good news, I seemed to be firmly on track for lower second class honours, followed by military service and a return ticket to Tyneside, perhaps as a secondary modern school teacher.

What saved me was the particular age structure of the LSE Economics department at that time. To the outsider the place was dominated by such luminaries as Roy Allan, James Meade, Frank Paish, Henry Phelps-Brown, Arnold Plant, Lionel Robbins, Richard Sayers, *et al.*. Robbins held an informal Friday afternoon seminar for third year specialists, which often took the form of a dialogue between him and my classmate Sam Hollander, whose intelligence and erudition were even then completely awe inspiring. I do, therefore, count Robbins among my teachers. As to the others, however, undergraduates like me only saw them, if at all, from a distance in large lecture theatres. Serious teaching was done in small groups (there were only about a dozen specialists in Economics Analytic and Descriptive in my year) by those known as 'the younger members of the staff': Chris Archibald, Bernard Corry, Bob Gould, Kurt Klappholz, Kelvin Lancaster, Dick Lipsey, Maurice Peston, not to mention Ed Mishan, Bill Phillips and Jack Wiseman, who belonged to this group in intellectual spirit if not quite in years. And further instruction was on offer in the Three Tuns (the School pub) at lunch time and in the early evening, particularly from Archibald, Corry and Lipsey. For this group, economics was a way of life, and an enjoyable one too, rather than merely an academic subject, and to someone like me, who was looking for just that, the example they set was irresistible. The fact that I was also beginning to see how economics might offer some answers to those conventional questions about the Depression was an added bonus. In my third year, with Bernard Corry as my tutor, I got interested in my studies.

The LSE's third year syllabus in Economics Analytic and Descriptive led to examinations in Economic Theory, Applied Economics, the History of Economic Thought, and two options; here I chose the 'Essay' paper – answer one question from a menu that covered the whole syllabus, and then some – and (I think) Public Finance. The emphasis was, in fact, on 'Economics Analytic' and we learned how to do economic analysis at what was then a pretty high level. Stigler's *Theory of Price* (1952 edn) was a Part I book, as was Hansen's *Guide to Keynes* (1953), and in the third year, in preparation for Part II, we read selections from the once ubiquitous American Economics Association (AEA) series of *Readings* in various topics, one or two monographs – for example Lerner's *Economics of Control*

(1944), and Patinkin's *Money, Interest and Prices* (1956), with important supplementary material from Archibald and Lipsey (1958) – and some up-to-date journal articles as well – notably by Phillips (for example, 1954) on stabilization issues. We also read every page (well, Sam Hollander did!) of the *Wealth of Nations*, and of Ricardo's and Marshall's *Principles*, and some of us read Thornton's *Paper Credit* as well.

The 'descriptive' part of the syllabus did not get much attention, and I do not recall that the format of examinations in Applied Economics or Public Finance required it. An examinee was probably well advised, other things equal, to find out which British industries were in public ownership, but on balance it was better to learn a little more about the virtues and limitations of the application of marginal cost pricing rules in the public sector – Jack Wiseman was disconcertingly persuasive, even to someone like me, who still held socialist views, on those limitations. Extra points were also to be earned by those able to paraphrase the Lipsey–Lancaster (1956) 'Second Best' theorem. And, on the macro side an appreciation of the implications of time lags for the feasibility of stabilization policies was a lot more prized than knowledge of the size and growth rate of the British national income, its composition, or any other set of mere facts.

All this was enormously appealing, and I acquired the knack of manipulating simple economic models. I also began to suspect that Economics was one of those subjects in which a little knowledge of the basic analytic tools would take one a long way. I was right; indeed it took me a lot further than I had expected. In the summer of 1959, to my utter astonishment, and to the amazement of a lot of other people too, no doubt, I graduated with first class honours – evidently, not all of life's arbitrary shocks are adverse. My old friends Archibald, Corry and Lipsey have often told me since, usually after a few beers, that my first was the most marginal ever awarded in the history of the LSE, and for all I know they have been telling the truth. It did not matter though, because in those days, a first was a first. My escape from Tyneside and the lower-middle classes was now permanent if that was what I wanted, and I did. I went to America.

Graduate school in America

My applications to American graduate schools had been sent off long before I took final exams. My teachers had told me that proper post-graduate training was only available in America, true enough at that time before taught Masters programmes were introduced in Britain; American schools would also give firm acceptances before degree results were out, which meant that, even with the forecast lower second, I might get one more year of deferment from military service; and besides, I had an American girlfriend. But it was not quite straightforward after all. My mediocre performance at Part I had presumably been noted in letters of reference, and of the half dozen or so schools to which I applied, only the University of Syracuse would take a chance on me.

My continued membership of the Socialist Society perhaps had something to do with the trouble I encountered in getting a visa. Past membership of the Young Conservatives turned out to have its uses after all, and Dame Irene Ward MP wrote on my behalf to the Embassy, presumably assuring them that I was unlikely to use either force or violence to overthrow the Government of the United States if I was allowed into the country for a year or so. I got the visa, but I was turned down for a Fulbright travel grant. The LSE loaned me the money for the fare, however, and off I went, on an elderly ship, named the *New York*, registered in Greece. Sam Hollander, whose first had been predicted, went to Princeton, crossing on the *Queen Mary*: I was a little jealous.

Syracuse is one of those middle rank American universities which Europeans always undervalue. It is more famous for its football team than its Economics department, but there was no nonsense about the MA programme that I followed. Its theory component repeated quite a lot of what I had done the year before, as it would have done at even the most prestigious schools, and I was finally forced to learn basic calculus, linear algebra and some statistics. All of this came too late to make me anything other than a very mediocre technician, but that was a good deal better than nothing. I could now at least read a lot more of the literature, and in due course teach it too. I also got used to the American routine of examinations two or three times a term rather than once or twice in a lifetime! Syracuse was close enough to New York City that I was twice able to visit the old Metropolitan Opera House. But the most exciting music of the year was at the university, a student performance of excerpts from *Susannah*, with, if I am not mistaken, Floyd Carlisle himself providing the piano accompaniment. Europeans, as I have said, undervalue universities like Syracuse.

But by now I had my first, and with compulsory military service abolished in Britain in the nick of time, I tried again for a place in one of the top American departments. The response was very different this time, except from Yale which refused me admission – another of life's arbitrary shocks, and one that perhaps explains why I am not a Keynesian – and I chose Chicago. At LSE I had attended Karl Popper's lectures on methodology, and the optional paper in Logic and Scientific Method had produced one of the few bright spots in my Part I results. I was completely convinced of the importance of testing economic theories against empirical evidence, as were most of my third year teachers who were then in the middle of a brief but fruitful flirtation with Popper's ideas. At Chicago too, as I knew from Milton Friedman's writings, they were interested in testing theories; and besides, Harry Johnson, whom I had never met but whom the younger LSE faculty who had taught me revered, was now there as well, having left Manchester a year or so earlier. And Chicago had then, as it still does, a most distinguished opera company.

My American girl friend and I got married in the summer of 1960, and set off for Chicago in my recently acquired second-hand Citroën 2cv. The marriage was not a good idea; it fell apart almost as quickly as did the car. Whatever each of us was trying to accomplish by marrying the other could certainly have been achieved by less self-destructive means, but we had to learn this and a number of other lessons the hard way; let us leave it at that. Fortunately, when we parted three years later, there were no children to worry about.

I was only physically present in Chicago for two years, because I took a year out of my studies in 1961–62 as a temporary assistant lecturer at LSE, but Chicago's impact on me was enormous. To begin with, the sheer quality of my fellow students restored some of the intellectual humility that getting a first had temporarily undermined. Eitan Berglas, Glen Cain, Martin Carnoy, Ed Feige, Giora Hanoch, Jim Holmes, Bob Lucas, G.S. Madalla, Sam Peltzman, Maurice Perlman, Sherwin Rosen and Neil Wallace, were among my contemporaries, and that is a list of names I am very proud to be able to drop! At Chicago, Economics was treated as a relevant and socially useful discipline, not a compendium of intellectual games to be played for the fun of it; but as such, as Al Harberger in particular managed to convey in his teaching, it could still be immensely enjoyable. Friedman taught me Price Theory (giving me the only B of my graduate career in the first term – I took more care in the second!). His style was to assume that we had already read his mimeoed lecture notes, soon to be published as *Price Theory – a Provisional Text* (1962) and to lecture rather discursively, sometimes reading out a quotation from *Time* or the *New York Times* as a prelude to suggesting 'Let's analyse this'. Once, probably because the Core Exams were approaching, I asked him when we were going to cover the Slutsky Equation, to which the friendly but pointed reply was, as I recall, 'When you've learned to read newspapers intelligently will be time enough'.

Monetary economics at Chicago for me was mainly a matter of Harry Johnson. He taught the PhD level course in 1960–61, and in 1962–63 he ran the workshop, because Friedman was on Sabbatical. Al Marty taught the course that year. Harry was a self-effacing teacher who insisted that his students should get to know 'the literature' and not just those bits of it that were being locally produced. Chicago then, and now, was said to inculcate narrow-mindedness in its students, 'brainwash' was the verb sometimes used, but seldom can a reputation have been less deserved than in the years I was there. Sceptics are referred to Johnson's (1962) *American Economic Review* (AER) survey of monetary economics: that is what we were taught in the formal course. And although Friedman and Meiselman presented their work on the relative stability of velocity and the multiplier at the Money workshop (see Friedman and Meiselman 1963) a guest called Allan Meltzer impressed upon us the importance of the rate of interest as a systematic influence on velocity (see Meltzer 1963) while a little later another, Grant Reuber, suggested that we think about the Phillips curve as a policy constraint subject to which a quantifiable social utility function could be maximized (see Reuber 1964). Joan Robinson's first visit to the United States was in 1961, and at Chicago, unlike anywhere else, she was granted classroom time to expound her views on capital theory to the graduate students. And it is worth mentioning that I, still a self-proclaimed socialist (although weakening fast) was supported in my final year (1962–63) by a fellowship in the personal gift of Friedman.

I absorbed one other important lesson in those years. I learned to take data seriously, from Margaret Reid, who was on my thesis committee, and from Anna Schwartz for whom I worked during the summer of 1961 as a research assistant on the *Monetary History of the United States* (Friedman and Schwartz 1963). They showed me that data were not merely items to be looked up in tables, should one ever stop talking about testing a theory and actually get down to doing so. I learned that data had to be created by somebody; that how that might be done was not independent of the purpose to which they were going to be put, and that anyone using data to test a theory would be well advised to spend a little time enquiring where they had come from in order to ensure their relevance to the problem at hand, and perhaps checking them for accuracy against their primary source, too. Finally, I learned that people who deal with data are just as thoughtful, intelligent and useful as are theorists. I am still appalled by the average academic economist's lack of respect for those who do the archival research and field work upon which the empirical basis of our discipline depends.

My year at LSE in 1961–62 was a welcome break from studies. I had finished my Chicago course requirements, passed the core and a field exam in Money, all in the previous year, and I was ready for a change of pace. My teaching duties in London were light, consisting mainly of giving back-up tutorials to Dick Lipsey's first year lecture course, from which his *Positive Economics* (1963) would soon emerge. Unfortunately the pay, £860 per annum, was well matched to the arduousness of the work, and the Laidlers were very poor. So was nearly everyone else, however, so it did not matter much.

The 'younger members of the staff' were still a very cohesive group, and had been joined by John Grant, Miles Kennedy, Max Steuer and Jim Thomas, while Bertie Hines and Vicky Chick, then both graduate students, were very much part of the circle. The M2T (methodology measurement and testing) seminar, the main outcome of the economists' flirtation with Popper's ideas, was still flourishing, with Frank Brechling and Dick Lipsey on trade credit (see Brechling and Lipsey 1963) and Chris Archibald on the predictive powers of maximizing models (see, for example, Archibald 1965) prominently on the programme. I remember going to lots of parties, and I remember leaving some of them – drink was very much part of the LSE economist's way of life in those days. But I did do some work, notably to prepare, with considerable help from Bernard Corry, for my remaining Chicago field examination in the History of Economic Thought which I took in absentia, and passed, in the early summer of 1962.

By the time I got back to Chicago in September all that remained was to write a thesis. My topic was 'Income Tax Incentives for Owner-Occupied Housing'. Al Harberger was my committee chairman, and given that I also participated in the Money workshop, then under Harry Johnson's temporary supervision, I discovered that drink could be very much part of the Chicago economist's way of life too. Indeed, I was a good year into my first appointment at Berkeley before I realized that economists' parties were not, in fact, always intended to be events at which everyone got a bit drunk, as a preliminary to offering frank criticism of everyone else's work: I am not sure what my Californian colleagues made of me, and I should prefer not to guess.

My thesis, which involved an empirical investigation of the positive and normative consequences of the United States failure to tax the imputed rental income yielded by owner occupied housing, did get finished, however (see D1). It may seem odd that someone destined to specialize in monetary economics, and who had already made a major intellectual investment in that field, should write a thesis in Public Finance, but it was not quite so strange then. Both LSE and Chicago, or at least the faculty with whom I had the privilege of working in those places, still encouraged their students to think of themselves as economists first, and specialists second; and the standard analysis of the demand for a durable good whose services-in-kind were subject to taxation or subsidy, on which my thesis was based, a few years later turned out to be applicable with virtually no modification to the analysis of inflation. So the thesis was not a detour after all.

Berkeley

The early 1960s saw a huge expansion of higher education, and those of us who had gone into graduate school in the expectation of living ever after in genteel poverty received a wonderful surprise when we came to look for jobs. They were there in abundance, and at high and rising salaries too, particularly in the United States. I had acquired a Green Card during the year back at LSE, and hence was a fully qualified participant in a very hot labour market. Partly at my wife's urging – we were by then separated, but on better terms than before as we planned our eventual divorce – I accepted an offer from Berkeley and we drove out there together in my new Corvair convertible, not a much better choice than the Citroën, as it turned out, but I had not heard of Ralph Nader then. I am not sure why Berkeley hired me. The department was very much a part of the East-Coast sphere of influence (a salt-water as opposed to fresh-water school as people would now put it) and people from Chicago were not usually invited in; but I am glad I was: permit me to drop a few more names, this time of my fellow assistant professors: Peter Diamond, Dan McFadden, Bernie Saffran, Oliver Williamson and Sidney Winter.

In the monetary economics field, things were not so good. Howard Ellis was about to go to Brazil on a State Department mission, and Hyman Minsky would soon leave for Washington University in St. Louis, although not before I had learned a lot from him about the nature of a monetary economy that helped me begin to make sense of some of the things Victoria Chick had been on about in London, but which would not find their way into my own work until much later. Tom Mayer was there, however, as a visitor for a while, but even when teaching at Davis he lived in Berkeley, and I saw a good deal of him. In due course I met Karl Brunner down at University of California at Los Angeles (UCLA), and he was usually to be found on the other end of the telephone if one called for advice, as I sometimes did. And Dale Jorgenson's expertise in applied econometrics was at the disposal of anyone who was interested. There were visitors too, among them at various times Dick Lipsey, Bob Gould and Bernard Corry. I was hardly isolated, then, and there were advantages in the thinness with which my own field was staffed. I became more quickly involved with graduate teaching than I otherwise would, and when Minsky left I also inherited the workshop (or continuing seminar as we called it) which he had set up and raised some funds for at about the time of my arrival. It met in the evening (Thursday, I think), and a willingness to visit a bar after the paper was the main prerequisite for membership.

Friedman's (1959) 'The Demand for Money – Some Theoretical and Empirical Results' had caused quite a stir. At a time when conventional wisdom took the liquidity trap doctrine for granted, it appeared to show that velocity might be essential independent of interest rates. Like anyone else teaching monetary economics, I needed to come to grips with this paper. I found two potential flaws in it. First, Friedman seemed to have some details of what he called the 'shock absorber' approach to the demand for money wrong; second, he seemed to have overlooked the possibility of there being a secular relationship between interest rates and velocity when he had designed the test which appeared to show that there were no cyclical interest rate effects at work. With the help of a National Science Foundation (NSF) grant, I got to work on what became my first two published papers (Cl and Chapter 1, below). I did not get the individual-market experiment distinction quite straight when dealing with shock absorber effects and, perhaps as a result, I did not return to those matters for nearly ten years, but I did better with the second issue. It was also at Berkeley that I began to investigate the dynamics implicit in the lagged dependent variables that empirical work suggested were so badly needed in some key structural equations. As a student of Popper, I had learned that the results of empirical work should be used to modify theories, with a view to generating further predictions, so this seemed a natural thing to do (Chapter 3). I also wrote a short paper on the Phillips curve with Bernard Corry (C3).

While all this was going on, I found time to remarry, this time more wisely. Antje was recently arrived from Germany and a trainee buyer in her uncle and aunt's fashion store. We lived on Telegraph Avenue and were early evening regulars at the Pic (Cafe Mediterraneum, formerly Piccolo Espresso) and later evening regulars at either the Steppenwolf or the Albatross where something a little stronger was on sale. This was Berkeley on the eve of the university's first round of troubles, before the Bay area drug scene got nasty, and before anyone had heard the word 'counterculture'. For a year or two we were part of a social circle whose willingness to live and let live may have been naive, but is still a joy to recall – even if one or two people did express a little surprise that Antje and I had made the effort to get married, while one or two others found our opera-going habits a bit exotic.

An unpleasant example of life's arbitrariness brought this existence to an abrupt end in the summer of 1966. By then the University of California had managed to radicalize its student body by attempting to prevent campus facilities being used for the organization of civil rights demonstrations in Oakland – some of these students had risked their lives in Mississippi, and they were not about to stand for petty nonsense from university administrators. The Vietnam War was expanding rapidly enough to attract attention too. On the personal front, a preliminary review of my academic progress had convinced the majority of my senior colleagues that my work 'lacked seriousness' – their phrase – and one of them had laughed out loud when I confessed that I was writing a paper on Thomas Tooke's views on Peel's 1844 Bank Act. It was probably time to leave, but I was not permitted the luxury of making up my own mind about that. Along with the acquisition of my Green Card in 1962 had gone the obligation to register for military service, which had not seemed to matter at the time. Student and faculty deferments were automatic and, besides, I would be over-age by 1963; but that was before the Vietnam War became serious. Early in 1966, my deferment was cancelled, and in July I was summoned to a pre-induction medical, which I passed with flying colours. No one in authority at the university seemed to want to know about these problems and, something I still find hard to excuse, I had the distinct impression that there was a reluctance to testify to the 'essential' nature of my work lest that testimony be used in a future tenure case.

Rather than risk induction, which usually followed the medical by a couple of weeks, I resigned my position at Berkeley at once. I spent a few nights on the telephone to friends in Canada and Britain. The academic market was still very much on the sellers' side, and within a few days Chris Archibald had offered me a lectureship (with tenure!) at Essex where he and Lipsey were in the process of building a brand new department. Antje's uncle and aunt, who knew a few things about hasty emigration decisions, having left Germany in 1933 and France in the early 1940s, gave us much support and help; we needed it, for, even in California, Vietnam was not, in 1966, the widely unpopular cause it was to become, and my departure had to be as quiet as it was quick. I made a brief visit to my parents, who were delighted to have me back in Britain, and then went to Wivenhoe to find housing (and to buy some Covent Garden tickets for October) before the autumn term began. Antje tidied up our affairs in California and, somewhat to the surprise of some of our Telegraph Avenue friends, who never took such things for granted, joined me just before term began.

Essex

No one could ever convict members of the Berkeley Economics department of not being completely dedicated to their discipline, but to my way of thinking the prevailing attitude there, particularly at the senior levels, had been excessively earnest. What had attracted me to Economics at the LSE, and had continued to do so at Chicago, were working atmospheres in which people not only thought that what they were doing was important, but in which they were evidently enjoying themselves as well. The Essex department in the late 1960s was another such place, not surprisingly perhaps, since it was the creation of Chris Archibald and Dick Lipsey, with some help from Frank Brechling.

The university as a whole had been set up to encourage easy informal interaction among faculty and students, and in the Economics department, where the faculty were young, that worked. Even though the university as a whole quickly acquired a well-deserved reputation for student radicalism and activism, excitement in the Economics department continued to be found, not at the barricades, but in the classroom, at workshops, and in various pubs, not least the Buck's Horns in Colchester, where department members attained standards in table football that were at least as high as those they reached in economics. There was lots of money for visitors, who came for a year or a term rather than a week or a day. Again, a little name dropping is in order. In the three years I spent at Essex, in addition to my permanent colleagues, who for various periods included, in addition to Archibald and Lipsey, Bob Clower, Gene Savin and Joe Ostroy, the following were long-term visitors: Carl Christ, Ed Feige, Art Goldberger, Herschel Grossman, Murray Kemp, Al Marty, Michio Morishima and Colin Simkin.

Most important as far as my own work was concerned, it was at Essex that Michael Parkin and I first became colleagues. Although we produced no joint work at that time, our interaction was continuous and enormously fruitful. I taught him the monetary economics that I had learned at Chicago and he taught me what I would have learned had I gone to Yale. He had begun to master the latter material while working in the relative isolation of Sheffield and Leicester, and he made it sound a good deal more sensible that anything I had heard from the newly minted Yale PhDs who had passed through Berkeley from time to time on job market tours.

On balance, though, Chicago won out in these encounters, the most intense of which invariably took place at the above-mentioned Buck's Horns.

Essex was as unstable as it was exciting. New universities had not been expected to challenge the intellectual standards prevailing at the old, but, in Economics at least, Essex had, and that was not altogether welcome among the British academic establishment. I was too junior to know just who was taking which decisions, and why, but by 1968–69 even I noticed that the funding needed to consolidate what had been achieved was beginning to dry up, and that Archibald and Lipsey might leave in frustration, as, in fact, they eventually did; so when, in quick succession, I was interviewed at Manchester for a Chair, and advised by Harry Johnson (who had by then replaced Lionel Robbins at the LSE) to accept it if offered, accept it I did. We moved to Manchester in September 1969. For the next six years, regular visits to the Free Trade Hall to hear the Hallé orchestra ensured that our musical tastes continued to expand, and English and Welsh National Opera touring productions ensured that we were not entirely deprived of opera either.

Manchester

Work had gone well at Essex. I had finished everything that I had started while in California (including my paper on Thomas Tooke, D7), I had written the first edition of my little book on the *Demand for Money* (Al), which was probably to do more for my reputation than any other single publication, and I had also written two papers (Chapter 4 and C6) that grew out of the 'Pesek and Saving controversy' (1967), one of the many attempts at that time to bring some further badly needed theoretical coherence to monetary economics in the wake of Patinkin's pioneering efforts in that regard. It was here that expertise in stock-flow analysis and some of its welfare applications, acquired during my PhD work on the demand for housing, came in handy. I write all this a little defensively. Although my CV as it stood in 1969 would probably be worth a tenured position in many respectable Economics departments even today, younger readers of this memoir will probably wonder what kind of standards, if any, were adhered to in making appointments to provincial chairs in Britain in the late 1960s. The problem, of course, from the point of view of those making the appointments, was that it was still very much a seller's market. Universities that were not willing to take chances on appointments that would have been regarded as premature in normal times simply did not fill their vacancies.

Not that I was welcomed with open arms at Manchester: Alan Prest, the Jevons Professor and Head of the Department of Economics, made it quite clear, with that consummate rudeness masked as courtesy which only graduates of the older British universities seem to be able to command, that I was not welcome in his department, and a number of my new junior (in rank but not in years) colleagues shared his views. I could not believe my luck when he announced that he was leaving for the LSE a few months after my arrival (and I hope because of it), not least because that created a vacancy which Michael Parkin might fill. Although some of the old guard in the Manchester Economics department were genuinely welcoming – Dennis Coppock, John Knapp and Richard Harrington in particular – I badly needed some support in an environment that was a lot more hostile than I had expected, and I had not entered it with my eyes closed.

The fundamental problem at Manchester was that it had three separate departments, Economics, Econometrics, and Agricultural Economics, the majority of whose members could barely talk intelligibly to one another. A single department would have been a great deal better. I knew all that before accepting my appointment, but I thought I had secured the support of the Professors of Econometrics (Jack Johnston) and Agricultural Economics (Wat Thomas) to move towards an eventual merger of the departments. I suppose 'eventual' is a vague term, but, in 1969 I had something a little earlier in mind than 1995 (when in fact such a merger finally took place). What had made my appointment at Manchester possible, and would make Michael Parkin's possible too, was that filling a chair there was a matter for a Senate Committee with relatively minor departmental representation. Michael and I were never fully accepted in the Department of Economics, and we created our own research environment through the 'Manchester Inflation Workshop'. This was a broadly based research programme on the 'Causes, Consequences and Cures' of inflation which, at the beginning of the 1970s, was becoming a pressing policy issue. Members of all three Economics departments, not to mention Accounting, could, and some did, participate; and since it was funded by a Social Science Research Council (SSRC) grant, we were able to support a few junior people of our own choosing as full-time researchers too.

The early 1970s saw a strong surge of interest in monetary economics in general, and in what came to be called 'Monetarism' in particular, in both Britain, and Western Europe. Alan Walters and his Birmingham colleagues Clive Barrett, Noel Kavanagh and David Sheppard had started to apply Chicago-style models to British monetary data in the mid-1960s (see Walters (1969) for a survey and relevant references) at about the same time that Harry Johnson had gone to the LSE and I had gone to Essex, but it took a few years for any of this to have a noticeable impact. In Britain, the Money Study Group (MSG) played a crucial role. It was founded immediately after the 1969 Hove Conference which Johnson had organized to celebrate the tenth anniversary of the Radcliffe Report, and its executive committee consisted of Johnson, Bob Nobay, Michael Parkin and myself. With a little help from David Worswick and Cathy Cunningham, the MSG soon obtained modest but invaluable SSRC funding. It ran workshops in London once or twice a term, to which academics, working in what were even then rather isolated provincial departments, could get their travel expenses paid, and it also organized occasional conferences that eventually evolved into annual affairs held at Oxford. The MSG was the prototype for similar organizations in other sub-disciplines.

On the continent, conferences organized by Emil Claassen and Pascal Salin at Paris–Dauphine, and, quite crucially, Karl Brunner's annual Konstanz seminar, which began in 1969 and is still going strong, provided the main organizational infrastructure through which intellectual contacts were made and ideas were transmitted. Michael Parkin and I did a lot of travelling in the early 1970s both to keep in touch with what others were up to, and also to present the results of our own ongoing work at Manchester. I will leave it to others to sort out just who contributed what to the spread of Monetarism in Britain, and indeed Europe, and when they did it. One thing I will insist on, however: although Monetarism was originally an import from America, the local product nevertheless quickly became distinct.

We did add considerable content to the doctrine, not least, I still like to think, at Manchester, and some of that content was re-exported too. No one did better work on assembling the evidence on the ineffectiveness of incomes policies than Michael Parkin and Michael Sumner (see Parkin and Sumner 1972) and although Harry Johnson and Alexander Swoboda with their London–Geneva group obviously had a lot to do with establishing Monetarism's relevance to the international economy, so did Michael, this time working in particular with George Zis (see Parkin and Zis 1976).

While still in Berkeley, I had worked out some implications for the properties of the *IS–LM* model of what we were learning empirically about the demand for money function, and I had sent a copy of my paper (Chapter 3) to Friedman. He was kind about the paper, but pointed out that it dealt with a fixed price level system. The real challenge, he suggested, was to get the interaction of output and inflation into such a model. He was, of course, drawing my attention to what later came to be called the 'missing equation' problem, and it became the central focus of my own contribution to the work of the Manchester Inflation workshop. I was then, and I still am, unable to understand why Friedman himself did not explore the potential of his own (1968) work on the expectations augmented Phillips curve in this role, but he did not. I did, and after a false start (C13), I followed the advice of Michael Parkin (offered, I distinctly remember, as we walked down the stairs to the cab-rank in Euston station) to forget about the full-employment\unemployment dichotomy, and concentrate on variations in output *per se*. I soon succeeded in combining a Phillips curve with a simple quantity equation to produce what must have been one of the first versions of the now commonplace *IS–LM* plus expectations-augmented-Phillips-curve macro-models (Chapter 7).

The *LM* curve of my model was vertical, which made the system very simple to analyse, but it also put many people off because that made it too monetarist for their taste. However, empirical work which I carried out during a brief visit to the St. Louis Fed., in early 1973 (made in the course of a longer stay at Brown) showed that the model held up remarkably well against US data. But the St. Louis Fed. people did not like the work either, because, as far as I could tell, a Phillips curve, even one incorporating expectations with an *estimated* long-run coefficient of unity, was too 'Keynesian' a device for their tastes. Having invited me to write up my work for their *Review*, they declined to publish it. The resulting paper ended up in the *Manchester School* (C16) with a spin-off in the *American Economic Review* (C18).

This little story is typical of the reception given at the time to my contribution to 'Manchester Monetarism'. It was too close to American Monetarism in its emphasis on the money supply, or domestic credit, as the main source of output and price level fluctuations to be acceptable among then orthodox Keynesians, particularly British Keynesians; but American monetarists disliked its emphasis on the Phillips curve as representing some sort of disequilibrium phenomenon. 'Equilibrium modelling' was even then becoming the new fashion in those circles. Still a Popperian of sorts, I thought of myself as trying to build small macro-models whose validity should be judged by their empirical content rather than their conformity to anyone's theoretical preconceptions, but I had quite a few uncomfortable workshop presentations during that period, particularly in the US in the first half of 1973, as a result of sticking to that agenda. An analytic paper analysing an open-economy system (see Chapter 7 for an outline) was also coolly received and, having been rejected by the *Journal of Money, Credit and Banking*, which sat on it for about eighteen months before doing so, appeared for the first time in my own contribution to the Manchester Inflation workshop's series of volumes *Essays on Money and Inflation* (1975) (A3).

Three essays reprinted here appeared in that collection. The first of these (Chapter 5) was an essay on the expectations-augmented Phillips curve and its policy implications, while the second (Chapter 6) was an informal exposition of the framework in terms of which I was then coming to think about inflation, delivered as the Lister Lecture to the British Association for the Advancement of Science (BAAS) in 1972. Quite how I came to be honoured with that lectureship is a mystery to me. It certainly had nothing to do with Joan Robinson, that year's President of Section F. Indeed, I suspect that I was smuggled on to her programme by a BAAS committee, which included Harry Johnson, with the express purpose of irritating her. If that was its intention, the committee certainly succeeded. In introducing me to the journalists, school children and interested lay people who made up my audience, she noted, first, that the Lister Lecture was supposed to be given by someone under thirty-five years of age who had made a distinguished contribution to the social sciences, and second, that I was indeed under thirty-five, and hence satisfied the first criterion. She then sat down!

The third of the above-mentioned papers (Chapter 8) marked a major turning-point in my work. In 1973, I was invited to a conference in Lund sponsored by the Arne Ryde Foundation, and my contribution was written in the summer of that year, immediately after the visit to the US during which my work had received such a rough ride, not least at St. Louis. The topic was loosely specified by the conference organizers – they wanted something on the economics of information – but the paper's content was the result of a self-conscious effort to answer the criticism that my version of Monetarism was *ad hoc* and lacking in proper theoretical foundations. That effort took me in exactly the wrong direction as far as my critics were concerned: this paper marks the first appearance in my writings of what has, ever since, been a constant theme: namely, that money is a social institution which is a substitute for, and not a complement to, the Walrasian market, so that conventional general equilibrium theory and monetary economics do not mix: shades of much earlier discussions with Vicky Chick and Hy Minsky, I now suspect, but I was not conscious of this at the time. I was, however, aware of the influence of Brunner and Meltzer (1971) and Axel Leijonhufvud, while Charles Goodhart was also thinking along similar lines (see Goodhart 1975).

The paper from my time in Manchester that attracted the most attention was none of these. Rather it was the (1975) 'Inflation – a Survey' (C19) which Michael Parkin and I prepared for the *Economic Journal*. It says something about the insularity of the Royal Economic Society in those years that, when Dick Lipsey suggested that Michael be asked to write such a survey, and when he in turn asked that I be invited to become a co-author, they did not have the faintest idea of what kind of a paper they were likely to get. This paper, not reprinted here, because it is rather long and readily available elsewhere, seems very middle-of-the-road now, but in 1975 in Britain it was a different matter. In that time and place, the doctrine of the 'new inflation' was at its most influential: that doctrine held that whatever may have been true in the past, the current inflation was not a monetary but a socio-political phenomenon, requiring a considerable extension of the corporate state to rein it in. Our survey claimed, to the contrary, that the evidence showed inflation still to be an economic phenomenon, and primarily a monetary one at that. Brian Reddaway, the editor of the *Economic Journal*, acted with great integrity: dislike our product though he did, he nevertheless published it. I am told, however, that the most he would say for it, if directly asked, was that it had not turned out to be quite as bad as he had, at one stage, feared!

By the time our inflation survey appeared, Michael Parkin and I were both in Canada. It had become clear that there was no room for further progress at Manchester; no-one but us wanted to merge its three departments of economics; funding for our work was getting tighter and tighter, and there was no prospect of keeping together anything but a skeleton of the team with which we had worked. My salary had never been high – after five years it was still well below the professorial average – and it was falling fast in real terms as a result of inflation. The red ink on the bank statement was becoming more prominent by the month, sometimes, indeed, there was no black to be seen. And on top of that, my heavily mortgaged house, bought new in 1969, had serious problems with its foundations which were not covered by the Housebuilders' Association guarantee, and I was involved in expensive litigation with the builder. So when Grant Reuber, whom I had met all those years earlier at the Chicago workshop, approached me about moving to the University of Western Ontario, and Harry Johnson encouraged me to take the bait, I did. I also drew attention to Michael's availability.

It was a hard decision to uproot myself from Britain. I had made a big investment, not just in Manchester but in the British profession at large. I had helped found, and was a member of the executive of the Money Study Group, and I was also on the Association of University Teachers of Economics (AUTE) executive. I had served on the SSRC and Council on National Academic Awards (CNAA) subject committees at a time when those bodies were helping to promote a new level of professionalism in economic research and teaching in universities, but also in polytechnics (now the new universities). I had acted as an editorial advisor to Philip Allan as he began to build up a list that significantly raised the quality of economics textbooks available to British readers, and I had done a great deal of external examining, both at universities and polytechnics.

I had also achieved a certain amount of visibility beyond the academic community as an exponent of the monetarist approach to the analysis inflation in particular, and of macro-policy in general. Indeed, I had begun to attract the attention of politicians after my evidence to the House of Commons Expenditure Committee in 1974 (El) ('Britain in "Economic Soup" says Professor' was one headline – see *Financial Times*, 27 June 1974). Robert Carr invited me to lunch at the House of Commons, and I had two or three private talks with Keith Joseph. I even received a letter from Margaret Thatcher. But although I had strong views on macroeconomic policy, which can be summarized by saying that the Quantity Theory of Money was a much greater threat to the Heath government than was the National Union of Mineworkers, I did not want to get too close to any of these. Academic economists who get too closely involved with political parties or particular politicians always seem to end up defending the indefensible on behalf of their friends, and in the process they damage not only their own credibility, but that of the discipline too.

Be that as it may, much as I enjoyed living in Manchester, my base at the university was becoming untenable, and red ink on the bank statements was pushing me into doing more in the way of paid outside work – a talk or broadcast here, a newspaper column there – than I knew would be good for me in the longer run. So I had to write off my investment in Britain in order to continue to function as an academic economist. With the law-suit against the builder settled (more or less in my favour) just in time, we left for Canada in July 1975. My parents had taken my remaining in Britain pretty much for granted, and they had gained much satisfaction from seeing my name in the newspapers or hearing me on the radio from time to time. They never quite understood my decision to emigrate. What was there to go to in Canada, when I was already a professor in Britain? And the move caused them considerable personal distress too, because it would deprive them of regular contact with our daughter, their only grandchild. Emigration, however, seemed the only way of ensuring that I could continue to be a full-time and productive academic economist, and that was, when all was said and done, the way of life I had chosen.

Western Ontario

The Western Ontario Department was already strong when Michael Parkin and I arrived in the summer of 1975, although it had not yet attained the level of visibility it deserved. Grant Reuber was by then moving up through the university administration and would soon leave to begin a distinguished career in banking and public service, and Ron Bodkin, whose work on the inflation–unemployment trade-off had attracted a good deal of attention, left just as Michael and I arrived – there was no causative relationship here, I hasten to add. But in macroeconomics, Tom Courchene and Joel Fried were there, while Ron Wonnacott and Jim Melvin had already established Western as an important place in International Trade. A number of the younger people who were to do so much to raise the department's reputation over the next decade were also already there in 1975: Russ Boyer in International Finance who pioneered the analysis of currency substitution, Jim Markusen, an important contributor to the integration of monopolistic competition and trade theory, and Peter Howitt, who for twenty years was to be my most valued colleague (see his essays on *The Keynesian Recovery* (Howitt 1990) to see why) were all untenured assistant professors in 1975. John Whalley, Knick Harley, Ron Wintrobe and Glen MacDonald, among others, were recruited shortly thereafter.

Don Patinkin was a regular short-term visitor to the department in the 1970s. He was then deeply involved in his studies of the origins of the Keynesian Revolution, and for those of us who were interested in this topic, Fried, Howitt and myself, he was the best colleague imaginable. It was Don, more than anyone else, who encouraged me to pursue my interest in the History of Economic Thought with more energy, and it was from him that I learned the importance of reading literature in the context of what its authors and their contemporaries knew, rather than of what we know nowadays. It is a hard trick, and no-one masters it completely, but it is surely one of the keys to good work in the area. Our professional interaction grew into a friendship that easily outlasted the end of his visiting arrangement at Western.

Western, like all Ontario universities, was well funded in the 1970s, and research support was readily available. Teaching loads were relatively light, and in any case the exceptional quality of the students in the graduate and honours BA programmes made those loads a pleasure to bear. I had emigrated because I very much wanted to combine being a full-time academic with providing a reasonable standard of living for my wife and daughter. Western made that possible, as it would not have been had I remained in Britain. Once in Canada, moreover, my wife was also able to do what she had always really wanted to do – go to art school and pursue a career in drawing and printmaking – and from London Ontario, it is only a 240-mile round trip to the opera in Toronto. I was approached discreetly about returning to the UK when the Thatcher Government was elected, but I had no difficulty in deciding to stay put.

Not that everything was now to be plain sailing in my academic life: the fact is that, from the mid-1970s onwards, things were pretty rough for those who, like myself, did not recant the views which had led the profession at large to pin the 'Monetarist' label on them. The attacks came from two sides. First of all, stability of the demand for money function had been the keystone of monetarist doctrine, and new empirical results were beginning to cast doubt upon it. Second, but more fundamentally, New-classical economics, based on explicit Walrasian micro-foundations, and incorporating the rational expectations hypothesis, was on the rise, and its exponents found my style of Monetarism unacceptably *ad hoc*.

The first of these lines of attack was, to a degree, unfair, but only to a degree. The money demand function that first began to break down in the early 1970s was Steven Goldfeld's (1973) well-known quarterly United States function, based on Gregory Chow's (1966) partial adjustment model. It was very much a short-run relationship, of the kind that had to be stable if monetary policy was to be used for fine-tuning; but Monetarism had never been about fine-tuning. If out of steady-state adjustment mechanisms were not stable, that presented an interesting phenomenon to be investigated, but it did not matter very much for monetarist policy prescriptions. Unpredictable shifts in the underlying long-run relationship were much more serious, however, because if they were occurring, then that undermined the case for reducing policy to a suitably chosen rule for the money growth rate. I worked on both sets of issues in the later 1970s, and presented my main results in a long (too long to be printed here) paper at a Carnegie-Rochester conference in 1980 (C35). Both kinds of problem seemed, in fact, to be at work, and so it became necessary to abandon advocacy of the money growth rule (see, for example, Chapter 9). To that extent, my Monetarism had to be toned down a bit in the face of empirical evidence around 1980.

Friends have sometimes commented that my viewpoint not just on monetary rules but on economics in general seemed to shift to the 'left' during my first ten years or so in Canada. That, I think, is largely an illusion created by two facts: I was never particularly right wing on many microeconomic policy matters to begin with (see D55 for the evidence); and in macroeconomics, under the influence of New-classical economics, a large number of other people were in fact shifting to the 'right' at that time, while I, apart from the matter of the money growth rule, was standing my ground as best I could.

I have already mentioned that, once I had begun to think about the matter (in around 1973), I came to the conclusion that Walrasian general equilibrium theory and money ought not to be mixed; but New-classical economics did just that, in a way that claimed to produce an altogether deeper theoretical case against policy activism than more traditional monetarist doctrine had ever developed. Erstwhile monetarists who joined the New-classical camp often seemed to believe that they were doing nothing more than putting the old monetarist superstructure on technically more secure microeconomic foundations. Michael Parkin was one of this group, and our intellectual differences now made it impossible to work as closely together as we had in the past. This is not the place to refight old battles. Let me just reiterate my long-held view that New-classical economics was indeed a radical new doctrine, not merely a mathematically tighter reformulation of Monetarism, and that it was also a doctrine whose empirical content was decidedly suspect from the very outset (see Chapters 9 and 12). At Western, I went on developing the ideas on which I had been working when I left Manchester.

Shortly after I had published my 'Information, Money …' paper (Chapter 8) I had met Peter Jonson, who was on leave from the Reserve Bank of Australia to complete a PhD at the LSE under Harry Johnson's supervision. He was interested in a style of macroeconometric model in which expenditure flows in goods, labour and asset markets responded to discrepancies between desired and actual stocks of assets, financial assets and money in particular. The econometric techniques needed to work along these lines had been developed by Rex Bergstrom and Clifford Wymer, both New Zealanders, although Bergstrom was at Essex and Wymer at the LSE. Their nationality was not quite irrelevant, however, because what they were doing was carrying forward the research programme on macro-stabilization issues which Bill Phillips had initiated, and to which I had been introduced as an undergraduate by his lectures (see Bergstrom and Wymer 1974).

Peter was already thinking about what kind of theoretical underpinnings would go with such applied work, and, upon reading my paper, he saw that our minds were moving in very much the same direction. His nowadays sadly neglected (1976) paper, published in *Kredit und Kapital*, bears witness to this. Peter also recognized that the empirical paper I had written at St. Louis in 1973 (C16) was not as compatible with those theoretical underpinnings as was the empirical work that he had in progress. He quickly convinced me of this – not a difficult task, given the relationship between those underpinnings and the Archibald–Lipsey (1958) extension of Patinkin's analysis which I had first encountered as an undergraduate – and also that the econometric tools that Wymer had developed were well suited to my own ambitions of building really small-scale macroeconometric models that had serious empirical content while remaining simple enough in their structure to be taken into the undergraduate classroom. Between 1975 and 1981 I put a good deal of time into working on such models, not least during the long and fruitful (northern hemisphere) summer vacation of 1977 spent at the Reserve Bank of

Australia. Patrick O'Shea, my research assistant there, had access to dress rehearsals at the Sydney Opera House, so our collaboration was doubly enjoyable. We produced a small econometric model of the UK (C33), and later, working with various research assistants, I would also build little models of the Canadian (D45) and United States (Chapter 10) economies along similar lines.

This work did not catch on widely. Partly, perhaps mainly, that was because models in this style ran very much contrary to New-classical principles in their lack of explicit microeconomic foundations; they were easy to criticize, therefore, in a knee-jerk sort of way, particularly for those who were more interested in scoring points than in understanding how the economy functions; it was hard to improve on those models' empirical performance, however, without moving to much more elaborate systems. Crucially, they predicted that 'unanticipated money' would affect real variables directly through real balance effects, rather than through the price fluctuations required by the New-classical framework, and which, as the data showed (and as Lucas (1996, p. 679) has now acknowledged), simply did not occur. There was, nevertheless, a straightforward empirical reason why I abandoned this line of work: the productivity growth slowdown that hit all Western economies in the mid-1970s played havoc with any empirical model, mine included, in which capacity output was represented by a simple time trend, and I did not have the faintest idea how to cope with this problem. If I was doing this kind of work nowadays, I would, I suppose, use some kind of explicit stochastic growth model to anchor the economy's supply side, and then try to superimpose monetary shocks upon it with their consequences for real variables amplified by a little price stickiness. As the currently fashionable real-business-cycle research programme expands to accommodate the investigation of monetary policy questions, it may well end up doing something of this sort.

Small econometric models were not my only effort to keep my own version of the monetarist research agenda going. My 1981 book *Monetarist Perspectives* (A4) tackled theoretical issues, and its second chapter (Chapter 11, below) filled two important gaps in that agenda. First, it reconciled some important stylized facts about the role of lagged dependent variables in the demand for money function with the mechanics of the monetary transmission mechanism which I was embodying in my small models; and second, in relating the presence of those lagged dependent variables to the whole transmission mechanism of monetary policy, it provided good reasons not to worry about the fact that their coefficients often proved econometrically unstable. My 1983 Harry Johnson Lecture (Chapter 13) carried these arguments further, putting them in a broader context, and in 1988 my Presidential Address to the Canadian Economics Association (CEA) (Chapter 14) tried to relate all this to the non-Walrasian vision of a monetary economy that I had first adopted in 1973.

In 1981 I agreed to take my turn as Department Chairman at Western. The fact that, in 1984, I ended a seven-year appointment after three years demonstrates that this venture into administration was not a success. The immediate reason for my early departure was straightforward: a student appealed a mark, and the mark went down on a colleague's re-reading; the student appealed to the Dean who proposed to restore the original mark without further assessment; I protested, and secured the

Dean's assent to have the paper read by an examiner external to the university; but when the external examiner awarded a grade consistent with the department's re-read, the Dean restored the original mark anyway, informing me only after he had informed the student. Someone had to go, and modern universities being what they are, it was the chairman. I stayed on for a year as a 'lame duck' so that my successor, Michael Parkin as it turned out, could be selected in an orderly fashion. The year 1983–84 was the most miserable one of my career.

I was not altogether sorry to be forced into resignation, however, for in the early 1980s I began to find myself increasingly at odds with some of my colleagues about appointments and tenure decisions. Western is a big department (close to fifty positions at that time) in a rather small country, and it seemed to me, as it still does, that it needed to accommodate considerable diversity of viewpoint and approach if it was to do its job properly; more, certainly, than any American department needs to, for any department there is 'small' relative to the size of the economics profession as a whole, which can and does provide for diversity among, rather than within, individual departments. However, my view that academic heaven was unlikely to be found in, shall we say, a department just like that at Rochester but three times the size, was not widely shared at Western and, inevitably, it was the majority who carried the day. At Berkeley I had been a bit discomfited by the way in which academic seriousness sometimes turned into a humourless earnestness; now at Western, particularly among some of the younger people whom I myself had helped hire and promote, that same seriousness bred self-righteous intolerance. In the view of some of them, anyone who doubted the verities of New-classical economics was not merely misguided, but professionally incompetent. I am told that, at about the time I gave up the chairmanship, I caused considerable offence to some of my colleagues by referring to them as the 'Thought Police'. I had not deliberately set out to offend them, but, all the same, and after due reflection, it was the least they deserved.

Western was by no means the only Economics department to suffer such stresses in the 1980s. Young academics are always inclined to take themselves a bit too seriously, as I am sure some of my older Manchester colleagues, even the friendly ones, must have remarked about me. But in the 1980s, demographic facts ensured that a large number of young people were entering an academic market that had turned against the seller at last. Their sheer numbers, and the extraordinarily competitive nature of the environment they encountered, were bound to make them aggressive and hard to get along with. This is a problem, I think, that the simple passage of time will take care of and, although it made life difficult for some of us for a few years, I doubt that it will turn out to have done any lasting damage to the discipline. It did do harm to the department at Western, however, because a number of talented people who simply could not be bothered with the constant sniping of some of their colleagues left for more congenial appointments elsewhere.

Another trend of the 1980s also did much to undermine the attractiveness of Western's academic environment, at least in my eyes; namely, the growing 'professionalization' of the university's administration, again a local manifestation of a widespread phenomenon. By the early 1990s, the university's President and Vice-Presidents – who at that time were multiplying like Cantillon's 'mice in a barn' – were straight-facedly referring to themselves as 'senior management', and to students as 'clients', while academic staff had become a sub-set of the institution's 'human resources' whose task it was to 'service' the above-mentioned 'clients'. Indeed, for a year or two the whole university was urged to dedicate itself to the provision of 'Total Quality Service', and 'Service Improvement Coordinators' – nouns always seemed to travel in trios at that time – were appointed here, there and everywhere to ensure that principles which allegedly had done wonders for Japanese manufacturing in the 1960s, were observed with suitable reverence.

All of this was comical, but I also found the attitude that underlay it, namely that a university's faculty, who actually do the job of creating, preserving and disseminating knowledge, are less important than its administrators, to be profoundly demoralizing. I am still waiting for a note of congratulations from senior management on having been elected President of the Canadian Economics Association for the academic year 1987–88; I still get angry when I pass the new buildings they had erected without making budgetary provision for such matters as heating, lighting and cleaning; and I get even angrier when I have to waste time typing and filing my own correspondence, emptying my own waste-bin, and so on as a consequence of the economies that the university subsequently, and quite foreseeably, was forced to make as a consequence of their decisions. More fundamentally, although I suppose that 'servicing clients' whose main aim in life is to become accountants or solicitors is one function of the tertiary education sector, that is not exactly what my generation of academics thought a university was for.

A few bright spots remain at Western, though. Our department still maintains a separate undergraduate honours programme, which offers a real education in economics to serious students who are willing to make the effort to acquire it; and despite the best efforts of the Thought Police, whose ranks are now considerably depleted, the department still attracts a few independently minded graduate students and junior faculty who, like the best of the honours students, seem to want to make economics their own way of life just as much as I did.

In the last ten years, my interests have become less directed towards monetary theory *per se*, and more towards its history. Even as I wrote my CEA presidential address (Chapter 14), I was conscious of using it more to sum up past work than to break new ground. I have taken the History of Economic Thought seriously from my undergraduate days onwards, but this is a field in which a great deal has to be read before anything of significance can be written, and the simple passage of time helps a great deal here. Also, I acquired mathematical technique far too late for it ever to have become a natural part of my way of thinking, and I long ago found that there is no fun to be had from learning new technical tricks solely for the purpose of being better able to teach economic models that I do not believe to be socially useful anyway. It is, therefore, mainly a matter of comparative advantage that I now work less on monetary theory and more on its history. Others can judge whether this move should really be called a 'retreat', as I am told by Al Marty some have done, or simply a natural consequence of getting older; and in any event, I try to ensure that my work is as accessible to monetary economists as it is to historians (see Chapter 16). The shift into history has added a nice touch of symmetry to my career, however, because Sam Hollander, my fellow undergraduate from the 1950s, and a member of the Department of Economics at the University of Toronto since 1964 is once again playing an important part in my academic life, this time as the co-organizer, with Margaret Schabas, of the York University–University of Toronto History of Economic Thought workshop which I try to attend regularly.

I also spend a good deal of time these days working on economic policy issues. Again, this is not a new activity, but like the History of Economic Thought, policy discussion gets relatively easier as one gets older, and in my case this effect is amplified by the fact that, although monetarist-style models are no longer academically fashionable, they remain very useful as tools for policy analysis (see Chapters 15, 17 and 18). Much of my policy-related work in the last six or seven years has been carried out under the auspices of the Toronto located C.D. Howe Institute, and in collaboration with Bill Robson – it is a small world, for Bill is the son of John Robson, whose John Stuart Mill project had much to do with first attracting Sam Hollander to the University of Toronto in 1964. Toronto is a pleasant city (with good and still improving opera!) so I do not mind spending a good bit of time there. I must confess, though, with some regret, that one reason I do so is that I am intellectually isolated at Western these days. Over the years, the efforts of the Thought Police and senior managers did take quite a toll on the quality of my working environment.

I have not yet retired. The excuse for this essay, and this volume, is that I am unlikely to do any further serious work in Monetary Economics *per se* and not that I have given up Economics. I hope that this is an acceptable reason for not concluding it with a long list of 'lessons that I have learned from life'. The fact is that I stumbled into academic economics almost by accident, not so much as a career, but as a way of life that appeared much preferable to the alternatives available in the late 1950s. I am not sure how I would have fared as a solicitor, accountant or secondary modern school teacher on Tyneside, but I cannot imagine that I would have had nearly as much satisfaction, not to mention fun, from such work as I have had from Economics, rough patches and all. So far, the balance of the arbitrary shocks to my life seems to have been comfortably positive.

References

Archibald, G.C. (1965), 'The Qualitative Content of Maximizing Models', *Journal of Political Economy*, **73**, February, 27–36.

Archibald, G.C. and R.G. Lipsey (1958), 'Monetary and Value Theory – a Critique of Lange and Patinkin', *Review of Economic Studies*, **26**, October, 1–22.

Bergstrom, A.R. and C.R. Wymer (1974), 'A Model of Disequilibrium Neoclassical Growth and its Application to the U.K.', London, LSE (mimeo).

Brechling, F.P.R. and R.G. Lipsey (1963), 'Trade Credit and Monetary Policy', *Economic Journal*, **73**, December, 618–41.

Brunner, K. and A.H. Meltzer (1971), 'The Uses of Money: Money in the Theory of an Exchange Economy', *American Economic Review*, **61**, December, 784–805.

Chow, G. (1966), 'On the Long-Run and Short-Run Demand for Money', *Journal of Political Economy*, **74**, April, 111–31.

Friedman, M. (1959), 'The Demand for Money – Some Theoretical and Empirical Results', *Journal of Political Economy*, **67**, June, 327–51.

Friedman, M. (1962), *Price Theory – a Provisional Text*, Chicago: Aldine.

Friedman, M. (1968), 'The Role of Monetary Policy', *American Economic Review*, **58**, March, 1–17.

Friedman, M. and D. Meiselman (1963), 'The Relative Stability of Monetary Velocity and the Investment Multiplier in the United States 1898–1958', in *Commission on Money and Credit: Stabilization Policies*, Englewood Cliffs, NJ: Prentice-Hall.

Friedman, M. and A.J. Schwartz (1963), *A Monetary History of the United States 1867–1960*, Princeton NJ: Princeton University Press, for the NBER.

Goldfeld, S.M. (1973), 'The Demand for Money Revisited', *Brookings Paper on Economic Activity*, **3**, 577–638.

Goodhart, C.A.E. (1975), *Money, Information and Uncertainty*, London: Macmillan.

Hansen, A.H. (1953), *A Guide to Keynes*, New York: McGraw-Hill.

Howitt, P.W. (1990), *The Keynesian Recovery and Other Essays*, Hemel Hempstead: Philip Allan.

Johnson, H.G. (1962), 'Monetary Theory and Policy', *American Economic Review*, **52**, June, 335–84.

Jonson, P.D. (1976), 'Money, Prices and Output – an Integrative Essay', *Kredit und Kapital*, **4** (2), 499–518.

Lerner, A.P. (1944), *The Economics of Control*, New York: Macmillan.

Lipsey, R.G. (1963), *An Introduction to Positive Economics*, London: Weidenfeld & Nicholson.

Lipsey, R.G. and K. Lancaster (1956), 'The General Theory of the Second Best', *Review of Economic Studies*, **24**, October, 11–32.

Lucas, R.E. jr. (1996), Nobel Lecture, 'Monetary Neutrality', *Journal of Political Economy*, **104**, August, 661–82.

Marshall, A. (1890), *Principles of Economics*, 8th edn, London: Macmillan, 1920.

Meltzer, A.H. (1963), 'The Demand for Money: The Evidence from the Time Series', *Journal of Political Economy*, **71**, June, 219–46.

Parkin, J.M. and M.T. Sumner (eds) (1972), *Incomes Policy and Inflation*, Manchester: Manchester University Press.

Parkin, J.M. and G. Zis (eds) (1976), *Inflation in the World Economy*, Manchester: Manchester University Press.

Patinkin, D. (1956), *Money, Interest and Prices*, New York: Harper & Row.

Pesek, B. and T. Saving (1967), *Money, Wealth and Economic Theory*, New York: Macmillan.

Phillips, A.W. (1954), 'Stablization in a Closed Economy', *Economic Journal*, **64**, June, 290–323.

Reuber, G.L. (1964), 'Empirical "Trade-offs" and the Reaction Function of the Authorities', *Journal of Political Economy*, **72**, April, 109–32.

Ricardo, D. (1817), *On the Principles of Political Economy and Taxation*, edited by P. Sraffa, Cambridge: Cambridge University Press, 1951.

Smith, A. (1776), *An Inquiry into the Nature and Causes of the Wealth of Nations*, edited by Edwin Cannan, New York: Modern Library, 1937.

Stigler, G. (1952), *The Theory of Price*, London: Macmillan.

Thornton, H. (1802), *An Inquiry into the Nature and Effects of the Paper Credit of Great Britain*, edited by F.A. von Hayek, London: George Allen & Unwin, 1939.

Walters, A.A. (1969), 'The Radcliffe Report – Ten Years After: A Survey of Empirical Evidence', in D.R. Croome and H.G. Johnson (eds), *Money in Britain 1959–1969*, London: Oxford University Press.

1 The rate of interest and the demand for money – some empirical evidence

Introduction

This was the second of two papers (C1 and C2) dealing with issues raised by Friedman (1959). It was written in Berkeley during early 1965. Friedman was highly (and rightly) critical of its first draft, which attributed to his paper a conclusion that velocity was independent of interest rates rather than a report of his inability to find convincing empirical evidence of such a relationship's presence in the data. The paper was initially submitted to the *Journal of Finance* whose referee rejected it with the extraordinary argument that it was illegitimate to base conclusions about the effects of changing the supply of money on evidence about the nature of the demand for money. I still do not know what that referee thought demand curves were for, but I did not argue. I sent the paper to the *JPE* which was about to print its companion, and after further refereeing, more constructive this time, it was accepted.

By the time the paper appeared in the December 1966 *JPE* (with obvious typographical errors in Table 4A) I was at Essex. For some reason, no one drew my attention to Friedman's October 1966 *Journal of Law and Economics* paper on the same topic while I was at work on this paper, and I did not discover it for myself until a couple of years later – too late to refer to it in the 1969 edition of my *Demand for Money* (A1).

References

Friedman, M. (1959), 'The Demand for Money – Some Theoretical and Empirical Results', *Journal of Political Economy*, **67**, June, 327–51.

Friedman, M. (1966), 'Interest Rates and the Demand for Money', *Journal of Law and Economics*', **9**, October, 71–85.

Reprinted from THE JOURNAL OF POLITICAL ECONOMY
Vol. LXXIV, No. 6, December 1966

THE RATE OF INTEREST AND THE DEMAND FOR MONEY—SOME EMPIRICAL EVIDENCE

DAVID LAIDLER*
University of Essex

I

THE relationship between the demand for money and the rate of interest is a key one in macroeconomic models, and recently a fair amount of effort has been expended on investigating it empirically. However, this effort has not, on the whole, been directed solely at problems arising from the rate of interest but has generally been part of a larger attempt to investigate the nature of the demand function for money as a whole. As a result, the evidence that we have about the role of the rate of interest in this function tends to be fragmentary and hard to assess. There are at least four issues involved. First, though many workers have found a relationship between the demand for money and the rate of interest, Friedman's (1959) inability to do so in terms of a quite subtle test is disturbing.[1] Second, even if we discount Friedman's result, the question as to whether the demand for money is more closely related to long-term or short-term interest rates remains open. Third, the estimates we have of the interest elasticity of the demand for money range from the region of − 0.1 to close to − 1.0.[2] Finally, it is important to find

* The work described in this paper was carried out with the financial assistance of the National Science Foundation to which I am deeply grateful. Thanks are also due to Bruce Boston and Gordon Harrington who carried out the statistical work involved. I am also indebted to Milton Friedman and Anna J. Schwartz for making data available to me. The comments of Professors Friedman and Harry G. Johnson as well as of the members of the University of California (Berkeley) Continuing Seminar in Money and Banking on earlier drafts of this paper resulted in substantial improvements in this version. All remaining errors and omissions are, however, my own responsibility.

[1] Friedman has no theoretical objection to including the rate of interest in the demand for money function (see Friedman, 1956), nor was he convinced by his empirical results that it was in fact unimportant. Rather, he saw them as reasons for further research on the matter (cf. Friedman [1959], p. 348). However, since Friedman makes a rate of interest effect in the shape of the rate of change of prices a centerpiece of his inflation analysis, it is a trifle surprising that he did not carry its investigation in the present context a little further. Note also that in Tobin (1965) some of Friedman's data were used to provide strong evidence of the existence of an interest elasticity of demand for money.

[2] Brunner and Meltzer (1963, 1964) and Meltzer (1963) used a long rate, while Teigen (1964) and Bronfenbrenner and Mayer (1960) preferred a short

out whether or not there is any evidence in favor of the textbook version of the liquidity-trap hypothesis. Many writers have commented that they find little evidence in favor of it, but their results have not been generated by tests designed to directly confront this proposition with facts, so that it is difficult to know how much weight to put on their conclusions.

It is the aim of this paper to bring more evidence to bear on these four issues, and its major conclusions are these: It is possible to find a stable relationship between the demand for money and the rate of interest in terms of a test procedure similar to Friedman's (1959); the relevant rate is a short one; the interest elasticity of the demand-for-money function is probably in the range of − 0.15 to − 0.20; there is little evidence of the existence of the liquidity trap as part of the structure of a stable demand for money function.

II

The demand equation for money balances chosen for the tests reported here may be written as $M_d = f(Y_p, r)$, where M_d is the demand for money, Y_p is permanent income, and r is the rate of interest.

Permanent income was selected as the appropriate "other" variable in the relationship mainly because it performed better than its two principal rivals—the level of non-human wealth and the level of measured income—in a series of tests which I have reported elsewhere (Laidler, 1966), but also because it was this variable that Friedman (1959) used in the tests whose results were least favorable to the rate of interest's role in the demand-for-money function.[3] The series used is Friedman's per capita expected real income.

The money definition employed includes time deposits at commercial banks, and it is cast in per capita real terms. Again, there is a dual reason for this choice, for in my earlier work, mentioned above, this definition yielded a more stable relationship than did a more conventional definition, while it was when using such a definition of money that Friedman (1959) failed to find any role for interest to play in determining the demand for money. Since this definition is not the one usually employed, most of the tests were also carried out with money defined as the sum of currency held by the public and demand deposits. These results are also reported, and the reader is thus enabled to judge for himself how much weight should be attributed to this choice of definition in assessing the conclusions. For all these variables, the price deflator employed is one for current prices rather than permanent prices.

Two interest rates had to be employed,

rate. Only Heller (1965) tried to discriminate between the two, and his conclusion that the short rate is preferable is somewhat vitiated by being based solely on postwar data. In fairness to these workers, it should be pointed out that they were more concerned with demonstrating the importance of some interest rate in the demand-for-money function than with selecting the best. Since long rates of interest have less variance than short rates, the matter is crucial when it comes to estimating the interest elasticity of demand for money. The lower estimates, due to Heller, use the short rate, while the upper one is found in Meltzer (1963, p. 225, eq. [3]) and uses a long rate. Note that most of Meltzer's estimates, however, are somewhat lower, being closer to − 0.5.

[3] Permanent income is one measure of return on wealth, and it might be argued that it confuses the two basic determinants of the demand for money, interest and wealth, in one variable, and hence may give misleading results. This objection is not sustainable, however, for it is income that is the actual return on wealth, while permanent income, in principle, at any rate, measures what the return on wealth would be if the rate of return were constant. Thus, permanent income does not confuse the measurement of *variations* in wealth and interest, which is the crucial point on deciding on the usefulness of the variable for regression analysis. This interpretation of permanent income is fully explored in Friedman (1963).

and here the short rate is represented by the rate of return on four-to-six month commercial paper, while the long rate is represented by the yield on twenty-year bonds. The choices were basically determined by the availability of these data for long time periods and are probably not of crucial importance. In principle, the demand for money is related to some index of the entire spectrum of interest rates, and the empirical problem is to discover whether this index is more heavily weighted with short or long rates. Any rate, short or long, will have its own special characteristics that cause it to deviate from the "ideal" short or long rate, and there is no way that I know of to ascertain a priori which rate is the best approximation of this ideal. The most that one can hope for is that the short rate used is reasonably representative of short rates in general and does not, by reason of some special characteristic, happen to behave more like a long rate. Similarly, one must hope that the long rate selected is a reasonably representative one.[4]

[4] Strictly speaking, one should use here the interest differential between bonds and time deposits or, when the latter are omitted from the money definition, the rate of interest on bonds and that on demand deposits. The absence of any reliable data on these variables for the full period 1892–1960 prevented me following this procedure. It should be noted that in Brunner and Meltzer (1963) it is argued that this lack of information leads to more problems when time deposits are included in the definition of money than when they are excluded. This argument must be based on the fact that explicit interest is paid on time deposits. However, over the period of this study, 1892–1960, interest was explicitly paid on demand deposits for many years, and is still paid implicitly, in the form of reduced charges on accounts with higher balances, more favorable loan treatment, and the like. Though interest paid on money holdings does raise a problem, it is hard to see why it should be more extreme in the case of money defined to include time deposits, simply because the interest payments on them are explicit while demand-deposit interest is paid less directly.

III

Many people have found evidence in favor of a relationship between the demand for money and the rate of interest using straightforward regression analysis, but Friedman (1959), using a more subtle approach, found none. I will now show that such a relationship can be found in terms of an experiment similar to Friedman's. The reader will recall the nature of his test. A function relating the demand for money to permanent income alone was fitted to cycle-average data, and using this relationship, annual, within-cycle projections of the velocity of circulation were made. It was found that this relationship predicted cyclical fluctuations remarkably well, and also that the errors involved in these predictions were almost completely unrelated to the level of interest rates (Friedman, 1959, p. 349).

Since most of the variation in interest rates is cyclical, and since this variable is usually called upon to explain cyclical rather than secular variations in velocity, this is hardly the result that one would expect. A relationship whose fitting abstracted from cyclical variations in money-holdings should have left errors in prediction explicable in terms of the interest rate when applied to cyclical data. There are two possible explanations for this result. One is that variations in the demand for money are not related to variations in the interest rate. The other is that there is some error in the secular relationship Friedman (1959) measures between money-holdings and permanent income. If his predictions of velocity are based on a false relationship, then their deviations from actual velocity need not necessarily be related to interest rates or indeed to any other variable.[5]

[5] In Latané (1960 p. 447) it is pointed out that the secular decline in interest rates observed over

Such a situation could arise if there were some secular correlation between permanent income and interest rates which caused permanent income to pick up part of the effect of interest rates in a regression from which the latter variable was omitted. In order to check on this possibility, cycle-average regressions were run for the time period 1891–1957 between money-holdings and permanent income, with the interest rate both excluded and included. The results of these regressions, performed in logarithmic terms, are set out in Table 1, and it will be noticed that even secularly the rate of interest is a significant explanatory variable of the demand for money. It will also be noticed that both the intercept of the regression and the coefficient of permanent income are somewhat altered by the inclusion of the rate of interest in the relationship.

TABLE 1

CYCLE-AVERAGE DATA, TROUGH TO TROUGH, 1891–1957*
(MONEY DEFINED TO INCLUDE TIME DEPOSITS)

$\text{Log}_{10} M = a + b_1 \log_{10} Y_p$, and $\log_{10} M = a + b_1 \log_{10} Y_p + b_2 \log_{10} r$†

a	b_1	b_2 (Short Interest Rate)	R^2	S.E.
−2.017......	1.618 (0.068)*	....	.978	0.037
−1.403......	1.430 0.044)	−0.158 (0.024)	.995	0.018

* Peak-to-peak averages were also tried, and this in no way altered the results. The series stops in 1957 because this is the last trough before 1960, the year in which my data end.

† In this test logs to the base 10 were employed to facilitate the prediction of annual observations. All other tests reported in the paper used natural logarithms.

These two equations were applied to predicting annual levels of per capita real money-holdings, and the first of them showed a mean error in prediction of \$33.53, while the second, which includes the rate of interest, reduced this statistic to \$16.02.[6] The errors in prediction arising from the first equation were also examined, and they did not appear to be very closely related to the interest rate, suggesting that the difference in the intercept and coefficient of the logarithm of permanent income that results from the omission of the interest rate is sufficient to produce misleading results on this score. On the basis of this evidence, it is probably safe to conclude that the rate of interest must be included in the demand function for money.

The reader will have noticed that a short rate of interest was used in the above test, and the appropriateness of

the past fifty years or so might account for the fall in income velocity that Friedman (1959) interprets as showing money, or rates its services to be a luxury. As may be seen from Table 1, this suggestion is only partially correct. Though the presence of an interest rate in the regression lowers the elasticity of demand for money with respect to permanent income, this parameter still remains greater than unity.

[6] Out of the sixty-four years between 1890 and 1960, omitting the war years, for which predictions were made, the inclusion of the rate of interest improved the prediction in forty-two cases. It should be pointed out that Friedman (1959) predicted velocity rather than money-holdings and also that this time series went back to 1869. The absence of interest data before 1890 prevented my duplicating his time period, but though my text is not an exact replica of his it does focus on its essential point, the distinction between secular and cyclical movements in the demand for money, and hence may safely be regarded as a refutation of his results.

this choice is confirmed by the next set of results to be discussed. Given that the interest rate is an important variable in the demand function for money, and given that movements of various interest rates are related to one another, one would expect almost any rate chosen at random to show some relationship to cash balances. In choosing the "right" rate, one is forced to ask which shows the closest relationship with money-holdings, that is, provides the highest coefficient of determination.

There is a further test, however, for though all interest rates are interrelated there is no reason to suppose that the nature of their interrelationship remains unchanged for all time. Thus, if the demand function for money is stable, one would expect the "right" interest rate to show the same relationship to the demand for money in different time periods while the "wrong" one need not. Whatever explanatory power this latter rate might have in a demand-for-money function arises from its acting as a proxy for a more appropriate interest rate. If its relationship to that more appropriate interest rate varies from time to time, this will show up in the form of variations in its relationship to the demand for money.

The tests performed were designed to look into both of these matters. In addition to fitting linear regressions to the logarithms of the data, and the first differences of the logarithms for the entire period 1892–1960 with 1917–18 and 1941–45 omitted, similar regressions with the time period subdivided into 1919–60, 1892–1916, 1919–40, and 1946–60 were also performed.[7] The results of these regressions are to be found in Table 2, and, as will be seen, there is little question of the superior explanatory power of the shorter interest rate. As far as the levels of the data go, it provides a higher coefficient of determination in every case save one, 1892–1916, and its coefficient has a range of variation between the three independent subperiods of between − 0.124 and − 0.142, while the coefficient of the long rate varies between — 0.303 and — 0.552. As to the first-difference results, the period 1892–1916 again is the only one in which the long rate shows slightly more explanatory power, while yet again the variation-of-regression coefficient between time periods is much less for the short rate. The first-difference results are of course less satisfactory than those obtained with the levels of the data, but this is only to be expected. First differencing almost automatically increases the role that measurement error can play in distorting measured relationships. The fact that the regression coefficients are almost uniformly lower for the first-difference regressions is surely explicable in terms of the existence of error in the independent variables.[8] Given these results, it is not difficult to come to some conclusions about the interest elasticity of the demand for money. If we discount the first-difference results for 1946–60, we are left with a range of − 0.088 to − 0.155 for

[7] The period 1919–60 was included here to facilitate comparison with the results obtained with a narrow money definition presented in Table 4.

[8] The fact that the use of first differences does not destroy the relationships obtained but only distorts them slightly seems to dispose of the criticism, sometimes expressed, that the good results obtained for demand-for-money functions with time-series tests on the levels of data are merely the results of data having a common, but in fact unrelated, upward trend. The low and insignificant coefficients obtained with both interest rates for the period 1946–60 are probably due to disequilibrium in the money market in those years. The postwar running down in cash holdings could well dominate the first-differenced data for this period, without also dominating their levels. This is not to mention the fact that interest rates were pegged until 1951.

TABLE 2

DEMAND FOR MONEY FUNCTIONS, ANNUAL DATA 1892–1960 AND SUB-PERIODS
(MONEY DEFINED TO INCLUDE TIME DEPOSITS)

A. $\log_e M = a + b_1 \log_e Y_p + b_2 \log_e r$

Time Period	a	b_1	b_2 (Short Rate)	b_2 (Long Rate)	R^2	S.E.
1892–1960	−3.003	1.394 (0.022)	−0.155 (0.010)	....	.992	0.048
	−3.650	1.514 (0.041)	....	−0.245 (0.067)	.967	.099
1919–60	−2.321	1.291 (0.027)	−0.149 (0.009)	....	.988	.039
	−0.117	1.034 (0.047)	....	−0.488 (0.045)	.974	.056
1892–1916	−4.547	1.636 (0.052)	−0.124 (0.051)	....	.982	.037
	−5.079	1.753 (0.054)	....	−0.303 (0.106)	.983	.035
1919–40	−2.088	1.254 (0.113)	−0.142 (0.010)	....	.940	.042
	−1.536	0.792 (0.171)	....	−0.552 (0.063)	.873	.061
1946–60	2.018	0.665 (0.214)	−0.142 (0.019)	....	.836	.025
	1.508	0.777 (.450)	....	−0.338 (0.103)	.530	0.042

TABLE 2—*Continued*

B. $\Delta \log_e M = a + b_1 \Delta \log_e Y_p + b_2 \Delta \log_e r$

Time Period	a	b_1	b_2 (Short Rate)	b_2 (Long Rate)	R^2	S.E.
1892–1960	0.006	1.216 (0.166)	−0.097 (0.020)	....	.514	0.038
	.011	0.928 (0.174)	....	−0.262 (0.081)	.427	.041
1919–60	0.005	1.111 (0.194)	−0.088 (0.024)	....	.527	.038
	.008	0.869 (0.206)	....	−0.212 (0.088)	.435	.042
1892–1916	0.003	1.528 (0.358)	−0.128 (0.042)	....	.493	.038
	.017	0.897 (0.351)	....	−0.713 (0.232)	.494	.037
1919–40	0.013	1.130 (0.244)	−0.095 (0.042)	....	.531	.042
	.021	0.835 (0.248)	....	−0.172 (0.149)	.441	.046
1946–60	.012	0.694 (0.400)	−0.039 (0.026)	....	.269	.027
	0.013	0.675 (0.442)	....	−0.064 (0.101)	.164	0.029

NOTE.—Numbers in parentheses are standard errors of the regression coefficients.

this parameter.[9] However, the possibility of error in the independent variable has been raised, and, inasmuch as a specific rate of interest is here being used as a proxy for a spectrum of rates, this is not a matter that can be ignored, so that these estimates must be regarded as putting some minimum bound on the parameter. Maximum estimates can be obtained by performing the logarithmic regression of the rate of interest on permanent income and the stock of money and inverting the coefficient of the latter variable. This was done for all regressions involving the short rate of interest, and the estimates obtained here ranged from a low of − 0.156 (levels of data 1919–40) to a high of − 0.588 (levels of data 1892–1916), with the levels of the data for 1892–1960 yielding a measure of − 0.192. It would be easy to get into involved discussions of whether the money-stock data are more subject to error than the interest-rate data and as to which subperiods are more likely to have their results influenced by such error. Suffice it to say, however, that I regard the results for the levels of the data over the total period 1892–1960 as being more likely to be reliable than those for shorter periods, if only because error is more likely to make up a relatively smaller part of the variance of the variables over such a long period. This is particularly true of the money stock, which is dominated by its long-run growth here. The most likely range for the interest elasticity of demand for money is therefore − 0.155 to − 0.192; and the absolute outside limits that one can put on the parameter are − 0.088 as a minimum and − 0.588 as a maximum.[10]

One problem remains to be tackled and that concerns the existence, or otherwise, of the liquidity trap. This hypothesis suggests that at some low level of the rate of interest the demand for money becomes infinitely interest elastic. The period 1892–1960 contains years in which the short rate of interest falls below 1 per cent and years in which the long rate is also unusually low. Thus, by dividing the sample between years where the relevant rate of interest was above its mean and years when it was below, one would expect to be able to find evidence of an increasing elasticity of demand for cash as the rate of interest falls, always supposing, of course, that the liquidity-trap hypothesis is true. This should be the case because the sample containing low-interest-rate observations would be weighted with those observations taken when the rate was, by any reasonable standard, "very low," while such observations would be excluded from the other sample.

The observations were divided as described above, both in terms of the long rate of interest and the short. Regressions were then performed for the separate samples on the logarithms of the data and on the first difference of the logarithms. In the latter case, an observation was allocated to its appropriate sample on the basis of the level of the interest rate at the end of the year over which the change was measured. The results of this test are set out in Table 3 and, as will be seen, the division of the data along these lines does nothing to

[9] It is worth pointing out that the elasticity estimates obtained for the long rate, using both money definitions, are close to those given in Meltzer (1963) where non-human wealth is the other independent variable. This suggests that the results presented here are not strongly dependent on the choice of permanent income as the other variable.

[10] The maximum estimates for each period were as follows, that for the levels of the data being the first of each pair—1892–1960: − 0.192, − 0.348; 1892–1916: − 0.588, − 0.428; 1919–60: − 0.166, − 0.308; 1919–40: − 0.156, − 0.441; 1946–60: − 0.175, − 0.251.

cast doubts upon the stability of the interest elasticity of the demand for money. Indeed, the elasticity with respect to the short rate seems to fall a little at low rates of interest, though the elasticity with respect to the long rate rises slightly at low interest rates. Neither discrepancy has any statistical significance, however. In addition, there is no sign that the relationship is a less reliable one when the interest rate is low, the ratios of the regression coefficients to their standard errors being roughly the same in both samples. The only exception here is in the opposite direction. In the regression using the short rate and the levels of data, the relationship is more significant at low levels of the rate of interest. Thus, the hypothesis of the liquidity trap, as it is usually presented, appears to be

TABLE 3

DEMAND FOR MONEY FUNCTIONS FOR SAMPLES WHERE r IS ABOVE AND BELOW ITS MEAN VALUE

(MONEY DEFINED TO INCLUDE TIME DEPOSITS)

$\text{Log } M = a + b_1 \log_e Y_p + b_2 \log_e r$, and $\Delta \log_e M = a + b_1 \Delta \log_e Y_p + b_2 \Delta \log_e r$

A. SHORT INTEREST RATE—LEVELS OF DATA

	a	b_1	b_2	R^2	S.E.
r above its mean ...	−3.446	1.464 (0.035)	−0.155 (0.051)	.987	0.049
r below its mean	−2.171	1.268 (0.037)	−0.129 (0.015)	.981	0.038

B. SHORT INTEREST RATE—FIRST DIFFERENCES

	a	b_1	b_2	R^2	S.E.
r above its mean ...	0.010	1.231 (0.306)	−0.113 (0.031)	0.401	0.038
r below its mean	0.000(4)	1.116 (0.209)	−0.085 (0.027)	0.607	0.038

C. LONG INTEREST RATE—LEVELS OF DATA

	a	b_1	b_2	R^2	S.E.
r above its mean ...	−0.791	1.166 (0.090)	−0.614 (0.198)	.925	0.071
r below its mean	−2.371	1.396 (0.060)	−0.702 (0.178)	.977	0.097

D. LONG INTEREST RATE—FIRST DIFFERENCES

	a	b_1	b_2	R^2	S.E.
r above its mean ...	0.014	0.858 (0.240)	−0.208 (0.122)	.341	0.045
r below its mean	0.002	1.147 (0.293)	−0.304 (0.108)	.539	0.037

NOTE.—The samples used for short and long interest rates differ slightly, because not each year found both rates uniformly above (or below) their own means. Numbers in parentheses are standard errors of the regression coefficients.

refuted, though this does not mean that more sophisticated versions of the same idea have also been disposed of.[11]

This brings to an end the account of the tests based on the broad definition of money. The worth of the tests depends, of course, on the appropriateness of this definition of money. To facilitate judgment on that question, I shall now describe the tests performed with a narrower definition of money since these are directly relevant to this matter.

IV

I did not repeat the first of the tests described above, that which dealt with Friedman's (1959) inability to find a relationship between the rate of interest and the demand for money. The others, however, were repeated with a more conventional definition of money, and the results are set forth in Tables 4 and 5. It should be noted that reliable data on demand deposits only begin in 1915, and the earliest year for which any data are used here is 1919.

It would be pleasant to be able to report that these results merely confirm those already described, but unfortunately matters are not so simple. The first-difference results in Table 4A do tend to confirm the short rate of interest as the correct one to include in a demand-for-money equation, and, though for the period 1946–60 the results contradict this conclusion, in this particular regression neither interest variable shows any significant explanatory power. The higher coefficient of determination here attached to the regression that uses the long rate of interest is due solely to the latter variable being slightly less insignificant, if one may use such a phrase, than the short rate. On the basis of these first-difference results, the assessment of the interest elasticity of demand for money as being a little in excess of − 0.1 also seems to stand.

The results obtained by using the levels of the data in Table 4B, however, present a more complicated picture. Here the short rate of interest provides the higher coefficient of determination in only one case, 1946–60, and the coefficient of income in this regression is far lower than those obtained for other time periods and is completely inconsistent with these other results. Thus, the superior performance of the short rate here cannot be taken too seriously. Otherwise, there is nothing to choose between the two rates over the entire period 1919–60, while the long rate is clearly to be preferred for the period 1919–40. If this were the only evidence available, one would tend to conclude, albeit tentatively, that the long rate was a better variable than the short rate and that the interest elasticity of demand for money was, as a minimum estimate, somewhere between − 0.5 and − 0.8 rather than in the range of − 0.1 to − 0.2.

We do have other evidence, however,

[11] The simple liquidity-trap hypothesis is about the nature of the demand function for money, and this version of it is dealt with by my test. However, it may also be modified to a hypothesis about the banking system's demand for free reserves at low levels of the interest rate. Here it becomes a theory of the responsiveness of the money supply to central banking policy, and this version of it is clearly not tested here. In another form, the hypothesis may be about the elasticity of demand for short-term securities with respect to the rate of interest on long-term securities. Here it is a hypothesis about the role of liquidity premiums in the term structure of interest rates and again is not dealt with by my test. It should also be noted that even my results imply that the demand for money becomes flatter, when drawn in arithmetic terms, at low rates of interest. There is yet another way of stating the liquidity-trap hypothesis, which says that the trap exists when the level of the interest rate is low relative to expectations, so that this "low" level can shift over time. This is really a proposition that the interest elasticity of the demand for money is unstable. It is hard to reconcile this view with the highly significant estimates of this parameter presented in this paper which, moreover, are stable between subperiods.

in the face of which I would tend to dismiss that just cited. The results obtained using a narrow definition of money are contradictory. Those obtained with the first differences of the data favor the short interest rate, and those obtained from their levels slightly favor the long rate. There is no obvious reason for preferring one set of results to the other, and, if one could be sure that he were using the appropriate definition of money here, this is not an outcome that would be expected. However, it would not be surprising if such results turned up in the context of an inappropriate definition of money, for if the dependent variable of the relationship is badly defined there is no way of knowing what results might be produced. The regressions employing a broad definition of money provide consistent results, while those under discussion at the moment do not. It is tempting, then, to conclude that the broader definition of money is the more appropriate one for the problems at hand and that the contradictory conclusions ob-

TABLE 4

DEMAND FOR MONEY FUNCTIONS, ANNUAL DATA 1919–60 AND SUB-PERIODS (MONEY DEFINED TO EXCLUDE TIME DEPOSITS)

A. $\Delta \log_e M = a + b_1 \Delta \log_e Y_p + b_2 \Delta \log_e r$

Time Period	a	b_1	b_2 (Short Rate)	b_2 (Long Rate)	R^2	S.E.
1919–60	0.002	0.953	−0.106	....	.412	0.046
		(0.235)	(0.029)			
	.005	0.638	....	−0.334	.382	.048
		(0.234)		(0.010)		
1919–40	.011	0.940	−0.125	....	.377	.052
		(0.299)	(0.051)			
	.019	0.501	....	−0.368	.337	.054
		(0.287)		(0.173)		
1946–60	− .024	0.820	−0.031	....	.318	.025
	− .024	0.820	−0.031	....	.318	.025
	−0.024	0.896	....	−0.119	.338	0.025
		(0.382)		(0.087)		

B. $\log_e M = a + b_1 \log_e Y_p + b_2 \log_e r$

Time Period	a	b_1	b_2 (Short Rate)	b_2 (Long Rate)	R^2	S.E.
1919–60	−4.243	1.526	−0.206	....	.970	0.074
		(0.051)	(0.017)			
	−0.989	1.145	....	−0.721	.970	.074
		(0.062)		(0.059)		
1919–40	0.095	0.085	−0.188	....	.933	.049
		(0.134)	(0.012)			
	5.229	0.200	....	−0.785	.952	.042
		(0.117)		(0.043)		
1946–60	6.030	0.044	−0.176	....	.844	.039
		(0.333)	(0.030)			
	3.145	0.523	....	−0.516	.787	0.045
		(0.484)		(0.111)		

NOTE.—Numbers in parentheses are standard errors of the regression coefficients.

tained with the narrower definition reflect only the fact that that definition is an unsatisfactory one.

The case may be made stronger. Tables 2 and 5 contain twelve pairs of regressions which differ only in the definition of the dependent variable. If they are compared in terms of which definition of money enables us to predict percentage variations in money-holdings more accurately, it will be found that the standard error of the estimate is smaller in the context of a broad definition of money in nine cases out of the twelve. Moreover, two out of the three of which the opposite is true are first-difference relationships fitted for the period 1946–60. I have tended to put little weight on

TABLE 5

DEMAND FOR MONEY FUNCTIONS FOR SAMPLES WHERE r IS ABOVE AND BELOW ITS MEAN VALUE

(MONEY DEFINED TO EXCLUDE TIME DEPOSITS)

$\text{Log}_e M = a + b_1 \log_e Y_p + b_2 \log_e r$, and $\Delta \log_e M = a + b_1 \log_e Y_p + b_2 \Delta \log_e r$

A. SHORT INTEREST RATE—LEVELS OF DATA

	a	b_1	b_2	R^2	S.E.
r above its mean	−2.608	1.267 (0.091)	−0.160 (0.089)	.959	0.03
r below its mean	−5.060	1.650 (0.064)	−0.237 (0.026)	.969	0.068

B. SHORT INTEREST RATE—FIRST DIFFERENCES

	a	b_1	b_2	R^2	S.E.
r above its mean	0.005	0.669 (0.598)	−0.111 (0.048)	.380	0.038
r below its mean	0.003	0.989 (0.289)	−0.105 (0.038)	.423	0.052

C. LONG INTEREST RATE—LEVELS OF DATA

	a	b_1	b_2	R^2	S.E.
r above its mean	−1.569	1.164 (0.115)	−0.402 (0.254)	.877	0.091
r below its mean	−0.791	1.117 (0.056)	−0.695 (0.104)	.967	0.051

D. LONG INTEREST RATE—FIRST DIFFERENCES

	a	b_1	b_2	R^2	S.E.
r above its mean	0.011	0.327 (0.277)	−0.181 (0.130)	.162	0.046
r below its mean	−0.011	1.257 (0.385)	−0.418 (0.131)	.653	0.042

NOTE.—The samples used for short and long interest rates differ slightly because not each year found both rates uniformly above (or below) their own means. Numbers in parentheses are standard errors of regression coefficients.

these postwar results in dealing with other issues, and there seems no reason why they should be accorded any more weight here. Though they cannot be ignored entirely, it is surely not going too far to suggest that they have a greater chance of being misleading than do those results obtained over longer periods. The evidence favoring a broad definition of money is, then, stronger than it looks at first sight, so that I am inclined to discount the problems raised by the tests just described and to stick to my initial conclusion concerning the "correct" rate of interest to use in the demand-for-money function, as well as those concerning the magnitude of the interest elasticity of demand for cash balances.

With respect to the liquidity trap, one's interpretation of the evidence given in Table 5 must also depend on his views as to the appropriateness of leaving time deposits out of the definition of money and on his view as to the "right" rate of interest to include in the demand-for-money function. Suffice it here to point out that the combination of a narrow money definition with a long rate of interest does, at least on the basis of the evidence from first differences, suggest that the elasticity of demand for money with respect to the rate of interest increases at the rate of interest falls. This is the only case in which such evidence does appear, and one's judgment of it must depend entirely on the way he regards the particular formulation of the demand-for-money function that produced it. My own inclination, as must be apparent from the preceding discussion, is to discount this particular result as the product of an inappropriately defined function.

V

One task now remains, and that is to fit these results into a broader framework than that of the theory of the demand for money per se. The first of my results, that a relationship exists between the demand for money and the rate of interest, should remove any final doubts that, in the context of a simple macroeconomic model, the Hicksian LM curve is positively sloped. This, in its turn, means that variations in consumer expenditure and investment that arise independently of monetary changes can have an effect not only on interest rates but also on the equilibrium level of income. Clearly, the same is true of fiscal policy. Whether these independent effects can be "significant," or "large," clearly depends upon the meaning that one cares to attach to such words. Suffice it to say here that the elasticity of demand for money with respect to the rate of interest seems to be small enough to put fairly narrow limits on the variations in velocity that could be induced by changes in saving and investing behavior. Thus, major fluctuations such as the 1929–33 downturn are probably best explained as largely monetary phenomena. Lesser fluctuations, however, could be produced independently of monetary changes.[12]

The conclusion that it is a short rate of interest, rather than a long rate, that is relevant for money-holding clarifies the nature of a problem rather than solves one. If investment is more sensitive to long rates of interest and if the first impact of a change in the money supply is on short rates, then in order to have a theory as to how changes in the money stock affect the economy, one must have a theory as to how interest rates of various terms are interrelated. Thus, instead of being a "fringe" subject in discussions of monetary theory and

[12] This conclusion is very much that reached in Friedman and Schwartz (1963, pp. 676–700).

policy, the theory of the term structure of interest rates comes to be a central topic, essential to any description of the mechanism by which changes in the money supply affect the real variables in an economy.

In the case of the liquidity trap, the results on the whole confirm the conclusions reached by others and hence suggest that the LM curve is never horizontal. How effective monetary policy can be, however, depends upon more than the LM curve, for the responsiveness of aggregate demand to changes in interest rates as well as the direct responsiveness of expenditure to changes in the quantity of money are just as important. To put it in Hicksian terms, we still need to know about the IS curve.[13]

Thus, when put into the broader context of macroeconomic theory, the results described in this paper, even if accepted as demonstrated beyond doubt, which is more than I would claim for them, are more conspicuous for the light they cast on unsolved problems than for the difficulties they settle. They do, however, clarify the nature of the problems to be solved and, in doing so, contribute something to the ultimate solution.

REFERENCES

Bronfenbrenner, M., and Mayer, T. "Liquidity Functions in the American Economy," *Econometrica*, XXVIII, No. 4 (October, 1960), 819–34.

Brunner, Karl, and Meltzer, Allan H. "Preceding Velocity: Implications for Theory and Policy," *J. Finance*, XVIII (May, 1963), 319–54.

———. "Some Further Evidence on the Supply and Demand Functions for Money," *ibid.*, XIX (May, 1964), 240–83.

Friedman, Milton. "The Quantity Theory of Money, A Restatement," in Milton Friedman (ed.). *Studies in the Quantity Theory of Money*, Chicago: Univ. of Chicago Press, 1956.

———. "The Demand for Money—Some Theoretical and Empirical Results," *J.P.E.*, LXVII (June, 1959), 327–51.

———. " 'Windfalls,' the 'Horizon,' and Related Concepts in the Permanent Income Hypothesis" in Carl F. Christ *et al. Measurement in Economics, Studies in Mathematical Economics and Electronometrics in Memory of Yehuda Grunfeld.* Stanford, Calif.: Stanford Univ. Press, 1963.

Friedman, Milton, and Schwartz, Anna J. *A Monetary History of the United States, 1867–1957*. Princeton, N.J.: Princeton Univ. Press (for the National Bureau of Economic Research), 1963.

Heller, H. R. "The Demand for Money—The Evidence from the Short-Run Data," *Q.J.E.*, LXXIX (May, 1965), 291–303.

Laidler, David. "Some Evidence on the Demand for Money," *J.P.E.*, LXXVI (February, 1966), 55–58.

Latané, Henry A. "Income Velocity and Interest Rates: A Pragmatic Approach," *Rev. Econ. Statis.*, XLII (November, 1960), 445–49.

Meltzer, Allan H. "The Demand for Money: The Evidence from the Time Series," *J.P.E.*, LXXI (June, 1963), 219–46.

Teigen, R. "Demand and Supply Functions for Money in the United States," *Econometrica*, XXXII, No. 4 (October, 1964), 477–509.

Tobin, James. "The Monetary Interpretation of History," *A.E.R.*, LV (June, 1965), 464–85.

[13] Direct effects may of course be looked upon as working through interest rates also. This is particularly the case when one considers the effect of monetary changes on expenditure on consumer durables.

2 The results and implications of recent empirical work on the aggregate demand function for money in the United States

Introduction

This paper, previously unpublished, was written in Berkeley in 1965–66, and was based on graduate lectures. It was submitted to a journal – let this one remain nameless – that acknowledged receipt of it and then seems to have lost the manuscript. Subsequent letters of enquiry about its fate were not answered. It provided the outline for the first edition of my book on *The Demand for Money* which I wrote in 1967–68, at the invitation of Ed Mock and Michael De Prano (an occasional participant in the Berkeley continuing seminar during my time there).

Four things strike me about the paper upon reading it now: (a) the naive confidence it displays in the robustness of empirical results; (b) the uncertain grasp that its author had of the earlier twentieth century literature on the quantity theory; (c) the way in which *IS–LM* analysis was deployed to illustrate the differences between what would later be called 'Monetarist' and other positions a few years before Friedman did so, to many people's surprise, in his *Monetary Framework* (see R.G. Gordon (ed.) 1974); and (d) the discussion it contains of whether and to what extent government bonds are net wealth. I did not claim then, nor do I now, any originality for the two latter features of the paper, but they do show that monetary economists were not quite as backward in the 1960s as it is sometimes thought.

I have corrected only typographical and spelling errors in the original manuscript. The bibliography, however, got detached and lost at some stage. What appears here is an *ex post* reconstruction. That is why publication details are given for papers which were only in working paper form when this was written.

Reference

Gordon, R.G. (ed.) (1974), *Milton Friedman's Monetary Framework*, Chicago: University of Chicago Press.

The results and implications of recent empirical work on the aggregate demand function for money in the United States*

I

To write any kind of survey in a field so soon after the appearance of one as clear and comprehensive as that of Harry G. Johnson (12) needs an excuse. Mine is this: when Johnson wrote his survey, the recent spate of empirical work on monetary economics was just beginning, and indeed it was his survey which first clearly defined the major empirical issues that needed to be settled. A great deal of quantitative work has been done in the meantime, and the first reason for the present paper is to show to what extent the important issues have been settled. My second reason follows naturally enough from this, for I shall also try to examine some of the implications of recent empirical work in monetary economics for macro-economic theory. The money market, after all is not the beginning and end of anything, but is part of a macro-economic model. Thus the ultimate issues of monetary economics are not the stability of the demand function for money and the arguments that should be included in it, but rather matters such as how effective and reliable monetary policy is likely to be, and to what extent one may rely on the money market to offset fluctuations in the real side of the economy. Before one can deal with the latter questions, he must know the answers to the former, and in this paper I shall try to deal with the results of empirical work in monetary economics in the context of these broader issues.

As far as possible, I shall try to avoid covering matters already dealt with by Johnson, though this will not always be possible.[1] First, I shall look at problems raised by various hypotheses of the money market in terms of a very simple static macro-economic framework. Then I shall go into the theoretical underpinnings of the various models of the demand for money that have been tested empirically. Finally, the empirical results achieved to date will be described, and looked at for the light they shed on the broader macro-economic issues mentioned above.

II

As has already been pointed out, the money market is but one part of a macro-economic model, and to assess the importance of any work in monetary economics *per se*, one must look at the light which it throws on the working of the macro-

* I am grateful to Thomas Mayer and Bernard Corry for their many helpful comments on an earlier draft of this paper. The criticism of the members of the University of California (Berkeley) Continuing Seminar in Money and Banking also resulted in many improvements in this version. Finally, I am grateful to the National Science Foundation for the financial support that made this work possible. All errors and omissions are, of course, my own responsibility.

economy. Thus, in this section of the paper, I shall sketch out what seem to be the most relevant of conventional static macro-economic theories, which differ in terms of their treatment of the money market, and describe the different roles the money market plays in them. In all of them, I shall assume that the money supply is exogenously determined.[2]

In the simplest of all so-called 'classical' models of the economy, the money market plays hardly any role at all. In such a model, full employment is automatically assured by the equilibrium of supply and demand in the labour market, and, with a given production function and stock of capital, the level of output is also determined. The allocation of output between investment and consumption is carried out by the rate of interest. Only the price level is left to be determined in the money market, and though this is an important matter in the context of an open economy, there are probably few economists today who would regard the matter of the external balance as important a policy consideration as the level of income and employment.

However, it takes the addition of but one assumption to this model to make the money market one of prime importance. This assumption is that of the downward rigidity of money wages. Price flexibility ensures that the real stock of money will always be compatible with the demand for it at full employment income so that in terms of the Hicksian framework the *LM* curve will always cut the *IS* curve at that level of income. If we introduce into this model some historically given level of money wages, then there is a maximum amount above which the real stock of money cannot rise without an increase in the nominal money supply. If this maximum amount should be less than what the public would demand at full employment then an equilibrium level of income lower than full employment income, rather than merely a lower price level, is the result. The addition of this one simple assumption of downward rigidity in money wages, then, brings the money market to the centre of the scene, and since it seems to be widely accepted that wages are sufficiently rigid downward in fact to make this assumption a good approximation of reality, I shall take it for granted that less than full employment equilibrium is a possibility.

Unemployment, even if it is possible, is hardly desirable, and since Keynes at least, economists have looked to macro-economic models to tell them how to avoid it. The answer that one gets depends on the model that he looks at, and there are at least three theories of the money market which produce different answers. The first is the crudest version of the Quantity Theory of Money, that postulates a constant velocity of circulation. In Figure 1, this is translated into the Hicksian framework, and involves a vertical *LM* curve. It thus implies that full employment can be reached *only* through monetary policy. Fiscal policy, which works by shifting the *IS* curve will succeed only in raising interest rates as resources are reallocated to the government from the private sector. This model of the money market also has implications for our understanding of business fluctuations, for it immediately rules out the possibility that variations in the marginal efficiency of capital can lead to variations in the equilibrium level of income. Again it is only the interest rate that is free to vary, and fluctuations in equilibrium income must all be explained in terms of monetary disturbance. In a model such as this one with an historically given

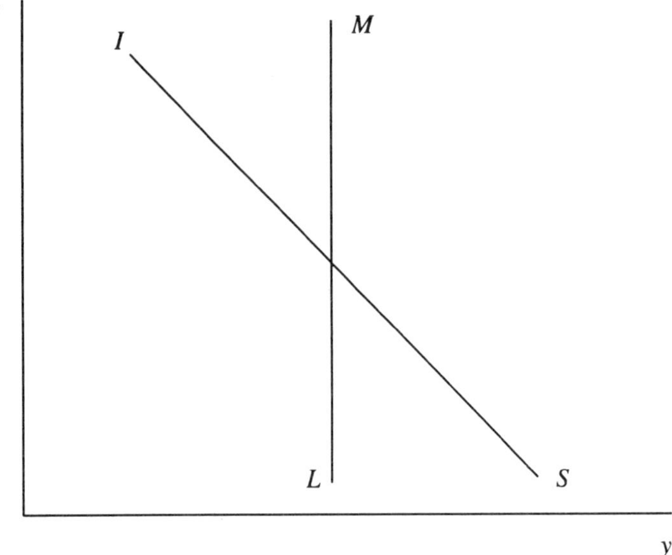

Figure 1

minimum wage level, the level of income and employment is determined solely by the nominal quantity of money.

Needless to say, there are more sophisticated versions of the Quantity Theory of Money than this and we may characterize them by saying simply that they allow the velocity of circulation to vary positively with the rate of interest. In terms of the *LM–IS* framework, they produce an *LM* curve which is positively sloped, as shown

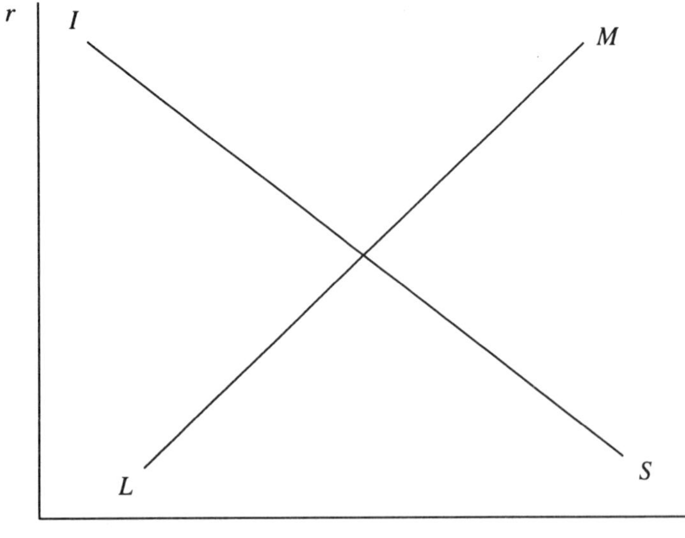

Figure 2

in Figure 2. Here, though the equilibrium level of income can be expanded by increasing the supply of money, this can also be accomplished by fiscal policy, since shifting the *IS* curve results in a combination of higher interest and higher income. Similarly, one cannot automatically conclude from a model such as this that the business cycle is a purely monetary phenomenon. Fluctuations in the level of income can arise from independent shifts of the *IS* curve. How 'big' such shifts can be and how 'effective' fiscal policy might be in such a world is clearly dependent upon the slope of the *LM* curve, or to put it another way, on the interest elasticity of the velocity of circulation.

A third possibility, involves, of course, the Keynesian hypothesis of the liquidity trap, the notion that at some 'low' level of the rate of interest, the *LM* curve becomes perfectly horizontal as shown in Figure 3. In a world in which this section of the *LM* curve is relevant, it is clearly impossible to increase the level of income by increasing the quantity of money, while it is equally obvious that fluctuations in income must be due solely to shifts of the *IS* curve.[3]

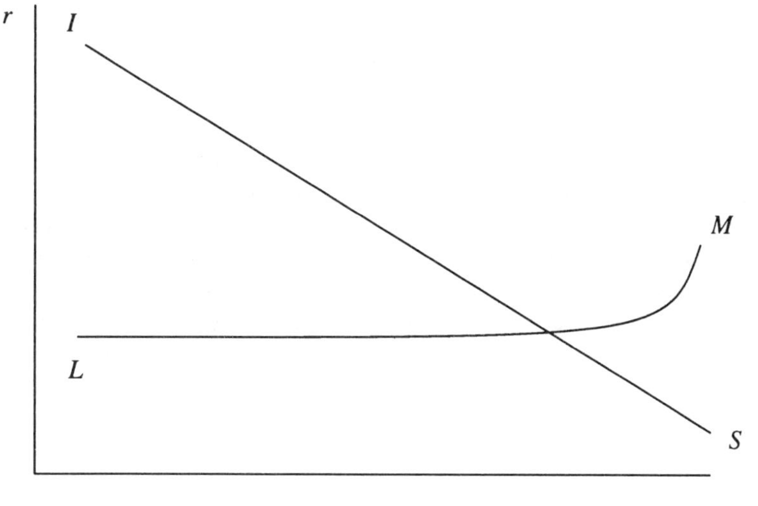

Figure 3

Thus, we have three possible hypotheses about the *LM* curve; that it is vertical, that it is positively sloped, and that it is, in certain possibly relevant regions, horizontal. Clearly, it is important to be able to pick the most relevant of these hypotheses. It is equally important to find out whether the *LM* curve may be drawn at all as a stable relationship, and this may only be done if some variable other than the level of income or the rate of interest is not an important one in the demand for money function. The simple static macro-economic framework set out here is an heroic abstraction of reality and it is only useful if it has picked out the variables that dominate the determination of income in the world. If for example the level of non-human wealth were to prove to be a more suitable variable for inclusion in the demand for money function than income, one would need a theory of the relationship between non-human wealth and income before such a function could be included in a model of the determination of income and employment. Such a model would clearly be more complicated than those set out here. More complexity in economic models is neither good nor bad *per se*, and how much complexity is needed is a matter to be settled in the context of whatever problems are to be solved. In terms of the problem of income determination, our current models are not very useful if the level of income is not an appropriate argument for inclusion in the demand for money function. This matter then, along with that of the responsiveness of the demand for money to the rate of interest, is clearly one that will bear empirical investigation.

In the rest of this paper, I shall go on to consider competing hypotheses of the demand for money, and then I shall consider them in terms of the available empirical evidence as to their relevance in order to see to what extent the matters raised here have been settled.

III

Money is usually described as a 'means of exchange' and a 'store of value'. It is useful to classify theories of the demand for money in terms of which of these aspects they stress, for though it is possible to get a 'general' theory of the demand for money which includes all possible aspects of the problem, theories which limit the matters they take into consideration have the great advantage of being more precise (though not necessarily more correct) in their empirical predictions.

Modern theories of the transactions demand for money, which stress the means of exchange function of cash, have their classical statement, in this century at least, in the work of Irving Fisher (5), and until the recent work of Baumol (1) and Tobin (21) have been somewhat mechanistic in outlook. It is probably not going too far in the way of simplification to say that Fisher who never explicitly formulated the problem in terms of a demand function regarded transactions as analogous to an output in whose production process money balances play the role of a factor used in fixed (though perhaps trend adjusted) proportion to output, at least in the long run. This view in turn led him to look for the factors that might influence the level of transactions velocity in the nature of the relevant production function; that is to say in the institutions and technology of the transactions making process. Thus, for example, he looked to the growth of money substitutes, and improvement in geographical communications to secularly lessen the need for money, and hence increase its transactions velocity. In discussing the transactions demand for money, Keynes (13) made little advance on Fisher. He did however make two changes that are worth noting. First, he stated the theory as one of the demand for money, rather than as a theory of velocity and hence of the price level; second for the volume of transactions, he substituted the level of income, thus implicitly postulating a stable transaction–incomes ratio. Despite these changes, however, the theory remained at least in its more popular expositions, since Keynes himself mentioned interest as an opportunity cost of holding transactions balances, as mechanistic as it had been with Fisher. It was left to Baumol and Tobin to explicitly introduce the notion of maximizing behaviour into this branch of monetary theory. Both were able to show that, for a given cost of transforming other assets into money, the transactions demand for money should be stably and negatively related to the rate of interest, and that it should increase less than in proportion to the volume of transactions.[4]

There is more variety to be found in theories of the demand for money conceived of as a store of value. This is not surprising for to take this view of money automatically places one in the framework of the theory of consumer choice since money is far from being the only store of value. The modern roots of these theories are, of course, to be found in the discussions of the so-called Cambridge *k* begun by Marshall and formalized by Pigou (19). They postulated that, 'other things being equal', the public's demand for money would be a constant fraction of its resources. It should be clear that this early work was more interesting for the questions it raised than for those it answered. Even the term 'resources' is a vague one, and it is never quite clear whether it is to be interpreted as wealth, a stock variable, or income, a flow variable.[5] Nor is there too much analysis of what the important 'other things' might be and how they might change. The rate of interest is one, since it is the opportunity cost of holding money, and the degree of uncertainty about the future course of events is another, but there is no sustained effort to analyse the effects that these might have on the demand for money, nor are they by any means the only factors mentioned.

It was Keynes's analysis (13) of the speculative demand for money that first picked out one factor for special emphasis and his choice was uncertainty about future levels of the rate of interest. This analysis takes as the dominant characteristic of money as an asset the fact that, unlike many other financial assets, it bears no coupon payment and hence is not subject to fluctuations in value arising out of variations in the interest rate. There is little point here in describing this well known analysis in any detail, though perhaps one point is worth making about it. It assumes either that there is a given volume of assets other than money in the economy, or a given level of wealth, so that one or the other of these variables belongs in the total Keynesian demand for money function along with the rate of interest and the level of income.[6] This is a point that seems to have been overlooked by some empirical tests of so called 'Keynesian' hypotheses of the demand for money and it will be taken up below.

The emphasis on money as an asset free from interest rate risk also underlies Tobin's application (22) of the theory of portfolio choice to the asset demand for money. This analysis is superior to that of Keynes in several respects. First, it introduces the expected yield on bonds over a finite period, the opportunity cost of holding money, explicitly into the demand for money function. In Keynes's work the interest rate that appears explicitly is the current ratio of coupon payment to market value on perpetual bonds whose level stands in the demand for money function as a proxy for the expected yield (including capital gains and losses) on these instruments over some finite holding period. Second, Tobin's analysis of expectations is more sophisticated. In Keynes's, expectations for the individual are single valued. Either the price of bonds is expected to rise or to fall or not to change, whereas in the Tobin model expectations about the yield on holding bonds are characterized as a probability distribution with a mean and a variance. The probability distribution is attached to the yield on bonds, and it is shown that the greater the proportion of the total portfolio held in bonds, the greater is both the portfolio's expected rate of return and the variance of that rate of return, for given expectations about the yield. The individual managing his portfolio is viewed as being risk averse and hence as trading off return against risk in deciding on its composition. This approach enables Tobin to derive a negative relationship between the demand for money and the expected yield on bonds for given riskiness of this yield, as measured by the variance of the distribution of expectations, and a given size of portfolio. Thus, the smooth relationship between the demand for money and the rate of interest which in a Keynesian world can only be gotten by aggregating over individuals with different single valued expectations is achieved for each individual in the Tobin model. It is also worth stressing that the volume of wealth, which hovers uneasily in the background in Keynes's approach is introduced explicitly in this more recent model. Despite these differences, though, the Tobin approach clearly belongs in the class of 'Keynesian' theories, for it differs from Keynes's analysis of the asset demand for money in the method of analysis only. Like the earlier theory it stresses the quality of money as an asset free from interest rate risk, and concentrates on this characteristic to the exclusion of others.

There is another offshoot of the Cambridge tradition in monetary theory, usually associated with the so called 'Chicago School', and in particular with Milton Friedman (6, 8) that descends from Marshall and Pigou through the work of Hicks (10) rather than that of Keynes. This approach views the demand for money as being determined by the same forces that would determine the demand for any capital good. Thus in its most general form this theory characterizes the demand for money as being the result of a budget constraint, wealth, a set of opportunity costs, yields on various other assets, and a utility function. It views money as yielding a direct flow of services to its owner, and hence as having more in common with a consumer durable than with a financial asset yielding interest. Thus it is hypothesized that the demand function for this asset, like that for any other consumer durable, should be constrained by total wealth, both human and non-human (for which permanent income is the usual empirical proxy), rather than by some narrower concept that might be thought more appropriate when money is regarded as a financial asset with rather special interest characteristics.[7] This approach does not, of course, deny the importance of money in the transactions making process, or that money may be regarded as an asset free of interest rate risk. Rather, it suggests only that an adequate theory of the demand for money can be constructed without paying explicit attention to these factors.

These then are the principal theories of the demand for money that have been advanced recently, and I will now go on to look at the empirical formulations of the aggregate demand function for money that have been based upon them for it is this function rather than any micro relationship that is relevant for the problems raised earlier.

IV

Though I have set out the foregoing theories of the demand for money as alternatives, it must be clear to the reader that none of them explicitly excludes the others. Money may be held in part as a transactions balance pure and simple, in part as a risk offsetting item in an efficiently managed portfolio, and, in part as a consumer durable for the flow of services it yields its owner. Moreover, it is quite obvious that these categories may overlap. Thus, in the present state of knowledge, it would hardly make sense to ask which theories have been refuted in the normal scientific sense. Nor would it be fair to their authors to do so, since Baumol and Tobin, if not Friedman, never claimed to be producing general theories of the complete demand function for money of an individual, let alone of the whole economy. However, it does make a great deal of sense to ask which set of considerations seem to suggest the best aggregate demand for money function. The alternative to using the simple theory that is most empirically relevant would be to use some complex 'generalized' model of the demand for money that has not yet been constructed. Moreover, it is impossible to tell how badly such a generalized model is needed until one has seen how well existing simple models of the demand for money perform in the face of empirical evidence.

Three empirical models of the total demand function for money in the economy have been put through extensive empirical tests, and they may be stated in their most general forms as follows:

$$M_d = f(Y,r) \tag{1}$$

$$M_d = F(W,r) \tag{2}$$

$$M_d = g(Y_p,r) \tag{3}$$

where M_d is the quantity of money demanded in real terms, Y is measured real income, W is real non-human wealth, Y_p is real permanent income and r is some rate, or rates, of interest.

Since all the theories discussed in the last section of this paper were couched in terms of individual behaviour, and the tests to be discussed below were performed with aggregate data, and since certain variables that appear in the discussions of the theories (e.g., the volume of transactions) do not appear in these empirical formulations, it would be as well to discuss the relationship between the underlying theories and these equations.

Though equation (1) is precisely the one that appears in all our macro-economics textbooks as the aggregate demand function for money, it is perhaps the most difficult one of all to relate closely to any of the foregoing theories. It has, however, been viewed as being related both to a Keynesian view of the demand for money, and as having something to do with the modern transactions approach to the problem. The difficulty with the first interpretations is easily seen, and has been alluded to earlier. Implicit in the Keynesian analysis of the speculative demand for money is the existence of a given stock of other assets in the economy, and though this may be regarded as being approximately constant in the short run and hence can be omitted from a short-run model in just the same way as Keynes omits the effect of new investment on productive capacity in his analysis of the real goods markets, it is not a matter that can be overlooked if the equation is to be fitted by regression analysis to time series data generated over a period of around half a century.[8] One may only interpret such tests as having to do with Keynesian theory if he will interpret measured income in this equation as standing as a proxy for the volume of assets as well as having something to do with the Keynesian transactions motive for holding money.

As to viewing equation (1) as having to do with the modern approach to the transactions demand for money, if one wishes to replace the volume of transactions with the level of income as an argument in the function he must postulate a stable relationship between these two variables, and again this is an assumption that is more likely to be true over short periods of time than over long ones. However, it is worth noting that there is no empirical evidence on this matter one way or another. There is another difficulty with this interpretation of equation (1). The Baumol theory predicts that the individual unit will experience economies of scale in money holding. Thus, for a given volume of transactions in an economy, the amount of money needed to finance them at a given rate of interest and cost of transforming income earning assets into money, will depend upon how they are distributed among the participants in the transactions making process. One individual making a given volume of transactions will need less money than two individuals undertaking half of that volume each. There is nothing in equation (1) to take account of this distribution factor, nor is there any variable that would measure possible variations in the 'brokerage fee' for transforming other assets into money. Thus one must conclude that the formal connection between equation (1) and a modern theory of the transactions demand for money is tenuous indeed. The best one can do in this connection is perhaps to regard equation (1) as an hypothesis that the total economy behaves with respect to money holdings 'as if' it were an individual whose ratio of transactions to income was constant. Tests of equation (1) can then be regarded as tests of this analogy. Despite these difficulties, equation (1) must ultimately stand or fall by its predictive powers, and it has been tested and interpreted in both the ways discussed above.[9] If one wishes further justification for its having been tested, he need only look at the chapter on the demand for money in any macro-economics text-book.

Equation (2) which has as its arguments the volume of non-human wealth and the rate of interest may be related to the Tobin approach to monetary theory, though it does not have to be, since, as noted above, there are suggestions in early Cambridge monetary theory that a formulation similar to this might prove fruitful, and Brunner and Meltzer tend to regard it as a variant of Friedman's approach. However, if it is to be so interpreted, it is worth noting that the Tobin approach would only predict a stable relationship of this kind for a given degree of riskiness of bonds. Otherwise some variable measuring this concept should be included in the function. Thus there is an implicit assumption of the constancy of this factor in equation (2). Moreover, it should be noted that there are many more types of risk in the world than those associated with the rate of interest on bonds, including, be it said, risks associated with holding money at times of fluctuating prices, so that there is yet another implicit assumption that it is the risks inherent in fluctuations in the interest rate on bonds that dominate here. Once more, then, there is something of a gap between the strict logic of the theory and the empirical formulation of the demand for money equation that is based on it. Nor is equation (3) any different in this respect, for Friedman's theory is really one of consumer behaviour, and in the aggregate economy firms also hold money. Thus there is an assumption that firms behave 'as if' they were households with respect to holding cash balances.[10] Here, too, as in equation (2), no attention is paid to possible effects of variations over time in the distribution of wealth on the aggregate demand for money function.

Thus, in no case, is there any easy logical series of steps between the basic micro-economic theories of the demand for money discussed in the preceding section of this paper, and the simple aggregative functions that have been tested empirically. This does not mean that the latter were not worth testing, however, since results based on them are clearly capable of casting some light on the macro-economic problems raised at the outset of this essay. Nor does it mean that the micro-theory is of no relevance, for it is far from obvious that these aggregate functions would ever have been conceived of had their outlines not been suggested by the basic theoretical work. In this case, the process of getting from the micro-economics to the aggregate hypotheses may have been more a matter of intuition than of logic, but it is no less important for that. The only thing that one must be careful of here, is interpreting any empirical results achieved as throwing direct light on the underlying micro-economic hypotheses. This would clearly be a misleading step to take.

There are more problems than these, however, in going from the underlying theories of the demand for money to the empirical tests, for none of them even in the forms in which they have been cast at the beginning of this section, tell us much about how to define the actual time series to be used in testing them. Even the correct definition of money has been, and indeed still is, a matter of dispute, for it is only in the context of a transaction approach to the problem of the demand for money that theory gives us any guide as to how to define money. Here, it is plain that the tests should be concerned with the demand for 'means of exchange' and hence, as far as the United States economy is concerned, the definition of money as currency in the hands of the non-bank public plus demand deposits at commercial banks is dictated by the theory.

This is hardly the case with the other approaches to the problem. Thus, if the similarity of money to a consumer durable is stressed, and it is viewed as an asset that yields services as a source of immediate purchasing power, a strong case can be made for including time deposits at commercial banks in the definition since they are, in effect, for the consumer sector if not always for firms, convertible on demand into either cash or demand deposits. A similar, and almost as strong case, can be made for deposits at Mutual Savings Banks and Savings and Loan Association shares. Similarly, if one stresses the fact that money is an asset whose capital value does not fluctuate with the interest rate, then from this point of view all the above mentioned assets are perfect substitutes.

At heart then, the problem of the correct definition of money is one to be settled in terms of how close the public regards the substitutability of these various assets, and of how precise are the predictions one wants out of his theory. These are largely empirical matters, and most workers have treated them as such, for though they have confined themselves generally to the liabilities of the commercial banks, most of their tests have been performed with money defined both to include and exclude time deposits. Below, it will be noted which tests were performed with which definition of money.

There has been little disagreement about the two income series. Measured income has almost always been defined as net national product, while the permanent income demand equation has always employed Friedman's expected real income, a series derived from his work on the consumption function.[11] Two concepts of non-human wealth have been used. Brunner (3, 4), Latané (16), Meltzer (17, 18) and Heller (9) have defined it as the net worth of the private sector including government debt outstanding. They thus treat the government as being 'outside' the private sector. This writer (14), however, used a saving relationship as a proxy for the first difference of non-human wealth, and since net national product minus consumption was the variable that the relationship was supposed to yield, implicit in its use is the postulate that any additions to the assets of the government are to be viewed as having the same effect as the demand for money as additions to the assets of the private sector.[12] Its use also implies that issues of government debt for the financing of government consumption are to be regarded as simultaneous additions to the assets and liabilities of the private sector. The question as to whether the general public do in fact look upon themselves as 'stock holders' in the government, regarding the income coming from government acquired assets as making future tax payments lower than they otherwise would be, and regarding new issues of debt as increasing future tax liabilities as well as future interest receipts, is a complicated one, and there is no space to go into it here. Suffice it to say that this writer, like Johnson (12) (pp. 342–3) finds the arguments in favour of this view quite convincing, while Brunner, Meltzer and Heller apparently do not.[13]

There has also been some disagreement about the appropriate interest rate to use. In principle, the role of the interest rate in any demand for money function is to measure the opportunity cost of holding money. It should then measure the yield on holding assets other than money over whatever is the average horizon for which plans are made to hold cash balances. In practice, two series are available for the United States economy over a sufficiently long period to make them usable in long time series tests. They are the yield on 20 year bonds and the yield on 4 to 6 month commercial paper, and different workers have made different choices between them. Again even though 20 years may seem an excessively long horizon for planning to hold money, the correct choice is ultimately an empirical matter, and the evidence on it will be discussed below. For the moment, it is sufficient to note that the two series are in fact so highly correlated with one another that the choice of interest rate is in no way critical for any of the qualitative results achieved.

In the context of the rate of interest it might also be pointed out that interest paid on assets treated as money, either explicitly as in the case of time deposits, or implicitly, in the case of demand deposits, has been ignored in all the tests dealt with here. The reason for this omission is no more that the absence of reliable data to measure these rates. The fact that good results have been obtained in the absence of data on such rates suggests that they have been fairly constant over time relative to other rates.

V

It was not until the last three or four years that work that sought to comparatively test the empirical relationships set out earlier was carried out. Earlier, Latané (16) showed that a variant of equation (1) fitted the monetary history of the United States fairly well since he was able to explain a good deal of the variation of the ratio of money holdings (defined to exclude time deposits) to income in terms of variation in the rate of interest. Teigen (20) also worked with a version of equation (1) and showed that it could be combined with a supply of money function to produce a good explanation of observed fluctuations in the velocity of circulation. Friedman (8) attacked the same problem in terms of equation (2) and demonstrated that cyclical fluctuations in the ratio of measured to permanent income could well be responsible for observed fluctuations in the velocity of circulation of money defined to include time deposits.[14]

Though this work of Friedman, Teigen and Latané clearly has value, its contribution lies in establishing the theories tested as worthy of further testing, rather than in establishing them as the 'best' theories of the demand for money. This can only be done by testing theories together against similar data and finding out which will explain most. This work has mostly been carried out by Karl Brunner and Allan Meltzer (3, 17), with one contribution from H.R. Heller (9), and another from this writer (14).

The results of these comparative tests are by no means unanimous in their selection of the best theory, though the evidence is fairly strong as to which is the worst. Only Heller, who worked with post World War II quarterly data found that equation (1) provided the most satisfactory explanation of the data and then only when a narrow definition of money was used, but he confined his work to equations (1) and (2), not testing the permanent income hypothesis of the demand for money.[15] However, my own tests, which used annual data, found that it was *only* in the post World War II period that equation (1) could be judged better than equation (2), and then only on the basis of the reasonableness of its regression coefficients rather than in terms of its explanatory power. Over the whole period 1892–1960, and for various other sub-periods, equation (1) was never the best performer on any criterion for either definition of money, and usually the worst. Brunner and Meltzer (3) and Meltzer (17) obtained similar results, and since a wide variety of tests and statistical techniques were used in this work it seems safe enough to give up equation (1); as safe, at any rate, as it ever is to give up an hypothesis in the face of empirical evidence in a subject whose experimental technique is as imprecise as is that of Economics.[16] It is safer still to give up the transactions demand analogy interpretation of this equation, since in no tests did anyone find convincing evidence in favour of this interpretation's prediction of economies of scale in money holding.[17]

As to equations (2) and (3), the matter is much more open. In my own tests (14), which fitted a demand function for money using regression analysis of the first differences of annual data for the period 1892–1960 and for various sub-periods, equation (3) proved the best performer for either definition of money. A broad definition, however, yielded the best of all results here in terms of the explanatory power of the independent variables and in terms of the stability of the parameters of the function between sub-periods, though equation (2) performed better when time deposits alone were taken as the dependent variable.[18] Brunner and Meltzer (3) obtained different conclusions, and the methods used by them differ enough from those of this writer to make it difficult to assess the reasons for this.

First, rather than fit a demand function for money directly, they chose to fit a function which explained velocity, based upon a demand function; second, they use log. linear regressions on the levels of the data, rather than the linear first difference technique employed by this writer; and third, rather than use orthodox statistical techniques to assess the relative explanatory power of the competing hypotheses, they used an ingenious test which works as follows.[19] They took the first ten years' observations of their total time period, fitted a regression to it, and used the parameters of this regression to predict the velocity of circulation for the eleventh year of their sample. They then took the second through eleventh years' data and predicted velocity for the twelfth year, and so on, all the way through their data. They compared the predictive errors of the competing hypotheses (in terms of the mean absolute percentage error and the root mean square percentage error) and judged the hypothesis with the lowest error of prediction to be the best. In these terms, as noted above, they found functions based on equation (1) to be inferior to those based on either equation (2) or equation (3), whatever the definition of money used, but they also found, contrary to my results, that equation (2) provided the sounder basis for predicting the velocity of circulation of money, however defined. Also, the narrower definition of money proved better than one which included time deposits. Though the differences involved here were only marginal ones, and did not always hold for shorter sub-periods within their sample, the same may be said of the results that this writer obtained.[20]

Thus, the choice between non-human wealth and permanent income as an argument in the demand function for money is one that is still to be settled. This writer has his own preference for permanent income here, but it is based on largely *a priori* reasons which will be taken up below. Here, I am concerned only with the empirical evidence and this, pending further work, must be regarded as inconclusive.

So far, I have said nothing about the rate of interest, apart from mentioning Latané's result. Only Friedman (8) found evidence to deny the importance of this variable. His method was to fit a regression of the logarithm of the money stock on the logarithm of permanent income to cycle average data and to use the relationship thus measured to predict annual variations in income velocity. He found that the errors in prediction arising from this approach were not closely related to any rate of interest variable. The present writer (15), however, duplicated Friedman's experiment but included the rate of interest in the initial regression equation. It was found that the variable was statistically significant and that the predictive performance of the equation for annual data was considerably improved.[21] Thus Friedman's tentative conclusion that the rate of interest was of minor significance in the demand for money function would seem to be disproved by this result.

Quite apart from this there is an enormous preponderance of evidence in favour of including the rate of interest in the demand for money function. All the tests of Brunner and Meltzer (3, 4), and Meltzer (17), Heller (9), and this writer (14, 15), find this variable to be significant, regardless of the particular interest rate series used, and as noted above there has been disagreement on the matter of which interest rate series is the most appropriate. Brunner and Meltzer used the yield to maturity on 20 year bonds in their empirical work, but as already mentioned this seems to imply an excessively long planned holding period for money. Heller (9) and this writer (15) tested the relative explanatory power of this rate and of the yield to maturity on 4–6 month commercial paper and both found that the latter on the whole performs better. However, as pointed out earlier, the two rates are so highly correlated with one another that the substitution of one for the other seems to make little difference to any of the qualitative results obtained. Only for the quantitative matter of estimating the interest elasticity of demand for money is there any difference. The variance of the long rate is smaller than that of the short rate and hence gives higher estimates of this parameter; between –0.5 and –1.0 rather than between –0.1 and –0.2 as obtained with the short rate (see (15)).

On the matter of the liquidity trap, there seems to be no evidence that it exists as part of a stable demand function for money. Bronfenbrenner and Mayer (2) tested for its existence by seeing if the elasticity of the ratio of money holdings to income with respect to the rate of interest increased as the interest rate fell, and could find no evidence of such a tendency. This writer (15) using both a short and a long rate measured the interest elasticity of the demand for money defined both to include and exclude time deposits for a sample of observations where the relevant rate of interest was below its mean value for the period 1890–1960 and a sample where it was above this mean value. Again there was no tendency for it to be greater in the former case. Brunner and Meltzer, in their prediction tests, were able to predict velocity in the 1950s with regressions based on samples heavily weighted with observations taken in the 1930s without any unusually large errors in prediction. Thus, it seems even safer to give up the notion of the liquidity trap as part of a stable demand for money function than it is to give up the idea that measured income is a variable that belongs in the function.

VI

We are now in a position to summarize the outcome of all this empirical work in the context of the problems raised at the beginning of this essay. As to the interest elasticity of demand for money, it seems that the two extreme possibilities raised there have no empirical support. Only Friedman was able to produce evidence as to the insignificance of the rate of interest for this relationship and everyone else has found evidence to contradict his conclusion. The notion of the liquidity trap, the other extreme possibility, does not seem to have even one piece of evidence in its favour. Thus, if one must choose between the models depicted in Figures 1, 2, and 3, he would be wise to select the second of these as being the one closest to reality. However, this model is, apparently, not as good as all that. The other issue raised, as to whether it was adequate to use a measured income variable in the demand function for money, has been settled in the negative. Though it is not yet clear which variable should replace it, there is a great deal of evidence that measured income is not the best one to use here. Thus, though there is much empirical work to be done in monetary economics, that which has been completed to date seems to have fairly decisively refuted the very model of the demand for money that forms the centrepiece of current textbooks of macro-economic theory, a function that is constrained by measured income and has, as a part of its structure, the liquidity trap. It is rather ironic that the most widely taught notions about the money market should prove to be those with the least empirical validity.

These conclusions, though certainly interesting and relevant, are rather negative ones. In order to deal with the more basic issues raised at the beginning of this paper as to the effectiveness of monetary and fiscal policy, and the like, we need more positive conclusions. As I noted above, though the empirical evidence is indecisive on the matter I prefer permanent income to non-human wealth as the variable with which to replace measured income in the demand for money function. My reasons are as follows.

The simple macro-economic model in terms of which this paper set out the problems of monetary economics has a real as well as a monetary side to it, and the consumption function makes up a part of it. That is to say, implicit in the *IS* curve is the proposition that consumption depends largely upon measured income. This hypothesis has also come under a good deal of empirical attack in the last few years, and it is now widely agreed that some form of permanent income is a better argument in the consumption function than is measured income. Though it is not the only variant of the permanent income concept that is available for the role, the Friedman version of this notion does perform very well here, and certainly does better than measured income.[22] Thus, on grounds of symmetry alone, it would be more convenient to use permanent income in the demand for money function than it would be to use non-human wealth. There is more to it than this though, for as was stressed earlier, macro-economics is primarily concerned with the determination of measured income, and if some variable other than measured income is included in the demand for money function, one needs some idea of the relationship between that variable and measured income in order to deal with the problem of income determination. There is nothing in the current literature that tells us what the relationship between income and non-human wealth might be. This is not the case with permanent income, for it is usually empirically defined as a weighted average of current and past measured income. At the very least this is a good empirical approximation of the relationship between the two variables, and hence is one that might be fruitful to use in the construction of a macro-economic model of income determination.[23] To replace measured income with permanent income in the consumption function and the demand for money relationship gives us a macro-economic model of the determination of permanent income. Moreover, if we are interested in what can cause *changes* in the level of measured income, and it was in terms of changes in income that the basic questions we expect macro-economics to answer were cast at the beginning of this paper, we know that the only way to get a change in the equilibrium level of permanent income at any particular time is for measured income to change in the same direction.

Thus, at the very least, qualitative answers to those questions are available.[24] The fact that there seems to be no evidence in favour of the liquidity trap hypothesis tells us at once that we may never rule out monetary policy as being ineffective (always presuming, of course, that changes in the interest rate affect the level of aggregate demand) and it tells us that in looking for the causes of fluctuations in the level of income, we must not neglect the money market as a possible source of such instability. At the same time, the fact that there is some interest elasticity to the demand for money implies that fluctuations in autonomous expenditure are also a potential factor here. This result also means that fiscal policy can be an effective instrument of economic control. In sum, the evidence tells us that the analysis of the history of economic fluctuations, or of current policy, requires a model which includes both monetary and real influence so that to concentrate solely on one or the other is likely to be misleading. Though this is perhaps what was suspected all along, it is comforting to have our suspicions confirmed by the evidence.

Notes

1. In particular, Section III of this paper which deals with competing theories of the demand for money covers ground that Johnson has already covered. For this reason it is rather brief.
2. Thus, I do not discuss anywhere in this paper the theory of the money supply. My reason for not doing so is that this branch of monetary economics seems to be on a different level to that of the theory of the demand for money, since it is a matter, not of the interacting choices of individuals, but of the legal institutions that surround the operation of the banking system. Thus, one would expect any theory of the money supply to be a good deal less general in its applicability to different times and places than a theory of the demand for money. Besides which, if one wishes to pursue monetary policy, it is helpful that the money supply be in the control of the monetary authorities so that any model which seeks to discuss the effectiveness of monetary policy would do well to include this assumption. One must be careful in applying such a model to the explanation of historical events however, for it is always possible that in the situation being analysed, the money supply was not fully exogenous to the rest of the system.
3. It might also be noted that, in a model with flexible wages and prices the liquidity trap is a barrier to the achievement of full employment, and it needs the introduction of a wealth effect to ensure that full employment and equilibrium are synonymous.
4. Baumol, explicitly applying inventory theory, showed that for a pattern of continuous payments and discontinuous receipts, or *vice versa*, with a brokerage fee on the sale of bonds but not on their purchase, that money holdings would be proportional to the square root of transactions and inversely proportional to the square root of the rate of interest. The introduction of brokerage fees on the purchase of bonds introduces a term in the level of transactions into this relationship, but the net effect is still to leave the demand for money as less than proportional to the volume of transactions.
5. The term 'resources' is Pigou's and he carries out his analysis in terms of a model in which the only good is 'corn', produced once a year. Thus, there is no clear distinction here between wealth and income over the period. As Johnson points out, nowhere in early Cambridge economics is there any analysis of the interrelatedness of wealth and income (see (12), p. 350).
6. One will get a different demand function for money depending on which assumption is made, of course, as has been pointed out by Meltzer, Turvey, and Brechling (see Johnson (12), p. 346). The constant level of wealth assumption would be more appropriate for analysing open-market operations, while the constant volume of bonds would be preferable in the context of the creation of fiat money. Keynes himself did not seem to see the need for making one assumption or the other very clearly.
7. In other words, this is but an application to a special case of Friedman's work on the determinants of consumption. It should be clear that what is 'consumed' here are the services of money that flow from the stock that is held.
8. Such as the tests of Brunner and Meltzer (3, 17), and Latané (16).
9. Brunner and Meltzer, and Latané associate this empirical hypothesis with a Keynesian approach to monetary theory. H.R. Heller, however, tends to associate it with a transactions approach.
10. Meltzer (18) has shown that firms' demand for money may be approximated as a linear relationship with sales. Inasmuch as for many firms, sales are equivalent to consumption on the part of the public, and inasmuch as consumption depends upon permanent income, we may rationalize the fact that this difficulty with the Friedman hypothesis does not seem to lead to problems in its empirical application.
11. Heller, however, used a gross national product variable for measured income, arguing that errors

in estimating depreciation were probably such as to make the gross series a better estimate of net national product for his purposes than the published measures of that series. Note that for purposes of fitting a demand for money function, it is accurate measurement of year to year fluctuations in the income series rather than of its level that is critical. Friedman's permanent income series is, of course, a geometrically weighted average of present and past levels of net national product. Its derivation is described in some detail in (7) pp. 143–8.

12. My proxy relationship took the following form. It was postulated that, since saving is the first difference of wealth, and since consumption seems to be a constant fraction of permanent income, saving could be measured by a constant fraction of permanent income plus transitory income. Thus, permanent income and transitory income were the two variables that actually entered the regression in lieu of the first difference of wealth. It should be pointed out that the use of an indirect measure such as this does not necessarily mean that it is less accurate than a direct measure, for there are many errors that can be made in attempting a direct measure of a concept like total non-human wealth.
13. However, it should be noted that Meltzer (17) did test his equation using a Goldsmith estimate of the same concept of wealth used by this writer. He found that it performed very badly, and I am unable to explain the discrepancy between his results and my own in this regard unless it arises from the fact that whereas my regressions were cast in *per-capita* real terms his used nominal values of the data not deflated for population.
14. Friedman used the money stock as a proxy variable for the demand for money, and this procedure has become a common one. It is to be defended by assuming first that the money market, as observed, is approximately always in equilibrium, and that at least some of the variables that appear in the demand function for money do not appear in the supply function. This matter is discussed in detail by Friedman (8). It is also worth noting that when Brunner and Meltzer fitted supply and demand equations for money simultaneously (4), they found no evidence to contradict results that Meltzer has obtained earlier (17) fitting a demand function alone, with the money stock standing as the measure of the demand for money.
15. The function which Heller fitted was cast in money, rather than real terms, and he used money income, rather than real income and the price level separately. Thus using a log. linear relationship he fitted

$$M \cdot P = a(Y \cdot P)^{b_1} \cdot r^{b_2}$$

rather than

$$M \cdot P = aY^{b_1} \cdot P \cdot r^{b_2}$$

which would be more in keeping with basic theory. Thus, his results are hard to assess, since there is a similar problem in his formulation of equation (2).

16. This writer used linear regression analysis of the first differences of the data; Meltzer used log. linear regression analysis of their levels, whilst Brunner and Meltzer used a prediction test described below.
17. Edward Whalen (23), who tested an empirical expression explicitly grounded in the Baumol hypothesis on data for a cross section of firms, where one might expect a transactions motive to be more likely to dominate money holdings, found no consistent evidence to support this notion either, nor indeed could he find much evidence for the stability of the function he fitted, with or without economies of scale in money holdings.
18. This anomalous result led me to conclude that though a broad definition of money was the better one to use time deposits seem to fulfil more than one role in the portfolio so that any definition of money could only be regarded as an approximation to the theoretical concept.
19. As mentioned earlier, the variable used to measure non-human wealth also differs. It should further be noted that in their formulation of equation (2), Brunner and Meltzer include the ratio of measured to permanent income as a variable which they interpret as a proxy for the rate of return on human wealth.
20. It should be noted that the criterion minimized by Brunner and Meltzer in fitting the function was, of course, the summed squared residuals of the logarithm of velocity. This is more akin to the root mean square percentage error of prediction than to the mean absolute percentage error, and on the basis of the former statistic the permanent income demand function, with money defined to include time deposits, proved to be the best of those they tested.
21. There are two minor differences in the tests. Friedman used data from 1869–1957, whereas this writer began with 1890 owing to the absence of interest rate data for earlier years. Also, whereas

Friedman predicted velocity, this writer predicted money holdings. The relationship with the rate of interest included predicted more accurately in 44 out of 65 cases.

22. The two principal rivals here are the Friedman hypothesis, and the Modigliani life cycle hypothesis. Recent work by Robert Holbrook (11) shows that both are better than a simple measured income function, and that, of the two, the Friedman version is slightly to be preferred.
23. It should be noted, however, that there is a slight difference in income concepts. Keynesian income is defined so as to equal the aggregate demand for goods and services. The Friedman concept includes such items as the flow of services coming from consumer duables which clearly has nothing to do with Keynesian aggregate demand. Thus, there is an added element of approximation arising from this factor in going from a permanent income model to one that tells us something about aggregate demand.
24. To get quantitative conclusions, however, which must be our ultimate aim, we obviously need much more evidence than we have at present. We would need a formal model of the relationship between permanent and measured income complete with measures of the lag patterns inherent in the process of going from one equilibrium to another. It should be noted that when I speak of equilibrium permanent income, I mean a value of that variable equal to measured income and hence not changing.

Bibliography

1. Baumol, W.J. 'The Transactions Demand for Cash – An Inventory Theoretic Approach'. *Quarterly Journal of Economics* **66** (November 1952): pages 545–56.
2. Bronfenbrenner, M. and T. Mayer. 'Liquidity Functions in the American Economy'. *Econometrica* **28** (October 1960): pages 810–34.
3. Brunner, Karl and Allan H. Meltzer. 'Predicting Velocity: Implications for Theory and Policy'. *Journal of Finance* **18** (May 1963): pages 319–54.
4. ——. 'Some Further Evidence on Supply and Demand Functions for Money'. *Journal of Finance* **19** (May 1964): pages 240–83.
5. Fisher, Irving. *The Purchasing Power of Money*. New York, 1911.
6. Friedman, Milton. 'The Quantity Theory of Money, A Restatement'. In *Studies in the Quantity Theory of Money*, edited by Milton Friedman. Chicago, 1956.
7. ——. *A Theory of the Consumption Function*. Princeton, NJ, 1957.
8. ——. 'The Demand for Money – Some Theoretical and Empirical Results'. *Journal of Political Economy* **67** (June 1959): pages 327–51.
9. Heller, H.R. 'The Demand for Money – The Evidence from the Short-Run Data'. *Quarterly Journal of Economics* **79** (June 1963): pages 219–46.
10. Hicks, J.R. 'A Suggestion for Simplifying the Theory of Money'. *Economica* **2** (February 1935): pages 1–19.
11. Holbrook, Robert. *Alternative Models of Consumer Behaviour: The Permanent Income Cycle and the Consumption Life Cycle*. University of California at Berkeley, Doctoral Dissertation, June 1965.
12. Johnson, Harry G. 'Monetary Theory and Policy'. *American Economic Review* **52** (June 1962): pages 335–84.
13. Keynes, J.M. *The General Theory of Employment, Interest, and Money*. London and New York, 1936.
14. Laidler, David. 'Some Evidence on the Demand for Money'. *Journal of Political Economy* **74** (February 1966): pages 55–68.
15. ——. 'The Rate of Interest and the Demand for Money'. *Journal of Political Economy* **74** (December 1966): pages 545–55.
16. Latané, H.A. 'Cash Balances and the Interest Rate – A Pragmatic Approach'. *Review of Economics and Statistics* **36** no.4 (October 1964): pages 477–509.
17. Meltzer, Allan H. 'The Demand for Money: The Evidence from the Time Series'. *Journal of Political Economy* **71** (June 1963): pages 219–46.
18. ——. 'The Demand for Money: A Cross Section Study of Business Firms'. *Quarterly Journal of Economics* **77** (August 1963): pages 405–22.
19. Pigou, A.C. 'The Value of Money'. *Quarterly Journal of Economics* **37** (November 1917): pages 38–65.
20. Teigen, R. 'Demand and Supply Functions for Money in the United States'. *Econometrica* **32** no.4 (October 1964): pages 477–509.
21. Tobin, James. 'Liquidity Preference as Behaviour Towards Risk'. *Review of Economics and Statistics* **25** (February 1958): pages 65–86.

22. ——. 'The Interest Elasticity of Transactions Demand for Cash'. *Review of Economics and Statistics* **38** (August 1956): pages 241–7.
23. Whalen, Edward. 'A Rationalization of the Precautionary Demand for Cash'. *Quarterly Journal of Economics* **80** (May 1966): pages 314–24.

3 The permanent income concept in a macroeconomic model

Introduction

I had learned from Karl Popper that scientists test theories, modify them in the light of what they learn, and then proceed to further testing. In the 1950s and 1960s, we had learned that consumption and the demand for money depended upon permanent income, so what was more natural than to modify *IS–LM* in the light of this new knowledge. The paper was submitted to the *American Economic Review* just as Donald Tucker's (1966) analytically similar, but conceptually somewhat different, paper appeared, so it was not accepted there. I was sufficiently upset that I could not get the title of the latter paper right when I acknowledged its existence in the version of this piece that was eventually accepted by *Oxford Economic Papers*. The relationship between this paper's results and that of a long line of subsequent literature in which overshooting effects occur as a consequence of time lags in structural relationships should be obvious to the reader.

Chris Archibald and Dick Lipsey were very critical of my use of geometry in this paper, suggesting that it showed an unacceptable lack of technical competence on my part. A subsequent paper (C12) on the same topic was written largely to prove that I could manipulate difference equations if people insisted that I did so, and it was no doubt more elegant. I was at Manchester, and working on other things altogether, by the time this second piece appeared; it did not add a great deal to my original results either, and what it did add about adjustment lags was, I now believe, wrong. (See Chapter 11, below.)

Reference

Tucker, D. (1966), 'Dynamic Income Adjustment to Money Supply Changes', *American Economic Review*, **56**, June, 433–49.

THE PERMANENT-INCOME CONCEPT IN A MACRO-ECONOMIC MODEL[1]

By DAVID LAIDLER

I

THOUGH the economist possesses many sophisticated tools for the analysis of the macro-economy, perhaps none is so versatile as the simple model which, having evolved from the *General Theory*, now forms the centre-piece of any course or textbook in basic macro-economics. However, increasingly in recent years, the behaviour relationships embodied in the model have become the object of empirical investigation and all of them, one way or another, have been modified in the light of accumulated evidence. Little has formally been done to put these modifications back into the framework of a complete model, to see how different it is in its implications from the original one and it is the object of this paper to begin the task on a simple level.

Here I shall concentrate on the consumption function and the demand for money function, setting to one side the problem of the demand for investment goods. The reason for this is simple enough. The basic framework of the Keynesian macro model is static in nature, and most modifications that have been suggested for the investment function involve some form of the accelerator relationship. This essentially dynamic concept is not one that can be easily forced into a static model. Thus, though there are still plenty of interesting models to be built that focus on the accelerator, I will not attempt to incorporate it in the analysis that follows.

The simple Keynesian consumption function makes consumption a function of measured income, and it is widely agreed that this formulation of the relationship is inadequate except as a first approximation. Economists now prefer to talk in terms of consumption being determined by some longer-run income concept, whether it be permanent income as suggested by Friedman, or life-cycle income as postulated by Modigliani.

[1] The work reported in this paper was done independently and in ignorance of the results recently reported by Donald Tucker in his 'Lagged Responses to Money Supply Changes' *American Economic Review* 1966. This paper differs from Tucker's in the following respects. It deals with responses to changes in autonomous expenditure as well as in the money supply, it is more concerned with the impact effects, rather than the long-run effects, of such changes, and finally it uses simple geometry and algebra rather than difference equations to obtain its results so that it should be accessible to more readers.

I am grateful to Mr. E. Neave of the University of California (Berkeley) and also to the members of the Continuing Seminar in Money and Banking of the same institution whose discussions of an earlier draft of this paper resulted in many improvements in the current version. Remaining errors and omissions are, of course, my own responsibility.

12 PERMANENT-INCOME CONCEPT IN A MACRO-ECONOMIC MODEL

Similarly, though there is wide agreement that the rate of interest belongs in the demand for money function as Keynes suggested, measured income has been found to be inadequate as the other argument. As with the consumption function there is no clearly 'best' replacement, for though both permanent income and non-human wealth perform better than measured income in the relationship, there is still room for debate about the relative merits of these two variables.

Thus, it is possible to construct various macro-economic models, but here I shall limit myself to one. I shall put together a model in which measured income is replaced by permanent income in both the consumption function and the demand for money function. Though future empirical work may show that this is not the best possible of all simple static models to construct, there is sufficient evidence accumulated already to enable us to have some confidence in its being better than existing models, inasmuch as the behaviour relationships included in it conform more closely to the evidence than do the simpler ones they replace.

In the next few pages, I shall follow conventional patterns of exposition by first of all dealing with the real goods market and the multiplier relationship in isolation. I shall go on to consider the money market, and finally I shall put the two sides of the model together in terms of a variant of the Hicksian *IS–LM* diagram. The analysis as far as possible will be geometric, though simple algebra will be used at one stage in order to clarify certain matters.

II

The basic problem which macro-economics seeks to handle is the determination of the level of income and employment, and it is current *measured* income which is important here. Since this variable does not appear in our behaviour relationships, we must have some notion about its relationship to its replacement, permanent income, before we can deal with such problems. Fortunately we do not have to look far for such a relationship, for Friedman has suggested that permanent income may be measured as a geometrically weighted average of present and past measured income:

$$Y_{p_t} = bY_t + b(1-b)Y_{t-1} \ldots b(1-b)^n Y_{t-n} \ldots \qquad \text{II (1)}$$

This definition is of course a measurable proxy for what is inherently an unmeasurable concept, but since it is this proxy that has been used for much of the empirical work that has been done on the permanent-income hypothesis, it is hard to see how we can go far wrong if we employ it in our model and I shall therefore do so.[1]

[1] Thus, the reader who does not find the permanent-income notion too appealing may regard this as a model in which the public responds to changes in income with a distributed lag.

It follows from II (1) that we may write the relationship between consumption and permanent income in two forms.[1]

$$C_t = kY_{p_t} \qquad \text{II (2)}$$

or

$$C_t = k(1-b)Y_{p_{t-1}}+kbY_t. \qquad \text{II (3)}$$

The first of these is the usual Friedman formulation of the function and the second is analogous to a Keynesian consumption function with an intercept whose value depends upon previous levels of income. However, both represent the same relationship. In Fig. 1 both forms of this relationship are graphed, for on the horizontal axis both permanent and current income are measured. Now it is in the nature of the weights of permanent income that if current measured income is equal to the previous period's permanent income then current permanent income is equal to both of them. From this it follows that in time t the measured income version of the consumption function must cut the permanent-income version at the level of permanent income ruling in time $t-1$.

Let us now add investment at some given level of the rate of interest to the model and assume that the economy is in equilibrium at level of income Y_t, which, in turn is equal to $Y_{p_{t-1}}$ and to Y_{p_t}. Now suppose that the rate of interest falls so that the level of investment rises. The effect of this is shown in Fig. 2. Both of the aggregate demand $(C+I)$ functions are shifted up by an equal amount, and if a multiplier process works itself out fully between times t and $t+1$, the initial effect on the economy will be to raise the level of income to Y_{t+1}.

This, however, can be only a temporary equilibrium, for permanent income in time $t+1$ is greater than it was in time t, so that in time $t+2$ the current-income version of the consumption function must shift up. It is easy to determine the amount by which it does so geometrically. The two aggregate demand curves show the same relationship between aggregate demand and permanent income, but it has been convenient to draw them in different forms. However, if we know the level of aggregate demand that rules with measured income of Y_{t+1} given previous permanent income of Y_{p_t} we know that the value of $Y_{p_{t+1}}$ must be such as to yield the same level of aggregate demand. It can, then, be located at $Y_{p_{t+1}}$ in Fig. 2. Thus the current-income version of the aggregate demand

[1] It should be noted that there is a slight difference between Keynesian consumption, usually regarded as being equivalent to expenditure by the consumer sector, and Friedman's consumption concept, which includes the flow of services from consumer durables but not their purchase. The latter are to be regarded as being determined by some sort of accelerator process, and hence are, as already noted, omitted from the model. It is worth pointing out that a simple accelerator which makes investment a function, say, of the first difference of permanent income could be written as $I_t = d(Y_{p_t}-Y_{p_{t-1}}) = d(bY_t-bY_{p_{t-1}})$ and included in a model like the one we are describing here. Its inclusion would, however, make the simple geometry employed here unusable.

curve that is appropriate for time $t+2$ will cut the permanent-income version at this point, and income in time $t+3$ will be determined. It should be obvious that this is a process that will continue indefinitely as measured and permanent income approach the point Y_p^*, approaching one another as they do so.[1]

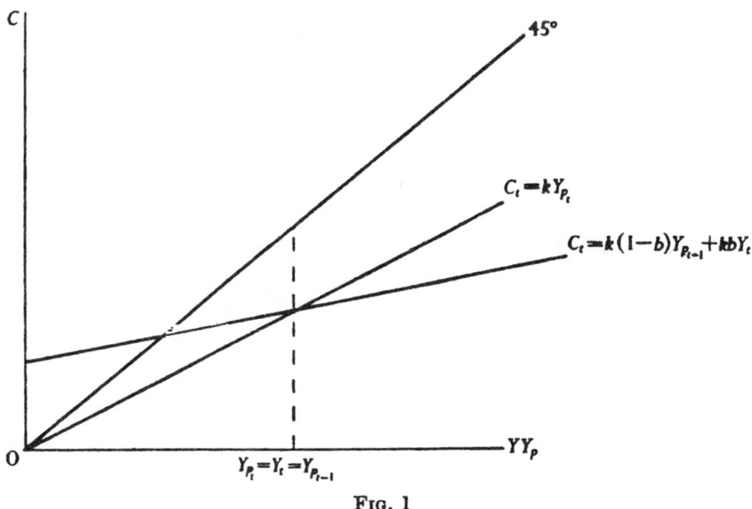

FIG. 1

The analysis of the money market in isolation is, if anything, even simpler than that of the real-goods market. Again one can make use of the fact that permanent income can be written as a combination of current measured income and past permanent income, and hence the demand for money function may be written as either

$$M_{d_t} = mY_{p_t} - lr_t \qquad \text{II (4)}$$

or as

$$M_{d_t} = m(1-b)Y_{p_{t-1}} + mbY_t - lr_t. \qquad \text{II (5)}$$

Both of these relationships are graphed in Fig. 3, for a given rate of interest r_t, with the market assumed to be in full equilibrium with permanent income equal to measured income at time t. Now suppose the rate of interest rises in time $t+1$. Both functions will shift in the manner shown in Fig. 3, and measured income must change to Y_{t+1} if the market is to be equilibrated. However, this involves the level of permanent income shifting to $Y_{p_{t+1}}$. Thus, by exactly similar reasoning to that used in the multiplier analysis, in time $t+2$ the measured-income version of the demand for money function will cut the permanent-income version at that level of

[1] Since the short-run consumption function cuts the long-run one at a point to the left of Y_p^*, and is sloped more shallowly, measured income can never exceed Y_p^*. Moreover, permanent income must always increase so long as measured income is above it, so that measured income must continue to rise toward some limit. Since any level of measured income to the left of Y_p^* is attainable and exceedable, this limit must be Y_p^*.

permanent income. Hence the market will be in full equilibrium at the end of two periods.[1]

III

The analysis of markets in isolation is not of much interest in itself, for it is the interaction of the money and real goods markets in the income-determination process that is the central analytic difficulty of macro-economics. The most widely used tool for dealing with this problem in a

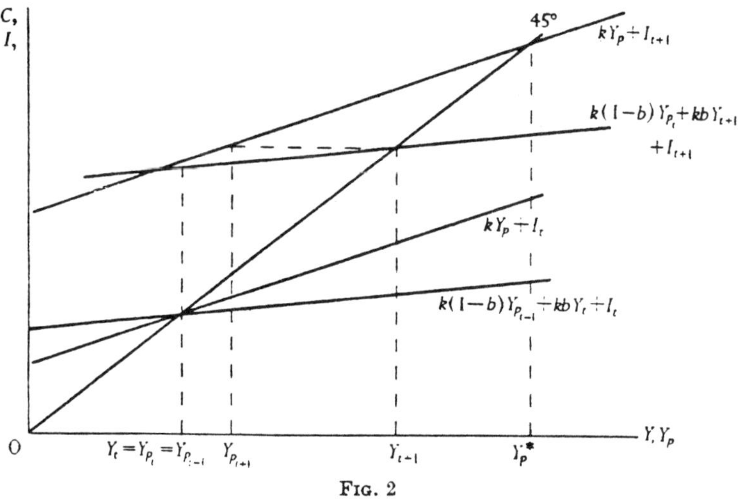

Fig. 2

comparative static framework is the Hicksian *LM–IS* curve diagram, and the permanent-income model we have here may be set out in these terms. From the real-goods market we may derive a long-run *IS* curve ($I_p S_p$ in Fig. 4) which shows the locus of levels of permanent income and the rate of interest that yield equilibrium in the real-goods market. We may also derive a short-run curve (*IS* in Fig. 4) which will show the equilibrium combinations of measured income and the rate of interest that must rule in the goods market given the previous period's permanent income. Since this relationship is based upon the short-run consumption function of Fig. 1, and since there is one such function for every level of permanent income, there will be a short-run *IS* curve passing through every point on $I_p S_p$. Moreover, since the short-run value of the multiplier is smaller than its long-run value ($1/1-bk$, as opposed to $1/1-k$) the short-run curve will be the steeper of the two.

[1] Though the real goods market is equilibrated over only an indefinitely long period the money-market analysis suggests that the latter can come to rest after but two periods. This is due to the fact that there is no circular flow mechanism like the multiplier process at work in the money market to keep it in motion. It should be noted that the choice of a linear demand for money function here has no particular significance for the qualitative nature of the results obtained.

16 PERMANENT-INCOME CONCEPT IN A MACRO-ECONOMIC MODEL

Long- and short-run curves, ($L_p M_p$ and LM in Fig. 4) may be derived from the analysis of the money market, and since a given change in the interest rate requires a bigger change in measured income than it does in permanent income to ensure that the money market remains in equilibrium with a given money stock, the short-run curve will be more shallowly sloped than the long-run one. Again, there is a short-run curve passing through every point on $L_p M_p$.

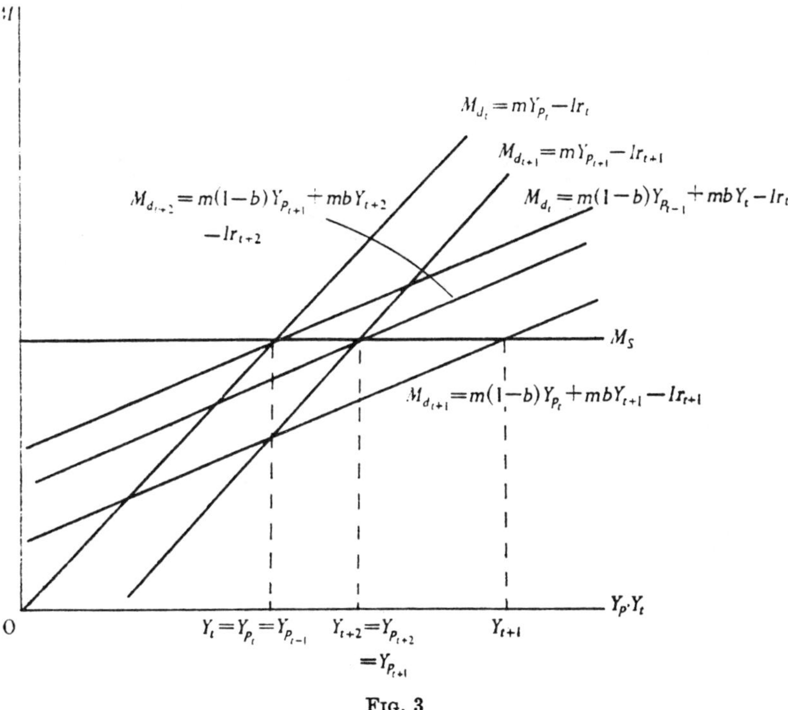

FIG. 3

With the aid of this apparatus we may analyse the effects of changes in the exogenous variables of the model in the usual way. Consider, for example, an increase in the supply of money. This will shift $L_p M_p$ to the right, and the final equilibrium of the system will be at Y_p^* in Fig. 5. However, we may also say something about the path to this new equilibrium by making use of the short-run curves. Immediately after the shift in the money supply in time $t+1$ the relevant short-run IS curve is that which cuts the long-run curve at Y_{p_t}, and the relevant short-run LM curve cuts the new long-run one at the same level of permanent income. Their intersection at Y_{t+1} gives us the first point on the path to final equilibrium. However, the short-run LM curve, which shows equilibrium combinations of income and the rate of interest in the money market, given the previous period's permanent income, is but another way of showing equilibrium combinations of permanent income and the rate of interest. Thus, in a manner exactly analogous to the way in which we found the new level of permanent income in the analysis of the multiplier, we may locate $Y_{p_{t+1}}$ on $L_p M_p$. Thus, in time $t+2$ the relevant short-run IS and LM curves cut the long-run ones at this level of permanent income, and a new level of measured income is determined. After a disturbance in one of the exogenous variables, permanent income moves along the $L_p M_p$ curve until

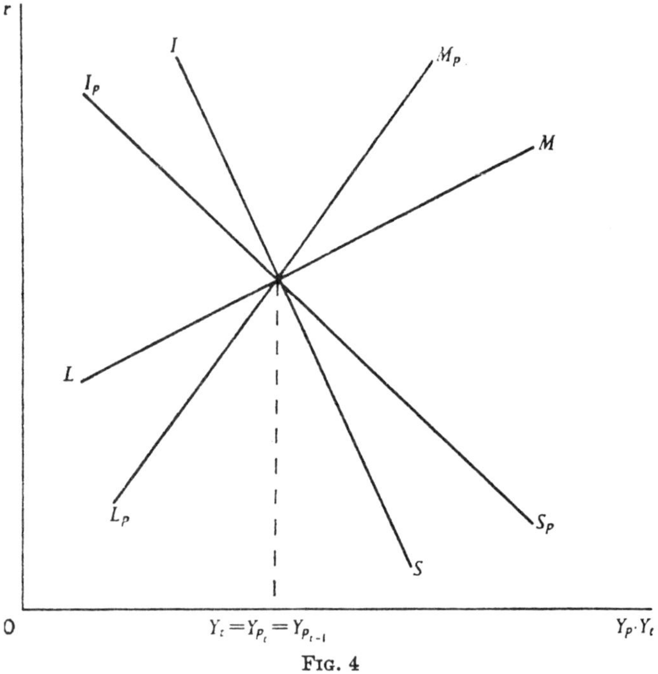

FIG. 4

Y_p^* is reached, since the shifting of the short-run curves period by period must be continued until measured and permanent income converge on each other. Clearly, this type of analysis may be carried out for rises or falls in either the money stock or the level of autonomous expenditure.

IV

Now it will be noted that the predictions of this model as to the behaviour of measured income in response to a change in one of the exogenous variables are not precise, for though income will unambiguously rise in the first period in response to say, an increase in the money supply, it can rise by more than the ultimate shift in the level of permanent and hence of measured income. Though the short-run IS curve lies to the left of the long-run one in the relevant region of Fig. 5, the short-run LM curve lies to the right of the long-run function so that whether their intersection lies to the right or the left of Y_p^* clearly depends upon their slopes. Thus, the impact effect of a change in one of the exogenous variables on the level of measured income may be greater than its final effect, for the ambiguity just mentioned arises in the case of shifts to either the left or right of both the *LM* and *IS* curves.[1]

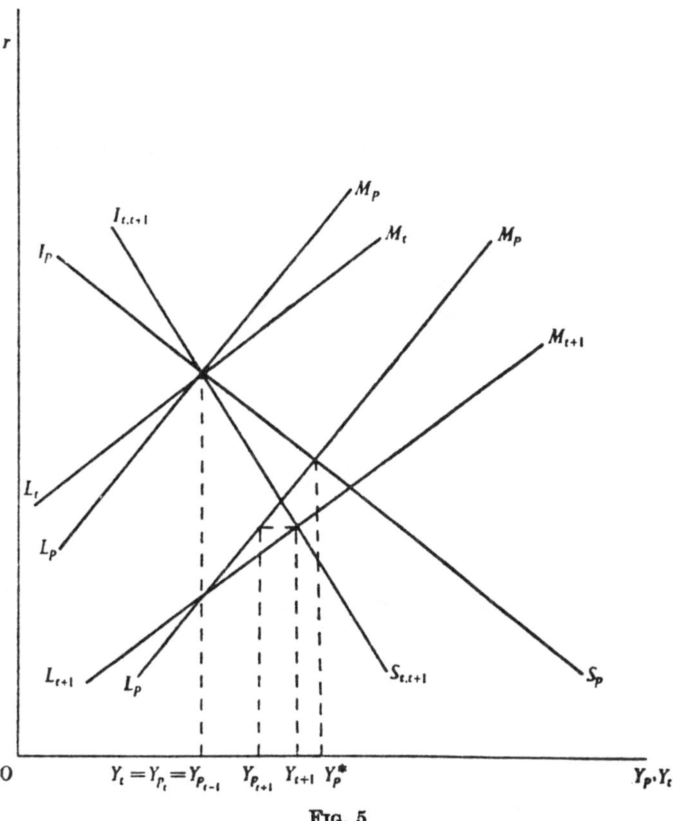

FIG. 5

To make this matter clear, consider the following analysis. The long-run version of the model we are dealing with here may be written as follows, in linear terms for the sake of simplicity.

$$C_p = kY_p \qquad \text{IV (1)}$$

$$I = A - ar \qquad \text{IV (2)}$$

[1] In his interesting paper 'Professor Friedman on the demand for money', *JPE* 73, pp. 545–51 (Oct. 1965), A. A. Walters obtained the result that if the demand for money depends upon permanent income, then the impact effect of a change in the money supply on the level of income will always be greater than the long-run effect. In terms of the model presented here, Walters's model is obtained if the parameter relating the demand for money to the rate of interest is set equal to zero. The fact that Walters could find little empirical backing for his prediction is probably to be interpreted as indicating that the rate of interest is in fact an important determinant of the demand for money.

$$Y_p = C+I \qquad \text{IV (3)}$$

$$M_d = mY_p - lr \qquad \text{IV (4)}$$

$$M_d = \bar{M}. \qquad \text{IV (5)}$$

From this we may derive the curve $I_p S_p$

$$r = \frac{A}{a} - \frac{1-k}{a} Y_p \qquad \text{IV (6)}$$

and $L_p M_p$

$$r = -\frac{\bar{M}}{l} + \frac{m}{l} Y_p. \qquad \text{IV (7)}$$

Combining these and solving for the equilibrium level of permanent income, we have

$$Y_p = \left(\frac{1}{(1-k)+(am/l)}\right)A + \left(\frac{1}{(l-lk/a)+m}\right)\bar{M} \qquad \text{IV (8)}$$

so that

$$\frac{\partial Y_p}{\partial A} = \frac{1}{(1-k)+(am/l)} \qquad \text{IV (9)}$$

and

$$\frac{\partial Y_p}{\partial \bar{M}} = \frac{1}{(l-lk/a)+m}. \qquad \text{IV (10)}$$

The short-run version of our model is

$$C_t = kbY_t + k(1-b)Y_{p_{t-1}} \qquad \text{IV (11)}$$

$$I_t = A_t - ar_t \qquad \text{IV (12)}$$

$$Y_t = C_t + I_t \qquad \text{IV (13)}$$

$$Md_t = mbY_t - lr_t + m(1-b)Y_{p_{t-1}} \qquad \text{IV (14)}$$

$$Md_t = \bar{M}_t. \qquad \text{IV (15)}$$

From this model we get, as a short-run *IS* curve

$$r_t = \frac{k(1-b)}{a} Y_{p_{t-1}} + \frac{A_t}{a} - \frac{(1-kb)}{a} Y \qquad \text{IV (16)}$$

and as a short-run *LM* curve

$$r_t = \frac{m(1-b)}{l} Y_{p_{t-1}} - \frac{\bar{M}_t}{l} + \frac{mb}{l} Y_t. \qquad \text{IV (17)}$$

Measured income then equals

$$Y_t = \left(\frac{k(1-b)}{1-kb+(amb/l)} - \frac{m(1-b)}{(l-lkb/a)+mb}\right)Y_{p_{t-1}} +$$

$$+\left(\frac{1}{1-kb+(amb/l)}\right)A_t + \left(\frac{1}{(l-lkb/a)+mb}\right)\bar{M}_t \qquad \text{IV (18)}$$

so that

$$\frac{\partial Y_t}{\partial A_t} = \frac{1}{1-kb+(amb/l)} \qquad \text{IV (19)}$$

and

$$\frac{\partial Y_t}{\partial \bar{M}} = \frac{1}{(l-lkb/a)+mb}. \qquad \text{IV (20)}$$

20 PERMANENT-INCOME CONCEPT IN A MACRO-ECONOMIC MODEL

Now, in these terms, the question as to whether the impact effect of policy is greater or smaller than its ultimate effect asks whether expressions (9) and (10) are smaller or greater than expressions (19) and (20) respectively. Since these expressions all have a numerator of unity, the answer depends only upon the relative values of their denominators. If the denominator of (9) is smaller than that of (19) then the ultimate effect of an increase of autonomous expenditures is greater than its initial effect, and vice versa. Similar implications about changes in the money supply follow from the relative magnitudes of the denominators of (10) and (20). Thus we must evaluate

$$\left(1-k+\frac{am}{l}\right)-\left(1-kb+\frac{amb}{l}\right) \qquad \text{IV (21)}$$

and

$$\left(\frac{l-lk}{a}+m\right)-\left(\frac{l-lkb}{a}+mb\right) \qquad \text{IV (22)}$$

which may be rearranged as

$$\left(k-\frac{am}{l}\right)b-\left(k-\frac{am}{l}\right) \qquad \text{IV (23)}$$

and

$$\left(\frac{lk}{a}-m\right)b-\left(\frac{lk}{a}-m\right) \qquad \text{IV (24)}$$

respectively.

These expressions may be positive, negative, or zero, depending upon the magnitudes of k, a, l, and m. Moreover, the sign of (24) will always be the same as that of (23). That is to say, if the impact effect of a change in the money stock is greater than the long-run effect, then the impact effect of a change in autonomous expenditure will be greater also than its long-run effect. Thus, if:

$$k-\frac{am}{l}=x \qquad \text{IV (25)}$$

where x has any arbitrary value, then

$$\frac{lk}{a}-m=\frac{lx}{a} \qquad \text{IV (26)}$$

so that if x is positive then so is this last expression, if x is zero or negative, then so again is this last expression.

If the impact effect of some policy change is greater than its long-run effect, we need some mechanism which will reverse the direction of change of income in subsequent time periods to bring it back towards its ultimate level. This is to be found in the influence of changes in permanent income on subsequent levels of measured income. From IV (18) we have

$$\frac{\partial Y_t}{\partial Y_{p_{t-1}}}=\frac{k(1-b)}{1-kb+(amb/l)}-\frac{m(1-b)}{(l-lkb/a)+mb} \qquad \text{IV (27)}$$

which may be rewritten as

$$\frac{\partial Y_t}{\partial Y_{p_{t-1}}}=\left(\frac{1-b}{(l-kb/a)+(mb/l)}\right)\left(\frac{k}{a}-\frac{m}{l}\right). \qquad \text{IV (28)}$$

The first term is clearly positive, and as to the second term, it follows from IV (25) that

$$\frac{k}{a}-\frac{m}{l}=\frac{x}{a} \qquad \text{IV (29)}$$

Thus, the impact effect of a policy change can only be greater than the long-run effect if the parameters of the model are such as to make the effect of a change in permanent income on subsequent measured income opposite in sign to the initial change in permanent income.

If the initial response of measured income to a shift in either the money supply or autonomous expenditure is to change by more than the ultimate equilibrium shift in permanent income, then the direction of change of measured income will be opposite in subsequent periods as the model approaches its final equilibrium.

V

So far, it has been shown that a macro-economic model built in terms of permanent, rather than measured, income may be used to determine the level of measured income. It has also been shown that such a model is simple enough to be dealt with in terms of geometry and elementary algebra. However, to be of any interest, the model must tell us something that we did not know before or raise some questions we had not thought of asking, about the process of income determination. I would claim that this model does so.

To begin with, it implies a time path for the adjustment of interest rates to a change in one of the exogenous variables that does not obviously follow from simpler models. Specifically, it shows that the initial effect of an increase in the money supply or a decrease in autonomous expenditure will be to lower interest rates by more than the amount by which they will ultimately fall. This follows from the fact that in the relevant regions of the *IS–LM* framework the short-run *LM* and *IS* curves lie unambiguously below the long-run relationships. An exactly opposite result holds for the effects of an increase in autonomous expenditure or decrease in the money supply. Thus, for example, the model tells us that there is nothing strange about the coexistence of rising interest rates and rising income after an expansion in the money supply for if the world is so structured that the impact effects of a change in monetary policy on income are less than the long-run effects, we would expect to observe, after an initial fall in rates, rising interest rates and rising income. The reader may easily derive the type of observations that would follow from other shifts of the exogenous variables.

The predictions which the model makes about the effects of shifts in the exogenous variables on the level of income have already been dealt with in some detail above, and it has been shown that it is only the direction of change of income in response to the initial impact of such a shift that is unambiguously predicted. Thereafter, the time path of income may reverse its direction.[1] This is interesting from two points of view. First, it shows to be totally erroneous the view that the effect of the permanent-income hypothesis of consumption, in stretching the multiplier process out over time, also implies that the effects on the level of income of some policy change will be spread out over time. The introduction of the money market explicitly into the picture destroys the logic of this position, except of course in the extreme case of the liquidity trap. More interesting than this, however, is the fact that the model's ambiguity on the time path of income poses an interesting empirical question that would certainly bear investigation, since it raises a new problem in the context of the important issue of the leads and lags with which an economy responds to policy changes. It should also be noted that the model is quite flexible in this regard, for though the analysis carried out in the last section was done in terms of the model being disturbed from a position of full equilibrium, there is no reason why one cannot manipulate it in order to analyse the effects of policy changes that occur while the economy is on the move from one long-run equilibrium to another. For example the model is quite capable of predicting that the level of income might respond to a decrease in the money supply by increasing less rapidly than it otherwise would have done rather than by actually falling, if the economy is already expanding to a new level of income in response to some previous policy change. Again, this is not an unambiguous prediction, for it will depend upon the amount by which the money supply is decreased, and upon relative magnitudes of the parameters of the model.[2] Once more it is seen that this analytic framework raises interesting empirical questions about important issues.

[1] This point has a rather interesting implication in the region of full-employment income, since it suggests that a policy shift, be it an increase in the money supply or an increase in government expenditure, which is not strong enough to bring the economy up to full employment as its final equilibrium, could nevertheless generate full employment and inflationary pressures initially.

[2] There is an intriguing sidelight here. The model implies that, with a given amount of autonomous expenditure, the level of income at any time will depend not only on the level of the money supply, but also on the amount by which it might have changed in previous periods. It is only the long-run equilibrium level of permanent income that depends solely on the level of the money stock. Thus there appears to be a good deal more sense in Friedman's practice of comparing changes in the rate of change of the money supply with changes in the level of income than some of his critics have been willing to allow. This is a point that would clearly bear further theoretical examination. It should be noted that Walters makes a similar observation.

Thus, the simple model presented in this paper appears to pass the final test for such an analytic framework, inasmuch as it does seem to tell us something that was not obvious before, and inasmuch as it does raise interesting empirical questions. Though I would not argue that it by any means exhausts what can be done in the way of incorporating the results of recent empirical work in macro-economics in a simple theoretical scheme, it would seem that it represents an interesting beginning to such an endeavour.

The University of Essex

4 Money, wealth and time preference in a stationary economy

Introduction

This paper grew out of the so-called Pesek and Saving (1967) controversy during which monetary economists painfully worked out the differences between accounting conventions and economic theory in the analysis of monetary policy. It deploys an analytic apparatus which derived from my PhD work on housing, and which I also used to analyse some welfare aspects of the gold standard at about this time (see C7).

This paper would perhaps have attracted more attention had it discussed variations in the inflation rate, and hence located itself in the context of debates about the super-neutrality of money. Instead it dealt with variations in the rate of return paid by the emitters of money on their liabilities, and placed itself in the context of parochial, but then quite important, British debates about making the banking system more competitive. These two matters are, of course, from the point of view of this kind of model, analytically identical, as I well knew at the time, but I did not know how to market my results. There should have been, but was not, a reference to Miguel Sidrauski's famous (1967) paper here, because this essay is, in essence, a geometrical representation of a special case of his analysis, albeit with the extra wrinkle of an endogenous time preference rate. I cannot explain this omission.

Finally, I note with some satisfaction that the demand for money in this paper is explicitly motivated in 'value of shopping time' terms – not bad for 1969, but hard to square with an equilibrium model, as I began to realize a few years later. (See Chapter 8, and D31.)

References

Pesek, B. and Saving, T. (1967), *Money, Wealth and Economic Theory*, New York: Macmillan.

Sidrauski, M. (1967), 'Rational Choice and Patterns of Growth in a Monetary Economy', *American Economic Review*, Papers and Proceedings, **57**, May, 534–44.

MONEY, WEALTH AND TIME PREFERENCE IN A STATIONARY ECONOMY*

DAVID LAIDLER *University of Manchester*

Monnaie, richesse et préférence temporelle dans un modèle statique de l'économie. L'analyse qui suit est conduite dans le cadre d'un modèle néo-classique simple avec population stable et secteur monétaire. Elle concerne les conséquences de l'introduction des versements d'intérêts en rapport avec les balances réelles, sur les propriétés de l'équilibre du secteur réel du modèle. Les secteurs réels et monétaires sont indépendants l'un de l'autre tant que l'on maintient certains postulats, particulièrement la constance du coefficient de préférence temporelle. Cette indépendance disparaît avec la définition d'un coefficient de préférence temporelle qui varie avec le degré de richesse; de plus, la nature des conséquences sur le secteur réel de l'introduction des versements d'intérêts en rapport avec la détention d'actifs sous forme monétaire, change suivant le caractère des formes de richesse que l'on retient comme facteurs de comportement.

Trois concepts de richesse sont retenus : la « richesse non-humaine, » y compris la monnaie évaluée à la marge comme flux de disponibilités (« money valued at its marginal rate of amenity flow »); le concept précédent, plus la valeur présente du revenu de travail; enfin, la définition exhaustive, qui inclut même la valeur présente du flux d'avantages intramarginaux que procure la monnaie comme flux de disponibilités (« the present value of the intra-marginal amenity flow accruing from money »). Dans le cas où le coefficient de préférence temporelle varie en fonction du degré de richesse, telle que définie en dernier lieu, la présente analyse nous amène à montrer que l'introduction des versements d'intérêts en rapport avec la détention d'actifs liquides a pour conséquence une diminution du rapport capital/travail de même que de l'output du secteur de la production. L'auteur prétend que cette conclusion est plus satisfaisante, de prime abord, que celles que l'on tire à partir de définitions plus limitatives de la richesse.

I

Recent work in monetary theory has caused us to revise quite radically our ideas about such matters as the inter-relationships between wealth and money and about the likely effects on other economic variables of paying interest on money.[1] This paper attempts to advance our understanding of these problems

*I am deeply in the debt of Harry Johnson, Allan Meltzer, Frank Hahn, and Michael Parkin whose most helpful comments on an earlier draft of this paper have greatly contributed to my understanding of the matters with which it deals. The paper was also read to the University of Essex Department of Economics Staff Seminar and received much useful criticism. All errors and misunderstandings that remain in this version are, of course, my own responsibility.

[1]The origin of much of the recent work on this problem is B. Pesek and T. Saving, *Money, Wealth and Economic Theory* (New York, 1967). Relevant recent literature includes E. Feige and D. Nichols, "Money, Wealth and Welfare," mimeograph (University of Wisconsin Social Science Research Institute, 1968); M. Friedman, "The Optimal Quantity of Money" in M. Friedman, *The Optimal Quantity of Money and Other Essays* (Chicago, 1969); Harry G. Johnson, "Inside Money, Outside Money, Income, Wealth, and Welfare in Monetary Theory," *Journal of Money, Credit and Banking*, I (Feb. 1969), 30–46; D. Laidler, "The Definition of Money: Theoretical and Empirical Problems," *ibid.* (forthcoming). However, basic contributions to this literature are M. Bailey, "The Welfare Costs of Inflationary Finance," *Journal of Political Economy*, 64 (April 1956), 93–110, and P. Cagan, "The Monetary Dynamics of Hyperinflation," in M. Friedman, ed., *Studies in the Quantity Theory of Money* (Chicago, 1956).

Canadian Journal of Economics/Revue canadienne d'Economique, II, no. 4
November/novembre 1969. Printed in Canada/Imprimé au Canada.

a little further by showing that the manner in which we define wealth can affect the predictions we might make about the consequences, for variables such as the capital-output-ratio, the level of output and the rate of interest, of introducing interest payments on money. As might be expected, the definition of wealth becomes important the moment we allow the stock of "wealth" to enter any of the behaviour relationships in the model.

For the sake of keeping what becomes a quite complex taxonomy as simple as possible, I deal only with the comparative statics of a model in stationary state equilibrium; this is quite sufficient to show the importance of the matters discussed.[2]

II

The economic model with which I shall deal is simple and quite conventional. The production sector turns out only one good which may be either consumed or used as a non-depreciating capital good to which there are diminishing returns. The population is of given and unchanging size and devotes a fixed proportion of its time to providing labour services to the production sector. This gives a labour force of fixed size and ensures that, in the absence of technical change, the economy's equilibrium is a stationary one. The balance of the population's time is spent either trading, which yields no utility in and of itself, or at valuable leisure. Real money balances are also used in the trading process and are a substitute for labour; they are assumed to be produced at zero social cost. They may be regarded as producing leisure and as yielding diminishing returns in the production of leisure. The marginal utility of goods is assumed constant throughout the analysis that follows. The reader may, however, if he wishes, add, as a reason for postulating a downward sloping demand curve for money, diminishing marginal utility of leisure to diminishing returns to money in the production of leisure. In either event, the assumption of a constant marginal utility of goods, and that of the independence of the marginal utilities of money and goods, permit us to use the area under the demand for money curve as an unambiguous measure, in terms of goods, of the amenity flow yielded by money holding.[3] As usual, distribution effects are assumed to be non-existent.

The foregoing assumptions will be maintained throughout the analysis. On the other hand, the supply-of-wealth-function, the analogue in a stationary model of the savings function of a growth model, will be allowed to vary in three ways. First, it will be assumed that the rate of time preference is independent of the level of wealth and constant; second, it will be assumed that greater wealth makes people *less* patient so that the rate of time preference

[2]Though, as is indicated below (n. 4) there is a growth model analogous to the model developed here so that the results are of potentially broader application.

[3]The Marshallian assumptions made here have the unfortunate property of implying a zero income elasticity of demand for money. However, the geometric technique used requires that these assumptions be made. They are necessary if the area under the demand for money function is to give an unambiguous measure of the amenity flow arising from money holding.

increases with wealth; finally, because it seems at least as reasonable to argue that people might become *more* patient as they get wealthier, the consequence of letting the rate of time preference fall as wealth increases will be investigated.[4]

Another assumption permitted to vary concerns what the public regard as their wealth: first the notion of wealth will be confined to marketable assets only – that is physical capital and money, and, where there are commercial banks of positive equity value, this equity also; second, the notion of wealth will be extended to include the present value of labour income from the production sector of the economy; finally, the present value of the flow of leisure money's use confers upon the population will also be included in the definition of wealth.

The experiment to be performed with these variations on the model is as follows. I shall compare a situation in which money bears no interest with one in which interest is paid on money at the equilibrium rate of return to physical capital and ask how this change affects the other variables in the model. The simplest case is that in which the rate of time preference is constant and I shall begin by considering it.

In Figure 1, wealth is measured along the horizontal axis in units of the one good that is produced. The rate of interest is measured vertically, and it is worth pointing out explicitly that, since the interest rate is a rate of flow, all areas in this and subsequent diagrams may be measured as flows of the single good. The curve *AE* is the marginal product of capital, whose quantity is measured from left to right, while the curve *CF* is the demand for money function, the quantity of money being measured from right to left. With the rate of time preference given at *R*, and no interest being paid on money, equilibrium is established with a capital stock of *OK*, a money stock of *KW*, *ABR* of labour income, and *CBKW* of amenity flow provided by money, *CBD* of this amount being consumer's surplus. This will be the equilibrium situation whether the money stock is the liability of the government or of a privately owned commercial banking system. If money exists by government fiat, the public hold the whole stock of physical capital directly, while if money is the deposit liability of commercial banks, these institutions must hold physical capital in the amount *KW* to balance their deposit liabilities. There is that much less physical capital for the public to own directly, but, because the banks pay no interest on their deposits, the value of their equity is just equal to the present value of the income they earn from holding this physical capital, and this, of course, is equal to *KW*. Part of the capital stock is owned indirectly in the form of bank equity but the public's non-human wealth position is the same as in the fiat money case.

If we introduce interest payments on money, real balances held will increase until the marginal amenity flow from them is zero; $FW = KW'$ of money will

[4]To assume constant returns to scale and exogenous population growth would turn our model into a neo-classical one sector growth model. The saving function analogous to this supply-of-wealth-function has two components, one which maintains the capital-output-ratio over time, between the actual and a desired rate of interest, the desired one being the rate of time preference and the actual one being the ratio of the marginal product of capital to a unit of capital. The latter ratio is referred to as simply the marginal product of capital throughout this paper.

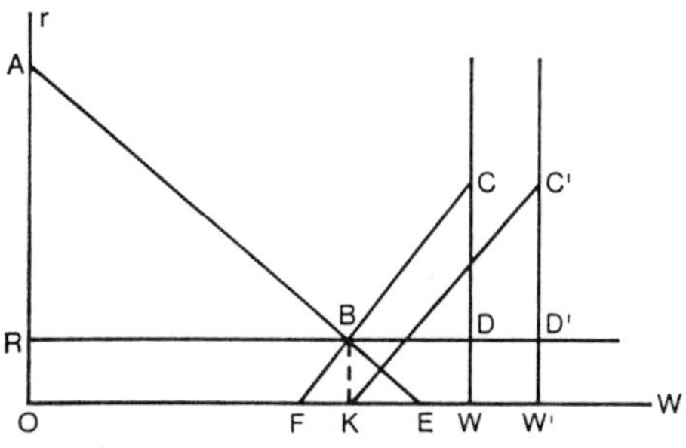

FIGURE 1

be held. Nothing will happen in the real sector of the model, because nothing has affected the constant rate of time preference to which the marginal product of capital is equated. Thus, welfare in the economy is clearly increased by paying interest on money, for physical output does not change and there is an unambiguous increase of *BFK* in the amenity flow yielded by real balances. What happens to "wealth," however, depends upon how it is measured, and how the interest payments on money are financed.[5] If we confine our notion of wealth to non-human wealth, then so long as interest payments on money are financed out of the income to physical capital, the introduction of such interest payments leads to a *fall* in wealth. In the commercial banking case, the equity value of the banks vanishes, and the money stock becomes an indirect way of holding a portion of the physical capital stock; wealth becomes *OK*, as opposed to an initial value of *OW*. If interest payments on fiat money were financed by levying lump-sum taxes on the income to capital, the result would obviously be identical, but if they were financed by taxing labour income, then wealth would increase, by the amount of extra real balances held, to *OW′*; this is because the government would in fact be turning labour income into a return to non-human wealth as far as the public were concerned, by reducing labour income and increasing the income to be earned by money holding.

If the present value of labour income *ABR* is included in our notion of wealth, then the introduction of interest payments on money, no matter how financed, reduces wealth.[6] Initially, when money bears no interest, wealth is equal to *OK* plus *KW* plus the present value of *ABR*. When money does bear

[5]The inter-relationships of measures of wealth with measures of welfare in a model very similar to this one are discussed at some length in Harry G. Johnson, *Essays in Monetary Economics* (London, 1967).

[6]Clearly the case in which labour income is not thought of as being a return to any kind of wealth and the case in which this income is capitalized at the same rate as the income yielded by physical capital are two limits to a continuously variable solution to a problem. When human wealth is not marketable, it is not unreasonable to argue that, at the very least, labour income might be discounted at a rate higher than the marginal product of capital. If it is, then even if we admit the notion of human wealth, the government's ability to tax labour income and pay it out as interest on money is equivalent to making human wealth marketable and hence more valuable. *KW′* is the maximum increase in wealth one can get by replacing a tax on income from capital with one on labour income to pay interest on money. So long as human wealth has some value, then there is some gain, albeit smaller, which falls to zero as the rate of discount applied to labour income approaches the marginal product of physical capital.

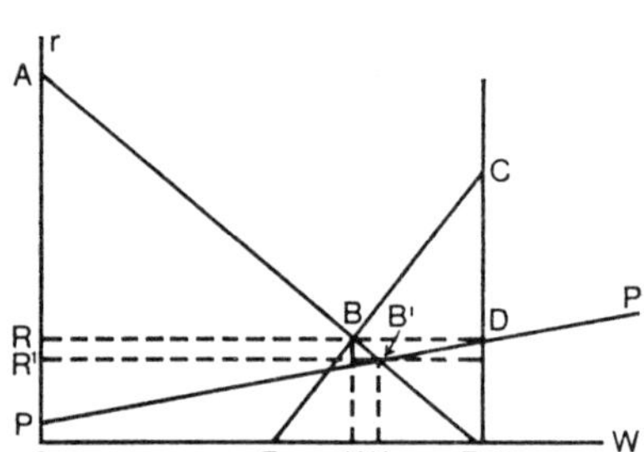

FIGURE 2

interest, the value of the money stock, KW' is just offset by the present value of the taxes that have to be levied to pay the interest; where they are levied or by whom, is of no importance. Finally, if the consumer's surplus arising from the use of money is included in the income discounted to obtain wealth, then wealth clearly increases by the amount ½ FK, which is the present value of BFK.

The last few paragraphs do not seem to have led very far, but the reader would be wrong to infer that they amount to no more than so much accounting. The assumptions of the model as they stand at present may be regarded as a set of sufficient conditions for equilibrium in the real sector of the economy to be independent of what happens in the market for real balances. The assumptions are very restrictive and little modification to them is needed to destroy this independence. If, for example, we were to drop the premise that the supply of labour services to the production sector is proportional to an exogenously given population, and instead permitted the public to choose simultaneously the proportion of their time spent at leisure, at trading, and at work, then the introduction of interest payments on money would presumably lead to more time being spent both at work and at leisure, and hence would lead to an increase in the productivity of capital and a higher equilibrium capital stock and level of output. More important from the point of view of this brief essay, however, we may destroy the independence of the real and monetary sectors in this simple model by letting the rate of time preference vary with the level of "wealth". As soon as we make this modification, the manner in which wealth is measured becomes of critical importance to the model's behaviour, as I will now go on to show.

Figure 2 differs from Figure 1 only in that the marginal rate of time preference increases with "wealth" along the line PP, so that equilibrium exists at a rate of interest R. Figure 2 is labelled exactly as Figure 1 and all distances and areas on it have the same interpretation in the initial equilibrium situation as do the similarly labelled distances and areas of Figure 1. Figure 2 may be used to analyze the effects of introducing interest payments on money, provided we make the additional assumptions that only marketable non-human wealth affects the rate of time preference, and that interest on money is either paid by commercial banks out of the return they earn on the physical capital they own, or, in the fiat money case, by lump sum taxes levied on the

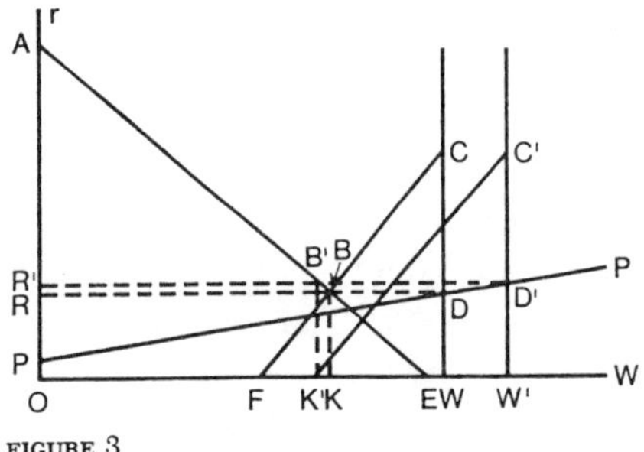

FIGURE 3

return to physical capital. Given these two assumptions, the introduction of interest payments on money will, as we saw above, reduce the public's "wealth" even though they come to be holding more real balances and receive more welfare. Such a reduction in wealth implies that, with an initial capital stock now equal to total wealth of *OK*, the rate of time preference is below the marginal product of capital. Saving equal to *KK′* will have to take place to restore equilibrium at a higher level of output, at a higher capital-output ratio, and at a lower rate of interest *R′*.

As we saw above, to pay interest on fiat money from a tax levied on labour income, when the public do not regard human capital as wealth, leads to an increase in "wealth". This case is analyzed in Figure 3, which is identical to Figure 2 as far as the initial equilibrium is concerned. As we have already seen in the constant time preference case, to pay interest on money out of a tax levied on labour income raises the level of wealth, and hence, in this instance, raises the rate of time preference above the marginal product of capital ruling in the initial situation. There is dissaving of *K′K* of physical capital in this case and the new equilibrium is one at which both output and the capital output ratio are smaller and the rate of interest higher than in the situation where money bears no interest. "Wealth" though ends up at the new higher level of *OW′*, the increase in this case being equal to *FK* minus *K′K*.

In the context of this model, and of the hypothesis that it is only non-human wealth that affects behaviour, there turns out to be a distinction to be made between money on which the interest paid comes from the return to non-human wealth and money whose interest is financed from a tax on labour income, a distinction analogous to that which economists used to make between inside and outside money. As soon as we start treating human wealth capitalized at the marginal product of physical capital as relevant to the rate of time preference, this particular distinction vanishes, as might have been expected. Deposit money and fiat money become identical, regardless of the source of interest payments on the latter. The analysis of this case, though, is not quite the same as that set out in Figure 2, for we must be careful to note that a change in the stock of physical capital changes the stock of human wealth as well, both because it changes the size of labour income and because it changes the rate of discount at which this income is capitalized.

This last effect is not hard to handle in terms of the graphical apparatus used

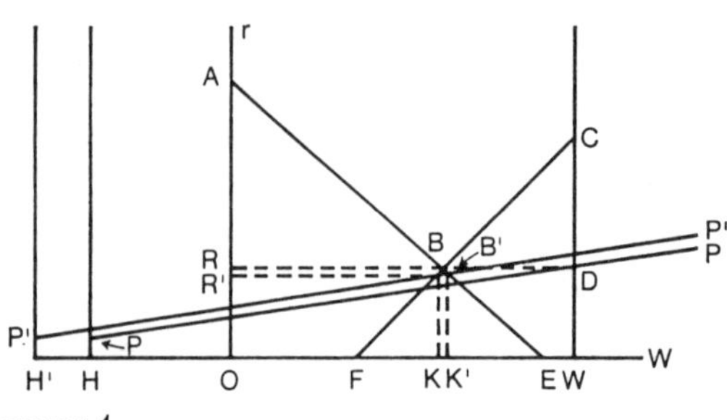

FIGURE 4

so far. We may produce the horizontal axis of Figure 2 to the left and measure human wealth from right to left along it. We then have Figure 4, and *OH* is the initial equilibrium stock of human wealth. The line *PP* now originates from a vertical axis at *H* rather than *O*, but as far as the initial equilibrium situation is concerned, matters are just as they are in Figure 2. When interest payments on money are introduced, the initial effect is to lower wealth and to produce an incentive to saving. As the capital stock increases from *K* toward *K′*, the stock of human wealth increases as well, both because labour income goes up and because the rate at which it is discounted falls. Human wealth approaches *OH′* in value and the line *PP* shifts to the left toward *P′P′*. The result of introducing interest payments on money is still to increase the capital-output-ratio, as well as output, and to lower the rate of interest, but not by as much as when non-human wealth alone enters into the determination of the rate of time preference and interest payments on money are financed solely from the income earned by physical capital.[7]

These conclusions about the behaviour of output, the capital-output-ratio, and the rate of interest are reversed as soon as we permit the present value of the amenity flow yielded by money to become relevant to the determination of the rate of time preference. Figure 5 deals with this case, and it differs from Figure 4 in two respects. First, *OM* measures (from right to left) the present value both of labour income and the amenity flow yielded by cash in the initial equilibrium situation in which no interest is paid on money. Second, because, in the no interest on money case, we have in the past been including *part* of this amenity flow in the computation of wealth (the area *BKWD* in Figures 1–4, whose present value is, of course, *KW*), we must be careful to note that total wealth in the initial situation portrayed in Figure 5 is *MK*, and not *MW*; *KW*, the market value of money holdings, is already included in *OM*. This initial equilibrium situation is characterized by a physical capital stock of *OK*, *KW* of money balances, and an interest rate of *R*. The introduction of interest payments on money initially *increases* wealth in this case (by ½*FK*, the present value of *BFK*) causing *M* to shift leftwards towards *M′* and *PP*

[7]But recall that human wealth being valued at a discount rate exactly equivalent to the marginal product of physical capital, as is implicit in Figure 4, and at zero, as in Figure 3, are limiting cases. If the interest on money is paid from a tax on labour income, then any solution between that given in Figure 3 and that produced by Figure 4 is possible depending upon the rate at which labour income is discounted, cf. n. 6.

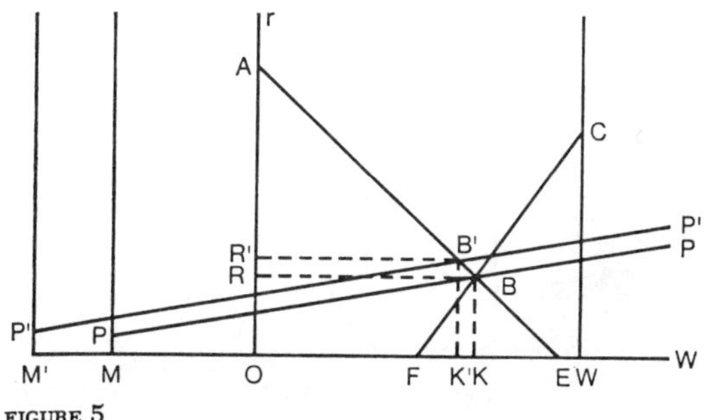

FIGURE 5

to move towards $P'P'$. This tendency of M to shift leftward is, of course, offset to some extent by the tendency of human wealth to fall as the stock of physical capital falls, but the final equilibrium must still be characterized by a smaller capital-output-ratio, with a capital stock OK', a lower level of output, and a higher rate of interest R', than prevailed in the initial situation.

The next step to be taken in this taxonomy is to let the rate of time preference fall with "wealth", and to examine this assumption's implications. However, to go through the mechanics of this in any detail would be needlessly repetitious, not to say tedious. Suffice it to state the obvious conclusion then, that all those results obtained with an upward sloping time preference schedule are reversed when it slopes downward, and to illustrate this point with one case only, that in which all income from whatever source is relevant as far as the calculation of wealth is concerned.

Figure 6 is just like Figure 5, except that the line PP slopes downward, and is drawn asymptotic to the horizontal axis to capture the reasonable enough notion that the rate of time preference, even if it may fall, can never become negative. The introduction of interest payments on money initially increases wealth by $\frac{1}{2}FK$ and shifts M to the left towards M' The resultant shift to the left of PP in this case is equivalent to a *downward* rather than an *upward* shift of the curve so that the marginal product of capital at OK comes to be above the rate of time preference. There is thus an increase in the capital stock to say nothing of a further shift leftwards of M as the stock of human wealth rises. This process continues until a new equilibrium is reached at a lower rate of interest, a higher level of output, and a higher capital-output-ratio.[8]

III

The most general conclusion to be drawn from the foregoing analysis is that the question of how to measure wealth is much more than a matter of choosing a convenient accounting convention. Arguments for and against the classification of the return to labour income as being a return on "human wealth" are well known, and there is little to be added to them here. It is worth noting

[8]This system is prevented from "running away" with a constantly increasing stock of wealth by the assumption that the rate of time preference is asymptotic to zero combined with the implicit assumption that the marginal product of capital can reach zero.

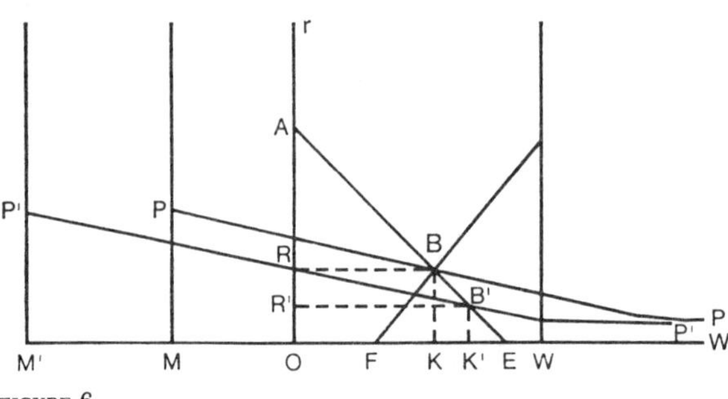

FIGURE 6

again, though, that if one does decide that the wealth concept is best limited to non-human wealth, then one must always be careful to specify the source of the income used to pay interest on money in a model such as the one analyzed above. There is, as we have seen, a useful distinction to be made between money whose interest is paid from income produced by capital (analogous to the old "inside money" notion) and money whose interest is paid from labour income (analogous to "outside money"). Indeed this distinction is useful anywhere when labour income is capitalized at a rate different to that applied to income yielded by physical capital.

Once the notion of human capital is admitted it seems plausible to this writer also to regard as relevant for behaviour the present value of the amenity flow coming from money. Leisure is just as much a good as any other, even though it cannot be marketed but must be consumed by its own producer. Indeed, not to capitalize this particular flow of income into wealth produces distinctly counter-intuitive results in the model I have analyzed. For time preference to increase with wealth means that current consumption gets more valuable relative to future consumption as wealth increases. Money is a capital good produced at zero opportunity cost and to introduce interest payments on it gives the community more of it, that is more future consumption, at no cost. It would be intuitively appealing to suppose that this would lead to some current consumption out of capital, future consumption having become relatively less scarce. The foregoing analysis leads to this conclusion only when the amenity flow from money is discounted and treated as wealth. If it is not, the model predicts a substitution *away* from current consumption into the accumulation of real capital as a direct result of the increase in real balances. This is a most peculiar result, and its peculiarity must be the property of the premise that yielded it; that premise is the exclusion of the amenity flow arising from cash balances from the stream of income discounted to calculate wealth.[9] Even though the question of the most useful definition of wealth is not one to

[9]A similar argument, though with all signs reversed, may be built around the properties of the model when the rate of time preference falls with wealth. One would expect that, when more of a capital good is acquired free, the fall in the relative desirability of present goods to future goods implied by the falling rate of time preference would lead to the acquisition of more capital. This will only happen if the amenity flow from cash balances is capitalized as a component of wealth.

be settled by *a priori* reasoning, this premise is one of which we ought at least to be most suspicious.

To put it shortly, the analysis presented in this paper shows that the difficulties in the concept of wealth revealed by recent work in monetary economics are much more than matters of accounting when "wealth" enters any behaviour relationship. The same analysis, however, in revealing the difference that various definitions of wealth can make to the behaviour of a quite conventional model, also suggests that, when dealing with questions having to do with the interaction of the real and monetary sectors of economic models, the most intuitively appealing results are produced by capitalizing all income, including the total amenity flow yielded by real balances.

5 The Phillips curve, expectations and incomes policy

Introduction

I had doubts about the policy trade-off interpretation of the Phillips curve from the mid-1960s onwards, but though Friedman had discussed expectations in this context while I was still a graduate student, I did not immediately see the importance of this, as my paper with Bernard Corry (C3) shows. I was, however, beginning to think about whether some variation upon the modelling of permanent income, as used in Chapter 3, above, but applied to the expected inflation rate, might help me understand these matters better when Phelps's (1967) paper appeared in *Economica*. I therefore recognized its importance, and that of Friedman's (1968) paper, very quickly.

The paper reprinted here was first presented at a Money Study Group conference in early 1971, by which time I had realized that the expectations-augmented Phillips curve could reconcile the phenomenon that came to be called 'stagflation' with a monetary explanation of inflation. On rereading it now, I am pleased by its discussion of the role of what we would now call 'credibility' in reducing the costs of anti-inflation policies, and I am pretty sure that this discussion derived from what I had been taught as an undergraduate about what used to be called the 'announcement effects' of policy. I am less pleased by my evident belief that a less than unit coefficient on lagged inflation implied the existence of a long-run, albeit steep, structural trade-off between inflation and unemployment. Although I never treated error learning as anything other than a first approximation to modelling inflation expectations, I obviously did have a few important things to learn from the subsequent development of the rational expectations idea.

References

Friedman, M. (1968), 'The Role of Monetary Policy', *American Economic Review*, **58**, March, 1–17.

Phelps, E. (1967), 'Phillips Curves, Expectations of Inflation and Optimal Employment over Time', *Economica* NS **34**, August, 254–81.

5. The Phillips Curve, Expectations and Incomes Policy

DAVID LAIDLER*†

I

The 'Phillips curve' made its first explicit appearance in the literature only thirteen years ago and has ever since played a central role in the analysis of inflationary situations.[1] Even though the basic concept is extremely familiar, it is worth discussing it briefly at the outset, for such a discussion will make it much easier to set out the way in which recent work on the role of price expectations in inflationary situations and on incomes policies fits in with the basic analysis.

Fig. 1 depicts a 'Phillips curve'. On the vertical axis is measured the percentage rate of change of money wages per unit of time ($\dot{W}$), and on the horizontal axis the percentage of the labour force unemployed (U). The curve itself depicts a smooth negative relationship between two variables and cuts the horizontal axis at a positive level of unemployment. Now there are three questions (at least) to be asked about the relationship depicted in Fig. 1. What economic theory predicts that it should exist? Does empirical evidence confirm that it does exist? Finally, what does the existence of such a relationship imply for the design of economic policy in the face of inflation?

A textbook of scientific method would suggest that these questions should be answered in the order they are posed above. However, the world is not so tidy, and in early work on the relationship it was the last two questions that received most

* David Laidler is Professor of Economics at the University of Manchester.

† I am grateful to Michael Parkin for his help at all stages of the preparation of this essay, and to George Zis for drawing my attention to a number of errors in the first draft. Remaining errors and omissions are, of course, my own property.

attention. In his original paper, Phillips (1958) paid only slight attention to questions of theory and concentrated on presenting a formidable body of evidence that, at least as far as the United Kingdom was concerned, a relationship such as that depicted in Fig. 1 did exist and indeed had existed unchanged since 1861.

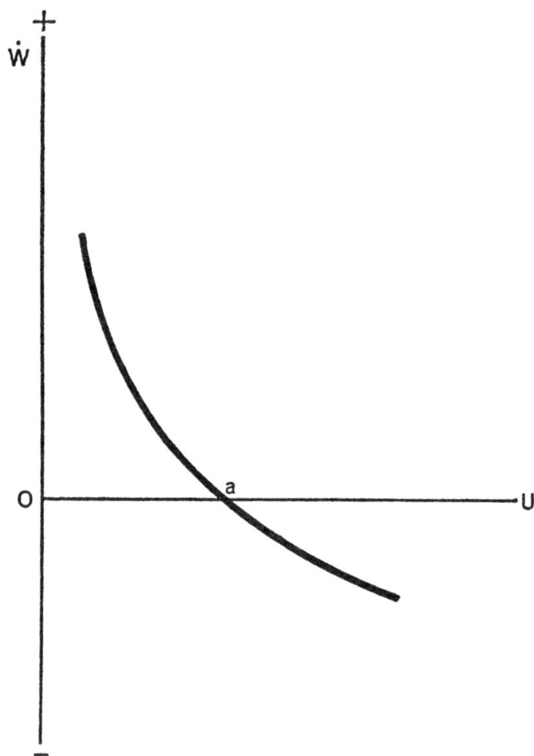

Fig. 1. The Phillips curve

The methods that Phillips used to estimate the form and slope of the relationship were unorthodox, but details of those methods need not in any case concern us here. The important thing to note is that in estimating his curve he applied those methods only to data drawn from before the First World War. He then showed that post-First World War data lay along the very same curve with the post-Second World War data apparently lying closest of all.[2]

Such stability as this in a relationship between two variables over such a long time period is rare indeed in empirical economics, and taken by itself is sufficient to explain a great deal about the rapidity with which economists accepted the Phillips curve. However, there are two other attractive features to the analysis. First, there is the matter of its policy implications. Up till the late 1950s the basic problem for macro-economic policy was thought of as being the simultaneous attainment of price stability and a high level of employment. Though early post-war pessimism about attaining high employment was not justified by events, price stability proved much more elusive.[3] The Phillips curve provided a ready-made explanation for the 'failure' of policy. It suggested that high employment and price stability were incompatible, and that the British economy could only have more of one at the expense of less of the other. To the positive question 'How can one have price stability and high employment?' the Phillips curve seemed to give the answer 'One can't'. It also suggested that it would be more to the point to ask the normative question 'Which combination of unemployment and inflation of those attainable is the most desirable?' Given that economists had been unable to answer the positive question, it is not surprising that they were (and are) attracted by a concept that suggested they were asking the wrong question in the first place.[4]

The final, but not necessarily the least important, attraction of simple Phillips curve analysis lies in the theoretical justification advanced for it. As it stands, Fig. 1 merely portrays a relationship between two variables; it is clearly impossible to carry out any analysis of that relationship unless one has an explanation of why it exists. Lipsey (1960) provided such an explanation. He argued that wages tend to fall in conditions of excess supply of labour and to rise in conditions of excess demand, and he also argued that unemployment varies systematically and inversely with the level of excess demand for labour.[5] Clearly, when labour is in excess supply, that excess supply will manifest itself in unemployed people seeking jobs. However, Lipsey also noted that a national labour market is far from frictionless: even when overall the supply of labour equals the demand for labour there will exist positive 'frictional' unemployment. Since supply and demand being in balance results in a steady wage rate'

Lipsey argued that this frictional unemployment was indicated by point *a* in Fig. 1, where the Phillips curve cuts the horizontal axis. He then argued further that he would expect the pressure of positive excess demand for labour to result in frictional unemployment falling below *a* because jobs become easier to find as the job vacancy rate increases along with the demand for labour.

Excess demand for labour can be produced either by shifts in the supply curve of labour or the demand curve, and is quite independent of the sources of those shifts. Thus Lipsey's theoretical explanation of the Phillips curve makes that analysis neutral as between 'demand pull' and 'cost push' theories of the inflationary process. One economist may regard inflation as being completely the result of bad monetary policy, and another can argue that it is solely the consequence of the activity of monopolistic trade unions, but either position leaves room for its proponent to accept the Phillips curve analysis as elaborated by Lipsey. In short, the Phillips curve and its policy implications seemed to provide an insight into the nature of the inflationary process about whose importance economists on all sides of debates about the likely causes and appropriate cures for inflation could agree.[6]

II

The simple theory of the Phillips curve described above, and its apparent policy implications, were absorbed with remarkable speed into the generally accepted corpus of macro-economics, and though the early and mid-1960s generated a large enough literature on the topic, in my judgement at least, nothing of basic importance was added by this literature to the fundamental contributions of Phillips and Lipsey.[7]

It was not until the late 1960s that two circumstances were to produce both new academic interest in the Phillips curve and genuine intellectual advance in our understanding of it. In Britain, the attempt by the late Government to influence the rate of inflation by way of a prices and incomes policy, whether or not it was prompted by a conscious effort to by-pass the inflation–unemployment trade-off implicit in the Phillips curve, was certainly amenable to interpretation and analysis as such. Incomes policy seems an important subject for study and the

Phillips curve a natural tool to use in the course of that study.[8] In the United States an important role in the resurgence of interest in monetary economics was played by the analysis, both positive and normative, of the relationships between expectations about the rate of inflation and the behaviour over time of the velocity of circulation of money. The variable proved particularly powerful in dealing with data drawn from inflationary situations. It was again a natural, not to say fruitful, extension of the analysis of price expectations to look at their role in the determination of the rate of money wage inflation.[9]

Now in empirically analysing recent British experience, Parkin (1970) has shown that it is helpful to deal simultaneously with the effects of incomes policy and inflationary expectations; both seem to have played a role in generating the relevant data so that the effects of both have had to be allowed for when the data are analysed. However, the two phenomena are analytically distinct, and it will be convenient initially to treat them separately here.

There is, as I noted earlier, an element of ambiguity in Lipsey's analysis of the labour market behaviour that produces the Phillips curve.[10] It starts from two propositions: that the supply and demand for labour determine the equilibrium wage level, and that the rate of change of the wage level in disequilibrium will depend upon the extent of the disequilibrium as measured by the excess demand for labour. Now the Phillips curve is an hypothesis about the behaviour of *money* wages while orthodox supply and demand analysis of the labour market is about the behaviour of *real* wages, and the two concepts are only interchangeable in conditions of price-level stability. If the excess demand for labour is inversely related to the level of unemployment and positively related to the rate of change of the *real* wage, then we may predict that there will exist a stable inverse relationship between the rate of change of *real* wages and the level of unemployment. However, this relationship is not the Phillips curve; to get from it to the Phillips curve we must introduce the expected rate of price inflation into our model.

We need the expected rate of inflation and not its actual current rate because individual wage bargains are struck at discrete intervals and, for any particular bargain, it is not the current price level that matters in determining the real wage that is being aimed at but the level of prices that is expected to rule over the period for which the bargain is being struck. Thus the rate at which the money wage rate will change between any two bargains will be influenced by how price expectations have changed between the times at which the two bargains are struck, and not *directly* by how the price level itself has changed

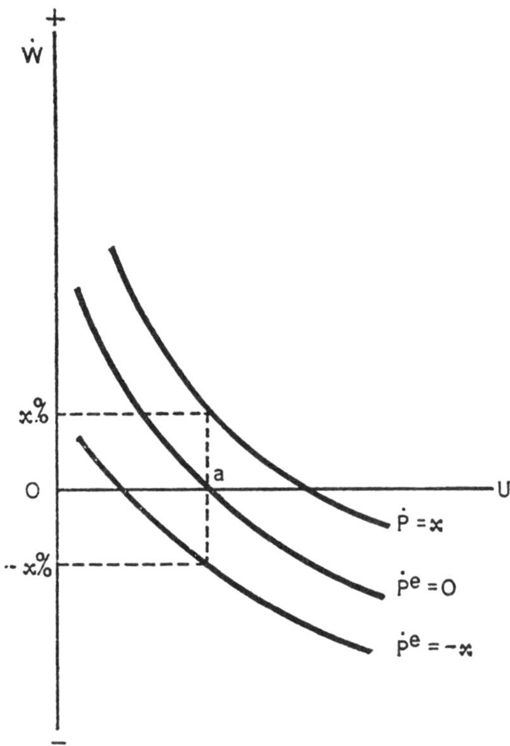

Fig. 2. A family of Phillips curves

over the same interval; though in practice one would expect expectations to be based at least to some extent upon actual recent experience. In any case, merely to keep the real wage constant when prices are rising will result in money wages rising at the expected rate of price inflation, and attempts to increase real wages will result in money wages rising faster than the expected rate of price inflation.

Once we insist that the supply of and demand for labour determine the real wage, and once we note that wage bargains get struck at discrete intervals so that it is expected and not current prices that enter into the determination of the relevant real wage, we find that, in terms of Fig. 1, there is a different Phillips curve for every expected rate of price inflation ($\dot{p}^e$). Representatives of a family of such curves are drawn in Fig. 2, and they have the characteristic implied by the above analysis that each level of unemployment corresponds to a unique rate of change of the *real* wage rate.

Now the foregoing argument implies much more than that there exists a variable, changes in whose value can shift the Phillips curve. Causation does not run only one way from the expected rate of price inflation to the rate of wage inflation. This becomes clear the moment one considers the way in which these variables are likely to interact over time, and, as we shall now see, the nature of their interaction is such as to lead to the conclusion that the trade-off between wage inflation and the level of unemployment implied by the Phillips curve is mainly a short-run phenomenon. Indeed, the strict logic of the argument that follows implies that the trade-off is *solely* a short-run phenomenon – that the 'long-run' Phillips curve is vertical – but this latter proposition, though it is the most contentious one in current academic debates about the role of price expectations in the Phillips curve, is not in my judgement fundamental to any of the implications of the analysis for anti-inflationary policy. The fact that the trade-off becomes steeper with the passage of time is what is important from this point of view, and everyone involved in these debates seems to agree that it does so.

Why this should be the case is best seen by way of an example. Let Fig. 3 depict the situation in an economy in which there is price stability – and expected price stability – and in which U_0 yields a rate of wage inflation $\dot{W}_0$ which is just compensated for by rising labour productivity. Now if the authorities in this economy were to decide that U_0 was too high a level of unemployment, that U_1 was preferable, they could initially achieve this level of unemployment by policies which would also lead to a rate of wage inflation of $\dot{W}_1$. However, with no change in productivity growth, prices would begin to rise at a rate equal to $\dot{W}_1 - \dot{W}_0$. Now so long as people form their expectations about inflation on the basis of current and past behaviour of prices, the price inflation thus induced would begin to become anticipated. It would continue at the same rate so long as the authorities pursued policies to maintain wage inflation at a rate of $\dot{W}_1$, and the longer it continued at that rate the closer to the

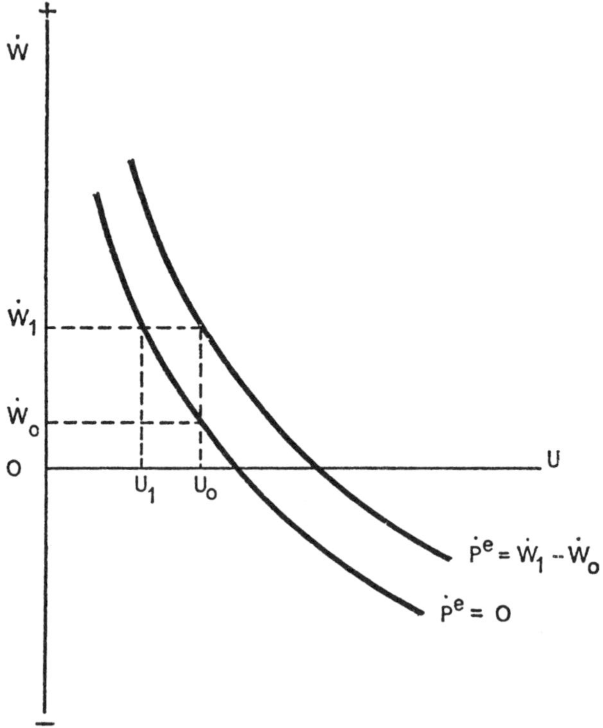

Fig. 3. Short- and long-run response of unemployment to the rate of wage inflation

actual rate of inflation would the expected rate move. Thus, the closer to its ultimate location (at $\dot{p}^e = \dot{W}_1 - \dot{W}_0$) would the short-run Phillips curve shift and the closer to U_0 would the level of unemployment compatible with the rate of wage inflation $\dot{W}_1$ become.

There have been a number of empirical investigations of the kind of wage–price spiral implied in the above example, and there seems to be abundant evidence that wage inflation which proceeds sufficiently fast to involve price inflation does lead the public to form expectations about price inflation that shift the traditional (what I am now calling the 'short-run') Phillips curve upwards. In the long run the trade-off between inflation and unemployment vanishes completely only if actual inflation becomes perfectly anticipated, and there does seem to be doubt as to whether the mechanism involved works quite as perfectly in practice as it does in the foregoing fairly abstract piece of economic analysis; nevertheless there is no disagreement that the trade-off becomes considerably less acute as time passes and people permit current inflation to influence their expectations.[11] This is an extremely important discovery from the point of view of the design of anti-inflationary policy, as we shall now see.

The Phillips curve as originally conceived presented policy-makers with a simple trade-off indeed: more unemployment for less inflation. The introduction of expectations into the analysis complicates the trade-off. Again an example is the best way to see this. Suppose the 'long-run' Phillips curve is such as is depicted in Fig. 4, and I have drawn it with a slope to emphasise the independence of what I have to say of extreme assumptions about perfect learning mechanisms being embodied in the model, and suppose we begin at point *X* on that curve with a given rate of inflation and a given level of unemployment. Suppose the Government of the day finds point *X* uncongenial and prefers point *Y*; how is it to get there? There are many routes, but a comparison of two of them will suffice to illustrate the nature of the policy trade-off involved in choosing a route.

First, suppose the Government attempts to attain at once the rate of inflation compatible with *Y*. This would involve taking policy steps to contract the excess demand for labour to such an extent that initially the economy would move to Y^1 on the short-run Phillips curve that passes through *X*. Clearly the actual rate of inflation would then be below that expected on the short-run Phillips curve passing through *X* and, as expectations were revised downwards, this short-run Phillips curve would shift to the left until point *Y* was reached.

Alternatively the authorities could choose to move immediately to the level of unemployment compatible with ultimate equilibrium at *Y*. This would involve shifting the economy to point Y^{11} on the short-run Phillips curve. Again, the actual inflation rate would fall below the expected one, and again the constant revision of expectations in the light of experience would eventually result in the economy reaching *Y*. However, inasmuch as people learn about the likely future rate of inflation from current experience, the bigger is the discrepancy between

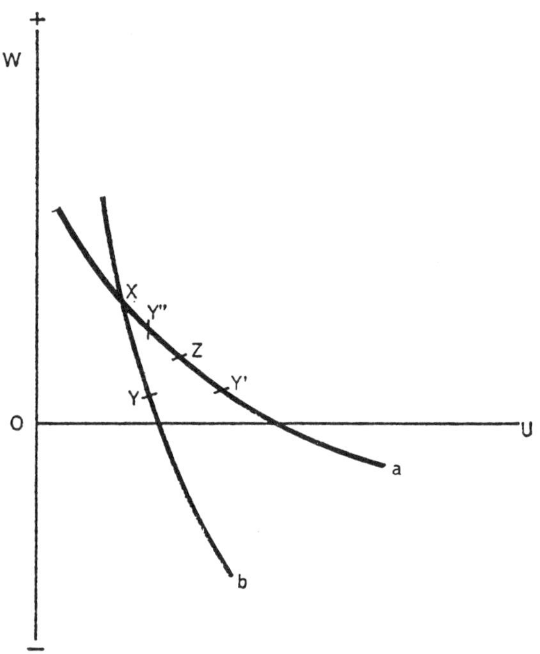

Fig. 4. Long- and short-run Phillips curves
a. Short-run curve
b. Long-run curve

experience and expectations, the faster are expectations likely to be revised. This is a well-tested proposition and in the present context it implies that the first route from *X* to *Y* considered will be a more rapid one than the second.

Now the decision to start the foregoing analytic example from a point of equilibrium on the long-run Phillips curve was a matter of expositional convenience only. In Britain at the moment, both the rate of inflation and the level of unemployment are high by standards of recent history. Phillips's original analysis suggested that a level of unemployment of just under 2½ per cent combined with productivity growth in the region of 2–3 per cent per annum would lead to virtual price stability! This fact suggests that the current British situation is best represented by a point on a short-run Phillips curve to the right of the long-run one, a point such as *Z*. Indeed, if inflation expectations are still catching up with experience the point *Z*, far from being static, might actually be moving upwards. However, this does not mean that the foregoing analysis is irrelevant. If the basic mechanism sketched out above is a good model of the effects of inflation in the labour market, it is still true that we may expect to reduce the rate of inflation only slowly if we maintain unemployment at its present level, and that if we seek a rapid end to inflation this must involve a higher level of unemployment than we have at present.

This comparison of routes whereby inflation may be ended is of course merely illustrative of a general proposition about the trade-offs implied by the introduction of inflation expectations into the Phillips curve, and that proposition is as follows. The more rapidly is the rate of inflation reduced, the higher will be the average level of unemployment while it is being reduced. One can bring inflation to a halt quickly by having more unemployment for a relatively short time, or slowly by having less unemployment for a longer time. This is the qualitative nature of the policy trade-off. I do not think we can yet say anything very precise about its quantitative nature other than to note that the experience of both Britain and the United States over the last few years suggests that, if unemployment rates are to be kept from rising any higher than they are at present, then the timetable for significantly reducing the rate of inflation must be conceived of in terms of years rather than months.

Indeed we need not confine ourselves to the evidence of the last few years on this matter. The analysis we have been discussing leads to the conclusion that any attempt to reduce the current rate of inflation below its expected rate will lead to an increase in the unemployment rate which, though 'transitory', may nevertheless endure for an uncomfortably lengthy period. There is no reason to suppose that this conclusion applied only to situations in which the relevant inflation rates are positive, and once this is grasped, the events of the later 1920s and 1930s in Britain and those of the 1930s in the United States may also be regarded as evidence of the consequences of rapid reductions in the rate of inflation relative to its expected level. One might also note that when viewed in this broader perspective, modern theories of the Phillips curve come to look like more general versions of Keynes's hypothesis about the downward rigidity of money wages. They predict, after all, that the rate of change of money wages is rigid downwards relative to the expected rate of price inflation, and a special case of this is a downward rigidity in the level of money wages when the expected rate of inflation is zero.

Now the analysis of the last few paragraphs assumes that price-level expectations are only influenced by data generated within a 'wage–price spiral', and that the workings of the labour market are not interfered with so as to alter the manner in which wages respond to market forces. Some form of incomes policy is frequently put forward as a means of breaking into the mechanism described above in such a way as to enable the economy to by-pass the sacrifices of output inherent in the unemployment generated by reducing the rate of inflation by conventional methods.[12]

There are two distinct ways in which incomes policy might break into this spiral. It might influence the way in which real wages respond to shifts in the supply of and demand for labour, or it may influence expectations about inflation independently of the current behaviour of prices. As we shall see in a moment, incomes policy as practised in the past seems to have been effective in interfering with the supply and demand mechanism in the labour market – not always with the results anticipated – but I must confess to having doubts about according any unique role to incomes policy as a means of influencing expectations; since I know of no study either published or unpublished on this particular issue, however, these doubts are not as firmly based as they might be.

There is no question that it would be highly desirable to have a tool with which expectations about inflation could be damped independently of a fall in the actual rate of inflation. In terms of Fig. 4 such a tool would shift the 'short-run' Phillips curve downwards and to the left independently of the wage–price mechanism described above and hence enable the rate of inflation to be reduced at a lower cost in unemployment than otherwise.

This shift of the short-run Phillips curve would not, in and of itself, reduce the rate of inflation of course. There is nothing in the foregoing analysis to suggest that changing expectations alone will have any influence on the rate of inflation; it simply suggests that if expectations about inflation can be changed independently of the influence of information transmitted by market forces, then a given rate of inflation will be attainable at a lower cost in transitory unemployment than otherwise. The Phillips curve analysis is, as I noted at the outset, silent and neutral on the appropriate policies with which to achieve a given rate of inflation.

Even so, a policy with the ability to change expectations would be a useful part of any anti-inflationary package, and incomes policy is often portrayed as being peculiarly suited to that role. However, I cannot see why. The key to breaking the expectations link in the wage–price spiral involves convincing those involved in wage bargaining that past evidence on price increases is not a reliable indicator of what is going to happen in the future. If the Government announces its intention to influence the future rate of inflation by way of an incomes policy, this will change expectations if incomes policy is expected to work. Equally, however, an announced intention to reduce the rate of inflation by reducing the rate of growth of the money supply will influence expectations if the policy proposal is credible. What is important is that the Government's willingness and ability to reduce the rate of inflation should be believed in and not the means by which this end is to be achieved. Since there is no reason to suppose that the public has more faith in the anti-inflationary powers of incomes policy than in those of more traditional policy tools, there is no reason why the recognition of the importance of the role played by expectations in the inflationary process should imply that incomes policies are peculiarly effective anti-inflationary devices.

There is another side to the case for using incomes policy to affect expectations, however, though it seems no better grounded. It can be argued that by actually imposing restraints on prices and incomes for a period, the actual rate of inflation will be reduced, the expected rate of inflation reduced, and the spiral broken. However, to have anything more than a temporary effect, such a policy would have to convince the public that the course of prices while it was in force was a good indicator of the likely course of prices when the policy was removed.

As I have already noted, there is a good deal of evidence to support the view that price expectations are on the whole largely based on past experience, but it is probably a mistake to apply this evidence to the very special circumstances of the transition from a period of prices and incomes control to one in which these controls are relaxed. It is at least a plausible hypothesis that this is the very time at which the public would regard past experience as a particularly bad guide to the future. If this hypothesis is true, incomes policy can, at best, interrupt the wage–price spiral for only so long as it is imposed. If the act of imposing the policy leads to a downward revision of expectations about inflation, then the act of removing it is as likely to lead to those expectations being revised upwards again – unless of course the end of incomes policy is accompanied by the introduction of other anti-inflationary mesuraes that the public expect to hold down the rate of change of prices. In that case, though, it is the public's belief in the efficiency of the new policies, rather than the legacy of an incomes policy, that holds down expectations of inflation. One cannot help but wonder if the so called 'wage–price explosion' that followed the relaxation of incomes policy by the late Government may not be explained by its failure to replace that policy with some other credible (and visible) any-inflationary measures.

Be that as it may, if incomes policy has no special virtue as a means of influencing expectations about the rate of change of prices, this does not imply that it is a generally ineffective anti-inflation weapon. Casual analysis might suggest, and indeed the view was quite widely held among economists until recently, that incomes policy would hold back the rate of wage inflation that might be experienced at any particular level of excess demand for labour; this because the imposition of incomes policy somehow involved introducing extra friction that forces tending to make money wages rise would have to overcome.

Incomes policy could be thought of as shifting the Phillips curve (presumably long-run and short-run, though the distinction was not current at the time that this view of incomes policy was at its most popular) and lessening the seriousness of the inflation–unemployment trade-off implied by it.

Early attempts to investigate the degree to which incomes policies had shifted the Phillips curve in post-war Britain suggested that they had had some success. There did seem to be evidence that some systematic shifting of the relationship had taken place upon the introduction of incomes policy.[13] However, this evidence rested on the assumption that the only effect of incomes policy was to shift the Phillips curve parallel to itself; Lipsey and Parkin (1970) found no difficulty at all in demonstrating that careful analysis of the theory underlying the curve did not in fact lead to the prediction that incomes policy would shift the curve parallel to itself. Rather they argued that an effective incomes policy would both shift and alter the slope of the relationship. Hence the evidence alluded to above was produced by misconceived tests and implied nothing at all about the effectiveness or otherwise of incomes policy.

Not only were Lipsey and Parkin able to show that incomes policy both shifted and altered the slope of the Phillips curve in principle, they were able to show (using statistical methods that have, admittedly, been much criticised) that it had apparently done so in practice, that the use of incomes policy seemed to have pivoted the curve until it became virtually horizontal, in the manner illustrated in Fig. 5. Their original work did not allow for the likely influence of inflationary expectations – surely the reason why their so-called 'policy off' results do not extrapolate well to present experience – but subsequent work by Parkin showed that to make explicit allowance for expectations did not in any way affect the conclusion that in the presence of incomes policy the rate of wage inflation is independent of the level of unemployment, and indeed of the level of excess demand for labour.

Now this suggests that incomes policy is a double-edged weapon. Applied at a low level of unemployment it decreases the rate of wage inflation, but applied at a high level it increases it. Moreover – with the single exception of the period 1947–50 in which price and wage controls were only part of a much larger array of restrictions imposed on market behaviour – Lipsey and Parkin found that incomes policy had been applied at times of relatively high unemployment so that it had, if anything, worsened rather than improved the situations with which it was supposed to deal.

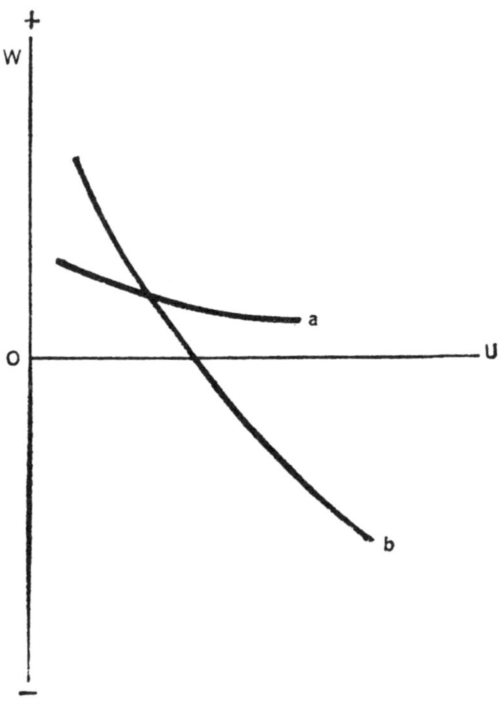

Fig. 5. The Lipsey–Parkin hypothesis about the effect of incomes policy on the Phillips curve

a. Incomes policy on Phillips curve.
b. Incomes policy off Phillips curve.

The interesting question about these results is what is it that determines the rate of wage inflation when it is not responding to the market forces of supply of and demand for labour. The answer advanced by Lipsey and Parkin, which has not been subjected to any independent testing and hence must not be regarded as anything more than a tentative hypothesis, is that, though enough of the national labour market is competitive to ensure that the market as a whole works approximately 'as if' it were competitive throughout in normal (policy off) times, there are important segments of the market, notably the public sector, where competitive theory is far from obviously applicable. Incomes policy affects the Phillips curve by disrupting the competitive sectors of the labour market. This leaves the other non-competitive sectors to set a 'norm' for wage increases that then tends to be widely adopted.[14]

This is not to say that non-competitive sectors of the labour market are unaffected by incomes policy, but since we have little idea about how they work in its absence there is no way of knowing whether or how they are in fact influenced. This is unfortunate because the implications of the Lipsey and Parkin results are clear enough. Either incomes policy is applied at periods of below-average unemployment or it will make matters worse rather than better. This conclusion can only be escaped if some way can be found of ensuring that wage increases in non-competitive sectors of the labour market are brought down to below what competitive forces would allow at times of above-average unemployment. Since we know so little about wage bargaining in non-competitive conditions, it is hard to see how such policies can be devised other than by a process of trial and error. Moreover, this presupposes that the trouble does stem from non-competitive sectors of the labour market in the first place: it is worth reiterating that this proposition is an as yet untested hypothesis.

One final *caveat* is in order before this discussion of incomes policy is brought to a close. Even if it did prove possible to devise an incomes policy that unambiguously could be seen to shift the Phillips curve downwards and to the left so that the rates of wage and price inflation could be reduced at a smaller cost in unemployment than in the absence of such policy, it would not follow that it was desirable to implement it. We regard unemployment as a 'cost' of reducing the rate of inflation mainly because unemployment involves loss of output. Output can be lost by misusing resources as well as by not using them. Fluctuations in relative wages in competitive labour markets are, in principle at least, the means whereby labour gets reallocated towards more productive uses. If incomes policy interferes with this mechanism, it is at least possible that it will produce, as a by-product, sufficient misallocation of the employed labour force as to impose losses that more than offset the gains that arise from having more of the labour force employed. In judging the effectiveness of incomes policy in reducing the costs of bringing down the rate of inflation, these potential allocative effects are just as important as the more obvious impact of the policy on the overall level of employment. However, since there seems to be no evidence that we know even how to use incomes policy in such a way as to reduce consistently the rate of inflation associated with a given level of unemployment, the lack of any work on the allocative effects of incomes policy does not perhaps represent such a serious gap in the literature as it otherwise might.

III

The conclusions that have been drawn in the foregoing discussion are easily summarised. The Phillips curve represents an hypothesis about the way in which the labour market behaves during inflationary situations. Neither in its original form nor in the more sophisticated versions that have been produced recently does it have anything to say about the causes of or cures for inflation. The Phillips hypothesis states that, if a lower rate of inflation is desired, then a higher rate of unemployment must be tolerated. Originally it appeared that the rate at which one variable was traded off against the other was independent of the time horizon over which policy was being designed, and of the past inflationary experience of the economy. More sophisticated analysis, both theoretical and empirical, has shown that the trade-off is more complex.

The amount of unemployment that will be associated with a given rate of inflation at any moment in time will be higher the more rapid has been inflation in the recent past, at least so long as past experience affects expectations about the future. Given that past experience has been of a higher rate of inflation, the longer a given rate of inflation is sustained the lower will be the level of unemployment associated with it. This is because expectations adjust to current experience and what we have termed the 'short-run' Phillips curve shifts so that unemployment and inflation rates approach equilibrium on a steep – in the ideal limiting case, vertical – 'long-run' Phillips curve. Thus the policy trade-off when seeking to reduce the rate of inflation is between a rapid reduction associated with a relatively short period of 'high' unemployment and a slow reduction associated with the existence of 'low' unemployment over a longer period.

It would undoubtedly be desirable to find a way around this trade-off if possible, and one method of softening it would be to influence expectations independently of the market information that normally goes into their formation. It would appear that incomes policy is neither better nor worse conceived to break into the wage–price spiral in this way than any other policy. An announced intention of bringing down the rate of inflation can persuade the public to discount past experience in forming expectations so long as it believed that the announcement will be followed by effective action. There is no reason to suppose that an announced intention to use incomes policy will be any more credible than an announced intention to use any other policy tool. Moreover, we know so little about the factors determining expectations that we cannot rule out as implausible the possibility that the removal of even a successful policy of incomes restraint might not itself lead to an increase in inflationary expectations, and a worsening of the terms of the inflation–unemployment trade-off.

Incomes policy can influence the inflationary spiral at another point by breaking the excess demand for labour/rate of change of (real) wages link in the causative chain. However, available evidence suggests that this has only been done once in the post-war period in such a way as to lower the rate of inflation; in all the other instances incomes policy seems to have increased the rate of inflation above what it otherwise would have been. We have no well-tested explanation of why the policy has worked this way, and hence can have little confidence in our ability to design an incomes policy that will not have a similar effect on the future. Moreover, nothing is known about the effects of such policies on the allocative efficiency of the labour market.

All in all, I would conclude that we know so little about how to design a successful incomes policy that it would probably be better to forget about it altogether, face up to the difficult policy choice inherent in modern versions of the Phillips curve, and, recognising that the time horizon for noticeably reducing the rate of inflation without further significant increases in unemployment in a matter of years and not months, set about designing a long-term strategy for dealing with the problem using more conventional tools of monetary and fiscal policy. Given the current state of the balance of payments, and given that Britain is far from being the only country facing inflation, it may even be the case that a policy of reducing the rate of inflation only very slowly can be carried through without exchange-rate depreciation. If it cannot, then the policy choice becomes more complicated still. To discuss this issue in any detail would take me far beyond the scope of this paper; for this reason, and not because prepared policy towards the exchange rate is an important element in the control of inflation, I shall not pursue this aspect of the problem any further.

NOTES

1. In Phillips (1958). Note, however, that the relationship was implicit in the model used in Phillips (1954).

2. Cf. Phillips (1958): Fig. 1 (1861–1913), Fig. 9 (1913–48), Fig. 10 (1949–57).

3. Hutchinson (1968), particularly chap. 1, provides a ready source of quotation from the pronouncements of economists on this problem in the immediate post-war period.

4. It has often been remarked that the Radcliffe Committee were unfortunate in that the period over which their report (1959) was prepared saw a revival of interest and faith in traditional monetary policy among academic economists so that the report was out of fashion by the time it appeared. It is also true that the idea of trade-offs between policy goals came to the forefront over the same period and the Radcliffe Report was totally uninfluenced by this concept. I suspect that this omission contributed just as much to the cool reception of the Report among academic economists as did its failure to note the 'monetarist revolution'.

5. The reader will note that there is an ambiguity about the term 'wages' here. The Phillips curve has to do with money wages and orthodox analysis of the supply and demand for labour with real wages. As we shall see below, it was precisely this ambiguity, and the desire to clarify it, that led economists to introduce expectations about inflation into the analysis of the Phillips curve. However, in 1961, the problem apparently went unremarked. We may, in retrospect, regard Lipsey as having produced a theory of the Phillips curve for the special case in which the expected rate of inflation is zero.

6. This argument presupposes that the 'cost push/demand pull' distinc-

tion is synonymous with the distinction between demand-side and supply-side disturbances. Matters are not quite so clear-cut, for as Michael Parkin has pointed out to me, the term 'cost push', when applied to wage inflation has sometimes been used to characterise circumstances in which wages rise independently of the concurrent existence of excess demand for labour. As we shall see below, expectations of inflation shared by both demanders and suppliers of labour can cause money wages to increase without there ever arising any excess demand for labour. Thus, recent Phillips curve analysis incorporating expectations about inflation can comprehend this other 'cost push' concept in a manner that earlier analysis could not.

7. A good deal of the 1960s literature had to do with the fact that, for the United States, a simple two-variable Phillips curve was far from stable over a long period. A glance at Fig. 1 of Samuelson and Solow (1960) will confirm the extent of this problem. The United States experience need not concern us here, but two aspects of British work ought to be noted.

First, Hines showed (1964) that the rate of change of trade union membership as a proportion of the labour force was a statistically significant variable, additional to the unemployment rate, indeed virtually swamping the unemployment rate, in explaining the rate of change of money wages. He argued that this variable was a proxy for union aggressiveness and that his result was evidence for the existence of 'cost push' inflationary pressures. However, he failed to explain why this aggressiveness did not operate through shifts in the supply curve of labour and hence have its influence taken account of, along with the many other factors that presumably influence the excess demand for labour, in the unemployment rate. Thus Hines's statistical relationship is difficult (if not impossible) to interpret in terms of Lipsey's rationalisation of the Phillips curve. At the same time Hines did not present clear alternative specification of labour market behaviour, so it is hard to know whether the interpretation he offers of the apparent importance of the rate of change of unionisation is reasonable.

Second, the point at which the Phillips curve cuts the horizontal axis (if we ignore inflationary expectations) is supposed to measure 'frictional' unemployment. Phillips' original curve implies a frictional unemployment rate of between 6 and 7 per cent. Lipsey argued that frictional unemployment was likely to be particularly high when there were large inter-regional discrepancies in the excess demand for labour – even though these cancelled out in the aggregate. This is because it is more difficult for the unemployed to move inter-regionally than intra-regionally to find work. This argument of Lipsey's thus suggests that the Phillips curve would tend to shift leftwards as inter-regional discrepancies in unemployment rates become smaller, and vice versa. Work by Archibald (1969) has tended to confirm this hypothesis and has potentially interesting implications for regional policy.

8. Principal contributions here are Smith (1968), Lipsey and Parkin (1970) and Parkin (1970).

9. Though the idea of an expected rate of inflation goes back at least as far as Irving Fisher (1896), it made its first explicit appearance in modern monetary economics in the work of Friedman (1956), Cagan (1956) and Bailey (1966). It was introduced into the Phillips curve literature by Phelps

(1967), who has also used the concept in work on monetary problems (1965), and Friedman (1968). The only study of which I am aware that uses the concept when dealing solely or even mainly with U.K. data on wage inflation is Parkin (1970). Cagan (1969) does, however, present some preliminary results for Britain.

10. Cf. note 5 above. This is not to say that the analysis that follows is free of ambiguities. To a demander of labour, the real wage is given by the ratio of the money wage rate to some index of the price of his output, while to a supplier it is given by the ratio of the money wage rate to some index of the price of the bundle of goods he typically consumes. In a closed economy in which relative prices were not changing, these two different price indices would necessarily move together, but not otherwise. I know of no work on this particular point, and hence cannot judge the extent to which the following analysis might be vitiated by ignoring the problems raised by it.

11. On this matter, see, for example, work by Cagan (1969) and Solow (1969) for the U.S., and, as already noted, Cagan (1969) and Parkin (1970) for the U.K. Of these, only Cagan's results might imply that the Phillips curve becomes vertical in the long run, though this writer has severe doubts about the methods by which Solow produced results implying that it did not (cf. Laidler, 1970).

12. Much in what follows hinges on what is meant by 'incomes policy'. I take it to mean direct intervention to control prices and money incomes, either by legal restraints or moral suasion, and would not term the mere setting of a target rate of growth of prices and money incomes an 'incomes policy'. Thus it is the choice of policy instruments that defines an incomes policy, not the choice of policy targets.

13. Smith (1968) is a typical example of such studies, which hinge on the inclusion in regression equations of an intercept shift dummy variable for 'incomes policy' on periods. This method is an adequate device for investigating shifts in functional relationships only if there is good *a priori* reason to suppose that the shift being investigated would be a parallel one if it occurred.

14. This explanation is set out by Lipsey and Parkin (1970) pp. 120–2. There is less emphasis there on the public-private sector division, and on the distinction between competitive and non-competitive segments of the labour market, than there is in my interpretation of the Lipsey–Parkin hypothesis. I am indebted to Michael Parkin for clarifying the original analysis along these lines.

REFERENCES

ARCHIBALD, G. C., 'The Phillips Curve and the Distribution of Unemployment', *American Economic Review, Papers and Proceedings*, LIX (May 1969).

BAILEY, M. J., 'The Welfare Cost of Inflationary Finance', *Journal of Political Economy*, LXIV (1966), 93–110.

CAGAN, P., 'The Monetary Dynamics of Hyperinflation', in Milton Friedman (ed.), *Studies in the Quantity Theory of Money* (Univ. of Chicago Press, 1956).

——, 'Theories of Mild Continuing Inflation: A Critique and Extension', in Stephen W. Rousseas (ed.), *Proceedings of a Symposium on Inflation: Its Causes, Consequences and Control* (Wilton, Conn.: The Calvin K. Kazanjian Economics Foundation Inc., 1969).

FISHER, I., 'Appreciation and Interest', Publications of the American Economic Association, 3rd ser., XI (Aug. 1896) 331–442.

FRIEDMAN, M., 'The Quantity Theory of Money: A Restatement', in Friedman (ed.), *Studies in the Quantity Theory of Money* (Univ. of Chicago Press, 1956).

——, 'The Role of Monetary Policy', *American Economic Review*, LVIII (Mar 1968) 1–17.

HINES, A. G., 'Trade Unions and Wage Inflation in the United Kingdom 1893–1961', *Review of Economic Studies*, XXXI (1964) 221–52.

HUTCHINSON, T. W., *Economics and Economic Policy in Britain 1946–1966* (London, Allen & Unwin, 1968).

LAIDLER, D., 'Recent Developments in Monetary Theory: Discussion Paper', in D. Croome and H. G. Johnson (eds), *Money in Britain 1959–1969* (Oxford Univ. Press, 1970).

LIPSEY, R. G., 'The Relation between Unemployment and the Rate of Change of Money Wage Rates in the United Kingdom, 1862–1957', *Economica*, n.s., XXVII (Feb 1960) 1–31.

——, and PARKIN, J. M., 'Incomes Policy: A Reappraisal', *Economica*, n.s., XXXVI (May 1970) 115–38.

PARKIN, J. M., 'Incomes Policy: Some Further Results on the Determination of the Rate of Change of Money Wages', *Economica*, n.s., XXXVII (Nov 1970) 368–401.

PHELPS, E., 'Anticipated Inflation and Economic Welfare', *Journal of Political Economy*, LXXIII (Feb 1965) 1–17.

——, 'Phillips Curves, Expectations of Inflation and Optimal Unemployment over Time', *Economica*, n.s., XXXIV (Aug 1967) 254–81.

PHILLIPS, A. W., 'Stabilization in a Closed Economy', *Economic Journal*, LXIV (June 1954) 290–323.

——, 'The Relation between Unemployment and the Rate of

Change of Money Wage Rates in the United Kingdom', *Economica*, n.s., xxv (Nov 1958) 283–99.

RADCLIFFE COMMITTEE (Committee on the Working of the Monetary System), *Report* (London, H.M.S.O., 1959).

SAMUELSON, P. A., and SOLOW, R. M., 'Analytical Aspects of Anti-Inflationary Policy', *American Economic Review*, L (May 1960) 177–94.

SMITH, D. L., 'Incomes Policy', chap. iii of R. E. Caves and Associates, *Britain's Economic Prospects* (Washington: Brookings Institution; London: Allen & Unwin, 1968).

SOLOW, R. M., 'Recent Controversies on the Theory of Inflation: An Eclectic View', in Stephen W. Rousseas (ed.), *Proceedings of a Symposium on Inflation: Its Causes, Consequences and Control* (Wilton, Conn.: The Calvin K. Kazanjian Economics Foundation Inc., 1969).

6 The current inflation – explanations and policies

Introduction

This is the original text of my 1972 Lister Lecture to the BAAS. It presents an informal version of what some came to call the 'Manchester Monetarist' interpretation of Britain's inflationary experience of the 1970s. It was written before the first oil price shock of 1973, but I thought at the time, and still do, that the significance of this event for the course of inflation in the 1970s was grossly exaggerated, and there is not much that I would have changed in the basic analysis set out here had the lecture been written two years later. In my view, Britain's 20 per cent plus inflation rate in 1975 was largely the consequence of incompetent monetary policy, and not of the behaviour of OPEC or the National Union of Mineworkers.

With hindsight, I am struck by how close we at Manchester had come to the idea of rational expectations by 1972, without actually getting there. Subsequent empirical work (D19 and C23) confirmed the importance of world inflation and exchange rate changes for the inflation rates of a number of open economies under the Bretton Woods System. Incidentally, my emphasis on the open economy taking its price level behaviour from the rest of the world undoubtedly had its origins in my work on Thomas Tooke (D7).

The Current Inflation – Explanations and Policies

David Laidler

Up to the mid-1960s the broad facts of British economic life were a low level of unemployment, a moderate rate of inflation, and an increasing tendency towards balance-of-payments deficits. The widely accepted interpretation of these facts was that they reflected an excess aggregate demand for goods and services which simultaneously resulted in pressure on the labour market – hence the low unemployment level, pressure on wages and prices – hence the moderate inflation rate, and, as a result of wage and price inflation, a gradual loss of competitiveness on the part of British exports and import substitutes which produced the balance-of-payments problem.

Experience and orthodox economics

The period since the devaluation of 1967, particularly the years since 1969, has seen a large and, until recently, increasing balance-of-payments surplus, a high and, until recently, increasing level of unemployment and an inflation rate far more rapid than any experienced since the end of the Korean war. It is widely held that this recent experience contradicts the orthodox economist's view that variations in the price level have their origins in variations in aggregate demand and hence can be dealt with by the traditional monetary and fiscal tools of demand management. The coexistence of rapid inflation and high unemployment is seen as evidence that the nature of the inflationary process has changed and that the source of price increases must be sought on the supply side of the economy. From this it follows that anti-inflation policy must concentrate upon holding down cost, and particularly wage, increases; hence the belief that a prices and incomes policy of some sort is essential to the solution of the current problem.

In this article I shall argue that recent experience is far from being unique, and that there is nothing in this experience to contradict the orthodox view that inflation is caused by excess demand, once it is realized that this orthodox view tells us not only that expectations are of importance but also, and crucially, that we should look to the world at large, and particularly the United States, if we wish to find the source of the current British inflation. It follows from this view that traditional demand management policies are perfectly capable of dealing with inflation provided they are co-ordinated with policy towards the exchange rate. Indeed, inflation will not be cured without resort to such policies, though the cure cannot be expected to be costless. Thus I shall conclude the article with a brief discussion of the factors that ought to be considered in designing an appropriate anti-inflation policy.

Effect of expectations

The view that the same theory cannot account for the course of inflation before and since 1969 stems from the fact that since 1969 both the inflation rate and the level of unemployment have increased dramatically. This evidence appears to be totally inconsistent with the theory that higher rates of inflation are associated with higher levels of excess demand for goods and services and hence with lower unemployment levels. But this theory, like any other in economics, makes its predictions on an 'other things equal' basis. In the 1950s and 1960s many of its staunchest proponents failed to state explicitly the circumstances under which one ought to expect its predictions to be true. In particular they failed to note that an important determinant of the rate at which any firm will raise its prices, and for that matter any firm and trade union will between them raise wages, must be the rate at which prices in general are expected to increase in the economy. Thus they failed to state explicitly that variations in the level of excess demand cause variations in the rate of inflation relative to the rate *which is expected* and hence are only systematically related to variations in the inflation rate when expectations are not changing.[1] Thus there is scope for at least two views about the recent course of inflation: that the nature of the inflationary process itself has changed, and that the basic process has remained the same but that the general public's expectations about the inflation rate have changed.

Now expectations are not directly observable. Virtually any price level behaviour, however unlikely, can be rationalized *ex post* by saying that expectations must have changed. However, it is possible to specify which variables other than the inflation rate itself change with inflationary expectations. It is also possible to formulate precise hypotheses about the factors which influence expectations. To be specific on these two counts is to turn the postulate that expectations must have changed from an *ex post* rationalization of no scientific value into a potentially falsifiable hypothesis.

Economic theory does predict that inflationary expectations affect matters other than wage and price setting. Indeed the

[1]The view that the inflation rate varies systematically with excess demand is of course the basis of Phillips curve analysis. There is no mention of expectations in Phillips' original paper (1958) nor in the work of Lipsey who developed Phillips' analysis further, cf. Lipsey (1960) and Lipsey and Parkin (1970). Note, though, that Parkin (1970) paid careful attention to expectations, and did find them to be important.

concept made its first appearance in economics – close to a century ago – not in the context of the theory of wages and prices at all, but as part of a theory of the behaviour of interest rates.[2] The prediction then, as now, was that the rate of interest on those assets whose value is fixed in nominal terms – typically bonds – would tend to exceed that on those assets which represent a claim on real physical assets – typically equities – by the expected rate of price inflation. I say 'tend' here because the yields would differ exactly by the expected rate of inflation only if the assets in question were otherwise exactly alike. Even so, on the basis of this theory one may predict that increases in the expected rate of inflation will lead to relative increases in the rate of interest on nominal assets. Inspection of Figure I reveals that the difference between the yield on ordinary shares, that is on equities, and the yield on preference stocks began to widen in late 1966 and opened up dramatically between the final quarter of 1968 and about half way through 1969, just before the 'wage explosion' began in earnest. This behaviour is certainly consistent with the predictions of the expectations hypothesis and, even if it

Figure I

Yields on preference stocks and ordinary shares in the United Kingdom 1962 II to 1971 IV

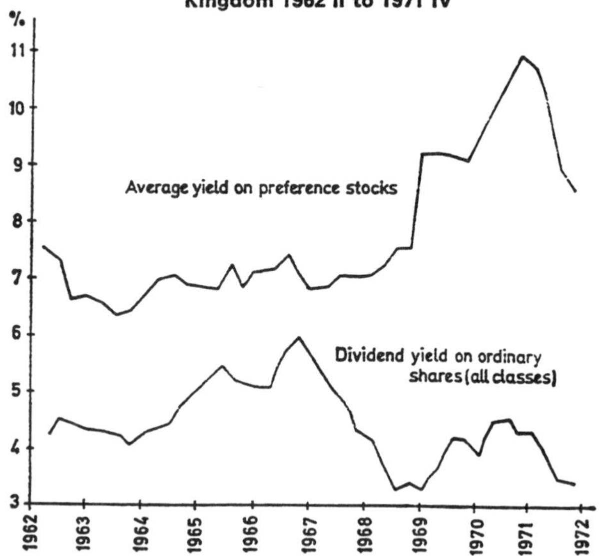

Source: Figures are for quarterly averages of monthly data taken from the 'Company Security Prices and Yields' tables in various issues of *Financial Statistics*.

[2]Cf. Irving Fisher (1896).

stops a long way short of establishing the truth of that hypothesis as an explanation of the increase in the inflation rate, it does at least raise it above the status of a mere *ex post* rationalization.

Now let us turn to the question of the manner in which expectations are formed. For well over a decade economists have found that a surprisingly simple theory of expectations gets them a long way in interpreting aggregate economic phenomena. The theory is that people form their expectation of the future value of some economic variable, in due course observe the actual value of the variable, and make their next prediction about it by revising their initial one by a fraction of the amount by which it was in error. This so-called 'error learning hypothesis' has been applied to income and interest-rate expectations, but its original application was to inflation theory and specifically as a component of an extremely successful attempt to explain the time path of prices during hyper-inflation.[3]

Now if people form their expectations by adjusting to their last error, and if past expectations have been similarly formulated, it will be intuitively obvious that the currently expected rate of inflation will depend upon all past values of the actual inflation rate. Recent values will have more influence than more distant ones; indeed it is easy to show that the error learning hypothesis implies that the expected rate of inflation is equal to a weighted average of current and past inflation rates, where the weights decline geometrically with time.[4] Thus it has the great advantage of enabling us to express a variable that cannot be directly observed in terms of observable phenomena, hence making the expected inflation rate an empirically useful concept. In particular, as I shall now show, it enables us to answer the question, what relationship ought we to observe between the rate of inflation and the level of excess demand when the expected inflation rate is not held constant?

Closed economy model

I mentioned at the outset of this article that I believe the openness of the British economy and events abroad to be crucial in any explanation of recent events. The easiest way to see that this is the case is first to consider what the relationship between the rate of inflation and excess demand ought to be in a closed economy in which the expected rate of inflation is generated solely by the error learning mechanism sketched out above, and in which the actual inflation rate departs from the expected rate solely in response to variations in the level of

[3]The hypothesis was first applied to income expectations by Friedman (1957) to interest rates by Meiselman (1962) and to the inflation rate by Cagan (1956).
[4]This is shown in Cagan (1956).

excess demand. A comparison of this extremely simple and abstract economic model's behaviour with that of the British economy yields what I believe are vital clues to understanding recent, and indeed not so recent, economic history.

This theory in fact tells us that the *rate of change* of the rate of inflation ought to be related, not only to the size of the gap between aggregate demand and potential full employment output, but also to the rate at which that gap is changing. According to this theory, when the level of economic activity is falling away from full employment the rate of inflation will slow down and, as it rises towards full employment, the rate of inflation will at first continue to slow down but will begin to speed up as expansion continues.[5] Thus, this extremely simple and orthodox model in which inflationary expectations respond only to past experience of inflation, and current inflation responds only to expectations and excess demand, tells us that it is the rate of change of the inflation rate and not its level that ought to be related to swings in output and employment, and makes reasonably precise predictions about the nature of that relationship.

Experience in the United Kingdom

In Figure II, I have plotted the time path of the rate of change of prices as it relates to the course of the business cycle in twentieth-century Britain. Now it would be surprising indeed if an extremely simple model of a closed economy were not to make some erroneous predictions about the rate of inflation in a complicated open economy such as Britain, particularly when it is granted a seventy-year time span in which to make errors. In fact, the model goes badly wrong in its predictions in 1925-27 when the rate of inflation failed to continue its upward trend, 1931-35 when it first began to rise too soon and then stopped rising at the very time when it should have begun to rise, 1949-50, 1960-62 and 1967-68 when in each case it was rising when the model predicts that it should have been falling.[6] In addition to these cases, there is some problem with the pre-1914 results inasmuch as a constant inflation rate tends to replace what should be a falling one. The extremely mild nature of the business cycle in these years, combined with the inevitably poor quality of the

[5] To show this requires some algebra. The problem is analysed in considerably more detail in Laidler (1972). Empirical work being carried out by my colleagues John Carlson and Michael Parkin suggests that a slightly modified expectations hypothesis in which people learn from their last two errors is more appropriate for dealing with inflationary expectations in Britain. This hypothesis, which is equivalent to saying that people take note not only of the size and sign of their predictive errors but also of the direction and rate of change of those errors, does not yield predictions that are qualitatively different from our earlier ones.

[6] My turning points are taken from Matthews (1969). Note that the NBER regard 1924-27 as having constituted a separate cycle, but that Matthews disagrees with this dating. There are no turning points given after 1964 but we are on safe ground, I think, if we assert that the economy was not on a cyclical upswing in 1967. If anything 1968 marked a trough.

Figure II **Rate of change of retail prices in the United Kingdom 1900-70 shown with business cycle peaks (↑) and business cycle troughs (↓)**

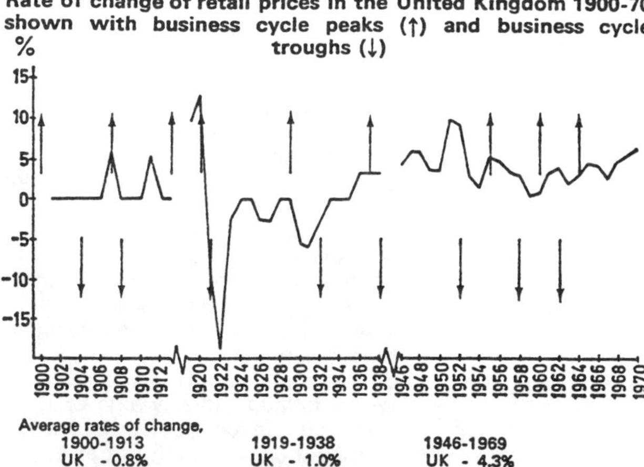

Source: Figures are percentage first differences of the retail price index data taken from Table E of the *British Economy Key Statistics 1900-1970.*

price level data for the period, suggests that this should not trouble us unduly.

There seem to me to be two major lessons to be learnt from Figure II. First, the period since 1967 is by no means the first time that orthodox inflation theory has failed to predict events in the British economy. This, I suggest, goes a long way towards undermining the view that recent experience is the result of some new causative mechanism that has never been at work before. Secondly, with the exception of 1960-62 (which I am unable to explain at present), every other false prediction comes in the wake of a major exchange rate change. The pound was revalued in 1925, devalued in 1931, effectively revalued by the American devaluation and realignment of exchange rates of 1933-34, devalued in 1949 and again in 1967. It would be hard to find a more striking confirmation than this of the importance of the openness of the British economy. Let us therefore see how our basic model can be modified to deal with an open economy.

Model for an open economy

Both components of the model must be altered somewhat when we come to consider an open economy with fixed exchange rates. In a closed economy, if demand exceeds supply, the rate of inflation rises relative to expectations, and if it falls short it falls. The same is true of an open economy with a flexible exchange rate. Inflation drives down the exchange rate ensuring both that import prices keep up with those of home-produced goods and that the price in terms of domestic currency received by exporters rises also. Deflation has exactly opposite effects.

The existence of fixed exchange rates means that the foreign-trade sector provides an alternative source of both supply and demand for goods at prices fixed by world market conditions. If demand exceeds domestic output, then an increase in imports and a diversion of goods from exports is a possible substitute for domestic inflation, while a shortfall of demand may equally be diverted into a 'favourable' change of the balance of payments. For a 'small' economy with a 'large' foreign sector where there are negligible costs of switching output between foreign and domestic markets, the tendencies just outlined would be sufficient to ensure that domestic prices never deviated from world prices so that the world inflation rate, whatever it might be, would be the domestic one too. Such an economy is, of course, very much a limiting case, though not an empirically irrelevant one, for we can get considerable insight into the problems of particular regions of Britain, for example, by regarding them as small open economies of this kind. For Britain as a whole, there probably are significant costs of moving between domestic and foreign markets that mean that the openness of the economy limits, rather than completely overwhelms, the tendency of the inflation rate to vary in the short run with the level of aggregate demand.

In the long run, and assuming fixed exchange rates, it is surely unreasonable to expect the British inflation rate to move too far from that ruling in general in the rest of the world. British producers of exportables cannot be expected to hold domestic prices constant when the prices of their goods on world markets are increasing, nor can the suppliers of British imports and import substitutes be expected to sell them below world market prices for any length of time.

Now all this amounts to saying that the openness of the British economy means that the domestic inflation rate is less sensitive to purely domestic disturbances than it would be were the economy closed, and that in the long run the inflation rate ruling in the rest of the world is going to have an important – perhaps dominant – influence. This at least is likely to be true so long as a fixed exchange rate remains fixed.[7]

[7]This argument suggests that firms initially choose the rate at which they change their prices as equal to the world inflation rate plus the amount they expect the British rate to differ from the world rate and then revise these plans in the face of excess demand or supply. This leads to a model which determines the rate of change of deviations in the British inflation rate from the world rate, rather than the rate of change of the inflation rate itself.

Results of devaluation

If there is a devaluation the domestic price of imports must rise, while the domestic price of exports too will rise as producers divert output towards the overseas markets made more profitable by the devaluation. Moreover, these effects will spread through factor markets and will influence the prices of goods not directly involved in foreign trade. These are the inevitable and obvious consequences of a devaluation and it is reasonable to suppose that those involved in fixing wages and prices will anticipate a period of accelerated inflation in the wake of a devaluation. Thus exchange-rate changes under a fixed rate regime must introduce an extra factor – independent of past experience – into the determination of the expected inflation rate, as well as setting in motion the events whereby the expectations in question are validated. This is surely a plausible hypothesis with which to explain the systematic failure of a closed economy model to predict the direction of change of the inflation rate in the period following exchange-rate changes.[8]

British and world inflation

Though it was the behaviour of the inflation rate after exchange-rate changes that first prompted consideration of the openness of the economy, the foregoing argument also tells us to look for another characteristic in the figures given with Figure II. It tells us that in the absence of exchange-rate changes, the British inflation rate would on average in the long run follow the world rate. If we take a long-run average of the United States inflation rate as an approximate measure of that world rate, and this is surely permissible given the dominance of the United States in world trade, then we may compare the average levels of the British and US inflation rates to see if this prediction has any empirical content. Inspection of Figure II will certainly confirm that, systematic though variations in the British inflation rate may have been, it has fluctuated around quite different average levels at different times. These average levels have not deviated far from the long-run world inflation rate, represented by the United States rate, as is also apparent from inspection of Figure II.[9] Only since 1949 has the British inflation rate been systematically above the US rate, but it has taken two devaluations to permit this, just as, incidentally, Germany's very low rate of inflation has had to be accompanied by an upward drift in the value of the mark.

The argument so far may be summarized. The long-run trend in the British inflation rate is given from the outside so long as Britain maintains a fixed exchange rate; and most fluctuations

[8] The empirical work of Carlson and Parkin mentioned earlier has addressed itself to this particular hypothesis and provides support for it.
[9] This is of course only a crude first test. The hypothesis in question here would certainly be worth much more careful investigation than this.

about this trend result from variations in the domestic level of aggregate demand. These variations cause the rate of inflation to differ from the expected level which, of course, will normally be dominated by the world rate. However, changes in the exchange rate exert a powerful independent effect on the expected rate of inflation so that a devaluation gives an upward impetus to the inflation rate and a revaluation a downward impetus independently of what is happening to aggregate demand and the level of employment. Furthermore, this analysis explains the broad pattern of events since 1900, a pattern into which events of the last few years are no more difficult to fit than any others.

Inflation in recent years

The abnormally high inflation rate of recent years may be interpreted as resulting from a combination of two circumstances. First, there was the attempt of the American authorities to finance a war in Vietnam and a war on poverty while simultaneously cutting Federal tax rates and attempting to keep interest rates down. This led to a greatly increased rate of monetary expansion after 1966 and to a substantial increase in the world inflation rate, an increase which was bound to affect the British rate of inflation (see Figure III). Secondly, the devaluation of 1967 led to an upward revision of inflationary expectations that was independent of and additional to the effect of the change in the world inflation rate. The combined effects of these two factors swamped the downward pressure being exerted on the inflation rate by the considerable excess supply in the economy until towards the end of 1971. No serious problem was noted until 1969, two or three years after the forces towards which this argument points were set in motion, but inspection of Figure II confirms that it was 1967 that saw the trough in the inflation rate. We noticed that we had a problem in 1969 because it was then that the rate of inflation reached an unusually high level, but it had already been rising steadily towards that level for two years; moreover Figure I suggests that the expected inflation rate began to move up sharply even before, and surely in anticipation of, the devaluation of 1967. These two facts lend further support to the view that one must look to the events of 1967 and before to find the origins of our current problems.

Now if it is the case that the current inflation may be explained in the terms set out in this article it follows at once that explanations that look to purely domestic causes of inflation – I am thinking here in particular of those explanations that centre on trade-union militancy – are quite simply too parochial in outlook and confuse the description of inflation with the analysis of its causes. Certainly there is ample room within the explanation I have advanced for trade unions to

Figure III **Rate of change of money supply and rate of change of consumers price index in the United States, 1955-1971 (quarterly figures, annual rates)**

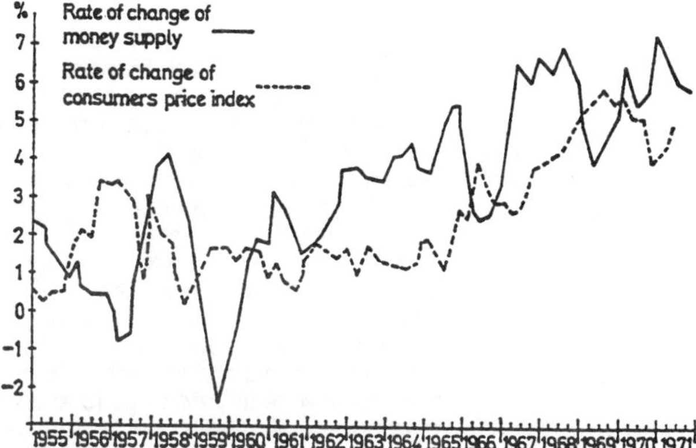

Sources: Figures are for deseasonalized annual rates of change based on data taken from various issues of the *Federal Reserve Bulletin*. The money supply is here defined as currency held by the public plus demand deposits.

demand large increases in money wages in a period in which large increases in prices are anticipated, and for employers to be willing to concede to such increases. I know of no evidence, however, that would compel disbelief in the assertions of trade union leaders that their 'militancy' in recent years has been the result of their desire to protect their members' living standards against erosion by an inflationary process neither of their creation nor under their control.[10]

Coping with inflation

How then are we to cope with inflation both in the long-run sense of avoiding the problem in future and in the short-run sense of dealing with the present situation. If my diagnosis of the evidence is correct, there is precious little Britain can do about inflation in the long run if she maintains a fixed exchange rate. She must simply accept the world rate and recognize that her own contribution to the determination of that rate is negligible. It might be noted in passing that if the enlarged Common Market does form a currency union, then Britain will, by the same argument, have to accept the European inflation rate. Whether or not this is the world rate depends upon whether the Common Market adopts a floating or fixed rate vis-a-vis the rest of the world. However, the rate

[10]The classic study of wage inflation that seemed to lend considerable support to the union militancy hypothesis is that of Hines (1964). The results of a recent study by Purdy and Zis (1972) go a long way towards undermining Hines' results. Even so, as Purdy and Zis show, even an uncritical acceptance of Hines' results enables us to put down only a small fraction of the inflation rate to union militancy.

of domestic price increase is surely a legitimate matter of domestic concern and there can be no presumption that the rest of the world will generate just that rate of inflation that the British population finds desirable; and to repeat, domestic control over the domestic inflation rate requires a flexible exchange-rate. The authorities now seem to have recognized this, but it ought to be stressed that the adoption of such an exchange-rate regime does not guarantee the achievement of the desired rate of inflation.[11] It merely makes it possible for Britain to have any rate of inflation she chooses regardless of what is happening elsewhere.

Though I have argued that recent inflation has to a significant extent been imported, the secular increase in the balance-of-payments deficit that took place throughout the period 1950-67 is strong evidence that Britain was importing price stability over this earlier period. To discuss in any detail what the appropriate inflation rate to aim for would be and how it might be maintained would require another one or two articles. Suffice it then to assert that I think there would be widespread agreement that the target rate of inflation should be lower than the present rate, and also to assert that the maintenance of a steady long-run rate of growth of the money supply at an appropriate rate must be a *sine qua non* of the policy that would achieve that rate of inflation. This, of course, is the one policy that successive British Governments have never tried. Let us now take up the more pressing problem of how to reduce the current inflation rate.[12]

Prices and incomes policy

It is a widely held view that a prices and incomes policy is an essential ingredient in any measures designed to reduce the current inflation rate, but I would reject this view for two reasons. First, the premise upon which the case for such a policy is based is that union aggressiveness is the root cause of the problem and I have already rejected that premise. This is not a decisive argument against an incomes policy for, inasmuch as large wage and price increases are a symptom of inflation, it is certainly possible that a policy of attempting directly to control them could relieve the symptoms if it did

[11] It might seem odd at first sight that I am arguing simultaneously that devaluations are inflationary and that the operations of a flexible exchange rate system will not lead to inevitable inflation when the rate falls. However, there is no inconsistency here. With a fixed exchange rate, a balance-of-payments deficit arises as a consequence of inflationary pressures *and instead of* domestic price increases. Devaluation may, crudely speaking, be regarded as forcing the price level to rise to the level it would have achieved in the first place had the earlier deficit not occurred. With a flexible rate, inflationary pressure results in rising prices which lead to a fall in the rate. When a new equilibrium rate has been reached to accommodate the new domestic price level that is the end of the story.

[12] The case for a steady rate of growth in the money supply is put most eloquently by Friedman (1960). I have given a non-technical account of the case in Laidler (1971) (item 8 in References p. 20) and discussed much of the work upon whose results the case is based in Laidler (1971) (item 8 in References p. 20).

not in and of itself cure the disease. However, the fact remains that quite exhaustive empirical investigation has failed to produce any evidence that such policies have in the past affected the rate of inflation, with the sole exception of the Cripps era when wage and price controls were accompanied by a battery of quantitative restrictions as well.[13] This of course does not mean that prices and incomes policies have no effect. Given that they are so much easier to apply to some sectors of the economy than others, they undoubtedly produce some inefficiency in the use of resources and considerable short-run inequities in the distribution of income. Thus, like orthodox policies, they impose costs on the community, but, unlike orthodox policies, there is no evidence that they succeed in reducing the overall rate of change of prices and incomes. In the face of these problems it is surprising that there is still such wide support for the reintroduction of prices and incomes policies, but it is worth noting that their proponents find it much easier to agree that some such policy should be used than to agree upon even the approximate form in which it should be implemented.

Be that as it may, there is no mystery as to how the rate of inflation may be reduced. Sufficiently stringent demand management policies can do that. Indeed, in the present state of knowledge these are the only policies available to us. The problem is that such policies simultaneously produce unemployment, so that reducing the rate of inflation is costly. The central prediction of the expectations theory of wage and price setting advanced earlier is that it is impossible to reduce the rate of inflation below its expected rate without simultaneously producing unemployment. To be sure, this same unemployment produces a downward pressure on wage and price inflation that eventually feeds back into expectations so that a lower rate of inflation can be enjoyed in the long run without a permanent rise in the unemployment rate; but this does not alter the fact that reducing the inflation rate is costly while the process of reduction is in progress. The same theory, though, suggests that the more time we are willing to take about reducing the inflation rate by a given amount, the less unemployment will we have to tolerate in the interim.[14]

Minimizing unemployment

Now it is deficient demand for goods and services, and hence for labour, that simultaneously slows down the rate of price and wage inflation and brings about unemployment. There is no natural law that there must be a unique relationship between excess supply and unemployment. Excess supply is not the only cause of unemployment. Structural imbalance in the economy, both as between industries and regions, is a

[13] For a survey of this evidence cf. Parkin, Sumner, and Jones (1972).
[14] I have discussed this issue in more detail in Laidler (1971) (item 7 in References p. 20)

source of unemployment as is the inevitable and closely related friction involved when the labour force is redeployed in the face of changes in the composition of output. If unemployment must be endured in order to reduce the inflation rate, then it is surely reasonable to expect governments to make an effort to minimize the amount necessary. This requires measures to make labour markets more efficient, both as transmitters of information about where job vacancies are and as providers of incentives and opportunities for individuals to equip themselves with the skills necessary to fill those vacancies, for these are the ways in which the frictional and structural components of unemployment can be reduced.

Reducing the burden of inflation

A similar argument must hold about inflation. If we must put up with more inflation than we would like for a significant period in order to minimize the unemployment problem, then there is a great deal to be said for minimizing the burden that it places on the population. Now, in an economy in which everyone always had perfect information about the future course of prices the cost of inflation would be relatively small.[15] Inflation would simply be one more factor to take into account when making decisions. Problems arise when information is less than perfect and mistakes are made. For example, people enter into private insurance and pension contracts with certain expectations about the future course of prices, the rate of inflation turns out to be higher than expected, and their real wealth is diminished. Or again, Parliament sets state pensions and income tax rates, presumably, with the intention of providing the old with a certain minimum standard of living and imposing a certain pattern of real tax burdens on the working population. Inflation at a faster than anticipated rate ensures that what Parliament intended does not come about; poverty among the old and excessive tax burdens upon the working population are the result.

One could multiply such examples without difficulty, but enough has already been said to illustrate the nature of the problems brought on by the recent increase in the inflation rate. They are essentially distributional problems and there is

[15]They would not exist at all if the information was free, and there were no costs to be incurred in adjusting plans in the light of new information. It is precisely because information is costly to obtain, and because remaking plans is expensive, particularly when binding contracts have been entered into, that even predictable inflation is costly. It is worth noting explicitly that distributional effects of the type discussed here occur at any time when the rate of change of prices deviates (either upwards or downwards) from the anticipated rate. They are not peculiarly the result of rising prices *per se*. I am grateful to John Foster for helpful discussion on these matters. The academically-minded reader will note that I am not dealing here at all with the welfare costs that arise during anticipated inflation from the failure of money to bear interest at competitive rates. It is my judgment that, over the last few years, these costs have been insignificant relative to the distributional effects on which I am here concentrating.

nothing inherent in the inflationary process that prevents them being tackled as such. There is no reason in principle why state pensions, and even tax rates, cannot be pegged to the cost of living.[16] There is no reason why holders of claims to private pensions cannot be compensated for the losses imposed upon them by an unexpected increase in the rate of inflation after they entered into their contracts. Similarly, but on the other side of the coin, there is no reason in principle why the debtors who gain from inflation – for example householders with mortgages – cannot be taxed on the windfalls which unanticipated inflation brings them.

How easy it would be to deal with any particular distributional inequity that has arisen or could in future arise from inflation cannot be assessed without a detailed study. However, I raise this general question not because I have ready-made answers to its many facets but because I find it surprising that, given that we have been living with inflation for so long, and given that so many people profess to be deeply disturbed by its adverse distributional effects, so little work has been done on devising the means whereby we could minimize these effects. Surely the most serious side effect of various governments' pursuit of incomes policies to reduce the inflation rate without increasing unemployment – always a futile pursuit since 1950 – has been to distract attention from the problems of making labour markets more efficient and of making it easier for the general public to live with inflation. After all, if one thinks that he has found a ready-made, rapid and costless cure for inflation there is no need to make the effort of investigating the means whereby the costs involved in curing it slowly by other methods may be minimized.

Policy implications Thus, the policy implications of my analysis can be stated very simply. Adopt a flexible exchange rate and rely on the rate of monetary expansion to achieve, in the long run, the rate of inflation desired. Recognize that the inflation rate can be reduced only at the cost of unemployment during the transition, so proceed slowly towards the target. Accept that the amount of unemployment needed to reduce the inflation rate by a given amount is smaller if labour markets are more efficient, and if there is less structural imbalance in the economy. Admit that much of the harm that inflation can do may be ameliorated by policies to compensate the losers;

[16]We are beginning to see some movement in this direction, albeit in an unsystematic way. Old age pension rates are now reviewed annually, while increases in the minimum money income at which households become liable for income tax seem to be becoming more frequent.

hence pay much more attention than hitherto to designing policies to deal both with the structure of the labour market and the distributional inequities produced by inflation. Above all, face up to the fact that inflation is not a problem for which some costless panacea is likely to be found just around the corner, and use the considerable knowledge that we already have of its nature to cure it. This cost, however, will not be zero.

This article is the text of the 1972 Lister Lecture delivered at the Leicester meeting of the BAAS. It is based on work currently being carried out under the auspices of the SSRC – University of Manchester Inflation Project. As will be apparent from the references it draws not only on the author's own research but on that of other members of the project. In particular the author would mention many helpful and stimulating discussions with John Foster, Michael Parkin, David Rose and George Zis. He is grateful to John Hargreaves for drawing the charts and collecting the data on which they were based. Nevertheless the author alone is responsible for the points of view expressed.

Biographical Note

Professor David Laidler studied at the LSE and in the United States. He has lectured at several universities and has held a Chair at Manchester since 1969.

References

1. P Cagan, 'The Monetary Dynamics of Hyperinflation' in Milton Friedman (ed.) *Studies in the Quantity Theory of Money*, Chicago, Ill, 1956.
2. I Fisher, 'Appreciation and Interest', *Publications of the American Economic Association*, third series II, Aug. 1896, pp. 331-442.
3. M Friedman, *A Programme for Monetary Stability*, New York, Fordham University Press, 1960.
4. M Friedman, *A Theory of the Consumption Function*, Princeton, N.J. 1957.
5. A G Hines, 'Trade Unions and Wage Inflation in the United Kingdom 1893-1961', *Review of Economic Studies* (31), 1964, pp. 221-252.
6. D Laidler 'The Influence of Money on Economic Activity: A Survey of Some Current Problems' in G Clayton, J Gilbert, and R Sedgwick (eds.), *Monetary Theory and Monetary Policy in the 1970's*, Oxford, Oxford University Press, 1971, pp. 75-135.
7. D Laidler, 'The Phillips Curve, Expectations and Incomes Policy', in H G Johnson, and A R Nobay (eds.), *The Current Inflation*, London, Macmillan, 1971.
8. D Laidler, 'Monetarism, Stabilisation Policy and The Exchange Rate', *The Bankers Magazine* No. 1531 (Oct. 1971) pp. 163-168.

21 The Current Inflation – Explanations and Policies

9. D Laidler, 'Simultaneous Fluctuations in Prices and Output: A Business Cycle Approach', mimeo, University of Manchester 1972. (Available from the author on request).
10. R G Lipsey, 'The Relation Between Unemployment and the Rate of Change of Money Wage Rates in the United Kingdom 1862-1957' in R A Gordon, and L R Klein (eds.) *Readings in Business Cycles,* Homewood, Ill, 1965, reprinted from *Economica,* Vol. XXVII (1960) pp. 1-31.
11. R G Lipsey, and J M Parkin, 'Incomes Policy: A Reappraisal', *Economica,* NS (36), May 1970, pp. 115-138.
12. R C O Matthews, 'The Post-War Business Cycle in the UK' in Martin Bronfenbrenner (ed.) *Is the Business Cycle Obsolete?* (Wiley International, 1969).
13. D Meiselman, *The Term Structure of Interest Rates,* Englewood Cliffs, N.J., Prentice Hall, 1963.
14. J M Parkin, 'Incomes Policy – Some Further Results on the Determination of the Rate of Change of Money Wages', *Economica,* NS (37), November 1970, pp. 386-401.
15. J M Parkin, M T Sumner, and R A Jones, 'A Survey of the Econometric Evidence on the Effects of Incomes Policy on the Rate of Inflation', mimeo, University of Manchester, 1972. (Available from the authors on request.)
16. D L Purdy, and G Zis, 'Trade Unions and Wage Inflation in the UK – A Reappraisal', mimeo, University of Manchester, 1972. (Available from the authors on request.)

7 Monetarist models of inflation in closed and open economies

Introduction

This working paper was presented at a Money Study Group seminar at the end of 1972, but was never submitted for publication. Its initial reception must have persuaded me that its results needed more motivation than they were given here if they were to 'sell', because one rather short paper in due course became two somewhat longer ones. Neither of these had any luck with journals, however, ultimately appearing as D21 (the closed economy case), and C15 and A3, Chapter 9 (respectively a conference abstract and a full exposition of the fixed exchange rate open economy case). The closed economy model formed the basis for an empirical study of US data (C16) carried out at the St. Louis Fed., whose reception is discussed in my memoir. A flexible exchange rate version of the open economy model, written shortly after my arrival in Canada appeared in *Economica* (C25).

I have chosen to print the original working paper here, rather than its later published derivatives, because it is brief and because it seems adequate to convey the analytic core of what I was up to at this time, namely combining the quantity theory of money (or a vertical *LM* curve version of the *IS–LM* model) with the expectations augmented Phillips curve to model stagflation in a closed economy, and combining a version of the monetary approach to balance of payments theory (or Tooke's discussion of a price-taking open economy if the reader prefers it) again with the Phillips curve, to do the same in a fixed exchange rate open economy.

Monetarist models of inflation in closed and open economies

Introduction

In recent debates about inflation, those who have been termed 'monetarists' have advanced particular interpretations of events both in the United States and Britain. These interpretations have had certain factors in common – an emphasis on the role of monetary variables in the economy, and on the role of inflationary expectations in shifting the Phillips curve – but there have also been differences of emphasis depending upon whether the relatively closed American economy or the relatively open British economy is under discussion. Thus, the British inflation is largely seen as being imported (from United States) while the American one is viewed as being internally generated by excessive monetary expansion.

Whatever the details of these interpretations they have commanded a good deal less than widespread support in both countries. One reason for this, particularly among academic economists, is the lack of explicit dynamic models of the inflationary process from which the monetarist propositions may be seen to follow. The major aim of this paper is to set out two such models, one for a closed economy and one for an open economy. They are built on monetarist premisses and yield monetarist conclusions. They are advanced not in the hope of making converts to the monetarist position, but with the more modest aim of making its basis – or rather a particular version of its basis – clear, so that the position, if it is not more widely accepted, will at least be more widely understood.

In addition to providing an explicit framework from which already well known propositions may be derived, these models also, I believe provide fresh insight on one or two aspects of inflation – particularly in an open economy. One cannot be more specific than this without explicitly considering the models in question and I now turn to the task of setting them out.

A closed economy model

The closed economy model is easily set out.[1] The variables are all measured in natural logarithms and are defined as follows: P is the price level, Y is real national income, Y^* is that level of real national income at which the supply and demand for labour are equal and the 'natural' level of unemployment prevails, while M is the nominal money stock. We define y as being equal to the difference between Y and Y^*; obviously this variable is inversely related to the level of unemployment and may stand as a proxy for that variable. The current value of a variable minus its previous period's value is indicated by the use of Δ as a prefix. A superscript e indicates the expected value of a variable, while time lags are denoted by subscripts $-1, -2$, etc.[2]

Two sets of simple equations describe the model. In the money market the quantity of nominal balances demanded is assumed proportional to the price level and to be a log. linear function of real income. In short the demand for money function is the simplest possible version of the Cambridge quantity theory.

There are two interpretations of the absence of some kind of rate of interest variable from this relationship. The first is that the demand for money balances does not respond to changes in the opportunity cost of holding them, and I would want to defend this interpretation on neither theoretical nor empirical grounds. The second interpretation however is that the opportunity cost of holding money does not change over the time period and ranges of values of variables to which the analysis refers. If money is the liability of a competitive banking system it will bear interest at a rate that will vary with rates on other assets – though not necessarily with a perfect one-to-one relationship – while changes in the expected rate of inflation will become incorporated in the return on money balance just as they will in the return on other nominal assets. In such a case the only scope for the opportunity cost of money to vary will arise from changes in the relative supplies of money and other assets, and if we assume that such variation is negligible, it becomes appropriate to omit the opportunity cost variable from our equation. To treat the banking sector as if it were competitive, and hence to assume that the opportunity cost of money holding is a variable whose value changes sufficiently little for it to be safely ignored, is in keeping with the spirit of monetarist analysis and this is what underlies my adoption of the Cambridge equation in this model.

With an exogenously given rate of change of nominal balances, and the usual equilibrium condition we have,

$$\Delta M_d = b\Delta Y + \Delta P = \Delta \overline{M} s \tag{1}$$

which we may rewrite as

$$\Delta \overline{M} s = b\Delta Y^* + b\Delta y + \Delta P \tag{2}$$

The other equations deal with price setting and describe a form of sophisticated Phillips curve.[3] It is assumed that the rate of inflation rises relative to its expected rate when unemployment is above its 'natural' level and falls when it is below that level. Thus, we have

$$\Delta P = gy + \Delta P^e_{-1} \tag{3}$$

Moreover, the expected rate of inflation is presumed to be generated by the usual error learning mechanism so that

$$\Delta P^e = d\Delta p + (1-d)\Delta P^e_{-1} \tag{4}$$

Now equation (3) is not altogether satisfactory, for the first term in it tells us that the rate of inflation will change in proportion to the difference between logarithm of actual income and that of full employment income. The usual non-linearity of the Phillips curve would imply that this relationship should also be non-linear, with the rate of inflation becoming increasingly sensitive to variations in the level of actual income the higher is that level. In short it would be desirable for the relationship to have the form depicted in Figure 1(a). In fact it has the form given in 1(b). The form adopted, however, gives us a large gain in simplicity, and provided

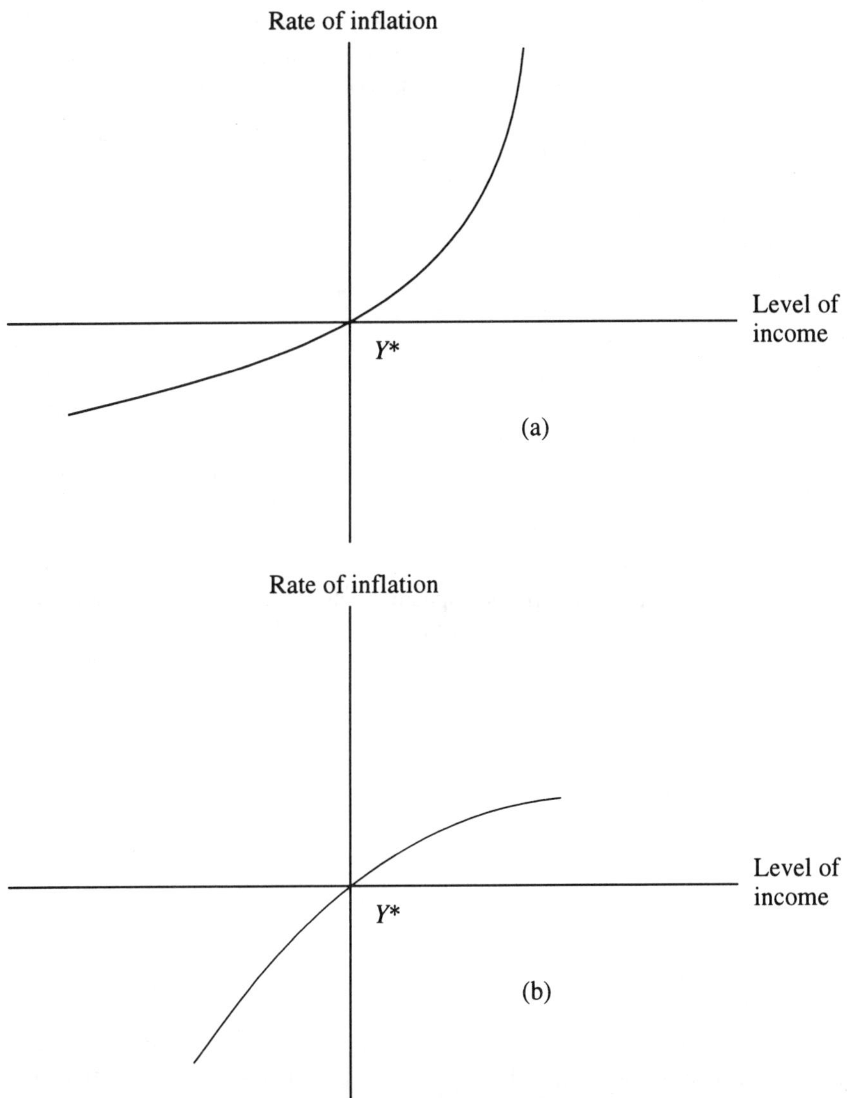

Note: Relationships between the inflation rate and income (*not* measured in logarithms) at a given expected inflation rate. (a) as implied by the Phillips curve. (b) as implicit in equation (3).

Figure 1

that we remember that it is only likely to hold as a good approximation in the neighbourhood of equilibrium there seems no reason to suppose that we will be seriously misled by the model's predictions, particularly as we are more concerned here with their qualitative than with their quantitative properties. This matter becomes more important when we deal with the open economy model, as we shall see below.

The foregoing equations between them determine the way in which the time paths of real income and prices interact. To derive the relevant expression, we eliminate the expected rate of inflation variable from equations (3) and (4). This is done utilizing the Koyck transformation and leaves us with

$$\Delta P = g\Delta y + dgy_{-1} + \Delta P_{-1} \tag{5a}$$

which may also be written as

$$\Delta P - \Delta P_{-1} = g\Delta y + dgy_{-1} \tag{5b}$$

The properties of equation (5) are of course quite independent of the monetary sector of the model with which I am dealing here. It represents a spelling out in terms of observable variables of a version of the sophisticated Phillips curve. In the form written as (5a), we find that both the size of the log. of income's deviation from full employment equilibrium and the rate of change of that variable, to say nothing of the lagged inflation rate, belong in the equation determining the rate of change of prices. If we remember that the variable y is inversely related to the unemployment rate it will be apparent that equation (5) is qualitatively similar to certain apparently theoretically *ad hoc* specifications of the Phillips curve used in early empirical work. The sophisticated theory of the Phillips curve, it turns out, requires that unemployment, the rate of change of unemployment and the lagged rate of inflation all be in the relationship.

Two things follow from this, as is most apparent from (5b). First neither the level nor the rate of change of income's deviation from full employment tell one anything about what the rate of inflation itself ought to be. It is the *rate of change* of the inflation rate that is related to these variables. Second, it is simply not true, as is apparently widely believed, that the existence of excess capacity in the economy ought, according to the sophisticated Phillips curve theory, to result in a slow-down of the inflation rate. The rate of change of excess capacity is also important, and the more rapidly output is expanding towards full employment, the more likely is it that the inflation rate will begin to accelerate before full employment is reached. This prediction of course includes the possibility of a negative inflation rate becoming positive before full employment is reached. It has not been widely enough recognized, I believe, that the sophisticated Phillips curve is capable of predicting that the rate of inflation is likely to increase when income expands towards full employment even in the absence of exogenous cost push factors and of production bottlenecks.

If we eliminate the rate of inflation variables from equations (2) and (5) we may derive an expression for the time path of income's deviation from full employment, and it is here that the nature of the monetary sector of this particular model becomes important. The relevant expression is

$$y = \frac{1}{b+g}\left(\Delta\overline{M}_s - \Delta\overline{M}_{s-1}\right) - \frac{b}{b+g}\left(\Delta Y^* - \Delta Y^*_{-1}\right) + \left(1 - \frac{dg}{b+g} + \frac{b}{b+g}\right) y_{-1} - \frac{b}{b+g} y_{-2} \tag{6}$$

If we assume that the growth rate of full employment income is an exogenous constant it is easy to show that the economy always converges on full employment income when the rate of growth of the money supply is constant. We have

$$y = \left(1 - \frac{dg}{b+g} + \frac{b}{b+g}\right) y_{-1} - \frac{b}{b+g} y_{-2} \tag{7}$$

and this equation is convergent if

$$\left|\frac{b}{b+g}\right| < 1 \tag{8}$$

$$1 - \frac{dg}{b+g} + \frac{b}{b+g} < 1 + \frac{b}{b+g} \tag{9}$$

clearly these two conditions always hold. Convergence may be cyclical if

$$\left(1 - \frac{dg}{b+g} + \frac{b}{b+g}\right)^2 < \frac{4b}{b+g} \tag{10}$$

and this inequality reduces to

$$d + \frac{1}{d} < 2 + \frac{4b}{g} \tag{11}$$

Apart from noting that the model is more likely to display cyclical properties the larger is d, the larger is b and the smaller is g, there does not seem to be a great deal that one can say on this issue in the absence of quantitative information on these parameters.

Clearly in the absence of a constant in equation (7) the steady state solution for y is zero so that the model converges on full employment. As for the steady state rate of inflation, equation (5) tells us that it will be constant at full employment while equation (2) may be solved to yield the familiar expression.

$$\Delta P = \Delta M - b\Delta Y^* \tag{12}$$

The steady state value of the rate of inflation will be equal to the rate of monetary expansion minus the income elasticity of demand for money times the growth rate of income. A different inflation rate is thus the only long run consequence of changing the rate of monetary expansion. The short run consequences involve fluctuations in both real income and the inflation rate as equations (5) and (6) indicate.

An open economy model

It is not difficult to extend the foregoing model to deal with the behaviour of prices and output in a simple open economy. The economy in question is one which produces and consumes both tradeable goods and non-tradeables. In the markets for tradeables it is a price taker both as a buyer and a seller. It is also sufficiently small relative to the world economy to have no discernible influence, whether direct or indirect, on the time path of world prices. In addition this economy does not participate as either a borrower or lender in world capital markets so that what happens to its balance of payments is given solely by the behaviour of the current account.

Our model must be modified in two ways to enable it to cope with the behaviour of such an economy. Both the assumption that the rate of monetary expansion is exogenous and the assumption that the price level's behaviour is completely determined by domestic forces must be abandoned.

Consider first the rate of monetary expansion. We know that the absolute rate of change of the money supply in an open economy is definitionally equal to the rate of domestic credit expansion plus the rate of change reserves. We also know that the percentage rate of change of the money supply may be approximated by a weighted average of the percentage rates of change of the two magnitudes. The weights in question are the proportions of the money stock matched by domestic credit and reserves in some base period. So long as the percentage rates of change of the two components are relatively small, or do not differ much from one another, the approximation in question is a good one, and we shall use it here writing

$$\Delta Ms = v\Delta\overline{C} + (1-v)\Delta R \tag{13}$$

where ΔC is the percentage rate of domestic credit expansion which may be treated as an exogenous variable, ΔR is the percentage rate of change of reserves, and v is a positive fraction.

The percentage rate of change of reserves, depending as it does solely on the balance of trade will be greater the lower is the relative price of non-tradeables (for a low price for non-traded goods encourages the use of resources in the production of tradeables for export and import substitution) and the lower is the level of income. Using a log. linear version of such a relationship we may write

$$\Delta R = B - ny - m(p - \pi) \tag{14}$$

where p is the price of non-traded goods and π the price of tradeables. The price of non-tradeables is the only price which can be set by domestic firms and instead of having equations (3) and (4) to determine the rate of change of the price level in general we replace them with analogous expressions to describe the behaviour of the price of non-tradeables. Thus

$$\Delta p = gy + \Delta p^e_{-1} \tag{15}$$

$$\Delta p^e = d\Delta p + (1-d)\Delta p^e_{-1} \tag{16}$$

The general price level in an open economy is obviously a weighted average of the prices of tradeables and non-tradeables, and the log. linear nature of the model being built here dictates that we should use geometric rather than arithmetic weights. Such weights have the property of yielding 'diminishing returns' in the value of the index for successive equal increments in the price of any category of goods given the price of the others. Hence they go some way to allowing for the fact of substitution against relatively high priced goods, and have a certain advantage over arithmetic weights quite independently of the properties of this particular model.

In any event, we may write

$$\Delta p = w\Delta p + (1-w)\Delta\pi \tag{17}$$

Where $\Delta\pi$ is the exogenously given proportional rate of change of the price of tradeables – the 'world inflation rate' – and w is a positive fraction. The open economy model is completed by the addition of a demand for money equation identical to that used in the closed economy case and an equilibrium condition.

$$\Delta Md = b\Delta Y^* + b\Delta y + \Delta P = \Delta Ms \tag{18}$$

It is convenient to look at this model's steady state characteristics first of all. If the rate of inflation for non-tradeable goods is to be constant, it follows from equations (15) and (16) that y must equal zero. Thus full employment is as much a characteristic of the open economy steady state as it is of the closed economy. As to the rate of inflation, equations (13), (14) and (18) yield

$$p - \pi = \frac{v}{(1-v)m}\Delta C + \frac{1}{m}B - \frac{b}{(1-v)m}Y^* + \frac{w}{1-v}\Delta p + \frac{(1-w)}{(1-v)m}\Delta\pi \tag{19}$$

Every term on the right hand side is a constant, and if $p - \pi$ is to be constant it follows that the rate of inflation of the price of non-tradeables, and hence of the domestic price level must equal that of the world price level. Thus the equilibrium rate of monetary expansion is determined endogenously to the system. Domestic monetary policy, operating through the rate of credit expansion is in the long run only capable of influencing the rate of change of the reserves, and the level – as opposed to the rate of change of – domestic prices. Moreover, given the rate of domestic credit expansion, there is only one equilibrium domestic price level, relative to that ruling in the rest of the world; in the long run an exchange rate change can influence nothing except the units in which prices are measured. In short, this model faithfully reproduces, as its steady state properties, the predictions of what is usually called the monetary theory of the balance of payments.[4]

How interesting all this is depends of course upon whether or not the model's dynamic properties are such as to cause it to converge on its steady state solution. We get, on the assumptions that ΔC, ΔY^*, and $\Delta\pi$ are constant, a third order difference equation of the form

$$y = \alpha_1 y_{-1} - \alpha_2 y_{-2} + \alpha_3 y_{-3} \tag{20}$$

where

$$\alpha_1 = \frac{3b + 2[wg + (1-v)n] - wdg + (g - dg)(1-v)m}{b + wg + (1-v)n + g(1-v)m} \tag{21}$$

$$\alpha_2 = \frac{3b + wg + (1-v)n - wdg}{b + wg + (1-v)n + g(1-v)m} \tag{22}$$

$$\alpha_3 = \frac{b}{b + wg + (1-v)n + g(1-v)m} \tag{23}$$

The necessary and sufficient conditions for the stability of such equations are[5]

$$\alpha_1 - \alpha_2 + \alpha_3 < 1 \tag{24}$$

$$-\alpha_1 - \alpha_2 - \alpha_3 < 1 \tag{25}$$

$$|\alpha_3| < 1 \tag{26}$$

$$\alpha_3(\alpha_3 - \alpha_1) + \alpha_2 < 1 \tag{27}$$

Inequalities (25) and (26) obviously hold, while (24) gives us

$$\frac{b + wg + (1-v)n + (g - dg)(1-v)m}{b + wg + (1-v)n + g(1-v)m} < 1 \tag{28}$$

which is also obviously always true.

(27) is less straightforward, but may be written as

$$bd(1-v)m < w^2 gd + wd(1-v)n + \left(1 + w + \frac{(1-v)n}{g} + (1-v)m\right)g(1-v)m \tag{29}$$

It is possible to conceive in principle of both n and g being sufficiently small for this inequality to be violated or for b to be sufficiently large, but this, in my judgement, is more a theoretical than a practical possibility. b is the income elasticity of demand for money; and we know that this parameter is unlikely to be far above unity in any actual economy, and is much more likely to be less. Moreover, the constancy of g is a convenient assumption rather than an accurate reflection of any actual economy's properties. In fact we would expect g to get larger as y increased, approaching infinity at some relatively small positive value for y. That at least would be the implication of treating Figure 1(a) as a reasonably accurate characterization of the relationship between the inflation rate and income. As to the cyclical properties of the model, it has proved too complex and general to permit their analysis. Since the closed economy model is a special case of this one, it is probably safe to assume that it can generate cycles.[6]

The dynamic properties of this model are such that it is virtually certain to converge upon its steady state. Thus it seems that the predictions of the monetary theory of balance of payments, embodied as they are in this steady state, are of some relevance. The foregoing analysis does not exhaust the information that can be culled from this model. A number of variables, notably the rate of domestic credit expansion and the world inflation rate, have been treated as constants for purposes of analysis, but are far from being so in practice. It is of interest to ask how the economy might respond to the initial impact of changes in these variables.

Equation (20) was derived on the assumption that ΔC, $\Delta\pi$ and ΔY^* were all constant. Relaxing this assumption yields

$$y = \gamma_1 \Delta\Delta\Delta C + \gamma_2 \Delta\Delta\pi + \gamma_3 \Delta\Delta\pi_{-1} - \gamma_4 \Delta\Delta\Delta Y^* + \alpha_1 y_{-1} - \alpha_2 y_{-2} + \alpha_3 y_{-3} \qquad (30)$$

where

$$\gamma_1 = \frac{v}{b + wg + (1-v)n + g(1-v)m} \qquad (31)$$

$$\gamma_2 = \frac{(1-v)m - (1-w)}{b + wg + (1-v)n + g(1-v)m} \qquad (32)$$

$$\gamma_3 = \frac{1-w}{b + wg + (1-v)n + g(1-v)m} \qquad (33)$$

$$\gamma_4 = \alpha_3 = \frac{b}{b + wg + (1-v)n + g(1-v)m} \qquad (34)$$

and α_1, α_2 and α_3 are defined as before.

Inspection of the parameters of the exogenous variables enables us to learn, not what the direction of change of y will be following a change in one of them, but at least where y will lie relative to where it otherwise would have been.

Consider first a change in the rate of domestic credit expansion. Since

$$\Delta\Delta\Delta C \equiv (\Delta C - \Delta C_{-1}) - (\Delta C_{-1} - \Delta C_{-2}) \qquad (35)$$

it follows that an increase in ΔC increases y initially but has an equal and opposite effect in the next period (and *vice versa* for a fall). These effects are not purely transitory for initial shocks have their impact perpetuated through the influence of the lagged y terms. The economic interpretation of the role of the lagged change in the rate of domestic credit expansion is that such a change has a smaller impact upon both income and the inflation rate in an open economy than an equal change in the rate of change of the money supply in a closed economy. The short run consequences of such a change for output and inflation are cushioned to some extent by the openness of the economy just as the long run consequences are completely cushioned. If the rate of domestic credit expansion increases, the economy immediately begins to send excess cash balances abroad via the balance of payments. The whole impact does not have to be absorbed in changes in output and the inflation rate as it would be in the case of a closed economy.

The initial direction of the impact effect of a change in the world inflation rate is ambiguous. An increase in the rate will initially lead to more or less unemployment depending on whether

$$(1-v)m \gtrless (1-w) \tag{36}$$

The economics behind this ambiguity is easy enough to set out. An increase in the world inflation rate means an increase in the domestic inflation rate and hence an increase in the rate of change of the demand for nominal balances. Other things equal, this leads to a fall in the demand for goods and services as people try to replenish their cash balances. However other things are not equal. The passage of time alone ensures that a higher relative price for tradeables ensues so that the balance of payments begins to provide the requisite monetary expansion independently of any decline in home demand. Thus the impact of the change in question also has an expansionary side. Indeed, output must eventually go above the full employment level in order to accelerate the rate of price inflation for non-tradeables up to that of world prices. This is the economic interpretation of the unambiguously positive effect of the lagged change in the world inflation rate on output. Though it takes us beyond what is directly implied by our formal model, whose time structure is extremely simple, it is probably fair to conclude that this ultimate effect will be longer delayed, rising unemployment being more likely to occur, the more rapidly does the demand for money respond to changes in the price level and the more slowly do resources shift between sectors in response to relative price changes. This may be an important matter when it comes to analysing actual runs of data for particular economies.

In principle this model may also be adapted to deal with the consequences of an exchange rate change. A devaluation would, within its structure, be equivalent to a sharp increase in the world inflation rate for one period followed by a return to the old rate of inflation in the next. Thus the impact of an exchange rate change would initially be like that of a change in the world inflation rate followed by an equal and opposite impact. To make economic sense of this again takes us outside the very constricted time structure of our formal model.[7] A devaluation with domestic credit expansion held constant will initially lead to either more or less unemployment depending upon whether the demand for money adapts quickly or slowly to the new world price level relative to the rate at which factors of production are reallocated between the non-tradeable and tradeable goods sectors. At some stage devaluation must produce greater than full employment output in order to have the price level of non-tradeables catch up with that of tradeables. Thereafter there is a tendency to unemployment as the domestic inflation rate, for a while running above the world rate, is brought back to equality with that rate.

The trouble here is that there is no mention of the likely effect of a devaluation upon expectations of inflation. In this model people blindly learn about the future course of inflation from experience of its past course and are not permitted to exercise their imaginations to the extent of predicting that an exchange rate change will lead to expectations so formed being unreliable. Thus the analysis in the previous paragraph must be taken with a large grain of salt, for it is almost certainly misleading particularly in its insistence that greater than full employment income is necessary at some time on the economy's time path to a new equilibrium. This would not be necessary if the expected inflation rate was given an exogenous push by the fact of devaluation.

Summary and conclusion

The preceding pages have contained quite a number of results and it is worthwhile bringing them together in summary form before concluding this essay. The closed economy model with which we began has the following properties:

(a) Real income tends to return to full employment equilibrium after a disturbance.
(b) Such an equilibrium is consistent with any constant *rate of change* of the money supply. In the long run, the rate of change of the money supply affects only the rate of price inflation.
(c) A change in the rate of change of the money supply initially affects both real income and prices.
(d) A particular level of income and employment may co-exist at a particular moment with any rate of price inflation. Expectations inherited from the past as well as the current level of excess demand affect the current inflation rate, so that the 'trade off' between inflation and unemployment is a short run phenomenon.

None of the foregoing propositions is new to the literature. They form the backbone of the 'monetarist' interpretation of inflation in a relatively closed economy such as the United States. Thus, such novelty as the closed economy model of this paper possesses lies not in the originality of its predictions but in the very fact that these predictions are derived from an explicit dynamic model.

If we turn to the open economy model we find that it also has properties (a) and (c). However the following properties set it apart from the closed economy model.

(e) The rate of inflation is in the long run determined from the outside. Only the rate of change of reserves and the domestic *price level* are affected in the long run by the rate of domestic credit expansion.
(f) Changes in the rate of domestic credit expansion affect both income and prices in the short run, but the impact of such changes is softened by the openness of the economy, relative to what it would be in a closed economy.

(g) Changes in the world inflation rate and the exchange rate, in and of themselves, will have impact effects on real income as well as upon prices. The nature of these impacts depends upon the relative size and speed of the reaction of the demand for nominal balances, and their supply (through the balance of payments) to changes in the world price level, and in its rate of change.

There is more novelty in these open economy results. Though (e) consists largely of well known predictions of the monetary theory of the balance of payments, that the equilibrium domestic *price level* (though not its inflation rate) will vary with the rate of domestic credit expansion is, I believe, a new prediction. (f) is not new, but again there is something to be said for having it explicitly derived from a formal model, while (g) does seem to scratch at new ground and raise particularly interesting questions.

Two *caveats* in conclusion: first the open economy model makes no provision for capital flows. Whether or not this is an important omission from the point of view of the predictions it makes can only be discovered by finding room for them in the model and seeing how its behaviour differs from that analysed here. Second, our analysis has made no provision for feedbacks through the international economy of the consequences of domestic changes. This omission puts another, potentially severe, limitation on the applicability of the results generated in this essay.

Notes

1. The basics of the monetarist position as it applies to a closed economy are to be found in Friedman (1968), Johnson (1971a and b) deals explicitly with inflation and extends the analysis to the open economy.
2. Clearly the first differences of Y^*, Y, and P may be regarded as percentage rates of growth. Note that in dealing with the dating of expected values of variables, the subscript refers to the time *at* which the expectation is formed and not that *for* which it is formed. Thus ΔP^E_{-1} is the rate of inflation expected at $t = -1$ to hold at $t = 0$.
3. Lipsey (1960) uses precisely these variables in some of his empirical formulations of the Phillips curve. There is nothing inherently monetarist about this version of the Phillips curve. I have elsewhere used it in a much more Keynesian framework than this (1972).
4. Cf. Johnson (1971a and b) for surveys of this theory.
5. This set of conditions is taken from Box and Jenkins (1970) p. 114.
6. I am indebted to David Rose for help and advice on this point.
7. Interpreting the results of this model is not straightforward, to some extent at least because it is formulated as a discrete time approximation. Thus we cannot distinguish cleanly between a change in the world inflation rate at a particular level of world prices on the one hand and a discrete shift in world prices with a constant inflation rate (i.e. an exchange rate change) on the other. Instead we have permanent and one period only changes in the inflation rate.

References

Box, G.E.P. and Jenkins, G.M. *Time Series Analysis: Forecasting and Control*. Holden Day. 1970.

Friedman, Milton 'The Role of Monetary Policy' *American Economic Review* (58) March 1968, pp. 1–17.

Johnson, H.G. 'The Monetary Approach to Balance of Payments Theory' Lecture delivered to Graduate Institute of International Studies, Geneva, Switzerland, February, 1971a.

Johnson, H.G. *Inflation and the Monetarist Controversy*, de Vries Lectures, Amsterdam, 1971b.

Laidler, D.E.W. 'Simultaneous Fluctuations in Prices and Output: A Business Cycle Approach', mimeo, University of Manchester 1972.

Lipsey, R.G. 'The Relation Between Unemployment and the Rate of Change of Money Wage Rates in the United Kingdom, 1862–1957', in R.A. Gordon and L.P. Klein (eds) *Readings in Business Cycles*, Homewood, Ill, 1965. Reprinted from *Economica*, Vol XXVII (1960) pp. 1–31.

8 Information, money and the macroeconomics of inflation

Introduction

I think that this is my best paper. As I have explained in my memoir, it was written in response to criticism of an alleged lack of micro-foundations for analysis of the type summarized in Chapter 7, above. As the reader will see, much of what later came to be called 'the buffer stock approach' to monetary theory is set out here: compelling evidence that this approach was not, as some people would have it, a defensive reaction to instability of empirical demand for money functions, but rather a positive attempt to provide microeconomic foundations for a particular kind of macroeconomics. The fact that this approach later turned out to be helpful in explaining short-run money demand instability was an *ex post* bonus. (See Chapters 11 and 13, below, and also C54.)

The arguments of this paper also show how much monetarists of my variety and post-Keynesians have in common, and I think that, in my case, this must have derived from much earlier discussions with Vicky Chick (1961–62), and Hy Minsky (1963–65), though I was not conscious of this link in 1973.

In addition to the Lund conference for which it was prepared, I also presented this paper at Keil, where Erik Lundberg was, for some reason, a member of the audience. He was very complimentary about it, which pleased me immensely, but which also should have warned me (though it did not) that my new line of argument was hardly going to appeal to the mainly American critics I was trying to mollify. As the reader will see, in 1973 I had not grasped the fact that Bob Lucas's version of the 'new microeconomics' was fundamentally and irrevocably Walrasian.

INFORMATION, MONEY AND THE MACRO-ECONOMICS OF INFLATION*

David Laidler

University of Manchester, Manchester, England

Summary

Traditional analysis of the price mechanism as a device for disseminating information is inadequate. It cannot explain the existence of unemployed resources, nor can it explain the role of money in the economic system. Money balances are held to economise on information gathering costs because information about prices themselves is imperfect. Moreover, money flows between economic agents carry information about the appropriateness of prices being set by them. Money therefore has a basic role to play in economic analysis on the micro level as well as on the macro level. The economics of allocation, unemployment and inflation are fundamentally one and the same thing. A system of macroeconomic theory consistent with this view is only now beginning to be built up, and is likely to cast in explicitly dynamic rather than comparative static terms.

I

Recent years have seen a spate of work on a set of inter-related problems; work that has gone under a variety of headings: "the economics of information", "the new microeconomics", "the re-interpretation of Keynesian economics" to name but three of the more popular titles.[1] It deals with one of the oldest problems in our subject: the way in which a market economy co-ordinates the activities of economic agents, each of whom is pursuing his own self-interest so as to produce a coherent social solution to the problem of scarcity.

In this paper, I shall describe how this work departs from older approaches to the problem, and show how a potentially far greater degree of integration between microeconomics and macroeconomics is permitted by the insights it yields, this integration hingeing on the role played by money in the economic

* This paper was prepared for the Symposium on the Economics of Information held at the University of Lund from 22nd to 24th August, 1973. I am grateful to John Foster, Malcolm Gray and George Zis for reading and commenting on an earlier draft.

[1] The basic ideas of this branch of the literature are chrystallised in two books: Leijonhufvud (1968) and Phelps (1969), but important papers by Clower (1965) and Stigler (1961) ought also to be mentioned. Once a particular viewpoint becomes clearly established in economics it is inevitable that particular aspects of it will be found to have been present in earlier writings. The new microeconomics is no exception but in this paper I hope to avoid dealing with the history of economic ideas for its own sake.

Swed. J. of Economics 1974

system. I shall then argue that such integration implies a considerable modification of prevailing macroeconomic orthodoxy and one that completely breaks down the distinctions between the economics of inflation and depression. I shall sketch out the salient features of this "new macroeconomics", particularly as it applies to the problem of inflation, showing how it permits an economic—as opposed to sociological or socio-psychological—explanation of this phenomenon, an explanation that assigns a key role to monetary factors. Thereafter, I shall not end with any set of neatly drawn conclusions, for, perhaps, the strongest theme of all those running through the following pages is that this new work puts us in possession, not of any new set of established truths, but of a set of insights which provide the foundations upon which much economics can be reconstructed. Such reconstruction has hardly begun.

II

The question of the dissemination of information has long been central to economics. It has seldom, if ever, been the case that a model of an economy has been built upon the explicit assumption of complete and costless information.[1] The "economic problem" concerns the allocation of scarce resources among competing ends. We want an economic system to solve for a set of quantities. Prices are of no intrinsic importance from this point of view. Consider Robinson Crusoe's economic life: he has to allocate the resources available to him in order to satisfy his wants, but he has no-one to trade with, no-one with whom he must co-ordinate his activities. The solution to his maximisation problem will, to be sure, yield a set of prices along with a set of quantities, but there is no question of those prices helping him to solve his maximisation problem. They simply exist as part of its solution. The economist looking from the outside at a general equilibrium system made up of many economic agents, and finding its equilibrium properties, will solve simultaneously for quantities and prices, and, since it is the quantities that go to satisfy wants, it is the quantities that are the important part of the solution. If every agent within the economy had the same information as that economist looking in from the outside, he could perform exactly the same calculation and immediately act in a way that was consistent with equilibrium overall.

Prices are important in the analysis of allocation precisely because information is not perfect in the sense just outlined. In traditional accounts of a market economy, prices convey both information and incentives to economic agents in order that they will act in a fashion that is consistent with general equilibrium in the absence of complete information about the nature of

[1] The analysis of "recontracting" based on Edgeworth's work involves economic agents being informed about allocations of goods and then accepting or rejecting such allocations. This analysis comes as close to assuming complete and costless information as does any. I am indebted to Alan Feldman for drawing my attention to this point.

that equilibrium. Analysis of Walrasian tâtonnement is, then, concerned not with the existence and stability of general equilibrium in a situation of complete knowledge, but in a situation of highly imperfect knowledge. There is no other way to justify the key role played by prices in that analysis. Each individual knows about the technology available to him and the resources with which his is initially endowed, but nothing about the endowments or tastes of other members of the economic system. It is solely through market prices that his activities are co-ordinated with the activities of others. The basic social role of prices is to economise on costly information about the possibilities open to economic agents, and to provide the incentives for them to harmonise activities.[1]

But Walrasian economics does not get to the root of the social problem of co-ordinating economic activity. One symptom of its inadequacy is the difficulty of reconciling the existence and use of money with such a view of the world. A numeraire, a unit of account, may be introduced on the grounds that it economises on computation costs, but in a Walrasian economy in static equilibrium, and trade takes place under no other circumstances in such an economy, it is difficult to see why an intermediate good should enter naturally into the process of exchange.[2] After all, one interpretation of static general equilibrium is that the same exchanges take place time and time again between the same agents. It is difficult to apply to such circumstances the usual arguments about the greater costs of direct barter, most of which stem from the costs of finding the appropriate set of trading partners; but even if some such artificiality as uncertainty about the precise timing of meetings between pairs of traders during the market period is introduced, this only opens up the possibility of intermediate trades taking place; it stops far short of explaining why it is sensible to hold inventories of any good, and money in particular, between market periods.[3] It only makes sense to do this if the individual sees some chance of his receipts in the market not being equal to his outgoings, and this possibility does not arise when all trades are taking place, and are known to be taking place, at equilibrium prices. Only if individuals come to market uncertain of the prices at which they are going to trade or uncertain about the likelihood of expenditures and receipts

[1] That prices are an economical way of conveying information and instructions is basic to the Lange-Lerner defence of the viability of a socialist economy. Frank Knight's still widely read account of the functions of a price system (1933) makes much of this point also. However, the author of *Risk Uncertainty and Profit* was by no means unaware of the problems that the passage of time and the difficulty of forecasting the future raise for the smooth functioning of a price system.

[2] The very role of a numeraire in economising computation is another example of the way in which Walrasian general equilibrium economics recognises the problem of economising on information costs.

[3] In trying to integrate money with a simple Walrasian analysis of exchange, Patinkin (1965) introduces the notion that though trades all take place on a particular day, the actual settling of accounts takes place between market days and with an uncertain time pattern. The very artificiality of this construction provides an excellent example of the difficulty of bringing money holding into Walrasian economics.

balancing does it become sensible to hold inventories of goods and money between visits to the market.[1]

We frequently talk about how supply and demand in the market determine prices but this is precisely what they do not do in Walrasian analysis. *Ex ante* supply and demand information are used by the auctioneer to determine prices and then the market opens up for trade. The prices of the Walrasian model economise information costs for participants in the market but they are not determined by anything, or anybody, within the economy. They are given, costlessly, from the outside. From an empirical viewpoint it is difficult to take seriously the proposition that a market economy functions with everyone aware of all the prices that are ruling, and it is even more difficult to believe that all the prices ruling at a particular moment are compatible with the market being cleared overall. As time passes, tastes and technology change, equilibrium quantities of goods and services change, and so does the structure of equilibrium prices. Beyond the question of whether, at a particular moment a set of prices exists, knowledge of which on the part of economic agents would cause them to act in a manner compatible with the existence of general equilibrium, lie the questions of how, or even whether, those prices are set in the first place, and how information about them is disseminated. The very existence of the phenomenon of unemployment among scarce resources makes it impossible to hold to the comfortable proposition that any market economy behaves "as if" equilibrium prices always rule and are known to all agents.

That the failure of prices adequately to convey information and incentives lies at the root of the problem of unemployment has long been a commonplace of macroeconomics. The reasons typically advanced for inappropriate price patterns have to do with institutional rigidities associated with monopoly and with various forms of irrationality that go under the general heading of "money illusion". In any case, these reasons have never been central to orthodox macroanalysis which concentrates upon the consequences rather than the causes of these rigidities. This analysis is enshrined in the LM-IS or Hicks–Hansen macro model. In its usual text-book formulation this model presents an account of the determination of an *equilibrium* situation in which, because of wage and price rigidities, real output lies below the maximum that would be permitted by the full employment of available resources.[2]

[1] This is not to say that there exists a particular degree of uncertainty beyond the control of the economic agent. The point is that he may both reduce uncertainty by devoting real resources to information gathering and reduce the costs of uncertainty by holding and trading with money. Money holding is up to a point a cheaper alternative to incurring search costs and this is an important reason why money holding is associated with the persistence of market uncertainty. On this matter see Brunner & Meltzer (1971). See also below pp. 8–11 where the role of money is further discussed.

[2] The typical contemporary textbook simultaneously contains an account of how the behaviour of prices is a key factor in ensuring an appropriate allocation of productive resources, and an account of a model premissed on the downward rigidity of prices, which if taken seriously, demonstrates that a market economy cannot even guarantee full employment of resources let alone an appropriate alocation of them: hardly a comfortable pair of positions to hold simultaneously and made no easier to reconcile by sometimes

The existence of money in the LM–IS model, as it is usually interpreted, is no easier to explain than it is in terms of Walrasian analysis. To say that prices are rigid does not mean that they are unknown to anyone, and to postulate that the economic system is in equilibrium, even at less than full employment, would appear to involve all participants in market activity being able to undertake all their planned exchanges of goods and services in a manner consistent with given expectations. All the factors that make it difficult to explain why money should exist in the context of a smoothly functioning Walrasian system are present in the LM–IS model even though its very structure, and many of the apparently most empirically relevant propositions that may be derived from that framework, are critically dependent on the existence of an asset that goes by the name "money" and purports to correspond to some easily recognised empirical counterpart.

That neither the Walrasian nor the Hicks–Hansen model can provide any compelling explanation for the existence of money is particularly disconcerting when we try to deal with the contemporary problem of inflation. A theory of inflation must explain variations in the ratio in which money exchanges for goods and services but neither of these models even explains *why* money should be exchanged for goods and services in the first place. It is hardly surprising that there is widespread doubt about the capacity of orthodox economics to deal with inflation. However, the new approaches, alluded to at the outset of this paper, to the problem of how a decentralised market economy goes about disseminating the information concerning the behaviour that is required for general equilibrium to prevail are putting us in a position to get to grips with the problem of inflation. The new microeconomics enables us to begin constructing a new macroeconomics whose relevance to the way in which a market economy deals with the problem of scarcity is far clearer than was that of the old macroeconomics.

III

This "new microeconomics" rests on three obviously true premisses, from which the old microeconomics, in its more rigorous formulations, nevertheless, abstracted. First, once they are committed to a certain course of behaviour, economic agents may not instantaneously and costlessly change that commitment; thus, the passage of time, and its irreversibility are matters of paramount importance in understanding economic activity. Second, prices are not "determined by markets" but are set by individual agents. Third, information about prices that currently rule is not freely available but must

being accompanied by a third view to the effect that, if by good luck or wise management, full employment does prevail, then the price mechanism can after all play its allocative role!

Finally, it should be noted that whether the Hicks-Hansen model is what Keynes "really meant" or not is not an issue which I wish to raise here. The way the model is utilised in orthodox analysis and not its historical origins is what matters in the current discussion.

actively be sought at a cost in real resources. Based on these premisses we have models in which members of the labour force remain unemployed while they seek information about wage levels in various employments, at each moment deciding to remain unemployed or not, depending upon whether the expected return from further search is enough to compensate for the income forgone by not taking the highest paying job currently known to be availble; we have models in which firms set prices on the basis of expectations about the time path of sales and hence of profits that various pricing policies will generate, and in which they adjust prices as those expectations fail to be fulfilled; we have models in which the costs of adjusting prices result in their being changed at discrete intervals rather than continuously; and so on.[1]

At present it is far from clear how these various models of individual behaviour might fit together into a coherent whole: indeed, it is not even clear that they do all fit together. However, certain themes run through them all. Most obvious is the paramount importance of expectations. To offer goods at a certain price, to accept employment at a certain wage, and so forth, all involve making commitments for the future and hence involve closing off alternatives. Such choices cannot be made in an uncertain world unless expectations about the future are formed; but because expectations cannot be formed with certainty, and because current and past experience is not a thoroughly reliable guide to the future, behaviour will not immediately respond to current changes in circumstances. A firm will not immediately cut its prices and reduce its output when demand falls since it is costly to do either and not immediately obvious that the fall in question is anything but temporary. Nor will a worker faced with a choice between a lay-off or a wage cut necessarily take the wage cut. It might, given his expectations of his earning power elsewhere seem to pay him to accept unemployment while looking for another job. Only if his search activity reveals to him that he was unduly optimistic about the alternatives will he become willing to accept a lower wage. We have a picture, then, of an economic system in which people form expectations, act upon them, and as a consequence of acting, receive information in terms of which they will eventually modify both their expectations and their future behaviour. Equilibrium in such a system thus requires not only that everyone's plans be compatible at a particular moment, but also that the outcome of everyone's action be what he expected. Only in this way is there no incentive for behaviour to change over time.[2]

It is relatively easy to rationalise the use of money in such an economic system. If the future pattern of prices is unclear, so that what any economic

[1] Labour market search analysis underlies the work of Alchian (1969), Lucas & Rapping (1969), Mortenson (1969) and Phelps (1972). Phelps & Winter (1969), Carlson (1972) and Barro (1972) deal with the pricing behaviour of firms. All except the last two cited pieces of analysis are to be found in papers included in Phelps & Winter (1969).

[2] Hicks defined equilibrium in this way as long ago as 1932. It is also worth noting that Robbins (1935) regarded uncertainty as a basic postulate of theories both of economic dynamics and of money.

agent might expect to realise from the sale of goods and services is uncertain, and if it is costly to change production and consumption plans, then it might pay to hold various buffer stocks rather than engage in the costly search activities needed to reduce uncertainty to negligible proportions. Moreover, it is not hard to see that a buffer stock of an asset that is readily exchangeable with anyone for anything is particularly desirable. Money is just such an asset since virtually every trade involves an exchange of goods and services against money. By holding money, the economic agent can reduce the amount of resources he devotes to generating information for himself since it reduces the costs which ignorance and errors impose upon him. For example, it enables him to undertake various market transactions at discrete intervals—to engage in indirect trade—rather than to devote time and effort to the costly business of seeking out just those people whose trading plans perfectly complement his own so that he may then engage in simultaneous direct barter. Once a general means of exchange is established in use, then, it pays everyone to maintain it in use and to hold inventories of it.[1]

Equally, it is reasonable for those fixing prices to fix them in terms of the item against which they exchange so that the unit of account and the means of exchange in the economy are usually the same asset. The basic fact of the allocative mechanism is not the determination of a set of relative prices by markets—which may, trivially, be converted to money prices by using a numeraire—but the fixing of money prices by economic agents—which may, of course, be converted into a set of relative prices whose significance is far from trivial. When put in these terms the difference in perspective between the new and the old microeconomics is sharp indeed. Money now enters at the beginning of the analysis with a fundamental role to play rather than entering at the end as an afterthought.

Money plays two interlinked roles in this new approach to economics. Individuals may economise on gathering information by holding money as an inventory of generalised purchasing power, while the volume of money that flows between agents conveys information to them about whether the expectations upon which they have planned their market activities were correct. Excess demand (or supply) for a good manifests itself as more money (or less) than expected being offered in exchange for it at the going price. The use of a price system and the use of money are inextricably linked up with the transmission of information between economic agents. To return to Robinson Crusoe for a moment, his economic life needs neither prices nor money. Both are social institutions whose role is to contribute to the co-ordination of economic acitvity where information is imperfect and costly.[2]

---

[1] The foregoing analysis of the role of money draws heavily on the analysis of Brunner & Meltzer (1971). Note that though it provides a rationale for the use of money, it does not explain how the use of money develops in the first place.

[2] Which is not to say that it is always preferable to use money in trading activities. Specialised dealers, for example in used cars, often find it appropriate to indulge in

All this points to money being a very special good indeed and suggests that to treat it in analysis as if it were no different to any other good is likely to be fraught with difficulties. In particular, it suggests that to treat the general price level, which is the inverse of the price of money, as if it were directly determined by the supply and demand for money just like the price of any other good is misleading. Even in terms of the new microeconomics one would expect an excess demand for a particular good to lead those selling it to revise upwards its price relative to what it otherwise would have been, but it is of the very essence of the foregoing analysis that no-one sets the "price" of money relative to goods in general. There is no unique market for money and its "price" emerges as the result of economic agents each setting the price of the particular good he is supplying in terms of money. Thus, there is no question of inflation being understood in terms of the supply and demand for money alone.[1] A satisfactory theory of inflation must take into account the factors that influence the price setting activities of individual agents *vis-a-vis* particular goods and services.

The very body of analysis that poses the problem of explaining price level fluctuations in these terms, however, puts us in a position to deal with it, as I shall now show. The resulting approach to macroeconomic disturbance still assigns a key role to money's behaviour, but not the least of its advantages over the old macroeconomics is that it explains why money should be so important. The importance of money for macroeconomic phenomena stems from its role in the transmission of information and incentives between economic agents.

IV

So long as macroeconomics is based on the postulate that factors such as monopoly and money illusion are the main determinants of price level behaviour, it cannot provide a coherent explanation of inflation in terms of economic factors. Sociological and socio-psychological explanations thus become popular for want of an alternative. It is the peculiar contribution of the new microeconomics to macroeconomics that it explains the time path of prices and their potential incompatibility with full employment as the result of rational behaviour in the face of the imperfect and costly information that is inherent in a market economy. It thus opens the way to a truly economic explanation of the inflationary process in which output and employment fluctuations play a key role. This is not to say that, in the current state of knowledge, such an explanation can explicitly and rigorously

---

barter. Moreover, when long established trading relationships exist the information that these provide about the reliability and probity of particular economic agents make the institution of trade credit a viable proposition. This is *not* to say that either used cars or trade credit are money, but only that they may substitute for money, the *general* means of exchange, in certain *specific* transactions.

[1] The argument here has something in common with earlier work on the validity of the so-called Classical Dichotomy; *cf.* Brunner (1951) and Patinkin (1965).

be deduced from the new microeconomic models referred to earlier. The discussion of aggregative policy problems will not wait for this difficult task to be accomplished; moreover the present generation of micro models which attribute imperfect information to individual agents also attribute to them unlimited and costless access to computational skills and, hence, is unlikely to represent anything like the last word to be said on the relevant problems at micro level.[1]

Nevertheless, it does appear to be possible to describe the process of inflation in a way that seems consistent with what we know of the microeconomics of price formation. The basic postulates about behaviour that underly the analysis of the allocative mechanism in the absence of costless knowledge about which prices are ruling and which prices it would be appropriate to set provide the ingredients of such a description. Firms set the money prices of both inputs and outputs. Their ability to do so implies that, over some relevant time horizon, they exercise both monopoly and monopsony power; along with the prices they set must go certain expectations about both the volume of sales that will be realised and the volume of factor services that will be offered to them for employment. Disappointed expectations about quantities cause prices to be revised upwards if more output is demanded or fewer factors supplied than expected and *vice versa*. Firms meet unexpected discrepancies between the volume of sales and that of factor payments by permitting inventories of goods and money balances to vary, and by varying the intensity with which inputs are utilised, thus gaining time to revise their price and output plans. Households search for prices and wage offers and revise their expectations about the terms that can be had in the light of that search; search activites are supported both by cutting down on current consumption expenditure and by running down assets, including money balances. An important factor in the determination of the wages and prices that firms think it appropriate to set at any moment, and households expect to find at any moment, is the recent history of wages and prices as perceived by the agents in question as a result of their search activities. Finally, both firms and households find it sensible to maintain, on average, (but obviously not at each and every moment) an inventory of cash balances whose purchasing power bears a stable relationship to the real volume of market transactions in which they expect to be involved.[2]

[1] The emphasis in these models is on the maximising behaviour of individual agents rather than on the interaction over time of the market behaviour of many such agents. To maintain rigour at the level of the analysis of the individual while dealing with market activity presents formidable technical problems, and hence it may be appropriate to characterise individual agents as operating by simple rules of thumb when dealing with market activity. Whether it is or not is basically an empirical question. I am indebted to Sidney G. Winter for helpful discussion on this point.

[2] A stable, and not a constant relationship is postulated here, and there is a great deal of evidence in favour of this. Not the least thing that we require from the new macroeconomics is that it explain and be consistent with the empirical evidence amassed to support the old.

The foregoing specifications are broadly drawn and, clearly, a wide variety of particular macro models could be constructed within the boundaries that they lay down. We may, nevertheless, make the following general observations about the nature of the inflationary process. When the rate of change of money wages and prices is just what economic agents expect it to be, and when it also just generate the volume of sales and availability of inputs that firms expect, then there will be no forces at play to cause those rates of change to vary over time.[1] Such an equilibrium rate of inflation—including a zero or negative one—is compatible with a certain level of unemployment, because one would always expect to find a certain fraction of the labour force involved in wage and price searching rather than in employment.[2]

Any rate of inflation may be an equilibrium rate provided that it is anticipated and generates the appropriate level of output and employment. However, for a given level of real output and transactions, and hence, for a given demand for real cash balances, a different inflation rate requires a different rate of growth of the nominal money supply. The proportionality of the rate of inflation to the rate of monetary expansion, a key proposition of the "old macroeconomics" as far as inflation is concerned, emerges from the newer framework as a proposition about *equilibrium* inflation.[3] Though the "old macroeconomics" usually had causation clearly running from money to prices there is no such direct implication in the foreging argument. Firms, on the basis of expectations, think it appropriate to raise prices; firms and households finding themselves with growing money balances attempt to exchange them for goods and factor services but the prices of these are rising at just that rate which absorbs the growth in money balances and keeps them at an equilibrium level. The flow of money between economic agents informs them that the expectations upon which they set prices and wages were valid. There is no suggestion of "demand pull" or "cost push" here: this traditional dichotomy has no meaning in the present context.

If an equilibrium inflation rate is one in which expectations are always justified, then a disequilibrium rate involves disappointed expectations. Suppose wages and prices are rising at the expected rate but that this is

---

[1] Again, there is a good deal of empirical evidence that people do form expectations about the rate of inflation and act upon them when it comes to money holding. The same expectations ought to inform the fixing of prices and money wages.

[2] This, of course, is the so-called "natural rate of unemployment" hypothesis. There is no need to think of this rate as a constant that never changes. Presumably the faster do tastes and technology change, the more worthwhile an activity will search be, while, given that people have memories, the more search there has been in the recent past, the less valuable might it be at present. Even though the "natural rate of unemployment" may be expected to vary over time, however, this does not seriously affect the current analysis. Phelps (1972) ch. 2 presents a most useful discussion of the determinants of the natural unemployment rate.

[3] Strict proportionality here is only a prediction in the case of a non-growing economy. In general the quantity theory prediction is that the rate of inflation will equal the rate of monetary expansion minus the income elasticity of demand for real balances times the growth rate of real income.

in excess of what can be supported by the current rate of monetary expansion. In order to maintain inventories of real cash balances at desired levels households just cut expenditure. Firms' inventories of goods will begin to accumulate unexpectedly and their cash balances will run down as households restore theirs. The shortfall of cash flowing into firms signals to them the desirablility of revising prices and wages downward relative to what was planned as well as the desirability of cutting output and employment. Lowered wage offers will persuade those engaged in job search to prolong that search, finance it in part by cutting back on expenditure, and thus reinforce the tendencies already set in motion by what amounts to the first round of a Keynesian multiplier process.

Now to cut prices, wages and employment is just what we require a firm to do when a shortfall of cash inflow signals that demand has shifted away from what it has to sell towards someone else's product. But a firm cannot immediately distinguish between a general fall in demand and one specific to its own product. Nor can a member of the labour force immediately distinguish between a shift in the structure of the demand for labour and a shift in its overall level. An overall fall in output and employment is thus an integral part of the mechanism whereby it is signalled to firms that their pricing policies have been inappropriate and to firms and households that their wage and price expectations have been erroneous, given the rate of monetary expansion. An exactly similar argument, but with signs reversed, goes through if we start with wages and prices rising too slowly for the rate of monetary expansion. Not the least appealing characteristic of this new approach to macroeconomics is that it enables us to use the same theory to deal with both inflation and depression. In disequilibrium prices and output fluctuate together. Even if it is output fluctuations that are important in a particular instance, it is impossible to analyse the behaviour of output without reference to the behavior of prices. Similarly, if price level behaviour is of most concern, it cannot be understood unless attention is paid to the time path of output. Instead of having an economics of depression and an economics of inflation we simply have macroeconomics.[1]

The framework which I have outlined in the last few pages is not irrevocably tied to any particular view of the original source of specific macroeconomic

[1] The foregoing can all be cast in LM–IS erms. So long as the rate of monetary expansion and the rate of inflation are equal — I assume zero real growth for simplicity—the LM curve is stationary, and if it intersects the IS curve at that level of real income at which the natural rate of unemployment prevails we have full macroeconomic equilibrium. If it does not, then disappointed expectations about sales and job prospects cause the rate of inflation to vary relative to the expected rate of inflation and relative to the rate of monetary expansion. Hence, the LM curve begins to shift and the level of real income to change affecting in turn the rate of inflation. The model as usually presented may then be re-interpreted as showing a point on a disequilibrium path at a moment in time rather than a situation of macro equilibrium. The so-called "full employment" version of the model becomes nonsense in terms of this analysis and the usefulness of the whole LM–IS system as an expositional device is sharply reduced.

disturbances, but it does assign a key role to the behaviour of the money supply. It tells us first of all that a necessary condition for there to exist an equilibrium rate of inflation is that there must be a constant rate of monetary expansion. But the properties of equilibrium inflation *per se* are, perhaps, of more academic than practical interest. Equilibrium inflation, being fully anticipated, has none of the socially disruptive consequences for the distribution of income and wealth that are the prime reason for regarding price level fluctuations as undesirable. As is well-known, the only consequences of having one equilibrium inflation rate rather than another is a tendency for equilibrium cash balances to be of a different order of magnitude and for this to be associated with a different long-run equilibrium capital stock. Even these consequences hinge upon cartel arangements in the banking system preventing a competitive rate of return being paid on money balances.[1] The predictions of the quantity theory of money then, an important component of the old macroeconomics, are, according to the new, likely to be consistent only with the facts of what is in many ways the least interesting aspect of the inflationary process.

Nevertheless, this new approach assigns money a key role in disequilibrium too. It views incompatibility between the rate of monetary expansion on the one hand and the actual and expected inflation rates on the other as lying at the heart of the process whereby output, employment and prices fluctuate together, while simultaneously suggesting that the very characteristics of this process will tend to distract attention from its fundamentally monetary nature. Suppose that, in a condition of full equilibrium, the rate of monetary expansion increases. There is no reason to believe that excess cash balances will initially spill over equally into each and every sector of the ceconomy, nor is there any reason to believe that, if such a disruption were to take place a number of times, the same sectors would be affected in the same order and to the same extent on each occasion. Much would depend on the way in which new money found its way into the system. Thus, it would be all too easy to infer from observation that the inflation rate was changing as a result of special circumstances affecting specific sectors of the economy at a particular moment. Such observations as these surely lie at the root of the widespread acceptance of structuralist explanations of inflation. The proximate cause of price and wage level changes is, after all, not some auctioneer declaring the price of money balances to be falling relative to goods and services, but the actions of specific firms in raising the prices of particular goods and the wages of particular classes of labour.[2]

---

[1] See Patinkin (1972) chs. 10 and 11 for a lucid exposition of the issues at stake in the analysis of the long run neutrality of money.

[2] Note though that the faster the pace of structural change in an economy, the higher will be the natural rate of unemployment. Hence a speedup of technical change combined with a policy of maintaining a given unemployment rate will inevitably prove inflationary. This point is made by Alchian (1969).

It is also an inherent property of a disequilibrium inflation in which the actual rate exceeds the expected rate that those whose money incomes are increasing are surprised to find that rising prices prevent real incomes from increasing at the same rate. This surprise is an integral part of the mechanism whereby inflationary expectations are brought into harmony with what is actually happening. While expectations are catching up with events, however, there is inevitable disappointment about realised real income levels.[1] It would be easy enough to take such a symptom of inflation for a fundamental cause and it is not surprising that competition over real income levels is often looked upon as lying at the root of the inflationary process. After all, it is another inherent property of disequilibrium inflation that real income and interest rates also fluctuate along with prices so that there is unlikely to be any close correlation between the rate of monetary expansion and the rate of inflation. The old macroeconomics would have us read such a lack of correlation as evidence against a monetary explanation of a particular inflationary episode, but not the new.[2]

It has already been observed that, in terms of the new analysis, the economics of inflation and depression are the same, and the arguments of the last two paragraphs are easily enough adapted to the case of an economy in the process of contracting as a result of a slowdown in the rate of monetary expansion. There is no reason to suppose that the impacts of such a slowdown should be equally spread across all industries, and again there is considerable potential for confusion of cause and effect: the reader hardly needs reminding that recessions are frequently attributed to causes specific to particular industries. There is also something to be said about the behaviour of income relative to expectations in economic contraction. Money incomes fall or fail to rise as quickly as before, but it is not immediately apparent to households that the behaviour of prices will tend to offset the effects of this on real income. Thus, expenditure plans are cut by more than is justified by events. In this light the "hoarding" that so often accompanies recession and is frequently regarded as being one of its causes is more appropriately regarded as a symptom.[3]

[1] This is a modern version of Hume's wages lag hypothesis. Though real wages do not necessarily fall, they do fail to rise as fast as was expected.

[2] One must be careful here not to carry this argument to the point of rendering a monetary explanation of inflation irrefutable. A well specified dynamic model would, of course, make precise predictions about the relationship between the inflation rate and the rate of monetary expansion that would be open to test.

[3] Note that this argument implies that income expectations are formed on the basis of expectations about money incomes and of expectations about price level behaviour, rather than being derived directly from past evidence on the behaviour of real income itself. The relationship betwen this argument and more usual formulations of the permanent income hypothesis would be well worth investigating.

Disappointed income expectations are one aspect of the more general distributional consequences of the actual inflation rate differeing from that which was expected. Such consequences, though their social importance has long been recognised, have occupied a rather minor role in the traditional economic analysis of inflation. The tendency has been to regard them as an unfortunate by-product of inflation about which economics has

Now the old macroeconomics does not confine itself to situations in which the major influence on economic activity is an *exogeneous* rate of monetary expansion. In the Wicksellian analysis of inflation the level of the so-called "money rate of interest" is set by the banking system at such a level as to result in excess demand at full employment. Prices rise and the money supply simultaneously expands to validate this. Where the monetary theory of the balance of payments is applied to a small economy operating a fixed exchange rate, the domestic price level rises in harmony with world-wide trends and the balance of payments instantaneously adjusts in order to provide the required expansion of the money supply. The new macroeconomics no more than the old can afford to ignore the relevance of the institutional assumptions that underly such pieces of analysis as these. However, it would stress that the validation of price level behaviour by that of the money supply is likely to be a state of affairs approached only in the long-run rather than something which can be relied upon to occur immediately.

In the Wicksellian case the initial response to the appearance of a discrepancy between the money rate of interest and the "natural" rate—which must now be redefined as that rate of interest compatible with the maintenance of the natural rate of unemployment—would be an increase in output followed by an increase in the inflation rate and only then by an increase in the rate of monetary expansion. Moreover, changes in inflationary expectations over time would alter the real value of the money rate of interest for a given nominal value, and hence the level of aggregate demand and the inflation rate itself. All in all, there would appear to be plenty of scope for both output and the inflation rate to fluctuate once the lags in behaviour inherent in the new macroeconomics are put into a Wicksellian framework.

The same can be said of the application of the monetary theory of the balance of payments to the problem of inflation in a small open economy. Instead of all firms being "price takers" in a competitive world market, it becomes appropriate to think of those firms selling abroad or buying from abroad searching out and taking account of world price level trends when forming the expectations upon which their own price and output decisions are made. There is no need to expect them to do this continuously, completely and accurately; while we might expect firms who deal only in the domestic market to be even slower in adapting their plans to what is happening in the world at large. Moreover, along with capital account adjustments, it requires a change in the composition of output between these two groups of firms to generate the balance of payments effects by which the rate of monetary expansion is adapted to change circumstances. The new macro-

little to say. The new analysis stresses that these distributional effects arise because economic agents act on faulty information and that they are likely to alter their expectations and future actions as a result. Thus, such distributional effects can influence the future course of the economy and should, perhaps, be assigned a much more central role in the analysis of macroeconomic disequilibrium than has usually been accorded them.

economics naturally focuses our attention upon the time required for the necessary re-allocation of productive resources to take place. This new analysis would seem to have an important role to play in illuminating the potentially confusing disequilibrium dynamic process whereby a small economy adapts its inflation rate to that ruling in the rest of the world.[1]

V

In this paper, I have tried to show that recent analysis of the way in which a market economy deals with the problem of disseminating information among economic agents puts us in a position to build a microeconomics of allocation and distribution and a macroeconomics of inflation and depression which are consistent with one another and which assign a key role to money. I have also sketched out some properties of the relevant macroeconomic system, arguing that the basic advance has been to make endogenous to the macroeconomy the behaviour of the general price level so that the problem of explaining price level behaviour becomes one of economic rather than sociological or socio-psychological analysis. Nevertheless, my account of this new macroeconomics has indeed been a sketch, and for reasons that are not hard to find. It has been fundamental to my argument that the appropriate formulation for a model of the macroeconomic system is a dynamic one in which the time paths of key variables interact over time. The precise behaviour of dynamic economic systems is notoriously dependent upon the quantitative as well as upon the qualitative characteristics of the structural relationships that it encompasses.

We would like to know how long it takes to get back to an equilibrium inflation rate after disturbance and we would like some idea of how large are the real income fluctuations relative to the fluctuations in the inflation rate that they accompany. There is always the possibility of outright instability in a dynamic system to say nothing of proneness to cyclical behaviour, and it would be desirable to know something of the circumstances under which any actual economy might display such characteristics. Such problems as these are immediately raised by the conclusion that the appropriate formulation of macroeconomics is dynamic. Only by building and analysing explicit models can we begin to get to grips with them but *a priori* analysis alone is hardly likely to prove enough. The general outlines laid down by the analysis set out in this paper would permit an extremely wide variety of models. The only way to narrow down the field is by the test of empirical

[1] Laidler (1972) presents one attempt to come to grips with this problem. The monetary theory of the balance of payments is really based on the proposition that the relevant market for analysing inflation is more widespread than the boundaries of a particular natiolna state. These boundaries are after all political rather than economic. The analysis of what happens in one small economy is inherently a partial equilibrium exercise which perhaps ought to be complemented by an analysis of the causes of inflation at the level of the world economy.

content. Thus, the building up of new macroeconomics is likely to be a process of formulating hypotheses about particular aspects of macroeconomic behaviour, testing them against available data, and ruling them out or including them in the new structure depending upon their performance. The basic theme of this paper has been that new work on the manner in which a market economy disseminates information has permitted a far greater integration of micro and macro analysis than did earlier approaches. Almost as important, it looks like requiring a much greater degree of integration between theoretical and empirical work in economics than has previously existed.

References

Alchian, A.: Information costs, pricing and resource unemployment. In *Microeconomic foundations of employment and inflation theory* (ed. E. S. Phelps). W. W. Norton & Co., New York, 1969.

Barro, R. J.: A theory of monopolistic price adjustment. *Review of Economic Studies 29*, 17–26, 1972.

Brunner, K.: Inconsistency and indeterminancy in classical economics, *Econometrica 19*, 152–73, 1951.

Brunner, K. & Meltzer, A. H.: The uses of money: money in the theory of an exchange economy. *American Economic Review 61*, (5), 784–805, 1971.

Carlson, J. A.: Elusive passage to the non-walrasian continent, University of Manchester Inflation Workshop (mimeo), May 1972.

Clower, R. W.: The Keynesian counter-revolution: a theoretical appraisal. *The theory of interest rates* (ed. F. H. Hahn and F. P. R. Brechling). Proceedings of an I. E. A. Conference, Macmillan, London, 1965.

Knight, F. H.: Social economic organisation, pp. 3–30 of Knight's *The economic organisation* (1933), Harper and Row, New York, 1951, reprinted as Reading 1 in Breit & Hochman, *Readings in microeconomics*, Holt, Rinehart and Winston, London, 1969.

Laidler, D. E. W., Price and output fluctuations in an open economy. University of Manchester Inflation Workshop paper No. 7301, Dec. 1972.

Leijonhufvud, A.: *On Keynesian economics and the economics of Keynes: a study in monetary theory*. Oxford University Press, New York, 1968.

Lucas, R. E. Jr & Rapping, L. A.: Real wages, employment and inflation. In *Microeconomic foundations of employment and inflation theory* (ed. E. S. Phelps), 1969.

Mortenson, D. T.: A theory of wage and employment dynamics. In *Microeconomic foundations of employment and inflation theory* (ed. E. S. Phelps), 1969.

Patinkin, D.: *Money, interest and prices: an integration of monetary and value theory*, 2nd ed. Harper and Row, New York, 1965.

Patinkin, D.: *Studies in monetary economics*. Harper and Row, New York, 1972.

Phelps, E. S.: *Inflation policy and unemployment theory: the cost-benefit approach to monetary planning*. Macmillan, London, 1972.

Phelps, E. S. & Winter, S. G., Jr: Optimal price policy under atomistic competition. In *Microeconomic foundations of employment and inflation theory* (ed. E. S. Phelps), New York, 1969.

Robbins, L. C.: *An essay on the nature and significance of economic science*, 2nd revised ed. Macmillan, London, 1935.

Stigler, G. C.: The economics of information. *Journal of Political Economy 69*, (3), 213–225, 1961.

9 Monetarism: an interpretation and an assessment

Introduction

I was not idle in the seven years which intervened between the writing of Chapter 8 and this one. A glance at the bibliography will show that I was very busy working on the Monetarist agenda which I had set out for myself while at Manchester, but the work by and large involved filling in empirical details, rather than breaking new ground.

This paper was written for a Royal Economic Society Conference, when Monetarism (of a sort) was at the height of its policy influence. As an academic doctrine it was already in eclipse, because the profession had decided that empirical details mattered less than clear Walrasian theoretical foundations. This was a fundamental methodological error in my view, and I wish that people like Milton Friedman, Karl Brunner and Allan Meltzer, who had real professional standing, had opposed it with more vigour than they did in the 1970s and early 1980s when they could have had some effect. Why they did not is a puzzle that future historians of this episode will have to investigate.

At the RES conference, the other main speaker was James Tobin, and we both came under attack from Patrick Minford, already Britain's leading exponent of New-classical doctrine. Patrick had been the resident 'Treasury Keynesian' (I hope he is not offended by the label) at Manchester, and it was not until after he had left us that he moved into the New-classical camp. Tobin was probably as intellectually uncomfortable as I was with our temporary alliance on that day, particularly because in his view, and quite contrary to mine, Monetarism and New-classical economics were essentially earlier and later versions of the same doctrine.

The Economic Journal, **91** (*March* 1981), 1–28
Printed in Great Britain

MONETARISM: AN INTERPRETATION AND AN ASSESSMENT*

Like beauty, 'monetarism' tends to lie in the eye of the beholder, and before it can be assessed it must be defined. Though there have been several valuable attempts over the years to specify monetarism's key characteristics,[1] I shall not rely upon them in this essay. Each of them has been heavily conditioned by its time and place of writing, and monetarism has evolved over the years in response to changing circumstances, and in different ways in different places, as new hypotheses have either been developed or absorbed. Thus, I will begin this paper with my own characterisation of monetarism. In my view, the key characteristics of monetarism are as follows:

(I) A 'quantity theory' approach to macroeconomic analysis in two distinct senses: (*a*) that used by Milton Friedman (1956) to describe a theory of the demand for money, and (*b*) the more traditional sense of a view that fluctuations in the quantity of money are the dominant cause of fluctuations in money income.

(II) The analysis of the division of money income fluctuations between the price level and real income in terms of an expectations augmented Phillips curve whose structure rules out an economically significant long-run inverse trade off between the variables.

(III) A monetary approach to balance-of-payments and exchange-rate theory.

(IV) (*a*) Antipathy to activist stabilisation policy, either monetary or fiscal, and to wage and price controls, and (*b*) support for long-run monetary policy 'rules' or at least prestated 'targets', cast in terms of the behaviour of some monetary aggregate rather than of the level of interest rates.

(I) Categorises the theoretical core of monetarism as it developed in the 1950s and 60s, (II) and (III) represent theory developed or absorbed by

* I have benefited greatly from the extensive comments of John Foster, Milton Friedman, John Helliwell, Geoffrey Kingston, Clark Leith, Thomas Mayer, Ronald Shearer and George Zis, none of whom is to be held responsible for the views that I espouse. The financial support of the Social Science and Humanities Research Council of Canada is gratefully acknowledged.

[1] See, for example, James Boughton (1977), Karl Brunner (1970), Nicholas Kaldor (1971), Harry Johnson (1972), Franco Modigliani (1977), Thomas Mayer (1978), Douglas Purvis (1980). This list is far from exhaustive.

monetarists since the mid-1960s, while (IV) summarises a view of macro-economic policy issues which, even though it is neither logically implicit in their positive analysis, nor their exclusive property, has remained reasonably constant among monetarists for the last quarter century.

Before discussing these characteristics of monetarism in detail let me deal briefly with two propositions that some might feel should be included in the above list. First, on the one hand monetarists have frequently been accused of failing to give any account of the transmission mechanism of monetary policy, and have had attributed to them a belief in some mysterious 'direct' influence of money on expenditure; on the other hand they have themselves sometimes referred to a characteristically 'monetarist model' of that same transmission mechanism cast in terms of portfolio substitution among a wide variety of assets including reproducible capital, and even perhaps non-durable consumption goods. I believe that this is and always has been a non-issue. The claim that monetarists have failed to specify their transmission mechanism has been untrue from the very outset (see, for example, Brunner (1961), Friedman and David Meiselman (1963), Friedman and Anna Schwartz (1963*b*)), and although the mechanism propounded in those papers is a good deal more sophisticated and better grounded in relative price theory than that embodied in the textbook macro-economic models of the 1950s, or in the econometric models of that vintage, there is no essential difference between it and that analysed for example by James Tobin and his associates.[1]

Second, monetarists are often said to prefer 'small' to 'big' econometric models, and their views about the importance of the quantity of money for the determination of the general price level have undoubtedly led them to take highly aggregated systems seriously. Moreover, early large-scale econometric models were not constructed so as to highlight any strong effects of money on economic activity. Monetarists criticised them, as much for being Keynesian, as for being 'big'. Even so, subsequent developments have clearly shown that 'big' models can easily take on some very monetarist characteristics, while the Albert Ando and Franco Modigliani (1965) and Michael De Prano and Mayer (1965) papers demonstrate that single equation reduced form techniques can as well produce 'Keynesian' as 'monetarist' results.[2] Empirical analysis of all sorts has been used by both sides in the monetarist controversy, and if there is a method of empirical research more frequently associated with monetarist work than Keynesian, it is not small model or single equation econometrics, but National Bureau techniques of business cycle analysis.[3] Thus though empirical techniques have in specific instances, provided something to argue about, there seems to me to be no clear dividing line between the statistical methodology of monetarists and their opponents about which one can usefully generalise.

[1] This is the judgment of Johnson (1962) and Brunner (1970), among others.

[2] Consider, for example, the London Business School model of the U.K. economy (see Jim Ball and Terry Burns (1976)). The Canadian RDX2 model also seems to me to fall into this category.

[3] See, for example, Friedman and Schwartz (1963*a*), Philip Cagan (1979). Note that such monetarists as Brunner and Meltzer, however, do not use National Bureau techniques. They are mainly associated with the Chicago branch of monetarism.

I. THE QUANTITY THEORY OF MONEY

It has often been said that Friedman's celebrated essay on the Quantity Theory could just as well have been called 'The Theory of Liquidity Preference – a Restatement'. Harry Johnson (1962) argued that Friedman's work on the demand for money should be viewed as a development of a fundamentally Keynesian capital theoretic approach to monetary theory and Don Patinkin (1969) later documented that it was indeed just that. However, I would stress the word *development* here, for 'Keynesian' though Friedman's model is, it is no more *Keynes*' model than Keynes' 'Marshallian' theory of income determination is Marshall's theory; and it differed from other developments of Keynes' theory of liquidity preference that appeared at about the same time in a number of ways.

First it abstracted from any specific characteristics that money might have because it is a financial asset; Friedman treated money instead 'as if' a service-yielding consumer durable to which the permanent income hypothesis of consumption could be applied, just as Margaret Reid (1962) applied it to housing, or the contributors to Arnold Harberger (1960) did to a variety of other durable goods. In this respect Friedman's approach stands in sharp contrast to the analyses of William Baumol (1952) and Tobin (1956) (1958) as it does in its claim to be a theory of the total demand for money in the macro-economy rather than of some component of that demand. Second, Friedman explicitly recognised inflation as an own rate of return on money and postulated a well determined functional relationship between the expected inflation rate and the demand for money, a relationship whose existence Maynard Keynes (and some of his disciples) explicitly denied. (See Roy Harrod (1971).)

Finally, and so obviously that the matter is usually overlooked, Friedman asserted that the demand for money was, *as an empirical matter*, a stable function of a few measurable arguments. Keynes did not believe that – his empirically stable relationship was the consumption function – and nor did (or perhaps do) many of his British followers.[1] Moreover, pre-Keynesian monetary theorists did not believe in an empirically stable demand for money function either. Though they often enough assumed a constant velocity of circulation that is by no means the same thing, and in any event, they typically did so in order to make their analytic points with the maximum of clarity, and not with the intention of stating a belief about the nature of the real world. It is only with the publication of Friedman's essay that statements to the effect that the velocity of circulation is, *as a practical matter*, a stable function of a few arguments become central to debates about monetary economics. Its stress on this hypothesis makes monetarism a very different doctrine from Classical and Neoclassical economics, no matter what other similarities there may be, though it should be noted explicitly that the econometricians among American Keynesians

[1] The Radcliffe Report (1959) is based on the proposition that the demand for money function is essentially nonexistent as a stable relationship. For a later statement of the same point of view see Kaldor (1971), or Joan Robinson (1970).

have not found it necessary to adopt a monetarist label as a result of contemplating the possibility of the empirical stability of the relationship.[1]

Ten years ago it was possible to argue that this characteristic monetarist belief in a stable demand for money function was well supported by empirical evidence as I did in Laidler (1971). However, the last decade has produced a good deal of evidence to suggest that the relationship has shifted in an unpredicted way in a number of countries. There is not space to go into details here, but I would be willing to defend the following assertions.[2]

First the instability in question is often presented, particularly in the United States, as a matter of a cumulative deterioration in the ability of the function to track data. This cumulative deterioration is largely an illusion stemming from the use of dynamic simulations of relationships containing a lagged dependent variable. A *one-time shift* of such a function will, as a matter of arithmetic, lead to a *cumulative deterioration* of its dynamic simulation goodness of fit that should not be read as implying a *continuous* tendency of the relationship to shift. On the other hand, I do not believe we can safely conclude that such one-time shifts in the demand for money function have not occurred, despite the fact, again particularly in the United States, that some formulations of the relationship turn out to deteriorate significantly less than others during the 1970s. When important issues like the stability of the demand for money function begin to depend, for example, on just which interest rate or rates one uses to proxy the opportunity cost of holding money, I believe that the correct conclusion is not that the variable which provides the best fit this time around is the 'right' one, but that our knowledge of the details of the relationship is more fragile than we thought. Finally, arguments to the effect that the demand for money function has not 'really' shifted, that we can restore its stability by taking note of institutional change and redefining 'money' so as to take account of its effects, need to be handled carefully. They are relevant to the interpretation of economic history, but the successful conduct of policy requires that specific actions be taken *vis à vis* precisely defined aggregates in order to achieve particular policy goals. To say, after the event, that our policy did not work because new assets evolved whose existence affected the outcome of our policies in a way that we could have forecast had we only been able to foresee their invention, may be true, but it is not very helpful in enabling us to do better next time, unless the evolution in question was, as it sometimes can be, the predictable outcome of some policy action or other.

Shifts in the demand measured for money function are not a new phenomenon. Evidence drawn from more than one country shows that the demand for money function shifted as the institutional framework evolved long before 1974. To cite but four examples: the income elasticities of demand for money seem to have fallen significantly in both the United States and Britain in the

[1] Note in particular that the Keynesian James Tobin was the author of a pioneering econometric study of the demand for money function. See Tobin (1947). See also his review of Friedman and Schwartz (1963*a*), Tobin (1965), where further econometric estimates of the demand for money function are presented.

[2] I have dealt with the matters taken up here in much greater length in Laidler (1980).

20th century (see Laidler, 1971), the abolition of interest payments on demand deposits in the United States in 1933 was associated with a change in the nature of the demand function for narrow money (see Charles Lieberman, 1980), as was the growth of Savings and Loan Associations in the 1940s (see Cagan and Schwartz, 1975), or in Britain, the introduction of 'Competition and Credit Control' in 1971. Such shifts in the demand for money function are not new, then, but they are important. Though two of the above examples were the result of policy changes and might have been predicted *ex ante*, two were not. In any event these effects of institutional change on the demand for money function have important implications for our views on the proper conduct of monetary policy, as I shall argue in Section IV below.

In the traditional vocabulary of economics, the phrase 'quantity theory of money' referred to a theory of (or better an approach to the analysis of) the relationship between the supply of money and the general price level. The characteristic monetarist belief that variations in the supply of money are the 'dominant impulse' (to borrow Brunner's phrase) causing fluctuations in money income is clearly related to this traditional version of the quantity theory, but modern monetarists are more clearcut in their attribution of a dominant causative role to the money supply than were quantity theorists of earlier vintages.[1] The difference here is surely attributable to monetarists' belief in a stable demand for money function, because earlier quantity theorists spent much of their time contemplating the empirical possibility of autonomous shifts in velocity. However, it takes more than a belief in a stable demand for money function to yield the monetarist view of these matters.

Setting aside the important complications that arise in the open economy, there are two ways in which a conventional analytic model of the IS-LM variety can be made to produce 'monetarist' results. First in its under-employment form, if, relative to expenditure, the demand for money is insensitive to interest rates then the quantity of money comes to dominate the determination of the level of real income. Now obviously a monetarist must deny that the interest elasticity of demand for money is infinite, and this has been done often and explicitly, but it is mainly in Britain that such a denial has been thought to amount to a distinctively monetarist statement. A number of textbook writers (including myself) have gone to the other extreme and used the assumption of a zero interest elasticity of demand for money to generate monetarist propositions from an under-employment IS-LM model. However, Friedman's (1959) study of the United States function is a notable exception to the general tendency of demand for money studies – including those of such monetarists as Brunner and Meltzer (e.g. (1963)) – to find a significant interest elasticity of demand for money, and his inability to find a relationship turned out to be the result of faulty statistical method (see Laidler, 1966, and Friedman, 1966). Thus, the existence or non-existence of a statistically significant interest elasticity of demand for money has not been a serious

[1] But as with all such blanket judgments as this there are important exceptions. Irving Fisher's empirical work on the relationship between money and prices presented in *The Purchasing Power of Money* (1911) is not so far removed from modern monetarism.

issue between monetarists and their opponents for at least fifteen years. If it had been, it is hard to see how monetarists, not least Friedman could have contributed to the analysis of the welfare costs of inflation, or how Friedman and Meiselman could have accepted their own evidence of the importance of autonomous expenditure as an influence on money income during the depression years with such equanimity.[1]

If we rule out the vertical LM curve, we can still get an IS-LM model to produce monetarist results if we assume full employment, and then postulate that the major source of disturbance is variations in the level – or rate of change of – the nominal money supply. With the determinants of velocity, except the expected rate of inflation, thus pinned down at full employment, and with fluctuations in money income thus reduced to fluctuations in the price level, the characteristics of the demand for money function – other than its stability and homogeneity in the general price level and its sensitivity to fluctuations in the expected inflation rate – become quite irrelevant to the relationship between the quantity of money and money income. A Keynesian of course would agree, as an analytic matter, with this proposition, but would probably deny what the monetarist would claim: namely that, if the IS-LM model is to be used as a framework for discussion at all – and there are some monetarists, notably Brunner and Meltzer, who would not want to use it at any price – then this full employment version of it is frequently the empirically relevant one.

To put matters this way is, in effect, to say that monetarists' belief in the quantity theory as a theory of money income boils down to the view that sustained inflation is caused by an expanding money supply. This is not too far from the mark, and much of the spread of monetarism in the last fifteen years stems from its ability to provide a readily comprehensible explanation of inflation along these lines. However, to cast the monetarist approach to the analysis of inflation in terms of a 'full employment' IS-LM model is difficult to justify except as a very first approximation. Though monetarists are among those who have written at considerable length about the interaction of the quantity of money and the price level in models where 'full employment' is the rule, the models in question have been long-run equilibrium growth models, not versions of short-run IS-LM analysis; in any event the 'money and growth' literature and, to a lesser extent, that dealing with 'money and welfare', even though it builds on Friedman's formulation of the relationship between the demand for real balances and the expected rate of inflation as a well defined inverse function, is properly viewed, not as an offshoot of monetarism, but as an extension of Patinkin's (1956) theoretical analysis of the classical dichotomy and the neutrality of money to deal with the *long-run* properties of a *growing* economy, in the presence of variations in the *rate of change* of the nominal

[1] But this of course is not to say that Friedman has always paid as much attention to the interest elasticity of the demand for money as his critics might have wished. See for example the various reviews of the monetary history of the United States, but note that the monetarist Allan Meltzer (1965) was as critical on this score as any other reviewer. What we are here dealing with is a characteristic of some of the work of one, albeit the most important, monetarist rather than of monetarism in general.

money supply.[1] In dealing with the interaction of the quantity of money, money income, and prices, the essential monetarist contribution has been to postulate the existence of stable relationships among these variables as an *empirical* matter, and to draw *practical* conclusions about the proper conduct of *short-run* stabilisation policy from studying their nature, and the 'money, growth and welfare' literature has next to nothing to say about these matters.

When it comes to empirical propositions about the relationship between money and money income, what was once monetarist heresy is now close to being received orthodoxy. In this respect monetarism has made an important positive contribution to macroeconomics. In the United States it seems now to be widely accepted that the correlation between the quantity of money and money income that long runs of time series data display is not just the result of coincidence, but does in fact constitute evidence for the existence of a causative relationship that has run primarily from money to money income rather than vice versa. The weight of the evidence produced by Friedman and his various collaborators (not to mention predecessors) and the persuasiveness of their arguments, has changed enough minds to warrant the conclusion that, in an important sense, 'we are all monetarists' now. Elsewhere in the world, not least in Britain, there has been a similar movement of opinion. Certainly one no longer hears much about velocity being variable 'almost without limit'. However, one does hear more about 'reverse causation' in Britain as an explanation of the correlation between money and money income than one does in the United States (I shall take this matter up below).

Even so, monetarist doctrine asserts not just that variations in the quantity of money lead to systematic variations in money income, but also, that those variations are primarily in prices rather than real income. Although, as I have already noted, much of monetarism's popular appeal stems from its claim to provide an easily comprehensible theory of inflation, that theory of inflation is by no means universally accepted. The view that the influence of money on money income falls on its real income component and not on prices has constituted a 'Keynesian' alternative to the monetarist position on these matters and the 'expectations augmented Phillips Curve' has provided a focus for debate about them.[2] That is why a particular set of beliefs about its nature is a vital ingredient of monetarist doctrine.

II. THE EXPECTATIONS AUGMENTED PHILLIPS CURVE

The notion of a trade off between inflation and unemployment was widely prevalent in Keynesian literature even before Arthur Brown (1955), William Phillips (1958) and Richard Lipsey (1960) formalised it in terms of what seemed

[1] Mayer (1978) argues, correctly I believe, that Patinkin should not be regarded as a monetarist. This of course is not to deny the important influence that Patinkin's work had on subsequent monetary analysis. See, for example, Jonson (1976*b*).

[2] There seems to have been a systematic shift in British opinion from the Radcliffe view that money does not matter at all, to the view that money matters for real income but not for prices. To trace this development is beyond the scope of this paper. However, the work of Richard Kahn shows clearly that it has taken place. Compare his evidence to the Radcliffe Committee with, for example, Kahn (1976).

to be an empirically stable functional relationship. Monetarists have long doubted its existence, instead asserting a belief in the 'inherent stability' of the private sector in the absence of policy induced monetary disturbances, by which they have usually meant nothing more complex than that the system tends in and of itself to operate at or near 'full employment', regardless of the inflation rate, if policy makers do not upset matters. The papers of Edmund Phelps (1967) and Friedman (1968) provided a framework in terms of which differences of opinion about these matters could be stated sharply enough to be confronted with empirical evidence. Although some commentators (e.g. Helmut Frisch, 1978) treat the Phillips curve as providing an alternative theory of inflation to the monetarist approach, this is surely a mistake. In its expectations augmented form, it emerged at the turn of the decade to provide what Friedman (1970) called 'the missing equation' in the monetarist model of inflation.

It is possible to derive this 'missing equation' from two very different theoretical bases, and disagreements here are of quite fundamental importance for macroeconomics, but the first round in the debate about the expectations augmented Phillips curve, and the one that was crucially relevant to monetarism, paid little attention to these matters. It was almost entirely empirical because the relationship in question enabled alternative viewpoints about important and pressing policy issues to be formulated and investigated in an easily manageable way. With Δp the inflation rate, Δp^e the expected inflation rate, and y some measure, either direct or indirect, of the deviation of output from its 'full employment' level, and v a 'catchall' vector of other influences, systematic as well as random, the general form of the relationship may be written as follows:

$$\Delta p = gy + b\Delta p^e + v. \tag{1}$$

A whole spectrum of beliefs about the nature of inflation may be expressed in terms of this simple equation, depending upon the values assigned to its parameters. Thus, the extreme 'sociological' view of the determination of the price level, that was widely prevalent in Britain in the early 1970s, would predict that the parameters g and b were essentially equal to zero, implying that monetary policies, if they had any effect on money income, would influence real income alone.[1] The behaviour of prices, in this view, was determined by exogenous factors that would all go into the catchall vector v. At the other extreme, the typical monetarist of the early 1970s would argue that g was positive, so that inflation would, relative to expectations, be low in a depressed economy, and high in an over-expanded one. He would also argue that the coefficient b on expected inflation would be equal to unity, and would supplement equation (1) with some formula for the formation of expectations, typically based on the error learning hypothesis, that ensured that, eventually, any constant actual inflation rate would come to be fully anticipated. For him, therefore, any trade off between inflation and deviations of output from full employment was a temporary one which vanished in the long run. The typical 'American Keynesian' of the same vintage would agree with the monetarist about the parameter g, and about the reasonableness of assuming that expecta-

[1] See Peter Wiles (1973) for a particularly extreme version of the sociological approach to inflation.

tions would eventually catch up with experience, but would assign a value of less than unity to the parameter b, thus ensuring that though the price in terms of inflation of increasing output was higher in the long run than in the short run, it did not, as the monetarist asserted, ever become infinitely high.[1] He might also argue that equation (1) omitted to mention explicitly many factors that in particular times and places might have an important influence on the inflation rate, and which it will suffice here to think of as being captured in v.

There is not space here to survey the extensive empirical literature that these issues generated, but its upshot may be summarised easily enough. The evidence that, other things equal, inflation varies with the level of aggregate demand is overwhelming. To the extent that differences of opinion here ever set monetarism apart from other points of view – and I think they probably did in Britain, though not in North America – then surely we have here another case of 'we are all monetarists now'.[2] There has also been a swing towards the typically monetarist belief that in the long run there is no economically significant inflation–output trade off. The more rapid inflation of the 1970s and the more sophisticated methods of modelling expectations developed over the same period have provided empirical evidence of a type that we did not have a decade ago to support this belief. There is still substantial disagreement though on the question of how fast the economy converges on the long-run solution. Finally there is more of a consensus about the importance of the influence of 'other' factors on the inflation rate than there was. Monetarists are willing to agree that factors such as the activities of OPEC, unexpected real shocks, or sudden changes in the level of indirect taxes, can affect the behaviour of the price level 'temporarily' against the background of long-run trends determined by monetary factors; Keynesians, particularly American ones, in their turn are now willing to agree that the long-run trend of inflation may well be determined by monetary factors while continuing to stress the importance of special factors for the short run. However, as we shall now see, there is much less of a consensus about the theoretical basis of the Phillips curve than there is about its empirical properties.

As originally analysed by Lipsey, the Phillips curve dealt with the reaction of the money wage to the existence of a general condition of excess demand for labour in the economy, and therefore of the general price level to the excess demand for goods. Excess demand was conceived of, not as a purely *ex ante* notion such as we meet in theoretical analyses of Walrasian tâtonnement, but as a realised quantity such as appears in models of economies made up of markets characterised by sticky prices. In their original critiques of the Phillips curve. Friedman (1968) and Phelps (1967) both concentrated on the point that disequilibrium in the labour market might be expected to bring pressure to bear on real wages rather than on money wages *per se*, and that what would happen to the latter would therefore be critically influenced by what was thought to be happening to the general price level. Each of them, though Phelps more explicitly so than Friedman, treated unemployment as a quantity

[1] I have in mind here, in particular, the work of Robert Solow (1969) and James Tobin (1972).

[2] See Anthony Santomero and John Seater (1979) for a recent and well-balanced survey of the evidence on these matters.

signal that conveyed to economic agents the desirability of varying prices, and hence seemed to be providing a crucial correction to what remained a fundamentally Keynesian approach to the analysis of wage and price stickiness.[1]

On the other hand, most of the contributors to the well-known Phelps (1969) volume started from a very different theoretical basis to provide an explanation of the interaction of output and prices, though the similarity of their conclusions to those stated by Phelps and Friedman at first distracted attention from what in retrospect was the much more important theoretical matter of different premises.[2] According to this alternative approach, which was anticipated by Irving Fisher (1911), the expectations augmented Phillips curve is in fact an aggregate supply curve. Equation (1) is derived from

$$y = (1/g)\,(p - p^e) \tag{2}$$

combined with the following definition of the expected rate of inflation

$$\Delta p^e \equiv p^e - p_{-1}. \tag{3}$$

Brunner and Meltzer were quick to adopt this interpretation of the expectations augmented Phillips curve. They had already developed a view of the transmission of monetary impulses in asset markets that stressed the role of relative prices as signalling devices, and found it easy enough to extend that line of reasoning to the markets for output and labour services as well (see Meltzer, 1969).[3] By now there can be no doubt that this aggregate supply curve interpretation of inflation employment interaction is the dominant one among monetarists. However, not all monetarists have accepted it (see, for example, Cagan, 1979), and as I shall now argue, it raises issues that go well beyond the traditional subject matter of the monetarist debate.

To say that the Phillips curve is an aggregate supply curve is to say that fluctuations in output and employment in response to price level variations represent the voluntary choices of individuals operating in markets which are continually clearing. Since voluntary choices made on the basis of erroneous expectations are by no means the same thing as choices that lead to the outcome which agents would have desired, this is not to deny that deviations of output and unemployment from the 'natural' levels they would attain if expectations were fulfilled represent a serious problem.[4] However, it is to

[1] Notice that in some of his subsequent writings on inflation-unemployment interaction Friedman adopts an aggregate supply curve interpretation of the Phillips curve. See, for example, Friedman (1975).

[2] See the papers by Armen Alchian, Robert E. Lucas and Leonard Rapping, Donald Gordon and Alan Hynes, and Dale Mortensen, all in the Phelps (1969) volume.

[3] In later work carried out by Brunner and Meltzer and their associates, a version of the aggregate supply curve in which the rate of change of output rather than the level of output affects the rate of inflation appears. This form of the relationship appears to stem from their tendency to treat the expected inflation rate as synonymous with the rate of change of the expected price level. See Brunner and Meltzer (eds.) (1978) and particularly the comments there by Bennett McCallum.

[4] Thus, though I agree with much of what Willem Buiter (1980) has to say about this theory of employment, I cannot accept his characterisation of it as 'The Macroeconomics of Dr. Pangloss'. It might be noted that in the aggregate supply curve interpretation of the Phillips curve, the natural unemployment rate becomes a long-run equilibrium concept. In the price reaction function interpretation of the relationship it seems to me to be synonymous with the Keynesian concept of the minimum feasible unemployment rate. For a perceptive discussion of some of the issues involved here see Thomas Wilson (1976).

locate the cause of unemployment, not in the failure of markets to bring together all willing buyers and sellers in *ex ante* mutually satisfactory trades, but rather in a failure of markets (and other social institutions as well perhaps) to convey sufficient information to enable the expectations upon which those trades are based to be formed accurately in an economy subjected to stochastic shocks.

If fluctuations in output and employment about their natural rates are the result of the failure of expectations to be realised, the manner in which expectations are formed must play a vital role in their analysis. That is why the "rational expectations" hypothesis is a natural supplement to the aggregate supply curve interpretation of the Phillips curve. If agents suffer losses in utility as a result of making expectational errors, they have an incentive to use all available information in forming their expectations up to the point at which the marginal benefit from improving their accuracy equals the marginal cost of doing so. The rational expectations hypothesis does *not* say that every agent's expectations are always as accurate (i.e. have as small a variance) as they would be if he were equipped with a 'true' econometric model of the economy in which he operates (though it is sometimes convenient to formulate it that way in analytic and empirical exercises), but it does say that his expectations will not be wrong *systematically* over time and to that extent will resemble those generated by such a 'true' model in being unbiased and serially uncorrelated. An agent who forms expectations in a manner that leads to systematic error will find himself persistently making the wrong choices; hence in the very course of his market activities, he will be provided *gratis* with the information necessary to eliminate that systematic error.

If each individual makes only random errors in forming expectations, two questions naturally arise: how does it happen that at a particular moment the expectations of a predominant number of agents in the economy should be in error in one particular direction so that aggregate output and employment come to deviate from their 'natural rates', and how does it happen that the fluctuations in output and employment which are observed in any actual economy come to display that pattern of serial correlation summarised in the term 'business cycle'? The answer to the first question given by Lucas (1972) is by now well known. If individuals have more up-to-date information about the money prices that rule in the markets in which they operate as sellers than about others, then in order to assess the pattern of relative prices upon which their quantity decisions rest, they must form expectations about the behaviour of other money prices. An unforeseen shock affecting the whole economy which leads to a change in the general price level will influence individual money prices, and will have its consequences everywhere misread as reflecting relative price changes. Hence quantities supplied will everywhere change.

If that was all there was to it, output and employment fluctuations would be random over time. However, if there are time delays in getting information to agents, if there are costs of adjusting output decisions once taken, or if some of the goods over-produced in error in the face of a positive unexpected shock to the price level are durable, then the effects of that shock will persist over time.[1] By the time its effects on output have petered out there will be too many durable goods in the economy – capital will be 'too deep' – and the marginal productivity of labour in terms of consumption in industries producing durable goods will fall. If workers prefer to take extra leisure when their marginal productivity is low, and if the price system operates so as to inform them of when that is the case, there will be a voluntary fall in the level of employment that will persist until the structure of the economy's capital stock is restored. The objection to this explanation of the cycle, that it predicts more wage variability than we observe in the real world, can be countered by arguments to the effect that firms and households find it mutually beneficial to enter into wage contracts under which wages do not instantaneously fluctuate in tune with the marginal productivity of labour, but under which firms are permitted to lay off workers in such a way that the latter still take more leisure at times when their marginal productivity is unusually low, even though the behaviour of wages no longer signals the fact.

Readers will find the last paragraph reminiscent of the Austrian business cycle theory of the 1920s and 1930s, and that is no accident. It is the Austrians, and not, as Solow (1980) has suggested, Pigou, who are the predecessors of Lucas, Sargent and their associates. Like Ludwig von Mises and Friedrich von Hayek, they have set themselves the task of producing a theory of the business cycle that is firmly based on the notion that all market phenomena represent the harmonious outcome of the voluntary choices of maximising individuals. However these neo-Austrians have gone beyond their predecessors to produce a theory in which output and employment as well as prices fluctuate as a result of such voluntary choices. Whatever we may think of the empirical relevance of that theory, and its proponents show an admirable, and un-Austrian, willingness to submit their ideas to empirical tests,[2] we must surely agree that its very construction represents an intellectual achievement of the highest order.

One can admire a theory without agreeing with it, and there are many including myself who would challenge the basic assumption upon which the analysis just discussed is based, namely that it is legitimate to model the economy 'as if' markets always clear. It is one thing to agree that commodity and asset markets dominated by specialist traders ought, and indeed do,

[1] I base the following arguments on the papers of Lucas (1975), Thomas Sargent (1976) and Lucas (1977). The first two of these papers are extremely technical and I am by no means sure that I am doing justice to them in the discussion that follows. Milton Friedman has pointed out to me that one can only say that errors are random or systematic if one is also specific about both the *time at* which expectations are formed, and the *period for* which they are formed. If one is now planning for, say a five-year horizon, then the rational expectations hypothesis permits the actual value of any variable to deviate systematically from its *ex ante* expected value over any interval of less than five years. This matter is clearly related to questions raised by adjustment lags, the durability of certain goods, and so on, since the horizon over which a decision taken now is likely to be binding is also presumably the horizon over which a rational agent would seek to form expectations about relevant variables. To the best of my knowledge, the published literature has not recognised this point explicitly, and it deserves much more attention than I have space to give it here.

[2] To comment on the empirical work in question, notably that of Robert J. Barro (1978), would take us beyond the scope of this essay.

display the characteristics associated with continuous clearing and rational expectations, and quite another to attribute similar characteristics to the markets for many components of final output, and above all to the labour market. One may follow Hicks (1974) in distinguishing between 'flexprice' and 'fixprice' markets, assign the labour market to the latter category, and argue that the interaction of inflation and unemployment is best analysed on the premise that the Phillips curve represents the disequilibrium response of prices to a mismatching of supply and demand.

Of course the 'neo-Austrians' are well aware that there is no Walrasian auctioneer to set prices, and no recontracting to ensure that trade only takes place at market clearing prices; but they do assert that individual agents – or their representatives – are acute enough in their bargaining to ensure that money wages and prices universally behave 'as if' markets operated along such Walrasian lines, that they perceive the possibility of realising mutual gains by adjusting wages downward when excess supply turns up in the market in which they are operating, and act upon that perception.[1] However one can have no difficulty accepting the proposition that, even in labour markets, if it is mutually beneficial to lower money wages (or their rate of change), agents will discover this and will agree to do so, but still find it hard to understand how the relevant information is conveyed to the agents in question without the intervention of quantity signals. In a Walrasian market, the auctioneer can discover that the price is too high by adding up notional supplies and finding out that they exceed notional demands, to use Robert Clower's (1965) terms, but how can participants in any actual labour market find out that money wages there are too high without some of them discovering first that they are unable to sell all the services that they would like at the going rate?

If adjustments in the level (or rate of change) of money wages and prices to aggregate demand shocks are anything other than instantaneous, then markets fail to clear, trade takes place at false prices, and quantity signals, perhaps amplified by multiplier effects, become an integral part of the mechanism whereby monetary changes are transmitted to the behaviour of the price level. This line of analysis is as 'Keynesian' in spirit as the clearing market approach is 'Austrian', and its existence permits one to subscribe to the expectations augmented Phillips curve without also being committed to a clearing market rational expectations approach to the analysis of economic fluctuations. Moreover, the approach in question does *not* differ from the clearing market view in denying that individuals perceive and then engage in all available mutually beneficial trades. It simply denies that they do so infinitely rapidly. I do not see why, as for example Barro (1979) has recently suggested, to postulate an infinite speed of price adjustment in the face of excess demand or supply is to conform to sound microeconomic principles,

[1] Robert J. Barro (1979) presents a particularly forceful and clearcut statement of what I am calling the 'neo-Austrian' view on these matters. Robert Solow (1979) might be regarded as providing a traditional Keynesian rebuttal of this line of argument. Note that questions of the relevant time horizon, raised in footnote 1, p. 12, are again relevant here.

and to postulate anything significantly slower is to propose an '*ad hoc* non-theory'.

The non-clearing market approach to analysing inflation employment interaction is not obviously incompatible with the notion of rational expectations. If output fluctuations convey information about the appropriate behaviour concerning price setting as this approach suggests, they can be regarded as constituting one of the ingredients of the expectations upon which such behaviour is based. In that case the term Δp^e in equation (1) can be thought of as summarising influences upon expectations *other than quantity signals*.[1] To say this begs the question of what those 'other influences' on expectations might be, but leaves open the possibility that the same type of information to which the rational expectations hypothesis draws our attention could be incorporated without difficulty into models based on the non-clearing market approach. Observations on the past behaviour of the money supply, for example, might well provide agents with information about the appropriate way to set prices, and might be included among those 'other' influences, as might, in an open economy, variations in prices ruling elsewhere in the world economy, variations in exchange rates, and so on.[2]

The non clearing-market interpretation of the Phillips curve needs to be reconciled with the basic facts of the business cycle. Once given, why do output signals not result in an immediate adjustment of prices to a market clearing level? The answer here is straightforward – a quantity signal will lead to a response in price behaviour only to the extent that agents believe that the shock which gave rise to it will persist into the future. Inability to disentangle short-term from persistent shocks will lead to a tendency to under-react to quantity signals, and hence to cause them to be drawn out over time. I would conjecture that the Austrian-style arguments about the role of errors made with respect to the production of durable goods in the business cycle can be superimposed upon this fundamentally Keynesian explanation of the persistence of output fluctuations should anyone wish to do so.[3]

Although theoretical analysis of the interaction of output, employment and prices in terms of an expectations augmented Phillips curve can thus proceed along two very different lines, it is a mistake to treat debate about these issues as simply the latest round in the monetarist controversy. Though monetarists and Keynesians are in much closer agreement than they were about the empirical stability of the demand for money function, and about the empirical nature of output-inflation interaction, they still take the same diametrically

[1] Alternatively, as Michael Wickens has suggested to me, we may think of Δp^e as being a rational expectation of inflation conditional upon information available at an earlier time than that at which the quantity signal is received.

[2] I base the foregoing discussion on conversations and correspondence that I have had with Marcus Miller and Peter Jonson on various occasions. See also Clements and Jonson (1979).

[3] A more extensive account of these matters is given in Laidler (1975), chapter 1. Note that Brunner, Alex Cuckeirman and Meltzer (1979) provide an analysis of persistent shocks within an aggregate supply curve framework. Note also that Peter Howitt (1979) argues that, once explicit attention is paid to the role of inventories in the price setting process, the contrast between clearing-market and non-clearing-market approaches to economic modelling becomes blurred, and to some extent semantic rather than substantive in nature.

opposed views on the proper conduct of macroeconomic policy that they did a quarter century ago, and divisions of opinion here do not, as I shall argue below, depend upon differences of views about the theoretical basis of price-output interaction. Since the policy debate is undoubtedly a continuation of the monetarist controversy, and since disputes about the theoretical basis of the Phillips curve clearly deal with a new set of issues, it seems to me to be misleading to treat what I have here termed the neo-Austrian view as synonymous with monetarism, as for example Frank Hahn (1980) does. I shall discuss the policy aspects of the monetarist controversy in Section IV, but before I do so, it will be convenient to discuss the place of the monetary approach to balance of payments and exchange rate theory in monetarist doctrine.

III. THE MONETARY APPROACH TO BALANCE OF PAYMENTS AND EXCHANGE RATE ANALYSIS

The monetary approach to balance of payments and exchange rate analysis represents in some respects a revival of the English Classical approach to these problem areas. However, the monetary approach differs in important ways from Classical analysis, and the very characteristics that thus distinguish it are borrowed from closed economy monetarism.[1] Most important, advocates of the monetary approach postulate the existence of a stable demand for money function, not just as a working simplification, but as an empirical hypothesis; it is this hypothesis that transforms the approach from an accounting framework into a body of substantive theory. Furthermore, in early statements of the doctrine, its proponents tied down the real income argument of that function by assuming full employment but they soon learned how to replace this assumption with an expectations-augmented Phillips curve approach to price-output interaction.[2] In effect the monetary approach to balance of payments and exchange rate analysis provided the means whereby these characteristically monetarist hypotheses were made relevant to economies other than the United States which, under the Bretton Woods system, was about as close an approximation to a closed economy that was also a separate political entity as the world has ever seen. Monetarism thus only came to be important outside the United States, not least in Britain, in alliance with the monetary approach to balance of payments and exchange rate analysis.

Until 1971 the world was on a system of fixed exchange rates against the United States dollar. Under such a system the existence of a stable demand for money function, whose arguments are beyond the direct control of the domestic authorities, implies that the money supply is an endogenous variable that must adjust to demand. Given this insight, evidence that suggests, for example in the United Kingdom in the 1950s and 1960s, that causation seems to have run predominantly from money income to money, rather than vice

[1] The locus classicus for pioneering work on the monetary approach to balance of payments analysis is, of course, Frenkel and Johnson (1975).

[2] See, for example, Laidler (1975), chapter 9, and Jonson (1976*a*).

versa, is no embarrassment to a monetarist provided that he is also willing to attribute most of the variation in money income to causative factors originating abroad. Moreover, although the expectations augmented Phillips curve tells us that in general we should expect to find no stable inverse trade off between inflation and unemployment, post-war United Kingdom data do display just such a well determined relationship down to 1967, and this fact needs explaining. The monetary approach to balance of payments analysis suggests two complementary reasons why this should be the case. First it notes that, so long as a fixed exchange rate is to be maintained, the prices of tradable goods sold domestically are going to be determined in the long run, not domestically, but on world markets, and from this it follows that the domestic price level's long-run behaviour is going to be constrained by the behaviour of prices in the world at large. Economic agents do not have to be more than merely sensible to perceive this fact and to incorporate it into their expectations. If world prices are relatively stable, and they were until the late 1960s, then so are inflation expectations, and our expectations augmented Phillips curve, equation (1), no matter how we interpret its microeconomic origins, will predict that the data will generate a stable inflation–unemployment trade-off.

This explanation of the existence of a stable inflation–unemployment trade-off in post-war Britain is an important component of what may fairly be called monetarist hypotheses, about the nature of the stop-go cycle in the 1950s and 1960s and about the degeneration of that economy's performance in the 1970s, which contrast strongly with conventional 'Keynesian' accounts of the same phenomena. The latter begin from the proposition that Britain has a peculiarly high marginal propensity to import, so that, under the Bretton Woods system, attempts to run the economy at a high degree of capacity utilisation, though they produced only a small and on the whole acceptable amount of inflation, were frustrated by balance of payments pressure which forced a reversal of policy. The monetarist hypothesis about stop-go, on the other hand, has it that high levels of demand were associated with high rates of domestic credit expansion which, under fixed exchange rates, generated balance of payments problems in large measure as an *alternative* to domestic inflationary pressure. The conventional view seemed to imply that Britain's economic performance could be improved by adopting exchange rate flexibility and allowing a depreciating currency to offset the balance of payments effects of a high propensity to import. With a flexible exchange rate, the economy could be run at a higher level of capacity utilisation and could grow more rapidly without interference from a balance of payments 'constraint'. According to this view a series of exogenous shocks and the autonomous activities of trade unions undermined a basically well-founded strategy when it was adopted in the 1970s. The monetarist view, on the other hand, argues that the adoption of exchange rate flexibility replaced a balance of payments problem with a domestic inflation problem when expansionary policies were pursued, and did nothing to influence the economy's ability to sustain either a higher level or rate of growth of real income. For the monetarist, therefore, the deterioration of British economic performance after 1972 was the predictable (and predicted) consequence of a policy of expanding aggregate demand against a background of exchange rate flexibility.[1]

Now the monetary approach to balance of payments analysis does far more than make monetarist analysis relevant to Britain. It also permits the explanation of the international spread of inflation in the late 1960s in terms of the repercussions in the world economy of United States monetary expansion, and it treats the breakdown of the Bretton Woods system as the culmination of this process. However, it is only fair to note that such analysis performs less well in the face of the behaviour displayed by the international monetary system since exchange rates began to float in the early 1970s. The prediction that the behaviour of exchange rates can be analysed fruitfully as if determined in efficient asset markets does seem to be supported by the data. However, a basic postulate of the monetary approach is that the equilibrium value of the exchange rate between any two currencies reflects purchasing power parity. Just as data generated under fixed rates show that the price levels of particular economies can display considerable autonomy for substantial periods of time, so under flexible exchange rates systematic and persistent deviations of exchange rates from purchasing power parity do seem to be possible. Though purchasing power parity considerations underlie the behaviour of long period averages of data, implying that, ultimately the terms of trade between countries are independent of monetary factors, there seems to be ample room for short run deviations from the long run pattern. Just why this should be the case, and what explains the patterns of such deviations as we observe, are important and, at the moment, open questions.[2]

Be all that as it may, the present regime of flexible exchange rates came into being because the authorities in various countries learned that they could not control such politically important variables as domestic inflation and unemployment while continuing to adhere to the Bretton Woods arrangements. The diversity of inflation rates among countries since 1971 supports the view that the adoption of flexible rates allows such variables to have their behaviour predominantly determined at home; and long before the 1970s, monetarists, not least of course Friedman, argued that the adoption of exchange rate flexibility was a necessary prerequisite to the pursuit of monetarist policies in individual countries. In the 1970s we have seen the emergence of conditions under which individual countries could implement independent monetary policies, and as I have suggested above, it is mainly on the matter of policy prescriptions that sharp differences between monetarists and their opponents persist. I shall therefore devote the penultimate section of this paper to a discussion of these matters.

[1] It is worth pointing out that I set out much of the foregoing argument in my 1972 Lister Lecture. See Laidler (1975), chapter 10, where the lecture is reprinted. The argument is developed in further detail in Laidler (1976*a*).

[2] Frenkel (1980) provides a useful and accessible overview of the issues involved here and the evidence on them.

IV. POLICY ISSUES

As we have seen, when it comes to propositions about the demand for money function, the relationship between money and money income, and output inflation interaction, there is a real sense in which 'we are all monetarists now'. The issues that nowadays distinguish monetarists from their opponents concern the conduct of economic policy. As he did in the 1950s the monetarist still wants fiscal policy to stick mainly to its traditional tasks of influencing resource allocation and the distribution of income and wealth, and monetary policy to adhere to some simple rule under which the monetary aggregates do not react to short-run fluctuations either in real output or prices; the Keynesian on the other hand is still a proponent of activist stabilisation policy.

These policy issues are not independent of the theoretical questions that we have discussed earlier, and indeed, much of the current popularity among monetarists of the neo-Austrian approach to the analysis of price-output interaction stems from the erroneous belief that it provides the only sound basis for scepticism about the effectiveness of activist stabilisation policies. Many Keynesians focus their attacks on that same piece of analysis in the belief, just as erroneous, that if they succeed in refuting it, they also succeed in restoring the case for activist stabilisation policy. Now the approach in question does indeed imply that output and employment can be influenced by policy only to the extent that it causes prices to vary in a way that agents in the private sector do not forsee, while the rational expectations hypothesis tells us that if such effects were systematic, the private sector would discover the fact, adapt to it, and thereby render policy ineffective. It follows at once that the only macroeconomic policy that can influence income and employment is a purely random one, and no supporter of 'fine tuning' could possibly recommend that.

The argument just sketched out is logically watertight. So is this counter-argument: if inflation–output interaction reflects the role of quantity signals in the mechanism whereby various shocks, including those imparted by policy, have their effects transmitted to prices, the way is opened for monetary and fiscal policy to exert a systematic influence upon output and employment. However, there is much more than this to be said about the feasibility and desirability of activist policies. If there was not, how could it be that Friedman (1960) was able systematically to state his views on policy more than a decade before Lucas (1976) and Sargent and Neil Wallace (1975) developed the theoretical arguments that are now so widely regarded as the only logical underpinning of those views? The Lucas–Sargent–Wallace analysis certainly provides a *sufficient* basis for monetarist policy prescriptions, but it is not a *necessary* basis for them: it is one thing to say that the world is so structured that policy can systematically influence output and employment in the short run, and another thing altogether to say that policy makers have enough knowledge to use that ability in a way that will be beneficial.

If it is agreed that in the long run the Phillips curve is essentially vertical – or perhaps even positively sloped if allowance is made for super-non-neutralities

– then that certainly does not rule out the possibility of the economy slipping below its natural rate of output in a short run that may be of considerable duration, or the possibility that there exists an appropriate menu of monetary and fiscal policies that might hasten its return to that natural rate without generating any serious costs during the transition. As a first step to exploiting this possibility though, those in charge of policy would need to know what the natural rates of output and employment actually are. As a second step, they would need accurate information upon where the economy actually is, and where it would move in the absence of a policy change, not to mention at what pace. Armed with this not inconsiderable amount of information, policy makers would know that they were in a position where it might be useful to deploy some policy measure or other. To design the policy would of course require them to know about the size and time path of the economy's response to the measures they might take, factors which even the loosest application of the rational expectations idea tells us are likely to be influenced by the policy measures themselves.

Now I will readily agree that we have the mathematical and statistical tools available for tackling the design of stabilisation policy along the foregoing lines, and I also agree that our econometric models contain answers to all the quantitative questions that I have just raised. However the conclusion that I draw from all this is that we are probably rather good at fine-tuning econometric models.[1] One can rest the monetarist case against activist policy on the proposition that markets always clear and that expectations are rational, but one can also rest it on the much more down-to-earth proposition that we are too ignorant of the structure of the economies we live in and of the manner in which that structure is changing to be able safely to implement activist stabilisation policy in the present environment, or in the foreseeable future.

Among the penalties for making errors in fine tuning that concern monetarists are those that come in the form of uncomfortably high and perhaps accelerating inflation that would result from setting over-optimistic targets for employment and output. Thus, if there is something in the policy environment that weakens the ability of the inflation rate to accelerate, the penalties for such errors are milder, and the case against fine tuning developed above can be softened a little. In the 1950s and 1960s, there can be little doubt that the British authorities did succeed in fine tuning income and employment variables within the rather narrow bounds laid down by what then appeared to be balance of payments constraints. The monetarist interpretation of that period implies that the background of monetary stability implicit in the commitment to a fixed exchange rate was the real constraint on how far fine-tuning policy could be pushed and also that it provided the necessary conditions for its limited success. However the fact remains that the experience in question does show that a limited degree of fine tuning is feasible if only a background of long-run price stability is assured, and is seen to be assured.

It is hard for a monetarist to see how one could avoid assigning to monetary

[1] John Helliwell has suggested to me that the application of policy optimisation techniques to such models is better regarded as a test of their validity than as a preliminary to actual policy making.

policy the role of providing that necessary assurance.[1] A fixed exchange rate regime is one way of tying down monetary policy, and the adoption of some sort of a money supply growth rule would be an alternative. But this means that fine tuning would have to be by fiscal policy. Such a conclusion will be of little consolation to American Keynesians who are forced by the inability of American institutions to deliver rapid changes reliably in fiscal variables to assign to monetary variables a far more important role in stabilisation policy than their British counterparts ever did. However it may do a little to cheer up the British, for whom a return to the days of 'never had it so good' might be a welcome relief from the consequences of 'going for growth'.

As should be apparent from the last few paragraphs, I regard the question of whether governments should or should not indulge in a limited amount of fiscal fine tuning as a secondary issue for monetarists.[2] Related questions concerning public sector borrowing and the share of the public sector in National Income are even more peripheral to the monetarist debate. No matter what the public perception of these matters might be, I insist that monetarist doctrine tells one that there are severe limits to the extent to which public sector borrowing can be financed by money creation, and beyond that has nothing to say about whether a 'high' or 'low' level of such borrowing is in and of itself desirable. Similarly monetarism offers no guidance as to how big the public sector of any economy ought to be. It is a macroeconomic doctrine and the issues at stake in debates about the size of the public sector, the welfare state, and so on are fundamentally microeconomic in nature.

Monetarism however has had a good deal to say about wage and price control policies. It has opposed them, not just for ideological reasons, but for the much more down to earth reason that they have not been expected to work.[3] This position has been mainly and justifiably defended on the basis

[1] It is worth noting that the Radcliffe Committee (1959) regarded the task of monetary policy to be the achievement of background stability for the economy. Their view differed from the monetarist approach to the same issue in putting interest rates at the centre of the policy making process rather than any monetary aggregate. In the kind of sociological theorising about inflation that was particularly popular in Britain in the early 1970s incomes policy was to be assigned the task of stabilising prices and expectations.

[2] I would emphasise that this is not a new position on my part. It is one that I have consistently taken. Of course the questions about the effectiveness of fiscal policy are important ones for macroeconomists, and the Brown Univesity Conference on Monetarism (see Jerome Stein, 1975) dealt almost exclusively with such issues. I accept Purvis' (1980) judgment that the outcome of that conference was to show beyond a reasonable doubt that 'fiscal policy matters' but also his judgment that in retrospect the debate about the effectiveness of fiscal policy has not been the most important one in the monetarist debate, however important an issue it might be in its own right for macroeconomics.

Finally note that the foregoing discussion ignores the question as to whether, even if we had enough knowledge to ensure that fine tuning could be used beneficially, the political process would permit it to be used in that way. This question, as Milton Friedman has pointed out to me, is a vital one in any practical debate about activist policies.

[3] Of course there has been a considerable ideological content to the monetarist debate and I would not deny that for a moment. Nor would I take the position that there is anything reprehensible about ideological debates *per se*. I play these issues down in this paper not because, from a broader perspective I would regard them as unimportant, but because my expertise as an economist does not put me in a position to say anything very useful about them.

of empirical evidence: in the post-Korean war period it is hard indeed to find any wage-price control scheme that has not produced disappointing results over any period longer than a few months. However monetarists have also sometimes opposed controls on theoretical grounds, particularly in the context of open economies. They have noted that under fixed exchange rates the behaviour of world prices and hence the domestic prices of traded goods cannot be controlled by domestic regulations, any more than can the money supply. They have also pointed out that under flexible rates, though the money supply is under control, neither the exchange rate nor world prices can be regulated separately. In either case in an open economy wage and price controls inevitably impinge upon 'the domestic component' of the price level and are hence policies towards relative prices. For that reason, they cannot for long influence the behaviour of the general price level, unless they are accompanied by a battery of quantitative restrictions, not least on foreign trade, that very few of their advocates have been willing to contemplate.

In the 1960s wage and price controls came to be regarded as an alternative to monetary policy in the control of inflation, and in the early 1970s serious attempts were made in both Britain and the United States to use them as such. In both cases the attempts failed sufficiently dramatically that the proponents of controls now regard them at best as supplementary devices to be deployed in harmony with more traditional demand side policies rather than as a serious alternative to such measures. Though such a viewpoint stops short of the blanket opposition to controls that, along with other monetarists, I would still be willing to defend, it does represent a substantial move in a monetarist direction from positions taken a decade ago. Here, as in other instances, much of the heat has gone out of the monetarist controversy.[1]

There is more to practical monetarism than scepticism about fiscal fine tuning and opposition to wage and price controls. Its key positive tenet is that monetary weapons should be assigned to the attainment and maintenance of long-run price stability, and hence that those same monetary weapons not be used for fine tuning purposes. In this respect, as with the other components of the doctrine which we considered earlier, there has been a considerable growth in the acceptance of monetarism. Propositions about the desirability of setting rules and targets for the growth of monetary aggregates are now commonplace in the statements of Central Banks. If monetarists complain – and they do – about the failure of Keynesian policies since the mid 1960s, then simple fairness requires them to say something about the lessons that they have learned about the viability of their own policy proposals from what many observers believe to have been widespread and sustained efforts to apply them during the 1970s.

[1] Michael Parkin, Michael Sumner and Robert Jones (1973) is still an admirable source of information about wage and price controls in the British economy. Michael Walker (ed.) (1976) contains much useful information on other countries. Note that the views that I state here about the importance of using wage and price controls, if they are to be used, in conjunction with monetary and fiscal policy, rather than instead of such policies, are those of the McCracken Committee. See McCracken *et al.* (1978).

The first thing to be said on this score is that the case for monetary growth-rate rules, as initially stated by Friedman (and Edward Shaw) was put in terms of the capacity of such a policy to *maintain* stability in an already stable economy – it was a policy prescription for *staying out* of trouble. However it has been only since our economies have found themselves deeply *in trouble* that monetarist policy proposals have attracted the attention of policy makers. There is much less unanimity among monetarists about how to tackle the problem of restoring stability than there is about how to maintain it. Though all monetarists would agree that a return to a modest growth rate of some monetary aggregate or other is the long-run goal, the neo-Austrians would favour a rapid return to such a rule, while those of us who take a more traditional view of the nature of the Phillips trade-off have advocated 'gradualism'.

Unless we take the cynical view that the rhetoric of central bankers bears no relationship to their intentions, we must conclude that in a number of places attempts have been made to implement gradualist policies. There are two questions to be asked about those attempts: first, is it the case that those attempts have resulted in a systematic and gradual reduction in the rate of growth of any monetary aggregate? and second, if such attempts have anywhere been successful, did that success lead to a reduction in the inflation rate? As is well known, policy has in the main failed on the first count. Only in Canada, to the best of my knowledge, have the authorities set, and on the whole succeeded in achieving, pre-stated monetary growth targets over an extended period. It is equally well known that the single most important reason for this failure, at least in the United States and Britain, has been the unwillingness of those in charge of monetary policy to give up setting interest rate targets when they adopted targets for the money supply, combined with a proclivity to stick with the interest rate target when the two came into conflict, as they inevitably had to sooner or later. This was not been universally the case, however. Germany and Switzerland have had difficulty sticking to money supply targets because of concern with the behaviour of the exchange rates rather than interest rates, as Sumner (1979) has noted, while political concern over the exchange rate and interest rates during the winter of 1979–80 posed a serious threat to the continuation of the Canadian experiment.

It would be easy enough to argue in the light of all this that recent experience offers essentially no test of monetarist gradualism, but that seems to be going too far. Monetarists have usually treated questions of income distribution and resource allocation as separate and distinct from those of monetary policy. This dichotomy is a useful one when the problem for monetary policy is to *maintain* already existing stability, but can all too easily lead one to neglect the way in which monetary policy interacts with allocation and distribution when its implementation requires sharp (albeit temporary) increases in interest rates. A key factor here is of course the political importance of the housing market, and of the behaviour of mortgage interest rates. In retrospect, it is clear that monetarists did not do a very good job of educating policy makers – both elected and otherwise – about the problems that adopting monetarist policies would generate in this area. Some of us did raise these matters, but apparently not loudly enough.[1] High interest rates have turned out to be more difficult for politicians to face up to than high unemployment rates, and that was not foreseen.

There are also technical problems with implementing monetarist policies. The manipulation of interest rates as the centrepiece of monetary policy long antedates the Keynesian revolution, and was quite appropriate in economies whose monetary rule was to maintain convertibility into gold or some other currency at a fixed price. However the day-to-day operating procedures of central banks, the very organisation of their decision making processes, not to mention the structure of the private markets in which they operate are all geared by force of tradition to making and implementing decisions about interest rates. Although monetarists have done a great deal of work on the basic economics of the money supply process under different policy regimes, and though some of them, notably Brunner and Meltzer, have frequently scolded their colleagues for neglect of these issues, hindsight suggests that they did not recognise the extent to which the problem of implementing a different monetary policy might require a basic overhaul of institutions if it was to be solved, an overhaul that might involve a considerable break with traditional practices, and hence be hard to implement, or that, if they did, they were unable to convince policy-makers to undertake that overhaul at the same time as they adopted monetarist rhetoric.

If central banks, apart from the Bank of Canada, have not in fact succeeded in smoothly slowing down monetary expansion rates in a sustained way, a number of them have nevertheless managed to create contractions in monetary growth rates that have been sharp and persistent enough to bite. Associated with these contractions, have been the 'shifts' of the demand for money function that I discussed earlier in this paper. As the reader will recall, I argued that these shifts were, in all probability, real phenomena, and not statistical artifacts, that such shifts were nothing new, and that they were probably to be explained, at least in part, by institutional changes which themselves might plausibly be interpreted as a response to monetary policy. I believe that these shifts of the demand for money function, relatively small though they have been, force us to reassess a fundamental tenet of practical monetarism, namely the injunction to fix *ex ante* a growth rate rule for the money supply, and then ensure adherence to it by taking away from the monetary authorities the discretion to do otherwise.

Objections to such a proposal have frequently been cast in terms of the question 'How are you going to define the money supply for purposes of implementing this policy?' The answer typically given has been that it does not much matter, because if the rate of growth of one monetary aggregate is pinned down, all the others will end up behaving consistently, at least on average over the kind of time periods for which stability in monetary policy is really important. That answer is surely valid if one is dealing with an

[1] See Laidler (ed.) (1976*b*), particularly chapters 7 and 9, for an earlier statement of my own views on the role of the housing market and its interaction with monetary policy and inflation. I readily acknowledge that the source is an obscure one.

economy in which there is no institutional change in the private sector, but that does not make it as adequate a response to the question as I once thought it did. Suppose we agreed to set a rule for the growth rate of M1 and that initially we could agree on what assets to include in that aggregate. What if after the rule had been implemented some new asset, for example a new kind of chequing account, evolved? Perhaps the demand function for M1 as initially defined would then shift, but if *ex post* we included the new asset in our definition of M1 we might still be able to show that the demand for narrow money had not 'really' shifted, after all.

Such problems would not arise if we were not too specific in laying down the precise definition of money that was to bind policy makers in the future. However, to do that would leave it open to the discretion of someone at some time in the future to decide just how to define the monetary aggregate whose rate of growth was tied down with a rule, and that amounts to giving them the discretion to ignore the rule in question. It is hard to resist the implication that it does not seem to be possible, let alone desirable, to eliminate all scope for discretionary policy in a world in which the monetary system is in a state of evolution. I hasten to add that this does not imply that attempts to implement short-run fine tuning of the economy by way of manipulating interest rates are all of a sudden alright, or that it is fruitless to require central banks to announce target ranges for monetary expansion over, say, one or two year time horizons. However it does imply that it is as a practical matter impossible to prevent policy makers doing the wrong things if they so wish by tying them down to a monetary growth-rate rule. Unless we can accurately foresee the path that innovations in the financial sector are going to take, someone somewhere is going to have to be granted the discretion to deal with them when they arise. The monetarist injunction not to use monetary policy for fine tuning is not affected by these considerations, but the proposal that the once and for all enactment of a simple rule can lead to that injunction being implemented is undermined. That seems to me to be a rather severe criticism of monetarist policy doctrine.

V. CONCLUDING COMMENTS

As the reader will by now have seen, it is my view that the core of monetarism has consisted of a series of empirical propositions and policy prescriptions, all of which are quite consistent with mainstream economic theory. One can approach the analysis of social questions in terms of the maximising behaviour of individual agents without believing in a stable demand for money function, or a vertical long-run Phillips curve, but evidence that such relationships exist need in no way disturb one's theoretical preconceptions. Although there have been episodes in the monetarist debate where the relevance of mainstream economics to the analysis of such social questions as inflation and unemployment has been vigorously questioned, particularly in Britain, it has mainly been about questions amenable to being settled with reference to empirical evidence, as Mayer (1978) has also argued.

Viewed in this light, I would suggest that, in all but one aspect, the monetarist debate is as close to being over as an economic controversy ever is. The demand for money function does seem to be more stable over time than the early critics of monetarism suggested, while shifts in it have been neither new phenomena, nor of sufficient magnitude seriously to undermine long-run relationships between money and money income. Puzzles about 'reverse causation' in the data for countries such as Britain cease to be puzzles when the openness of the economy and the nature of the exchange-rate regime are taken account of. There is now much less disagreement about the empirical nature of the interaction of real income and inflation: there is a short-run trade off between inflation and unemployment and it does seem to vanish in the long run. Though we should not under-rate the importance of the consensus that has been achieved on the foregoing issues – or neglect to mention explicitly that the consensus in question is not universal – this does not mean that there is now no controversy in macroeconomics. As we have seen two areas remain contentious.

First, one aspect of the monetarist debate remains alive, and that concerns the proper conduct of monetary policy. I doubt that my own view, that the case for governing monetary policy by rules is impossible to sustain in the face of careful consideration of the influence of institutional change on the behaviour over time of the demand for money function, will find a great deal of support among monetarists at present, while I would be surprised to find it regarded as sufficient of a concession to 'fine tuning', and it really is no such thing, to satisfy the Keynesians. Thus, I would expect debates about this matter to keep the monetarist controversy alive for a while yet.

The other, and in my view far more important, issue has to do with the market-theoretic foundations of macroeconomics. The issues raised by Lucas and his collaborators are not the issues that have traditionally concerned participants in the monetarist debate and it is misleading to approach them as if they were. The debate about the assumptions of clearing markets and rational expectations as a basis for macroeconomics is a new one, and as Brian Kantor (1979) has suggested is really about whether Keynes' *General Theory* carried economics forward or took it on a fruitless detour. Though it has very little to do with monetarism, it nevertheless concerns issues of fundamental theoretical importance for macroeconomics. Let us hope that this new controversy proves to be as fruitful as the monetarist controversy has been.

University of Western Ontario D. LAIDLER

Date of receipt of final typescript: August 1980

REFERENCES

Ando, A. and Modigliani, F. (1965). 'The relative stability of monetary velocity and the investment multiplier.' *American Economic Review*, vol. 55 (September), pp. 693–728.

Ball, R. J. and Burns, T. (1976). 'The inflationary mechanism in the U.K. economy.' *American Economic Review*, vol. 66 (September), pp. 478–84.

Barro, R. J. (1978). 'Unanticipated money, output and the price level in the United States.' *Journal of Political Economy*, vol. 86 (August), pp. 549–81.

—— (1979). 'Second thoughts on Keynesian economics.' *American Economic Review*, vol. 69 (May), papers and proceedings, pp. 54–9.

Baumol, W. J. (1952). 'The transactions demand for cash: an inventory theoretic approach.' *Quarterly Journal of Economics*, vol. 66 (November), pp. 545–56.

Boughton, James M. (1977). 'Does Monetarism Matter' in Elmus Wicker (ed.). *Lilley Conference on Recent Developments in Economics April 21–23*. Bloomington, Indiana, Indiana University.

Brown, Arthur J. (1955). *The Great Inflation 1939–1951*. London: Oxford University Press.

Brunner, K. (1961). 'The report of the Commission on money and credit.' *Journal of Political Economy*, vol. 69 (December), pp. 605–20.

—— (1970). 'The monetarist revolution in monetary theory.' *Weltwirtschaftliches Archiv*, vol. 105, pp. 1–30.

—— (1978). 'Issues of post-Keynesian monetary analysis.' In Thomas Mayer (1978).

—— Cukierman, A. and Meltzer, A. H. (1979). 'Stagflation, persistent unemployment and the permanence of economic shocks.' Carnegie–Mellon University (mimeo).

—— and Meltzer, A. H. (1963). 'Predicting velocity: implications for theory and policy.' *Journal of Finance*, vol. 18 (May), pp. 319–54.

—— —— (eds.) (1978). *The Inflation Problem*. Carnegie–Rochester Public Policy Conference Series. Amsterdam: North-Holland.

Buiter, W. H. (1980). 'The macroeconomics of Dr. Pangloss: a critical survey of the New Classical Macroeconomics.' ECONOMIC JOURNAL, vol. 90 (March), pp. 34–50.

Cagan, P. (1978). 'Monetarism in historical perspective.' In Thomas Mayer (1978).

—— (1979). *Persistent Inflation*. New York: Columbia University Press.

—— and Schwartz, A. J. (1975). 'Has the growth of money substitutes hindered monetary policy?' *Journal of Money, Credit and Banking*, vol. 7 (May), pp. 137–60.

Clements, K. W. and Jonson, P. D. (1979). 'Unanticipated money, disequilibrium modelling and rational expectations.' *Economic Letters*, vol. 2, pp. 303–8.

Clower, R. W. (1965). 'The Keynesian counterrevolution: a theoretical appraisal.' *The Theory of Interest Rates* (ed. F. H. Hahn and F. P. R. Brechling). London: Macmillan.

De Prano, M. and Mayer, T. (1965). 'Tests of the relative importance of autonomous expenditure and money.' *American Economic Review*, vol. 55 (September), pp. 729–52.

Fisher, I. (1911). *The Purchasing Power of Money*. New York.

Frenkel, J. (1980). 'Flexible Exchange Rates in the 1970s', in Laurence H. Meyer (ed.). *Stabilisation Policies Lessons from the 70s and Implications for the 80s*. St. Louis, Washington University and Federal Reserve Bank of St. Louis.

—— and Johnson, H. G. (1976). *The Monetary Approach to Balance of Payments Theory*. London: George Allen and Unwin.

Friedman, M. (1956). 'The quantity theory of money: a restatement.' In *Studies in the Quantity Theory of Money* (ed. M. Friedman). Chicago: University of Chicago Press.

—— (1959). 'The demand for money: some theoretical and empirical results.' *Journal of Political Economy*, vol. 67 (June), pp. 327–51.

—— (1960). *A Program for Monetary Stability*. New York: Fordham University Press.

—— (1966). 'Interest rates and the demand for money.' *Journal of Law and Economics*, vol. 9 (October).

—— (1968). 'The role of monetary policy.' *American Economic Review*, vol. 58 (March), pp. 1–17.

—— (1970). 'A theoretical framework for monetary analysis.' *Journal of Political Economy*, vol. 78 (March–April), pp. 193–238.

—— (1975). *Unemployment Versus Inflation*. London: Institute of Economic Affairs.

—— and Meiselman, D. (1963). 'The relative stability of monetary velocity and the investment multiplier in the United States, 1898–1958. Commission on Money and Credit. *Stabilization Policies*. Englewood Cliffs, New Jersey: Prentice-Hall.

—— and Schwartz, A. J. (1963*a*). *A Monetary History of the United States, 1867–1960*. Princeton, New Jersey: Princeton University Press for the NBER.

—— —— (1963*b*). 'Money and business cycles.' *Review of Economics and Statistics*, vol. 45 (February), supplement, pp. 32–64.

Frisch, H. (1977). 'Inflation theory 1963–1975: a second generation survey.' *Journal of Economic Literature*, vol. 15 (December), pp. 1289–317.

Hahn, F. H. (1980). 'Monetarism and Economic Theory'. *Economica* NS 47 (February), pp. 1–18.

Harberger, A. C. (ed.) (1960). *The Demand for Durable Goods*. Chicago: University of Chicago Press.

Harrod, R. F. (1971). 'Discussion paper.' In *Monetary Theory and Monetary Policy in the 1970's*. (ed. G. Clayton, J. C. Gilbert and R. Sedgewick). London: Oxford University Press.

Hicks, J. R. (1974). *The Crisis in Keynesian Economics*. Oxford: Basil Blackwell.

Howitt, P. W. (1979). 'Evaluating the non-market-clearing approach.' *American Economic Review*, vol. 69 (May), Papers and Proceedings, pp. 60–4.

Johnson, H. G. (1962). 'Monetary theory and policy.' *American Economic Review*, vol. 52 (June), pp. 335–84.

—— (1972). *Inflation and the Monetarist Controversy.* DeVries Lectures, 1971. Amsterdam: North Holland.

Jonson, P. D. (1976*a*). 'Money and economic activity in the open economy, the United Kingdom 1880–1970.' *Journal of Political Economy*, vol. 84 (October), pp. 979–1012.

—— (1976*b*). 'Money, prices and output: an integrative essay.' *Kredit und Kapital*, vol. 9, pp. 499–518.

Kahn, R. F. (1976). 'Inflation: a Keynesian view.' *Scottish Journal of Political Economy*, vol. 23 (February), pp. 11–5.

Kaldor, N. (1970). 'The new monetarism.' *Lloyd's Bank Review* (July), pp. 1–18.

Kantor, B. (1979). 'Rational expectations and economic thought.' *Journal of Economic Literature*, vol. 17 (December), pp. 1422–75.

Laidler, D. (1966). 'The rate of interest and the demand for money: some empirical evidence.' *Journal of Political Economy*, vol. 74 (December), pp. 545–55.

—— (1971). 'The influence of money on economic activity: a survey of some current problems.' In *Monetary Theory and Monetary Policy in the 1970's* (ed. G. Clayton, J. C. Gilbert and R. Sedgwick). London: Oxford University Press.

—— (1975). *Essays on Money and Inflation.* Manchester: University of Manchester Press; Chicago: University of Chicago Press.

—— (1976*a*). 'Inflation in Britain: a monetarist analysis.' *American Economic Review*, vol. 76 (September), pp. 485–500.

—— (1980). 'The demand for money in the United States: yet again' (ed. K. Brunner and A. H. Meltzer). Carnegie-Rochester Conference Series. *The State of Macroeconomics.* Amsterdam: North Holland.

—— (*et al.*) (1976*b*). *Study on the Possible Part Played by Certain Primary Non-employment Incomes in the Inflationary Process in the United Kingdom.* Commission of the European Communities, Brussels.

Lieberman, C. (1980). 'The long-run and short-run demand for money revisited.' *Journal of Money, Credit and Banking.*

Lipsey, R. G. (1960). 'The relationship between unemployment and the rate of change of money wage rates in the United Kingdom, 1862–1957.' *Economica*, vol. 27, pp. 1–31.

Lucas, R. E., Jr. (1972). 'Expectations and the neutrality of money.' *Journal of Economic Theory*, vol. 4, pp. 103–24.

—— (1975). 'An equilibrium model of the business cycle.' *Journal of Political Economy*, vol. 83 (November–December), pp. 1113–44.

—— (1976). 'Econometric policy evaluation: a critique.' *The Phillips Curve and Labour Markets* (ed. K. Brunner and A. H. Meltzer). Carnegie-Rochester Conference Series. Amsterdam: North Holland.

—— (1977). 'Understanding business cycles.' In *Stabilization of the Domestic and International Economy* (ed. K. Brunner and A. H. Meltzer). Carnegie–Rochester Conference Series. Amsterdam: North Holland.

Mayer, T. (1978). *The Structure of Monetarism.* New York: W. W. Norton.

McCracken, P. *et al.* (1977). *Towards Full Employment and Price Stability.* (The McCracken Report.) Paris: OECD.

Meltzer, A. H. (1965). 'Monetary theory and monetary history.' *Schweizerische Zeitschrift Volkswirtschaft und Statistik*, (spring), pp. 409–22.

—— (1969). 'Money intermediation and growth.' *Journal of Economic Literature*, vol. 7 (March), pp. 27–56.

Modigliani, F. (1977). 'The monetarist controversy, or should we forsake stabilization policies?' *American Economic Review*, vol. 67 (March), pp. 1–19.

Parkin, J. M., Sumner, M. T. and Jones, R. A. (1972). 'A survey of the econometric evidence on the effects of incomes policy on the rate of inflation.' In *Incomes Policy and Inflation* (ed. J. M. Parkin and M. T. Sumner). Manchester: University of Manchester Press.

Patinkin, D. (1965). *Money, Interest and Prices*, 2nd ed. New York: Harper Rowe.

—— (1969). 'The Chicago tradition the quantity theory and Friedman.' *Journal of Money, Credit and Banking*, vol. 1 (February), pp. 46–70.

Phelps, E. (1967). 'Phillips curves expectations of inflation and optimal unemployment over time.' *Economica*, N.S., vol. 34 (August), pp. 254–81.

—— (*et al.*) (1969). *Microeconomic Foundations of Employment and Inflation Theory.* New York: W. W. Norton.

Phillips, A. W. (1958). 'The relation between unemployment and the rate of change of money wage rates in the United Kingdom, 1861–1957.' *Economica*, N.S., vol. 25 (November), pp. 283–99.

Purvis, D. D. (1980). 'Monetarism – a review.' *Canadian Journal of Economics*, vol. 1 (February), pp. 96–121.

Radcliffe Committee (Committee on the Working of the Monetary System) (1959). *Report.* London: HMSO.

Reid, M. (1962). *Housing and Income.* Chicago: University of Chicago Press.

Robinson, J. (1970). 'Quantity theories old and new.' *Journal of Money, Credit and Banking*, vol. 2 (November), pp. 504–12.

Santomero, A. M. and Seater, J. J. (1978). 'The inflation–unemployment trade-off: a critique of the literature.' *Journal of Economic Literature*, vol. 16 (June), pp. 499–544.

Sargent, T. J. (1976). 'A classical macroeconomic model for the United States'. *Journal of Political Economy*, vol. 84 (April), pp. 207–38.

—— and Wallace, N. (1975). 'Rational expectations, the optimal monetary instrument and the optimal money supply rule.' *Journal of Political Economy*, vol. 83 (April), pp. 241–54.

Solow, R. M. (1968). Recent controversies on the theory of inflation: an eclectic view.' In *Symposium on Inflation – Its Causes, Consequences and Control* (ed. S. Rousseas). New York: The Calvin K. Kazanjian Economics Foundation.

—— (1979). Alternative approaches to macroeconomic theory: a partial view.' *Canadian Journal of Economics*, vol. 12 (August), pp. 339–54.

—— (1980). On theories of unemployment.' *American Economic Review*, vol. 70 (March), pp. 1–11.

Sumner, M. T. (1980). The operation of monetary targets.' In K. Brunner and A. H. Meltzer (eds.): *Monetary Institutions and the Policy Process*. Carnegie–Rochester Public Policy Conference Series. Amsterdam: North-Holland.

Stein, J. (1976). *Monetarism*. Amsterdam: North-Holland.

Tobin, J. (1947). Liquidity preference and monetary policy.' *Review of Economics and Statistics*, vol. 29 (May), pp. 124–31.

—— (1956). The interest elasticity of transactions demand for cash.' *Review of Economics and Statistics*, vol. 38 (August), pp. 241–7.

—— (1958). Liquidity preference as behaviour towards risk.' *Review of Economic Studies*, vol. 25 (February), pp. 65–86.

—— (1965). 'The monetary interpretation of history.' *American Economic Review*, vol. 55 (June), pp. 464–85.

—— (1972). 'Inflation and unemployment.' *American Economic Review*, vol. 62 (March), pp. 1–18.

Walker, M. (ed.) (1976). *The Illusion of Wage and Price Control*. Vancouver, B.C.: Fraser Institute.

Wiles, P. (1973). 'Cost inflation and the state of economic theory.' ECONOMIC JOURNAL, vol. 83, pp. 377–98.

Wilson, T. (1976). 'The natural rate of unemployment.' *Scottish Journal of Political Economy*, vol. 23 (February), pp. 99 107.

10 A small macro-model of the post-war United States

Introduction

This paper sets out one of a series of small macro-models of various economies that, very much under the influence of Peter Jonson, I worked on with a number of research assistants in the late 1970s. (See C33 and D45 for other examples.) The first draft was completed in early 1981, and it was presented at an LSE sponsored conference where it drew from its discussant Robert J. Barro a tirade about the futility of *ad hoc* empirical work and the utter necessity of sound microeconomic foundations which was spectacular even by the standards he had already famously established. I leave it to the reader to decide how much of a point he had.

On rereading this paper, I am struck by its finding that fiscal policy matters, which runs counter to most monetarist empirical work. I am less impressed with its treatment of the money supply as an exogenous variable. It is quite possible to combine endogenous money with buffer stock effects on expenditure, as Bill Robson and I (cf. D100) have recently shown. I also draw attention to the fact that the use of full information maximum likelihood estimation here and elsewhere in work of this type, demonstrates that it was not just New-classical economists who, in the 1970s, became uncomfortable with econometric models of the 1960s vintage, which were built one equation at a time, with no attention paid to linkages among them. (See Lucas 1996, p. 671.) Our way of handling this problem, however, was non-Walrasian and hence, from a Walrasian viewpoint, *ad hoc*.

Reference

Lucas, R.E. jr. (1996), Nobel lecture – 'Monetary Neutrality', *Journal of Political Economy*, **104**, August, 661–82.

A SMALL MACRO-MODEL OF THE POST-WAR UNITED STATES*

by
DAVID LAIDLER†
University of Western Ontario
and
BRIAN BENTLEY†
University of Waterloo

I Introduction

Some years ago, one of us developed a small scale model of the interaction of output and the inflation rate in a closed economy. (See Laidler, 1973.) The model in question consisted of only three equations, but turned out to have considerable empirical content when tested against data generated by the post-Korean War United States. Thus, unlike the vast majority of "classroom sized" analytic models, it could be defended against charges of "oversimplification" by noting that, though many important elements of the real world were omitted, enough key features seemed to have been left in to ensure that it was nevertheless of some practical relevance. The model consisted of a demand for real money balances function, log linear in the level of real income, but containing no opportunity cost variable, an expectations augmented Phillips curve, and an equation defining the expected rate of inflation as being determined by a first-order error learning process. It was driven by but two exogenous variables, the nominal money supply, and the "full employment" or "natural" level of output, which was for empirical purposes determined by a log linear time trend. Its real side was thus a "vertical LM curve" short-run income determination model which permitted nothing but money to influence the level of aggregate demand.

In this paper we present a more sophisticated version of the same type of model from which the most objectionable features of its prototype have been removed. An opportunity cost variable is permitted to enter the demand for money function, and the role of the expected rate of inflation in determining the value of this opportunity cost is explicitly recognized. Also variables other

*Manuscript received 1.10.82; final version received 17.2.83.

†We are grateful to the SSHRCC for financial support, and to Charles Adams, Bob Barro, Michael Burns, Jeff Carmichael, Peter Jonson, Bill Poole and Rob Trevor for helpful comments on an earlier paper dealing with this model, and to Michael Artis and two anonymous referees for constructive criticism of the previous version of this essay.

than the quantity of money, such as government expenditure, taxes, and what we may loosely term the marginal efficiency of capital, are permitted to influence the level of aggregate demand. Interest rates, which were completely omitted from the earlier model, are included here and determined within the system. The "full employment" level of income is still treated as exogenous in what follows, but this is hardly an uncommon property for a short-run macro-model. As did its prototype, this model turns out to have considerable empirical content. We will show that it fits post-Korean War United States data reasonably well, and that it is rather robust in the face of an extension of the data back to 1946. Moreover, we shall also show that it fits this longer set of data about as well as Robert J. Barro's "new-classical model" of price and output determination (see Barro, 1978), despite being in most respects a simpler structure. Before turning to these empirical results we will present the basic model for which they have been generated.

II The Model

Our model consists of six equations, determining output, the demand for money, the inflation rate, a nominal interest rate, a real interest rate, and the expected inflation rate. The first of these is the most complex, being in effect the reduced form of a simple Keynesian income-expenditure system.[1] Aggregate output is treated as responding immediately and passively to satisfy aggregate demand, which in turn consists of private sector expenditure and government expenditure. Real government expenditure on goods and services, G, is treated as exogenous, while real private sector expenditure, E, is determined in the following way. With Y^* real permanent income, R the real rate of interest, T the tax rate, Ms the quantity of nominal money supplied, Md the quantity of nominal money demanded in the "long run" (the term will be more precisely defined in a moment), and subscripts -1 referring to time lags, we write

$$E = k[R_{-1}, T_{-1}, Ms/Md_{-1}]Y^* \qquad \text{......(1)}$$

So that, with Y real current output, we have

$$Y = G + k[\ ]Y^* \qquad \text{......(2)}$$

If we treat the term in parentheses in equation (1) as having the form

$$R_{-1}^{a_6'} \cdot T_{-1}^{a_3'} \cdot (Ms/Md_{-1})^{a_1'}$$

[1]The output equation which we are about to discuss is closely related to that used by Laidler and O'Shea (1980) in their small model of the U.K. economy under fixed exchange rates. Its lag structure is the same as that used in their earlier paper and was imposed on the model, without data mining, from the outset. A version of it, that did not include fiscal policy variables, was also used by Laidler (1980) to explain quarterly U.S. data. Some might think of it as a form of "IS" curve, but the presence of a monetary disequilibrium term means that investment is not always equal to saving. Therefore we prefer not to use this terminology.

then a log linear approximation to equation (2) is given by

$$y = \alpha_1(ms - md)_{-1} + \alpha_3 t_{-1} + \alpha_4 g + \alpha_6 r_{-1} \quad \text{......(i)}$$

In equation (i), which is the output equation of our model, the variables have the following meanings:

y	log Y/Y^* or the transitory component of the logarithm of output
t	the deviation of the logarithm of the tax rate from its steady state value
g	the deviation of the logarithm of government expenditure from its steady state value
r	the deviation of the real rate of interest from its steady state value
ms	the logarithm of the money supply
md	the logarithm of the quantity of money demanded in the "long run".

In the steady state, the supply and long-run demand for money are equal to one another, so the term $(ms - md)$ also measures the deviation of that variable from its steady state value.

The parameters of equation (i) are to be interpreted as follows

$$\alpha_1 = k\alpha_1' \quad \text{......(3)}$$

$$\alpha_3 = k\alpha_3' \quad \text{......(4)}$$

$$\alpha_4 = (1 - k) \quad \text{......(5)}$$

$$\alpha_6 = k\alpha_6' \quad \text{......(6)}$$

As will be apparent, equation (i) is obtained by linearizing equation (1) about the steady state values of the logarithm of its variables, on the assumption that the steady state value of national income is given by Y^*, so that this "natural" level of output is treated as equivalent to the "permanent" real income variable which influences private sector expenditure.[2] If output always converges upon the same natural level, its value represents an expectation of income that is, in the "long run", rational. However, this does not mean that complete long-run "crowding out" is necessarily imposed upon this equation. Y^* could vary with the steady state values of G and T, but our model has nothing to say about this matter.[3] In any event, equation (i) leaves fiscal policy's temporary effects on real income open to empirical investigation,

[2]The precise procedure is described by Wymer (1976).

[3]However, for purposes of our empirical work, long-run crowding out *is* imposed by the way in which we measured the "steady state" values of the relevant variables. It is worth noting that in the work of Jonson and his various associates on the RBA 76 model of the Australian economy, the steady state properties of the system are generated by what amounts to a neoclassical growth model embedded in the system. That model, of course, is far more complex than the one we present. See Jonson, Moses and Wymer (1976).

while the same may be said of the influence of interest rate fluctuations.[4]

The most unusual argument in equation (i) is the term $(ms - md)$, though there are by now several precedents for including this "real balance effect" term in such an equation.[5] Recall to begin with that the term md represents the logarithm of the "long-run" quantity of money demanded. By this phrase we mean exactly what Gregory Chow (1966), and others writing since him, meant; namely the quantity of money which agents would hold, given the values taken by the arguments in the demand function, if there were no costs involved in instantaneously adjusting cash holdings to their desired level. The term $(ms - md)$ represents the difference between the quantity of money in circulation, which therefore *must* be held by agents, and this long-run demand for money.

The proposition that there might be a difference between the amount of money in circulation at a particular moment and the long-run demand for money at that same moment is a commonplace of the literature on the demand for money. It is one of the premises upon which the conventional "adjustment cost" argument for including a lagged dependent variable in the function when modelling the "short-run" demand for money is based. However, in an economy in which the nominal money supply is exogenous to the variables determining the demand for money, it is incorrect to postulate that the money supply adjusts slowly towards a long-run target value; but that is just what the usual adjustment cost based lagged dependent variable formulation of the demand for money function implicitly does. If the exogenous money supply differs from the quantity of money that agents wish to hold, then their attempts to adjust their cash holdings must cause their expenditure flows to take a value different from those implied by whatever values other factors affecting expenditure might take. In short, there is a real balance effect on expenditure when the economy is "off" its long-run demand

[4]Moreover, the possibility that short-run fluctuations in output might themselves influence expenditure, thus generating a multiplier process, could easily be allowed for by adding a lagged transitory income term to the right-hand side of equation (i). Its absence there does not reflect any *a priori* judgement on our part. Indeed we tested for the importance of this variable in the course of our empirical work, but, with the annual data that we used, found no role for it to play. The reader might note that the parameter α_5 was reserved for this lagged dependent variable in our work, and that is why it does not appear in the version of the model presented. Similarly α_2 has been reserved for future use to investigate terms of trade effects on aggregate demand. The fact that lagged y was not significant suggests that to include it as an argument in the demand for money function in a model as simple as this would be unhelpful.

[5]See, for example, Bergstrom and Wymer (1974); Jonson (1976); Jonson, Moses and Wymer (1976); Laidler and O'Shea (1980); and Laidler (1980). The reader should note that, although we here stress money and neglect other assets, as do the papers cited, we do not mean to imply that disequilibrium in other stocks is necessarily unimportant. However, it would take a more elaborate model than this one to investigate this question.

for money function, and the term $\alpha_1(ms - md)$ in equation (i) represents an attempt to capture it in simple algebraic terms.[6]

Had the phrase not already been appropriated by the "new-classical" economists, and given a different meaning, it might have been convenient to refer to the term $(ms - md)$ as "unanticipated money": it does, after all, refer to the amount of money in circulation to which the arguments of the long-run demand for money function have not adjusted. Moreover, to include this term in an output-determining equation is to say that "unanticipated money leads to changes in output". However, in the work of Barro (1978), unanticipated money is money to which the *price level* has not fully and proportionately adjusted. It influences output by way of effects on the general price level which individual agents misread as reflecting relative price changes. For us "unanticipated money" refers to money to which the arguments of the long-run demand for money function have not adjusted, and its effect on output arises not from a supply side response to price changes, but from a real balance effect on expenditure to which output then responds.

The long-run demand for money in our model is given by the following, quite conventional, log linear relationship

$$M_d = \delta_0 + \delta_1 y^* + \delta_2 r_n + p \qquad \text{......(ii)}$$

The only variables here not yet defined are r_n, which is the logarithm of some nominal interest rate, p the log of the general price level, and y^* the log of Y^*. As will become apparent in a moment, the nominal interest rate responds, within the model, to expected inflation, so the latter variable's influence on the demand for money is captured here.

Our initial choice for an equation determining price level behaviour is a conventional expectations augmented Phillips curve. The reader should not interpret this as being some sort of "aggregate supply" function. We have already used a Keynesian 45° aggregate supply curve in deriving our output equation, and cannot now resort to introducing a second such relationship, inconsistent with the first, into our model. Rather, we treat our Phillips curve as a price setting equation.[7] Where Δp is the first difference of the logarithm of the price level, Δp^e the expected inflation rate, and y the deviation of the logarithm of income from its "natural" level, and hence a proxy for excess demand, we write

$$\Delta p = \beta y_{-1} + \Delta p^e_{-1} \qquad \text{......(iii)}$$

Equations (i) and (ii) contain a nominal interest rate representing the opportunity cost of holding money, and a real interest rate which is thought of as exerting a negative influence on the flow of expenditure. According to

[6]This matter is discussed in much greater detail in Laidler (1982, Chapter 2).

[7]This alternative interpretation of the Phillips curve is discussed in Laidler (1982, Chapter 4) and contrasted with the aggregate supply curve interpretation.

Irving Fisher, the nominal interest rate ought to equal the real interest rate plus the expected rate of inflation, at least on assets that are otherwise similar. Thus we write, using capital letters to denote natural values of the variables[8]

$$Rn = R + \Delta p^e \qquad \text{......(iv)}$$

With our interest rate variables thus linked by equation (iv), we need only to add an equation to determine one of them in order to complete our model. In deriving equation (i), we postulated the existence of a steady state value for the real rate of interest, arguing that temporary deviations of the rate from this steady state value would influence aggregate demand. It is reasonable to think of this steady state value as being determined by underlying "long-run" forces of "productivity and thrift" which will generate long-run supply and demand curves for loanable funds. One fact which might produce short-run fluctuations in the supply and demand for loanable funds, and hence influence the real rate of interest, is surely an excess supply or demand for money. If the economy as a whole is trying to adjust its money holdings towards some target value determined by the long-run demand for money function, then existing assets as well as currently produced goods and services would presumably be one of the objects of the resulting flows of expenditure. To the extent that such expenditure flows had the effect of driving interest rates, both nominal and real, away from the steady state values, variations in the real rate of interest in our equation (5) would capture a further channel of influence on expenditure of the quantity of money, rather than represent an independent factor affecting aggregate demand.

Here we postulate that the real rate of interest is determined by an equation such as

$$R = \phi_0 + \phi_1(ms - md) + \rho \qquad \text{......(v)}$$

where the parameter ϕ_0 is an estimate of the steady state value of the real rate of interest, where ϕ_1 is expected to be negative and where ρ is a "catchall" vector of other influences on the real rate of interest, representing fluctuations in the marginal efficiency of capital. Equation (v) is more conventional than it initially appears. Although the real rate of interest appears explicitly on its left-hand side, rather than the nominal rate, this is purely a matter of expositional convenience: equation (iv) would permit us to write equation (v) as explicitly determining the nominal interest rate, provided that we added the expected inflation rate to its right-hand side. To have the nominal rate of interest respond to the flow supply and demand for loanable funds, with an excess stock supply of money contributing to increase the flow supply of loanable funds, is hardly an unusual notion, but that is the idea embodied in

[8] We will discuss the problems raised by mixing logarithms and natural values of interest rates in our system in due course.

equations (iv) and (v).[9]

Of course, many textbook expositions of macroeconomics tell us that the rate of interest always moves to equate the supply and demand for money. In fact, that variable is set by traders in the bond market. If an excess stock supply of money generates an increased flow demand for bonds, then those traders will presumably lower the interest rate until a matching flow supply of bonds is generated. There is no reason that we can think of for the resulting change in the interest rate to be just such as to equate the stock supply and demand for money. When we concentrate on static equilibrium in macroeconomics, we know that "liquidity preference" and "loanable funds" theories of the interest rate are equivalent. Here we are attempting to model the disequilibrium dynamics of the macro economy, and as Harry Johnson (1951–52) warned us long ago, the two approaches are not equivalent in such circumstances. He also suggested that, out of equilibrium, the loanable funds hypothesis might be more plausible. That is the suggestion which our equation (v) embodies.[10]

We use the error learning hypothesis to determine the expected rate of inflation, and make no apology for this. Although this hypothesis is much criticized for its mechanical nature, it performs well empirically, and its use imparts to our model an element of inertia in price level behaviour that commentators as otherwise diverse in their views as Tobin (1980) and Cagan (1980) have each argued is an important factor in the inflationary process in modern economies. Since we include the expected inflation rate in both our price equation and that linking nominal with real interest rates, when we estimate our model we do use the information contained in the interest rate variables to discipline the estimation of the parameter of our error learning process. Though this will hardly satisfy exponents of the rational expectations hypothesis, it does at least introduce an element of forward-looking behaviour into our treatment of expectations. Thus the expectations equation which completes our model is given by

$$\Delta p^e = d\Delta p + (1 - d)\Delta p^e_{-1} \qquad \text{......(vi)}$$

Although the logarithms of the two interest rate variables appear in

[9]Because our model is to be estimated by full information techniques, with all constraints implied by the model's structure imposed, it makes no difference to our parameter estimates whether we write our interest rate equation as (v) or whether we use the nominal rate as the dependent variable with the expected inflation rate added to the right-hand side. If we were to use OLS, or some similar technique, this proposition would, of course, no longer hold.

[10]Artis and Lewis (1976) postulated that the rate of interest does not move at once to clear the money market, and found this hypothesis supported by U.K. data. However, they did postulate that the supply and demand for money determine the rate of interest towards which the system tends to move and hence their formulation, though in the same spirit as that advanced here, does differ from it.

equations (i) and (ii), it is the natural values of these variables which appear in equations (iv) and (v). Because we wish to estimate our model as a "complete" system, using full information techniques in order to exploit the many links among its components, this will not do. Hence for estimation purposes we use the natural value of interest rates throughout the model, approximating the log linear relationships with semi-logarithmic formulations wherever appropriate. Later we will report the results of such single equation estimates designed to check on the extent to which the approximation under discussion here distorts our results.

The model as a whole may now be written as follows:[11]

$$y = \alpha_1(ms - md)_{-1} + \alpha_3 t_{-1} + \alpha_4 g + \alpha_6^1(R_{-1} - \phi_0) \qquad \ldots\ldots(\mathrm{i}^1)$$

$$md = \delta_0 + \delta_1 y^* + \delta_2^1 Rn + p \qquad \ldots\ldots(\mathrm{ii}^1)$$

$$\Delta p = \beta y_{-1} + \Delta p^e_{-1} \qquad \ldots\ldots(\mathrm{iii})$$

$$Rn = R + \Delta p^e \qquad \ldots\ldots(\mathrm{iv})$$

$$R = \phi_0 + \phi_1(ms - md) + \rho \qquad \ldots\ldots(\mathrm{v})$$

$$\Delta p^e = d\Delta p + (1 - d)\Delta p^e \qquad \ldots\ldots(\mathrm{vi})$$

III The Data

Our model was initially estimated for the period 1954–1978 using annual data for the United States. It was also fitted for the years 1946–1976. Barro's (1978) new-classical model was fitted for this latter period and, inasmuch as it deals with the behaviour of prices and output, generated results with which ours are directly comparable.[12] Our choice of data is reasonably straightforward. Real income is gross national product, and the price level the GNP deflator. Government expenditure is real purchases of goods and services by federal, state and local governments, while the tax rate is given by the ratio of federal, state and local taxes (net of transfers) to GNP. The money supply variable is nominal M2, and this choice is important. The results reported below do not, in every respect, hold up if M1 is used instead.[13] The three-month

[11]The stability properties of the model as written here were investigated, but it proved too complex for us to extract any readily interpretable economic content from the analysis. If interest rates are dropped from the model, its dynamic structure becomes identical to that of the model described in Laidler (1973), though the interpretation of the parameters is a little different. This special case of our model is, on plausible parameter values, dynamically stable, though prone to cycles.

[12]We also estimated our model for the period 1946-1978 but, because the extra two years of data made no significant difference to any of our results, we do not report the outcome of these particular experiments.

[13]Using M1, we are unable to get well-determined estimates of the real permanent income elasticity of demand for money from our system, though other elements of the output equation hold up. We suspect that this problem arises from our choice of trend real income as the scale variable in our demand for real balances function. This is a very "long-run" variable, and Meyer and Neri (1975) have suggested that the demand for M1 is more closely related to current transactions. Note that Laidler (1980) reports similar problems when using quarterly data to estimate a version of our equation (i) by ordinary least squares.

Treasury Bill rate is the nominal interest rate in our demand for money function. "Steady state" real income and government expenditure were generated as simple log linear time trends fitted to the relevant series for the period 1946–1978. For the tax rate, there seemed to be no well determined trend, so the steady state value of this variable is represented by its mean.[14] We did not follow such a procedure with the real rate of interest. Rather, we used the level of this variable in our empirical work, including its "steady state" value (ϕ_0) in the intercept of our output regression and permitting the parameter in question to be estimated.

We chose the dividend price ratio to represent the real interest rate, partly because we believe that variations in this variable will capture those elusive shifts in the marginal efficiency of capital to which we have referred above. If an excess supply of money was the only factor causing the real interest rate to fluctuate, then its inclusion in equation (i) would be redundant. However, if there are autonomous fluctuations in expectations about the future profitability of investment, then, for a given current rate of flow of dividend payments, these would presumably be reflected in fluctuations in stock prices. These fluctuations would occur independently of variations in monetary variables, and there might then be enough independent variation in the dividend price ratio for it to play a role of its own in equation (i) even in the presence there of $(ms - md)$. We could think of no way of measuring these marginal efficiency of capital variations independently of the dividend price ratio; in fitting equation (v) we treated ρ as being part of the equation's error term, and used $(ms - md)$ as the sole explanatory variable in that expression.

Initially we had trouble getting equation (v) to perform well, though the rest of the model was not affected by these difficulties. We "solved" this problem with a little data mining. The addition of a shift dummy variable for the years 1973 onwards to this equation was all that was required to get it to perform well. The success of this procedure implies that there was a sustained exogenous downward shift in the marginal efficiency of capital in 1973.[15] The

[14]It should be noted that it is these measurement procedures which impose the assumption of long-run crowding out upon our model. It is also worth noting explicitly that we did a considerable amount of work to explore the consequences for our model's performance of using different time periods to generate the relevant trends and means, and confirmed that our results were not sensitive to this particular choice of period.

[15]An alternative interpretation of this "shift" is that there was a change in the steady state value of the real interest rate in 1973. In that case, it would be appropriate to add the same shift dummy to the intercept of equation I. We did experiment along these lines and found that very little difference was made to our results by doing this, though the significance of the real interest rate as an argument in the output equation was affected, particularly when the equation was estimated in isolation by ordinary least squares.

relationship between real and nominal interest rates as specified in equation (vi) is valid for the case of assets that are otherwise identical, but there are many differences between common stock and Treasury Bills apart from one being a real and the other a nominal asset. We attempt to capture the effects of all these differences in a constant "liquidity premium", γ_0, which we expect to take a negative value. As to the timing of our data, output, government expenditure, and taxes are measured by annual rates of flow, centred at mid-year. The money supply and interest rate variables are end-year figures, being averages of the 4th quarter observation and the 1st quarter of the following year. The price level is also an end-year figure, being a 4-quarter average centred at the end of December.[16]

IV Empirical Results

The model set out at the end of Section II of this paper cannot be estimated as it stands. Two of its equations, those determining the long-run demand for money, and the expected inflation rate, have non-observable dependent variables. When these are substituted into the appropriate places, and the minor modifications discussed in the last section are made, our model reduces to the following four-equation system:

$$y = -(\alpha_1\delta_0 + \alpha_6^1\phi_0) + \alpha_1(ms - p)_{-1} - \alpha_1\delta_1 y^*_{-1} - \alpha_1\delta_2^1 Rn_{-1} + \alpha_3 t_{-1} + \alpha_4 g + \alpha_6^1 R_{-1} \quad \text{......(I)}$$

$$\Delta p = \beta\Delta y_{-1} - d\beta y_{-2} + \Delta p_{-1} \quad \text{......(III)}$$

$$Rn = d\gamma_0 + \Delta R + dR_{-1} + d\Delta p + (1 - d)Rn \quad \text{......(IV)}$$

$$R = \phi_0 - \phi_1\delta_0 + \phi_2 D_{1973\text{-}78} + \phi_1(ms - p) - \phi_1\delta_1 y^* - \phi_1\delta_2^1 Rn \quad \text{......(V)}$$

Our *a priori* expectations about the values of the parameters of this system are as follows:

$$\alpha_1, \alpha_4, \delta_1, \beta, \phi_0, \phi_2 > 0$$
$$0 < d < 1;\ \alpha_3, \alpha_6, \delta_2, \phi_1, \gamma_0 < 0$$

A number of over-identifying restrictions on parameter values are implicit in the above model, and it was estimated with all of these being imposed, using the discrete time versions of the full information maximum likelihood programmes developed by Dr. Clifford Wymer. Table 1 contains the results of

[16]This choice was made so as to ensure that our results on the price equation were as comparable as possible to Barro's, which are based on annual price level observations, though centred on June. We explicitly checked to confirm that the substitution of a two-quarter average made no essential difference to our results. As far as the output equation was concerned, it did not, but the use of a one-year average measure of prices rather than a six-month average did lead to considerable improvement in the price equation's performance. From 1947 until 1978 our price level variable is a four-quarter average of quarterly values of the deflator. For earlier years quarterly data were not available and so we use a two-year average of annual observations because our data need to be centred at end-year. This procedure affects only one or two observations when we apply our model to the longer of the two periods for which it was estimated.

this exercise for the years 1954–1978. The results presented there seem to us to be satisfactory, on the whole. All parameters take the sign that was *a priori* expected. Furthermore, only the parameter relating output to the tax rate fails to be different from zero at conventional levels of statistical significance; but even this parameter is sufficiently large relative to its standard error that it would be unwise to dismiss the possibility that tax rate variations did have a significant short-term impact on output in the 1954–1978 period on the basis of this evidence.

Variations in the real rate of interest have an important direct effect on expenditure in equation (I), but they are themselves in part the result of a real balance effect, as the statistically significant negative value for the parameter ϕ_1 implies. This means that interest rate variations are an important indirect channel of monetary effects on output, and that there are also enough non-monetary sources of variation in the dividend price ratio to enable the parameter α_6^1 to be separately estimated. This, in turn, suggests that our conjectures, about fluctuation in the marginal efficiency of capital being an independent source of output variation, are not without foundation.

It might be argued that, because our real interest rate variable is derived from the stock market, and because the stock market processes and reflects all relevant information about future economic activity, the good performance of that variable in equation (I) arises merely from its being a good leading indicator of economic activity. If this was the case, it would be hard to explain why the other variables in the equation retain their explanatory power in its presence. The stock market presumably does not ignore information about monetary and fiscal policy and if all we had here was a leading indicator of output, one would expect it to swamp any variables whose effects it already incorporated in a regression explaining output. In fact, it does not, nor does its omission from equation (I) make any important change to the values of the parameters attached to the remaining variables, as work which we do not report in detail here shows.

The parameter estimates reported in Table 1 make quantitative as well as qualitative sense. The parameters of the demand for money function are well within the range of what one might have expected on the basis of a wide range of studies—though the implied interest elasticities do seem to be a little on the high side given some recent work (e.g., Lieberman, 1980). Above all, the well-determined values for α_1 and ϕ_1 suggest that the adjustment of real balances towards their desired long-run values has a pervasive and systematic influence on the macroeconomy. Such a result has already been well documented for the United Kingdom by Jonson (1976), for Italy by Spinelli (1979), and for Canada by Laidler *et al.* (1982). It is, therefore, of considerable interest to have such strong confirmation of the importance of real balance effects for the United States as well.

The next step in our investigation of the empirical properties of our model involved fitting it to data for 1946–1976. Before we discuss the results of this exercise which are presented in Table 2, two points should be noted. We have already referred to difficulties encountered in obtaining a satisfactory performance from our interest rate determining equation, and noted that the problems involved were "solved" by introducing the shift dummy parameter ϕ_2 into the relationship. An extra dummy variable had to be added to the real interest rate equation to "solve" problems encountered with the 1946–1976 time period. In Table 2, ϕ_2 is to be interpreted as before, while ϕ_3 is attached to a dummy variable which takes the value unity for 1946–1953 and zero thereafter.[17] More importantly, the period between the end of the Second World War and 1953 was one in which nominal interest rates were pegged. For this period, it is nonsense to suggest that the Fisher equation (IV) represents an appropriate way of modelling the behaviour of the Treasury Bill rate. Hence, with appropriate use of dummy variables, we limited the period for which the parameters of equation IV were estimated to 1954–1976, simply treating the nominal interest rate as a constant K for earlier years.

These relatively minor modifications were the only ones made in order to generate the results presented in Table 2. The most notable difference between those results and the estimates given in Table 1 lies in δ_2, which measures the interest sensitivity of the demand for money. As we shall argue when we discuss ordinary least squares estimates of our expenditure equation, this problem seems to stem in part from the use of a semi-logarithmic formulation of the demand-for-money—interest-rate relationship, which was adopted in the first place as an approximation designed to maintain the linearity of our model. Over the period 1946–1953 the Treasury Bill rate was maintained approximately constant at a level well below that ruling on average after 1953, so that the addition of these years to the data set might be expected to do particular damage here if the relevant relationship was in fact mis-specified.[18]

[17]The reader should note that the arguments presented in footnote 15 are equally relevant here and that similar experiments with dummies to those described there were carried out for this longer time period and with similar results.

[18]The reader might note that, if the rate of interest vanishes from our demand for money function, it becomes possible to eliminate equation IV from our system. We also experimented with dropping both interest rate variables altogether. In that case, equations I and III themselves form a real income and price determining model that is a special case of the more elaborate system being described here. In fact, such a simplified model performs quite well, with the parameters of remaining variables changing very little when the interest rates are removed. However, the model does lose explanatory power. One might have expected all this, given that the model is thus reduced to a structure which is much like that estimated by Laidler (1973).

The strength of the fiscal policy variables, implied by the results presented in Table 2 is noteworthy. There is no doubt here about the statistical significance of tax rate changes as a short-run influence upon aggregate demand. The quantitative importance of this variable, and of government expenditure, is also considerably greater, too much so for the comfort of anyone wishing to claim *quantitative* stability for the model's parameters in the face of the additional data used in the generation of Table 2. Indeed, these parameters are not the only ones whose estimates change quite a lot in the face of additional data.[19] However, all parameter estimates presented in Table 2 remain of the *a priori* expected sign, and are of reasonable orders of magnitude as well. Our model is at least qualitatively robust. To say this is not to claim all that much for it, perhaps, but it is more than can be claimed for many models when extra data are added to the sample for which they were originally estimated, particularly data like these, dominated by the aftermath of the Second World War and by the Korean War.

V A Comparison With Barro's Model

Though the results reported above are surely strong enough to support the claim that our model should be taken seriously, they do nevertheless concern its performance taken in isolation. However, it is possible to compare the performance of our model with that of an alternative, widely cited, framework. One of our dependent variables, the deviation of the log of output from trend, is the same as that explained by Barro's (1978) new-classical model of the United States while one other, the inflation rate, differs only in the timing of observations: Barro's inflation rate is centred at end-year and ours at mid-year. Barro presents the residuals from his equations, and a direct comparison of them with ours can therefore be made. Of course, it should be clear that the comparison here is of goodness of fit of competing models and not of their capacity to make *ex-ante* forecasts. The timing of the data on the right-hand side of the relevant equations precludes this latter interpretation.

Table 3 presents the relevant information as far as output is concerned. The residuals from Barro's output equation, as fitted by ordinary least squares, are reported in the first column, and subsequent columns report residuals from our model. The second column of the table presents the residuals from our equation when it is fitted as part of the complete system, whose results are reported in Table 2. The third column presents the residuals

[19]The intercept of the demand for money function δ_0 changes a good deal with the addition of the earlier years. Any variable omitted from the model that has a non-zero average effect on output would have its effects taken up in this parameter because of the way we estimate it.

from an ordinary least squares estimate of our own equation which we shall discuss in a moment. We also present statistics for the mean absolute value of these residuals.

As far as explaining output is concerned, there is essentially nothing to choose between Barro's model and ours. Even when all the constraints on parameter values implicit in the structure of the complete system are imposed upon our output equation, its mean absolute error is but one-tenth of one per-cent worse than that of Barro's equation. However, the latter is an ordinary least squares estimate of a single equation taken in isolation and, furthermore, one in whose construction a distributed lag scheme was determined by the data.[20] Information contained in the rest of the model was taken into account in arriving at our estimate, which would tend to worsen its fit relative to that of an ordinary least squares estimate. Also the extremely simple lag pattern with which the construction of the model began was maintained throughout the exercise; it was imposed upon the data *a priori*, and they were not permit-ted to determine its form.

The last column of Table 3 contains residuals from an ordinary least squares estimate of our output equation, further details of which are given in Table 4. The residuals are from a completely log linear specification of the equation, derived from equation (i) and a log linear demand for money function.[21] Their mean absolute value is the same as that generated by Barro's model. Though the absolute sum of the residuals is marginally smaller (.336 as opposed to .346) it is inappropriate to draw conclusions from this, given the data from which these sums derive have been rounded to 3 places initially. The standard error of the regression, σ, presented in Table 4 has, as far as we know, been calculated by the same formula as Barro's and is marginally smaller than that for his equation, which was .016. The Durbin-Watson statistic for our equation is a "borderline" value, suggesting that autocorrelation in the residuals of our output equation is not a serious problem for the 1946–1976 period. This is a point of some importance, because Wymer's programmes do not contain any error term diagnostics and in this respect there must always be an element of doubt about the results that they

[20]According to Barro's results, "unanticipated" money takes three years to have its full effects on output and about a further year to have all its effects on prices.

[21]We also fitted the version of the equation with natural values of the interest rates by ordinary least squares and found that the results here were essentially the same as those generated by full information techniques. In particular, the nominal interest rate did not appear to be a significant variable in the demand for money function. As the reader will see, this particular problem vanishes when a log linear formulation is used while the goodness of fit of the log linear relationship is also slightly better. Unfortunately, the output equation when estimated in log linear form for the 1954-1978 period produces an insignificant coefficient on the log of the nominal interest rate. We must, therefore, conclude that the demand-for-money—interest-rate relationship is one of the more fragile ones in our model.

generate. We did re-estimate our equation, using ordinary least squares with the Cochrane-Orcutt adjustment for the first order serial correlation, and confirmed that, for the period 1946–1976, there were no serious problems here. The result we obtained was:

$$\begin{array}{l} y = \underset{(0.176)}{-\,0.388} + \underset{(0.048)}{0.430\,ms_{-1}} - \underset{(0.055)}{0.344 y^{*}_{-1}} - \underset{(0.044)}{0.138\,t_{-1}} + \underset{(0.034)}{0.293\,g} \\ \quad - \underset{(0.014)}{0.063\,r_{-1}} + \underset{(0.010)}{0.016\,rn_{-1}},\ R^2 = 0.875,\ \sigma = 0.013,\ \rho = \underset{(0.175)}{0.271}, \\ \quad DW = 2.189 \end{array}$$

As is apparent, first order serial correlation of the residuals is not statistically significant in this equation, and that is why we use the OLS version of it, without the Cochrane-Orcutt adjustment in our comparisons with Barro's model.[22]

The fact that the least squares parameter estimates for the output equation are very like those yielded by the complete model suggests that much of the strength of that model's overall performance derives from this equation. This conclusion is supported by further work, not worth reporting in detail, which shows that our real interest rate determining equation generates nonsense results, of no statistical (or economic) significance, when attempts are made to estimate it in isolation. This is true for both the 1954–1978 period and for 1946–1976. The price equation, however, does not perform so badly in isolation, as we shall now see.

Table 5 compares the residuals from Barro's price equation and from ours. It should be noted that, because Barro's price level data are centred at mid-year and ours at end-year, the residuals here are not strictly comparable. The "complete model" form of our expectations augmented Phillips curve produces a mean absolute error that is but a tenth of a percent greater than Barro's equation. The years 1946 and 1947 produce exceptionally large residuals for Barro. Indeed his price equation was actually fitted for the period 1948–1976 because the presence of these two earlier years in his sample made nonsense of estimates of the equation for the entire period. There are two ways of judging this matter. The first is to argue that the very fact that our equation fits a sample including these earlier years shows its superiority. The second is to suggest that, on the contrary, a comparison which includes residuals for 1946 and 1947 is unfair to Barro, who did not claim to be able to explain these two years in the first place. Because our model fits the Korean

[22]However, the reader should note that OLS estimates of the relevant equation for the 1954-1978 period suggest that serial correlation is a more important problem in the shorter period, thus lending further support to the conclusion that we have already drawn above, namely that the robustness of our model in the face of data from various time periods lies more in its qualitative nature than in the quantitative values of its parameters.

War period badly, if we start the comparison with Barro in 1950, his equation wins easily enough. If we drop the Korean War years, our equation is back in contention again.[23]

In short, just whose equation is the better here depends very much upon the choice of periods, but 1946–1976 is Barro's chosen period, not ours. Moreover, his residuals come from an equation fitted in isolation, with a rather complex lag structure generated by the data; and he had considerable difficulty in reconciling the lag structures of his output and price equations when he came to fit them simultaneously by full information methods.[24] Our residuals, on the other hand, come from an equation estimated as part of a complete system as well as in isolation, and it gains little from being estimated in isolation as far as goodness of fit is concerned, as the results presented in Table 6 confirm.

In any event, Barro's model, with which we are here comparing our results, is widely cited and, despite all its shortcomings, our model does perform about as well as his for the time period that he selected. Moreover, it does so without the aid of distributed lag patterns generated by the data; with fewer difficulties in satisfying implicit cross-equation constraints upon parameters; and while treating the nominal interest rate, which is exogenous in Barro's system, as an endogenous variable, at least for the bulk of the period. This is not to mention the fact that, with perhaps the exception of the way in which the real balance effect is formulated, our model is little more than an empirical application of a textbook style post-Keynesian model.

VI Conclusions

The model we have presented in this paper is analytically simple, and although it has fallen a good way short of perfection in its ability to explain empirical evidence, the tests to which it has been subjected have nevertheless been stringent ones. It has been tested against data for two, albeit overlapping, time periods, and has been compared in explanatory power to another, widely cited, model. Whether it may be said to have "passed" these tests is ultimately a subjective matter, but we would claim that its performance has been at least strong enough to warrant taking the model seriously. Though some bits of the system have given us trouble, notably those that

[23]And the reader might note that Barro's model fits the years 1973-74, when the OPEC price shock was coming through, suspiciously well for a system that pays no attention to this event.

[24]Indeed, Barro's results, taken at face value, tell us that "anticipated" money, that is, that which is expected to be created, has an instantaneous effect on prices, while that which is known to exist already takes four years to change prices if its creation was not foreseen. Perhaps we are not alone in finding these implications of his results peculiar.

deal with the determination of real and nominal interest rates, and their influence on other variables, this is hardly surprising. These variables are notoriously difficult to model empirically.

We should not permit problems here to distract us from the robustness of other aspects of the model. The role of "real balance effects" in influencing output, and perhaps the real rate of interest, gets support from our work. The output relationships, which are well determined here, were originally developed using data for other countries, the United Kingdom and Australia, not to mention Canada and Italy, and our results therefore represent a "replication" of other experiments in the true sense of the word, and a successful replication at that. Moreover, in generating our results on the influence of fiscal policy we were involved in replicating an experiment originally carried out for other countries and, again, the replication was in good measure successful. Given that when monetary variables have in the past been used in simple models of the United States, notably in the St. Louis model, fiscal policy has appeared to be irrelevant as far as the determination of real income is concerned, these results are especially noteworthy.

Whether our model should be called "Keynesian" or "Monetarist" is hard to say. In the importance it accords to the interaction of the supply and demand for money in determining income and prices it is well within the "Monetarist" tradition. However, in its stress upon disequilibrium effects, and upon aggregate demand as being the prime determinant of current output, it is more "Keynesian" in nature, and this is not to mention the importance attached to fiscal policy by our results. Whatever adjective the reader may care to bestow upon it, however, the model is undoubtedly *not* in the "new-classical" tradition represented by the empirical work of Barro. The fact that it is more straightforward than Barro's model, and copes about as well with the same data as does that structure, suggests that there is as yet no pressing empirical reason to abandon traditional modes of macroeconomic analysis in favour of this radical new alternative. Perhaps that is the most important implication of our work.

TABLE I

Full Information Maximum Likelihood Parameter Estimates 1954–1978

	(a) Value (Figures in Parentheses are Asymptotic Standard Errors)
δ_0	0.445 (0.294)
δ_1	0·817 (0·045)
δ_2^1	– 0·986 (Implied elasticity (0·491) at mean – ·045)
α_1	0·327 (0·053)
α_3	– 0·053 (0·048)
α_4	0·131 (0·043)
α_6^1	– 2·085 (0·305)
β	0·266 (0·091)
d	0·266 (0·091)
ϕ_0	0·034 (0·001)
ϕ_1	– 0·061 (0·021)
ϕ_2	0·012 (0·003)
γ_0	– 0·025 (0·010)

TABLE 2

Full Information Maximum Likelihood Parameter Estimates 1946–1976

	(a) Value (Figures in Parentheses are Asymptotic Standard Errors)
δ_0	1·635 (0·312)
δ_1	0·636 (0·049)
δ_2^1	− 0·027 (0·702)
α_1	0·323 (0·039)
α_3	− 0·184 (0·041)
α_4	0·339 (0·030)
α_6^1	− 1·189 (0·297)
β	0·288 (0·132)
d	0·402 (0·117)
ϕ_0	0·034 (0·011)
ϕ_1	− 0·038 (0·012)
ϕ_2	0·008 (0·002)
ϕ_3	0·024 (0·002)
γ_0	− 0·027 (0·006)
K	0·011 (0·004)

TABLE 3

Residuals from Various Equations Explaining the Deviation of the log of GNP from Trend

	Barro	Laidler-Bentley "Complete" Model	Laidler-Bentley OLS
1946	·006	− ·024	− ·021
47	·001	− ·002	·001
48	·002	·034	·022
49	− ·012	− ·010	− ·025
50	·007	·018	·007
51	− ·006	·021	·014
52	− ·015	− ·002	− ·002
53	·014	− ·008	·005
54	− ·007	− ·008	− ·003
55	·015	·008	·018
56	·012	·018	·016
57	·011	·015	·011
58	− ·025	− ·017	− ·015
59	− ·019	− ·024	− ·024
60	− ·006	− ·007	− ·014
61	− ·004	− ·015	− ·005
62	·002	− ·015	− ·010
63	·005	− ·005	·001
64	− ·003	·010	·011
65	·009	·015	·015
66	·024	·010	·007
67	·017	·000	·001
68	− ·001	− ·012	− ·013
69	− ·032	− ·003	− ·008
70	·004	·013	·007
71	− ·005	− ·002	·003
72	·004	·000	·007
73	·028	·025	·023
74	− ·010	− ·005	− ·009
75	− ·029	− ·009	− ·007
76	·011	− ·019	− ·011
Mean Absolute Error	·011	·012	·011

TABLE 4

*Parameters of the Output Equation 1946–1976 and 1954–1978 as Fitted by Constrained Least Squares**

(Figures in Parentheses are Asymptotic Standard Errors)

	1946–1976	1954–1978
Intercept	− 0·366 (0·188)	− 0·425 (0·230)
α_1	0·366 (0·048)	0·477 (0·078)
δ_1	0·770 (0·069)	0·780 (0·067)
δ_2	− 0·057 (0·026)	0·015 (0·026)
α_3	− 0·190 (0·044)	− 0·101 (0·710)
α_4	0·319 (0·037)	0·193 (0·068)
α_6	− 0·049 (0·014)	− 0·054 (0·017)
σ	0·015	0·014
D.W.	1·563	0·959

*Note that these results are for a completely log linear form of the equation, and that the parameters having to do with interest rates are not comparable to those presented in Tables 1 and 2. The parameters of the model are just identified in this output equation and so ordinary least squares estimates of this equation are identical to those using constrained techniques, except that the latter yield estimates of the asymptotic standard errors of δ_1 and δ_2.

TABLE 5

Residuals from Various Equations Explaining the Inflation Rate 1946–1976

	Barro	Laidler-Bentley "Complete" Model	Laidler-Bentley OLS
1946	– ·189	·030	·019
47	– ·073	– ·006	– ·016
48	– ·001	– ·054	– ·055
49	– ·016	– ·042	– ·041
50	·003	·088	·089
51	·016	– ·041	– ·038
52	·001	– ·025	– ·024
53	– ·006	– ·010	– ·011
54	·009	– ·003	– ·005
55	– ·004	·021	·014
56	·000	·001	·001
57	·003	– ·012	– ·013
58	·005	– ·002	– ·003
59	– ·010	·014	·014
60	·012	– ·011	– ·009
61	– ·003	·008	·009
62	– ·011	·009	·010
63	– ·006	– ·004	– ·002
64	·000	·005	·005
65	·015	·005	·006
66	·015	– ·002	– ·002
67	·002	– ·006	– ·007
68	– ·015	·007	·005
69	– ·016	·001	– ·001
70	– ·012	– ·007	– ·009
71	·013	·001	– ·000
72	·003	– ·000	– ·000
73	·000	·026	·026
74	– ·003	·019	·018
75	·009	– ·025	– ·027
76	– ·002	– ·001	– ·001
Mean 1946–76	·015	·016	·015
Absolute Error 1950–76	·007	·013	·013

TABLE 6

Parameters of Price Equation 1946–1976, 1954–1978

As Fitted By Constrained Least Squares

(Figures in Parentheses are Asymptotic Standard Errors)

	1946–1976	1954–1978
β	0·283	0·308
	(0·137)	(0·101)
d	0·558	0·179
	(0·240)	(0·242)
σ	0·025	0·030
D.W.	2·333	2·216

References

Artis, M. J. and Lewis, M. K. (1976). "The Demand for Money in the United Kingdom 1963–1973", *The Manchester School*, Vol. XLIV, No. 2, pp. 147–181.

Barro, R. J. (1978). "Unanticipated Money, Output and the Price Level in the United States", *Journal of Political Economy*, Vol. LXXXVI, No. 4, pp. 549–581.

Bergstrom, R. and Wymer, C. (1974). "A Model of Disequilibrium Neo-classical Growth and Its Application to the United Kingdom" in R. Bergstrom (ed.), *Statistical Inference in Continuous Time Econometric Models*, Amsterdam, North-Holland.

Cagan, P. (1980). "Reflections on Rational Expectations", *Journal of Money, Credit and Banking*, Vol. XII, No. 4, Part 2, pp. 826–832.

Chow, G. (1966). "On the Long Run and Short Run Demand for Money", *Journal of Political Economy*, Vol. LXXIV, No. 2, pp. 111–131.

Clements, K. W. and Jonson, P. D. (1979). "Unanticipated Money, Disequilibrium Modelling and Rational Expectations", *Economics Letters*, Vol. II, No. 4, pp. 303–308.

Johnson, H. G. (1951–52). "Some Cambridge Controversies in Monetary Theory", *Review of Economic Studies*, Vol. XIX, No. 2, pp. 90–104.

Jonson, P. D. (1976). "Money and Economic Activity in the Open Economy", *Journal of Political Economy*, Vol. LXXXIV, No. 5, pp. 979–1012.

————, Moses, E. R. and Wymer, C. R. (1976). "A Minimal Model of the Australian Economy", *Research Discussion Paper 7601*, Sydney, Reserve Bank of Australia.

Laidler, D. (1973). "The Influence of Money on Real Income and Inflation—A Simple Model With Some Empirical Tests for the United States 1953–72", *The Manchester School*, Vol. XLI, No. 4, pp. 367–395.

——— (1974). "Information Money and the Macroeconomics of Inflation", *Swedish Journal of Economics*, Vol. LXXVI, No. 1, pp. 26–41.

——— (1980). "The Demand for Money in the United States Yet Again" in K. Brunner and A. H. Meltzer (eds.), *The State of Macroeconomics*, Carnegie-Rochester Conference on Public Policy Series, Vol. XII.

——— (1982). *Monetarist Perspectives*, Deddington, Philip Allan, and Cambridge, Mass., Harvard University Press.

——— and O'Shea, P. (1980). "A Small Macromodel of An Open Economy Under Fixed Exchange Rates: The United Kingdom 1954–1970", *Economica*, Vol. XLVII, No. 2, pp. 141–158.

———, Bentley, B., Johnson, D. and Johnson, S. T. (1982). "A Small Macroeconomic Model of an Open Economy—The Case of Canada" in E. M. Claassen and P. Salin (eds.), *Recent Issues in the Theory of Flexible Exchange Rates*, Amsterdam, North-Holland.

Lieberman, C. (1980). "The Long Run and Short Run Demand for Money Revisited", *Journal of Money, Credit and Banking*, Vol. XII, No. 1, pp. 43–57.

Meyer, P. A. and Neri, J. A. (1975). "A Keynes-Friedman Money Demand Function", *American Economic Review*, Vol. LXV, No. 4, pp. 610–623.

Spinelli, F. (1979). "Fixed Exchange Rates and Monetarism—The Italian Case", *Research Report 7915*, University of Western Ontario, mimeo.

Tobin, J. (1980). "Are New Classical Models Plausible Enough to Guide Policy?", *Journal of Money, Credit and Banking*, Vol. XII, No. 4, Part 2, pp. 788–799.

Wymer, C. R. (1976). "Linearization of Non-Linear Systems—Supplement No. 15", *Computer Programs*, London School of Economics, mimeo.

11 On the demand for money and the real balance effect

Introduction

My (1982) book *Monetarist Perspectives* (A4) contained two reprinted (but revised) chapters, (Chapter 9, above, and C27) and three new ones. When I wrote it, I thought of its core as lying in a chapter entitled 'On Say's Law, Money, and the Business Cycle', which was a sustained critique of New-classical economics in general and its clearing markets' assumption in particular, a critique which made use of the ideas first set out in Chapter 8, above. As far as I can tell, no one ever read that chapter, but this one, which actually began life as a paragraph in the other, but kept on growing, has had some attention paid to it.

Although overstated here, I believe that the basic case made, that what we would now call the 'error-correction' process which we associate with the 'short-run' demand for money function is in fact a manifestation of the whole transmission mechanism of monetary policy, rather than of the portfolio adjustment costs that face money holders, is both fundamentally correct and still insufficiently appreciated. In retrospect, I should probably have sent this piece to a journal, where it might have had more of an impact – always assuming of course that it would have been accepted.

On the Demand for Money and the Real Balance Effect

1. THE LONG- AND SHORT-RUN DEMAND FOR MONEY

No proposition in macroeconomics has received more attention than that there exists, at the level of the aggregate economy, a stable demand for money function. When we say that the demand for money function is stable we mean at the very least that money holdings, as observed in the real world, can be explained, to conventionally acceptable levels of statistical significance, by functional relationships which include a relatively small number of arguments. We also mean, or should mean, that the same equation is capable of being fitted to samples of data drawn from different times and places, without it being necessary to change the arguments of the relationship in order to achieve satisfactory results, and also without the estimated quantitative values of the parameters changing too much.

Now of course a cavalier treatment of the requirements that the number of parameters be 'relatively small', and that parameter values not change 'too much' when the data are changed, could permit claims to be made on behalf of the stability of almost any relationship, but, in this case, there is no need to abuse the English language. In practice a 'small' number of arguments has meant three or four – typically including a scale variable such as income, permanent income or wealth, an opportunity cost variable such as a nominal interest rate or some measure of the expected inflation rate, and, if nominal balances have been the dependent variable, the general price level. The requirement that parameters not change 'too much' has meant not only that they have been expected to take their theoretically predicted sign, but also to stay within reasonable quantitative ranges as well, in the region of 0.5–1.0 or a little greater for the real income elasticity of demand for money, somewhere around −0.1−−0.5 or less for the interest elasticity depending upon the interest rate, not to mention the definition of money, utilised, and since economic theory predicts that the demand for money is a demand for 'real' balances, a price level elasticity of demand for nominal balances of close to 1.0.

I have surveyed empirical work on the demand for money elsewhere (Laidler 1977, 1980), and there is no need to go into detail about these matters again here. It will suffice to note that, although not every test on every set of data has proved satisfactory, the demand for money has turned out to be 'stable' in the sense in which I have used the word above quite often enough to convince the majority of monetary economists, some of whom twenty years ago were quite sceptical (see e.g. Modigliani 1977), of the importance of the relationship for our understanding of macroeconomic phenomena. One characteristic of the results generated by empirical work on the demand for money which seems to be rather general is that, unless one is dealing with data which are highly aggregated over time – business cycle phase averages for example (see Friedman 1959) – or which cover such a long period of time – fifty years or more, say – that the variation in the data used is dominated by secular changes, it has proved necessary to distinguish between the 'long-run' and the 'short-run' demand for money in order to achieve satisfactory results.

The long-run aggregate demand for money function may be thought of as being generated by the outcome of the following thought experiment: consider an economy in which, given the values of the various arguments in the function, the aggregate of agents desire to hold a certain quantity of money and are able to do so; then ask how much money they would be observed to hold in various *alternative* circumstances in which the variables that determine money holding took different values. If the tastes of agents *vis à vis* money holding did not change over time, and if there were no barriers to their moving instantaneously from holding one amount of money to another, the outcome of this experiment would be the same as that generated by varying the values of the arguments of the demand for money function over time and then observing the changes in cash balances associated with those variations. However, if agents face any costs of adjusting their money holdings, so the argument goes, they will not move immediately to a new point on their long-run demand for money function when one of its arguments changes. They will begin to move towards that point, but the speed of the approach will be determined by their response to the adjustment costs involved in getting there.

It will help with the clarity of the argument to put all this into a familiar algebraic form at this point. It is convenient to work with a log linear (constant elasticity) form of the demand for money function, and to divide time up into discrete periods, Hicksian 'weeks' say. Thus, with X a vector of factors determining the demand for real balances, p the log of the general price level, m^* the log of the quantity of money demanded as determined by the long-run function, we write

$$m^* = f(X) + p \qquad (1)$$

which is the long-run aggregate demand for money function.

Following practices which I shall in due course criticise, we may also write, with the subscript -1 denoting a one-period time lag and with m the log of nominal money demanded,

$$m - m_{-1} = b(m^* - m_{-1}) \qquad 0 < b \leq 1 \qquad (2)$$

which tells us how much of the gap between actual and ultimately desired money holdings will be closed during one period. Together these equations yield the short-run demand for money function

$$m = b\{f(X) + p\} + (1-b)m_{-1} \qquad (3)$$

An equation such as (3), or something very like it, has been used in an enormous number of studies of the demand for money, and the lagged dependent variable has almost invariably proved an important addition as far as increasing the relationship's explanatory power is concerned. The addition in question has usually been regarded as quite innocuous, because the kind of adjustment cost argument which I have just sketched out has been widely applied, not just to the demand for money, but to the consumption function as well, not to mention the demand for various durable goods (see Harberger 1960). Indeed, one well-known, and still frequently cited, article on this particular aspect of the demand for money (Chow 1966) was explicitly an application to money of techniques which its author had used when working on the demand for automobiles, techniques which, in essence, give econometric content to the Marshallian distinction between the long-run and short-run response of quantity demanded of some good to a change in some argument of its demand function, a distinction which seems at first sight to be universally applicable.

The bulk of this essay will be devoted to elaborating upon the proposition that, notwithstanding the widespread practice of adding a lagged dependent variable to the demand for money function, the belief implicit in this practice that the demand for money *in the aggregate economy* can be modelled in the long and short runs 'as if' money was a consumer durable good, is fallacious. It will also examine some of the implications of this proposition for what we do and do not know about the aggregate demand for money. The phrase 'in the aggregate economy' is italicised, because the problem to be discussed arises at the level of what Patinkin (1956) called the market experiment, and not at the level of the individual experiment at all. It will nevertheless be helpful to begin the argument with an examination of the relevant individual experiment.

2. THE INDIVIDUAL EXPERIMENT AND THE REAL BALANCE EFFECT

Though it was a controversial matter at one time, it is by now as near to universally accepted as anything in economics ever is that once the relevant object of choice is recognised to be 'real balances' (money holdings measured in constant purchasing power terms), and once their durability is taken account of, the individual agent's demand for money can, and indeed should, be analysed along with his demand for everything else. The amount of real balances which he will hold will be the outcome of the interaction of his utility function with his budget constraint, just like the quantity of anything else he will demand. It was at one time widely questioned whether it made sense to argue that money yielded 'utility' to the individual in the same way as other goods, but it is by now well established that, from the point of view of the individual experiment, the 'story' which one tells about this matter makes no critical difference.

One may argue that, by holding real balances, the individual agent is able to avoid the embarrassment of being unable to pay up promptly when unexpectedly called upon to meet his obligations in cash (Patinkin 1965, Ch. 5); one may argue that he is enabled to cut down on the transactions costs involved in liquidating income earning assets when cash is required (Baumol 1952, Tobin 1956); one may argue that the agent can avoid the uncertainties about future command over resources inherent in holding variable capital value assets such as bonds (Keynes 1936, Ch. 15, Tobin 1958); and so on. What is postulated here turns out to make no difference to our ability to integrate the analysis of the demand for money with that of other aspects of the agent's choices, any more than the motives we attribute to the owners of automobiles make any difference to our ability to apply choice theory to analysing the demand for that durable good.

What is important, as Patinkin (1965, Chs 5–7) showed quite clearly, is that agents *do* desire to hold real balances, and not *why*. This is not to deny that if we formulate some precise hypothesis about the nature and source of the 'utility' which money holding yields the individual, we might thereby put ourselves in a position also to formulate more precise hypotheses about the quantitative nature of the agent's demand for money function than generalised choice theory would yield. After all, the Baumol–Tobin 'square root rule' is an example of just this possibility working out in practice. However, if the qualitative predictions yielded by the basic theory of choice are sufficient for any particular purpose, then there is no need to ask why cash balances yield utility before applying that theory to analysing the demand for money. This is *not* to say that, when we engage in economic analysis, we never need to pay attention to those special characteristics of money as a social institution which facilitate the processes of exchange; but it is to say that, when considering the money holding behaviour of an individual agent acting alone, it will suffice to treat real money balances 'as if' they are a service-yielding consumer durable.

Using the same symbols as before, but attaching to them, where appropriate, the subscript i to indicate that we are indeed dealing with an individual, we may write the individual agent's long-run demand for money function, where 'long run' is defined in a manner analogous to that already used above, as

$$m_i^* = f_i(X)_i + p \tag{4}$$

Here, it is as well to note explicitly that m_i^* refers to the quantity of nominal balances the individual will plan to end up holding at the end of the current period, given the price level and the values of the variables included in X that rule during the period, if he faces no costs of adjusting his money holdings. If we are willing to entertain the possibility of our agent being off his long-run demand for money function over a time span longer than one period, and we should be, if only because Archibald and Lipsey (1958) established one set of mechanisms that make this a reasonable postulate, we might also argue that he moves back towards it slowly according to

$$(m_i - m_{i-1}) = b(m_i^* - m_{i-1}) \tag{5}$$

Once again then, we can derive a short-run demand for money function of the conventional form

$$m_i = b\{f_i(X)_i + p\} + (1-b)m_{i-1} \tag{6}$$

Here m_i is the amount of money the agent *actually* plans to hold at the end of the current period, and m_{i-1} is the amount of money with which he *begins* the current period; as we shall see in a moment, m_{i-1} may or may not be the amount of money he *chose* to hold in period -1. Be that as it may, the adjustment parameter b is easily enough motivated in the individual experiment. If, by the end of the period for which he is choosing his cash holdings, our agent is not on his long-run demand for money function, he obviously enjoys less utility, or incurs greater costs somewhere or other, than he otherwise would. Suppose, however, that in moving back towards that long-run relationship over the period in question he also incurs transactions costs of some sort. Call the first cost K_1 and the second K_2, and let them be determined in the following way:

$$K_1 = \alpha_1(m_i^* - m_i)^2 \tag{7}$$

$$K_2 = \alpha_2(m_i - m_{i-1})^2 \tag{8}$$

The agent seeking to minimise the sum of these costs will adjust his cash balances over time according to equation (5) where

$$b \equiv \alpha_1/(\alpha_1+\alpha_2) \tag{9}$$

The above cost functions are undoubtedly arbitrary; their quadratic form has much more to do with the fact that this enables us to derive a linear, and therefore easy to handle, adjustment process, than with any well thought through microeconomic analysis; also, the existence of an adjustment cost function such as (8) for the individual is not easily reconciled with the lump sum adjustment costs which are sometimes used in deriving the long-run demand for money function (when, for example, the Baumol–Tobin inventory approach is used), but such criticisms are not of any great importance for present purposes. Nothing fundamental in the arguments which follow depends upon the linearity of the adjustment process, but the simplicity of the argument is enhanced if we make the arbitrary assumptions which have to be made in order to keep the individual's short-run demand for money function in the form given by (6), not least because that is the form which is usually thought of as underlying the similar relationship used in empirical work on aggregate data.

Equation (6) tells us that the amount of nominal money we will observe our individual holding at the end of any time period will depend upon the general price level at which trade takes place during the period, whatever factors we might put in X – let us say, real income and a representative nominal interest rate over the period – and the quantity of nominal money he held at the beginning of that period. Such an equation makes perfectly good economic (and econometric) sense. The price level and nominal interest rates are quite beyond the individual's control, as is real income – unless we go into a model in which the labour–leisure choice is endogenous; and if we did that we ought to put the real wage, and some endowment of labour power, into the relationship instead. Beginning of period money is also exogenous from the point of view of current period behaviour, however it may be determined. The only endogenous variable in the equation is indeed the one which appears on its left-hand side.

Equation (6) is a meaningful, if rather trivial, expression, which can form the basis for a series of equally meaningful, and equally trivial, individual experiments. We can start our individual out on his long-run demand for money function, face him with changes in his real income, the interest rate, or the price level, and use equation (6) to generate the resulting time path of his nominal money holdings. In this case, note that m_{-1}, beginning of period money holdings, will be given by the value taken by the dependent variable of equation (6) in period −1. We can also present our individual with a windfall gain in nominal money holdings (perhaps as a result of the passage of a helicopter, cf. Friedman 1969), hold interest rates, prices and his income constant, and once again use equation (6) to tell us about his reaction. In this case, of course, beginning period money will not be equal to the individual's money holdings at the end of period −1.

We do not usually come across this latter experiment in the discussions of the demand for money, finding it instead in discussions of the 'real balance effect' where the influence of money on expenditure flows is at the centre of attention. However, it is a point too often taken for granted, and perhaps for that reason not fully enough appreciated, that, in the individual experiment, whenever there arises a discrepancy between desired long-run money holdings and actual money holdings, for no matter what reason, there must be accompanying effects on expenditure flows, either on current consumption goods and/or on the acquisition of other assets. The change in money holdings on the left-hand side of equation (5) must have its counterpart in the agent's expenditure if his budget constraint is to be satisfied. That is to say, when we talk of the adjustment over time of the agent's money holdings towards their long-run equilibrium, we are also talking about what is, to all intents and purposes, a real balance effect, or as Chick (1973, pp. 76–77 following Mishan 1958) called it, a 'cash balance effect'. This is true whether the experiment we are describing is set in motion by a variation in the arguments of the agent's long-run demand for money function, or by a change in his endowment of nominal money.

I am here using the phrase 'real balance effect' in a rather broader sense than did Patinkin (1956), because he reserved the term to characterise only wealth effects. He used the phrase 'substitution effect' to describe the consequences of those disturbances to the individual which required him to change only the composition of his assets. Here I am bringing both types of reaction under the one heading as Patinkin himself tended to do (1967). Moreover, this analysis of the dynamics whereby desired long-run money holdings are reached, presented above, is different from the account offered by Archibald and Lipsey (1958) to which I have already alluded, in their extension to the multi-period case of Patinkin's (1956) analysis of the operation of the real balance effect in the individual experiment. However, these differences reflect the fact that the foregoing analysis has started from the literature on the Demand for Money, rather than that which deals with the integration of Monetary Theory and General Equilibrium Theory. They do not imply that the conclusions which have been stated above about the relationship between monetary adjustments and expenditure flows are in any way misplaced. Thus, we may use the insights yielded by Patinkin's and Archibald and Lipsey's work to illuminate the connection between the individual and market experiments in the analysis of the role of adjustment costs in the demand for money function. This is a matter of considerable importance because, as Patinkin showed, the operation of the real balance effect in the market experiment is very different from its operation in the individual experiment. I now turn to a discussion of these issues.

3. THE MARKET EXPERIMENT WITH EXOGENOUS NOMINAL MONEY

The way in which a market experiment having to do with the demand for money, the real balance effect, and so on, works out must obviously depend on the nature of the market in which it is performed. It is convenient to begin here with the kind of economy analysed by Patinkin (1965, Chs 10 and 11): that is, one in which perfect competition reigns throughout, prices are perfectly flexible, tastes, technology and resource endowments are given and held constant over time, the money supply consists of tokens whose nominal quantity is exogenously given at the beginning of each period, and individual agents face no portfolio adjustment costs. In such a case, one conceivable source of disturbance would be a change in the nominal money supply: given perfect price flexibility (and setting aside distribution effects), the outcome of the operation of the real balance effect in the market experiment would be an *instantaneous* change in the price level. Its effect as far as the demand for money is concerned would be to keep the economy on its *long-run* function.

This does not imply that in empirical work it would be appropriate to substitute the logarithm of actual money supply for m^* on the left-hand side of equation (1), and estimate that relationship as a demand for money function, because, with the money supply exogenous and the price level endogenous, these two variables ought to change places. However, because the price level is endogenous in this economy, so are real balances and it would be appropriate to re-write the long-run demand for money function as

$$m^* - p = f(X) \tag{10}$$

Then, provided there was some exogenous variation over time in the factors included in X, a long-run demand for real balances function could be estimated in this form if m_s was substituted for m^*.

All this is somewhat academic, since we have noted already that the kind of quarterly and annual data which we use in our empirical work on the demand for money will not permit us successfully to estimate such a long-run relationship. We have also noted that it is usual to deal with this problem by adding a lagged dependent variable to the demand function, and that this practice is often defended by referring to the existence of adjustment costs. Suppose that we attempted to introduce these costs into the kind of economy we have briefly described above. Could we account for the presence of a lagged dependent variable in our aggregate demand for money function in these terms? We could not, as I shall now argue. To begin with, recall that equation (3) pictures nominal balances adjusting slowly over time in response to a change in some argument or another of the demand for money function, and note that in the economy I have just described it is the nominal money supply which changes to disturb agents' money holdings, and exogenously at that. In such an economy, where prices are perfectly flexible, individual adjustment costs would have no observable consequences for aggregate behaviour in the face of an exogenous change in the nominal money supply.

The latter assertion seems to fly in the face of certain conclusions which have a well established place in the existing literature of monetary economics. As long ago as 1966 Donald Tucker embedded an aggregate demand for money function, essentially the same as equation (3), in an IS–LM model, and showed that the presence of such an equation in a model of that type implies that at least one of the arguments of the demand for money function overshoots its long-run equilibrium value as an instantaneous response to a change in the money supply. This result is *mathematically* coherent, but it is *logically* incompatible with the existence of the individual adjustment costs on which the presence of a lagged dependent variable in the demand for money function is usually supposed to be based.

To see why, consider how Tucker's result would apply to an economy in which all the arguments of the demand for real balances (X) are held constant (at their 'full employment' levels, perhaps) and in which, therefore, only the price level can adjust to absorb a change in the quantity of money. In such an economy, let the nominal money supply be increased by a certain amount. If there is no lagged dependent variable in the demand for money function, that change in the quantity of money will lead to an equi-proportional change in the price level as a result of the pressure of demand exerted on goods markets as all agents try to restore their cash balances. The algebra here is trivial: from (1), if we postulate that the demand and supply of money are to be in equilibrium, we have

$$m_s = m^* = f(X) + p \tag{11}$$

and

$$p = m_s - f(X) \tag{12}$$

so that

$$\partial p / \partial m_s = 1 \tag{13}$$

Now suppose that we maintain the 'supply and demand for money are in equilibrium' assumption, but add a lagged dependent variable to the demand for money function. When the nominal money supply changes, a *greater than proportional* change in the price level *seems* to be required. From (3) we have

$$p = \frac{1}{b} m_s - f(X) - \frac{1-b}{b} m_{-1} \tag{14}$$

from which it *seems* to follow that

$$\frac{\partial p}{\partial m_s} = \frac{1}{b} > 1 \tag{15}$$

This is a very strange result indeed. Faced with portfolio

adjustment costs, the individual experiment tells us that the typical agent in the economy is prepared to take time about getting back to equilibrium, and that he therefore changes his demand for goods by less than he would in the absence of such costs when he receives an addition to his holdings of money. Yet we are asked to believe that the aggregate effect of this *smaller* increase in demand, this *weaker* real balance effect, is to cause the price level to change by a *greater* amount than it otherwise would. The conclusion is obvious nonsense.

The problem here has arisen because we have given the wrong interpretation to the variable m_{-1} in the aggregate demand for money function. The individual experiment which must underlie the market experiment we are discussing here is one in which the typical agent receives a windfall gain in money holdings and sets in motion expenditure which enables him to adjust his money holdings towards their long-run equilibrium level. As we have seen, in this individual experiment it is crucial to distinguish the cash balances the individual agent chose to end up holding at the end of period −1 on the one hand, and those with which he begins the current period on the other, because these two amounts are not the same when the individual's holdings of nominal money are exogenously disturbed. If he faces portfolio adjustment costs, the individual attempts to move his holdings of nominal money part of the way from where they are at the *beginning* of the period to the value given by his long-run demand for money. That is the meaning of equation (6). The individual can always do this, but when the nominal money supply is exogenous, the whole economy can not. In the aggregate, the money which is available to be held must be held.

But does not equation (15) tell us by how much the price level must change in order for the increased stock of nominal money to be held willingly? It does not, and the reason why it does not may be seen by considering equation (6), the individual short-run demand for money function. The aggregate demand for money is, of course, obtained by adding up the latter expression over all individuals in the economy. However, in the experiment we are considering we must substitute the individual's beginning of period money holding for the variable m_{i-1} on the right-hand side of (6). Therefore, the *current period's money supply* rather than the *previous period's aggregate demand for nominal money* ought to be substituted for the variable labelled m_{-1} on the right-hand side of equation (3). If we do this, equation (14) becomes

$$p = \frac{1}{b} m_s - f(X) - \frac{1-b}{b} m_s \qquad (16)$$

which of course reduces to the long-run equation

$$p = m_s - f(X) \qquad (12)$$

so that we have

$$\partial p / \partial m_s = 1 \qquad (13)$$

Thus, the 'overshoot' effect is non-existent, and the economy is always on its long-run demand for money function even in the presence of portfolio adjustment costs.

A similar argument can be mounted against Tucker's (1966) analysis, where output and interest rates, rather than prices, respond to the change in the money supply, and indeed William White (1978, 1981) essentially does just that. I shall return to this point below, but for the moment let it be clear that what is at stake here is not whether Tucker's results follow from the model which he writes down, because they do, but whether the experiments he carried out with his model are compatible with the underlying adjustment lag assumptions used to justify the presence of a lagged dependent variable in the aggregate demand for money function. An alternative motivation for lags in the demand for money function, for example one based upon sluggishness on the part of expectations to respond to experience, in a world in which the demand for money depends upon the expected rather than actual values of the arguments in the function, would be quite consistent with Tucker's market experiment. His results retain their interest even if we quarrel with one set of premises from which they might be derived. The results are in fact very similar (though not identical) to those discussed in Laidler (1968) where the existence of lags in the demand for money function, and elsewhere, is justified, following Friedman (1959), along expectational lines.

The above qualification is of some importance, because a good deal of work on the demand for money function has been devoted to investigating whether or not expectation lags are, in fact, a better explanation of the need to distinguish between a short-run and a long-run demand for money function in our empirical work than are adjustment lags. Specifically, it is well known that, if we substitute the logarithm of real permanent income y^*, and the logarithm of some interest rate r, for X in equation (1), and generate permanent income according to the log–linear error learning formula

$$y^* - y^*_{-1} = q(y - y^*_{-1}) \quad (17)$$

then, with the δs being the parameter of the long-run demand for money function, the short-run demand for money function is given by

$$m = q\delta_0 + q\delta_1 y + q\delta_2 r + qp + (1-q)m_{-1} - (1-q)\delta_2 r_{-1} - (1-q)p_{-1} \quad (18)$$

If this were the true short-run demand for money relationship, we would need to posit no adjustment lags in the individual experiment; agents could always be thought of as holding just the quantity of money they desired, and the long-run–short-run distinction, upon which successful empirical work seems to depend, would hinge upon discrepancies between current and permanent income.

However, it does not seem possible to defend the proposition that (18) is the true form of the demand for money function in the face of available empirical evidence, even though Feige's (1967) seminal paper on this subject seemed to show that it was. To begin with, Feige used annual data and did not rule out the possibility that quarterly data might reveal a role for adjustment lags. Subsequent work with quarterly data does seem to show that they have a role to play even in the presence of expectation lags, or at least Laidler and Parkin (1970) claimed that this was the case for the United Kingdom. Stephen Goldfeld (1973) went further and concluded that a lag structure of the type captured in equation (3) left nothing for expectations lags to explain in the context of recent United States quarterly data. Furthermore, with similar data, also for the United States, Laidler (1980) found that equation (18) systematically performed worse than an adjustment lag formulation of the function (though not of quite the same form as Goldfeld's, as we shall see in a moment). He found that this result held up with annual data too. Moreover, none of this is to mention that recent work on the notion of Rational Expectations must imply that equation (17) is a very dubious formulation of the relationship between permanent income and current income.

In short, appealing though the expectations lag hypothesis is as a solution to the problem of linking individual and market experiments while maintaining the distinction between the short- and long-run demand for money functions, the empirical evidence in favour of this solution is weak. Equations like (3) do fit the data rather well, but if that was because they were really good approximations to equation (18), then the latter would fit even better; and it does not do so on any systematic basis. However, this does not alter the fact that, in an exogenous money supply world, portfolio adjustment costs cannot be used to motivate the long-run–short-run demand for money distinction.

There is yet a third explanation of the presence of the lagged dependent variable in the aggregate demand for money relationship to be found in the literature on the demand for money. The explanation involves the 'real' (as opposed to 'nominal') adjustment model of the short-run demand for money. The model is usually written in the following way:

$$m-p=bf(X)+(1-b)(m_{-1}-p_{-1}) \qquad (19)$$

It is then estimated on the assumption that $m_s=m$. By way of comparison, consider equation (3) once more and substract from both sides of it the logarithm of the current value of the general price level. This yields an expression which differs from equation (19) only in the timing of the value of the price level observation by which lagged nominal balances are deflated.

$$m-p=bf(X)+(1-b)(m_{-1}-p) \qquad (20)$$

With this equation too, for empirical purposes the money supply is substituted for the quantity of money demanded. Clearly, if one of these expressions fits a particular data set well, so will the other, unless the price level series is extremely erratic; but in practice the series is highly autocorrelated. It was this real adjustment form of the function which Laidler (1980) found to fit better than that derived from an expectations lag, and in this study it also turned out that the real adjustment form performed better than its nominal counterpart, in the sense of providing an estimate of $(1-b)$ that was less than unity. Benjamin Friedman (1977) also obtained this result.

At the level of the individual experiment, the 'real' adjustment notion is, to say the least, decidedly odd. To apply it to the individual experiment is to argue that, if the general price level varies, the typical agent will instantaneously adjust his nominal balances in order to keep his real money holdings constant, but that a change in any other argument of the long-run function will meet with a lagged response. The price level is quite as exogenous as any other variable in the individual experiment, and any adjustment of real balances must involve the agent acquiring or running down nominal balances. It is therefore hard to see why this should be the case. However, when it comes to the market experiment, equation (19) perhaps makes more sense, because it tells us that real balances, rather than exogenous nominal balances, adjust slowly to any disturbance. As we have already noted, real balances are endogenous at the level of the market experiment even when nominal balances are not, and Alan Walters suggested as long ago as 1965 that an equation like (19) might be interpreted as a price level adjustment equation in an economy where nominal balances are exogenous.

In fact equation (19) is not quite accurately specified as a price level adjustment equation, as I shall now show. If we have, as our aggregate demand for money function,

$$m^* = f(X) + p \tag{1}$$

then with an exogenously given money supply, the equilibrium value for the price level p^* is given by

$$p^* = m_s - f(X) \tag{21}$$

Suppose that, for some reason, the structure of the economy was such that the price level moves slowly over time towards equilibrium according to

$$p - p_{-1} = b(p^* - p_{-1}) \tag{22}$$

Then, substitution of (22) into (21), and the addition of m_s to both sides of the equation, yields, with a little rearrangement,

$$m_s - p = bf(X) + (1-b)(m_s - p_{-1}) \tag{23}$$

This expression is very like both (19) and (20), and if it was in fact the true relationship describing the way in which the money supply and the arguments of the demand for money function interact over time, one would expect that the other two relationships would display considerable explanatory power as well. Indeed, econometrically speaking, if the 'true' relationship was

$$m_s - p = bf(X) + (1-b)(m_s - p_{-1}) + \varepsilon \tag{24}$$

then this would imply, for the 'real' adjustment model when m_s is substituted for m,

$$m_s - p = bf(X) + (1-b)(m_{s_{-1}} - p_{-1}) + u \qquad (25)$$

where

$$u = \varepsilon + (1-b)\Delta m_s \qquad (26)$$

and for the 'nominal' adjustment model

$$m_s - p = bf(X) + (1-b)(m_{s_{-1}} - p) + \eta \qquad (27)$$

where

$$\eta = \varepsilon + (1-b)\Delta(m_s - p) \qquad (28)$$

The importance of the presence of lagged dependent variables in empirical work on the aggregate demand for money function can then be explained in terms of price level stickiness, and this seems to me to be the best available explanation. The portfolio adjustment cost explanation is logically invalid, as we have seen, and the expectations lag explanation does not consistently stand up to empirical testing. However, if this conclusion is accepted, other problems immediately arise, problems which imply that attempts to bring empirical evidence to bear on this issue simply by attempting to fit equations (24), (25) and (27) to data would be unsatisfactory.

If the price level is sticky, then macroeconomics tells us that such variables as interest rates and real income will tend to change as the money market attempts to clear itself, but these are exactly the variables that one might expect to find in the vector (X). This in turn means that the use of single equation econometric techniques to estimate relationships such as (19), (20) or (23) in an economy where the nominal money supply is believed to be exogenous, is at the very least open to criticism for ignoring simultaneity problems. Jonson (1967a) has much to say about this matter in arguing that the demand for money function is best estimated as part of a complete macro system, rather than in isolation, and Cooley and Leroy (1981) have recently raised related issues in discussing the identifiability of the demand for money function.

Econometric questions are undoubtedly important, and it is not my intention to belittle them in any way when I say that, nevertheless, they are not central to the issues which I am attempting to tackle in this paper. The latter are economic in nature. I have shown in the last few pages that adjustment costs at the level of the individual demand for money experiment will produce no observable consequences at the level of the market experiment in an economy in which the nominal money supply is exogenous to the arguments of the demand for money function. It follows from this conclusion that there is something badly wrong with our habit of motivating the long-run–short-run demand for money distinction in terms of the existence of such adjustment costs. Nevertheless, we seem to need this distinction if we are to deal with a wide variety of real-world data on the determinants of money holding in a more or less satisfactory way.

I have argued that the best way out of this impasse is to interpret the typical short-run demand for money function as a slightly mis-specified price level adjustment equation. If this suggestion is accepted, it follows that the equation which we call a 'short-run demand for money function' is not a structural relationship at all, but a mixture of structural relationship (the long-run demand for money function whose parameters may or may not be being properly estimated if we use single equation techniques) and some reduced form of the whole economy. In particular, the adjustment parameter *b* must be interpreted as encapsulating the workings of those mechanisms whereby the price level moves slowly towards equilibrium after a monetary disturbance.

The fact that the adjustment speeds which are typically discovered in studies of the aggregate demand for money are very slow – it is not uncommon for money holdings to appear to move less than half way towards their long-run value within a year – has often puzzled monetary economists; but in the light of the above arguments, this fact would appear to tell us that sluggish price adjustment is an important fact of real-world economic life. This in turn means that the real balance effect is not just a factor which causes prices to change in some 'meta-time' when markets are clearing along Walrasian lines, but is an important empirical phenomenon underlying the generation of real-world data.

This conclusion might at first sight seem implausible, because it implies that the supply and demand for money can remain out of equilibrium for rather long periods of time, while the notion that the money market clears quickly is a commonplace of elementary macroeconomics. It is one thing to argue, however, that it is easy for the individual agent to rid himself of (or to acquire) cash, and quite another thing to argue that the economy as a whole can do so. In the latter case, as I have already pointed out, if the nominal money supply is exogenous, then any adjustment to the stock of real balances requires a price level change.

More to the point, even though, in the presence of price level stickiness, it is *possible* that the rate of interest can move to equate the supply and demand for money, it does not follow that this will in fact happen. In the standard classroom exposition of what Chick (1973, Ch. 3) has so aptly called the 'pseudodynamics of IS–LM', it is true that a change in the quantity of money is portrayed as causing a change in the rate of interest sufficiently large to keep the supply and demand for money in equilibrium, with changes in income and prices coming later. Nevertheless, there is no empirical basis for the proposition that in the real world the interest rate change in question is sufficient to establish money market equilibrium. All that is required to get the so-called 'transmission mechanism' to start working is that a change in the quantity of money move the interest rate away from a value which equates saving and investment at the current level of income, and not that the interest rate should attain a value which will equate the supply and demand for money. In any event, as White (1978, 1981) argues, interest rate changes are every bit as exogenous to money holders as price level changes. If the real world did indeed work as the above-mentioned 'pseudodynamics' suggest, we would never observe anything but a 'long-run' demand for money function. Hence this particular piece of analysis seems to be incompatible with the facts. However, this conclusion holds only for an economy in which the nominal money supply is determined independently of the demand for nominal money. As we shall now see, matters are more complex if the money supply is endogenous.

4. A DIGRESSION CONCERNING ENDOGENOUS NOMINAL MONEY

The arguments developed in the last few pages apply to an economy in which the nominal money supply is exogenous to the variables which determine the demand for it. It is sometimes suggested that, in many economies, not least in the United States and the United Kingdom, the actual conduct of policy in recent years has been such as to make it appropriate to think of the nominal money supply as responding passively to demand side factors in a manner which is reasonably captured by a nominal adjustment version of the short-run demand for money function similar to equation (3) or (20). That view is defended in the following way. Whatever changes there may or may not have been in the targets and indicators of monetary policy in the post-war period, its instruments have consistently been interest rates. The monetary authority has attempted to achieve whatever may have been its ends by standing ready to buy and sell securities at a price which, although not necessarily constant over time, is exogenously given at any moment. If over any reasonably short period – say a quarter – real income and prices may be regarded as predetermined, and if the monetary authority, and hence the banking system, stands ready to buy and sell securities at a given price, then there is no obstacle in the way of the economy as a whole adjusting its nominal money holdings towards a desired level at a pace of its own choosing. Given this view of the money supply process, equation (3) is sometimes defended as an appropriate and correctly specified tool for investigating the demand for money.

The argument just presented seems to me to be fallacious, or at least too simple. It rests upon a version of what Brunner and Meltzer (e.g. 1976) have termed the 'money market hypothesis' of the generation of the money supply, adapted to a situation in which the interest rate is the policy instrument; and they have argued that this hypothesis, though widely accepted, is crucially deficient. What Brunner and Meltzer term the 'credit market' hypothesis differs from it in correctly insisting that the non-bank public's supply of securities to the banking system is not simply the mirror image of its demand for the liabilities of that system. This is because the non-bank public also holds income-earning assets of a type distinct from those which it supplies to the banks when it borrows from them. It is convenient (but not logically necessary) to think of this third asset as reproducible physical capital. To see the significance of this characteristic of the credit market hypothesis for the issues under discussion here, it is helpful to begin with a situation of full portfolio equilibrium on the part of the banking system and the non-bank public, and then ask what happens, according to the two hypotheses, when the monetary authorities raise the price at which they are willing to buy securities.

The 'money market' hypothesis implies that the public will want to hold more cash balances, and will attempt to acquire them by offering securities to the banking system. It also tells us that any influence on output and prices will come later as a consequence of the effect of the lower interest rate on the level of aggregate demand for goods and services; and that, as output and price level changes materialise, more money will be forthcoming from the banking system as the public demands it. In short, the nominal stock of money will passively adjust to changes in the arguments of the demand function. If the money market hypothesis is true, nominal money will be just as much an endogenous variable in the market experiment as in the individual experiment, and equation (3) might indeed be an appropriate formulation.

The 'credit market' hypothesis leads one to tell a different story. Certainly a rise in security prices will lead the public to attempt to increase money holdings, but it will also, according to this hypothesis, lead agents to attempt to substitute physical capital for securities. In the market experiment, the whole of the non-bank public will try to make such a substitution, and the trick can only be accomplished by selling securities to the banks and taking the proceeds to buy physical capital – but of course the proceeds of such a sale of securities take the form of money, newly created, not because the non-bank public as a whole wants to hold it, but because each individual member of that public wants to use money to offer in exchange for capital. Once created, that money must be held, but its creation will coincide with, or even precede, the setting in motion of streams of expenditure which in turn will have consequences for the other arguments of the demand for money function, namely output and prices.

Eventually, the economy will end up with new long-run levels of income, prices, money holdings and so on, which may differ little from those which would be predicted by a model which ignored the distinction between securities and physical capital. However, we are here concerned with short-run adjustment, with the *process* whereby this equilibrium is approached, and that is critically different. It involves excess money operating upon expenditure flows which tend to force the arguments of the demand for money function to move towards new values; that is to say, it involves real balance effects. This is not to deny that money will also be created and extinguished in such a world in response to changes in the arguments of the demand for money function and in that sense be endogenous, but it is to argue that cause and effect will not run in the simple one-way manner from other variables to money which would be implied by the money market hypothesis, and which would justify equation (3) as a basis for empirical work.

The foregoing arguments fail to touch on yet another reason for not treating the nominal money supply as merely passively responding to the behaviour of the arguments of the demand for money function, even when the monetary authorities treat the interest rate as their principal policy instrument, namely that it is not only the extension of credit to the private sector, but also to the fiscal authorities, which leads to the creation of money. Even if, at a particular rate of interest, the values of income, prices, the rate of return on capital and so on are such as to render the supply of money and bank credit compatible with portfolio equilibrium on the part of the banking system and the non-bank public, that in no way guarantees either that the fiscal authorities' budget is in balance, or that, if it is not, the private sector will be willing to absorb just the right number of new government bonds to finance whatever deficit is being incurred. A fiscal deficit can therefore become an independent source of monetary expansion when the monetary authorities are treating the interest rate as their policy instrument. Once again, cause and effect will run from money creation to variations in the arguments of the demand for money function as well as *vice versa*, and real balance effects will be at work in influencing the outcome of any market experiment.

Closely related to the matters which I have just discussed are considerations having to do with the linkages between the balance of payments and the nominal money supply in an open economy operating a fixed exchange rate. It is true that the balance of payments can provide a channel whereby the nominal money supply will passively adjust to exogenous changes in the arguments in the demand for money function, and that, in a sample of data in which the only, or to put it more practically the major, source of money market disturbance lies in exogenous changes in those arguments, an equation such as (3) might be found to fit the data. In such a case, the parameter b would not be capturing the effects of adjustment costs which face individual agents attempting to re-arrange their portfolios; rather it would be summarising, in one statistic, the structure of the economy's balance of payments mechanism, and in particular the influence of real balance effects on that mechanism. This, however, is only part of the point. In a fixed exchange rate open economy, domestic monetary policy can obviously be an independent source of short-run disturbance to the domestic money market, while any shocks originating in the world economy which have balance of payments side effects can also lead to changes in the money supply which are exogenous to the arguments of the demand function. To say that, in such an economy, the nominal money supply is endogenous, is to say that variation in the nominal money supply is one equilibrating factor at work in the system. To this extent, the monetary behaviour of a fixed exchange rate open economy is different from that of the textbook closed-economy-with-an-exogenous-money-supply model, which we considered in the previous section of this essay; but the fact of long-run endogeneity of the nominal money supply stops far short of establishing the general validity of modelling the short-run demand for money along the conventional partial stock adjustment lines embodied in equation (3).

As to the flexible exchange rate case, here we are back to a system which is similar to the closed economy model, at least as far as the relationship between the factors governing the supply of money and the arguments of the demand for money function are concerned. Though the transmission mechanism for the effects of monetary changes to the price level may differ in this case from that to be found in a closed economy (see Essay 4, pp. 148–9, below), it is nevertheless that transmission mechanism, and not simply the portfolio adjustment costs facing individual agents, which must underlie any short-run deviation of actual money holdings and those predicted by the long-run demand for money function.

5. CONCLUSIONS

The arguments presented in this essay have been rather taxonomic, but it is nevertheless possible to draw certain general conclusions from them, conclusions which in their turn yield important implications about our empirical knowledge of the properties of the demand for money function in particular and of the macroeconomy in general. The basic purpose of this essay has been to argue that the simple portfolio adjustment cost model, on which the distinction between the short-run and long-run demand for money hinges in the individual experiment, will not do to motivate that same distinction at the level of the economy as a whole. In an economy in which the nominal money supply is exogenous, it is possible for the individual agent to change his holdings of real balances by adjusting his holdings of nominal money; but the whole economy can only accomplish this by changing the general price level. If such an economy is kept 'off' its long-run demand for money function by adjustment costs, and the data seem to tell us that this is a pervasive phenomenon, then I have argued that the relevant costs are those of changing prices, not those involved in portfolio adjustment.

I have nevertheless argued that, for an economy in which it is believed that the nominal money supply is exogenous to the variables determining the demand for money, various widely used forms of the 'short-run' demand for money function *might* deal adequately with the data. They will do so if the complex transmission mechanism, which lies between money and prices, happens to be such that its dynamics can be captured in that single parameter b; if the simultaneity problems, which must arise here in principle, turn out to be unimportant in practice; and if the money supply and the price level are sufficiently highly autocorrelated that the mis-specifications involved in using the 'wrong' lagged dependent variable (cf. equations (19), (20) and (23)) are also unimportant.

In the case of economies in which the nominal money supply might reasonably be thought of as sometimes adjusting to the arguments of the demand for money function, rather than *vice versa*, either because of the way in which monetary policy is conducted, or because of the exchange rate regime, the above argument cannot be made as a general proposition. In such economies, whether nominal money does in fact predominantly adjust to demand side factors, or *vice versa*, depends upon the nature of the shocks to which the economy is being subjected. Even here though, where the shocks in question are such that the nominal money supply is a passively adjusting variable, any slowness on the part of the economy to get back 'on' its long-run demand for money function, after being driven 'off' it, will not simply be a matter of the adjustment costs facing individual money holders. Instead, it will involve the operations of the financial system, and perhaps of the balance of payments mechanism as well.

All this implies that the adjustment parameter *b*, which in empirical work on the aggregate demand for money plays such an important role in enabling us to get 'satisfactory' econometric results, must in general be thought of as summarising the dynamics of a good part of the economic system, and not merely the structural dynamics of the demand for money function itself. In the market experiment, a demand for money function which contains a lagged dependent variable can only be interpreted as being a structural relationship in and of itself if the presence of that variable is justified in terms of expectations lags; and as I have argued, such a justification is hard to sustain as the whole story – though it may be an important component of the story – in the face of available empirical evidence.

The question must arise as to what we are to make of all the empirical evidence which we have on the demand for money function in the light of the foregoing arguments. First, it must not be forgotten that there have been studies of the aggregate demand for money, using long time period samples, and/or data with a high degree of time aggregation, which have not invoked the 'short-run–long-run' distinction, and which have generated more or less satisfactory results (e.g. Friedman 1959, Meltzer 1963, Laidler 1966). Second, and this is important, the vast majority of studies of the 'short-run' demand for money *have* produced implicit estimates of the parameters of the 'long-run' relationship which are reasonably consistent with those derived from the studies just cited. On this basis, I am inclined to argue that, although the interpretation of short-run dynamics which has usually accompanied studies of the short-run demand for money is inappropriate and misleading, nevertheless, for most of the data which have been used, the practice of adding a lagged dependent variable to the function, crude and arbitrary though it is, has turned out to be an adequate way of allowing for the fact that the economy is not always in long-run equilibrium when we observe it.

The above argument presents a conjecture, not a well established truth, and it should not lead anyone to conclude that all is well with our empirical knowledge of the demand for money function. In order to find out whether the argument is true, we would have to construct explicit macroeconomic models, which permit the economy in general and the money market in particular, to deviate from long-run equilibrium; and then explicitly investigate the relationship between the structure of those models and the functional forms which typically have been fitted in studies of the short-run demand for money. The parameter *b*, it has been argued above, is a 'black box' parameter which summarises what we may loosely refer to as the dynamics of the real balance effect, and we do not currently know just what is buried in it.

A number of writers, notably Jonson (1967a) and Mervyn Lewis (1978) have noted that those samples of data that seem to give us the most trouble, as far as finding a stable demand for money function is concerned, are drawn from times and places where the monetary system has been subjected to particularly large shocks, for example the United Kingdom or the United States in the 1970s. They have speculated that the difficulties involved here have stemmed from inadequacy in our modelling of the dynamics of the monetary system. That too is a conjecture, but it is one which follows naturally from the arguments advanced in this paper, and it too could be investigated by carrying out the type of experiment suggested above. The work of Jonson and his associates, which builds upon that of Bergstrom and Wymer (1974), has involved the construction of complete econometric models in which expenditure flows of various sorts are explicitly modelled as responding to real balance effects (see e.g. Jonson 1976b, Jonson, Moses and Wymer 1976, Jonson and Trevor 1980) and could provide a framework in terms of which such an investigation could be carried out.

Be that as it may, the arguments which I have advanced imply a severe criticism of much econometric modelling of the conventional post-Keynesian sort. For example, in the FMP model of the United States economy as described by Modigliani and Ando (1976), a demand for money function complete with lagged dependent variable is estimated independently of the rest of the system, and is treated as a structural relationship to be included in the model, which is then put through all manner of simulation exercises. If the coefficient of the lagged dependent variable of that demand for money function is in fact capturing, in some approximate and unspecified fashion, aspects of the dynamic behaviour of the economy as a whole, then to treat the relevant function as if it were a structural relationship, and to use it in complete model simulation exercises, is inappropriate. When this is done, the economy's structure is being utilised twice, once in 'black box' form in the coefficient of the lagged dependent variable in the demand for money function, and once explicitly in terms of the rest of the model. This criticism, which of course applies to far more pieces of work than the FMP model, is in fact a variation on the argument advanced above when we commented on the incompatibility of Tucker's (1966) model with the adjustment lag hypothesis so often used to motivate its structure. There is no need, therefore, to repeat it here in any detail; enough has already been said to make the seriousness of its implications for much of our econometric work quite obvious.

The basic conclusion to be drawn from the arguments of this essay is very simple. In treating money as if it were just another durable good in our empirical work on the aggregate demand for money, we have overlooked the critical distinction between the individual and market experiments which Patinkin made so clearly in his theoretical work on the real balance effect. In doing so, we have used reasoning which should only be applied to the individual experiment when dealing with the market experiment. As a result, much of our empirical work on the demand for money, particularly on the 'short-run' relationship, has no proper theoretical basis in terms of which it can be interpreted, and our knowledge of that relationship is therefore much less robust than we might have thought. We do, already, have the basic tools with which we can set about remedying this state of affairs in the shape of those pioneering macro models which explicitly try to get to grips with the dynamics of real balance effects, but the work of developing those models and applying them to the issues raised here has only just begun.

References

Archibald, G.C. and Lipsey, R.G. (1958) 'Monetary and Value Theory: A Critique of Lange and Patinkin' *Review of Economic Studies*, **26** (69) (January), 1–22.

Baumol, W.J. (1952) 'The Transactions Demand for Cash – An Inventory Theoretic Approach' *Quarterly Journal of Economics*, **66** (November), 545–56.

Bergstrom, R. and Wymer, C.R. (1974) 'A Model of Disequilibrium Neo-Classical Growth and its Application to the United Kingdom' London School of Economics International Monetary Research Programme (mimeo).

Brunner, K. and Meltzer, A.H. (1976) 'An Aggregative Theory for a Closed Economy' in J.L. Stein (ed.), *Monetarism*, North-Holland.

Chick, V. (1973) *The Theory of Monetary Policy*, Basil Blackwell.

Chow, G. (1966) 'On the Long-Run and Short-Run Demand for Money' *Journal of Political Economy*, **74** (April), 111–31.

Cooley, T. and Leroy, S. (1981) 'Identification and Estimation of Money Demand' *American Economic Review*, **71** (December), 825–44.

Feige, E. (1967) 'Expectations and Adjustments in the Monetary Sector' *American Economic Review*, **57** (May), papers and proceedings, 462–73.

Friedman, B. (1977) 'The Inefficiency of Short-Run Monetary Targets for Monetary Policy' *Brookings Papers in Economic Activity*, **2**, 293–335.

Friedman, M. (1959) 'The Demand for Money – Some Theoretical and Empirical Results' *Journal of Political Economy*, **67** (June), 327–51.

—— (1969) 'The Optimum Quantity of Money' in *The Optimum Quantity of Money*, Macmillan.

Goldfeld, S.M. (1973) 'The Demand for Money Revisited' *Brookings Papers on Economic Activity*, **3**, 577–638.

Harberger, A.C. (ed.) (1960) *The Demand for Durable Goods*, University of Chicago Press.

Jonson, P.D. (1976a) 'Money, Prices and Output: An Integrative Essay' *Kredit und Kapital*, **4**, 499–518.

Jonson, P.D. and Trevor, R.G. (1980) 'Monetary Rules: a Preliminary Analysis' Reserve Bank of Australia Discussion Paper 7903 (revised September 1980), Sydney (mimeo).

Jonson, P.D., Moses, E.R. and Wymer, C.R. (1976) 'A Minimal Model of the Australian Economy' Reserve Bank of Australia Discussion Paper 7601, Sydney (mimeo).

Keynes, J.M. (1936) *The General Theory of Employment, Interest and Money*, Macmillan, London.

Laidler, D. (1966) 'The Rate of Interest and the Demand for Money – Some Empirical Evidence' *Journal of Political Economy*, **74** (December), 545–55.

—— (1980) 'The Demand for Money in the United States: Yet Again' in Brunner, K. and Meltzer, A.H. (eds), *The State of Macroeconomics*, Carnegie-Rochester Conference Series on Public Policy, Vol. 12, North-Holland.

Laidler, D. and Parkin, J.M. (1970) 'The Demand for Money in the United Kingdom 1956–67 – Preliminary Estimates' *Manchester School*, **38** (September), 187–208.

Lewis, M. (1978) 'Interest Rates and Monetary Velocity in Australia and the United States' *Economic Record*, **54** (April), 111–26.

Meltzer, A.H. (1963) 'The Demand for Money: The Evidence from the Time Series' *Journal of Political Economy*, **71** (June), 219–46.

Mishan, E.J. (1958) 'A Fallacy in the Interpretation of the Cash Balance Effect' *Economica*, NS**25** (May), 106–18.

Modigliani, F. (1977) 'The Monetarist Controversy or, Should we Forsake Stabilization Policies' *American Economic Review*, **67** (March), 1–19.

Modigliani, F. and Ando, A. (1976) 'Impacts of Fiscal Action on Aggregate Income and the Monetarist Controversy: Theory and Evidence' in J.L. Stein (ed.), *Monetarism*, North-Holland.

Patinkin, D. (1956) *Money Interest and Prices* (1st edn), Row-Peterson New York.

—— (1965) *Money Interest and Prices* (2nd edn), Harper & Row.

—— (1967) *On the Nature of the Monetary Mechanism: The 1967 Wicksell Lectures*, Almqvist & Wicksell, Stockholm.

Tobin, J. (1956) 'The Interest Elasticity of Transactions Demand for Cash' *Review of Economics and Statistics*, **38** (August), 241–7.

—— (1958) 'Liquidity Preference as Behaviour Towards Risk' *Review of Economic Studies*, **25** (February), 65–86.

Tucker, D. (1966) 'Dynamic Income Adjustment to Money Supply Changes' *American Economic Review*, **56** (June), 433–49.

Walters, A. (1967) 'Lags and the Demand for Money' *Journal of Economic Studies*, **2** (1), 3–22.

White, W.H. (1978) 'Improving the Demand for Money Function in Moderate Inflation' IMF *Staff Papers* (September), 564–607.

—— (1981) 'The Case For and Against Disequilibrium Money' IMF (mimeo).

12 Did macroeconomics need the rational expectations revolution?

Introduction

In the early 1980s I wrote three papers criticizing New-classical economics – 'On Say's Law, Money, and the Business Cycle' (A4, Chapter 3), a paper that appeared in the *Banca Nazionale del Lavoro Quarterly Review* (D58) and this one, which was presented at a conference held at the University of Manitoba in honour of Clarence Barber. I have chosen it for inclusion here because, of the trio, it is the least accessible in other sources.

The paper largely speaks for itself. My main complaint against New-classical economics has always been its incompatibility with empirical evidence, a point that is now more widely accepted than it was when I began to make it; though I am bound to say that I do not find real business cycle theory an improvement in this regard, while I suspect that calibration is a technique well calculated to hide the empirical weaknesses of the models to which it is applied.

In the early 1980s I took to referring to New-classical economics as 'Neo-Austrian', on the grounds that the work of Lucas, Sargent, *et al.* on the business cycle bore far more resemblance to the interwar work of von Hayek than to anything that more obvious 'classics' such as Marshall or Pigou had ever produced. I still think that there is something to this judgement, which I defended at some length in D82, but not enough to justify the irritation that my terminology provoked in some quarters, so I dropped it. However, I was using the Neo-Austrian label when I wrote this paper, and the reader's tolerance of the usage is requested.

Did macroeconomics need the rational expectations revolution?

I

If any development in economic theory has attracted more attention in the last decade than the rational expectations hypothesis, it seems safe to say that macroeconomists at least have not heard about it. Some authors (e.g. Begg 1982) are now referring to a 'rational expectations revolution' in the discipline and claims are being made on behalf of that revolution not unlike those which, once upon a time, were made on behalf of the Keynesian Revolution.

As its title suggests, this essay is devoted to assessing such claims from the standpoint of macroeconomics. This particular focus is important for two reasons. First, as Begg's readers are well aware, the rational expectations hypothesis has found, and continues to find, applications well beyond the conventional boundaries of macroeconomics *per se*, and I shall not be concerned, for example, with judging the significance of the hypothesis for the theory of asset market behaviour in this essay. Second, and as Begg's readers are also well aware, many of the more striking results associated with the 'rational expectations revolution' in macroeconomics have involved not one hypothesis but two: the rational expectations hypothesis *per se*, and the proposition that the economy may usefully be modelled as if it were made up of a series of continuously clearing competitive markets. It is these two hypotheses which together form the core of what is often, somewhat misleadingly, called 'New Classical' macroeconomics. I prefer the label 'neo-Austrian' and shall use it in this essay.[1]

The two above-mentioned hypotheses are logically independent of one another, as the following examples ought to convince the reader. In a deterministic world, the proposition that agents hold rational expectations about the future time path of prices reduces to the assumption of perfect foresight about prices, and that assumption is present, albeit more often implicitly than explicitly, in virtually all the fixed price level *IS–LM* analysis which permeated the last generation of macroeconomics textbooks. At the same time some of Robert E. Lucas's pioneering work on inflation–unemployment interaction in a world of clearing markets (e.g., Lucas and Rapping 1969) utilized a mechanical error learning mechanism to model expectations in experiments which rendered expectations formed in that way systematically erroneous. Nevertheless, it is the combination of these two hypotheses which gives neo-Austrian macroeconomics its particular flavour. When I pose the ques-

A paper prepared for a conference on 'Economic Policies for Canada in the 1980s' to be held in Winnipeg, Manitoba in October 1982 in honour of the 65th birthday of Clarence Barber. I am grateful to Peter Howitt, Costas Nicolau, Michael Parkin and Tom Rymes for their comments on an earlier draft. None of them, however, is to be held responsible for the views I express in the following pages.

tion 'did macroeconomics need the rational expectations revolution?' I am really asking whether or not this branch of our subject needs to be reconstructed root and branch on the basis of these two hypotheses. Since such neo-Austrians as Barro (1979), Lucas and Sargent (1981) seem to be arguing unequivocally that just such a reconstruction is necessary, I do not believe that I am erecting a straw man in posing the issue in this way.

There are many ways of stating the rational expectations hypothesis. At one extreme the phrase may signify nothing more than what Friedman and Schwartz (1982, p. 630) have called the 'ancient idea' that, in making their decisions, agents will use all relevant and available information. Put in this way, the hypothesis is at best innocuous and at worst vacuous. All its content lies in the meaning one might attach to the words 'relevant' and 'available'. The neo-Austrians attach very specific meanings to these words. To begin with they attribute to agents correct knowledge of the structure of the economy in which they operate. If such knowledge is complete and there is no inherently stochastic element to the economy's structure, then this amounts to assuming perfect foresight, but if it is incomplete or if there is an inherently stochastic element to behaviour whose distribution is known, then it involves agents in making unbiased econometric forecasts of relevant variables. Furthermore, in arguing that, even though agents do not literally engage in sophisticated econometric forecasting exercises, they nevertheless behave 'as if' they did so, the neo-Austrians gloss over the distinction (of which they are nevertheless aware) between expectations and anticipations, and postulate that the information which they attribute to agents will be acted upon. Furthermore, for neo-Austrians the world of whose structure agents in question have so much knowledge is made up of clearing competitive markets.

As the reader will surely agree, when fleshed out in this way, the 'ancient idea' of rational expectations is anything but vacuous, but it is also far from innocuous. Even if, for some people, the idea might lose much of its *a priori* plausibility and appeal, this is not a reason to criticize it. Quite the contrary: to specify the hypothesis in this way is to deny the empirical relevance of an enormous variety of *a priori* plausible and possible patterns of behaviour, and that makes the hypothesis a powerful scientific proposition. Whether it makes it a correct proposition in the sense that the empirical predictions which it yields are not refuted by available empirical evidence, however, is a different matter, and it is this issue of correctness that I shall mainly be discussing in the body of this paper.

II

Proponents of the 'rational expectations revolution' argue that their approach to macroeconomics is not only superior to the 'Keynesian' alternative on theoretical and empirical grounds, but also that it provides a sounder guide to the analysis of macroeconomic policy. On the theoretical plane, the claim is one of superior microeconomic foundations, and I shall now briefly discuss this claim. Though I have grave doubts about it, they stem only partially from disagreement concerning the criteria that one might apply in forming judgements here. Economics seeks to explain a wide variety of phenomena, some of them micro and others macro in nature, and I would not deny that the fewer basic hypotheses the subject needs to cope with these phenomena the better. The argument that the hypothesis of the rational maximizing agent, be it a firm, a household, or a biological individual, is a basic element in economic analysis does not bother me either. If a body of theory dealing with issues which we usually classify as macroeconomic – the determination of the level of employment, prices, etc. – can be shown to be compatible with this basic hypothesis, then so much the better, and if it cannot, then so much the worse.

Now it is certainly true that the behaviour relationships proposed by Keynes in the *General Theory* (1936) – notably the consumption function – were presented by him more as 'laws' describing observable empirical regularities, than as consequences of individual maximizing behaviour. In its beginnings, macroeconomics did, particularly if judged by the standards of the 1980s, seem to lack firm micro-foundations. However, long before anyone had heard the phrase 'rational expectations', work was underway to counteract this defect. Whether or not we nowadays would approve of the details of particular studies, there can still be no denying that Friedman (1956, 1957), Modigliani and his associates Brumberg and Ando (1954) (1963), Jorgenson (1967), Eisner and Strotz (1963), Baumol (1952) and Tobin (1958), to name a few important contributors, were all attempting to provide a basis in maximizing behaviour for relationships which, taken together, make up what we would usually recognize as a standard 'Keynesian' *IS–LM* macro model; nor can there be any reasonable doubt that they largely succeeded in doing so. There is, that is to say, no fundamental incompatibility between the component parts of the standard *IS–LM* model and the maximizing postulate. To this extent, it does not lack micro-foundations.

There is, however, more to macroeconomics than isolated behaviour relationships. Any body of theory which deals with the economy as a whole must be concerned with the way in which individual agents, and groups thereof, interact with one another. It must have a foundation not just in the theory of individual maximizing behaviour, but also in the theory of markets. It is *here* that the microeconomic foundations of the two approaches to macroeconomics under discussion differ, and it is not hard to make the case that each one of them is, in its own way, unsatisfactory in this respect. The body of analysis pioneered by Patinkin (1965) Chapter 13, and Clower (1965) and brought to fruition, in various forms, by Leijonhufvud (1968), Barro and Grossman (1976) and Malinvaud (1977) was directed to showing that, if prices are slow, relative to quantities, to respond to shifts in demand, then quantity changes rather than price changes will play the role of equilibrating factors in markets generating Keynesian multiplier processes, which lead the economy towards 'income constrained' positions of rest. In their turn, these positions of rest can be shown to be equilibrium positions of an *IS–LM* model.[2]

Thus there *is* a clearly specified market-theoretic foundation for standard 'Keynesian' macroeconomics. We did not need a 'rational expectations revolution' because this was lacking. Rather, the proponents of its neo-Austrian form ask us to embrace their revolution because they regard that foundation as unsatisfactory, resting as it does on a postulate which directly contradicts the market theory to be found in most microeconomics textbooks. There it is price changes which are the equilibrating factors in markets rather than quantity changes. If the flexible price general equilibrium model is the norm against which all other constructions are to be judged, then the sticky price postulate which underpins Keynesian macroeconomics certainly appears to be '*ad hoc*'.[3]

On the other hand, I doubt if it would be difficult to find people to agree to the proposition that the assumption of complete price flexibility is also *ad hoc*. Certainly, if one is to make it, he must ignore the factors to which such economists as Keynes (1936), Hicks (1974), Tobin (1972) or Lipsey (1981) have pointed as providing a basis for price stickiness notably in the labour market, a basis, be it explicitly said, which treats such stickiness as the outcome of the rational maximizing behaviour of the agents operating in that market. According to this just mentioned body of work, the labour market does not conform to the competitive norm. Monopoly elements may be present, or, more fundamentally, externalities which stem from relative wages as well as their absolute level being an argument in individuals' utility functions. If factors such as these are admitted into the analysis, one cannot then develop a macro-theory by simple aggregation of individual experiments: instead interaction effects among agents become important. If the aim is to deduce macroeconomic predictions solely from propositions about individual behaviour, and that is, according to Lucas (1981), a key aim of his work, the competitive assumption must be maintained. His ignoring the micro-foundations of price stickiness is not therefore capricious, but is a necessary component of his research strategy, as it is of those other aspects of contemporary economic theory discussed by Rymes (1982) which treat the notion of externalities as vacuous.

Some theorists find a difficulty here, though. Frank Hahn (1982) in particular has argued that a model of competitive equilibrium with all markets always clearing is not the easiest in which to justify a role for money. This might make a fastidious economist uneasy about using such a model as the basis for the analysis of the macroeconomic consequences of monetary disturbances. Of course it can be done, because money can always be introduced into such a model by assumption. Such a procedure however is yet again open to the charge of being *ad hoc*. Although attempts by such workers as Karekan and Wallace (1981) and Bryant and Wallace (1980) to find a foundation for monetary theory in the overlapping generations model of Samuelson (1958) represent an attempt to avoid this particular pitfall, whether these attempts will prove successful or not must be a moot point at the moment, though the arguments of Hahn (1982) and McCallum (1982) to the effect that the model in question does not capture money's essential role as a means of exchange, and hence cannot be used as a foundation for a theory of money, seem to me to be very powerful.

That well-known term of disapproval '*ad hoc*' has turned up three times in the last page or so. The lesson here is surely straightforward: the market-theoretic foundations of macro-theories of all varieties are, in the current state of knowledge, shaky. We did not need the rational expectations revolution because the micro-foundations of existing macro-theory were nonexistent or widely perceived to be hopelessly flawed, though they were, and remain, incomplete. However, although the micro-foundations of the new macro-theory are certainly different from those of its older rival, and are more appealing to anyone whose training in micro-theory has stressed the competitive Walrasian model, they too can fairly be termed incomplete. The question of whether or not they are 'better' is not to be settled on *a priori* grounds. It seems to me to be an empirical matter.

Before I turn to empirical issues, a word should be said about the arguments that Lucas and his associates have advanced for the superiority on theoretical grounds of the 'rational expectations' notion *per se* over the mechanical extrapolation schemes that have so often been used to generate expectations variables in Keynesian models. Here I find little to argue about. It is of the very essence of macroeconomics that we need to understand the behaviour of the economy over time, and any macroeconomic model therefore needs a theory of expectations. Also, there is something very wrong with attempts to construct such a theory which arbitrarily assume that agents ignore information which is available to them, whose relevance they can perceive, and upon which they are able to act. To the extent that macroeconomists had to be reminded of these simple truths, and we did, we certainly needed the 'rational expectations' revolution.[4] The question, however, is whether, if we accept this part of the new doctrine, we also need to adopt what it offers us in the way of market-theoretic foundations for macro-theory. It is to this, as I have already argued, empirical question that I now turn.

III

As we have seen, the micro-foundations of the macroeconomics propounded by exponents of the rational expectations revolution are certainly different from those underpinning any 'Keynesian' alternative. Though that gives us no reason in and of itself to prefer the newer doctrine, it does require us to take it seriously. Surely no one would argue with the proposition that it is healthy for macroeconomics that there be available alternative approaches to explaining the key variables with which it deals. If there do exist such alternatives, then their explanatory power ought to be compared wherever that is possible. From such comparisons we might expect to learn something both about our theories and about the world we live in.

It has been a frequent claim of the exponents of neo-Austrian macroeconomics that the experience of the 1970s – particularly in the United States, though experience has been sufficiently similar elsewhere to suggest that the claim might be more broadly based – has constituted a crucial experiment in which Keynesian economics has been decisively refuted.[5] The particular facts to which they have pointed are the co-existence of high, and indeed, on average, rising inflation with rising unemployment and slow and declining rates of economic growth. These facts, we are told, are not what would have been or were predicted by the macroeconomic orthodoxy prevailing at the beginning of the decade. Rather, high and rising inflation was expected to coincide with low and falling unemployment, and with more vigorous real growth.

The first thing to be said about this claim is that whether it seems true or not depends upon one's perception of just what constituted prevailing macroeconomic orthodoxy in the 1960s. To be fair to Lucas and his associates, they are explicit about this, and always refer to a style of macroeconomics, based on what Samuelson referred to as the 'Neoclassical synthesis', which is exemplified by virtually all large scale US macroeconometric models. Nevertheless, this particular style of analysis does not exhaust the Keynesian legacy. Those who, in the 1960s, believed that inflation was a cost-push phenomenon caused by real income growth failing to keep up with the rising aspirations of the labour force would undoubtedly have predicted that a slow-down of real growth, such as the seventies witnessed, should be accompanied by high and rising inflation; and they would have predicted that attempts to control that inflation by demand side policies would have led to rising unemployment.[6]

I do not refer to this particular brand of 'Keynesian' economics because I am a sudden convert to it. I am not: I believe that certain other facts generated by the 1970s make it hard to accept. Even so I draw attention to it in order to make the point that the evidence cited by Lucas and his associates refute only one, albeit once widely accepted, version of Keynesian macroeconomics, namely that in which price level and output behaviour are linked through a Phillips curve whose structure is such as to permit a permanent inverse inflation–unemployment tradeoff. Such a relationship was certainly believed to exist by many during the 1960s and 1970s. However it was not an essential feature of Keynesian macroeconomics; nor, crucially, is it a necessary implication of the price adjustment mechanisms postulated by the Neoclassical synthesis.

As Lucas (1980) has explicitly noted, perhaps the most careful exposition of that particular brand of macroeconomics is Patinkin's [1956] (1965) *Money, Interest and Prices*. One of that book's numerous virtues was the care which Patinkin took to remind his readers that many of the results he generated were conditional upon expected prices being equal to current prices. Given his purposes, there was no need for Patinkin to modify this assumption, but anyone seeking to use his work as a basis for analysing the macroeconomics of inflation should have seen the need to do so. To put the same point in another way, when Lipsey (1960) set out the underlying micro-theory of the Phillips curve, using the same Samuelsonian price dynamics as did Patinkin, he should have recognized that the relevant price for his labour market analysis was not the money wage but the real wage. However he did not.

The upshot of this elementary but pervasive error was that, for a while, many economists analysed the endogenous dynamics of inflation on the basis of an implicit assumption that all agents believe inflation be an exogenous constant! However, and the point is not sufficiently appreciated, this error was revealed and corrected by Phelps (1967) and Friedman (1968) *before* the 1970s generated any experiments, crucial or otherwise. No one who had read and accepted the basic thrust of those articles found anything in the 1970s to unnerve him, nor did he need feel any uneasiness about adopting as the market-theoretic basis of his macroeconomics the kind of analysis advanced, say, by Leijonhufvud (1968). What the 1970s experience did refute was the particular assumption implicit in far too much of the macroeconomics of the 1960s that money illusion can be a permanent phenomenon. That assumption should never have been a central characteristic of Keynesian economics, or of any other kind of economics for that matter.

Phelps and Friedman both made the basic point that inflation expectations would not remain constant during an inflationary episode, and in suggesting that those expectations would tend in fact to respond to experience, they also rendered existing orthodox models capable of generating that set of stylized facts known as 'stagflation'. However, in modelling expectations, the only nod that Phelps and Friedman made in the direction of any kind of rational behaviour was in imposing the requirement that an ongoing constant inflation rate would eventually become fully anticipated. In terms of the error learning scheme which they adopted, they insisted that the weights accorded to past inflation in forming expectations about the future sum to unity. Even this *a priori* requirement was too much for some exponents of the neoclassical synthesis, who subjected it to empirical test, found it apparently refuted, and so concluded that the long-run Phillips curve, though steeper than the short-run curve, still permitted an inverse inflation–unemployment tradeoff.[7]

Be that as it may, the claim of Lucas and his associates that early attempts at modelling expectations were mechanical, and their claim that maximizing principles can usefully be applied in this area are amply justified, although one should note that much of the work in which adaptive expectations were used abounds in informal warnings about taking that particular hypothesis too literally or seriously. It was often presented as no more than a convenient first approximation to the modelling of endogenous expectations, not suitable for use in all circumstances, and probably inadequate at times when policies were changing.[8] But, and this is the crucial point, such warnings and qualifications did not impinge upon formal modelling exercises, and those who gave them showed no signs of appreciating that they were dealing with special cases of a general phenomenon which lent itself to formal modelling. To say, therefore, that those who used adaptive expectations did not take the hypothesis very seriously and recognized that there were many cases in which it was inadequate, is not to say that they understood the notion of rational expectations or appreciated its implications for macro modelling: they patently did not. Here we have a clear instance in which Economics undoubtedly needed one of the key ingredients of the rational expectations revolution.

IV

To say that agents will: use all information that is freely available to them; will take steps to acquire any other information for which the benefit outweighs the cost of acquisition; will act upon such information to the extent that they are free to do so; and hence will not, in a long run when they are free to act on all their information, make systematic errors, is not also to say that: the world behaves as if all markets are competitive and continuously clearing; all agents understand the workings and interaction of markets to the extent of being able correctly to forecast the outcome for the economy of any new exogenous shocks of whose nature they are aware; and that all real fluctuations are the result of random errors in forecasting exogenous variables. The former set of propositions is a very general statement of the notion of rational expectations to which any reasonable person might assent, and the latter is a very specific application of that general notion, hedged around with particular assumptions both about the nature of the economy, and about agents' knowledge of it, at which that same reasonable person might baulk.

Nevertheless, as I have already noted above, it is the latter set of propositions which forms the basis of neo-Austrian macroeconomics, and it should require more than the observation that one particular alternatively grounded macroeconomic model has failed to cope with a particular set of stylized facts to persuade us of the desirability of embracing the rational expectations revolution which it embodies. We need to know that there is no third or fourth option available among macro-theories which can explain those same facts as well as the 'revolutionary' model, or that, if there is, there exist other facts which enable us to reject those other options, before we can reasonably be expected to embrace that revolution.

We have already seen that, if explaining the stylized facts of the stagflation of the 1970s is all that is required, third and fourth options are readily available, though, of course, the 'revolutionary' model also can explain both stagflation and its cyclical character. Nevertheless we need to look at other facts if we are to make further progress in selecting the most satisfactory model from the menu now available. I have already referred to that particular offshoot of Keynesian economics in which money wage, and therefore price level behaviour is treated as a sociological cost-push phenomenon, and noted that such a model has no difficulty coping with the broad outlines of the stagflation of the 1970s. Though this branch of macroeconomics is not central to the topic of this paper, it is worth pointing out that my reasons for rejecting it are not – I hope – ideological, but empirical. Space will not permit me to do more than assert those reasons: namely the silence of this approach in the face of the clearly cyclical nature of the time path of both inflation and output, and its apparent contradiction by the outcome of policy experiments such as that embodied in Mr Anthony Barber's 1972 budget for the United Kingdom. Then an attempt to use fiscal and monetary stimuli to break through into sustained growth accompanied by lower inflation resulted instead in a short-lived real boom and a dramatic increase in the inflation rate. The Mitterrand government in France seems recently to have provided us with a little more evidence of a similar character, this time uncontaminated by an oil price shock.

Be that as it may, let me now turn to the empirical evidence with which it is sufficiently difficult to reconcile the macroeconomics associated with the 'rational expectations revolution' as to persuade me to reject that doctrine. As I have argued in considerable detail elsewhere (Laidler 1982, Chs 2–3) certain stylized facts generated by the voluminous literature on the demand for money function create difficulties for the rational expectations revolution, particularly those aspects of it whose crucial basis is the clearing competitive markets hypothesis. As we all know, the empirical work on the aggregate demand for money function which uses annual and quarterly data systematically demonstrates the need to postulate some kind of lag effect in the adjustment of actual cash balances to their long-run equilibrium level if conventionally acceptable criteria of goodness-of-fit and so forth are to be satisfied. It is also apparent that it is very difficult indeed to explain such lagged adjustment solely in terms of expectations formation, though this may well be part of the story.

The difficulty is that the kind of costs of portfolio adjustment which are usually used to justify such lagged adjustment effects would have no observable consequences in a model in which the supply and demand for money can be brought into equilibrium by the variation of a flexible price level. Price level changes cause real balances to vary for the individual agent without him encountering any adjustment costs. If the world really was made up of continuously clearing competitive markets, we would never observe anything but a long-run demand for money function (except for the consequences of expectation effects and distribution effects too). On the other hand, if the price level is slow to adjust, then it is easy to show that the long-run short-run distinction will be important as far as the observed behaviour of the demand for money function is concerned.[9] The facts I am citing are not quite fatal to the clearing markets' rational expectations model, because sufficient ingenuity in manipulating distribution effects and expectations effects could reconcile it with the evidence (see Laidler 1982, Ch. 3). It is in difficulty however, in the face of stylized facts which are very easy to explain once price stickiness is postulated.

The basic facts of money–output–price interaction over the course of the business cycle also present problems. Neo-Austrian economics predicts that 'anticipated' changes in the time path of the money supply, will affect only prices. 'Unanticipated' changes on the other hand, though they too will cause prices to vary, will have output and employment effects as well as a result of individual agents misreading the signals being conveyed to them by prices. Thus, over the course of the cycle we might expect the consequences of changes in the monetary growth rate to manifest themselves predominantly in price level behaviour and only to a lesser extent in the time paths of real variables. Moreover because all quantity changes in a neo-Austrian model are responses to signals given by prices, we should also expect quantity changes to be contemporaneous with or perhaps even to lag a little behind, price changes.

There is surely no better established stylized fact than that, over the course of the cycle, the first effects of changes in monetary growth rates are concentrated upon quantities with their effects on prices coming through only later. Despite this, attempts have been made to show that the neo-Austrian model is consistent with observed price–output behaviour. Thus the results generated by Barro (1978) are widely cited in this context. However, for him, 'anticipated' money is the forecast of a regression equation heavily weighted with lagged values of the money supply, and it therefore varies very little when the actual money supply changes. Current fluctuations in the money-growth rate are thus modelled as being mainly unanticipated. Boschen and Grossman (1980) have argued that, because agents can read newspapers, contemporaneously published data on the money supply ought to form the basis of the anticipated money concept used to test neo-Austrian predictions. Anyone who finds this argument persuasive must regard Barro's anticipated money series as inappropriately constructed, and hence his evidence as suspect. Moreover, he must also agree that Boschen and Grossman's results, which show that money supply fluctuations that are reflected in contemporaneously published data nevertheless seem to cause changes in output and employment, while those that are not do not do so, weigh heavily against the neo-Austrian view of things.

Now with sufficient ingenuity in distinguishing between money supply changes which are observed but expected to be temporary and those which are observed and expected to be permanent, and in distinguishing between prices which are posted and those which are 'really' charged, and so on, it would surely be possible to defend the neo-Austrian model against not only Boschen and Grossman's particular tests, but also against the general charge that it is incompatible with the stylized facts to which I have drawn attention. However, there is another problem arising from the nature of the demand for money function which ought to be raised at this point.[10] It is commonly accepted that the expected inflation rate is an important component of the opportunity cost of holding real balances, and it has been well known, at least since the seminal work of Cagan (1956) that, ignoring real growth, when, in an inflationary environment, the rate of growth of the nominal money supply is cut, two consequences must follow if equilibrium is to be restored in the long run. First, the rate of inflation must fall, and second, the quantity of real balances must rise, which is the same thing as saying that the ratio of the price level to the nominal money supply must fall. It follows that, on average, between the initial situation and the new long-run equilibrium, the inflation rate must be below the rate of monetary expansion. The question arises whether we can say anything more definite than this about the time path of prices, and the answer is that we can. However what we predict here is very different depending upon whether or not we postulate continuously clearing markets and rational expectations.

If agents' expectations are rational, in the sense that they understand the relationships between the money supply and the price level which I have just outlined; if they are aware of the change in the monetary expansion rate and expect it to persist; if all markets are to clear continuously; and if we insist on the economy ending up in equilibrium with a positive but finite stock of real balances; then the outcome of the experiment we are considering is well known. The price level will fall at once to a value compatible with the long-run equilibrium quantity of real balances determined by the new lower expected inflation rate and will thereafter rise at that rate, which is, of course, equal to the rate of monetary expansion.

Now I am not suggesting that anyone should take the above, very special, conceptual experiment literally, but it is nevertheless instructive. In particular, it reminds us that any anticipated change in the rate of monetary growth will have consequences not just for the ongoing inflation rate but also, if markets clear, it should cause a step change in the price level. For a number of reasons, this is awkward for the advocates of the rational expectations hypothesis. To begin with, if the step change in the price level was itself anticipated, that variable would be taken, by market forces, instantaneously to zero in the case of a cut in the monetary expansion rate or to infinity in the case of an increase. To insist, as they do, on confining the outcome of such experiments to situations in which a finite positive equilibrium demand for real balances exists, rules out the anticipation of step changes in the price level. However it does not also obviate the necessity for the step change in question to take place. If a new inflation rate is fully anticipated, the stock of real balances *must* change.[11] It goes almost without saying that, in the real world, we do not observe anything which remotely resembles such step changes in the price level, even in situations in which it can be asserted beyond any reasonable doubt that the rate of monetary expansion has been cut, is widely known to have been cut, and is widely expected to remain at its new lower level. The current situation in Canada is a clear case in point, as is that in both the United States and Britain. In this respect the outcome of the real-world experiments bears absolutely no resemblance to the predictions of the model advanced by advocates of the rational expectations revolution.

Sadly, the outcome of those experiments bears a great resemblance to the predictions of a model in which prices are sticky relative to expectations and expectations respond slowly to experience: in such a model the first consequence of tight money is lower output and the inflation rate falls only slowly. Once again, with sufficient ingenuity and sufficient hedging around of the basic model with special assumptions, one would probably be able to rescue the neo-Austrian approach. Indeed, the Liverpool econometric model of the United Kingdom in which monetary contraction leads to large increases in voluntary unemployment (see, e.g., Minford 1980) represents among other things, an attempt to mount just such a rescue. Nevertheless we find that once again it is exceedingly awkward to defend the desirability of the rational expectations revolution in the face of evidence which gives the alternative theoretical framework no trouble at all.

V

It would be a short step from the foregoing comments about the relevance of evidence generated by recent policy experiments in Canada and elsewhere for neo-Austrian economics to the conclusion that the 'rational expectations revolution' has made at best no contribution, and at worst a negative one, to our understanding of economic policy. However, it would be a great mistake to take such a step, because it is precisely in this area that the 'revolution' has something of lasting importance to offer macroeconomics. As I have already repeated several times, neo-Austrian economics rests on two hypotheses, not one, and the empirical difficulties I have been discussing above arise more from the postulate of continuously clearing markets and its interaction with the notion of rational expectations than from the latter idea *per se*. As I shall now argue, the rational expectations postulate makes a key contribution to our understanding of policy problems quite independently of its association with the idea of clearing markets.

No result in neo-Austrian economics has attracted more attention than the Sargent–Wallace (1976) conclusion that a fully anticipated change in the time path of the nominal money supply will have no effect on real income but only on prices. At the same time, there is no result whose true significance has been more widely misunderstood, A fully anticipated change in money supply behaviour is first of all one that is known to be taking place, and one whose long-run implications for the behaviour of equilibrium prices are fully understood by economic agents. However, there is more to it than that. If the change is to be anticipated, rather than just influence expectations, agents must be free to act instantaneously upon their newly acquired information, secure in the knowledge that their activities will be coordinated by markets in such a way that they will be able to fulfil their plans.

There is no reason to believe that a real-world experiment, in which politicians announce a policy change, and then follow through on their announcement, ought to bear any close relationship to the conceptual experiment of Sargent and Wallace. Why should agents believe politicians? Why should they expect the policy change to be sustained? What evidence is there to suggest that they understand the quantity theory of money? How many of them are free to act on new information even if they wish to do so? and so on? The policy ineffectiveness proposition does not have to be read as a proposition about the real world, however. Rather, it may be read as an eye-catching counterexample to a pervasive approach to the analysis of economic policy which has, often unwittingly, taken for granted certain things that had no business being taken for granted.[12]

The approach in question is, in essence, an application of the standard analysis of the individual maximizing agent, the agent under study being the policy maker who is endowed with, or entrusted with the care of, a social utility function whose arguments are various policy targets. He is pictured as having control of certain policy instruments which he manipulates in order to maximize the utility function in question, subject to a set of constraints given by the structure of the economy with which he is concerned. The matter of the design of economic policy then naturally breaks down into three steps. First, the social utility function must be discovered or devised; second, quantitative information about the structure of the economy must be sought; and third, a straightforward mechanical exercise in the application of the principles of constrained maximization yields the right settings for the policy instruments.

I shall touch briefly on the thorny questions surrounding the concept of a social utility function in a moment, but the neo-Austrian critique of this approach to policy analysis concentrates on the nature of the structure of the economy and the appropriateness of treating it as an unvarying constraint on the conduct of policy. Sargent and Wallace's analysis, and, of course that of Lucas (1976) remind us of the elementary fact that the 'structure' of the economy is nothing more than the outcome of the systematic behaviour of individual agents. Each one of them is engaged in exactly the same type of utility maximizing exercise as the policy maker, subject to a constraint, however, part of whose structure is the systematic behaviour of the policy maker himself, not to mention the reactions of other agents to the conduct of policy. Even if the typical agent bases his behaviour upon 'rules of thumb' he is likely to adapt those rules to perceived changes in this environment. Thus, as the conduct of policy varies, so in general will the 'structure' of the economy. An approach to the analysis of policy which ignores this proposition is, according to Lucas and his associates, hopelessly flawed. The Sargent and Wallace policy ineffectiveness theorem may be regarded as a vivid illustration of this flaw, even if it is not treated as a serious prediction about how the real world works.

The most important implication of the neo-Austrian insight into the nature of economic policy as far as macroeconomics is concerned is that it provides a much stronger and more general basis than previously existed for the case against discretionary policy. Thus Friedman (1960) rested his case for a monetary rule on the existence of long and variable time lags in the transmission mechanism of policy whose nature and structure were ill-understood. Implicit in his argument was the possibility that, with the passage of time and the growth of knowledge, discretionary policy might come to be more effective than a rule. The neo-Austrian insight considerably weakens this particular line of reasoning by warning us that knowledge of the economy's structure, generated under one policy regime, may not be relevant under a new one. Moreover it bases this warning not on a general worry that in human affairs, things might after all be different tomorrow from what they are today, but on a very precise reason for believing that this might be the case. The possibility of isolating those aspects of the economy's structure which do not depend upon expectations remains, so advances in knowledge may still enable policies to be improved. However the scope for such improvement now seems much smaller, and the difficulty of attaining it much greater, than they did two decades ago.

Of course the neo-Austrian insight leaves at least as many questions open as it answers. Changes in the policy regime are far from being the only source of disturbance to the structure of the economy. Thus the often heard admonition to adopt a policy rule, and a simple one at that, does not really solve many problems. For example, it may or may not be wise to stick to a *k%* money growth rule while the private sector is learning to adapt its behaviour to a change in the relative price of energy, but to settle this issue, one would have to know about how the economy's behaviour would change while it was absorbing information about a change in energy prices and in the conduct of policy. A modelling exercise which imposes the rational expectations hypothesis, and perhaps that of clearing markets too, is to some extent useful in coping with such questions, inasmuch as it tells us – if we take stability on faith – where the economy is likely to end up in the wake of such a disturbance. However, it tells us nothing at all about the time path towards this ultimate solution. If agents take time to learn, and markets take time to clear, this is an important omission. However, if the rational expectations revolution has not solved the questions of how agents learn about changes in their environment and about how the economy behaves while they are learning, it has nevertheless made a significant contribution simply by enabling us to formulate those questions.[13]

There is another area in the analysis of economic policy which has been as much overlooked by the neo-Austrians as by those whom they have criticized. It is an obvious fact that policy makers and the general public do not simply communicate with one another through behavioural signals given anonymously in the market-place. They are in constant touch with one another through the political process as well. Private sector agents do vote, and they do organize into lobbies which try to influence the conduct of policy in ways which will favour them. Politicians do seek votes, and do seek to influence public opinion. Public sector bureaucracies do have interests of their own to protect. Such matters have not been neglected by macroeconomists – see, for example, Johnson (1972) or Meltzer and Richard (1981) – but they have not yet been integrated into the neo-Austrian analysis, which is still concerned more with the technical question of how to maximize a social utility function than with understanding how the political process copes – the word is borrowed from Gordon (1980) – with the continuous and conflicting pressures out of which a consistent social utility function may or may not arise in the first place.

Nevertheless, it is unfair to criticize people who have been working hard at the analysis of one genuine and difficult problem for failing to get to grips at the same time with another. As I noted at the outset of this section, the contribution of the 'rational expectations revolution' to policy analysis has lain in deepening our understanding of the nature of the constraints that the structure of the economy places upon the conduct of policy and its contribution there has been a real one. Moreover, though proponents of the revolution have linked the notion of clearing markets to that of rational expectations in their writings on policy matters, if one treats what they have had to say as a series of counterexamples to a prevailing orthodoxy, rather than as a series of predictions about how policy will actually work out in practice, then their contribution in this area is one which should be taken notice of by anyone concerned with the analysis of policy, regardless of his views on the appropriateness of assuming clearing markets.

VI

The reader will by now realize that I do not think that there is any straightforward and unequivocal answer to the question 'Does macroeconomics need the rational expectations revolution?'. From the point of view of pure theory, there can be no doubt that this revolution embodies the most successful attempt that we have seen to link microeconomics to macroeconomics, though the novelty lies not in finding a basis in individual maximizing behaviour for the components of conventional macroeconomics, but in showing that a model made up of clearing competitive markets can reproduce at least some of the main characteristics of that complex of macroeconomic phenomena known as the business cycle. To the extent that any branch of any subject is healthier when it is forced to entertain more than one explanation of the behaviour with which it deals, macroeconomics certainly benefited from the 'rational expectations revolution'.

However, I would stress here that the revolution did indeed add one more alternative explanatory framework to the corpus of the discipline. Though its proponents have sometimes given the impression of believing that their approach alone could deal with the stylized facts of the 1970s, in rather the same way that Keynes produced a unique explanation of the 1920s and 1930s, this simply is not the case. The brand of economics which could not cope with the facts of stagflation, and it certainly existed, was, as I have argued, one which treated money illusion as a permanent phenomenon. There always were, and remain, a number of alternative approaches to macroeconomic analysis which do not suffer from this fault, and neo-Austrian economics is only one of them. I have also argued that when confronted with certain stylized facts – the presence of lag effects in empirical aggregate demand functions, the time path of prices and output in the wake of monetary changes, and so on – the neo-Austrian approach does not fare too well. I have no doubt that given sufficient ingenuity, its proponents can cope with these objections, just as those who insist that the earth is the centre of the universe can explain all observations in terms of epicycles, but I have also pointed to the relative ease with which models which incorporate an hypothesis of price stickiness can cope with the same facts.

From the empirical point of view, then, except in the not unimportant sense that it has generated good questions, I am inclined to argue that macroeconomics did not need the rational expectations revolution at least in its neo-Austrian form. However, as I pointed out at the very beginning of this paper, that form of the revolution rests on two hypotheses and not one: rational expectations and clearing markets. As I hope is clear from the arguments advanced in the course of this essay, the source of the empirical difficulties is overwhelmingly the second of these. That is why, despite my doubts about the empirical content of the 'revolution' I nevertheless judge it to have made an important contribution to policy analysis. In that context, the role of the clearing markets' postulate is to facilitate the construction of vivid and telling counterexamples to a prevailing orthodoxy. Their real force comes from the rational expectations notion itself, and hence they are important far beyond the boundaries of the particular conceptual experiments which generate them. In short, my conclusion is that macroeconomics did, and does, need the rational expectations hypothesis, but that it does not need the rational expectations revolution. We need to absorb the implications of that hypothesis into our already existing macroeconomic framework, rather than throw the latter overboard in favour of neo-Austrian theory.

Notes

1. I have explained this choice of label elsewhere – Laidler (1982) – in terms of the methodological individualism and reliance on the competitive general equilibrium model which characterizes this body of work. The opportunity cost doctrine, discussed by Rymes (1982) at this conference, is also a hallmark of Austrian Economics, and the reader will recognize that some of the specific policy issues discussed below are special cases of the more general analytic issues which Rymes discusses. The reader should note that there is now emerging a body of analysis which, in combining the notions of rational expectations with overlapping contracts, rather than clearing markets, promises to provide an alternative to the neo-Austrian approach. See, e.g., Fischer (1977), Taylor (1979). For a textbook treatment, see Parkin (1982) Ch. 25.
2. On this matter, see Barro and Grossman (1976), Ch. 3.
3. It is a frequent theme in the writings of Lucas (e.g. 1980) that Keynesians invalidly criticize his models because their predictions fail to conform, not to observed behaviour, but to the predictions of Keynesian models. In this complaint he is quite justified, but the tendency displayed by neo-Austrians to characterize any postulate about price behaviour that departs from the competitive norm as *ad hoc*, also sometimes comes perilously close to criticizing someone else's model for failure to conform to the conventions of one's own.
4. Anyone who believes that those who used the adaptive expectations hypothesis in their work nevertheless fully appreciated its limitations in this regard should consider the accelerationist hypothesis of Friedman and Phelps. This hypothesis has agents forming expectations about inflation in a manner which, in the long run, is appropriate only for a situation of constant inflation in an experiment whose outcome involves ever increasing inflation. I am grateful to Don Patinkin for this striking example of the slowness with which our profession grasps the full implications of new ideas.
5. This claim is stated with no equivocation by Lucas and Sargent (1981). However Lucas (1980) is much more tentative in advancing arguments along these lines.
6. Indeed, Clarence Barber and his associate John McCallum (1980) have advanced just such an interpretation of Canadian experience in the 1970s and have cited just such evidence as I here mention in support of their position.
7. See for example Robert Solow (1968).
8. My own work of the early 1970s comes to mind as an illustration of this. See Laidler (1975), Chs 3 and 10. Nevertheless, the ifs and buts that there permeate my verbal discussion find no counterpart in my formal modelling.
9. The alert reader will note that interest rate flexibility could do as well as price level flexibility in making adjustment costs irrelevant in the aggregate demand for money function. This point suggests that we understand a good deal less about the role of money in the aggregate economy than we thought we did, given the manifest importance of the long-run, short-run distinction in empirical work. On these issues see Laidler (1982) Ch. 2.
10. The following passage draws heavily on discussions with Michael Parkin, who is not, however, to be implicated in the conclusions which I draw.
11. The problem under discussion here was well known to those working in the area of money and economic growth in the 1960s and 1970s, not least to Sargent and Wallace (1973) who explicitly assumed that step changes in the price level are unanticipated. Robert Barro (1978) sidesteps the issues involved here in his empirical study of the roles of anticipated vs. unanticipated changes in the monetary growth rate in influencing prices and output by inappropriately treating the nominal interest rate as an exogenous variable.
12. Sargent and Wallace's own attitude to their analysis is ambivalent. The first part of their paper

presents their experiment as an example of the power of the rational expectations idea to generate novel predictions, but the closing pages of the same paper invite the reader to regard their analytic results as empirically relevant.

13. The reader should note that Lucas and Sargent's (1981) account of criticisms of the neo-Austrian approach shows that they are well aware of these issues.

References

Ando, A. and Modigliani, F. (1963), 'The "Life Cycle" Hypothesis of Saving: Aggregate Implications and Tests', *American Economic Review* (53), March, pp. 55–84.

Barber, C. and McCallum, J. (1980), *Unemployment and Inflation, The Canadian Experience*, Toronto: Canadian Institute for Public Policy.

Barro, R.J. (1978), 'Unanticipated Money, Output and the Price Level in the United States', *Journal of Political Economy* (86), August, pp. 549–81.

Barro, R.J. (1979), 'Second Thoughts on Keynesian Economics', *American Economic Review* (69), May, Papers and Proceedings, pp. 54–9.

Barro, R.J. and Grossman, H.I. (1976), *Money, Employment and Inflation*, Cambridge: Cambridge University Press.

Baumol, W.J. (1952), 'The Transactions Demand for Cash – An Inventory Theoretic Approach', *Quarterly Journal of Economics* (66), November, pp. 545–6.

Begg, D. (1982), *The Rational Expectations Revolution in Macroeconomics*, Deddington: Philip Allan Publishers; Baltimore, Maryland: Johns Hopkins University Press.

Boschen, J.F. and Grossman, H.I. (1980), 'Tests of Equilibrium Macroeconomics Using Contemporaneous Monetary Data', NBER Working Paper # 558.

Bryant, J. and Wallace, N. (1980), 'A Suggestion for Further Simplifying the Theory of Money', Staff Report No. 62, Federal Reserve Bank of Minneapolis.

Cagan, P. (1956), 'The Monetary Dynamics of Hyperinflation', in Milton Friedman (ed.), *Studies in the Quantity Theory of Money*, Chicago, Illinois: University of Chicago Press.

Clower, R.W. (1965), 'The Keynesian Counter-Revolution: A Theoretical Appraisal', in F.H. Hahn and F.P.R. Brechling (eds), *The Theory of Interest Rates*, London: Macmillan.

Eisner, R., and Strotz, R. (1963), 'Determinants of Business Investment', in Commission on Money and Credit, *Impacts of Monetary Policy*, Englewood Cliffs: Prentice Hall.

Fischer, S. (1977), 'Long Term Contracts, Rational Expectations and the Money Supply Rule', *Journal of Political Economy* (85), February, pp. 191–206.

Friedman, M. (1956), 'The Quantity Theory of Money, A Restatement', in Friedman (ed.), *Studies in the Quantity Theory of Money*, Chicago, Illinois: University of Chicago Press.

Friedman, M. (1957), *A Theory of the Consumption Function*, Princeton, New Jersey.

Friedman, M. (1960), *A Programme for Monetary Stability*, New York: Fordham University Press.

Friedman, M. (1968), 'The Role of Monetary Policy', *American Economic Review* (58), March, pp. 1–17.

Friedman, M. and Schwartz, A.J. (1982), *Monetary Trends in the United States and the United Kingdom*, Chicago: University of Chicago Press for the NBER.

Gordon, H.S. (1980), *Welfare Justice and Freedom*, New York: Columbia University Press.

Hahn, F. (1982), *Money and Inflation*, Oxford: Blackwell.

Hicks, J.R. (1974), *The Crisis in Keynesian Economics*, Oxford: Blackwell.

Johnson, H.G. (1972), *Inflation and the Monetarist Controversy* (De Vries Lectures 1971), Amsterdam: North-Holland.

Jorgenson, D.W. (1967), 'The Theory of Investment Behaviour', in Ferber (ed.), *The Determinants of Business Behaviour*, New York: NBER.

Karekan, J. and Wallace, N. (1981), 'On the Indeterminacy of Equilibrium Exchange Rates', *Quarterly Journal of Economics* (96), pp. 207–22.

Keynes, J.M. (1936), *The General Theory of Employment, Interest and Money*, London and New York: Macmillan.

Laidler, D. (1975), *Essays on Money and Inflation*, Manchester: University of Manchester Press; Chicago: University of Chicago Press.

Laidler, D. (1982), *Monetarist Perspectives*, Deddington: Philip Allan Publishers, Ltd.; Cambridge, Massachusetts: Harvard University Press.

Leijonhufvud, A. (1968), *On Keynesian Economics and the Economics of Keynes*, London: Oxford University Press.

Lipsey, R.G. (1960), 'The Relation Between Unemployment and the Rate of Change of Money Wage Rates in the United Kingdom, 1862–1957', *Economica* (27), pp. 1–31.

Lipsey, R.G. (1981), 'Presidential Address: The Understanding and Control of Inflation: Is There a Crisis in Macroeconomics?' *Canadian Journal of Economics* (14), November, pp. 545–76.

Lucas, R.E., Jr. (1976), 'Econometric Policy Evaluation', in K. Brunner and A. Meltzer (eds), *The Phillips Curve and the Labour Market*, Carnegie-Rochester Conference Series, Vol. I, Amsterdam: North-Holland.

Lucas, R.E., Jr. (1980), 'Methods and Problems in Business Cycle Theory', *Journal of Money, Credit and Banking* (12), November, Part 2, pp. 696–715.

Lucas, R.E., Jr. and Rapping, L.A. (1969), 'Price Expectations and the Phillips Curve', *American Economic Review* (3), Vol. 59, June, pp. 342–50.

Lucas, R.E., Jr. and Sargent, T.J. (1981), 'After Keynesian Economics', in *After the Phillips Curve, Persistence of High Inflation and High Unemployment*, Boston: Federal Reserve Bank of Boston.

McCallum, B.T. (1982), 'The Role of Overlapping Generation Models in Monetary Economics', Carnegie-Mellon University (mimeo).

Malinvaud, E. (1977), *The Theory of Unemployment Reconsidered*, Oxford: Basil Blackwell.

Meltzer, A.H. and Richard, S.F. (1981), 'A Rational Theory of the Size of Government', *Journal of Political Economy* (89), October, pp. 914–27.

Minford, P. (1980), 'A Rational Expectations Model of the UK Under Fixed and Floating Exchange Rates', in K. Brunner and A.H. Meltzer (eds), *The State of Macroeconomics*, Carnegie-Rochester Conference Series on Public Policy, Vol. 12, North-Holland.

Modigliani, F. and Brumberg, A. (1954), 'Utility Analysis and the Consumption Function: An Interpretation of the Cross Section Evidence', in K. Kurihara (ed.), *Post Keynesian Economics*, Rutgers University Press.

Parkin, J.M. (1982), *Modern Macroeconomics*, Scarborough, Ontario: Prentice Hall, Canada.

Patinkin, D. (1965), *Money Interest and Prices*, 2nd edition, New York: Harper & Row (first edition 1956).

Phelps, E.S. (1967), 'Phillips Curves, Expectations of Inflation and Optimal Unemployment Over Time', *Economica* (34), August, pp. 254–81.

Rymes, T.K. (1982), 'Keynesian and Neoclassical Value Theories: Some Implications for Policy', Carleton University, Ottawa (mimeo).

Samuelson, P.A. (1958), 'An Exact Consumption Loan Model of Interest with or without the Social Contrivance of Money', *Journal of Political Economy* (66), pp. 467–82.

Sargent, T.J. and Wallace, N. (1973), 'The Stability of Models of Money and Growth with Perfect Foresight', *Econometrica* (41), November, pp. 1043–8.

Sargent, T.J. and Wallace, N. (1976), 'Rational Expectations and the Theory of Economic Policy', *Journal of Monetary Economics* (2), May, pp. 169–83.

Solow, R.M. (1968), 'Recent Controversies on the Theory of Inflation: An Eclectic View', in S. Rousseas (ed.), *Symposium on Inflation: Its Causes, Consequences and Control*, New York, pp. 6–17.

Taylor, J.B. (1979), 'Staggered Wage Setting in a Macro Model', *American Economic Review* (69), May, Papers and Proceedings, pp. 108–13.

Tobin, J. (1958), 'Liquidity Preference as Behaviour Towards Risk', *Review of Economic Studies* (25), February, pp. 65–8.

13 The 'buffer stock' notion in monetary economics

Introduction

The early 1980s was not an easy period for me, as my memoir has explained, so the invitation from the by then combined Royal Economic Society and Association of University Teachers of Economics to deliver the annual lecture named in memory of so dear a friend as Harry Johnson meant a lot to me. I used the opportunity to provide a survey of the area of monetary economics to which I had been trying to contribute, and to relate my own work to that of others who had been pursuing similar lines of investigation.

One remaining problem, it seemed to me, was to show how an economy could stay 'off' its long-run demand for money function if the demand for money depended upon the rate of interest, for the latter was obviously very much a flexible price. How appropriate that I found an answer in Harry Johnson's own (1951–52) observation that liquidity preference and loanable funds were only equivalent theories of the interest rate in equilibrium.

Some of my colleagues at Western disliked this paper very much indeed, and one rumour that came back to me at the time was that they wanted me to be discouraged from presenting it outside of the department lest their reputations for New-classical orthodoxy were thereby damaged by association. Rumours being what they are, I cannot vouch for the truth of this tale, but on an 'as if' basis it had a certain plausibility. It might have been this rumour that caused me to recall, and put into departmental circulation, George Orwell's phrase, 'Thought Police'.

Reference

Johnson, H.G. (1951–52), 'Some Cambridge Controversies in Monetary Theory', *Review of Economic Studies*, **19** (2), 90–104.

THE 'BUFFER STOCK' NOTION IN MONETARY ECONOMICS*

by

David Laidler

Not the least of Harry Johnson's contributions to our discipline was the series of survey papers on aspects of monetary economics which he produced during the 1960s and 1970s. It is no exaggeration to say that the way in which the literature of monetary economics is organised even now follows the design which Johnson first set out in (1962) and built on in the subsequent decade. Nevertheless, the subject has not stood still, and one of the more interesting developments of the last few years has involved the introduction of what has been variously described as the 'disequilibrium money', 'shock absorber' or, as I prefer to call it, the 'buffer stock' notion into monetary economics.

The development of this line of thought was getting underway before Johnson's untimely death, much of it indeed under the auspices of his own research programme at the LSE. Even so this did not happen early enough for the relevant ideas to be put in their proper niche by Johnson himself, and the buffer stock approach is not yet fully integrated into the mainstream of monetary economics. Much of the relevant literature is empirical, concerned with modelling particular aspects of the monetary experience of specific countries: hence it is fragmented, and contains few papers which attempt a coherent account of just what this approach is and how it relates to other approaches to monetary analysis. Although essays by Goodhart (1982*a*, *b*), and Judd and Scadding (1982*a*) contain important discussions of these issues, to the best of my knowledge only Jonson (1976*a*) and Knoester (1979*a*) have devoted entire papers solely to this central issue, and these are relatively inaccessible and hence less widely known than they deserve to be.

In this lecture, I shall attempt to give a brief account of the essentials of this approach. First I shall sketch out its microeconomic background, and then I shall discuss those theoretical characteristics which differentiate it from the 'neo-Austrian' analysis of Robert E. Lucas Jr. and his associates, as well as from the conventional 'Keynesian' approach to monetary economics. Last, but by no means least, I shall argue that it yields simple theoretical insights into important empirical and policy-related issues which are troublesome for alternative approaches. In short, my tribute to Harry

* The 1983 Harry Johnson Lecture presented on April 12, 1983 at Oxford University to the Joint Annual Conference of the Royal Economics Society and the Association of University Teachers of Economics.

I am grateful to Bob Clower, Peter Howitt, Patrick Minford, Bob Nobay, David Peel, Baldev Raj and Franco Spinelli for comments which have helped me in revising this paper, but exonerate them of contributing to any of the errors it may still contain.

Johnson on this occasion involves me in the dangerous business of trying to emulate him, by offering a survey of a new and interesting body of analysis. I hope that my failure to match his standards of clarity and incisiveness in this lecture will not deter those who hear or read it from taking the subject matter seriously.

I. THE MICROECONOMIC BACKGROUND

Exponents of the notion of money as a 'buffer stock', and of the body of macroeconomic analysis associated with it, imagine the typical economic agent to operate in what is commonly called a 'market economy', but markets in the everyday sense of the word are conspicuous, if not by their absence, then at least by their rarity in such an economy. Trade does not take place at one time and place, and at prices known to all agents; nor does it consist of a series of bilateral exchanges of goods and services between agents, each of whom is intent on consuming what he receives in each transaction. Instead, trade is multilateral with one party to each bilateral exchange typically accepting some asset, not because he desires it for its own sake, but because he confidently expects someone else to accept it from him in due course in exchange for something else.

The buffer stock approach thus presupposes the existence of a system of monetary exchange. Such a system, considered as a social institution, is a substitute for the kind of Walrasian market which, more often implicitly than explicitly, provides the basis of so much macroeconomic theory.[1] Though barter transactions occasionally take place, and although trade credit arrangements also exist, the typical would-be buyer, whether a firm seeking labour, or a household seeking consumption goods, must as a matter of social convention offer in exchange money, or a credible promise to deliver money in the near future, in order to be able to transact. Moreover, given that there are costs to finding a buyer for assets when money is required, the individual agent might be expected to hold a fraction of his wealth in money as a 'temporary abode of purchasing power', to use Milton Friedman's phrase, even if it yields a lower explicit return to him than do other stores of value.

Theorising about the demand for money typically takes arguments such as these for granted, and answers questions about what determines how much money the individual agent will want to hold, and about how that quantity varies with its determinants. The relevant 'quantity of money demanded' here is not an entirely straightforward concept. The phrase does not refer to an amount of money which an agent will want to hold at each and every

[1] This does not mean that advocates of the buffer stock approach regard the explanation of the evolution of monetary exchange as either uninteresting or impossible, but they do not regard it as central to the issues which particularly concern them. The reader is referred to Jones (1976) and Niehans (1978) Chapter 6, for analyses of this matter. It might be noted that, in his (1971) textbook Chapter 2, Douglas Fisher made some play with the notion that a monetary system is a substitute for, rather than a complement to, the institution of a market. In stressing money's role as a means of exchange, the buffer stock approach has much in common with Hicks' (e.g., 1982) Chapter 19, analysis of money as a 'running asset'. This stands in contrast to Tobin's (e.g., 1969) stress on money as a store of value.

moment, but rather to an amount which he will want to hold on average over some time interval. The phrase 'quantity of money demanded' denotes, that is to say, the average or target value of an inventory, of a *buffer stock*, of cash balances.

The foregoing proposition is true even about the demand for money of an agent who is always able to fulfil his plans, and for whom trading activities bring no surprises; but it is also true about the demand of one whose income is subject to unforeseen variations, or whose expenditure is on goods the availability of which cannot be taken for granted, or the prices of which fluctuate unexpectedly.[1] To hold a buffer stock of generally acceptable purchasing power prevents, at least in part, surprises in markets where the agent is a seller from impinging upon his buying activities, and *vice versa*. Indeed the matter goes deeper: an agent's chances of being surprised in his market activity are not independent of the time and effort he puts into seeking and processing information relevant to those activities. If money holding enables him to endure the consequences of surprises at lower cost than would otherwise be the case, then money becomes a substitute for information. Thus the very existence of a monetary system which enables him so to protect himself will cause the agent to be more prone to surprises. Hence fluctuations in holdings of money about their target value are of the very essence of economic activity co-ordinated by monetary exchange.[2]

The individual agent's target demand for money might itself be expected to vary over time. The conceptual experiments which we perform at the level of the individual agent when teaching the theory of the demand for money usually involve the postulate that he is faced with some exogenous shift in one or more of the determinants of his demand for money – an interest rate, the price level, or his level of permanent income, say. We then trace out the consequences of that change for the agent's target holdings of nominal balances. Sometimes we complicate our experiment with an account of the effects of rising marginal adjustment costs on the path which money balances follow over time as they are brought towards that target level. When we do this, we refer to the target level as the 'long-run' demand for money, and to intermediate steps along the adjustment path as points on various, essentially Marshallian, short-run demand for money functions.

The experiments to which I have just referred are typical of the literature, but, in an economy characterised by monetary exchange, the windfall gains and losses which the agent experiences from time to time might well manifest themselves in unexpected variations in his cash holdings. A discrepancy between actual and long-run target money holdings can just as well arise from

[1] The inventory theoretic approach to the demand for money, as epitomised in the work of Baumol (1952) and Tobin (1956), has the individual's cash holdings fluctuating about an average value in a completely certain environment. Much of the basic analysis of the demand for money in a stochastic framework is surveyed by Orr (1970), where once again the concept of the 'demand for money' is explicitly an average over time or target quantity. The models to which I am referring here all deal with individual experiments, and their extension to the market experiment is far from a trivial business. Clower and Howitt (1978) deals with the market experiments which might arise from the Baumol–Tobin style of analysis and in this sense represents a pioneering contribution to the buffer-stock approach upon which others might build.

[2] The notion that money holding in a substitute for devoting resources to the generation of information is developed at some length in Laidler (1975) Chapter 1. It is also discussed by Brunner and Meltzer (1971).

this source as from changes in the arguments of the agent's long-run demand for money function, and there is no reason to believe that the way in which he responds to such a discrepancy depends in any way upon what generates it. Given that a discrepancy exists, the agent will attempt to move towards his long-run target demand for money by altering his current rate of flow of expenditures on goods, services, and asset accumulation. That is to say, for the individual agent, a discrepancy between actual and desired cash balances will set in motion a real balance effect.[1]

I make no claim for any novelty in the microeconomic aspects of the buffer stock approach to monetary analysis which I have just described. Apart from a few nuances of emphasis, mainly having to do with trade being a matter of monetary exchange rather than simultaneous barter, and with the characterisation of the agent's long-run quantity of money demanded as being a target or average-over-time value of an inventory, rather than a fixed amount observable at any moment, there is nothing in the last few paragraphs which is not a commonplace. Nevertheless, these apparently unimportant nuances, which so much of the literature of monetary economics ignores, form the basis of the buffer stock approach.

II. THE MARKET EXPERIMENT, EQUILIBRIUM, AND DISEQUILIBRIUM

We are not concerned with the individual agent for his own sake in monetary economics. We are interested in macroeconomic phenomena, with the way in which changes in the money stock interact with the real side of the economy to influence income, employment and the price level, not to mention the balance of payments and the exchange rate in open economies.[2] The notion of an aggregate demand for money function is central to the analysis of these issues, and we study the individual agent mainly to get some insight into the nature of this aggregate relationship. Typically, indeed, that is all we do; and the aggregate function is often treated as being simply a scaled-up version of the demand function of some representative agent.

It is hard to deny that such a simple approach to studying money in the aggregate economy has been fruitful, but nevertheless, when we follow it, we downplay the very properties of money stressed in the foregoing discussion of the individual agent. In particular we treat the aggregate demand for money as

[1] This line of reasoning of course goes back to Patinkin (1965) and Archibald and Lipsey (1958). Its relationship to the buffer stock approach is developed by Jonson (1976*a*) and Laidler (1982) Chapter 2. Note that Carr and Darby (1981) represents a recent attempt to incorporate ideas such as this into an empirical study of the aggregate demand for money function.

[2] In the context of the macroeconomics of the open economy, the buffer stock approach is a natural complement to the monetary approach to balance of payments and exchange rate analysis. There is not space to take up these issues in this lecture. See however Jonson and Kierzkowski (1975) and note that this and several other important papers dealing with the buffer stock approach, for example Jonson (1976*b*), Knight and Wymer (1975), were written as contributions to the SSRC-Ford Foundation London-Geneva Research Programme on International Monetary Economics supervised by Harry Johnson and Alexander Swoboda.

determining a quantity of cash balances which the economy as a whole will wish to hold, not just on average over time, but at any moment; and we also assume that market mechanisms somehow operate to ensure that the demand for money thus determined is kept equal to the quantity of money in circulation. There is no other way to justify the almost universal use of the quantity of money in circulation as the dependent variable in empirical studies of the demand for money function, regardless of the period of observation to which the data appertain.

The procedures to which I have just referred may or may not be safe, but to criticise them effectively we must show that the factors which they ignore are important for the real world phenomena about which monetary economics makes predictions. The buffer stock approach claims that, in treating money 'as if' the economy had a well determined stock demand for it which is realised at each and every moment, conventional treatments of monetary analysis do indeed leave out of account factors whose absence detracts from their empirical content.

The above criticism is levelled at both conventional 'Keynesian' macroeconomics and at the 'neo-Austrian' analysis of Robert E. Lucas Jr. and his associates. These two bodies of macroeconomics are very different from one another, and the latter has much less in common with the buffer stock approach than does the former, as we shall see in due course. Nevertheless, both proceed 'as if' the observed demand and supply for money were always equal to one another. In the Keynesian approach it is interest rate flexibility which guarantees this, and in the neo-Austrian framework, general wage and price flexibility. In each case, however, the economy is treated as being always 'on' its aggregate demand for money function. It is this property of both types of model which the buffer stock approach challenges; that is why it is sometimes referred to, somewhat misleadingly, as the 'disequilibrium money' approach.

The notions of 'equilibrium' and 'disequilibrium' which are creeping into the discussion, had better be clarified. By 'full equilibrium' I mean a situation in which each agent is able to carry out all his plans vis-à-vis buying and selling goods, services, and assets, and in which the *ex ante* expectations upon which those plans are based are fulfilled *ex post*. The buffer stock approach is not differentiated from others merely by the suggestion that the world we live in occasionally might depart from such a full equilibrium state. Indeed that branch of neo-Austrian analysis called 'equilibrium business cycle theory' relies for most of its content on a careful analysis of the consequences of the last mentioned condition being systematically violated across agents. The models which that theory generates are nevertheless 'equilibrium' models, in the more limited sense that all agents' *ex ante* plans are executed in markets where prices are free to vary in order to reconcile any initial inconsistencies among those plans before trading takes place.

Such equilibrium models are constructed so that all agents in them can and do at each and every moment achieve, among other goals, their target levels of money holdings. Once one begins to think of money explicitly as a buffer stock, it becomes a distinct possibility that such a notion of equilibrium might be too restrictive. It is of the very essence of such a stock that the agent should expect, and even perhaps plan, to be away from his desired average holdings of it from time to time; but when he is, it might reasonably be argued that he is hardly 'out of equilibrium' in the sense of being unable to carry out his plans. Furthermore, an equilibrium business cycle theorist would be unlikely to attach much significance to this point. An economy in which the supply and demand for money were equal to one another in the aggregate would behave in the same way, regardless of the state of individual money holdings, unless there were systematic distributional effects at work, and it is customary not to rely on such effects in macroeconomics.[1] Thus the equilibrium business cycle theorist could argue that the buffer stock idea was only significant for individual behaviour at best, and irrelevant for understanding events at the level of the economy as a whole.

The buffer stock approach does not in any *a priori* way imply either the theoretical or empirical irrelevance of the idea of an equilibrium between the aggregate demand and supply of money. However it does stress the possibility that, at certain times and places, and over certain time intervals, because time aggregation too could eliminate them, discrepancies between the actual and desired money holdings of individuals might not cancel out upon aggregation over agents.[2] More specifically, it asserts that the kind of quarterly and even annual macroeconomic data which we use in our empirical work are sometimes usefully analysed in such 'disequilibrium' terms and that therefore, the above-mentioned defence of equilibrium methods of analysing such data is suspect. For this to be the case it is necessary that wages and prices be less than perfectly flexible, but this postulate is not sufficient to guarantee the relevance of the buffer stock approach. I shall now take up these points in more detail.

III. PRICE STICKINESS AND THE ROLE OF THE RATE OF INTEREST

The difference between the buffer stock approach and neo-Austrian equilibrium economics concerns the interpretation of a simple stability experiment of the following kind.[3] Suppose a closed economy is initially in full equilibrium, in the sense defined above, and suppose, for the sake of simplicity, that money in this economy is non-interest bearing fiat currency. Then let its

[1] To put matters in terms of the well-known analysis of Archibald and Lipsey (1958) to which Jonson (1976*a*) and Jonson and Kierzkowski (1975) pay particular attention, so long as the tastes of all agents vis-à-vis goods and money are identical, the aggregate demand for goods and money at any moment will be independent of the distribution of the money stock. Thus every agent can be 'off' his long-run demand for money function without there being any macroeconomic consequences, provided that the price level is such as to generate the appropriate aggregate quantity of real balances.

[2] The papers of Akerlof (1973) and Tucker (1971) represent early attempts to come to grips with the analytic implications of this possibility in the context of macro general equilibrium models. I discussed related issues in Laidler (1982) Chapters 2 and 3, but when writing those chapters, I was unaware of the relevance of these earlier papers to my own work. Since I had read both papers at their time of publication, I owe their authors an apology for failing consciously to recall and acknowledge them before now.

[3] The differences which I here analyse are between currently available versions of these two approaches. Peter Howitt (1979) has suggested that these distinctions became blurred once inventories of goods are introduced as objects of choice into a neo-Austrian framework. (Also see Kawasaki *et al* (1983).)

nominal quantity be unexpectedly increased by a certain amount. At the instant immediately after this increase, but before any response to it, a state of disequilibrium characterised by an excess supply of money and an (on average) excess demand for everything else would obtain.

The equilibrium theorist and the buffer stock exponent would agree upon what must happen to remove this disequilibrium: prices must rise as must output, and interest rates must fall, in some combination.[1] For the equilibrium theorist, however, the requisite changes would take place in *meta* time; for him the very fact that it can be shown that the new quantity of money is incompatible with existing prices and quantities is sufficient reason to conclude that they cannot co-exist. For the buffer stock advocate, the incompatibility in question is removed over actual time as the streams of expenditure which it sets in motion influence first interest rates and output, and then prices. For the neo-Austrian, the real balance effect which lies at the heart of our stability experiment guarantees that a discrepancy between the supply and demand for money will not persist for any interesting time interval: for the buffer stock advocate, the same effect is made manifest in the movement over time of the macro variables in which he and every other macroeconomist is interested.

Though the buffer stock approach is vulnerable to the usual charges of ad hocness in its reliance on unexplained wage-price stickiness, it does suggest a possible line of defence against this charge. If individual agents find it costly to vary money wages and prices, and to gather the information upon which to base such changes, then the availability of a buffer stock of money which softens for them the consequences of making errors about these matters will itself be a source of wage and price stickiness. The agent will trade off the cost of holding money against the costs of obtaining information and of changing prices. This argument would surely repay more careful attention than I have space to give it here.[2]

Be that as it may, the buffer stock approach differs from orthodox 'Keynesian' theory too, even though the latter also relies upon price stickness. For the Keynesian, interest rate flexibility suffices to keep the supply and demand for money in equilibrium.[3] In his view, an increase in the supply of

[1] We are here dealing with the first round impact of a change in the money supply. The particular combination in which the foregoing variables will change in a neo-Austrian model will depend upon the extent to which the effects on the price level of the initially unexpected change in the money supply are misread by individual agents as reflecting changes in the relative prices of the particular goods and services which they sell. On this see Lucas (1972). I have dealt at length with the role of expectations in the transmission mechanism in Laidler (1982) Chapters 3 and 4. I neglect this issue here, not because it is unimportant, but because it is not central to the matters I am dealing with and because space does not permit me to discuss it to any useful extent.

[2] Note that Kawasaki *et al* (1983) have shown, in the context of the behaviour of the individual firm, how the possibility of holding inventories of goods may lead to price stickiness in the face of what the firm perceives as transitory demand shifts.

[3] In particular this is a characteristic of the approach of Tobin and his many associates and followers. See, e.g., Tobin (1969). Note that Tsiang (1982), whose work is highly relevant to the buffer stock approach, has criticised Tobin in particular for insisting on maintaining asset market equilibrium at all points in his analysis of the transmission mechanism.

money such as we have just postulated will immediately drive down the rate of interest until the supply and demand for money are equal. As a consequence, the present value of the streams of returns expected to be produced by existing capital goods rises above the current supply price of newly produced capital goods. The flow demand for capital goods therefore increases, as does their output. Increased demand spreads throughout goods markets as a result of incipient multiplier effects, and prices begin to rise. In turn, interest rates begin to increase too, and ultimately, if there are no more disturbances, the economy moves to a full equilibrium not too different from the eventual outcome of the neo-Austrian version of this experiment. It does so, however, by way of a process during which the supply and demand for many items, but not for money, are either unequal or are kept in equality by quantity rather than price fluctuations.[1]

Because the buffer stock approach relies on price stickiness as much as does orthodox Keynesian analysis, its account of the later stages of the transmission mechanism is essentially the same as the one just sketched not. Indeed the only, but far from trivial, difference between the two approaches concerns whether the initial impact on the rate of interest of an increase in the money supply is sufficient to bring the supply and demand for money into equilibrium immediately. In the Keynesian model it is, and in the buffer stock approach it is not. This is a small enough difference, but it is an important difference for explaining empirical evidence. It is also a difference of some theoretical interest for it turns out to be a manifestation of the distinction between 'liquidity preference' and 'loanable funds' approaches to the analysis of the rate of interest, as I shall now argue.

It is usual to defend the postulate of price stickiness by noting that Walrasian markets do not in fact exist in the real world, so that it takes time for new information to be digested and acted upon by the endogenous agents who in fact set the prices at which trade takes place. Nevertheless it is also usual to argue that, in markets dominated by specialist traders whose major role is to gather information and translate it into price changes, prices do in fact behave very much as they would if they were determined by a continuous auction, in which supply and demand were always held equal. Prominent among these Hicksian 'flex price' markets are those for financial assets such as bonds. However, even granted that the rate of interest is a 'flex price', and granted that a sufficiently large change in it could keep the supply and demand for money in equilibrium, it does not follow that those who set the rate of interest will in fact cause it to change by a sufficient amount to accomplish this in the face of a change in the supply of money: those who set the rate of interest are proximately concerned with the supply and demand for bonds, and not money.

To put it in the traditional language which I have already used, the theory of the interest rate which underlies the buffer stock approach is a loanable

[1] The sequence of events which I have just described is in effect what Chick (1973) aptly termed the 'pseudo dynamics of IS-LM'.

funds theory and not a liquidity preference theory. Now of course, in an economy in full equilibrium, the interest rate, not to mention all other prices, takes a value at which savings and investment and the supply and demand for money are simultaneously equal. However, the notion of money as a buffer stock is at its most relevant when the economy is not in equilibrium, and there is no reason to suppose, as Harry Johnson (1951–2) long ago pointed out, that liquidity preference and lonable fund theories of interest are equivalent in such circumstances.[1] It is only in equilibrium models that questions about which prices convey what information and incentives to whom are irrelevant. Leijonhufvud (e.g. 1981) in particular has continually reminded us that they are of the very essence when dealing with the social process whereby information is transmitted and individual activities co-ordinated in the presence of frictions which prevent a state of general equilibrium continuously obtaining.

Consider, in the light of these factors, the effects on the interest rate of an increase in the quantity of money. The buffer stock approach has it that the efforts of agents to rid themselves of excess money holdings lead, among other effects, to a stepped-up flow demand for bonds in the economy. This in turn puts downward pressure on the rate of interest as bond dealers attempt to prevent their inventories of bonds being exhausted. Such a lower interest rate might make agents in general more willing to hold money, and might even induce bond dealers to increase their own inventories of money at the expense of bonds as a speculative measure. However, the proximate cause of this lower interest rate is an increase in the flow demand for bonds induced by an excess stock supply of money. It is hard to see how it could be sustained if it were large enough immediately to eliminate the very excess stock supply of money which had induced it in the first place.[2]

The matter at issue here is even more clearcut in the limiting theoretical case in which the demand for money is independent of the rate of interest. Here the supply and demand for money can only be equilibrated by an increase in real income or prices. If it is granted that these variables change sluggishly, then after a change in the money supply there must persist a discrepancy between the supply and demand for money while the economy moves to a new full equilibrium; by assumption, no fall in the rate of interest can eliminate that discrepancy. In the 'vertical LM curve' case, then, the buffer stock approach has much *a priori* appeal.

[1] This line of reasoning has been a continuous and important theme in the work of Tsiang. See, for example, (1956 and 1982).

[2] The argument here is at first sight similar to that of Artis and Lewis (1976) but it is, in fact, crucially different from theirs. They made the *rate of change* of the rate of interest vary with the excess supply of money, while here I am arguing that it is the *level* of the interest rate relative to some underlying long-run equilibrium value which depends on the excess supply of money. Artis and Lewis achieved promising empirical results with U.K. data, but subsequent work by Laidler (1980) suggests that their formulation does not fit United States data. I am inclined to think that this lack of robustness on the part of the Artis and Lewis formulation reflects the fact that it misspecifies the relationship between excess money holdings and the interest rate.

So long as money constitutes, on the margin, net wealth to the economy, many would agree that, in the presence of price stickiness, real balance effects will have a direct and observable influence on expenditure on goods and services. In such circumstances it is not hard to argue that the case for the buffer stock approach has a certain plausibility. However, where money is an 'inside' asset and is not net wealth, the real balance effect is reduced to a matter of asset substitution working solely through the rate of interest. If we set aside the possibility of agents substituting directly from money into such real assets as consumer durables, the case in which monetary policy works solely through interest rates is one in which the capacity, or lack thereof, of the rate of interest to equilibrate the supply and demand for money becomes crucial to judging the relevance of the buffer-stock approach. If the interest rate can instantaneously equilibrate the supply and demand for money in such a case, then at the very least, the approach in question loses generality.

When Gurley and Shaw (1960) coined the term 'inside money', they applied it to the monetary liabilities of a privately owned banking system; they also argued that experiments of the kind I have been discussing, having to do with variations in the quantity of 'outside' fiat money, were virtually irrelevant for understanding the workings of any modern economy in which money is overwhelmingly bank money. Anyone who accepts this view, and who also regards the limiting 'vertical LM curve' case as more of an analytic curiosity than a serious empirical possibility, will regard the arguments which I have so far developed for the buffer stock approach as being rather tenuous. He would be wrong to do so. The extended and tortuous debate which followed the publication of Pesek and Savings' (1967) *Money Wealth and Economic Theory* established that Gurley and Shaw's version of the inside-outside distinction was quite misleading.

The debate in question established instead that the appropriate distinction is between interest bearing and non-interest bearing money: specifically, regardless of whose liability it is, any money which bears interest at a market rate is not net wealth on the margin, and any money which does not bear such interest is net wealth.[1] This it is changes in the quantity of competitive interest bearing money whose influence is transmitted purely by interest rate changes; but obviously an economy which uses such money is characterised by something approximating a vertical LM curve. The very economy in which the real balance effect is reduced to a matter of asset substitution is therefore one in which changes in the rate of interest alone are unlikely to be able to eliminate a discrepancy between the supply and demand for money. On the other hand, the economy in which the demand for money is responsive to market interest rates, so that interest rate changes might conceivably eliminate such a discrepancy, is an economy in which money is net wealth on the margin and in which real balance effects fall directly on goods markets. In such an economy the role of the interest rate in the monetary transmission mechanism

[1] Among the articles which helped establish this conclusion are Johnson (1969). Marty (1969) and Patinkin (1969).

is less crucial to establishing the *a priori* plausibility of the case for the buffer stock approach.[1]

The reader may or may not find the above arguments convincing, but even if he is willing to entertain the idea that the interest rate changes which come in the wake of a change in the money supply are not sufficient to equilibrate the supply and demand for money, he might still be inclined to downplay the significance of the point. Certainly, it differentiates the buffer stock approach from conventional Keynesian ideas in a somewhat less fundamental way than the notion of price stickiness distinguishes these two bodies of theory from neo-Austrian analysis. Nevertheless, this theoretical difference is of considerable practical importance, because it leads to very different empirical predictions and to very different perceptions about what monetary policy can and cannot accomplish. That is to say, the case for the buffer stock approach ultimately rests as much upon its empirical content as upon *a priori* reasoning.

IV. EMPIRICAL QUESTIONS

The key empirical difference between the conventional Keynesian and the buffer stock approaches has to do with the existence, or otherwise, of a 'short-run' aggregate demand for money function. At the level of the individual agent, there is no problem. If some argument or other in the function determining the agent's long-run 'target' level of money holding changes, one needs only to suggest that he encounters increasing marginal costs in adjusting his cash balances in order to derive for him a Marshallian 'short-run' demand function, or rather an array of such functions, each one defined with respect to a different period of time elapsing after the initial disturbance. However one cannot treat the economy as a whole 'as if' it were just like one representative agent with regard to such an experiment: the individual agent can always change his nominal money holdings by making market transactions, but the economy as a whole cannot usually do so.[2]

Suppose once more that the nominal stock of fiat money in an economy was exogenously increased. In that case, there would emerge initially excess money holdings for the typical agent and for the economy as a whole. The buffer stock approach tells us that such an excess of money leads to positive real balance effects in all markets. The typical agent undertakes expenditure flows designed to take him along a path towards a new long-run target level of real balances. Interest rates are pushed down, and output increases, but though the gap between them is narrowed, there still persists at this first stage in the transmission mechanism a discrepancy between the amount of money

[1] It might be noted that in this lecture I am using the phrase 'real balance effect' in the rather broader sense adopted by Patinkin in (1967). In *Money Interest and Prices* (1956) he used the term only to refer to the wealth effects of increases in the supply of flat money. The question of whether the authorities can in fact vary the quantity of money in a 'vertical LM curve' economy is addressed below.

[2] A fixed exchange rate open economy can of course do just that. Even here though the relevant costs have to do with balance of payments functions, and not those associated with individual portfolio adjustments.

which agents in the economy wish to hold in the long run and the amount in circulation.

Suppose, however, that markets work in a Keynesian fashion, so that the rate of interest continues to fall so long as agents try to reduce their money holdings at any positive rate.[1] In this case, as White (1981) has argued, the rate of interest must move instantaneously to a value at which the *long-run and not the short-run* quantity of money demanded absorbs existing cash. This must happen because the costs which agents face in adjusting their cash holdings, and which underpin the short-run/long-run distinction at the level of the individual experiment, are never in fact encountered. When any incipient flow of cash into the bond market causes the rate of interest to move downwards, this latter movement is exogenous to the individual agent. Hence it does nothing to eliminate his incipient flow of expenditure on bonds. The latter continues until its source has been eliminated, and the source in question is the difference between his actual and long run desired money holdings.

With interest rate flexibility, then, the long-run/short-run distinction is empirically irrelevant, and a lagged dependent variable in the aggregate demand for money function is hard to justify; but as everyone knows, this variable is, as a matter of fact, much utilised and apparently badly needed.[2] Cycle phase average data, such as used by Friedman and Schwartz (1982), and data drawn from time periods long enough to be dominated by secular variations, have been used to estimate demand for money functions without resort to lagged dependent variables. However, with quarterly data, and even annual data drawn from rather short time periods – fifteen to twenty years say – it is usual to invoke adjustment costs and the Marshallian long-run/short-run distinction so as to achieve satisfactory econometric results. In recent years, though, such satisfactory results have proved harder and harder to obtain even with the use of such an expedient: hence the growing concern among economists and policy makers alike about instability in the demand for money function.

The buffer stock approach claims to be able to account for the presence of a lagged dependent variable in empirical demand for money functions, and also yields suggestions about the causes of recently observed instability in the relationship. As I have shown elsewhere (Laidler 1982, Ch. 2) a demand for money function with a lagged dependent variable may be interpreted

[1] The argument here is exactly parallel to that set out in Laidler (1982) Chapter 2 which shows that in the presence of price level flexibility, a short-run demand for money function would not be observed. Lane (1983) pp. 112 *et seq* develops a more general version of this argument. Note that White (1981) argues that in the case of an economy with a well developed financial system, the rate of interest will in fact always move quickly to eliminate a discrepancy between the supply and demand for money, and that therefore, there can be no "disequilibrium" money holdings. White does not, however, go on to show how lagged dependent variables in empirical demand for money functions can be reconciled with this conclusion.

[2] Note that I here say 'hard' and not 'impossible' to justify. If one tries hard enough one can probably reconcile any observation with the postulate that the demand and supply of money are maintained in constant equilibrium. Cf. Laidler (1982) pp. 51–2 and 96–101 for a more detailed discussion of this and related issues.

as a particular way of writing down the relationship between changes in the money supply and subsequent changes in prices, in which the entire transmission mechanism is approximated by a single 'black box' parameter which is equal to unity minus the coefficient of the lagged dependent variable. The fact that such an expression can be derived from the buffer stock notion shows that this approach can, in principle at least, account for the empirical success of so-called short-run demand for money functions.

At the same time we have here an obvious starting point for an explanation of why such short-run demand functions have been less successful in recent years. It is well known that the transmission mechanism of monetary policy is complex and subject to long and variable time lags, and yet in the case of single equation 'demand for money' studies, the buffer stock approach implies that the mechanism is embedded in one constant parameter. Would it be surprising if such a procedure proved satisfactory enough when dealing with periods of monetary tranquillity, but turned out to be inadequate when faced with the unstable money supply behaviour of periods like the 1970s? If this conjecture is true, it might imply that the apparent fragility of the demand for money function in recent years stems not from problems with that relationship, but is rather a statistical artifact generated by inadequate modelling of the transmission mechanism.[1]

Providing a possible solution to the puzzle of instability of the demand for money function is not the only way in which the buffer stock approach tends to re-instate the importance of money for the behaviour of contemporary economies. It is often suggested that developments in financial markets have lately rendered money less interest elastic in demand than it once was, and hence less controllable by the authorities. In the limiting, zero elasticity, case, so it is argued, the authorities cannot change the quantity of money at all by way of open market operations: if changes in the price of bonds have no effect upon the public's demand for money, how can such changes cause the quantity of money in circulation to vary? If one takes the view that the economy is 'on' its demand for money function at each and every moment, it is hard to resist this argument.[2] However, the buffer stock approach enables one to counter it in terms of what amounts to a dynamisation of Brunner and Meltzer's (e.g., 1976) analysis of the money supply process.

Brunner and Meltzer have long, and correctly, argued that, when the authorities raise the price which they offer for bonds, the public does not

[1] Of course this is not to deny a role to institutional change in shifting the long-run demand for money function in the 1970s. The question is not whether some of our problems arise from this source, but whether all of them do. For a thorough discussion of these issues particularly as they arise in the context of recent United States experience, see Judd and Scadding (1982*a*).

[2] This argument appears to have its roots in a certain passage of the *General Theory*. See Keynes (1936) p. 197. It was advanced as long ago as (1965) by Gramley and Chase, but has not been too popular, at least in an explicit form, in the North American literature since then. However, it frequently turns up in British Keynesian writings: see for example Hahn (1971), Kaldor (1980) and Hicks (1982) pp. 262–4. The counter-argument which I sketch out here has been developed at greater length by Howitt and Laidler (1979), Judd and Scadding (1982*a*) and Artis and Lewis (1981) among others.

sell bonds to them because it wishes to hold more money. Rather the public sells bonds because it wishes to substitute higher yielding assets, such as physical capital, for them in its portfolio. The quantity of money in circulation is thereby increased, not because anyone wishes to hold extra cash, but because he must obtain it as an intermediate step to purchasing capital equipment, and because, if all agents in the economy are simultaneously trying to do this, the cash in question can only be obtained by selling bonds to the authorities. Thus money, which no one wishes to hold, is nevertheless created by open market operations. So long as the public's demand for bonds responds to interest rate changes, in Brunner and Meltzer's terms so long as there is a non-zero interest elasticity of demand for credit, open market operations can lead to the quantity of money in circulation changing, even though the demand for money is totally interest inelastic. This can only happen because the public's desire to substitute physical capital for bonds in its portfolio makes it willing, as an intermediate step, to accept money from the authorities over and above its long-run demand for that asset. It can only happen, that is to say, because money is a buffer stock.

V. CONCLUDING COMMENTS

The conclusions to be drawn from this lecture are easy enough to summarise. It is natural to think of the money holdings of the individual agent fluctuating over time around their long-run desired level, but if prices in general are flexible then such fluctuations will not have any observable consequences at the level of the economy as a whole. Nor will they have such consequences if the interest rate always moves to keep the aggregate supply and demand for money in equilibrium.

In either case, if not impossible, it is at least difficult: to understand why lagged dependent variables are required in empirical work on the aggregate demand for money function; to explain why such functions began to display instability in the 1970s; and to see how open market operations can be used to control the quantity of money in a world where so many assets which play the role of money bear interest at competitive rates. To these puzzles the buffer stock approach offers a simple solution based on the straightforward suggestion that fluctuations in money of holdings around their desired level characterise market experiments as well as individual experiments.

Quite apart from the qualitative aspects of the case for taking the buffer stock approach seriously, upon which I have concentrated in this lecture, there exists, as I noted at the very outset, a large and growing body of successful quantitative work based upon it. There is space here only to mention some representative studies. As far as the demand for money function *per se* is concerned, the issues which I have raised in this paper have been investigated for the United States by, among others, Lewis (1978), Laidler (1980), Coats (1982) and Judd and Scadding (1982*b*), for the United Kingdom by Artis and Lewis (1976) and for Finland by Kanniainen and Tarkka (1983). The buffer stock approach gets support from this work, particularly the more recent studies.

Single equation experiments such as I have just cited are not altogether adequate for investigating the buffer stock approach. It is, after all, a postulate about the transmission mechanism of monetary policy and this mechanism involves the whole economy, not just the demand for money function. In this context too, the approach has already generated a substantial body of literature. For the United Kingdom, one may point to the models of Jonson (1976*b*), Knight and Wymer (1975) and Coghlan (1981) not to mention the less formal analysis of Goodhart (1982*b*); for the Netherlands we have the work of Knoester (1979*b*), and for Australia the RBA 76/78 models of Jonson and his associates (e.g. 1976, 1980). To cite the above work does not imply that all of it is in every respect unquestionably satisfactory. No doubt careful scrutiny of any of the above-mentioned studies would lead to important questions requiring further work to resolve them. Such a comment is always true, however, when new ideas are being developed and tested, and in any event, one can already see where further questions might in particular arise.

To begin with there is nothing unique in principle about discrepancies between the supply and demand for money when it comes to setting in motion streams of expenditure. Excess supplies of other financial assets too might be important because, as for example the analysis of Gray and Parkin (1973) shows, in a multi-asset world, money is simply the most liquid of assets held as a buffer stock and is not otherwise unique in this respect. Moreover, Purvis (1978) has explicitly analysed an economy with multiple financial assets, showing how the real balance effect associated with discrepancies between the supply and demand for money is in fact a special case of a more general asset disequilibrium (if I may be permitted the phrase) effect. This work is of particular interest in as much as it uses a model in the Tobin (1969) tradition but argues that Tobin's practice of linking financial markets and goods markets solely through interest rates is misconceived. In addition to holding financial buffer stocks, economic agents also hold inventories of raw materials and finished goods. The interaction of the demand for inventories with the behaviour of stocks of financial assets is well worth investigating, both theoretically and empirically. The importance of inventory fluctuations over the course of the business cycle suggests that such interaction would have to play a central role in any 'buffer stock' model of the cycle which was to prove a satisfactory alternative to the currently available neo-Austrian explanations of Lucas (1975), Sargent (1976), and Barro (1978).[1] Indeed, Howitt (1979) has argued that, in the presence of inventories, the distinction between models in

[1] Indeed it is hard to see how one can avoid according inventory fluctuations a central role in further analyses of the buffer stock approach. If, when there is an excess supply of money, expenditure in the economy exceeds the level it would otherwise attain by an additional flow driven by a real balance effect, elementary national income accounting tells us that this expenditure will either not be satisfied at all or must be satisfied by running down inventories.

which markets do or do not clear, is largely semantic. If that argument is accepted, the model whose future existence I am conjecturing here might turn out to be as much an extension of these explanations as an alternative to them.

In short, the theoretical basis of the buffer stock approach to monetary analysis is well developed and simple, and it has already withstood a good deal of empirical testing. In his last survey paper on monetary economics, presented just ten years ago to a Conference of the Money Study Group held at this university, Harry Johnson urged us to develop ideas which are '... scientifically robust and sufficiently simple to be communicable to ... students and policy makers and the general public.' (1974). The buffer stock approach already has these characteristics, and as I claimed at the outset of this lecture, ought to be taken seriously, not least by those looking for a starting point towards further progress in monetary economics.

University of Western Ontario, Canada

References

Akerlof, G. A. (1973), 'The demand for money: a general-equlibrium inventory-theoretic approach,' *Review of Economic Studies*, vol. 40 (January), pp. 115–30.

Archibald, G. C. and Lipsey R. G. (1958), 'Monetary and value theory: a critique of Lange and Patinkin,' *Review of Economic Studies*, vol. 26 (69) (January), pp. 1–22.

Artis, M. J. and Lewis, M. K. (1976), 'The demand for money in the United Kingdom,' *Manchester School*, vol. 44 (June), pp. 147–81.

——and ——(1981), *Monetary Control in the United Kingdom*, Deddington: Philip Allan.

Barro, R. J. (1978), 'Unanticipated money, output, and the price level in the United States,' *Journal of Political Economy*, vol. 86 (August), pp. 549–81.

Baumol, W. J. (1952), 'The transactions demand for cash – an inventory theoretic approach,' *Quarterly Journal of Economics*, vol. 66 (November), pp. 545–56.

Brunner, K. and Meltzer A. H. (1971), 'The uses of money – money in the theory of an exchange economy,' *American Economic Review*, vol. 61 (December), pp. 784–805.

——and ——(1976), 'An aggregative theory for a closed economy.' In Stein, J. L. (ed.) *Monetarism*, Amsterdam: North-Holland.

Carr, J. and Darby, M. (1981), 'The role of money supply shocks in the short-run demand for money,' *Journal of Monetary Economics* (September), pp. 183–200.

Chick, V. (1973), *The Theory of Monetary Policy*, Oxford: Basil Blackwell.

Clower, R. and Howitt, P. W. (1978), 'The transactions theory of the demand for money: a reconsideration,' *Journal of Political Economy*, vol. 86 (June), 449–66.

Coats, W. L. (1982), 'Modeling the short run demand for money with exogenous supply,' *Economic Inquiry*, vol. 20, (April), pp. 222–39.

Coghlan, R. (1981), *Money, Credit and the Economy*, London: Allen and Unwin.

Fisher, D. (1971), *Money and Banking*, Homewood, Ill.; Richard Irwin.

Friedman, M. and Schwartz, A. J. (1982), *Monetary Trends in The United States and the United Kingdom: Their Relation to Income, Prices and Interest Rates, 1867–1975*, Chicago: University of Chicago Press for the NBER.

Goodhart, C. A. E. (1982*a*), 'Monetary trends in the United States and the United Kingdom: a British review,' *Journal of Economic Literature*, vol. 20 (December), pp. 1540–51.

——(1982*b*), 'Disequilibrium money – a note,' Bank of England (mimeo).

Gramley, L. and Chase, S. B. (1965), 'Time deposits in monetary analysis,' *Federal Reserve Bulletin*, vol. 51 (October), pp. 1380–406.

Gray, M. and Parkin, J. M. (1973), 'Portfolio diversification as optimal precautionary behaviour' in M. Morishima *et al. Theories of Demand, Real and Nominal.* London: Oxford University Press.

Gurley, J. and Shaw, E. (1960), *Money in a Theory of Finance*, Washington, D. C.: Brookings Institution.

Hahn, F. H. (1971), 'Professor Friedman's views on money,' *Economica*, vol. 38, pp. 61–80.

Hicks, J. R. (1982), *Money, Interest and Wages: Collected Essays in Economic Theory, Vol. 11*, Cambridge Mass.: Harvard University Press.

Howitt, P. W. (1979), 'Evaluating the non-market clearing approach,' *American Economic Review*, vol. 69 (May), Papers and Proceedings: pp. 60–4.

——and Laidler, D. (1979), 'Recent Canadian monetary policy – a critique,' in Purvis D. and Wirick, R. (eds.), Proceedings of Queen's University Conference on Economic Policy, Queen's University (mimeo).

Johnson, H. G. (1951–52), 'Some Cambridge controversies in monetary theory,' *Review of Economic Studies* vol. 19 (2), pp. 90–104.

——(1962), 'Monetary theory and policy,' *American Economic Review*, vol. 52 (June): pp. 335–84.

——(1969), 'Inside money, outside money, income, wealth and welfare in monetary economics,' *Journal of Money Credit and Banking*, vol. 1 (February), pp. 30–45.

——(1974), 'Major issues in monetary economics,' *Oxford Economic Papers*, vol. 26 (July), pp. 212–25.

Jones, R. A. (1976), 'The origin and development of media of exchange', *Journal of Political Economy* vol. 84 (August), Part 1, pp. 756–75.

Jonson, P. D. (1976*a*), 'Money, prices and output: an integrative essay,' *Kredit und Kapital* (4), pp. 499–518.

——(1976*b*), 'Money and economic activity in the open economy: The United Kingdom, 1880–1970,' *Journal of Political Economy*, vol. 84 (September/October), pp. 979–1012.

——and Kierzkowski, H. (1975), 'The balance of payments: an analytic exercise,' *Manchester School*, vol. 53 (June), pp. 105–33.

—— Moses, E. R. and Wymer, C. R. (1976), 'A minimal model of the Australian economy,' Reserve Bank of Australia Discussion, Paper 7601, Sydney.

and Trevor, R. G. (1980), 'Monetary rules: a preliminary analysis,' Reserve Bank of Australia Research Discussion Paper 7903, mimeo.

Judd, J. and Scadding, T. (1982*a*), 'The search for a stable money demand function,' *Journal of Economic Literature*, vol. 20 (September), pp. 993–1023.

——and ——(1982*b*), 'Dynamic adjustment in the demand for money: tests of alternative hypotheses,' Federal Reserve Bank of San Fransisco (mimeo).

Kaldor, N. (1980), 'Memorandum of evidence ... ,' Treasury and Civil Service Committee, Session 1979–80, *Memoranda on Monetary Policy*, London, HMSO.

Kanniainen, V. and Tarkka, J. (1983), 'The role of capital flows in the adjustment of money demand: the case of Finland,' University of Helsinki Working, Paper No. 188 (mimeo).

Kawasaki, S., McMillan, J. and Zimmerman, K. F. (1983), 'Inventories and price inflexibility', *Econometrica*, vol. 51 (May), pp. 599–610.

Keynes, J. M. (1936), *The General Theory of Employment, Interest and Money*, London and New York: Macmillan.

Knight, M. and Wymer, C. (1975), 'A monetary model of an open economy, with particular reference to the United Kingdom' International Monetary Research Project Discussion Paper (mimeo).

Knoester, A. (1979*a*), 'Theoretical principles of the buffer mechanism, monetary quasi-equilibrium and its spillover effects,' Institute for Economic Research, Discussion Paper Series 7908/9/M, Erasmus University, Rotterdam.

Knoester, A. (1979*b*), 'On monetary and fiscal policy in an open economy,' *De Economist*, vol. 127 (1), pp. 105–42.

Laidler, D. (1975), *Essays on Money and Inflation*, Manchester: Manchester Universsty Press; Chicago: University of Chicago Press.

——(1980), 'The demand for money in the United States: yet again,' in Brunner, K. and Meltzer, A. (eds.), *The State of Macroeconomics*, Carnegie–Rochester Conference Series on Public Policy, vol. 12, Amsterdam: North Holland.

——(1982), *Monetarist Perspectives*, Deddington: Philip Allan; Cambridge, Mass.: Harvard University Press.

Lane, T. (1983), *Essays on Monetary Control*, unpublished Ph.D. Thesis, University of Western Ontario.

Leijonhufvud, A. (1981), *Information and Coordination*, Oxford: Oxford University Press.

Lewis, M. (1978), 'Interest rates and monetary velocity in Australia and the United States,' *Economic Record* (April), pp. 111–26.

Lucas, R. E. Jr. (1972), 'Expectations and the neutrality of money,' *Journal of Economic Theory*, vol. 4 (2), pp. 115–38.

——(1975), 'An equilibrium model of the business cycle,' *Journal of Political Economy*, vol. 83 (November/December), pp. 1113–44.

Marty, A. (1969), 'Inside money, outside money, and the wealth effect,' *Journal of Money, Credit and Banking*, vol. 1 (February), pp. 101–11.

Niehans, J. (1978), *The Theory of Money*, Baltimore: Johns Hopkins University Press.

Orr, D. (1970), *Cash Management and the Demand for Money*, New York and London: Praeger.

Patinkin, D. (1965), *Money Interest and Prices*, 2nd edition, New York: Harper Row.

——(1967), *On the Nature of the Monetary Mechanism: The 1967 Wicksell Lectures*, Stockholm: Almqvist and Wicksell.

——(1969), 'Money and wealth – a review article,' *Journal of Economic Literature*, vol. 7, pp. 1140–60.

Pesek, B. and Saving, T. R. (1967), *Money, Wealth, and Economic Theory*, New York: Macmillan.

Purvis, D. D. (1978), 'Dynamic models of portfolio behavior: more on pitfalls in financial model building,' *American Economic Review*, vol. 68 (June), pp. 403–9.

Sargent. T. J. (1976), 'A classical macroeconomic model for the United States,' *Journal of Political Economy*, vol. 84 (April), pp. 207–38.

Tobin, J. (1956), 'The interest elasticity of transactions demand for cash,' *Review of Economics and Statistics*, vol. 38 (August), pp. 241–7.

——(1969), 'A general equilibrium approach to monetary theory,' *Journal of Money, Credit, and Banking*, vol. 1 (February), pp. 15–29.

Tsiang, S. C. (1956), 'Liquidity preference and loanable funds theories, multiplier and velocity analysis: a synthesis,' *American Economic Review*, vol. 46, pp. 539–64.

——(1982), 'Stock or portfolio approach to monetary theory and the Neo-Keynesian school of James Tobin,' *IHS-Journal*, vol. 6, pp. 149–71.

Tucker, D. (1971), 'Macroeconomic models and the demand for money under market disequilibrium, *Journal of Money, Credit and Banking*, vol. 3 (February), pp. 57–83.

White, W. H. (1981), 'The case for and against "disequilibrium" money,' *IMF Staff Papers* (September), pp. 534–72.

14 Taking money seriously

Introduction

It should go without saying that I was delighted to take on the Presidency of the Canadian Economics Association for the year 1987–88. The appointment is not exactly a sinecure, for the president elect is expected to organize the programme for the annual meeting of the Association at which he takes office. That meeting took place at McMaster University in June 1987, where I duly caught a virus that put me in bed for the following week, missing a conference in Europe as a result. My reward came twelve months later at Windsor, where I was allowed to harangue the membership for fifty minutes or so on my, by then, none too fashionable views on monetary economics, with no questions or comments from the audience allowed!

I hope this paper still speaks for itself. It was an attempt to sum up, in one place, the things that I had been working on for the previous fifteen years or so. It does repeat points made in earlier chapters, particularly 8, 9, 11, 12 and 13, for which I make no apology. That is what it was meant to do.

A little later, after I had brought out a collection of essays under the same title as this lecture (A5) a journalist (I have long forgotten who) somehow got wind of said title, and wrote that economists must be the only people stupid enough to need to be urged to take money seriously. If only he knew …

Taking money seriously

DAVID LAIDLER University of Western Ontario

Abstract. This survey paper argues that Walrasian markets and monetary exchange are alternative, not complementary, arrangements for co-ordinating economic activity; that if we realize this, many informational anomalies and price rigidities which appear 'irrational' in a Walrasian context can be understood as the outcome of maximizing behaviour in a monetary economy; and that the precautionary approach to modelling the demand for money takes on a particular importance in this way of looking at things. Empirical evidence on the demand for money is cited in support of this point of view, which tends to reinstate the quantity of money as an important economic variable, in contrast to the New-Classical vision of the economy which downgrades money's importance.

Prendre la monnaie au sérieux. Ce mémoire-synthèse suggère que les marchés walrasiens et l'échange monétaire ne sont pas des arrangements complémentaires de coordination de l'activité économique mais des arrangements de rechange; que, si on se rend compte de ce fait, plusieurs anomalies informationnelles et rigidités de prix qui semblent 'irrationnelles' dans un contexte walrasien peuvent être interprétées comme le résultat de comportements de maximisation dans une économie monétaire; et que l'approche à la modélisation de la demande de monnaie en termes de motifs de précaution devient particulièrement importante dans cette perspective. Des résultats empiriques de calibration de la demande de monnaie sont cités à l'appui de ce point de vue, qui tend à redonner à la quantité de monnaie un rôle de variable économique importante, par opposition à la vision de l'économie des Nouveaux Classiques qui pour sa part réduit l'importance de la monnaie.

The 1988 Presidential Address to the Canadian Economics Association, delivered in Windsor, Ontario on 4 June 1988. During the past year I have had fruitful discussions with Karl Brunner, Axel Leijonhufvud, Bennett McCallum, Allan Meltzer, Edmund Phelps, Thomas Sargent and John Taylor about many of the issues dealt with here, and I owe a special debt to Joel Fried and Peter Howitt for reading and commenting in great detail on earlier drafts of this paper. I have also benefited from the comments of Paul Anglin, Keith Cuthbertson, Steve Holland, Seppo Honkapohja, Brian Loasby, Alvin Marty, Michael Parkin, Tom Rymes, and George Stadler. It should be more than usually apparent, however, that harmonious though these discussions were, they did not always end in agreement, and none of the above should be held responsible for the views that I express. I am grateful to Mr. Paul Gomme for help in preparing diagrams.

Canadian Journal of Economics Revue canadienne d'Economique, XXI, No. 4
November novembre 1988. Printed in Canada Imprimé au Canada

0008-4085 / 88 / 687-713 $1.50

INTRODUCTION

There are many parallels between the 'Keynesian Revolution' and the 'Monetarist Counter-Revolution,' but surely the strangest of them is this: both were set in motion by economists who were convinced of the central importance of money to the economic processes they were investigating, and both ended up evolving views of the world in which money has but a minor role to play. This parallel did not arise entirely fortuitously. Whatever Keynes may have intended, what came to be called Keynesian economics soon came to rely on a version of Walrasian general equilibrium analysis in which market mechanisms exist and function independently of the behaviour of the supply and demand for money; and monetarism took over the same theoretical foundations.[1]

In this paper I shall argue three points: that such Walrasian analysis does not permit money to be taken seriously; that if we do take money seriously in the sense of regarding monetary exchange as an alternative, instead of a supplement, to Walrasian mechanisms for co-ordinating economic activity, many of the apparently anomalous rigidities upon which predictions about money's importance appear to hinge can be understood as the outcome of maximizing behaviour; and that if we also take money seriously in the sense of paying attention to the empirical evidence we have on the nature of the economy's demand for money function, we find that some of it does indeed point to the desirability of looking at monetary exchange in just this way.

MONEY IN KEYNESIAN, MONETARIST AND NEW-CLASSICAL ECONOMICS

In the economics of Keynes, as in Classical economics, money was a means of exchange; and textbook macro-economics even now refers to 'transactions' and 'precautionary' motives for holding money, which are said to derive directly from that role. However, when monetary economists adopted Walrasian general equilibrium, in its IS-LM disguise, as their basic vision of economic activity, they adopted a model that could not generate such motives internally. Whatever the vocabulary of the monetary economics that developed after the publication of the *General Theory*, its logical structure came to treat money as an asset pure and simple; and the emphasis that Hicks (1935) and Keynes (1930, 1936) placed on money's role as a short-term speculative asset represented an important contribution to monetary economics precisely because it laid the foundations for a theory of the demand for money as a store of value, and because such a concept of money was the only one which could be accommodated comfortably within a Walrasian frame of reference.

1 The parallels between the Keynesian Revolution and the Monetarist Counter-Revolution were analysed by Johnson (1971) in a lecture whose occasionally ad-hominem character should not to distract its reader's attention from its underlying seriousness. The standard reference on the distinction between 'Keynesian Economics' and 'The Economics of Keynes' is Leijonhufvud (1968).

The monetarist counter-revolution was an attempt to change perceptions about empirical phenomena, not to create a new theoretical structure. It therefore did nothing to interrupt the process, already close to completion in the 1950s, of integrating monetary theory with Walrasian value theory.[2] The further this process was pushed, the more the representative model of a monetary economy came to resemble one of a barter economy in which there happened to exist a peculiar asset called 'money' whose 'real' (i.e., 'utility'-yielding) quantity varied in inverse proportion to its price in terms of goods. The utility in question was said to arise from money's role as a means of exchange, of course, but there was no such role for it to play within the logical structure of the representative macro-economic model. Although that model was undoubtedly useful as a starting point for empirical work, it was also very vulnerable to theoretical criticisms such as those I have been summarizing here. Clower (e.g., 1965, 1967), Hahn (e.g., 1965), and Tsiang (e.g., 1966), for example, had articulated them by the mid 1960s, but although the end of that decade saw much interest in the micro-economic foundations of monetary economics, this particular line of argument was to become, and indeed remain, something of a minority taste among macro-economists. The reason for this was the success of new-Classical economics.

The original aim of Robert E. Lucas and his collaborators was to provide a micro-foundation for monetarist predictions about the short-run non-neutrality of money, and Friedman's (1968) long-run 'natural unemployment rate' hypothesis. The nature of that endeavour initially attracted attention to the supply side of the economy in general and the labour market in particular; only later (though surely inevitably) were new-Classical economists forced to face up to the fact that the Walrasian framework with which they had continued to work does not provide an internally coherent justification for the existence of money. Their resolution to this difficulty has taken two forms. Some, the proponents of what Hall (1982) has called the 'new monetary economics,' have pushed the money as a store of value view to new limits, and have concluded (correctly as far as the world described by their model is concerned) that, if money is dominated in rate of return (as it is in the real world) no one would hold it unless the government compelled them to do so.[3] Others, notably Lucas (e.g., 1984), have reintroduced money's means of exchange role into a dynamic, but still essentially Walrasian, model in the shape of an arbitrary 'cash in

2 The publication of the first edition of Patinkin's *Money, Interest and Prices* in 1956 was of course a major landmark here.

3 Hall cites papers by Black (1970) and Fama (1980) as being key contributions here, but the contributions to this literature that have attracted most attention are probably those of Wallace (1981) and Sargent and Wallace (1983). Note that Bennett McCallum (1983) criticizes this stream of the literature, particularly the part of it that explicitly relies on Samuelson's (1958) 'overlapping generations' framework, for neglecting money's means of exchange role, and in (1987) shows how adapting an 'overlapping generations' model to accommodate this phenomenon changes its properties. Wallace (1988) provides a non-technical survey of the 'legal restrictions' theory of money that remains useful despite the fact that it systematically ignores any work that is critical of the approach.

advance' constraint which derives directly from the work of Clower and Tsiang (although the rescue of Walrasian style macro-economics was hardly what the latter intended that idea to accomplish).

Protagonists of the approaches in question would no doubt argue that they are still exploring matters of logic, and that their theories should not yet be expected to meet the test of empirical relevance. Even so, the widespread adoption of these approaches has opened up a yawning gap between theoretical and applied work on monetary issues. In either type of new-Classical model, monetary shocks can cause price level fluctuations, but their assumptions of competitive equilibrium and rational expectations ensure that the amount of real harm which results is trivial. Setting aside issues of superneutrality, it is the fundamental prediction of new-Classical theory that only unanticipated changes in the money supply have consequences for real variables. Given the amount of information available in the real world about the behaviour of monetary aggregates, and the speed with which it becomes public, it is impossible to account for the magnitude of observed cyclical fluctuations in real income and employment in such terms. That is one reason why new-Classical economics, mainly at the prompting of Kydland and Prescott (1982), is in the process of spawning 'real business cycle theory' as an alternative, completely non-monetary, explanation of economic fluctuations.[4]

'Keynesian' arguments about the minor relevance of money for the behaviour of prices, output, and employment were, of course, very different from those of new-Classical economics. They involved assertions about the existence of liquidity and investment traps, and of sociological influences on money wages and prices so strong as to swamp the effects of conventional market forces. Monetarism rebutted these arguments with empirical evidence about particular functional relationships, and also about broader-based associations among the quantity of money, the price level, and output. Such evidence continues to accumulate, and those of us concerned with applied problems in general, and policy issues in particular, remain convinced that, in the real world, 'money matters' as much as ever.

To support this proposition, let me present two scatter diagrams of data taken from the FRB St Louis *International Economic Conditions (Annual Edition)* (June 1987). Figure 1a plots the relationship between average inflation rates ($\dot{p}$) and average nominal-money-less-real-income growth rates ($\dot{m} - \dot{y}$) for eleven countries over the period (roughly) 1970–85. Figure 1b plots the year-by-year relationship, for each of those same countries, between the

4 Thus Barro's (1978) work, which seemed to confirm new-Classical predictions about the importance of 'unanticipated money' and the irrelevance of 'anticipated money' for real economic variables is now regarded with considerable scepticism mainly as a result of the work of Mishkin (1982) and Boschen and Grossman (1982). Note that another reason for the current popularity of real business cycle theory is the finding of Nelson and Plosser (1982) that the time path of United States real income is satisfactorily characterized as a random walk. This finding seems fragile, however, if recent work by John McCallum (1988) and Pierre Perron (1987) is taken into account.

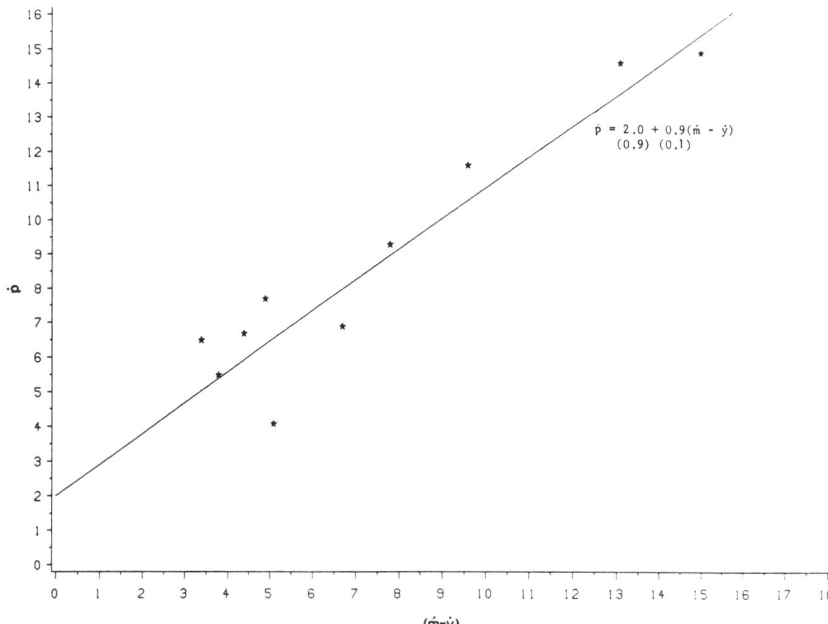

FIGURE 1a

deviation over a two-year period of real income growth from its long-run average value ($\hat{y}$) and the deviation in the first of those years of nominal money growth from the average value prevailing over the previous three years ($\hat{m}$). These scatters reveal two empirical relationships central to monetarist doctrine, namely, a long-run one between money growth and inflation and a short-run one between changes in money growth and subsequent real income growth.[5]

The inflation-money-growth relationship appears to be the stronger of the two, but figure 1b nevertheless indicates that changes in money growth rates significantly increase the probability of subsequent variations in real income

5 The data utilized in figure 1 are for the following North American and European countries and time periods: United States 1971–85, Germany 1974–85, Canada 1970–84, United Kingdom 1970–84, Italy 1971–84, Japan 1971–84, Sweden 1971–85, Spain 1971–83, Switzerland 1970–85, Belgium 1970–84, and the Netherlands 1971–84. France is omitted because of a major break in its money supply series. In each case the money supply is 'narrow' money, real output is GNP, and the price level is the GNP deflator. Each scatter has plotted with it the relevant least square regression line, with the standard error of its coefficients given below them in parentheses. The possibility that the money-growth-output relationship is the result of 'reverse-causation' can never be completely ruled out, although the plausibility of this explanation is reduced by the time lag inherent in figure 1b. Historical analysis of particular episodes, such as that employed by Friedman and Schwartz (1963) on the Great Depression, or Howitt (1986) on more recent Canadian experience seems to me to provide the best means of countering this line of argument.

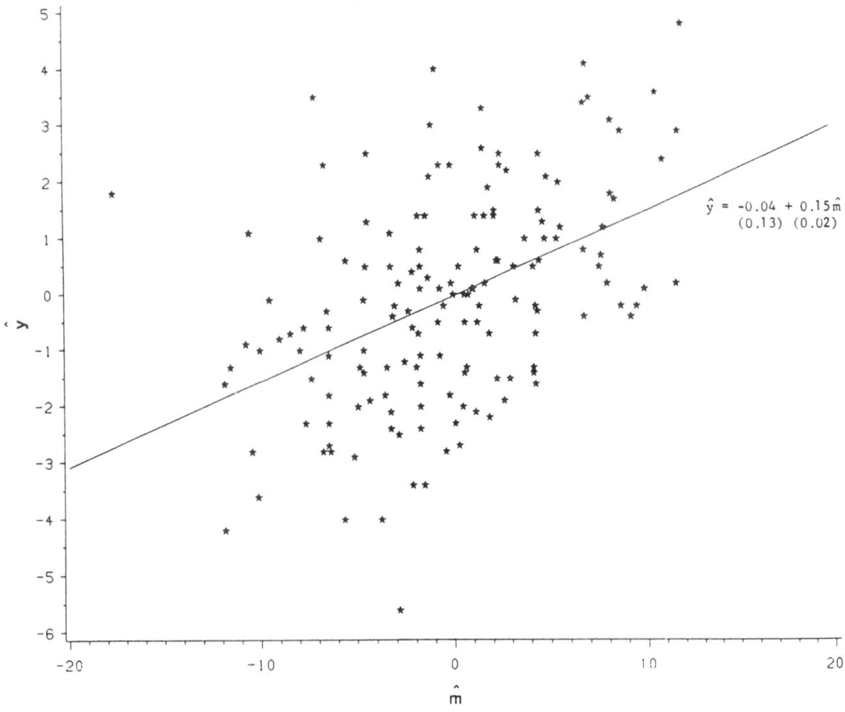

FIGURE 1b

growth. Brunner and Meltzer (1987) have recently recanted their view that monetary shocks are the dominant impulse driving economic fluctuations in the light of their reading of the evidence generated by the 1970s and 80s, and they are now more inclined to take an eclectic view of the mechanisms underlying the cycle such as that long advocated by Leijonhufvud (e.g., 1986). The data I present here certainly leave room for a substantial non-monetary component among the factors driving the cycle, but they are also consistent with the view that, if not dominant, monetary impulses have nevertheless remained systematically important over the very period in which popular opinion would have it that monetarism was being discredited.

I do not present these data as 'proving' anything about the real world. Rather my intention is to show that the 1970s and 80s have generated no crucial empirical experiment that would force an impartial observer to abandon monetarist doctrine.[6] The rise of new-Classical economics has been based on

6 Parkin (1987) has reported empirical work based on data related to, but not identical with, those I have used here. He claims his results to be inconsistent with a 'sticky-price Keynesian' view of cyclical fluctuations, but consistent with a new-Classical view. To accept Parkin's interpretation of the data requires us to (a) treat changes in relative commodity prices as reflecting solely the influence of productivity and taste shocks, and as occurring in-

theoretical, not empirical, arguments and it is surely ironic that a body of doctrine, whose immediate motivation was to provide a tight theoretical rationale for monetarist generalizations about the short-run empirical importance of money for real variables, has ended up re-establishing the Classical doctrine of 'Neutral Money' on firmer theoretical foundations than ever. As I shall now go on to argue, new-Classical economics, despite its great theoretical clarity and rigour (I judge it here by the standards of macro-economics), is at best unhelpful, or at worst downright misleading, in empirical applications, because its models, even those which employ a cash-in-advance constraint, do not encompass the basic facts of economic life that require economies to make use of a means of exchange in the first place. They do not take money seriously from a theoretical point of view, and that is why they cannot take it seriously empirically.

MONEY AND ALTERNATIVE MARKET MECHANISMS

New-Classical concerns with the micro-foundations of macro-economics did not arise in an intellectual vacuum. Lucas's (1972) paper grew out of his earlier contribution (with Leonard Rapping) to the celebrated (1969) Phelps et al. volume, *The Microeconomic Foundations of Employment and Inflation Theory*. Moreover, the late 1960s and early 1970s saw widespread efforts to find a satisfactory micro-foundation for the theory of money per se. I have already alluded to the work of Clower, Hahn, and Tsiang, and mention ought to be made, too, of the contributions of Hicks (1967), Leijonhufvud (1968), Niehans (1971), Brunner and Meltzer (1971), Ostroy (1973), Melitz (1974), Howitt (1974), Goodhart (1975), Jones (1976), and Alchian (1977), among others. Certain common themes ran through this otherwise heterogeneous collection of work. All of it drew attention to the enormous costs of generating and processing the information needed to co-ordinate the activities of individual agents in that complicated set of social arrangements we call an economy, and all of it argued that the institution of monetary exchange should be understood as a device to deal with them.[7] Such ideas have many antecedents in Classical economics, because, for 200 years at least, it was recognized that a barter economy would be so costly to operate that it could hardly be expected to exist

---

dependently of demand side disturbances; (b) ignore the work of Boschen and Grossman (1982) and accept that maximizing agents are unable to use information accruing during a year to influence their behaviour until the subsequent year; and (c) agree that sticky price models always yield the implications that monetary innovations 'Granger-cause' (i.e., unambiguously lead) innovations in real variables in annual data. Although it might be sensible to take any of these steps in the face of particular data sets and in the context of specific models, there is no general reason to do so. Thus, Parkin's interpretation of his results claims more for them than they can really support.

7 Brian Loasby has drawn my attention to the strong similarities between such a treatment of money and Coase's celebrated (1937) analysis of the firm as a social institution. To discuss this insight here is beyond the scope of this essay, but the parallel is well worth following up.

outside the economist's imagination, except in extremely primitive (at least in material terms) societies.

Within the Walrasian economy from which the contributors to the above-mentioned literature were trying to escape, information and incentives sufficient to co-ordinate the activities of otherwise isolated and self-interested agents are provided by the structure of relative prices. These have to be equilibrium prices because only in their presence can agents come to market secure in the knowledge that what they bring with them will be just sufficient to purchase what they wish to take away. Furthermore, if we assume that supply and demand for every good and service always match, perhaps it is also harmless to assume (it is certainly usual) that the Walrasian market is a place where agents can costlessly find willing trading partners as well. Now the information and co-ordination problems that the 'market' solves in this Walrasian story include those with which 'money' deals in traditional accounts which begin with the inconvenience of barter. That is why monetary theory based on Walrasian general equilibrium analysis either treats money as an asset pure and simple, or has to introduce monetary exchange in an apparently arbitrary fashion by appealing to a cash-in-advance constraint. It is also why the lines of enquiry opened up in the literature to which I have referred above still deserve the attention of monetary economists.

The Walrasian auctioneer solves the problem of co-ordinating economic activity by performing three distinct tasks: setting market clearing prices, informing agents about them, and bringing suppliers and demanders together so that trades can go through. In contrast, the adoption of a common means of exchange in an initially non-Walrasian barter economy simplifies co-ordination problems but does not eliminate them. Long transactions chains are ruled out if agents with something to sell take money in exchange and, when it comes to buying, offer money. It takes two parties to strike a single bargain, however; and even in a monetary economy, agents offering specific goods or services for sale still have to find someone who wants to buy them, agents offering money in exchange for specific goods or services still have to find sellers, and buyers and sellers have to find a mutually acceptable price. Some degree of market uncertainty and associated search and transactions costs, which would be completely absent from a Walrasian set up, therefore remain in money-using economies.

Some contributors to the literature to which I referred earlier, notably Howitt (1974, 1979), have found it helpful, and realistic, to note the existence of specialized agents, dealers, or middlemen, who play a key role in coping with these remaining co-ordination problems. These dealers (who may or may not also be producers) act as specialized traders, located at specific places and open for business at specific times. They hold inventories of goods ready for sale and set their prices too. Consumers are thought of as coming to these dealers' places of business during working hours, purchasing goods from them, and (if the dealers are also producers) as selling factor services to them as well. Monetary exchange, in the view of market mechanisms to which I here refer, is an institution that naturally complements the dealer. If sellers are specialized in the sense of offering for sale a well-defined class of goods, then it is clearly sensible to think of their being willing to take in return a commonly acceptable means of exchange, and also as posting their prices in terms of that means of exchange. Moreover, dealers must buy goods to replenish their inventories, and producers must pay the suppliers of their inputs. It is also sensible to expect that these trades will be mediated by money.

Now note that this vision of the trading process amplifies traditional accounts of how monetary exchange deals with the inconveniences of barter by cutting down on long transactions chains and saving 'shopping time.' In a dealer economy, a consumer wanting something specific does not have to search the market for some other agent who has it for sale. It will suffice to go to the right dealer. Money does little to save the consumer's shopping time in this view of the world. Its main function is to simplify the act of exchange per se (although of course the combined effect of dealer-mediated trade carried on with money is to reduce the many inconveniences of barter). This point is of some theoretical importance, because it is possible to conceive in principle of an economy that replaces the Walrasian auctioneer with dealers and monetary exchange in one of his three roles, that of bringing buyers and sellers together, but maintains that entity to set market-clearing prices and to keep agents informed of them.[8] Furthermore, if the auctioneer's capacity for conveying information to agents about market-clearing prices is limited to telling them about their selling prices, then such a set-up takes on a familiar new-Classical aspect, becoming in effect Lucas's version of a cash-in-advance economy.

A model of this type, though, is unusually artificial, even by the standards of macro-economics. Dealers are not just a useful fiction like the auctioneer: they exist; and it is awkward to work with a system that relies on both entities simultaneously, one to justify the existence of money and the other to set prices and inform agents about them. Once they are introduced, it is natural to have dealers set prices and also, along with their customers, collect and process the data on which market activities are premised. If prices are set by individual dealers, however, they may differ for the same goods at different places in the economy. Although consumers may not have to spend time looking for

8 An economy which only partially dispenses with the auctioneer's role is nevertheless a particularly useful fiction in order to simplify the modelling of the evolution of a means of exchange from an initial condition of barter. Most attempts to find a microfoundation for money are content to explain what it does, without concerning themselves about how it comes into being. Jones (1976) and, more recently, Kiyotaki and Wright (1987) are notable and important exceptions here. The latter paper is of particular interest in the current context because, in the model it analyses, dealers and monetary exchange emerge simultaneously as complementary phenomena.

suppliers of what it is they want, they will nevertheless find that it pays to search for a favourable price. Dealers too face problems that would not arise in a simpler world. Presumably they wish to maintain their prices at market-clearing values, but they must devote resources to calculating those prices. Sales volume will convey some information about whether or not prices are right, but if consumers are shopping around, it will have a stochastic character. Price setters who start off with the right price must therefore distinguish between random fluctuations in sales and those that signal a lasting shift in demand, and respond only to the latter.

All this gives money a more complicated role to play than it has in a simple cash-in-advance economy. If consumers find it worthwhile to shop around for favourable prices, the timing of their transactions, as well as those of dealers, becomes stochastic. They will therefore find it convenient to hold inventories of goods to smooth out discrepancies between the timing of acts of consumption and purchase. Dealers too will need inventories of goods in stock to absorb discrepancies between sales of goods and purchases from suppliers, whether these arise from random sources or from the possibility that it takes time to solve signal extraction problems before prices are changed. Where trade is carried on by money, however, movements of goods inventories must involve complementary fluctuations in the pattern of cash inflows and outflows, and these in turn must be absorbed by an inventory of cash balances, (or, depending upon the sophistication of the economy and the costs of trading in financial markets, of liquid assets). In short, if we dispense with the auctioneer entirely and have prices set endogenously, we create a world in which a precautionary demand for money becomes of the essence.[9]

THE PRECAUTIONARY DEMAND FOR MONEY AND PRICE STICKINESS

The traditional textbook model of the precautionary demand for money begins with individual agents who inhabit an economy much like that sketched out above. The model takes it for granted that transactions are mediated by money, and that, because of market uncertainty, agents face a stochastic pattern of cash inflows and outflows. It also takes the existence of other financial assets for granted and argues that, if there are costs of transforming other assets into cash, agents not only use money as a means of exchange, but also hold a 'buffer-stock' of cash to reduce the frequency with which they incur the costs of trading other assets for means of exchange in order to permit their transactions in markets in goods and services to go through. Such a model leads to a conventional formulation of the 'long-run' demand for money function, in which the demand for real balances rises with some scale variable measuring

9 The analysis of the preceding two paragraphs draws rather heavily on arguments that I set out in Laidler (1974). The reader's attention is drawn to papers by Leijonhufvud (1973) and Jonson (1976) which also explore these and related aspects of money's 'buffer-stock' role.

the real volume of market activity and falls as the opportunity cost of holding money rises.[10]

Now it is of the very essence of a demand for precautionary balances that, in the individual experiment, its value should fluctuate around an average or target level as the agent encounters those unpredicted fluctuations in the pattern of payments and receipts against which the balance is held in the first place; and such an approach to modelling the demand for money also enables us to predict the existence, in the market experiment, of a reduced (or quasi-reduced) form equation describing the short-run behaviour of real balances which displays the key characteristic of what we call (misleadingly, if this explanation of the phenomenon is correct) the 'short-run demand for money function,' namely, a lagged dependent variable on its right-hand side or, more generally, strongly serially correlated residuals. However, as I have shown elsewhere (Laidler, 1988), a necessary (not sufficient) condition for this result to arise in the context of a 'buffer-stock' model of the demand for money is that there exist a degree of price stickiness in the system; and, of course, the existence of price stickiness also produces just the kind of short-run non-neutrality that, I have argued above, provides a strong empirical incentive to take money seriously.

It is a commonplace that price stickiness can arise, quite mechanically, from inertia in expectations, from the existence of nominal contracts of significant length, or indeed from price-setting agents facing non-trivial costs of changing them; it is also a commonplace that the twin assumptions of Walrasian equilibrium and rational expectations which underpin modern new-Classical monetary theory rule out this phenomenon. However, if we take the proposition that monetary exchange reduces, but does not eliminate, uncertainty from market transactions, we are not only led to postulate the precautionary model of money holding referred to above. We are also led to take a more benign view of price stickiness assumptions, whether we motivate them in terms of systematic expectational errors or institutional rigidities. Both precautionary money holdings and price stickiness arise from the same source, namely, the informational imperfections that characterize an economy in which activity is co-ordinated by monetary exchange.

Consider in this context the rational expectations idea. The proposition that maximizing agents will make full use of all information economically available to them is irresistible, but how much information is that? New-Classical models have no explicit theory of the costs and benefits of information but are constructed as if they implicitly assume that marginal cost of generating relevant information rises in one step from zero to infinity. Information and

10 A particularly simple version of such a model was developed by Weinrobe (1972), and forms the basis of my own exposition of the precautionary motive in my book on *The Demand for Money* ... (Laidler, 1985) wherein the reader will also find references to other, more complex, treatments of this topic.

computing power are either free or completely unavailable, and scarcity of information occurs because the marginal cost of acquiring it becomes infinite before some theoretically ideal maximum amount of information (that which would guarantee the achievement of full Walrasian equilibrium) is reached, not because more information is to be had at a finite price. One can easily accept the rational expectations idea while simultaneously denying the relevance of this special case, and from a more general viewpoint, that idea does no more than compel us to think of agents gathering and utilizing information up to the point at which the marginal cost to them of acquiring it equals the marginal benefit that its possession confers.[11]

In a money-using economy, the marginal benefit from acquiring information must be the reduction in transactions costs that agents gain by being better informed. Such a reduction will be achieved by a closer matching of cash receipts and cash outlays so as to avoid the need to engage in costly trade in financial assets; but, as we have seen, the precautionary demand for money arises precisely from its capacity to reduce those same costs. If information enabling agents better to match up their cash inflows and outflows is to be had at zero marginal cost, they will of course acquire it, use it, and hold a smaller precautionary balance than they otherwise would; but if it comes only at rising marginal cost, and if money holding is a cheap buffer against the consequences of ignorance, those agents' decisions will, as a matter of rational choice, be based on less information than the economist looking into the economy from the outside would regard as available to them. Moreover, as Galbraith (1988) has recently shown, such 'economically rational' expectations are capable of generating serially correlated errors which agents do not find it worthwhile to eliminate.

Information gathering and money holding do not exhaust the avenues open to agents wishing to reduce the costs imposed upon them by the existence of a stochastic element in the time pattern of their payments and receipts. The money price at which they stand ready to deal is under agents' control, and the effects on their cash flow of fluctuations in demand and supply which they encounter may be reduced by varying it. However, haggling over prices in and of itself takes time and trouble which can be avoided if agents enter into contracts with one another to deal at preset prices, or, in the absence of continuing relationships among specific agents, if sellers simply state prices at which they stand ready to deal over non-trivial time intervals. Nominal price flexibility in goods markets is therefore a means of reducing transactions costs in asset markets, albeit a costly one. The degree of price flexibility in an economy should be higher, the higher are the costs of its substitutes, namely information and money holding; and the existence of precautionary money

11 When we put matters this way, it becomes clear that we are dealing with ideas first advanced in Stigler's seminal (1961) paper on the 'Economics of Information' and discussed in the context of monetary economics by, among others, Brunner and Meltzer (1971) and Laidler (1974). Brunner and Meltzer have recently taken up this theme again in (1987) and develop it along lines very similar to those I am following here.

holdings should be associated, not only with a degree of ignorance on the part of agents, but also with markets characterized by a degree of price stickiness.

In a money-using economy the extent of the gaps, between complete price flexibility and the amount that actually characterizes markets, and between 'all available' information and the amount gathered and utilized, will, moreover, vary. I am not only referring here to the possibility of exogenous technical progress in communications and data processing, although in a secular perspective these matters are surely important. I am also thinking of the endogenous responses of agents to variations in money's effectiveness in mitigating the consequences of ignorance and inflexibility. If money holding is a cheap and reliable buffer, then agents will find that it pays to remain relatively uninformed about the processes affecting the variability of their net receipts and will be relatively unwilling to undertake any costly measures that might render them either more predictable or controllable. If, on the other hand, money holding itself is a costly or unreliable source of insulation from such uncertainty, then the expenditure necessary to acquire and utilize extra information is more likely to be made.

Both the costs of using money as a buffer against market uncertainty and its reliability in that role have to do with the behaviour of the general price level. As is well known, expected changes in money's purchasing power are an important component of the opportunity cost of holding it. If money holding's capacity to act as a buffer against costly consequences of market uncertainty and inflexibility is available only at a high price, agents have a strong incentive to minimize those costs by other means. Hence, the foregoing argument suggests that anticipated inflation both discourages money holding and encourages expenditure on information and the maintenance of price flexibility on the part of agents. From the private point of view, such a response is presumably optimal, but from a social perspective it is wasteful. It involves devoting real resources to the reduction of costs that would, in conditions of price stability, have been offset by holding money; and, so it is usual to argue, once we leave a commodity money world, real balances are, on the margin, socially cheap (indeed perhaps free) to provide.[12]

It is worth drawing explicit attention to the fact that the informational problems encountered in a monetary economy of the type I am discussing here are rather different from those met up with in a new-Classical system. There, sellers are presented gratis with all available information about their own market, in the shape of a given money price for their output, but they have to extract an estimate of the general price level (in order to compute a relative price) from other data. With endogenous price setting, the information most needed by agents concerns the state of the market in which they are dealing.

12 Anyone who has participated in informal discussions about recent inflationary episodes in countries such as Argentina or Israel will have heard anecdotes about the sophistication their ordinary inhabitants develop about market processes. Instead of admiring this sophistication, as we so often seem to do, we might equally well deplore it as a manifestation of resource misallocation induced by irresponsible policy.

Data on the general price level are not irrelevant here, but it is hard to believe that they are of primary importance relative to local factors. Hence the fact that agents apparently do not make use of readily available information about the money supply, so puzzling to a new-Classical economist, is easily reconciled with the rationality postulate in an economy with endogenous price setting and information that is costly on the margin.[13]

However, the degree of priority given by agents to generating information about the general price level's behaviour will itself be endogenous. Anticipated changes in the price level influence the cost of obtaining money's services and unanticipated changes reduce the quality of those services; while, crucially, the extent to which price level variations are anticipated or unanticipated will itself depend upon the resources agents devote to gathering data on the matter and analyzing them. Fluctuations in the price level thus create incentives to acquire expertise not just about local market conditions but also about the monetary system. The larger those fluctuations, the more productive (privately) does it become to gather the latter kind of information and to act upon it.

There is, though, an externality here. Monetary instability encourages individual agents to acquire information and to gain flexibility, so that they may vary their own prices to counter its effects. Such price flexibility tends to be self-generating, however, because the more other prices vary, the more it pays the individual dealer to maintain and utilize the capacity to vary his own. To give one example of this phenomenon, Holland (1988) has shown, over the period 1965–86, that the degree of wage flexibility in the United States has systematically increased in response to the intensity of price-level fluctuations. At the level of the economy as a whole, these tendencies reduce money's usefulness, and so, as Keynes (1936, 269) long ago noted, price flexibility may not be quite the unmixed blessing that economists sometimes think it to be. One of its effects is to undermine money balances' capacity to act as a substitute for costly information gathering and processing.[14] It is perhaps not surprising that the political popularity of replacing decentralized and largely unregulated monetary exchange with alternative dirigiste schemes for co-ordinating economic activity tends to be greatest in periods of monetary instability.

13 Thus, anyone seeking a micro-economic story about inflation-unemployment-output interaction to complement the monetary economics I am here expounding should look to the work of Phelps (1969, 1972) as a starting point, rather than to the 'aggregate supply curve' analysis of new-Classical theory.

14 Both positive and normative aspects of these matters deserve a great deal more attention than I have space to give them here. Klein (1977) argued that price level uncertainty could cause the demand for money either to rise or to fall, depending upon whether agents decided to hold more or less money in the face of a fall in the volume of services produced by a unit of it. His empirical evidence seemed to show a mild positive relationship here, but subsequent work by Laidler (1980) showed that data for the 1970s reversed this result. More recently Friedman (1984) has conjectured that instability in the rate of money growth (which is related but by no means identical to price level uncertainty) ought to lead to a higher demand for money, a conjecture that receives some support from evidence recently published by Hall and Noble (1987). I conjecture that monetary instability, to the extent that it leads

SOME IMPLICATIONS FOR MACRO-MODELLING

The foregoing analysis has implications for how we should model price formation mechanisms in general and expectations mechanisms in particular. The new-Classical assumption that economic agents understand the structure of the economy and use that understanding to make optimal forecasts of the variables that concern them was never intended to be taken literally. Rather its proponents would have us think of agents as operating by 'rule of thumb,' and discarding rules that systematically mislead them until they find one that works, 'as if' its forecasts were being generated by a correct model of the economy they inhabit.

But how close to a 'correct model' need a rule of thumb be for agents to be satisfied with it? It would presumably suffice if its forecasts produced no systematic errors with consequences costly enough to make it worth agents' while to devote resources to reducing them. Economies in which money is cheap to hold and stable in its purchasing power give fewer incentives for simple and potentially erroneous rules to be weeded out. They are, therefore, likely to be inhabited by agents whose 'rational expectations' about the price level yield errors with a higher variance and are less robust in the face of changes in the pattern of shocks impinging on the economy than those with a history of inflation and monetary instability. A simple example (based on the assumption that monetarist analysis is broadly correct) will illustrate some possible implications of such a view.

In a small open economy operating a fixed exchange rate on a world economy characterized by price level stability, the rule of thumb that tomorrow's price level will be close to its average value over some past period will give essentially the same prediction as one that has it moving in proportion to the nominal-money-real-GNP ratio, or indeed as the forecast of some more complex 'true' model of the economy. An economist modelling such an economy would have equal predictive success by attributing to its inhabitants any of the above means of forecasting price level behaviour. If those inhabitants were using the first rule of thumb, however, they would be ill equipped to cope with the adoption of flexible exchange rates and unstable discretionary monetary policy. They might discover a more general rule in due course, but, as Parkin's (1977) analysis suggests, the economist modelling the

to fluctuating expenditure flows will increase the demand for money, and, to the extent that it increases price level uncertainty, will reduce it. I also conjecture that Klein's ambiguous prediction about the latter relationship arises from his having used a model in which there exists no substitute for 'money services.' If such a substitute does exist, in the form of resources devoted to information generation, it seems to me more likely that a reduction in money's capacity to perform its services will lead to a reduction in the demand for it. Finally, I suspect that the normative significance of fluctuations whose effects may be offset by increased money holdings will, upon analysis, prove to be quite different from that to be attached to instability that undermines money's capacity to function as an information substitute.

transition between regimes would be in trouble if he ignored the learning process and simply attributed his version of the 'true' model to them at all times. At the same time, if agents did learn to monitor the money supply and as a consequence adopted a rule of thumb a step closer to the 'true' model, then they would have little difficulty in forming expectations relevant to a transition back to a fixed rate or some similar regime, nor would an economist have trouble predicting their behaviour.

It is a mistake to treat 'expectations' as purely psychological phenomena when engaged in macro-modelling. What proximately matters for the way economies function is not what people expect, but how they act; and agents who have new information and understand its significance but are not free to act upon it, may as well be ignorant. Nominal rigidities may be the result of desirable resource economizing arrangements in an economy in which cash balances efficiently and cheaply buffer agents against the consequences of any imbalances in money flows that those rigidities may provoke; but they can cause real problems if circumstances change so as to reduce money's capacity to play that role. To return to the previous illustration, under a fixed exchange rate the success of the simple rule of thumb that the price level will tend to maintain a stable average level will encourage agents to engage in fixed nominal price contracts for significant time periods. Moreover, the length and rigidity of those contracts will have more to do with uncertainties about conditions in the market for the particular item being traded than with the likely course of the purchasing power of money. Under a discretionary monetary regime, when price-level behaviour becomes an issue, we might expect to find shorter contracts and more indexing, even though they involve more transactions costs. Moreover the transition from the fixed rate to discretionary policy would likely be more difficult than the reverse change because of this contrast in institutional starting points.

Now I do not intend the particular piece of elementary conceptual history running through the preceding paragraphs to be taken literally. I do, however, intend to be taken seriously the general message it illustrates: namely that it is dangerous uncritically to model agents' behaviour on the assumption that they form their expectations using the same model of their economy as the economist who studies them. Maximizing agents should not always be expected to act like that. Rather they will utilize only the information that the history of their economy has provided them with an incentive to acquire. Properly understood, however, this argument does not lead to the conclusion that new-Classical analysis is always and everywhere misleading. Economies in which agents' rules of thumb are consistent with the processes driving the behaviour of critical variables will look very much as if they are inhabited by well-informed rational agents of the textbook variety. Those rules of thumb are likely to be rather sophisticated in economies where the incentives to develop them have been strong, and the institutional flexibility needed for agents to respond quickly to new information is also likely to be present in such economies. Furthermore, ignorance and nominal rigidities, which characterize economies with a history of monetary stability, will be quite irrelevant to predicting their behaviour so long as that monetary stability prevails. New-Classical models should cope rather well with data generated by either type of economy.

Our analysis also warns us, however, that models that postulate that agents act 'as if' they understand the structure of the economy are unlikely to work well during transition periods, particularly those that involve a reduction in money's capacity to provide a cheap hedge against ignorance and inflexibility. If agents' rules of thumb mimic in their predictions the economy's true structure only in a particular policy environment but create systematic errors in another, then agents will have to experience those errors and the costs they impose before they can be expected to begin to correct them. Far from being ruled out by the postulate of rational behaviour therefore, systematic error would seem to be required by its application to learning processes. Hence, instead of refusing to take seriously explanations of particular historical episodes that rely on systematic errors on the part of agents, or price rigidities that are 'irrational' in prevailing circumstances, we should look askance at any account of the onset of instability that does not pay due attention to these phenomena. Moreover, because the period over which any individual is in a position to take important economic decisions (about such things as pricing policies, for example) is a good deal shorter than a lifetime, and because the intergenerational transmission of knowledge is an uncertain process, neither should we rule out the possibility of 'errors' being repeated. A good deal of older work on business-cycle history and related topics might regain respectability from this observation.

Now although the idea that old rules of thumb and institutional arrangements persist in new environments with which they are incompatible might help us understand the earlier stages of episodes of monetary instability, we must also recognize that the later stages will surely be characterized by the discovery and adoption of new ones. It is much easier to draw attention to the problem of how to embed an account of learning in an economic model than to solve it. Let me simply observe here that attempts to model agents' learning processes 'as if' they were econometricians seeking information about the economy by statistical induction seem to me to be of limited usefulness. Many of my colleagues would probably be delighted to see me proved wrong here, because if we could formulate an empirically robust theory along such lines, it would enable us to use the postulate of rational maximizing behaviour to cope with transition periods as well as with times of stability and hence to extend the area of experience to which new-Classical analysis can usefully be applied.[15]

There are two interrelated problems here. First, on my reading of the history

15 Recent examples of this type of analysis include Marcet and Sargent (1987) and Howitt (1987).

of our discipline, economic knowledge seems to evolve by a process much more akin to that which Karl Popper characterized as 'conjecture and refutation' than any other; and second, there is an inherently creative and hence unpredictable element to the process of conjecturing hypotheses about how the economy operates.[16] It is only if we envisage an end to the development of *qualitative* economic knowledge, so that learning need be concerned with only *quantitative* matters, that techniques of statistical inference will enable us to model all relevant aspects of learning satisfactorily. However, there is considerable comfort to be found in this, at first sight, nihilistic observation. Rymes (1979) and, more recently, Sargent (1984) have drawn our attention to the fact that it is all too easy to be led into an essentially vacuous type of economic determinism if we push ideas of rationality and foresight too far. To introduce an inherently unpredictable element into our vision of economic life, in the shape of a postulate about how learning takes place, enables us to avoid this particular trap. Perhaps it is the social scientist who believes that everything can and must be explained as the outcome of carefully calculated rational behaviour who is the real nihilist in this instance.[17]

PREDICTIONS ABOUT THE DEMAND FOR MONEY

Now the vision of market mechanisms underlying the foregoing arguments focuses on money's means of exchange function and argues that money holding should be viewed as an essentially precautionary phenomenon. To the extent that this rather specific view of money's role in economic life gets support from empirical work, those arguments are strengthened and begin to lose their predominantly a priori character. Empirical work on the aggregate demand for money function began in earnest in the late 1950s as a result of a change in the basic question that monetary economists asked. Instead of 'why do people hold money?' the issue became 'given that they do, what determines how much they will hold?' and Friedman's (1956) bold postulate that the aggregate demand for money was a stable function of but a few arguments was the starting point in settling it. The 'money-as-if-a-consumer-durable' approach adopted in much empirical work yielded large dividends in quantitative knowledge by modelling the aggregate demand for real balances function as the sum of the demand

16 I do not wish to be thought of as a supporter of a naïve view of scientific method that has the individual economist conjecturing new ideas and then disinterestedly seeking to refute them. The process here is a social one, in which self-interested individuals try as hard as they can to refute the conjectures of their competitors while simultaneously defending their own.

17 An emphasis on the limits of rationality as a foundation for economic analysis is a pervasive theme of 'post-Keynesian' macro-economics. See Chick (1983) and Foster (1987) for recent examples of work along these lines. Note also that New-Classical economists are not ignoring this problem at least as it arises in the context of transitions in the state of knowledge. See for example Lucas (1986) for a penetrating discussion of the issues involved, a discussion in which, let it be emphasized, he shows himself to be extremely sympathetic to the notion that there are limits to the explanatory power of the rationality postulate.

functions of individual agents who treated money as a source of purely private utility-yielding services. It ignored the nature of those services, not because they had not been analyzed, but because the empirical questions being asked did not seem to require that attention be paid to them.

Even so, it was soon pointed out, notably by Fried (1973), Dutton and Gramm (1973), Karni (1974), Diewert (1974), and Phlips (1978) that models of the demand for money that incorporate brokerage fees, as precautionary models inevitably do, may rather easily be made to yield the prediction that the demand for money should depend upon the real wage level. The key step here is to characterize this 'fee' as representing the time that agents must spend to turn other assets into cash.[18] This prediction was confirmed by evidence presented in the last four of the above-mentioned studies and has more recently been confirmed again by Dowd (1985). Also, as Fried stressed, when the prediction in question is combined with the observation that, at the level of the economy as a whole, real income and real wages tend to move together, it implies that regressions that include only the former variable will yield an upward biased estimate of its coefficient. This argument is important because it reconciles the characteristic prediction of precautionary demand models that the income elasticity of demand for money is below unity with the frequent occurrence of empirical estimates of this parameter in the region of unity.[19]

Evidence that it pays empirically to take explicit note of money's means of exchange function has thus long been available, but while it seemed possible to obtain good empirical performance from simpler functions that ignored this detail, this evidence had little impact. We can no longer be confident that it is safe to ignore the role money plays in the economy when we model the demand for it. Problems of empirical stability are neither illusory, nor confined to recent data. Closer inspection of already well-analyzed historical time series has revealed shifts in what initially seemed to be stable relationships. Recent work on these matters has exploited ideas about money that stress its means of

18 Of course brokerage fees also play a prominent role in Baumol (1953) and Tobin (1956) transactions demand models. Those models concentrate on money's means of exchange role and hence are close to the spirit of the approach to monetary economics that underlies this lecture. Indeed, Clower and Howitt (1976) may be regarded as an exploration of how the Baumol-Tobin model should be modified in the context of a non-Walrasian economy.

19 Lucas (1988) has shown that one such function with a unit elasticity, namely, that proposed and estimated by Meltzer (1963), still seems to be discernible in United States data, and he has also shown how such a relationship can be interpreted as part of the structure of an almost Walrasian (i.e., market clearing prices, rational expectations, plus a cash-in-advance or credit constraint) economy. Hence it is important for any advocate of the approach to money taken in this paper to be able to reconcile such evidence with that view. Note that Svensson (1985) and Hartley (1988) introduce a precautionary element into the demand for money in a version of Lucas's system by altering the timing with which information is made available to agents and by permitting cash to be used in a wider (but overlapping) range of markets than credit. They thus attribute to cash the capacity to generate market 'flexibility' of a type first analysed by Goldman (1974). All this analysis treats the provision of information as exogenous, and hence differs crucially from the approach taken here, but it nevertheless represents a step towards closing the gap between Lucas's approach to the analysis of money and that advocated in this lecture.

exchange role. Thus, Bordo and Jonung (1987), invoking the essentially Classical analysis of Knut Wicksell (1906) as a starting point, have investigated the effects of institutional factors such as better communications, easier access to banking facilities, and so on, on the demand for money and have found them to be systematically important. Such explanations of specific shifts in the demand for money function seem both plausible and natural in the light of the arguments presented earlier. Bordo and Jonung's work thus gives us further cause to treat money's means of exchange role, and the closely related precautionary nature of money holding, as being of considerable empirical relevance.

I noted earlier that the dynamics of the 'short-run demand for money function' may be derived from postulates about the degrees of price stickiness and expectational sophistication prevalent in the economy. Thus the precautionary approach to modelling the demand for money enables us to explain this aspect of the empirical evidence without resort to postulates about portfolio adjustment costs or measurement error, but as a natural characteristic of a monetary economy. Furthermore, in this view, short-run instability in velocity can be explained as the consequence of variations in price stickiness and informational characteristics, both between economies and over time. Such an approach to this important empirical problem once more follows immediately from the vision of money's role in the economy advanced above, a vision which has proved to be a fruitful foundation for empirical work on the demand for money.

The work in question, usually referred to as 'buffer-stock modelling,' is not, of course, without its critics. Thus Milbourne (1988) has recently prepared a careful survey of much of the literature to which I am here alluding and points to three types of problem. First, he notes, correctly, that some models rely on the dubious assumption that nominal money is a completely exogenous variable to generate their predictions. The assumption in question is certainly helpful to exposition, but fortunately it is not essential, as work by, for example, Gordon (1984) shows. Second, he argues that there are severe econometric problems with attempts to test buffer-stock ideas using single-equation techniques. Not everyone (e.g., Carr, Darby, and Thornton, 1985) accepts this criticism, but that work which follows the lead of Bergstrom and Wymer (1974) and Jonson, Moses and Wymer (1976) in taking a complete model approach to estimation is in any event immune to it. Finally, Milbourne notes, citing Cuthbertson and Taylor (1986), that, when it is combined with the new-Classical version of the rational expectations idea, which treats information and data processing as free goods, the buffer-stock approach runs into real empirical difficulties because the data appear to reject the restrictions on parameter values implied by the resulting model. However, more recent work by Cuthbertson and Taylor (1987), which was not available to Milbourne, shows that this problem may be dealt with by attributing what we might term 'sensible' rather than fully rational expectations to agents. The arguments of this paper strongly suggest that the existence of a significant precautionary element in the demand for money is likely to be incompatible with any extreme categorization of expectations, and hence gain support from these more recent results.[20]

A number of other predictions about the demand for money follow from the ideas set out in this lecture. For example, they imply that we should not think of the individual's precautionary demand for money as being underpinned by a stochastic pattern of payments and receipts generated by some exogenously given structure. Far from being exogenously given, that stochastic pattern is, if only within limits, controllable. Its dispersion can be reduced by devoting more resources to gathering market information, and by devoting more resources to maintaining the capacity to act flexibly in the market. Moreover, the incentive to devote resources to these ends varies systematically with the cost of holding money. When this cost is high, resources will be devoted to reducing the dispersion of cash flows, and vice versa. Hence *movements along* a demand for precautionary balances function derived on the assumption of a given structure of information will be accompanied by systematic *shifts of* that function. Note also that those shifts will not be reversible to the extent that information, once acquired, or new contractual arrangements once put in place, are durable. Ratchet effects in the demand for money-interest rate relationship, which figured prominently in the empirical work on the alleged instability of the U.S. demand for money function surveyed by Judd and Scadding (1982), might repay further investigation in the light of this argument.

The foregoing analysis also suggests that complications, in the form of interdependencies among agents' money holdings, might arise in getting from the individual to the market demand curve for money. Such interdependencies will exist in principle because a time and trouble cost of obtaining cash in exchange for other assets is basic to any model of the individual's precautionary demand for money. The cost to any one agent, however, of obtaining cash will surely vary with the amount of cash that other inhabitants of the economy hold. The more money held by others, the lower will be, to any particular agent, the costs of finding a willing cash buyer for some other asset, and, therefore, the less money will that agent hold. Thus, as the nominal interest rate rises, and each individual reduces cash holdings, the fact that all other agents simultaneously do the same produces forces which offset, though not of course entirely, this negative movement. The aggregate demand for money function will, then, be more steeply sloped with respect to the rate of interest than the sum of the individual relationships.[21]

20 Even so, the ideas under discussion here are difficult to test directly and definitively, because, as Milbourne's survey suggests, only a properly specified complete macro-model provides an appropriate vehicle for investigating them. There is obviously much room for debate about what such a model would look like and hence considerable scope for creating alibis for particular results.

21 I discussed this externality in Laidler (1977). Note that it bears a strong family resemblance to the externalities in search processes that produce the multiple equilibria that characterize the models of Diamond (e.g., 1984) and Howitt (1985) and have been analyzed more generally by Drazen (1987).

Now this last prediction can hardly be tested directly. To do so we would need data in which the opportunity cost of holding money varied for an individual while it remained constant for the rest of the economy. However, it might be indirectly tested by noting that cross-section data on the demand for money as a function of real income tell us something about how an individual's money holdings vary when those of all other agents remain constant, while aggregate time series evidence on the same relationship tells us about the same relationship when the money holdings of others are simultaneously changing. The externality just discussed would be held constant in the former case and at work in the latter, so the cross-section income elasticity of demand should be the higher of the two. The general presumption about income effects is that cross-section studies yield lower parameter estimates, so it is not without interest that the only systematic survey of evidence on this question of which I am aware (Feige and Pearce, 1977) does in fact find cross-section estimates to be higher on average. The difference here is not statistically significant and the work surveyed did not pay attention to brokerage fee effects, so one should not make too much of this result. Even so, the question is surely worth more detailed examination than it has so far received.

CONCLUSION

Now it can be argued that the predictions about the demand for money function discussed above, both those that have been tested and confirmed and those that for the moment remain conjectures, are of rather minor importance. So indeed they are as far as the demand function itself is concerned. They represent at best rather small embellishments to our knowledge of this relationship. However, I have taken the time to discuss them here, not because of what they tell us about the appropriate empirical specification of the demand for money function per se, but because of what their empirical confirmation suggests, or would suggest, about the motives underlying the behaviour that function summarizes.

As I have remarked above, where trading at false, and perhaps sticky, prices set on the basis of less than 'all available' information is of the essence, serially correlated fluctuations in output and employment, not to mention prices and real balances, naturally arise. In such a world, money is significantly non-neutral, and monetary policy is important. Although it was at one time taken for granted that any satisfactory macro-economic model would display such characteristics, the recent fashion for building upon Walrasian micro-foundations has undermined any consensus about such matters. I have argued in this lecture that an alternative, non-Walrasian, vision of the workings of the economy can be used to defend a traditional approach to macro-economic modelling, and that a precautionary view of money holding is central to that vision. Thus, if evidence that the precautionary model of the demand for money has explanatory power over real world data makes a trivial difference to our beliefs about the properties of the demand for money function, it ought nevertheless to have a profound effect on the way we think about the workings of market economies. That is the most important reason of all for taking money seriously.

REFERENCES

Alchian, A.A. (1977) 'Why money?' *Journal of Money, Credit and Banking* 9, 133–40

Barro, R.J. (1978) 'Unanticipated money, output, and the price level in the United States.' *Journal of Political Economy* 86, 549–815

Baumol, W.J. (1952) 'The transactions demand for cash: an inventory theoretic approach.' *Quarterly Journal of Economics* 66, 545–56

Bergstrom, A.R. and C.R. Wymer (1974) 'A model of disequilibrium neoclassical growth and its application to the United Kingdom.' Mimeo, LSE

Black, F. (1970) 'Banking and interest rates in a world without money: the effects of uncontrolled banking.' *Journal of Banking Research* (Autumn) 8–28

Bordo, M.D. and L. Jonung (1987) *The Long-Run Behaviour of the Velocity of Circulation* (Cambridge: Cambridge University Press)

Boschen, J. and H.I. Grossman (1982) 'Tests of equilibrium macroeconomics using intertemporal data.' *Journal of Monetary Economics* 10, 309–33

Brunner, K. and A.H. Meltzer (1971) 'The uses of money: money in the theory of an exchange economy.' *American Economic Review* 61, 784–805

— (1987) 'Money and the economy: issues in monetary analysis.' *The 1987 Raffaele Mattioli Lectures*. Mimeo, Carnegie-Mellon University

Carr, J., M. Darby, and D. Thornton (1985) 'Monetary anticipations and the demand for money: a reply.' *Journal of Monetary Economics* 8, 251–8

Chick, V. (1983) *Macroeconomics After Keynes* (Oxford: Philip Allan; Cambridge MA: MIT Press)

Clower, R.W. (1965) 'The Keynesian counterrevolution: a theoretical appraisal.' In F.R. Hahn and F.P.R. Brechling, eds, *The Theory of Interest Rates* (London: Macmillan for the IEA)

— (1967) 'A reconsideration of the microfoundations of monetary theory.' *Western Economic Journal* 6, 1–8

Clower, R.W. and P.W. Howitt (1978) 'The transaction theory of the demand for money: a reconsideration.' *Journal of Political Economy* 86, 449–66

Coase, R. (1937) 'The nature of the firm.' *Economica* NS 4, 386–405

Cuthbertson, K. and M.P. Taylor (1986) 'Monetary anticipations and the demand for money in the U.K.: testing rationality in the shock-absorber hypothesis.' *Journal of Applied Econometrics* 1, 355–65

— (1987) 'Monetary anticipations and the demand for money: some evidence for the U.K.' *Weltwirtschaftliches Archiv* 183, 509–20

Diamond, P.A. (1984) *A Search Equilibrium Approach to the Micro-Foundations of Macroeconomics* (Cambridge, MA: MIT Press)

Diewert, W.E. (1974) 'Intertemporal consumer theory and the demand for durables.' *Econometrica* 42, 497–516

Dowd, K. (1985) 'The demand for money, consumption and real wages.' Mimeo, University of Western Ontario

Drazen, A. (1987) 'Reciprocal externality models of low employment.' *European Economic Review* 31, 436–43

Dutton, D.S. and W.P. Gramm (1973) 'Transactions costs, the wage rate, and the demand for money.' *American Economic Review* 63, 652–65

Fama, E. (1980) 'Banking in the theory of finance.' *Journal of Monetary Economics* 6, 39–57

Feige, E.L. and D.K. Pearce (1977) 'The substitutability of money and near-monies: a survey of the time-series evidence.' *Journal of Economic Literature* 15, 439–69

Foster, J.I. (1987) *Evolutionary Macroeconomics* (London: Allen and Unwin)

Fried, J. (1973) 'Money, exchange and growth.' *Western Economic Journal* 11, 285–301

Friedman, M. (1956) 'The quantity theory of money: a restatement.' In M. Friedman, ed., *Studies in the Quantity Theory of Money* (Chicago: University of Chicago Press)

—(1968) 'The role of monetary policy.' *American Economic Review* 58, 1–17

—(1984) 'Lessons from the 1979–82 monetary policy experiment.' *American Economic Review* 74, papers and proceedings, 397–400

Friedman, M. and A.J. Schwartz (1963) *A Monetary History of the United States 1867–1960* (Princeton, NJ: Princeton University Press for NBER)

Galbraith, J.W. (1988) 'Modelling expectations formation with measurement errors.' *Economic Journal* 98, 412–428

Goldman, S.M. (1974) 'Flexibility and the demand for money.' *Journal of Economic Theory* 9, 203–22

Goodhart, C.A.E. (1975) *Money, Information and Uncertainty* (London: Macmillan)

Gordon, R.J. (1984) 'The short-run demand for money: a reconsideration.' *Journal of Money, Credit and Banking* 16, pt. 1, 403–34

Hahn, F.H. (1965) 'On some problems of proving the existence of equilibrium in a monetary economy.' In F.H. Hahn and F.R.P. Brechling, eds, *The Theory of Interest Rates* (London: Macmillan for the IEA)

Hall, R. (1982) '*Monetary Trends in the United States and the United Kingdom*: a review from the perspective of new developments in monetary economics.' *Journal of Economic Literature* 20, 1552–5

Hall, T.E. and N.R. Noble (1987) 'Velocity and the variability of money growth: evidence from Granger causality tests.' *Journal of Money, Credit and Banking* 19, 112–16

Hartley, P. (1988) 'The liquidity services of money.' *International Economic Review* 29, 1–24

Hicks, J.R. (1935) 'A suggestion for simplifying the theory of money.' *Economica* 2, 1–19

—(1967) 'The two triads.' In *Critical Essays in Monetary Theory* (London: Oxford University Press)

Holland, A.S. (1988) 'The changing responsiveness of wages to price-level shocks: explicit and implicit indexation.' *Economic Inquiry* 26, 265–79

Howitt, P.W. (1974) 'Stability and the quantity theory.' *Journal of Political Economy* 82, 133–51

—(1979) 'Evaluating the non-market-clearing approach.' *American Economic Review* 69, papers and proceedings, 60–4

—(1985) 'Transactions costs in the theory of unemployment.' *American Economic Review* 75, 88–100

—(1986) *Monetary Policy in Transition: A Study of Bank of Canada Policy 1982–85* (Toronto: C.D. Howe Institute)
—(1987) 'Wicksell's cumulative process as non-convergence to rational expectations.' Mimeo, University of Western Ontario
Johnson, H.G. (1971) 'The Keynesian revolution and the monetarist counter-revolution.' *American Economic Review* 61, papers and proceedings, 91–106
Jones, R.A. (1976) 'The origin and development of media of exchange.' *Journal of Political Economy* 84, pt. 1, 756–75
Jonson, P.D. (1976) 'Money, prices and output: an integrative essay.' *Kredit und Kapital* 4, 499–518
Jonson, P.D., E.R. Moses, and C.R. Wymer (1976) 'A minimal model of the Australian economy.' Reserve Bank of Australia Discussion Paper 7601
Judd, J.P. and J.L. Scadding (1982) 'The search for a stable money demand function.' *Journal of Economic Literature* 20, 993–1023
Karni, E. (1974) 'The value of time and the demand for money.' *Journal of Monetary Economics* 6, 45–64
Keynes, J.M. (1930) *A Treatise on Money* (London: Macmillan)
—(1936) *The General Theory of Employment, Interest and Money* (London: Macmillan)
Kiyotaki, N. and R. Wright (1987) 'Money as a medium of exchange.' Mimeo, University of Pennsylvania
Klein, B. (1977) 'The demand for quality adjusted cash balances: price uncertainty in the U.S. demand for money function.' *Journal of Political Economy* 85, 691–716
Kydland, F. and E. Prescott (1982) 'Time to build and aggregate fluctuations.' *Econometrica* 50, 1345–70
Laidler, D. (1974) 'Information, money and the macroeconomics of inflation.' *Swedish Journal of Economics* 76, 26–41
—(1980) 'The demand for money in the United States: yet again.' In K. Brunner and A.H. Meltzer, eds, *The State of Macroeconomics* Carnegie Rochester Conference Series vol. 12 (Amsterdam: North-Holland)
—(1977) 'The welfare costs of inflation in neoclassical theory.' In E. Lundberg, ed., *Inflation Theory and Anti-inflation Policy* (London: Macmillan for the IEA)
—(1985) *The Demand for Money: Theories, Evidence and Problems*, 3rd ed. (New York: Harper and Row)
—(1988) 'Some macroeconomic consequences of price stickiness.' *Manchester School* 56, 37–54
Leijonhufvud, A. (1968) *On Keynesian Economics and the Economics of Keynes* (London: Oxford University Press)
—(1973) 'Effective demand failures.' *Swedish Journal of Economics* 75, 27–48
—(1986) 'Real and monetary factors in business fluctuations.' *The Cato Journal* 6, 409–20
Lucas, R.E., Jr (1972) 'Expectations and the neutrality of money.' *Journal of Economic Theory* 4, 103–24
—(1984) 'Money in a theory of finance.' In K. Brunner and A.H. Meltzer, eds, *Essays on Macroeconomic Implications of Financial and Labour Markets and Political Processes*, Carnegie-Rochester Conference Series vol. 21 (Amsterdam: North-Holland)
—(1986) 'Adaptive behaviour in economic theory.' *Journal of Business* 59, pt. 2, s401–26

— (1988) 'Money demand in the United States: a quantitative review.' In B.T. McCallum, ed., Carnegie-Rochester Conference Series (forthcoming)

Lucas, R.E., Jr and L.R. Rapping (1969) 'Real wages, employment and inflation.' In E.S. Phelps et al. *The Microeconomic Foundations of Employment and Inflation Theory* (London: Macmillan)

Marcet, A. and T.J. Sargent (1987) 'Convergence of least squares learning in environments with hidden state variables and private information.' Mimeo, Carnegie-Mellon University

McCallum, B.T. (1983) 'The role of overlapping-generations models in monetary economics.' In K. Brunner and A.H. Meltzer, eds, *Money, Monetary Policy and Financial Institutions*, Carnegie-Rochester Conference Series, vol. 18 (Amsterdam: North-Holland)

— (1987) 'The optimal inflation rate in an overlapping-generations model with land.' In W.A. Barnett and K.J. Singleton, eds, *New Approaches to Monetary Economics* (Cambridge: Cambridge University Press)

McCallum, J. (1988) 'The persistence of output fluctuations.' Mimeo, McGill University

Melitz, J. (1974) *Primitive and Modern Money* (Reading, MA: Addison-Wesley)

Meltzer, A.H. (1963) 'The demand for money: the evidence from the time series.' *Journal of Political Economy* 71, 219–46

Milbourne, R. (1988) 'Disequilibrium buffer stock models: a survey.' Mimeo, Queen's University

Mishkin, F.S. (1982) 'Does anticipated monetary policy matter? An econometric investigation.' *Journal of Political Economy* 90, 22–51

Nelson, C.R. and C.I. Plosser (1982) 'Trends and random walks in macroeconomic time series.' *Journal of Monetary Economics* 10, 139–62

Niehans, J. (1971) 'Money and barter in general equilibrium with transactions costs.' *American Economic Review* 61, 773–83

Ostroy, J.M. (1973) 'The informational efficiency of monetary exchange.' *American Economic Review* 63, 597–610

Parkin, J.M. (1977) 'The transition from fixed exchange rates to money supply targets.' *Journal of Money, Credit and Banking* 9, 228–42

— (1987) 'What do we know about business cycles?' The 1987 Timlin Lecture (Saskatoon, University of Saskatchewan)

Patinkin, D. (1956) *Money, Interest and Prices*, 1st ed. (New York: Harper and Row)

Perron, P. (1987) 'The great crash, the oil price shock and the unit root hypothesis.' Mimeo, Université de Montréal

Phelps, E.S. (1969) 'Introduction: the new microeconomics in employment and inflation theory.' In E.S. Phelps et al., *The Microeconomic Foundations of Inflation and Employment Theory* (London: Macmillan)

— (1972) *Inflation Policy and Unemployment Theory* (New York: Norton)

Phelps, E.S. et al. (1969) *The Microeconomic Foundations of Inflation and Employment Theory* (London: Macmillan)

Phlips, L. (1978) 'The demand for leisure and money.' *Econometrica* 46, 1025–43

Rymes, T.K. (1979) 'Money, efficiency, and knowledge.' This JOURNAL 12, 575–89

Samuelson, P.A. (1958) 'An exact consumption-loan model of interest with or without the social contrivance of money.' *Journal of Political Economy* 66, 467–82

Sargent, T.J. (1984) 'Autoregressions, expectations, and advice.' *American Economic Review* 74, papers and proceedings, 408–15

Sargent, T.J. and N. Wallace (1982) 'The real bills doctrine and the quantity theory: a reconsideration.' *Journal of Political Economy* 90, 1212–36

Stigler, G.C. (1961) 'The economics of information.' *Journal of Political Economy* 69, 213–25

Svensson, L.E.O. (1985) 'Money and asset prices in a cash-in-advance economy.' *Journal of Political Economy* 93, 919–44

Tobin, J. (1956) 'The interest elasticity of the transactions demand for cash.' *Review of Economics and Statistics* 38, 241–7

Tsiang, S.C. (1966) 'Walras' law, Say's law and liquidity preference in general equilibrium theory.' *International Economic Review* 7, 329–45

Wallace, N. (1981) 'A Modigliani-Miller theorem for open-market operations.' *American Economic Review* 71, 267–74

— (1988) 'A suggestion for oversimplifying the theory of money.' *Conference Papers*, supplement to the *Economic Journal* 98, 25–36

Weinrobe, M.D. (1972) 'A simple model of the precautionary demand for money.' *Southern Economic Journal* 39, 11–18

Wicksell, K. (1906) *Lectures on Political Economy* vol. 2 (tr. 1935 E. Claassen) (London: Routledge and Kegan Paul)

15 What remains of the case for flexible exchange rates?

Introduction

Any economist who writes on macroeconomic policy has to worry about international monetary relations. I have always found arguments about optimal currency areas and the like to be somewhat other-worldly. I was exposed to Friedman's 'Case for Flexible Exchange Rates' (1953) at a very early stage in my training, probably as an undergraduate, and I have always found the basic political argument he made there utterly convincing. Monetary policy does have an irreducible political element to it, so the boundary of the best currency area is that to which the authority of a single political authority reaches. In the world as it is, that is the border of the nation state, and to try to push a single currency further than that, or even to peg exchange rates between single national currencies, is to ask for trouble.

I claim no originality for this position, but it is one that seems to require continual defence, and I have expounded it in a number of places (for example, 40, D34, D44, D54, D56, D74). This essay, delivered as a lecture to the Pakistan Society of Development Economists in January 1988, is representative of the way I have gone about putting the case. I hope that Adam Smith will forgive me for forgetting the need for police in order to enforce justice. (See p. 429.)

Reference

Friedman, M. (1953), 'The Case for Flexible Exchange Rates', in *Essays in Positive Economics*, Chicago: University of Chicago Press.

The Pakistan Development Review
Vol. XXVII, No. 4 Part I (Winter 1988)

Invited Lecture

What Remains of the Case for Flexible Exchange Rates?

DAVID P. LAIDLER*

1. INTRODUCTION

In the 1950s and 1960s, there was much support among academic economists for abandoning the Bretton Woods System in favour of a system of flexible exchange rates. Such proposals had their opponents, of course, some of whom, for example Robert Triffin (1960), believed that, if anything, the Bretton Woods System granted too much, rather than too little, scope to individual national governments to vary their exchange rates. Nevertheless, at that time, the weight of professional opinion was against them, and when exchange rate flexibility was adopted in the 1970s, economists by and large welcomed it. This change in policy regime was not, however, the outcome of reforms undertaken in the light of academic arguments; although these did have some influence in some places, not least the United Kingdom.[1] Nevertheless, the single most important factor leading to the demise of the Bretton Woods System was not the acceptance of any academic arguments about how to make the international monetary system function more smoothly. It was something much more down to earth, namely the unwillingness of certain governments, notably that of West Germany, to accept the balance of payments and hence domestic inflationary consequences of United States fiscal and monetary policies associated with the Vietnam War.

Though the introduction of flexible rates was widely expected to usher in a period of international monetary stability, the fact is that the system was not introduced in auspicious circumstances. It was not created by careful design, but as

*The author is Professor of Economics, University of Western Ontario, Canada. This paper was written during his tenure of an appointment as Faculty of Social Science Research Professor during the academic year 1988-89. He is grateful to the University of Western Ontario for making this position available to him. Russell Boyer has kindly provided comments on an earlier draft of this paper.

[1] There, in his 1972 budget speech the Chancellor of the Exchequer Mr Anthony Barber explicitly committed himself to allowing the sterling to float should balance of payments problems look like interfering with the experiment in generating demand led growth he was then setting in motion. A fuller account of this episode is given in Laidler (1976).

an *ad hoc* response to pre-existing instability, which a fixed rate system had failed to discipline and with which it was incapable of coping. It is not surprising, therefore, particularly if we give ourselves the benefit of a little hindsight, that experience with flexible rates has proved something of a disappointment to many of their advocates. Even if we allow for the difficult circumstances in which the system was introduced, however, we must still recognize that exchange rates have, from the very outset, moved around far more than shifts in relative domestic price levels could possibly justify. There is still room to argue that the exchange rate system has simply amplified disturbances originating elsewhere, rather than being in and of itself a source of instability, but there can be no denying that such amplification has nevertheless in and of itself created enormous difficulties. For example, fluctuations in the international value of the dollar in all likelihood had their origins in the conduct of United States fiscal and monetary policies, rather than in any instability inherent in international financial markets, but that has been small comfort to countries who have had to cope with the effects of such fluctuations on the real value of their international indebtedness.

The exchange rate regime may well be the messenger who brings bad news, rather than the cause of that news, but it has nevertheless turned out to be an extremely tactless messenger, small wonder, then, that there is by now considerable disillusionment with flexible exchange rates, and that the system has become something of a minority taste among practical politicians and bureaucrats. The European Monetary System has been far more successful than its opponents originally expected precisely because European politicians, seeing advantages in exchange rate stability which they had earlier failed to appreciate, are willing to put its maintenance high on their policy agenda. On a wider scale, participants in Economic Summit after Economic Summit regularly pay lip service to the merits of greater exchange rate stability, and may, as did the Europeans, in due course begin to match their words with policy actions.

Perhaps then, if the world does move away from exchange rate flexibility in the next few years, that will have as much to do with practical matters and as little to do with academic fashion as did its adoption in the first place. But the academic debate has not stood still in the last two decades, and here too the case for exchange rate flexibility has not fared well. Many of the older elements in that case are now in disrepute, and a whole array of new considerations arising from recent developments in pure monetary theory appear to cast doubt on the fundamental viability of such a system. If the academic defenders of fixed exchange rates looked like a rather old fashioned minority in the 1960s, then so perhaps now do the academic defenders of exchange rate flexibility. In this lecture it is my purpose to outline these developments in academic opinion. I shall discuss, in turn, traditional elements in the fixed versus flexible exchange rate debate, the idea of "currency substitution" which lies at the heart of its modern version, and the relevance of the so-called "legal restrictions" approach to monetary theory. Finally, and at the risk of myself appearing a little old fashioned, I shall suggest that there is, after all, still something to be said for exchange rate flexibility.

2. TRADITIONAL ARGUMENTS

It has long been recognized that, as far as pure economic theory is concerned, the best monetary system would involve the use of a single currency. The argument here is no less valid for being straightforward. It may be cast in terms of a simple, and well known, *reductio ad absurdam.* If the use of separate currencies whose relative prices can fluctuate is the best form of monetary arrangement among nations which trade with one another, why is it not also the best arrangement among regions of the same nation; among towns of the same region; among sections of the same town; among streets of the same section; or among individuals living on the same street? It is when this last question is put that the nature of the argument becomes clear. The very idea of transactions among individuals using as many monies as individuals is ridiculous. The whole point of the existence of money is to facilitate exchange, to overcome the well-known difficulties of barter, and to that end a single unit of account and means of exchange which all parties to a system of exchange may use is surely of the essence.

A single unit of account economises on record keeping and communications costs associated with trade; a single means of exchange economises on the search costs that would, in its absence, be incurred in finding willing partners with whom to engage in barter; and further cost savings may be realised by using the means of exchange as a unit of account, hence reducing by half the number of relative prices in the economy. Furthermore, a "nation" is a political entity with no self-evident significance for economics. As far as pure economic theory is concerned, trade is trade, and that which happens to take place across political boundaries is no different from any other kind. Computational and transactions costs are smaller the smaller the number of separate currencies involved in mediating trade, regardless of whether it is domestic, international, or a mixture of the two. It follows, then, as was asserted at the outset, that, from the point of view of economic efficiency, the best monetary arrangement for a world-wide economy is a single currency.

Now a single world currency is too much to expect, but the argument just presented suggests that it behoves those responsible for designing international monetary arrangements to approximate this ideal as closely as possible; and it is evident that a system of national currencies freely convertible as fixed exchange rates is a closer approximation than an otherwise similar system in which exchange rates are flexible, and hence subject to variation. To be sure foreign exchange transactions are not costless even at fixed rates of exchange, but when the rates in question are indeed fixed, a potentially important source of uncertainty to whose reduction real resources would otherwise be devoted is removed. Only if the uncertainty associated with flexible exchange rates was entirely a reflection of problems which would manifest themselves elsewhere under fixed rates would this argument be invalid. The tendency of flexible rate systems to amplify certain disturbances alluded to above, and to be discussed again later, makes this defence of exchange rate flexibility a dubious one, to say the least, and I do not wish to rely on it here.

Now the logic of the foregoing arguments is indisputable. Hence any case that might be made for flexible exchange rates must either rest on some assumptions about market frictions that are not normally made in fundamental discussions of the advantages of monetary exchange, or have an important non-economic component to it. In fact both elements were present in traditional arguments for flexible exchange rates. In particular there was always, and of necessity, a strong political undertone to them, stemming from the simple fact that they took as their starting point a world economy made up of nations.[2] To recognize the existence of these political entities in a debate about an apparently economic issue is to introduce extra-economic considerations into that debate from the outset, because, as we have already noted, the nation is not an economic concept. Furthermore, traditional arguments for flexible exchange rates all begin, more often implicitly than explicitly, by denying that economic activity co-ordinated by monetary exchange functions "as if" the economy was entirely made up of a system of interlinked perfectly competitive markets. To assume the contrary is also to assume the relevance of that famous theorem concerning the Pareto optimality of competitive equilibrium, and hence (if one accepts the Pareto criterion as laying down appropriate standards for the conduct of policy) to assume as well that whatever the *political* role of government in the organization of the nation state, it has no *economic* role.

Those departures of real world economies from the *textbook* competitive ideal, which provide an essential part of the case for flexible rates, are well understood. They come into view the moment one considers the institutional arrangements required to render a competitive economy a viable form of economic organization in anything resembling the real world. For voluntary exchange to take place, there must exist well defined property rights that can be exchanged, a rule of law which ensures that such rights cannot be transferred by the application of physical force or deception, and so on. At the very minimum, then, a competitive economy requires the support of a so-called "night-watchman state". Furthermore, if there exists more than one such state in the world, the means of ensuring that property rights cannot be violated by outside invaders must also be put in place in each of them. The

[2] The political element in the case was, more often than not, left implicit. It is worth emphasising, therefore that Milton Friedman's famous 1953 essay on this topic paid careful and explicit attention to it.

competitive model either ignores these problems altogether, or assumes that they are solved without encroaching upon the economy's endowment of productive resources. Even a night-watchman state, however, would in fact use up resources with an opportunity cost in the market economy which it supports, resources which must be provided from within the system. In short, as Adam Smith knew very well, the state can only provide "Justice and Arms" if it has command over "Revenue".[3]

In levying taxes, the state cannot avoid questions about the ethics of distribution. There are principles which enable these questions to be settled, but choices nevertheless have to be made of the principles themselves. A tax system designed according to the "benefit" principle will not be the same as one based on "ability to pay" criteria, and within these broad categories there is enormous scope for detailed variations among alternative schemes. And none of this is to mention all those other economic problems which require the state's attention, and which provide staple topics of that branch of our discipline known as Public Finance – public goods, externalities which cannot be dealt with by tinkering with the nature of property rights, the weighting and representation of the interests of future generations, etc. Considerations such as these imply that, while a minimal state is all that is absolutely necessary to any form of economic organization remotely resembling the textbook competitive model, something considerably more than that is both conceivable, intellectually defensible, and, crucially, likely to be encountered in practice.

Economic analysis postulates that agents are self interested, and it should also postulate that they carry that self-interestedness into their political activities as well. There is no analogue in political science, however, to the economist's competitive model which deals with a uniquely best design for a set of social mechanisms guaranteed to convert the pursuit of individual self-interest into the creation of some collective good. In the world of nation states, which is the only one in which it makes sense to discuss international monetary arrangements in the first place, there obviously exist different political systems (even within the western liberal tradition, which hardly exhausts the possibilities). In the absence of any criterion to select the "best" solution to such problems, these systems in turn are likely to mediate the distributional conflicts which must arise over the design of public policy in different ways. It is therefore sensible to put some premium on accommodating differences among national policies when designing the institutional framework of international relations; and it is precisely at this point that the principles of the Classical theory of public finance, which do not usually loom large in discussions of international monetary arrangements, turn out to be quite basic to one of the few elements in the traditional case for flexible exchange rates which still retains validity in the light of modern macroeconomic theory.

[3] The reference here is, of course, to Adam Smith's celebrated "Glasgow lectures" of 1763.

Those principles note that seignorage is a potential source of revenue to any government, and hence tell us that the question of how much, if any, revenue should be raised from the inflation tax ought not to be settled in isolation from the design of the tax-expenditure system as a whole. However, different political systems are likely to yield different choices about tax-expenditure systems, and hence about inflation.[4] Such different choices in turn can only be accommodated within an international monetary system which permits exchange rates to move in order to reconcile them. This is not to deny that a case can be mounted to the effect that, for a particular country, it might be unwise to choose an inflation rate different from that ruling elsewhere, or even to deny that the citizens of such a country might, through their political processes, choose to give up inflation as a flexible source of government revenue by adopting a fixed exchange rate on the currency of some other country. It is, however, to argue that, so long as the design of the tax-expenditure system is a matter of legitimate political concern within a nation state, so must be the choice of the inflation rate, and this argument represents a valid element in the traditional case for maintaining exchange rate flexibility.

Very few economists would argue that the need for the minimal institutions of the night-watchman state is the only departure of real world economies from the textbook competitive ideal that we need to take notice of. As was noted earlier, various frictions, usually assumed away in discussions of the fundamentals of monetary theory, have an important place in the traditional case for flexible exchange rates. The frictions in question are those which provide the subject matter of short-run macroeconomics. Price and wage stickiness, and/or information problems, are of the essence in macroeconomic models in the "Keynesian" tradition, whose policy applications take it for granted that some, or all, of such problems characterize actual economies and require government action to offset their consequences. When such short-run analysis is applied to open economies, an array of arguments about the merits of flexible exchange rates naturally emerge, and indeed they played a larger role in the traditional case in favour of exchange rate flexibility than those having to do with optimal taxation. All of the arguments in question are nowadays controversial, and, in my view, some of them are, indeed always were, downright dangerous.

The most dangerous argument of all at one time played a central role in the case for flexible exchange rates. It starts from the simple fact, already noted, that such a system permits individual nations to choose their own inflation rates through their political processes. I have argued that, *as far as the design of tax-expenditure systems is concerned,* this is a virtue of flexible rates, but the matter has, more often in the past than nowadays, been carried much further than that. If one believes that the unemployment rate is a legitimate target of macroeconomic policy, and crucially,

[4]Marty (1976) presents a pioneering analysis of inflation in the context of the theory of optimal taxation.

if one also believes, as most economists did in the 1960s, that it varies systematically with the rate of inflation, then it follows at once that the authorities are faced with a policy menu in which inflation and unemployment may be traded off against one another. If different nations' political processes, for good or bad reasons, result in different combinations of inflation and unemployment being selected, then exchange rate flexibility is required to reconcile those choices internationally.

The flaw in this argument for exchange rate flexibility was fully exposed by Sumner (1976) and is by now widely recognized. It lies in the idea that the inflation-unemployment trade-off, the "Phillips curve", is a permanent component of the economy's structure. It is now twenty years since Phelps (1967) and Friedman (1968) pointed out that, if expectations about inflation respond to experience, and tend to catch up to reality, then this trade-off will be at best a temporary phenomenon; and it is more than ten years since Sargent and Wallace (1976) building on the seminal work of Lucas (1972), showed that even a temporary trade-off would vanish if economic agents came rationally to anticipate the conduct of macro-stabilization policy. If there are no gains to be made on the unemployment front, though, from varying the inflation rate, there is no benefit along such lines to be had from maintaining an appropriate exchange rate regime. One very important component of the case for flexible exchange rates, as it used to be presented, no longer stands.

One other aspect of the traditional case for maintaining exchange rate flexibility, stemming from concerns about unemployment as a macro-policy goal nevertheless remains, but, as I shall argue, its strength depends upon certain empirical judgements, rather than on the logic of any economic model. It rests upon the observation (whose validity is by no means universally accepted) that money wages and output prices are much more costly to change, and hence slow to move in the face of shocks, than is a market determined exchange rate.[5] The latter is said to be, to use Hicksian terminology, a "flex-price", while the former are judged to include a significant proportion of "fix-prices". If we accept this proposition, even if only for the sake of argument, it is easy to show that an open economy will respond to various shocks in different ways, depending upon the exchange rate regime it has adopted. In particular, the susceptibility of unemployment to real shocks will be diminished, and to monetary shocks enhanced, by a flexible exchange rate.

Consider the impact of some real shock – a foreign taste or technology change for example – that renders a country's exports less marketable. Regardless of the exchange rate regime, domestic real income, and particularly the real incomes of factors employed in export industries, must be reduced. Under a fixed exchange rate regime, this must involve a fall (certainly relative to where they would have been, and perhaps absolutely) in money wages and in some prices too. If these are

[5] Thus new-classical analysis in the spirit of Lucas and Sargent and Wallace denies the relevance of such rigidities.

sticky, the adjustment process might be accompanied by transitional, but not necessarily trivial, unemployment. Under a flexible exchange rate some at least of the burden of adjustment will be thrown into the foreign exchange market, and real incomes will be reduced by the relatively painless mechanism of an exchange rate depreciation. Two caveats, however, must immediately be offered here. First, it cannot be claimed that all adjustment will be thrown onto the exchange rate; real shocks usually require a change in the structure of domestic relative wages and prices and these may prove difficult even under flexible rates. Second, the argument hinges crucially upon rigidities being in *money* wages. In an economy characterized by *real* wage rigidity, the response of money wages to exchange rate changes is to move to eliminate their real effects. Such an economy would be thrown into a vicious circle of inflation and depreciation if it attempted to adjust to a negative real shock by varying its exchange rate, and hence would be better off maintaining a fixed rate. Here though, if real wage resistance persisted, it would be the unemployment rate which would have to bear the brunt of any adjustment.

Even if these last two qualifications to the argument are judged relatively unimportant, and flexible exchange rates are regarded as helpful in dealing with the impact of real shocks on an economy characterized by money wage and price stickiness, it must also be recognized that the very characteristics that are helpful in this context create problems in the face of a monetary shock. The exchange-rate "overshooting" effects which Dornbusch (1976) analysed arise from precisely the same differential in speeds of adjustment of the exchange rate and domestic money prices which renders a flexible exchange rate so helpful in the case of a real shock. The argument is usually cast in terms of a country whose monetary authorities cut back on the rate of monetary expansion in order to slow their inflation rate. Such a country will, under flexible exchange rates (and capital mobility) see its currency appreciate in anticipation of the lower domestic inflation that such a policy will generate, particularly since the initial impact of monetary tightening on domestic interest rates will be to drive them up relative to those ruling abroad. As a result, export and import competing industries, hampered by an inability to adjust money wages to cope with this premature appreciation, will find themselves at a temporary, but not necessarily unimportant competitive disadvantage during the transition to a new long run equilibrium. They would not encounter such a disadvantage under a fixed exchange rate.[6]

[6] Note that the case of "overshooting" proper, in which the exchange rate moves immediately to a value beyond its ultimate equilibrium value is a special case which may, but need not necessarily, arise in the case of wage and price stickiness. However, the tendency for the exchange rate to move ahead of wages and prices as all three adjust to a new equilibrium is a more general phenomenon, and always creates the kind of short-term, but not necessarily trivial, competitive problems referred to here.

Now to put the overshooting argument in this way can easily leave the impression that such unfortunate consequences of wage and price stickiness can be avoided if only the domestic authorities refrain from inflicting shocks on their own economy. However, this impression is misleading. The crucial factor which sets in motion overshooting effects is a change in the relative degrees of monetary tightness ruling at home and abroad. Such a change can surely arise from domestic policies, but it can also be instigated abroad. Thus an *easing* of monetary policy abroad, associated with an expected speedup of foreign inflation, will have exactly the same effects as a similar degree of *tightening* of domestic policy. Thus, this analysis of "exchange rate overshooting" provides a formal basis for the observation, made earlier, that a system of flexible exchange rates tends to amplify the effects of certain shocks, now as we may more precisely say, monetary shocks; or, to put the same point another way, it demonstrates that the alleged capacity of a flexible rate system to insulate the home economy from foreign shocks is at best limited to the long run effects of monetary shocks and the short run effects of real shocks. Such a regime can do nothing about the long-run consequences of real changes in tastes and technology, while it actually makes some of the short run effects of foreign monetary instability worse.

Now one could go into considerably more detail about the traditional case for flexible exchange rates than I have in the last few pages, but my purpose has not been to produce a detailed survey of what are, after all, well known arguments, but simply to remind the reader of their general nature. When all is said and done, the traditional case for flexible exchange rates amounts to the following: a nation which wishes to have control over its own inflation rate must operate a flexible exchange rate. If it does so, it might also benefit from an enhanced ability to adjust more (though not perfectly) smoothly to real shocks, although this must be traded off against the possibility that monetary shocks will have their temporary real effects enhanced. Whether these latter considerations contribute or detract from the case for flexible rates must depend upon a judgement about the likely relative frequency of real and monetary shocks, about the degree of wage-price stickiness that characterizes the economy, and about the extent to which the stickiness in question is of money rather than real wages and prices.

If there were no more to the debate about exchange rate regimes than this, it would hardly have been worthwhile to write this lecture. However, in recent years, certain new ideals have entered the literature of monetary economics, have been applied to questions concerning the international monetary system, and do, I believe, lead to certain fresh insights into the old debate about flexible exchange rates. Central to these ideas, which have had the label "New Monetary Economics" attached to them, is the notion of "currency substitution", and it is to this topic that I now turn.

CURRENCY SUBSTITUTION

The notion of currency substitution originated in an unpublished 1973 paper by Russell S. Boyer entitled "Nickels and Dimes", and the arguments which he presented there remain the most useful in explaining its fundamental characteristics.[7] Boyer imagined a simple closed economy in which trade was mediated by monetary exchange, and noted that, according to usual neoclassical maximising principles, there would exist in that economy a well defined demand for a stock of real money balances. He went on to point out, again quite conventionally, that given a certain stock of nominal fiat money, the price of goods in terms of that money would be determined by the interaction of the nominal money supply with the above-mentioned demand for real balances.

At this point, however, Boyer posed a deceptively simple question: namely, what would happen if there existed in this economy two, instead of one, forms of fiat money, called, as the title of his paper suggests, nickels and dimes respectively? Clearly, the demand for real balances would not be affected by this change, so that, given exogenously fixed nominal quantities of the two monies, and, utterly crucially, *with a fixed relative price between them,* the nominal money stock would be determined interchangeably in units of one or the other. The price level too would then be determined in units of both monies. What, however, Boyer went on to ask, would determine the relative price ruling between the two fiat monies, which has to be fixed for the above argument to go through? In the simple economy which he imagined, the answer was: "Nothing". Any price of nickels in terms of dimes between zero and infinity would be equally compatible with overall equilibrium between the supply and demand for money.

Boyer's analysis must have seemed to readers in the early 1970s to be quite other-worldly but it turns out to be an extremely useful starting point for a search for a deeper understanding of the issues involved in the debate about flexible exchange rates than is to be had from the conventional arguments outlined earlier in this lecture. As I have already noted, a nation is a political, not an economic, entity, so it does no violence to Boyer's analysis to think of his closed economy as consisting of two nations, each with a domestic fiat money, called, shall we say "dollars" and "yen". If we recast the vocabulary of his analysis in this way, we do not change its logical properties. However, we now see that Boyer's model predicts that, under a flexible regime, the exchange rate between the two currencies, and the price levels of goods in terms of them, are completely indeterminate. The only variables which the model ties down are the world-wide stock of real balances and its distribution

[7] The basic ideas of this paper were incorporated in Boyer (1978), but only became widely known with the publication of Girton and Roper (1981), a paper which explicitly and generously acknowledged Boyer's contribution.

between the two countries. Now one must be careful about how one interprets the significance of these conclusions. Boyer certainly did not intend them to be treated as predictions about the world we live in. Rather he sought to raise questions about what factors, ignored in his model, might nevertheless be at work in the real world to remove, or at least mitigate, the tendency to exchange rate indeterminacy that he had uncovered.

The most obvious possibility here is the intervention in the foreign exchange market which, in the real world, monetary authorities do indeed undertake. We have already seen that, with the relative price of two nominal monies pegged, Boyer's framework becomes an almost trivially simple, not to say conventional, neoclassical model of price level determination. The real world analogue of such pegging in his model is of course a fixed exchange rate regime, so one way of reading his results is as a warning that a fundamental indeterminacy is inherent flexible rates but not under a fixed exchange rate system. Interpreted this way, Boyer's analysis of currency substitution provides a new component for the case against exchange rate flexibility. The indeterminacy in question here, be it noted, is in the static equilibrium value of the exchange rate, but an argument about the dynamic properties of the exchange market may be mounted which tends to remove this indeterminacy in a rather special way, as we shall now see.

Recall that the demand for any asset depends, among other things, upon its own rate of return relative to that yielded by close substitutes, and recall too that, in the basic currency substitution model, nickels and dimes (dollars and yen) are perfect substitutes for each other. Suppose we start off at some historically given relative price between the two monies, and assume that, once more as a result of unanalysed past events, the price levels in terms of each of them stand at their equilibrium levels. Then suppose we set in motion a version of a quite standard stability experiment. Specifically, let us disturb the initial equilibrium by forcing some exogenous change on the relative price of the two monies while leaving their prices in terms of goods unchanged, (though free to move). Clearly, to restore the initial equilibrium, one money would have to appreciate and the other depreciate. If agents came to expect that to happen, however, they would also change their estimates of the yields to be earned by holding the two monies. *Given perfect substitutability between them,* there would be an immediate and complete flight from the depreciating to the appreciating money, and the model would go to a solution in which one nominal money was quite valueless. In short, if we begin with two monies, and do not peg the exchange rate between them (thereby artificially creating one money) we create a world in which the slightest disturbance to any equilibrium in which two monies exist will immediately take us to a single money equilibrium. Of the infinite array of static equilibrium solutions to Boyer's model, then, only two corner solutions turn out to be dynamically stable. If we take this result seriously, then, the choice of exchange rate regime seems to boil down to one between pegged rates or a single currency for the international economy.

It would, however, be premature to stop at this point, because there are other ways of modifying Boyer's analysis than those so far taken.[8] Thus, we could note that, the above-mentioned implications of Boyer's analysis notwithstanding, we do encounter in the real world cases of exchange rate flexibility among fiat monies in which the currencies in question continue to co-exist despite differences, and variations in the differences, among their own rates of return. From the point of view of the *mechanics* of the Boyer model, the accommodation of this observation is easy to achieve and quite uncontroversial. All that is required is the postulate that the two currencies be less than perfect substitutes for one another, that the elasticities of demand for each them with respect to the rate of return differential ruling between them be less than infinite. This modification is enough to produce separate real demands for the two currencies and therefore, for given nominal quantities of the two, a determinate exchange rate between them. It is, in short, sufficient to convert Boyer's model into a simple version of the conventional two-country framewrok for studying flexible exchange rates which, with various further extensions, produces all of the conventional results outlined in the first substantive section of this paper. The mechanics here may be uncontroversial, but there is scope for a great deal of debate about the source of the imperfect substitutability that underlies those mechanics, debate which is of considerable relevance to questions about the desirability of flexible exchange rates.

LEGAL RESTRICTIONS

Perhaps the most radical development in monetary theory in recent years has

[8] Although it is of more historical than current interest, it is worth noting explicitly that we could replace Boyer's (realistic for the late twentieth century) assumption of competing fiat monies with one (extremely relevant to the economic history of the 19th century and earlier) of competing commodity monies. In this case, considerations of moving the commodities in question between their monetary and non-monetary uses, and of altering their overall quantities by current production enter to complicate matters. Even so, it is worth noting that Gresham's law, which states that, *with their relative mint price fixed,* the bad (overvalued relative to its cost of production or value in some other non-monetary use) metal will drive out the good, so that a bimetallic system will degenerate to monometalism, is closely related to the proposition that substitution between fiat currencies will, *when their relative price is not fixed* lead to one of them becoming dominant. I do not have space in the paper to deal with these matters, but the reader who is interested in following them up will find that the extensive late 19th–early 20th century literature dealing with the determination of exchange rates between gold and silver standard countries, and the properties of fixed-mint-price gold and silver bimetallism has analysed them thoroughly. Alfred Marshall's 1887-88 evidence to the Gold and Silver Commission, and Chapter VII of Irving Fisher's (1911) *Purchasing Power of Money* between them provide an admirable survey of the principle results achieved there.

been what Hall (1982) has called "the New Monetary Economics", henceforth to be referred to as NME, whose most visible exponents are Thomas J. Sargent and Neil Wallace (1982) and their associates. They take the co-existence of a non-(or low-) interest bearing asset such as money with other income earning securities to be a key fact that monetary theory must deal with, and they offer two basic explanations of the phenomenon. In the case of money which itself represents a claim, either on some real resource or income stream, current or deferred, its desirability is said to stem from the desirability of this "backing". This strand in the NME harks back to the turn of the century anti-quantity-theory analysis of J. Lawrence Laughlin, although the stress which Sargent and Wallace lay on the viability of the fiscal regime as a determinant of the quality of money's backing gives an original twist to their treatment of this idea.[9]

Even so, questions of the relevance of money's backing do not arise in the case of pure fiat money. Here the NME, particularly as articulated by Wallace (1988), attributes the existence of a distinct demand for money to the existence of "legal restrictions" imposed by government on the otherwise voluntary market activity of individuals. Commercial banks are required to hold central bank money as a reserve against their own liabilities; legal tender laws force agents to transact in terms of central bank money, or commercial bank liabilities directly convertible into it; tax regulations specify that liabilities to the government may only be discharged by transferring these assets; and so on. Such restrictions exist, so it is suggested, in order to enable government to collect revenues through seignorage, and play no role in promoting the economic welfare of individuals. Because governments are at best national in scope, each country has its own regulation-created money for which there exists a distinct, again regulation-created, demand. Thus, the demand for money function as we know it, perhaps the most intensely studied of all empirical relationships is the product, not of any fundamental economic process, but of government intervention in market activity.

If this argument of Wallace is valid, it is of profound significance for our conventional treatment of the flexible versus fixed exchange rates debate. This debate does, after all, concern the desirability of alternative forms of government intervention (or lack thereof) in market transactions involving the use of national monies. The nature, and stability, of the aggregate demand for real balances function contained in the models of national economies we use to address these issues is often crucial to their behaviour. If that function itself is the creation of government intervention in market processes, then it is inappropriate to assume that it is invariant to changes in regulations involving trans-border monetary transactions; economic

[9] See Girton and Roper (1978) for an accessible account of Laughlin's work. Knut Wicksell's (1906) *Lectures . . . (vol. 2.)*, Irving Fisher's (1911) *Purchasing Power of Money*, as well as Ludwig von Mises (1912) *Theory of Money and Credit* all contain rebuttals of it, which are (in my view at least) both effective and still worth reading.

models which do so are at best irrelevant to, and perhaps misleading about, questions concerning the design of the international monetary system; and our best guide to understanding the issues is the "deeper" (so-called) *a priori* analysis of the NME. That analysis, though, as Karekan and Wallace (1978) have explicitly argued, tells us that, in the absence of legal restrictions which, as such things usually do, disturb the Pareto optimality of the economy's equilibrium, we are back in Boyer's world of perfect currency substitution whose static properties yield indeterminate equilibrium exchange rates, and whose dynamics produce a single dominant currency.

Now I find the "legal restrictions" version of the NME a hard doctrine to swallow. It is, as Wallace has suggested, an "oversimplification", and I would add, as he would not, a misleading one. Nevertheless, one must be careful in criticising it. Its weakness is not that the factors upon which it focusses are irrelevant in the monetary systems which we encounter in the real world. Rather it is that the approach focusses on them alone, to the exclusion of other relevant matters. Just as the "backing" theory of the value of money converts one relevant influence on money's current desirability – in this instance its expected future command over utility yielding resources – into the sole relevant influence, so too does the legal restrictions hypothesis. No one could, or should, deny that reserve requirements affect the demand for central bank liabilities, or that laws forbidding domestic residents to hold bank accounts denominated in anything other than domestic currency affect the demand for bank deposits; nor should they deny that changes in such regulations have the potential to shift empirically estimated demand for money functions. To the extent that the NME has reminded economists who had forgotten that the prevailing legal framework affects the demand for money function, so that the "Lucas critique" is as potentially relevant there as anywhere else, it is valuable.[10] To the extent that it treats national laws and regulations as the sole source of demand for distinct national currencies, however, it goes, as I shall now argue, too far.

When applied to questions about the international monetary system, the legal restrictions approach starts by picturing the world economy as an integrated competitive entity, upon various regions of which different monetary regulations are imposed by *dei ex machina* called "governments"; but the actual international economy, and the monetary system which goes with it, did not evolve in this way.[11] To the extent that the history of that economy is important to understanding its current configuration, so too is the contrast here between theory and practice. To put it crudely, theory starts with an integrated world economy but economic history

[10] But I hasten to add that those engaged on empirical work on the demand for money have not neglected the influence of changing regulations on the stability of the relationship, as a glance at Judd and Scadding's well known (1982) survey paper will soon confirm.

[11] See Haberler (1980) for a commentary on the empirical relevance of Karekan and Wallace's application of currency substitution ideas to the fixed versus flexible exchange rate issue which deals in more detail with some of the issues raised here.

tells us that the world economy has evolved, in fits and starts to be sure, from a collection of rather self contained entities towards an integrated whole. Moreover the evolution of monetary institutions was both piecemeal and local. In large measure, the restrictions which interfere with the attainment of the textbook ideal of a-single-money-for-a-single-economy ideal were already there before anything much resembling a single world economy evolved. Moreover the institutional characteristics defined by formally legal restrictions were not usually created by them. The role of law here, as Menger (1892) long ago argued, has more often been to codify practices and obligations which had already evolved as social conventions.

In my view, the real problem facing those seeking to understand the international monetary system and to comment on its appropriate configuration is to understand why the pattern of growing integration among national economies over time has not found a closer parallel in the integration of their monetary systems. The evolution of institutions surrounding the provision and regulation of the means of exchange (and which ought not to be confused with asset markets in general) seems to parallel that of political rather than other economic institutions. To oversimplify the last thirty years or so of history, the world economy (or at least the western world economy) became more integrated as far as trade and goods and services is concerned. However, with the slow decline of United States' political dominance, the world polity became more fragmented. So too did the international monetary system, as the United States Dollar based Bretton Woods System gave way to the current flexible exchange rate regime. A proponent of the legal restrictions approach would presumably put this latter development down to a growing desire on the part of national governments to maintain, and indeed extend control over their seignorage income. As I shall now go on to argue, the reason why monetary developments have mimicked political rather than other economic changes is perhaps deeper than this, lying in the public-good nature of money, and the tendencies to natural monopoly inherent in its provision, factors which the NME ignores.

MONEY AS A PUBLIC GOOD

The NME has one important feature in common with the Monetarist and Keynesian economics which preceded it: whatever the words accompanying its theoretical arguments might say about money's role in mediating market transactions, the theoretical arguments themselves treat money as a store of value pure and simple. Though modern monetary economists, no matter what specific doctrines they might subscribe to, will always in their verbal arguments identify money's means of exchange role as crucial, the logical structure of their models tells a different story altogether. In Keynesian or Monetarist models, just as much as in the more precise constructions of the NME, the individual agent's demand for a stock of money is treated as the demand for an asset pure and simple, and its quantity is derived by considering its private return relative to that on other stores of value. The benefits derived by agents from holding money are thus treated as being purely private in nature. If the services yielded by money are treated like this, however, any government action which impinges upon individual choices about holding money cannot help but appear as an (economically) unwarranted interference with maximizing behaviour. But money *is*, after all, a means of exchange, and a system of monetary exchange *is* in every bit as fundamental to the operation of any economy based on voluntary trade as is a system of well defined and protected property rights. The fact that our conventional models of the demand for money do not take account of this fact do not make it any the less true.

Individual agents cannot each choose their own monetary system; they do have to participate in a common set of arrangements; and it is also true that particular individuals cannot be excluded from using the system once it is in place. The monetary system does appear, therefore, to have the requisite characteristics to be analysed as a "public good".[12] To say that a monetary system is a public good does not mean that the *provision* of a means of exchange should be included automatically in the functions of the "night-watchman" state. The theory of public goods tells us only that the demand for them must be articulated collectively. It does not also say that they must be collectively provided, or that their provision should be regulated. Indeed the literature dealing with the competitive provision of money, usually associated with the names Friedrich von Hayek (1976) and Laurence White (1984), which has much in common with the NME, argues that private sector competitive provision of the economy's means of exchange is quite feasible. To say that a particular solution to a problem is feasible, however, is not to say that it is also the best solution available. As I shall now argue, there are good reasons to suppose that, in the specific case of money, government participation in its supply and control is defensible, and that the imposition of certain legal restrictions on the monetary system, far from being unjustifiable and welfare reducing, are economically desirable.

To begin with, monetary exchange involves agents in surrendering their property rights in utility yielding goods and services for money, in the expectation that the money in question will in due course be accepted as payment for other goods and services, and the acceptability of money is overwhelmingly a matter of social convention rather than law. Nevertheless, part of the problem of ensuring that the property rights which are traded in a market economy are well defined involves clear specification of what acts do and do not constitute their transfer, so that disputes can be settled in a non-arbitrary fashion as and when they arise. A clear legal definition of what action does, or does not, suffice to discharge a debt is of the

[12] See Weldon (1973) for an early and much neglected analysis of money along these lines.

essence here, and legal tender laws offer just that. Those laws do not prevent agents voluntarily contracting to discharge obligations in other ways, but they do prevent one party to a bargain being coerced into such contracts, and they do help define what agreements are and are not enforceable at law in the event of a failure of one party or another to comply with them. Legal tender laws are thus part of the framework which defines property rights and hence help to make voluntary exchange feasible. They play a role similar to that of a government guarantee of weight and fineness stamped on a gold coin in a commodity money system in increasing the informational efficiency of the economy's exchange mechanisms.

Modern work on competitive money, such as that of White, recognizes that a system in which the means of exchange consists mainly of the liabilities (whether notes or deposits) of a competitive banking system requires some primary money to serve as the reserve base of the system. While such a reserve asset could be defined by social convention, it would, as the foregoing arguments suggest, be better if that convention became clearly defined in law. Moreover, in a fiat money world, it is hard to see that the provision of base money would not be a natural monopoly. After all, its primary function is to settle clearing balances among the institutions who provide the public with a means of exchange, and it has been well known since the work of Edgeworth (1888) on "The Mathematical Theory of Banking" that there exist economies of scale in this activity, stemming from the law of large numbers. It is surely uncontroversial that a necessary (though not of course sufficient) condition for a natural monopoly to promote the public rather than the private good, is that it be regulated, or operated directly by, government. A private profit maximising organization that had a monopoly over the provision of primary money would be a seignorage maximizer, aiming to generate a rate of inflation which would drive the nominal interest rate to a level at which the elasticity of demand for real balances was equal to -1. There is no reason whatsoever to believe that the resulting inflation rate would a socially desirable one.[13]

Now the reader will note that to argue, as I do here, that one base money is better than more than one is to present a variation on the theme encapsulated in the *reductio ad absurdam* with which the second section of this paper began. That same reader will also note that to argue that the rate of seignorage generated should be a prime consideration in judging the activities of whatever agent provides that base money is to restate what I have earlier termed the one valid element in the traditional case for flexible exchange rates. However, the discussions of the last few pages have, I believe, done more than merely repeat old arguments. They have also provided those arguments with deeper and more secure foundations. I have argued that money's means of exchange and unit of account functions, unlike the

[13] And this is not to mention that the provider of base money also has a role to play as a lender of last resort.

pure store of value role stressed by modern monetary theory, lend a public character to the services it provides. If this insight is accepted, then it follows that government becomes involved in the provision of money not simply because the inflation tax is a useful source of revenue (though it might be), but because the provision and regulation of the monetary system is a basic function of even the night-watchman state, and that the evolution of the monetary system tends to follow that of political, rather than economic activity, because its maintenance presents problems which cannot by their very nature be dealt with by the decentralized market activities of individual agents.

The implications of the foregoing, somewhat esoteric, arguments for the fixed versus flexible exchange rate debate are easily drawn out. They amount to the proposition that the provision of a monetary system requires the intervention of government. Since effective governments exist at the level of the nation state, rather than of the world as a whole, we should expect to observe a series of national currencies rather than one world money. It would be going too far, however, to build on this observation a case that an international monetary system *must* be based on national monies linked by flexible exchange rates. Monetary nationalism may be a natural and obvious choice for an individual government, but it is not the only one open. The provision of police services is a proper function for local government, but that does not mean that every town and village should organize its own force; and "contracting-out" the provision and regulation of primary money to some other government, either by adopting its currency outright as in the case of one or two countries with the U.S. dollar, or by the more usual adoption of a fixed exchange rate on some other country is a viable option.

If we look at the operation of a fixed exchange rate system as a form of contracting out government services, however, we put debates about the shoice of exchange rate regime in a useful perspective. This point of view first of all enables us to see that, in the absence of some supra-national entity whose legitimate authority is recognized by the nation states of the world, the idea of a single world money will remain just that: an idea. It also forces us to consider the possibility that, just as the extent of the contracting out of services among private parties, firms, local governments, and so on depends upon the ease with which contracts can be enforced, and the degree of trust existing among the parties, so does the viability of arrangements to contract-out the provision of monetary services among nations by way of fixed exchange rates among national currencies. Given the absence of an effective supra-national monetary authority to enforce good behaviour on the international suppliers of primary monies (which are called key currencies when they are provided to an international as opposed to domestic market), it is hard to imagine many governments entering into irrevocable arrangements to fix their exchange rates. If there is to be exchange rate pegging in the real world then, the peg is going to be adjustable, and the less trust there is in the future good behaviour of the authority providing a potential key currency, the more adjustable will it be. A flexible exchange rate is simply the limiting, no contracting out for want of trustworthy suppliers, case of this general tendency.

CONCLUSIONS

One conclusion of this paper is that very little indeed remains of the traditional case for flexible exchange rates. Their alleged capacity for permitting individual countries to exploit an inflation unemployment trade-off, which did so much to make flexible exchange rates attractive in the 1960s, has long since been shown to be non-existent. Though they can help an open economy cope with certain types of real shocks in the presence of money wage and price stickiness, their operation also turns out to amplify the consequences of monetary disturbances elsewhere in the world. Any preference for flexible exchange rates that stems from their insulating properties, then, must hinge upon an empirical judgement about the likely sources and sizes of disturbances in the world and domestic economies, and not upon any general theoretical proposition.

Nevertheless, there is another conclusion to be drawn as well, namely that there exists a strong, though by no means overwhelming, political presumption in favour of a flexible exchange rate regime. To maintain a flexible exchange rate is to retain domestic control over a matter of inherent political importance, namely the conduct of monetary policy, and to move towards exchange rate fixity is to begin to entrust the conduct of such policy to others. Where supranational political bodies which deal with economic policy exist and are respected, and/or where a consensus develops between countries as to what constitute desirable goals, then the "contracting out" of monetary policy becomes feasible. That is why the European Monetary System has proved viable in recent years. It also becomes feasible where there exists trust that a particular country will conduct its policy in a responsible fashion. That is why the international gold exchange standard (based on the pound sterling) flourished before the First World War, and the Bretton Woods System (based on the U.S. dollar) worked so well after the Second. However, in the absence of trust among nations in the responsibility with which their monetary policies will be conducted, fixed exchange rates are impossible. It is in this observation that the remaining, but still considerable, strength of the case for flexible exchange rates resides.

REFERENCES

Boyer, R. S. (1973). "Nickels and Dimes". Board of Governors, Federal Reserve System. (Mimeographed)

Boyer, R. S. (1978). "Currency Mobility and Balance of Payments Adjustment".

In B. H. Putnam and D. S. Wilford (eds.), *The Monetary Approach to International Adjustment.* New York: Praeger.

Dornbusch, R. (1976). "Expectations and Exchange Rate Dynamics". *Journal of Political Economy.* Vol. 84. (Dec.). pp. 1161–1176.

Edgeworth, F. Y. (1888). "Mathematical Theory of Banking". *Journal of the Royal Statistical Society.*

Fisher, I. (1911). *The Purchasing Power of Money.* New York: Macmillan.

Friedman, M. (1968). "The Role of Monetary Policy". *American Economic Review.*

Girton, L. and D. Roper (1978). "J. Laurence Laughlin and the Quantity of Theory of Money". *Journal of Political Economy.* Vol. 86. (Aug.). pp. 599–626.

Girton, L. and D. Roper (1981). "Theory and Implication of Currency Substitution". *Journal of Money Credit and Banking.* Vol. 13 (Feb.). pp. 12–30.

Haberler, G. (1980). "Flexible Exchange Rate Theories and Controversies Once Again". In J. S. Chipman and C. Kindelberger (eds.), *Flexible Exchange Rates and the Balance of Payments – Essays in Memory of Egon Sohmen.* Amsterdam: North Holland.

Hall, R. (1982). "Monetary Trends in the United States and the United Kingdom – A Review from the Perspective of the New Monetary Economics". *Journal of Economic Literature.* Vol. 20 (Dec.). pp. 1552–1555.

Hayek, von F. A. (1976). *Denationalising Money.* London: IEA.

Judd, J. P. and J. I. Scadding (1982). "The Search for a Stable Money Demand Function". *Journal of Economic Literature.* Vol. 20 (Sept.). pp. 983–1023.

Karekan, J. and N. Wallace (1978). "International Monetary Reform, the Feasible Alternatives". *FRB of Minneapolis Quarterly Review.* (Summer). pp. 2–7.

Laidler, D. (1976). "Inflation in Britain – A Monetarist Perspective". *American Economic Review.* Vol. 66 (Sept.). pp. 485–500.

Lucas, R. E. Jr. (1972). "Expectations and the Neutrality of Money". *Journal of Economic Theory.* Vol. 4 pp. 103–124.

Marshall, A. (1926). *Official Papers of Alfred Marshall.* In J. M. Keynes (ed.). London.

Marty, A. (1976). "Real Cash Balances and the Optimal Tax Structure". In M. J. Artis and A. R. Nobay (eds.), *Essays in Economic Analysis.* Cambridge: Cambridge University Press.

Menger, C. (1892). "On the Origin of Money". *Economic Journal.* Vol. 2 (June). pp. 239–255.

Mises, von L. (1912). *The Theory of Money and Credit* (2nd 1924 ed. tr H. E. Batson London, 1934. Reprinted New Haven, Yale University Press, 1953).

Phelps, E. S. (1967). "Phillips Curves, Expectations of Inflation and Optimal Unemployment Over Time". *Economica.* NS 34 (Aug.). pp. 254–281.

Sargent, T. J. and N. Wallace (1976). "Rational Expectations and the Theory of

Monetary Policy". *Journal of Monetary Economics.* Vol. 2 (May). pp. 169–183.

Sargent, T. J. and N. Wallace (1982). "The Real Bills Doctrine versus the Quantity Theory: a Reconsideration". *Journal of Political Economy.* Vol. 90 (Dec.). pp. 1212–1236.

Smith, A. (1763). *Lectures on Revenue Justice and Arms (The Glasgow Lectures).*

Sumner, M. (1976). "European Monetary Union and the Control of Europe's Inflation Rate". In J. M. Parkin and G. Zis (eds.), *Inflation in the World Economy.* Manchester: Manchester University Press.

Triffin, R. (1960). *Gold and the Dollar Crisis.* New Haven: Yale University Press.

Wallace, N. (1988). "A Suggestion for Oversimplifying the Theory of Money". *Conference Papers* supplement to the *Economic Journal.* Vol. 98 (March). pp. 28–36.

Weldon, J. C. (1973). "Money as a Public Good". McGill University. (Mimeo).

White, L. H. (1984). *Free Banking in Britain, Theory, Experience and Debate 1800–1845.* Cambridge: Cambridge University Press.

Wicksell, K. (1906). *Lectures on Political Economy.* Vol. 2 (tr. 1935 E. Claassen) London: Routledge and Kegan Paul.

Comments on "What Remains of the Case for Flexible Exchange Rates?"

In an important and influential paper written in 1953, Milton Friedman made the case for flexible exchange rates. Professor Laidler returns to this question in a beautifully-written paper that is well-worth serious study even for economists who are not specialists in monetary theory. The influential work of Dornbusch, Friedman, Lucas, Phelps, Sargent and Wallace is summarized and seen from a unified perspective that includes earlier, more classical work of Smith, Marshall, Edgeworth and Wicksell; as well as more recent and largely unpublished work of Boyer, Sumner and Weldon. However, for me, the nicest aspect of the paper is the broad use it makes of general economic theory, particularly capital theory and the theory of public finance. I would like to cofine this brief comment to these applications.

In his section on *Currency Substitution*, Professor Laidler discusses Boyer's question as to the consequences of more than one kind of fiat money in a given economy. He emphasizes that there is nothing in the model that determines the price ratio between the two kinds of money and that under any parameter shock, "there would be an immediate and complete flight from the depreciating to the appreciating money [and] . . . the choice of exchange rate regime seems to boil down to one between pegged rates or a single currency for the international economy". Here the literature of the early Seventies on the so-called Hahn Problem may have something to offer. In the version of Shell-Stiglitz (1969), for example, there are two capital goods in an otherwise standard Solow-Swan growth model. One has to designate kind of capital good the homogeneous commodity is to be turned into in each period and since this process is assumed to be costless, there is an indeterminacy of portfolio choice if the prices of the two goods are identical. If not, investment in only one kind of capital good is undertaken. The authors then ask, like Boyer and Laidler, whether there are any endogenous forces which will steer the economy towards a balanced growth path in which both assets are produced and held. They emphasize the crucial role of expectations and show how perfect myopic foresight can lock a competitive economy into trajectories in which an asset with a lower marginal product is nevertheless held because of capital gians and the no arbitrage condition. Further work has of Caton, Burmeister, Ross, Shell and others has introduced uncertainty into the model and has also relaxed the assumption of production costs of the two capital goods being identical.

Next, I turn to the insight that "the monetary system does appear . . . to have the requisite characteristics to be analyzed as a *public good"*. Professor Laidler also adds that "it has been known since the work of Edgeworth . . . that there exist economies of scale in this activity [and that] it is surely uncontroversial that a necessary (though not of course sufficient) condition for a natural monopoly to promote the public rather than the private good, is that it be regulated, or operated directly by government". This raises a host of interesting issues which, in my view are worth pursuing in light of recent advances in general equilibrium theory with increasing returns; see Cornet's (1988) introduction for an overview and detailed references. In particular, the recent work on Lindahl-Hotelling equilibria (Khan-Vohra (1987)) shows the viability of an equilibrium concept which considers both the presence of public goods as well as the fact that these public goods are produced under increasing returns to scale. Essentially, the concept uses Hotelling's prescription whereby the production of commodities produced under increasing returns are regulated and marginal costs at these production levels are given to the convex sector to be taken as parameters. If these commodities are also public goods, then one relies on personalized prices as advocated by Wicksell, Lindahl, Allais and Samuelson, to cover the marginal costs of producing these commodities. Of course, as is well understood, there is the "free rider" problem under which individual agents have an incentive to misrepresent their preferences and understate their demand for the public good. Presumably, this is lees acute in the context of the creation of a monetary authority. At any rate, there have been impressive recent advances in the theory of mechanism design and this literature may be relevant here; see Maskin (1985) for a survey. However, even abstaining from these difficulties, it is far from clear whether production should be regulated at marginal cost prices or, as advocated by Boiteaux, at average cost prices. Vohra (1988) has some interesting examples in this connection.

In summary, I learnt a lot from Professor Laidler's paper from thinking, even at this superficial level, on issues raised by him.

M. Ali Khan

The Johns Hopkins University,
USA

REFERENCES

Cornet, B. (ed.) (1988). "General Equilibrium Theory and Increasing Returns". *Journal of Mathematical Economics*. Vol. 17.

Khan, M. Ali and R. Vohra (1987). "On the Existence of Lindahl-Hotelling Equilibria". *Journal of Public Economics*. Vol. 34. pp. 143–158.

Maskin, E. (1985). "The Theory of Implementation in Nash Equilibrium". In L. Hurwicz, D. Schmeidler and H. Sonnenschein (eds.), *Social Goals and Social*

Organization: Essays in Honor of Elisha A. Pazner. New York: Cambridge University Press.

Shell, K. and J. E. Stiglitz (1967). "The Allocation of Investment in a Dynamic Economy". *Quarterly Journal of Economics.* Vol. LXXXI.

Vohra, R. (1988). "Optimal Regulation under Fixed Rules for Income Distribution". *Journal of Economic Theory.* Vol. 45.

Comments on "What Remains of the Case for Flexible Exchange Rates?"

Professor Laidler's paper is thought provoking, timely and has far reaching implications not only to the economies of the developed nations but, more importantly, to the World Monetary System at large. This paper raises some very crucial and important questions regarding the desirability and the effectiveness of the fixed versus flexible exchange rate systems in the present day politico-economic world.

Professor Laidler starts his paper by arguing that an international monetary arrangement with currency unification (or single world currency) promotes economic efficiency and that a fixed exchange rate rather than a flexible exchange rate system is the one largely closer to a world economy with a single currency, and therefore a monetary arrangement with a fixed exchange rate would be economically efficient. He further argued that since it is difficult to achieve, and even more difficult to sustain, a monetary union without political integration, a currency unification and hence a fixed exchange rate would be impracticable if not impossible. Therefore, he finally concluded that the desirability and sustainability of the current flexible exchange rate system "is much more a matter of what is politically feasible than economically desirable". (p. 19).

Professor Laidler's lengthy discussion on his disenchantment with the views proposed by the proponents of the school of "New Monetary Economics (NME)" on the issues of "Currency Substitution" and the "Money as Public Good" are very refreshing, philosophical and have implications which I believe are significant contributions to the literature. My comments are therefore, focused on these two issues.

On the issue of "currency substitution", Professor Laidler noted that under the flexible exchange rate system, if two (or more) international currencies are perfect substitutes, then there is an indeterminacy of exchange rate. In order to solve this possible instability in the exchange rate determination, he proposed that the two currencies be assumed to be less than perfect substitutes. In his paper he, however, did not provide, any explanation as to how the two currencies could be made less than perfect substitute. Tobin (1978), on the other hand suggested, "to throw some sand in the wheels of our excessively efficient international money markets" to introduce imperfections in the substitutability of the currencies. Tobin particularly proposed a uniform proportional tax on all spot rate conversions of the currencies.

This proposal, to a large extent, is expected to eliminate massive short term capital flows and thus allow the basic balance to determine the exchange rate. Although Tobin's *tax proposal* to avoid exchange rate indeterminacy seems simple and attractive, it has also been criticized by Dornbusch (1983) on the grounds that such a proposal may have limited applicability. In particular, Dornbusch (1983) argued that the increase in interest rate in the presence of Tobin's tax would be much higher for a country which is experiencing a current account deficit and it wishes to adopt an interest rate policy to eliminate current account imbalances. Consequently, as Dornbusch (1983), p. 72 notes that such a country would now "suffer the burden of financing the deficit and the Tobin tax".

I agree with Professor Laidler's argument with respect to the *public-good* nature of money and that the role of government should be a factor to take into consideration in the provision and regulation of the monetary system. It is also true that without some "supranational" government a global fixed exchange rate system is impracticable. But when considering the current problems of the international monetary system, we however, observe the dominant role played by the large industrialized countries (specifically, the G7 countries) creating an environment with strong implications for the process of negotiating a monetary regime as well as for the interplay of monetary policies under a given monetary regime. In situations such as this, the economic theory of perfect competition would be inadequate to solve the complex problems of the international monetary system. In fact, as suggested by Hamada (1985), one has to take into account explicitly the "political process of adopting and reforming the international monetary system endogenously". I think it is in this context that Professor Laidler concluded his paper stating the success of a given regime "is much a matter of what is politically feasible than economically desirable."

M. Aynul Hasan

Acadia University,
Canada

REFERENCES

Dornbusch, R. (1983). "Exchange Rate Economics: Where Do We Stand?". In J. Bhandari and B. Putnam (eds.), *Economic Interdependence and Flexible Exchange Rates*. Cambridge, Mass.: MIT Press. pp. 45–83.

Hamada, K. (1985). *The Political Economy of International Monetary Interdependence.* Cambridge, Mass.: MIT Press.

Tobin, J. (1978). "A Proposal for International Monetary Reform". *Cowles Foundation Discussion Paper 506.* New Haven, Conn.: Yale University.

16 The quantity theory is always and everywhere controversial – why?

Introduction

Although this is a collection of essays in monetary economics rather than in the history of economic thought, Mark Blaug persuaded me to include this piece with the simple but true observation that in monetary economics of all areas, the boundaries between current theory and its history are anything but sharply defined. I can claim to have been rather quick off the mark in arguing for a monetary explanation of Britain's inflationary problems in the early 1970s, and though that obviously had a lot to do with my having been trained at Chicago, it was not unrelated to the fact that, when I was an undergraduate, Lionel Robbins made sure that I read Thornton's *Paper Credit* (1802).

Even in the 1970s, I was to some extent conscious that I was refighting an old battle, and as I have gone more deeply into the history of the subject I have become ever more aware of the way in which debates about the quantity theory recur time and again and thrash out the same issues without ever being settled. So an essay that explores the reasons for this should have something to say even to monetary economists with no particular interest in history.

Michael Parkin has told me that he does not recall suggesting the title of this essay, but he did, in a brief conversation beside the water cooler outside the department office at Western.

Reference

Thornton, H. (1802), *An Inquiry into the Nature and Effects of the Paper Credit of Great Britain*, edited by F.A. von Hayek, London: George Allen & Unwin, 1939.

The Quantity Theory is Always and Everywhere Controversial—Why?*

'. . . the "quantity theory" of money . . . seems, like a cat with nine times ninety lives, however many times discredited, never to die.' J.C.R. Dow, *The Management of the British Economy 1945–1960*, p. 308.

DAVID LAIDLER
Department of Economics,
University of Western Ontario,
London, Ontario N6A 5C2
Canada

Controversy about the Quantity Theory has been marked by common themes since the 18th century. These include the definition of money, the relationship between correlation and causation, and the transmission mechanism. Controversy has continued because of the technical difficulty of sorting out the direction of causation running between money and prices, and, on a deeper level, because ideological concerns about the viability of market mechanisms are at stake in the controversy.

I Introduction

Of all the elements in a typical economics syllabus, that dealing with the relationship between money and the general price levels has the longest pedigree. In modern times the issue has been under more or less continuous discussion since the 16th century. Moreover, a particular view of this matter, encapsulated in what is usually called the 'quantity theory of money', has been central to that debate. Though the name did not become current until the late 19th century (it is an abbreviation of some such phrase as 'the quantity of money theory of the purchasing power of money') rudiments of the analysis to which it refers occur in the writings of Jean Bodin on the European inflation that followed the Spanish conquest of Central and South America, while a remarkably complete account of it was published by David Hume in 1752. Hume's work too came in the wake of an inflationary episode, namely the Mississippi Bubble; and ever since, whenever there has been inflation, debate about the quantity theory has been rejoined.[1] A version of it, many of whose features Hume would recognize, is central to, though not synonymous with, that body of doctrine commonly known as 'monetarism', and the monetarist controversy about the inflation of the 1970s was in some respects

* This is a revised version of the State Bank of South Australia Lecture, presented to the 1989 Conference of Economists, University of Adelaide, 10 July 1989. I am indebted to Joel Fried, Peter Howitt, Clark Leith, and Michael Parkin for helpful comments on an earlier draft of this paper, and especially to the latter for suggesting its title. This paper has grown out of a research project on the history of monetary economics undertaken with the aid of a grant from the Social Science and Humanities Research Council of Canada whose support is gratefully acknowledged, and was written during my tenure of a Faculty of Social Science Research Professorship at the University of Western Ontario. The usual disclaimers about responsibility for its content do of course apply.

[1] A selection from Bodin's writing is to be found in Monroe (1924) pp. 123 et seq. Note also that important elements of what we now think of as Human analysis are to be found in Richard Cantillon's *Essai sur la nature du commerce en general*, written before Hume's essays and heavily influenced by the Mississippi bubble, but not published until the late 1750s, and then little read. The classic account of the early development of the quantity theory is still to be found in Viner (1937).

simply the latest round in a centuries old debate.[2]

One cannot study the history of the quantity theory even briefly without being struck by the common themes that have run through the debate about it, or without being puzzled by economists' failure to settle the issues involved once and for all over a period of two or three hundred years. In this essay, I shall address this puzzle. First I shall briefly describe the quantity theory, and set out the main lines along which it has been criticized. Then I shall discuss the principal empirical elements of the ongoing debate, and attempt to identify the ambiguities here which have made it possible for reasonable people to take different views about the contemporary relevance of the quantity theory for so long. Finally, I shall offer some suggestions as to why the debate has continued to attract so much attention and generate so much energy.

II The Quantity Theory of Money

A doctrine which has been controversial for centuries is unlikely to have remained unchanged over the years, and so it is with the quantity theory. Nevertheless, the degree of continuity which it has displayed is quite remarkable. To illustrate this continuity it is helpful to begin in the middle of the story, with the quantity theory as it stood just before World War I. Two distinct ways of formulating the theory were then in circulation, the more widely known version (at that time) finding systematic expression in Irving Fisher's *Purchasing Power of Money* (1911). Fisher's version of the quantity theory starts from an accounting identity, the *equation of exchange*, which states the obvious truth that, in any economy, the volume of money expenditure made must equal the volume of money payments received. The former is the product of the quantity of money, M, and the transactions velocity of circulation, V; the latter of the volume of transactions which physically take place, T, and the average money price involved in them, P. The equation of exchange

$$MV = PT \qquad (1)$$

is not the quantity theory of money, but it provides a useful vehicle for setting out that theory, which was expressed by Fisher, as follows.

> The price level . . . normally var[ies] directly with the quantity of money (and with deposits which normally vary in unison with the quantity of money), provided that the velocities of circulation and the volume of trade remain unchanged, and that there be a given state of development of deposit banking. This is one of the chief propositions concerning the level of prices or its reciprocal, the purchasing power of money. It constitutes the so-called quantity theory of money. The qualifying adverb 'normally' is inserted in the formulation in order to provide for the transitional periods, or credit cycles [1911, p. 320].

Questions about bank deposits and credit cycles will be discussed later. For the moment, note that, for Fisher, the quantity theory of money states that, *other things equal, the price level varies in proportion to the quantity of money* (by which he meant what we would call currency). Note also that this is a theory, not a tautology, both because Fisher specified what these 'other things' are, and because elsewhere in the *Purchasing Power of Money* he went to great lengths to argue that, though they did in fact vary over time, their variations were (except in 'transitional periods, or credit cycles') independent of the movements of money and prices. Finally, note that such formulations of the relationship between money and prices occur continuously in the literature of monetary economics from the 18th century onwards. David Hume (1752) was, perhaps, less mathematically precise than Fisher in stating the quantity theory:

> It seems a maxim almost self evident, that the prices of everything depend on the proportion between commodities and money, and that any considerable alteration in either has the same effect, either heightening or lowering the price. Increase the commodities, they become cheaper; increase the money, they rise in their value [p. 298].

[2] There seems to me to be at least two aspects of monetarism, that are not, properly speaking, essential to the quantity theory *per se*. The first is its advocacy of a money-growth rate rule, and the second is its adoption of the expectations-augmented Phillips curve as a core analytic device. The latter, it seems to me, is a useful supplement to the quantity theory's account of the transmission mechanism, as I shall explain below. Note that Friedman (1987) defines the quantity theory more broadly than do I, to make this relationship one of its components. Differences here are, I think, mainly semantic, and the important point is to note that I am here treating the phrase 'quantity theory' to refer only to that component of modern monetarism that characterizes the relationship between money and the price level.

But anyone who cares to read the three famous essays in which Hume laid the groundwork for all subsequent expositions of the quantity theory will soon conclude that this has more to do with his style of exposition than the depth of his understanding. By 1911, that is to say, the quantity theory, as it was then understood, was well into the second century of its life.

But what of more recent literature? The essential continuity of contemporary 'monetarism' is with the 'Cambridge version' of the quantity theory, which is also a product of the pre-World-War-I period.[3] This approach argued that, given the stock of money available in the economy, its purchasing power would depend upon the economy's demand for a stock of money to hold. In the most precise formulation of the theory (that of Keynes, 1923), the demand was said, other things equal, to vary in proportion to nominal income.[4] Hence, where Y is *real* national income and P an appropriate price index, if we require equilibrium between the supply and demand for money, we have, as the Cambridge equation

$$M = kPY \tag{2}$$

which may be written

$$M(1/k) = PY. \tag{3}$$

If there is a stable relationship between the volume of transactions in the economy and real national income, there must also be a stable relationship between Fisher's transactions velocity of circulation V, and the Cambridge *income velocity* $1/k$. Pigou, a leading exponent of the Cambridge approach, pointed this out in (1917) and remarked, in direct reference to Fisher, 'It is thus evident that there is no conflict between my [Cambridge] formula and that embodied in the quantity theory' (p. 174).

Even so, the Cambridge formula proved more manageable (as Pigou said it would) largely because national income is a great deal easier to measure than the volume of transactions, and because price indices relevant to national income are easier to construct than those relevant to transactions. There is an obvious and direct relationship between this version of the quantity theory of money, particularly as expressed in equation (3), and Milton Friedman's (1987) proposition that:

> For both long and short periods there is a consistent though not precise relation between the rate of growth of the quantity of money and the rate of growth of nominal income. If the quantity of money grows rapidly, so will nominal income, and conversely [p. 30].

The continuity between Friedman's monetarism and the quantity theory is even more evident in another of his statements, namely that the 'real quantity of money demanded [i.e. kY in terms of (2)] is not affected by the price level' (p. 31) for this proposition is implicit in equation (2). Finally note that Friedman's version of the central proposition of 'monetarism', namely that '*inflation is always and everywhere a monetary phenomenon*' (1987, p. 32 Friedman's italics) also follows directly from the quantity theory, as may be confirmed by applying either to equation (3) or (1) the experiment of permitting M to grow exogenously while treating $(1/k)$ (or V) and Y (or T) as variables which move only slowly (if at all) and whose behaviour is given independently of that of either M or P.

In short, the quantity theory of money is, and has been for more than two centuries, a theory of the behaviour of the general price level which identifies variations in the quantity of money as the key (but not the sole) factor causing it to change. If it is to be empirically satisfactory, two things must be established: first that, with due allowance being made for the influence of explicitly specified 'other things', there can indeed be observed a proportional relationship between money and prices; and second that causation can indeed be shown to run from money to prices and not vice versa. Just as the quantity theory has existed in a recognizable form for more than two hundred years, so have its critics denied one or both of the foregoing propositions for nearly as long, as we shall now see.

III Criticisms of the Quantity Theory

At no time was the quantity theory in greater

[3] Although the Cambridge version of the quantity theory did not receive a systematic published exposition until Pigou (1917), it had in fact been worked out in all its essentials by Alfred Marshall as early as 1871 in a manuscript not published until 1975. On all this see Laidler (1988). I stress the Cambridge ancestry of modern monetarism's version of the quantity theory because of both groups' reliance on a stock supply and demand formulation of that theory.

[4] I choose Keynes (1923) here, rather than Pigou (1917) because the latter referred to what we would now call the 'scale variable' of the demand for money function not as income or indeed wealth, but with considerable ambiguity as 'resources'.

disrepute than during the two decades following World War II, though the source of this disrepute was not the war itself but the depression which preceded it, and the accompanying Keynesian 'revolution' in economics. Being a theory of the price level, the quantity theory had nothing to say about the depression, and by the early 1950s textbook writers dealt with it (if at all) only in passing, and then usually to suggest that it had never been more than a useless tautology.

British Keynesians in particular argued explicity that the concept of velocity had no behavioural significance, and was irrelevant to the analysis of monetary policy. Thus in his evidence to the Radcliffe Committee (Committee on the Working of the Monetary System) of 1958-59, Richard Kahn described velocity as 'an entirely bogus concept', and Nicholas Kaldor explained to the same committee that

> . . . the velocity of circulation . . . is not determined by factors that are independent either of the supply of money or the volume of money payments; it simply reflects the relationship between these two magnitudes.

This extreme position was not quite without historical precedent—similar views are expressed in Sir William Petty's *Verbum Sapienti* written in about 1665—but it was nevertheless something of a novelty, and indeed a short-lived one, in the debate under discussion in this paper. Though the Radcliffe Committee uncritically accepted Kahn and Kaldor's views, it ought not to have done so, since empirical evidence presented to it showed velocity in pre- and post-war Britain to be systematically related to the nominal rate of interest, and hence to have independent behavioural significance.[5]

Though evidence that velocity varies inversely with the rate of interest disposes of the particular objections of Kahn and Kaldor to the quantity theory, it does not establish its validity. Neoclassical economic theory, accepted by (all) quantity theorists and (many) anti-quantity theorists alike, has recognized, since the late 19th century, that interest is foregone when money is held, and that the nominal interest rate rises with the expected inflation rate. The groundwork of this analysis was in fact laid by Alfred Marshall (1887) and Irving Fisher (1896), the pioneers respectively of the 'Cambridge' and 'Transactions' versions of the quantity theory discussed above, but it was not fully and precisely articulated until Friedman did so in (1956), using a development of the Cambridge theory of the demand for money whose explicitly capital theoretic formulation owed a considerable debt to Keynes's (1936) treatment of liquidity preference.[6]

The analysis in question leads to the prediction that velocity varies systematically and positively with the inflation rate, or more precisely the expected inflation rate, and hence with nominal interest rates to the extent that the latter variables are market determined, but says nothing about the quantitative magnitude of the effect. This latter point is of crucial importance, because if velocity is *sufficiently* sensitive to inflation, the latter, once started, can accelerate without limit even in the absence of any monetary expansion. Conversely, if some factor, unrelated to the current behaviour of the money supply, ties down expectations of what the general price level will be in the future, a sufficiently high sensitivity of velocity to expected inflation also ensures that the quantity of money currently in circulation can be varied with essentially all effects being absorbed by velocity shifts rather than price level variations. Any tendency for the current price level to vary relative to its expected future value will change the expected inflation rate and hence have a largely (in the limit completely) offsetting effect on velocity. This implication, which bears a striking resemblance to the Keynesian doctrine of the liquidity trap, has only been developed clearly by

[5] Petty's essay is reprinted in Hull (ed.) 1899, Vol. 1. Note that the views expressed to the Radcliffe Committee by Kahn and Kaldor are to be found in their writings from the late 1930s onwards. On this see Tavlas (1981). The evidence to the Radcliffe Committee on the relationship between velocity and the interest rate was presented by Christopher Dow and Frank Paish. On this see Laidler (1989).

[6] In particular Friedman's precise capital-theoretic formulation of the demand for money function as a portfolio choice problem owes much to Keynes, as Patinkin (1969) pointed out. This fact does not, however, in my view undermine the claims of Friedman's work, taken as a whole, to lie directly in the ongoing tradition of the quantity theory, as my discussion of it above should make clear. It should be noted explicity that, as far as the influence of interest rates on velocity is concerned, it is the nominal rate that is important, according to the quantity theory. This does not mean, however, that the behaviour of the real interest rate is of no relevance to the quantity theory. On the contrary, this factor is crucial to the behaviour of the money supply, and hence to the question of whether money causes inflation or *vice versa*. This issue is discussed below in the section entitled 'The transmission mechanism and the cycle'.

Thomas J. Sargent and Neil Wallace (e.g. 1982) in the past ten years. The important point here is that the prediction of the quantity theory which is crucial to contemporary monetarism, namely, that (rapid enough) monetary expansion is necessary and sufficient for inflation to occur, turns out not to be a logically necessary implication of neoclassical monetary theory. For it to be true, the inflation (or interest) elasticity of velocity (or equivalently of the demand for money) must not be 'too high'.

It is worth noting that many monetary economists in the 18th and 19th century departed from the quantity theory when they analyzed systems based on commodity money for reasons that, with benefit of hindsight, look a little like those which Sargent and Wallace advance against modern monetarist doctrine. The economists in question were far from being radical dissenters from the mainstream of their subject, and include Adam Smith (1776) as well as Thomas Tooke (e.g. 1844) and his associates in the so-called Banking School. These, and many others, subscribed to the idea that the value of a commodity money, or paper money convertible into a commodity, was determined by the commodity's cost of production relative to that of goods.[7] They usually agreed that the value of *inconvertible* paper money would vary with its quantity, but they accorded validity to the quantity theory of money only in this special case. In Tooke's (1844) words:

> Every fresh issue [of inconvertible paper] beyond the point at which former issues have settled . . . is soon followed by a further rise of commodities and wages, and a fall in the exchanges . . . [convertible notes] are issued to those only who, being entitled to demand gold, desire to have notes in preference; and it depends upon the particular purpose for which the notes are employed, whether a greater or less quantity is required. The quantity, therefore, is an effect, and not a cause of demand [for goods. p. 69]

J. Laurence Laughlin, the principal American academic opponent of the quantity theory at the turn of the century, went even further than this. For him, an important factor determining the current purchasing power of an even *inconvertible* paper was the probability of its *future* redemption in terms of gold. He related fluctuations in the value of Greenbacks during the Civil War to the fortunes of the Union armies, and explained the deflation leading up to the resumption of gold convertibility in 1879 as reflecting the effect of anticipations of that redemption rather than the influence of any movements in the quantity of money. For Laughlin it was thus variations in the *quality* of money's *backing*, actual or prospective, that determined its current purchasing power, and variations in velocity ensured that variations in the quantity of money would always be rendered compatible with that purchasing power. Readers familiar with the recent writings of Sargent and Wallace will recognize the essential similarity of their position on this matter to that advanced by Laughlin.[8]

Tooke and the Banking School did not deny that the quantity of money and the price level generally move together. Rather they questioned the direction of causation running between these variables, arguing that prices cause money, rather than vice-versa. In this respect, their work embodies an important element continuously present in anti-quantity theory thinking. The Banking School confined what is nowadays called the 'reverse causation' or 'endogenous money' hypothesis to the case of a convertible currency and, as we shall see below when we come to discuss the quantity theory debate in the context of open economy analysis, there is much to be said for their position. Other proponents of reverse causation, though, both before and after the 1840s did not qualify their position so carefully. Thus, between 1797 and 1821 the convertibility of Bank of England notes into bullion was suspended, and there were two bouts

[7] The Banking School, that is to say, treated the cost of production theory of value as an alternative to the quantity theory. Later in the 19th century it was more usual to treat the two theories as complementary, the former as relevant to the long run and the latter to the short run. By the early 20th century, quantity theorists such as Fisher (1911) or Pigou (1917) had come to treat cost of production considerations as simply one factor affecting the supply of money under commodity convertibility.

[8] Sargent and Wallace's views differ somewhat from Laughlin's to the extent that they stress the role of fiscal policy, rather than some commitment to gold convertibility as being crucial to agents' views on the quality of money's backing. Laughlin's own most systematic account of his views is (1903), and Girton and Roper (1978) provide a recent and accessible account of his critique of the quantity theory. Note that such quantity theorists as Fisher and Wicksell (e.g. 1915) explicitly addressed Laughlin's critique, arguing that the effects he discussed were logically possible, but could be encompassed within the quantity theory framework as factors influencing velocity, and hence covered by the theory's 'ceteris paribus' clause.

of inflation during this period (1800–1801, 1808–1809). Quantity theorists, then known as 'bullionists', attributed these to excessive money creation on the part of the Bank, but its directors and their defenders put it down to supply side factors such as bad harvests and trade disruption associated with the progress of the war with France. Furthermore, these anti-quantity theorists argued that, provided the Bank regulated its note issue by discounting only good quality short-term commercial paper (known as real bills) in any quantity offered to it, the quantity of money in circulation would be the consequence and not the cause of prices, *even in the absence of bullion convertibility*.

Walter Bagehot (1873) was later to refer to the Bank directors' statements to this effect as 'almost classical in their nonsense', but this did not prevent the 'real-bills doctrine' enjoying recurring bouts of popularity throughout the 19th and well into the 20th century.[9] More generally, even if it is not linked explicitly to the real bills doctrine, the reverse causation hypothesis is still widely held today. The so called 'new view' of money propounded by James Tobin (e.g. 1969) and his associates, which still underpins the moderate Keynesianism of such commentators as Christopher Dow and Ian Saville (1988), stresses the capacity of modern banking institutions to provide the liabilities their customers wish to hold, and hence its potential for accommodating fluctuations in prices arising from other sources. The more extreme Cambridge disciples of Keynes, cited earlier as asserting in the late 1950s that velocity was infinitely malleable, had retreated to this more defensible position by the 1970s. Moreover, to the question of what then determines the price level, the most distinguished of them, Joan Robinson (1970), offered the following answer:

> The main moral of the *General Theory* can be expressed by saying that the general price level in terms of money is not a monetary phenomenon; its movement depend [sic] mainly upon money wage bargains; that is to say, it is very largely a political phenomenon [p. 512].

Setting aside the extraordinary misrepresentation of the subject of Keynes's (1936) masterpiece with which this statement begins, it is nevertheless telling; for it illustrates how, in modern controversy, the reverse causation hypothesis about the connection between money and prices goes hand in hand, as it did almost two centuries ago, and as it has usually done in the intervening years, with the view that inflation is a matter of independent cost push factor. And of course, this view is by no means confined to Cambridge Keynesians. In the 1970s, various versions of the cost-push hypotheses were widely held among what was then the mainstream opposition to monetarist doctrine, as a glance at Laidler and Parkin's (1975) survey of the literature on inflation will readily confirm.

The cost push factors to which particular importance has been attached at any time and place have of course varied over the years. During the French Wars, as has already been noted, the state of the harvest, and war-time disruption of trade were usually cited as driving British inflation by those who denied that monetary factors had a causative role to play; Laughlin (1909, pp. 266–71) singled out tariffs, and the operation of trusts as well as trade unions, as non-monetary causes of rising prices in the United States; while wage push was given pride of place in the Britain of the 1970s as the above quotation from Joan Robinson makes plain. But the menu from which such specific selections have been made has been remarkably consistent over time. Modern advocates of cost push may pay more attention to trade unions than did their 19th-century predecessors, but the latter did not ignore these organizations; nor have harvest failures and war time disruptions been entirely neglected by 20th-century advocates of cost push. The (1977) OECD McCraken Report on *Price Stability and Full Employment* cites harvest failures (including the harvest of Peruvian anchovies), political instability in the far east and middle east, as well as the activities of trade unions and monopolies, as factors contributing to inflation during the early 1970s.

IV *What is Money?*

The points of contention outlined above are susceptible to empirical investigation, and debates about the validity of the quantity theory have from the outset had an important explicitly empirical

[9] The real bills doctrine was to become particularly influential in German monetary thought, where the quantity theory was something of a minority taste, and played a role in underpinning the policies that led to the great Weimar hyper-inflation. Ellis (1936) remains the standard English language source on German monetary thought before 1933. The role that the doctrine played in the 'Bullionist Controversy' is documented by Fetter (1965), as is the 'cost push' explanation of price level fluctuation associated with it at that time.

element to them. The details of the empirical debate have obviously changed as data and statistical techniques have improved over the years, but certain themes and problems have been present in it from the beginning. The first, and most obvious, of these is partly semantic, and partly a matter of substance, namely the difficulty of giving empirical content to the concept of money. Usage has never been uniform at any moment, but it is a fair generalization that, with the passage of time, the set of assets referred to as 'money', and whose quantity is supposed by the quantity theory to determine the price level has systematically broadened. Hume (1752), for example, tended to use the word 'money' to mean gold (or silver) coin, though he agreed that 'paper credit', by which he meant bank notes, could also influence prices. By the middle of the 19th century, bank notes, but not other components of what was usually called 'the circulating medium' had come to be classified as money, and the mainstream quantity theory position at that time was that money so defined, and only money so defined, affected prices.

In Britain this position was held by the so-called 'Currency School' which promoted, and was successful in having enacted, the Bank Charter Act of 1844. The Act's major provisions involved forcing the quantity of bank notes in circulation to vary in lock-step with the Bank of England's holdings of bullion by imposing a 100 per cent marginal reserve requirement against them, while leaving the Bank entirely free to emit deposits as it saw fit through an essentially unregulated 'Banking Department', and were explicitly justified by reference to this erroneous notion.[10] The Act's opponents, the Banking School, based much of their opposition to this piece of legislation in particular, and the quantity theory of money in general, on their belief that:

> Whatever influence may be ascribed to bank notes, whether on prices, or on the rate of interest, or on the state of trade, cannot be denied to cheques or to the substratum, deposits payable on demand [Tooke 1844, p. 25].

This position had earlier been developed with great subtlety by Henry Thornton (1802), who though nowadays regarded as one of the most important exponents of the quantity theory of his own or any other time, was in the mid-19th century viewed as having been unduly sympathetic to the Bank of England during the early stages of the bullionist controversy, not least because of his sensitivity to just such institutional details as this.[11] Even so, the position on this issue which he bequeathed to the Banking School was so clearly correct that, their political defeat of 1844 notwithstanding, it became the orthdox one in subsequent decades, and the quantity theory as it was then understood came under considerable suspicion. Thus Mill, having told readers of successive editions of his *Principles* that 'the amount of goods and of transactions being the same, the value of money is inversely as its quantity multiplied by what is called the rapidity of circulation' (p. 513) immediately qualified this conclusion as follows:

> When credit comes into play as a means of purchasing, distinct from money in hand, we shall . . . find that the connection between prices and the amount of the circulating medium is much less direct and intimate, and that such connection as does exist no longer admits of so simple a mode of expression [pp. 513–14].

Mill's handling of the implications of the existence of widespread deposit banking was uncertain, but by the end of the 19th century, two distinct and clearly articulated approaches to the problems involved here were evident in the quantity theory literature.

The first of them, usually taken by, for example, the Cambridge quantity theorists before World War I was to treat bank deposit liabilities, not as money, but as an important factor affecting its velocity.[12] This approach seems innocuous enough, but in practice it led to velocity fluctuations taking pride of place over variations in the quantity of

[10] The standard accounts of the Currency School-Banking School debate are Viner (1937) Ch. 4, and Fetter (1965) ch. 6.

[11] Indeed, Thornton was not widely cited in the 19th Century, and it was only with the work of Viner (e.g. 1937) and von Hayek (1939) that his true stature came to be recognized. The tendency to regard him as an apologist for the Bank of England is evident in McCulloch (1845) and persists in the work of Hollander (1911). The quantity theorist among Thornton's contemporaries most widely cited before the 1930s was, of course, David Ricardo, whose first publication (1809), both post-dates Thornton's, and was a good deal less subtle in its analysis.

[12] The monetary theory set out in Pigou (1912) is an exception. Here, unlike the better known (1917) account, Pigou treats bank deposits as does Fisher, as another form of money, rather than as an influence on the velocity of currency. The difference here is essentially one of semantics.

'money' in empirical applications of the quantity theory. Knut Wicksell (1898), who regarded himself as an, albeit critical, exponent of the quantity theory, pushed this line of reasoning to the theoretical limiting case of what he called 'a pure credit economy', by which he meant an economy in which all exchange was mediated by the transfer of bank deposits. He concluded that, in such a case, the quantity theory would cease to be relevant. Though Wicksell himself attached little contemporary empirical significance to this special case, it was a different matter with subsequent generations of Swedish economists, and Bertil Ohlin (1936) was to characterize Wicksell as having ' ... successfully escaped from the tyranny which the concept "quantity of money" ha[d] until recently exercised on monetary theory' (p. xiv). In the hands of Wicksell's successors then, whose influence spread far beyond Sweden, Wicksellian monetary theory was completely purged of its roots in the quantity theory and ended up providing the theoretical basis for much modern analysis of the irrelevance of money, and of the reverse causation hypothesis discussed earlier.[13]

The second approach to coping with the role of banks received a clear statement from Irving Fisher, who defined 'money as *what is generally acceptable in exchange for goods* ... ' (1911, p. 8) (Fisher's italics), and (with superscript prime referring to deposits), extended his quantity equation to read

$$MV + M'V' = PT. \tag{4}$$

Fisher thus effectively assimilated into the quantity theory an idea that had earlier been regarded as quite antithetical to it. He also set an example for much subsequent work in the quantity theory tradition. As financial systems have continued to develop, disputes about what is and is not money, and whether or not the quantity theory remains relevant, have been ongoing, and considerable flexibility about which aggregates are relevant to that theory has often marked the work of its exponents. Friedman (1987) has recently summed up the matter as follows:

> There is no unique way to express ... the quantity of money ... Despite continual controversy over the definition of 'money', and the lack of unanimity about relevant theoretical criteria, in practice, most monetary economists have generally displayed wide agreement about the most useful counterpart, or set of counterparts, to the concept of 'money' at particular times and places [p. 2].

The first sentence of this statement is not controversial, but the second surely is. Thus a recent technical report from the Bank of Canada (Hostland, Poloz and Storer, 1989) investigates the properties of no fewer than 46 alternative ways of specifying the money supply. This is an extreme, but by no means atypical, example of how problems with the definition of money continue to plague debates about the quantity theory.

It is my main aim here to describe controversy about the quantity theory, rather than to argue one side of it. Even so, I would suggest that, as far as the modern debate goes, questions about the definition of money are most usefully addressed, as Will Mason (1976), certainly no monetarist, argued, by recalling that money's principal function is that of means of exchange. This suggestion does not in and of it itself settle matters precisely because there must always arise the question of how close a substitute must an asset be for a means of exchange before it may as well be treated as one. It does, however, rule out money definitions that are clearly very narrow—e.g. the monetary base in the case of economies where bank deposits are the principal means of exchange—and clearly very broad—e.g. those that include significant amounts of large wholesale notice deposits. It hence narrows down the area of debate about what is or is not money.

It must nevertheless be recorded that modern quantity theorists, myself included (see Laidler, 1969) have not usually taken this position in the past. Rather they have argued that money is best defined as that aggregate for which the most stable demand function exists, and have hence made themselves vulnerable to a charge of circular reasoning; they have, in effect, chosen as the appropriate definition of money only that which will confirm the theory they are purporting to test. To accept this point of Mason's though, as I now would be inclined to, and rely instead on a functional definition of money does not defuse all debate about this question. Those who, like Tobin (1969) or Hicks (1990), writing in a Keynesian

[13] I conjecture in this context that Richard Kahn's role as the translator of the (1936) English version of *Interest and Prices* was crucial. Notions of the malleability of velocity and reverse causation play a much more central role in Wicksell's analysis that in that of Keynes's *General Theory*, and yet they were to become under Kahn's influence, central tenets of what is usually thought of as English Keynesian economics.

tradition in which 'money's' role as a liquid store of value (as opposed to a means of exchange) is paramount, are naturally led to doubt the suitability of any single aggregate as a basis for monetary theory, and prefer to employ disaggregated portfolio analysis which is quite antithetical to the quantity theory.

Here is not the place to attempt to argue this matter to a conclusion. Suffice it to note that some exponents of the quantity theory, including this author, have found themselves in an untenable position on the question of the definition of money, as did their predecessors in the 1840s (albeit for different reasons), and therefore accept that on this score, the quantity theory has proved particularly vulnerable to criticism. Though my own expectation is that the theory will nevertheless survive the effects of recent institutional changes on the appropriate definition of money, as it did in the past, I readily agree that this is not a judgement that all readers of this paper will share.

V *Correlation and Causation*

As far as *long runs* of relatively highly time aggregated data are concerned, the conclusions that variations in money income and money are closely correlated, that, when allowance is made for variations in real income, money and prices move roughly in proportion to one another, and that velocity is systematically but rather insensitively related to interest rates, find an overwhelming amount of support.[14] Moreover, and in the light of the foregoing discussions crucially, such support is not usually sensitive to the definition of money chosen. Thus the extreme anti-quantity theory position of Kahn, Kaldor, and Radcliffe Committee, that velocity is no more that the ratio of two independently determined variables, is impossible to take seriously. Moreover, the Sargent and Wallace prediction about the malleability of velocity is certainly not generally true either (nor, for reasons to be discussed later did they ever claim it would be).[15] Correlation is *not* causation, however, and such evidence as I refer to here, though consistent with the quantity theory, does not prove it to be true. Even so, correlations are all that we can ever observe, and it is not surprising that differences of opinion about their causal significance have been central to debates about the quantity theory. Two types of evidence have been brought to bear on this issue of causation, having first to do with the timing of variations in data, and second with the mechanisms that are said to link money and prices.

To say that one factor causes another is to say that the occurence of the cause is *both necessary and sufficient* for the effect to take place. In a social science, at least, it is *not* also to say that the occurence of the cause must *temporally precede* the effect: rational agents might forecast the causing variable, and act in anticipation of it. This obvious point is of considerable importance in the context of the quantity theory, because it has from the outset been well understood that, in an open economy using a commodity currency in common with a wider world economy (the 18th-century case), or adhering to an international gold or silver standard (the 19th-century case), the domestic price level and quantity of money are in the long run simultaneously determined by the workings of the balance of payments. In 1752 Hume described the basic mechanisms involved here in the following terms:

> Suppose 4/5 of all the money in Great Britain to be annihilated in one night . . . Must not the price of all labour and commodities sink in proportion . . . What nation could then dispute with us in any foreign market . . . In how little time, therefore must this bring back the money which we had lost, and raise us to the level of all the neighbouring nations? Where, after we have arrived . . . the further flowing in of money is stopped by our fullness and repletion . . . Now, it is evident, that the same causes which would correct these exhorbitant inequalities, were they to happen miraculously, must prevent their happening in the common course of nature, and must forever in all neighbouring nations, preserve money nearly proportionate to the market industry of each nation. All water, wherever it communicates, remains always at a level [p. 318].

A century and a half later, Irving Fisher (1911) used the same hydraulic analogy to argue that:

> An individual country bears the same relation

[14] The reader might consult the bibliography of Friedman (1987) for references to the relevant literature.

[15] In certain episodes, involving hyper-inflation, it might have more content, as Sargent (1986) has argued. Note also that Bruce Smith (1985 a and b) has claimed to find some support for the Sargent-Wallace doctrine in the 18th-century colonial American data. The results of, and methods employed in, these two studies have, however, been vigorously disputed by Ronald Michener (1987), and Michael Bordo and Ivan Marcotte (1987) and are best treated as inconclusive by the non-expert in colonial history.

to the world that a lagoon bears to the ocean. The level of the ocean depends, of course, on the quantity of water in it. But when we speak of the lagoon, we reverse the statement, and say that the quantity of water in it depends upon the level of the ocean [p. 123].

Moreover, the endogeneity of the quantity of money in the fixed exchange rate open economy here conceded has more recently been a central proposition of the so-called 'monetary approach' to balance of payments analysis associated with the work of Harry Johnson (1972) and Robert Mundell (1971).

An increase in the quantity of money may well be as necessary and sufficient for prices to rise in a fixed exchange rate open economy as in any other; but, as quantity theorists have known since the 18th century, if the balance of payments of such an economy is disturbed by events in the world economy, then it is appropriate to think of the domestic price level and quantity of money as *both* responding to the disturbance in question. Though the relevant transmission mechanism for such a distrubance *might* run through the balance of payments to the domestic money supply and thence to prices, modern economic analysis which emphasizes the role of expectations tells us that there is no logical necessity that it must do so in each and every instance. Economic agents perceiving the distrubance in question and acting in anticipation of its ultimate consequences might well cause prices to change in advance of the money supply.

Even this argument is not a new one, however. To give but one example, when Wicksell (1915) considered the effects of an inflow of gold on the price level of a country on the gold standard, he first observed that 'It is frequently supposed that the newly imported gold only gradually, after arrival, causes a rise in prices'. In this he echoed, without explicitly referring to, the conclusions that had been drawn by Cairnes (1859-1860) and Jevons (1863) from their empirical studies of the effects of the Californian and Australian gold discoveries on British prices in the 1850s; but Wicksell went on to note, that:

> A rise in prices may be conceived as due to increased demand *even before the cases of gold have been received in payment for exported goods* . . . since even the preparations for gold mining require large amounts of . . . goods which will only be paid for in the future by newly mined gold . . . [1915, p. 164, my italics].

Under the gold standard, then, and indeed under any other kind of fixed exchange rate regime, an effect in the form of rising prices can precede the necessary and sufficient condition for its occurrence, namely an increasing money supply, and such a sequence of events has long been understood to be quite possible. Indeed, the Banking School's claim that, under gold convertibility, it is the cost of production of gold that determines the price level, to which the quantity of the money must than adjust, a claim to which I drew attention earlier, may be regarded as an early version of this argument, and one which is not, of logical necessity, incompatible with the quantity theory.[16]

Arguments about reverse causation have not always taken place in the context of fixed-exchange rate open economy assumptions. As I noted above, the reverse causation idea has often been associated with the proposition that inflation is a 'cost-push' phenomenon. No quantity theorist has ever denied that factors specific to particular sectors of the economy can, and sometimes do, drive up *particular prices*, but it has always been insisted that such effects will be offset by price falls elsewhere unless they are accommodated by a rising money supply. To put matters in terms of modern analysis, in the absence of such accommodation, the initial impact of a particular price increase on the general price level will be to generate an excess demand for money, and hence downward pressure on the overall level of demand in the economy.

If particular price increases are accommodated, however, then quantity theorists would argue, and indeed have long argued, that the necessary and sufficient condition for an increase in *the general price level* has taken place, and that monetary expansion has indeed 'caused' inflation, even though price level changes have preceded money supply increases. Thus, the suspension of the bullion convertibility of sterling between 1797 and 1821 placed Britain on what was essentially a flexible exchange rate. In a *Report*—see Cannan (1919)—that is universally regarded as one of the landmarks of the literature of the quantity theory, the House of Commons Committee set up to investigate

[16] Though the Currency School would not have accepted this argument, and certain modern exponents of the quantity theory have also attached considerable importance to showing that domestic money supply movements do precede price level movements even in fixed exchange rate open economies. On this matter see, for example, Friedman and Schwartz (1982) and Darby, Lothian *et al.* (1983).

Britain's inflationary problems of 1809–1810 (of which in the absence of price indices, the exchange rate was the agreed indicator) argued as follows:

> Your Committee however, on the whole, are not of the opinion that a material depression of the exchanges has been manifestly traced in its amount and degree to an augmentation of notes corresponding in point of time. They conceive, that the more minute and ordinary fluctuations of exchange are generally referable to the course of our commerce; that political events, operating upon the state of trade, may often have contributed as well to the rise as to the fall of the exchange; and in particular, that the first remarkable depression of it in the beginning of 1809, is to be ascribed . . . to commercial events arising out of the occupation of the north of Germany by the troops of the French Emperor. The evil has been, that the exchange, when fallen, has not had the full means of recovery under the subsisting system [for regulating the money supply] . . . the reduction of paper seems . . . the chief, if not the sole, corrective, to be resorted to [p. 35].

An essentially identical debate took place in the United States in the 1970s over the potentially inflationary (in the eyes of quantity theorists) consequences of the policy of accommodating oil price increases with monetary policy, a policy supported by such Keynesians as Modigliani (see 1977, p. 14–15). Here, as in 1810, the test of the quantity theory position, at least as set out by its exponents, lay not in evidence on the timing data, but in the outcome of a counter-factual experiment: what would happen to prices if the time path of the money supply were different? Quantity theorists would argue that the price level increases would either not have occurred in the first place, or would have quickly reversed themselves, while advocates of 'reverse causation' would either expect prices to have risen regardless, with output and/or velocity moving in place of the money supply, or would assert the impossibility of holding the money supply constant in such circumstances, hence denying the relevance of the counterfactual experiment. There is, of course, no way of performing such an experiment on real world data. In economics, counter-factual experiments are necessarily conceptual, and it is precisely the impossibility of bringing empirical evidence directly and unambiguously to bear on questions concerning the feasibility of non-accommodative policy and, if feasible, upon its consequences for prices, which lies at the heart of continuing controversy about the quantity theory.

VI The Transmission Mechanism and the Cycle

Economists are continuously carrying out conceptual experiments to deduce the consequences of this or that shock of policy. That is what economic models are for, and if the individual building blocks of the models which we use in such experiments are well supported empirically, we may have some confidence in their predictions. Thus, if we cannot directly observe causation running from money to prices, or indeed in the opposite direction, we can at least construct models of the transmission mechanism linking these variables and empirically investigate their component parts. Supporters and opponents alike of the quantity theory have long accepted the relevance of addressing the issues at stake in their debate in this way. Once more there is considerable continuity among the accounts that quantity theorists have offered over the years of the transmission mechanism whereby monetary causes have price level effects, and among the objections that their opponents have raised.

Hume (1752) asserted that '. . . though the high price of commodities be a necessary consequence of the increase in gold and silver, yet it follows not immediately upon that increase' (p. 293) and that ' . . . money, when increasing, gives encouragement to industry, during the interval between the increase of money and the rise of prices' (p. 324). He thus gave an early statement of an idea that, a little over two centuries later, was to reappear in the work of Friedman (1968) as the key to understanding the breakdown of money income changes between their real and price level components. This idea, sometimes formalized as an 'expectations augmented Phillips curve', has it that money supply changes affect real variables in the short run, but only prices in the longer run. Hence it is an essential compliment to the quantity theory if the latter is to be relevant to the long run. Hume also recognized that in some circumstances an increase in the quantity of money might involve ' . . . an increase of lenders above the borrowers [which] sinks the [rate of] interest . . . ' during this same transition. Furthermore we have already noted his understanding that, in an open economy operating as a part of a wider commodity money system, the price level was ultimately determined by world-wide conditions, and that the quantity of money would adjust to it through the balance of payments; but Hume also knew that, in the presence of inconvertible bank paper (the 18th-century equivalent of a flexible exchange rate regime), it would be the exchange rate that would move to reconcile domestic prices with those ruling elsewhere. We have here, in embryonic form at least, all the components of modern accounts of the links between money and prices in both closed and open economics.[17]

Nevertheless there are also important differences in emphasis between Hume's analysis and that which came after it. First of all, the expectations augmented Phillips curve is, in modern analysis, a central feature of the monetarist model of the business cycle, but there is no trace of any recognition of a cyclical element in macroeconomic fluctuations in Hume's work. The discovery of the cycle was an accomplishment of 19th-century economics. Second, his comment that an increase in the quantity of money might sometimes, and temporarily, lower the rate of interest was offered as a minor qualification to an argument mainly devoted to establishing the essential independence of the rate of interest of the quantity of money. It was only as banking developed that interest rate fluctuations came to play a central role in quantity theorists' accounts of the transmission mechanism. That is why we must turn to Thornton (1802) for the first clear statement, indeed the clearest statement until that of Wicksell (1898), of the proposition that, if the rate of interest at which the banking system stands ready to lend is below the rate of profit available to borrowers, credit and money creation will take place continuously, driving up the price level in the process.

Although this interest rate mechanism is widely regarded as central to the transmission of monetary shocks, it can come into play *either* because of a fall in the lending rate *or* because of an increase in the rate of profit. In the latter case, which Wicksell (1898), for example, thought to be the typical one, money creation will clearly be an endogenous process, accommodating the price level consequences of more fundamental causative factors; and money can then only be said to be a cause of prices in the sense that it is the failure of the bank lending rate to adjust at once to the new profit rate that permits the monetary expansion necessary for inflation to take place.

[17] I have discussed the issue of the transmission mechanism from the perspective of contemporary macroeconomics at some length in Laidler (1982), Ch. 4.

As we have noted, the discovery of the cycle was a 19th-century accomplishment, and neither Thornton nor Wicksell applied this analysis to cyclical fluctuations; but other quantity theorists did so in due course, and the potential for hypotheses about the transmission mechanism to become thoroughly intertwined with those about the causes of cyclical fluctuations in such real variables as output and employment was thoroughly realized by the start of the 20th century. To complicate matters further, very few quantity theorists have been willing to accord money as dominant a role in driving the cycle as they attribute to it in determining secular price level behaviour.[18] For Irving Fisher and Ralph Hawtrey (1913), not only was inflation a monetary phenomenon but the cycle too was mainly 'a dance of the dollar', but this view was very much that of a minority earlier this century, as it still is nowadays, the energetic support of Milton Friedman and other monetarists notwithstanding.[19]

Many economists, both past and contemporary, who would support the long-run validity of the quantity theory have put themselves in the awkward (but not logically inconsistent) position of simultaneously arguing that the theory in question is a good explanation of long-run price level fluctuations, but that the cycle is better understood as a response to variations in real variables, a response accommodated, and at most amplified, by the behaviour of the banking system, rather than being caused by that behaviour. Moreover, though the expectations augmented Phillips curve, or its new-classical counterpart, the Lucas (1972) aggregate supply curve, is a *necessary* component of a monetarist explanation of the cycle, it can play a role in other, more eclectic accounts of the cycle too. The work of its co-discoverer Edmund Phelps (1967) shows this quite clearly.

Even the adherents of a completely monetary theory of the cycle have conceded some empirical content to the reverse causation idea in this context. Recall that when discussing the quantity theory Fisher made something of an exception of 'transitional periods or credit cycles'. He did so because he believed that, within the cycle, the

[18] Thus the Currency School never regarded monetary factors as predominant in causing, as opposed to propagating the cycle. Nor did such Cambridge quantity theorists as Marshall and Pigou.

[19] This latter phrase is, of course, Irving Fisher's (1923). Note, however, that with the advent of the Great Depression, Fisher abandoned a purely monetary impulse theory of the cause of the cycle.

direction of causation among the variables in the equation of exchange became more complex than it was between cycles. For Fisher it was not permissible to claim either that the price level was caused, but not a causing variable, or that velocity and transactions volume (it would be real output in the Cambridge version) were independent of the behaviour of the quantity of money within the cycle. He also believed that the nominal rate of interest did not fully adjust to inflation over the course of the cycle, and that the volume of bank deposits therefore responded endogenously to price level fluctuations as the business community were led by the resulting fluctuations in the real interest rate to vary their bank borrowing. Whatever might set the upswing going, and Fisher took as his standard case a money supply shock, once it was in motion mutual interaction between bank money, prices and interest rates, as well as real output was of the essence.

> It has been seen that rising prices tend towards higher nominal interest . . . but that in general the adjustment is incomplete. With an initial rise of prices come an expansion of loans, owing to the fact that interest does not at once adjust itself. This produces profits for the enterpriser-borrower, and his demand for loans further extends deposit currency. This extension still further raises prices, a result accentuated by a rise in velocities though somewhat mitigated by an increase in trade [pp. 71-2].

And Fisher is not, as I have already stressed, the only quantity theorist to concede that reverse-causation between money and prices is an integral part of the transmission mechanism. Henry Thornton's (1802) *Paper Credit*, not to mention the 1810 *Bullion Report* (see Cannan, 1919), neither of which dealt with cyclical phenomena *per se*, nevertheless argued that reverse causation between prices and money is inevitable if the banking system follows the precepts of the real-bills doctrine in regulating its activities, and hence ignores the importance of varying the rate of interest at which it lends. Also, a major purpose of the Bank Charter Act 1844 was to constrain the behaviour of the Bank of England and to prevent an endogenous response to shocks to economic activity on the part of bank lending which might lead to the creation of currency. And so, when Friedman and Schwartz summed up one of the principal findings of their *Monetary History of the United States* (1963) as follows:

> While the influence running from money to economic activity has been predominant, there have clearly also been influences running the other way, *particularly during the shorter-run movements associated with the business cycle* [p. 695, my italics].

They were reiterating a position that had been taken by economists working in the quantity theory tradition for more than a century and a half.

In short, even those economists who have argued that the cycle is predominantly a monetary phenomenon have always accepted that a richer framework than that provided by the quantity theory is required for its analysis.[20] And in the history of business cycle theory, as has already been stressed, such economists have been in a minority. Marx, Schumpeter, and multiplier-accelerator theorists have sought the explanation of the cycle in the essentially non-monetary process of capitalist growth; and 'real' business cycle theorists, from Jevons with his sunspot theory, to Kydland and Prescott (1982), have attributed it to exogenous shocks to productivity. For all of these, the monetary aspects of the cycle are symptoms of deeper forces at work, playing at most a permissive role. One does not need to take much licence to let Marx (1867) speak for this whole group on the subject of monetary theories of the cycle.

> The superficiality of political economy shows itself in the fact that it looks upon the expansion and contraction of credit, which is a mere symptom of the periodic changes in the industrial cycle as their cause. As the heavenly bodies, once thrown into a certain definite motion, always repeat this, so it is with the social production as soon as it is once thrown into this movement of alternative expansion and contraction [p. 694].

Now it is not my purpose here to take a position on the right way to do business cycle theory. Rather the point I wish to make is this. If data on timing

[20] And indeed, Friedman's (1956) 'restatement' of the quantity theory as first and foremost a theory of the demand for money which must be supplemented with other hypotheses before it yields predictions about the behaviour of the macroeconomy amounts to an explicit concession of just this point by the quantity theory's leading exponent in the second half of this century. Note too, that Karl Brunner and Allan Meltzer have recently (1987) recanted their view that money is the dominant impulse driving the cycle in the light of recent American macroeconomic experience.

cannot be used to establish the direction of causation running between money and prices, then a more detailed examination of the transmission mechanism might help to do so. The moment one becomes concerned with the empirical aspects of such an examination, however, one becomes involved with the business cycle as well, because that is how the world happens to generate our data. It is possible to construct conceptual experiments in which the only factors at work are money supply changes, but others, equally logically coherent, can also be constructed in which the impulses originate elsewhere and money plays a more permissive role. Moreover, given the way in which modern banking systems behave, even a purely monetary explanation of the cycle finds it impossible to avoid conceding a role to reverse causation.

The cycle, then, is complicated and controversial in its own right. The mechanisms linking money and prices, all important for the quantity theory, are only one set of factors at work within it. Nor do cyclical experiments take place in a laboratory. There is considerable variety among cycles, and there is no particular reason to believe that the same forces will be of the same degree of importance in each one of them. All this is platitudinous, no doubt, but it does explain why detailed empirical study of the transmission mechanisms linking money and prices has failed to settle the question of the predominant direction of causation between these variables in a definitive way. The data are too complex to provide us with unambiguous answers to the questions which we would like to put to them.

VII Why Has Controversy Persisted?

Enough has been said by now to demonstrate the initial claim of this paper that the quantity theory of money, a recognizable doctrine for more than two hundred years, has been the subject of criticism with its own recognizable central themes for just as long, and that the ongoing debate about the theory has displayed an extraordinary degree of continuity. These facts raise three questions, which I shall now discuss in turn. Why does the quantity theory continue to command assent from a significant number of economists? Why, nevertheless, does it remain possible to disagree about its validity after so much debate? And finally, why do economists still find that debate worth pursuing when it has remained unresolved for so long? I would suggest that three characteristics of the quantity theory explain its longevity.

First, it is a simple theory about an important phenomenon. The fact that price level behaviour, and in particular inflation, is a matter of abiding political concern ensures that any explanation of it is likely to attract attention not only within, but also outside of, the scholarly community; and a simple, easily grasped explanation, such as the quantity theory offers is always going to find adherents among the general public. Hence it is going to be advanced and debated wherever inflation becomes an important political issue.

Second, as it has evolved over the years, the quantity theory has shown a remarkable capacity to absorb the good arguments of its critics. Consider for example the issue of what is or is not money. There can be no doubt that in particular times and places, quantity theorists have taken firm positions on this question, and that sometimes they have been wrong. A notable example of this was the denial, referred to earlier, by members of the Currency School that, in the Britain of the 1830s and 1840s, bank deposits and similar instruments could influence the price level. The failure of the quantity theory associated with this error did not discredit it in the longer run, but simply caused its exponents to incorporate their critics' arguments in their own position. The quantity theory has also, as I have argued above, proved flexible in its capacity to deal with questions concerning the timing of the data, and their relationship to the idea of reverse causation.[21] There is a fine line to be drawn between a robust and useful theory that proves capable of fruitful modification, and one which is flexible to the point of being vacuous. The quantity theory seems to have remained on the right side of this line, inasmuch as its central propositions about the influence of money on the price level has always continued to follow from its modified versions; but I must at once concede that its modern critics would be unlikely to agree with this judgement.

The third property of the quantity theory which has guaranteed its longevity is the extent of the empirical evidence consistent (notice that I do not say *uniquely* consistent) with its predictions. The associations over a wide variety of times and places between long-run variations in money, money income, and prices mentioned above are remarkable, and are consistent with the quantity

[21] Another example, also referred to earlier, is the way in which Friedman sharpened up the quantity theory by restating it in a fashion that owed much to certain insights of Keynesian economics. cf. fn. 6, above.

theory. It really is the case that there has never been a well-documented and important inflation unaccompanied by a monetary expansion, or a well-documented and important monetary expansion unaccompanied by inflation. The overwhelming weight of the evidence is, then, consistent with the quantity theory and inconsistent with certain extreme criticisms of it. To the extent that one comes to this evidence with a prior belief that the quantity theory is a plausible doctrine, that belief is strengthened by it.

The trouble is that this long-run evidence is also consistent with the alternative hypothesis that prices cause money rather than vice versa. I have already discussed this line of argument at considerable length, and it is easy enough to draw out of that discussion the central feature which keeps it both alive and interesting. Whether the reverse causation idea is or is not plausible in any particular instance depends, among other things, on monetary insitutions, on what plays the role of money in the economy, on how policy is conducted, and so on. Monetary institutions are continuously evolving, however, so that no matter how much evidence there might have accrued about the direction of causation between money and prices which has dominated the earlier episodes, it is always possible to argue that, this time around, things might be different. To the extent that economists take their pretensions to empiricism seriously (and I do) they are forced to 'wait and see' in each instance before they are able to claim that their position has or has not been validated by the evidence. Moreover, usually there is, as I have already pointed out, much more going on at any time than the interaction of money and prices, so that the evidence in question is likely to be hard to read. These two circumstances are surely enough to permit debate to be continued in an intellectually respectable way by those who have a stake in doing so, particularly at times when inflation becomes a problem, and hence when the quantity theory is likely to be advanced as a policy relevant doctrine.

And this brings me to the final question that I wish to take up in this essay. Why have economists had a stake in keeping this same debate going for more than two centuries? The answer, I conjecture, lies in ideology. Let me stress that I do not intend to imply here that debates about the quantity theory have been in and of themselves 'unscientific'. There have been, and remain, matters of logic and fact at stake in them, about which we would all be able to agree, in principle at least, regardless of our ideological stance. Rather what I mean is that ideology keeps us interested in this particular debate rather than a dozen others in which we could engage instead. It is not the quantity theory itself that is central here, but rather the body of theory to which it is complementary. Joan Robinson, who argued that inflation is not a monetary, but a political phenomenon, believed that the quantity equation should be read, as she put it in (1970), from right to left, with money income causing money. However, she argued:

> The reason why the equation was read left handed [by quantity theorists] was that it grew up side by side with a body of doctrine couched in 'real' terms which consisted mainly of an exposition of the conditions of equilibrium. Employment, accumulation, real wages, and the production and consumption of commodities were looked after in volume I of the *Principles of Economics* and there was nothing left to discuss in volume II except the supply of money and the general price level [p. 505].

But of course, those conditions of equilibrium, as much in today's *Principles* as in its 19th-Century version, are determined by the 'market', by the operations of the 'invisible hand'. The quantity theory, which has real variables determined independently of the monetary sector (at least outside of the cycle) is thus part and parcel of the intellectual underpinnings of economic and political liberalism. There is nothing wrong with that, I hasten to add. Indeed my personal position is that there is a great right with it. But so long as economic and political liberalism must compete with more collectivist ideologies, so will the quantity theory of money be an object of suspicion among those subscribing to the latter and that suspicion is likely to lead to vigourous debate.

But arguments about the quantity theory are not a simple matter of left and right. Conservative collectivists are just as suspicious of the quantity theory as are socialists. Moreover, the economic liberal tradition of which the quantity theory is a component is not an extreme one. It was heavily influenced by Utilitarianism, and accords an important role to those collective institutions we call governments, not least in regulating the monetary sector. It is not surprising then, that the quantity theory is also attacked from the libertarian right. In the 1830s and 1840s, there was a strong element of 'free banking' (so-called) thought in the arguments of the Banking School, as there is nowadays in the analysis expounded by Sargent and Wallace.[22] Here the argument is that the monetary system left to itself would be benevolently self-regulating. For Sargent and Wallace the very empirical regularities that are cited in support of the quantity theory by its supporters, and form the practical basis for granting government a role in regulating the monetary sector, are themselves better interpreted as a result of that regulation. That is why they do not regard the empirical regularities in question as undermining their own anti-quantity theory position.

To sum up, then: for the quantity theorist such as Friedman the market solves many problems, provided the monetary sector is properly looked after—I do not have space to discuss his views on what is 'proper' here—by some collective agency; for the collectivist critic such as Joan Robinson, it doesn't solve nearly as many problems and the behaviour of the money supply is beside the point as far as economic policy is concerned: and for those like Sargent and Wallace working in the 'free banking' tradition, government creates problems in the monetary sector with which, if left to itself the market could cope. When a doctrine is so neatly placed between ideological extremes as in the quantity theory, it is going to be under attack whichever one of them is intellectually fashionable. That, I believe, is why the quantity theory of money has been, is, and is likely to remain, always and everywhere controversial.

REFERENCES

Bagehot, W. (1873), *Lombard Street—a Description of the Money Market*, London.

Bordo, M. D. and Marcotte, I. A. (1987), 'Purchasing Power Parity in a Colonial America: Some Evidence for South Carolina 1732-1744, a Comment on the Michener Paper' in K. Brunner and A. H. Meltzer (eds), *Empirical Studies of Velocity, Real Exchange Rates, Unemployment and Productivity*, Carnegie-Rochester Conference Series vol. 27, North-Holland, Amsterdam.

Brunner, K. and Meltzer A. H. (1987), 'Money and the Economy: Issues in Monetary Analysis', *The 1987 Raffaele Mattioli Lectures*, Carnegie-Mellon University, mimeo.

Cairnes, J. E. (1859-1860), *Essays Towards a Solution of the Gold Question*, reprinted in *Essays in Political Economy*, Macmillan, London (1873).

[22] See White (1984) for an account of the early 19th-century debate about free banking, and Dowd (1988) for a modern discussion.

Cannan, E. (ed.) (1919), *The Paper Pound of 1797-1821: The Bullion Report*, P. S. King, London.

Cantillon, R. (1728), *Essai sur la nature du commerce en general*, tr. and ed. by H. Higgs, Macmillan, London (1931).

Committee on the Working of the Monetary System (the Radcliffe Committee) (1959), *Report*, HMSO, London.

Cowen, T. and Kroszner, R. (1987), 'The Development of the New Monetary Economics', *Journal of Political Economy* **95** (June), 567-90.

Darby, M., Lothian, J. *et al.* (1983), *The International Transmission of Inflation*, University of Chicago Press for the NBER, Chicago.

Dowd, K. (1988), *Private Money*, IEA, London.

Dow, J. C. R. and Saville, I. D. (1988), *A Critique of Monetary Policy—Theory and British Experience*, Oxford University Press, Oxford.

Ellis, H. E. (1936), *German Monetary Theory 1905-1933*, Harvard University Press, Cambridge, Massachusetts.

Fetter, F. W. (1965), *The Development of British Monetary Orthodoxy*, Harvard University Press, Cambridge, Massachusetts.

Fisher, I. (1896), 'Appreciation and Interest,' *Publications of the American Economic Association*, 3rd series II, 331-442.

—(1911), *The Purchasing Power of Money*, Macmillan, New York.

—(1923), 'The Business Cycle—Largely a Dance of the Dollar,' *Journal of the American Statistical Association* **18** (Dec), 1024-28.

Friedman, M. (1956), 'The Quantity Theory of Money—a Restatement' in *Studies in the Quantity Theory of Money*, University of Chicago Press, Chicago.

—(1968), 'The Role of Monetary Policy', *American Economic Review* **58** (March), 1-17.

—(1987), 'The Quantity Theory of Money' in J. Eatwell, M. Millgate and P. Newman (eds), *The New Palgrave* reprinted in *The New Palgrave—Money*, Macmillan London (1989).

—and Schwartz, A. J. (1963), *A Monetary History of the United States*, N. J. Princeton University Press for the NBER, Princeton.

—and Schwartz, A. J. (1982), *Monetary Trends in the United States and the United Kingdom*, University of Chicago Press for the NBER, Chicago.

Hawtrey, R. (1913), *Good and Bad Trade*, London, Constable.

Hayek, F. A. von (1939), 'Introduction' to H. Thornton (1802).

Hicks J. R. (1990), *A Market Theory of Money*, Oxford University Press, London.

Hollander, J. (1911), 'The Development of the Theory of Money from Adam Smith to Ricardo,' *Quarterly Journal of Economics* **25** (May), 429-70.

Hostland, D., Poloz, S. and Storer, P. (1989), 'An Analysis of the Information Content of Alternative Monetary Aggregates', Bank of Canada Technical Report No. 48, Ottawa.

Hume, D. (1752), 'Of Money', 'Of Interest' and 'Of the Balance of Trade', in *Political Discourses* reprinted in

Essays Moral Political and Literary, republished Oxford University Press (1963), London.

Hull, C. H. (ed.) (1899), *The Economic Writings of Sir William Petty*, reprinted Augustus Kelley, New York (1963-64).

Jevons, W. S. (1863), 'A Serious Fall in the Value of Gold . . . ' in H. S. Foxwell (ed.), *Investigations in Currency and Finance*, Macmillan (1884), London.

Johnson, H. G. (1972), 'The Monetary Approach to the Balance of Payments' in *Further Essays in Monetary Economics*, Allen & Unwin, London.

Keynes, J. M. (1923), *A Tract on Monetary Reform*, Macmillan, London.

—(1936), *The General Theory of Employment Interest and Money*, Macmillan, London.

Kydland, F. and Prescott, E. (1982), 'Time to Build and Aggregate Fluctuations', *Econometrica* **50** (Nov.), 1345-70.

Laidler, D. (1969), 'The Definition of Money: Theoretical and Empirical Problems,' *Journal of Money, Credit and Banking* **1** (Aug.), 508-25.

—(1982), *Monetarist Perspectives*, Phillip Allan, Oxford.

—(1989), 'Radcliffe, the Quantity Theory and Monetarism', in D. R. Cobham, R. Harrington and G. Zis (eds), *Money, Trade and Payments, Essays in Honour of Dennis Coppock*, University of Manchester Press, Manchester.

—(1988), 'Alfred Marshall and the Development of Monetary Economics', UWO, mimeo.

—and Parkin, J. M. (1975), 'Inflation—a Survey', *Economic Journal* **75** (Dec.), 741-809.

Laughlin, J. L. (1903), *Principles of Money*, Scribner, New York.

— (1909), 'Gold and Prices 1890-1907', *Journal of Political Economy* **17** (May), 257-71.

Lucas, R. E. Jr (1972), 'Expectations and the Neutrality of Money', *Journal of Economic Theory* **4**(2), 115-38.

Marshall, A. (1871), 'Money' published in J. Whitaker (ed.), *The Early Economic Writings of Alfred Marshall*, Vol 1, Macmillan (1975), London.

—(1887), 'Remedies for Fluctuations in General Prices', *Contemporary Review*, reprinted in A. C. Pigou (ed.), *Memorials of Alfred Marshall*, Macmillan (1925).

Marx, K. (1867), *Das Kapital* tr. from 3rd German edition by S. More and E. Aveling, edited by F. Engels (1883).

Mason, W. (1976), 'The Empirical Definition of Money—a Critique', *Economic Inquiry* **14** (Dec.), 525-38.

McCulloch, J. R. (1845), *The Literature of Political Economy*, London.

McCracken P. *et al.* (1977), *Towards Price Stability and Full Employment* (the McCracken Report) Paris, OECD.

Michener, R. (1987), 'Fixed Exchange Rates and the Quantity Theory in Colonial America' in K. Brunner and A. H Meltzer (eds), *Empirical Studies of Velocity, Real Exchange Rates, Unemployment and Productivity*, Carnegie-Rochester Conference Series Vol. 27, North-Holland, Amsterdam.

Mill, J. S. (1848 and subsequent edns), *Principles of Political Economy with Some of Their Applications to Social Philosophy*, London, reprinted in J. M. Robinson (ed.), 2 vols, University of Toronto Press (1965), Toronto.

Modigliani, F. (1977), 'The Monetarist Controversy or, Should we Forsake Stabilization Policies', *American Economic Review* **67** (March), 1-19.

Monroe, A. E. (1924), *Early Economic Thought*, Harvard University Press, Cambridge, Massachusetts.

Mundell, R. (1971), *Monetary Theory*, Goodyear, Pacific Palisades.

Ohlin, B. (1936), 'Introduction' to 1936 English translation of Wicksell (1898).

Patinkin, D. (1969), 'The Chicago Tradition, The Quantity Theory, and Friedman', *Journal of Money, Credit and Banking* **1** (Feb.), 46-70.

Phelps, E. (1967), 'Phillips Curves, Expectations of Inflation, and Optimal Unemployment Over Time', *Economica* NS. **37** (Aug.), 254-81.

Pigou, A. C. (1912), *Wealth and Welfare*, London, Macmillan.

— (1917), 'The Value of Money', *Quarterly Journal of Economics*, reprinted in A.E.A. *Readings in Monetary Theory* (Ch. 10), Allen & Unwin, London (1952).

Ricardo, D. (1809), 'Contributions to the *Morning Chronicle*', reprinted in P. Sraffa (ed.), *Works and Correspondence of David Ricardo*, Vol. III, Cambridge University Press (1951), Cambridge.

Robinson, J. (1970), 'Quantity Theories Old and New', *Journal of Money, Credit and Banking* **2** (Nov.), 504-12.

Sargent, T. J. (1986), 'The Ends of Four Great Hyperinflations', in *Rational Expectations and Inflation*, Harper & Row, New York.

—and Wallace, N. (1982), 'The Real Bills Doctrine Versus the Quantity Theory—a Reconsideration', *Journal of Political Economy* **90** (Dec.), 1212-36.

Smith, A. (1776), *An Inquiry into the Nature and Causes of the Wealth of Nations*, London.

Smith, B. (1985a), 'American Colonial Monetary Regimes: The Failure of the Quantity Theory and Some Evidence in Favour of an Alternative View', *Canadian Journal of Economics* **18** (Aug), 531-64.

— (1985b), 'Some Colonial Evidence of Two Theories of Money: Maryland and the Carolinas', *Journal of Political Economy* **93** (Dec.), 1178-1211.

Tavlas, G. S. (1981), 'Keynesian and Monetarist Theories of the Transmission Process: Doctrinal Aspects', *Journal of Monetary Economics* **7** (May), 317-37.

Thornton, H. (1802), *An Enquiry into the Nature and Effects of the Paper Credit of Great Britain*, London, reprinted and edited with an introduction by F. A von Hayek, Allen & Unwin, London (1939).

Tobin, J. (1969), 'A General Equilibrium Approach to Monetary Theory', *Journal of Money, Credit and Banking* **1** (Feb.), 15-29.

Tooke, T. (1844), *An Enquiry into the Currency Principle*, London, reprinted London School of Economics (1959).

Viner, J. (1937), *Studies in the Theory of International Trade*, Harper, New York.

Wallace, N. (1988), 'A Suggestion for Oversimplifying the Theory of Money', *Conference Proceedings*, supplement to *Economic Journal* **98** (March), 25-36.

White, L. (1984), *Free Banking in Britain: Theory, Experience, Debate 1800-1845*, Cambridge University Press, Cambridge.

Wicksell, K. (1898), *Interest and Prices*, tr. by R. F. Kahn with an introduction by B. Ohlin, Macmillan for the RES, London (1936).

—(1915), *Lectures on Economics* (Volume 2 of 2nd Swedish edition), tr. by E. Claassen, Routledge & Kegan Paul, London (1935).

17 Price stability and the monetary order

Introduction

Price stability, inflation targeting, Central Bank autonomy, and all the rest of it are nowadays all the rage, and so much the better for the countries where they are in my view. It is a sobering thought that, in most countries, inflation in the 2–3 per cent range, which would once have been regarded as an appalling performance, is a brand new experience in the adult life of anyone under 40. The Bank of Canada was early on the scene in the inflation control business (see John Crow 1968) and I became deeply engaged in the debate that followed. I have taken an editorial decision that contributions dealing specifically with the Canadian situation are perhaps too parochial to be of general interest, so I have not included any of them here. The interested reader can consult A7, A9, D71, D79, D91, D95, D101, E8, E9, E11 and E12.

This chapter was originally prepared for a conference sponsored by the Bank of Japan and it presents a representative sample of what I have had to say on these matters recently, but in rather general terms. As with my paper on flexible exchange rates, to which this is in some respects a companion piece, I make no claims to great originality for what is said here, but I make no apology for that either. The case set out is one that seems to require constant repetition if it is to be sold in the political market place.

Reference

Crow, J.W. (1988), 'The Work of Canadian Monetary Policy', *Bank of Canada Review*, February.

10 Price Stability and the Monetary Order

David Laidler

I. INTRODUCTION

William Stanley Jevons remarked that the study of money sometimes seemed to stand in the same position to economics as that of perpetual motion to physics, or squaring the circle to mathematics.[1] That was in 1875, but the capacity of monetary economists, not always from the fringes of the discipline, to generate extraordinary ideas did not diminish in the twentieth century. Whatever Keynes may have meant to tell his colleagues in the 1930s, by the 1960s his name had become associated with the idea that government stimulus to aggregate demand, accommodated by monetary expansion, could create a permanent increase in the economy's level of output (and perhaps its rate of growth too), at a negligible cost in inflation, which was in any event largely a non-monetary phenomenon, and economically benign into the bargain. The world economy is still recovering from the great inflation which these ideas helped to create.

Monetary economics is now going through the painful process of rediscovering and refining ideas about money and inflation in the tradition that Jevons defended. The first stage of this enterprise, named by Johnson (1971) 'The Monetarist counter-revolution', was largely associated with the work of Milton Friedman (e.g. 1960) and Karl Brunner and Allan Meltzer (e.g. 1963). Monetarism re-established inflation as an important policy problem, reinstated the intellectual respectability of the view that fluctuations in the value of money probably had a great deal to do with the behaviour of the supply and demand for it, and gave fresh impetus to the study of monetary policy as a means of generating price stability. Monetarism is now regarded as rather 'old hat' by academic monetary theorists, but in the policy area, where it is surely more important to be right than original, many monetarist ideas are still current.

This chapter, then, though critical of certain monetarist ideas, is nevertheless firmly in their tradition. It begins with a brief discussion of the desirability of price stability, defending the monetarist position on this matter with some rather non-monetarist arguments. It then argues that the traditional monetarist policy proposal, to achieve price stability into the indefinite future by legislating a policy rule to bind the monetary authorities once and for all, is indefensible in the face of the facts of institutional evolution in the monetary system. It goes on to develop the case that, because discretionary powers are needed to preserve price stability, the problem of designing the monetary order involves shielding those endowed with such powers from incentives to misuse them, and exposing them to incentives to behave appropriately. The 'free banking' solution to this problem in institutional design is rejected as unworkable, and an alternative approach, which recognizes the important role of the central bank, but emphasizes the importance of ensuring its independence of short-term political influence is instead defended. Finally, certain difficulties posed by the fact that central banks tend to be institutions of the nation state, while the problem of monetary stability impinges on the international economy, are explored in the light of those ideas of currency competition which also underlay the literature on free banking.

II. THE CASE FOR PRICE STABILITY

Monetarism re-established our understanding that inflation is a monetary phenomenon, but very little in monetarist analysis such as was expounded, for example, by Friedman (1969), enabled one to make the case that inflation did, after all, present a serious economic problem. The hypothesis that money could be treated 'as if' a consumer durable good, and that the public's demand for it could be modelled as a stable function of a small number of arguments, one or more of which measured the opportunity cost of holding it, led immediately and naturally to treating inflation as a tax on money's services, and to the assessment of the social damage it might do in terms of the welfare analysis developed in the literature on public finance to measure the welfare costs of indirect taxation: inflation increased the costs of holding real balances, led to less of them being held, and the value of the services thus given up could be measured as the area of a triangle (or trapezium) under the demand for real balances function. This analysis applied only to fully anticipated inflation. Unanticipated variations in the purchasing power of money would, it was readily conceded, have disruptive effects on the distribution of wealth, and might, depending on one's view of the justice or otherwise of its pre-existing distribution, be regarded as costly; but since the public could be relied upon to learn how to forecast an ongoing steady inflation rate, these would not arise if inflation was stable. And although the welfare costs of fully anticipated hyperinflation were recognized to be severe, those of moderate inflation seemed tolerable.

Monetarism did not confine its analysis of inflation anticipations to money holding behaviour. It also noted that wage and price formation processes were affected by them, and particularly when they were modelled in an adaptive, and therefore backward-looking fashion, it predicted output and employment losses from any attempt to lower the anticipated inflation rate. If anticipated inflation at moderate rates imposes rather low social costs, and if attempting to remove it is expensive, it is difficult to resist the temptation to settle for living with such inflation, and to devote scarce economic talent to working on more serious (and apparently distinct) problems, such as achieving and sustaining higher growth rates. Monetarists did not take this position, but they found it hard to argue against it when others urged it upon them; and when a naive version of the forward-looking rational expectations hypothesis, which predicted that the reduction of anticipated inflation would be essentially costless provided that the measure was pre-announced, failed badly in the early 1980s, their position was further weakened.

We now understand that the difficulties encountered by monetarists in earlier debates about the costs and benefits of inflation stemmed from an inadequate analysis of the role of money in economic life, and, closely related, an inadequate appreciation of just what would be involved in 'anticipated' inflation.[2] The 'money-as-if-a-consumer-durable' analogy, so useful as a starting point for positive econometric investigation of the demand for money function, is hopelessly misleading when carried over to the normative analysis of inflation. It treats money as an asset which yields a purely private flow of services to the agent holding it, and in so doing abstracts from its social functions as a means of exchange and unit of account. But the private services which a stock of real balances yield to their owner are not like those to be had from a refrigerator. They are more like those yielded by a telephone which arise from the instrument being used in conjunction with a piece of public capital, namely a telecommunication network.[3] Money provides services to the agents who hold it because it enables them to participate *with other agents* in the system of monetary exchange; and inflation not only makes it more expensive for them to hold real balances, it also undermines the efficiency of that system, particularly as a vehicle for cheaply conveying information about relative prices. Money's role as a unit of account is central here, as I shall now explain.

A 'fully anticipated' inflation, so easily analysed in an abstract model economy, is not just one that agents expect, it is also one to which their behaviour is fully adapted. Thus, in a fully anticipated inflation, all contracts, all accounting systems, all taxes, and so on, are fully and continuously indexed, so that changes in the purchasing power of money affect only the own real rate of return on cash balances; and if money itself is fully indexed – a possibility that it is easy enough to conceive of in principle – then such an inflation does not even impose the simple welfare costs referred to earlier. Such a fully anticipated inflation, which underlay the monetarist analysis of the 1960s and 1970s, can, however, *only occur in an economy in which money has ceased to function as a unit of account.*

Because it is relative prices which matter for the operation of markets, it is unsurprising that explicit analysis of the microeconomics of price setting and contracting seems to lead to the conclusion that indexation will arise as a matter of course, and that a fully anticipated inflation will have no allocative consequences; and indeed triple and quadruple digit inflations do tend to produce the abandonment of the inflating currency as a unit of account. The recent phenomenon of 'dollarization' in Israel and a number of Latin American countries amounted to just that. But in the face of lower inflation rates, nevertheless quite high enough to be damaging, pre-existing arrangements are remarkably durable. Local money remains the unit of account, and indexation does not spread beyond random ad hoc arrangements.[4] Price lists, tax codes, accounting practices, insurance, pension, and mortgage contracts, not to mention wage and salary agreements, continue in nominal terms long after everyone involved with them understands that the purchasing power of money is falling, is likely to continue to fall, and will profoundly affect their real implications.

When the value of money is falling, nominal prices change at discrete and unco-ordinated intervals, so that the structure of relative prices at any moment is distorted. And, though nominal interest rates adjust in the presence of inflation, this does not eliminate capital market distortions if taxes are levied on nominal interest income and on nominal capital gains, if debts continue to be discharged with constant nominal payment streams, if accounting conventions require inventories to be valued at acquisition cost, etc. Such multifarious distortions present all manner of private profit opportunities to those with special knowledge of financial and legal conventions. Human capital, like any other input, is scarce; and the more of it that is devoted to searching out and exploiting such gains, the less is available to help generate profit by other means, including the creation of new goods or better methods for producing existing ones. And human capital does not work alone. It collaborates with less skilled labour, with office space, and other physical capital to generate its output. Privately, the reallocation of scarce resources induced by inflation may be profitable, but socially it is costly. To devote resources to exploiting the private profit opportunities created by imperfectly anticipated inflation is to join, not a zero, but a negative sum game.

The upshot of all this is by now well known. There is no such thing as a fully anticipated inflation, and ongoing steady inflations are a great deal more costly than was once believed. Variability of the inflation rate does cause problems of its own that are well worth avoiding, and rapid inflation is more disruptive than low inflation, so that low and stable inflation is undoubtedly to be preferred to the high and variable variety. Price level stability is better yet, however, and by a significant amount, for the simple reason that it provides circumstances in which scarce resources are more likely to be devoted to increasing output and, indeed, to raising its rate of growth into the bargain. Price stability is neither necessary nor sufficient for economic growth, but it helps. Indeed, if estimates such as those of Jarrett and Selody (1982) for Canada, which suggest that a permanent one percentage point reduction in inflation is associated with a permanent one third of a percentage point increase in the rate of productivity growth, are given credence, it evidently helps a lot. And even if one regards such an estimate as implausibly high, Howitt's (1990) survey of the issues involved here shows that the cumulative value of much more modest gains can make a significant addition to any quantitative estimate of the benefits to be had from eliminating inflation.

To say that price stability is desirable, though it may be the end of one story, is merely the beginning of a number of others. For economies which are not already experiencing such a state of affairs – the United States, Canada, or the United Kingdom for example – the question must immediately arise as to whether the long-term benefits of stable prices are worth the costs of achieving it. Even if any slowdown in activity is strictly temporary, lost output is lost for ever; nor can one discount *a priori* the possibility that hysteresis effects might introduce an element of permanence into the fall in output and employment that seems to be the inevitable accompaniment to any attempt to lower inflation. This chapter will not address these matters in detail. Suffice it to note that I find arguments about the high and permanent nature of the costs of even moderate inflation sufficiently convincing, and those about the likelihood of a gradualist anti-inflation policy permanently damaging the economy's productive capacity sufficiently unconvincing, that I am firmly in favour of making the move to price stability. I deal with this matter by assertion, rather than careful argument, not in order to avoid intellectual difficulties, but for the simple reason that another set of questions raised by the desirability of price stability, namely how to achieve and sustain it, will easily occupy the space remaining in one chapter.[5]

III. THE MONEY GROWTH RULE AND DEMAND FOR MONEY INSTABILITY

We have seen that Monetarism's identification of price stability as a desirable policy goal has been rendered much more secure by further analysis of the mechanics of inflation. Other elements of the doctrine as it stood, say twenty years ago, have fared less well. Monetarism taught that, although variations in the behaviour of the money supply could have powerful effects on the time path of real income and employment, these operated with sufficient uncertainty as to their timing – with 'long and variable lags', to adopt the usual vocabulary – as to render them unhelpful for counter-cyclical policy. Since it also taught that the business cycle was mainly the result of monetary impulses in the first place, however, the very avoidance of money-supply shocks was, in and of itself, a powerful stabilization policy. A legislated quasi-constitutional rule, setting money growth at an 'appropriate' rate would simultaneously achieve secular price stability and largely eliminate the cycle. To modern eyes so simple a policy doctrine appears naive.

To begin with, a pair of oil price shocks have convinced most observers, including some prominent monetarists, that though monetary impulses are often important sources of cyclical disturbance, they are far from unique.[6] This observation does not undermine monetarist policy doctrines but it reduces expectations about what following them might accomplish. Stable money growth may not enable us to avoid cycles, but it could still provide a potentially powerful built in stabilizer to mitigate their severity. Or it might were it not for the instability which in the 1970s became apparent in the demand for money functions of a disturbingly large number of economies. Such instability is a potential source of cyclical disturbance in its own right, and threatens to undermine secular price level stability into the bargain. The task of monetary policy in its presence is to offset shifts in the demand for money with variations in the money supply, and the pursuit of price stability becomes technically an altogether more difficult matter.

I referred above to the *apparent* instability of demand for money functions, and my choice of this adjective was not gratuitous. As I shall now argue, the problem in question, though far from irrelevant to this chapter's topic, needs to be kept in perspective.[7] The relationship did not so much collapse as turn out to be rather more complicated than we had thought; and, a good deal of the problem arose from the tools we used to analyse the data, rather than with the economic processes generating them. The economic theory of the 1950s told us quite a lot about what to expect about so-called long run, or steady state, relationships among money and the variables determining the demand for it, but it was clear from very early on that more than these long-run relationships were at work in generating our data. For a while it seemed possible to deal with this issue by postulating the operation of 'short-run' adjustment dynamics, whose observable consequences could be captured by modifying the long-run relationship to accommodate distributed lags, often encapsulated in a single lagged dependent variable. The theoretical justification for this modification was at best flimsy and – this point is important – the accuracy of our estimates of the parameters of the underlying long-run demand function depended upon its appropriateness. In the 1970s, the data began to tell us that we had mis-specified the short-run demand for money function, but they did so in a way that opened up the possibility that the long run demand for money function was unstable as well. With traditional econometric methods for dealing with adjustment dynamics, one could not tell.

New techniques, involving studies of so called 'co-integration', and closely related 'error correction mechanisms' enable us to study the empirical properties of underlying long-run relationships without having to make prior commitments to specific ways of modelling short-run adjustment dynamics. As these have been applied to data on the demand for money function, a number of conclusions have emerged. First, adjustment dynamics are far too complex for it to be appropriate to model them with simple regressions involving a lagged dependent variable; second we understand next to nothing about the market processes generating them; third, once adjustment dynamics are cleared out of the way, steady state relationships that look very like stable long-run demand for money functions begin to re-emerge; but finally, the latter do appear to shift from time to time as a result of institutional change in the financial system. This final conclusion receives considerable corroboration from historical studies of institutional influences on the demand for money such as those of Bordo and Jonung (e.g. 1990), and also from Barnett's work on aggregation (e.g. 1990) which shows that, at least for the United States, Divisia aggregates whose construction takes account of the influence of institutional change on the relative liquidity of various components of monetary aggregates, appear to have more stable demand functions than do simple sum aggregates.

Each of these conclusions in turn has implications for what we can and cannot expect of monetary policy. In the 1970s, when discretionary implementation of money growth targeting (which should not be confused with adherence to a legislated money growth rule) was fashionable, the so-called short-run demand for money function was widely seen as the key to such implementation. The function in question was estimated on, say, a quarterly or even monthly basis, the values of its real income, price level, and lagged dependent variable arguments assessed, and then the one remaining argument, the rate of interest was set by the authorities in order to achieve the desired value for the left-hand side variable, the money stock. When the relationship broke down, so did the possibility of accurate control of money growth by these means. Though some commentators argued that it would be more appropriate to attempt to control money growth by way of a money supply function which linked that variable to base growth by way of a money multiplier, whose empirical properties were susceptible to econometric modelling, such arguments did not convince policymakers.[8] Furthermore, the fact of shifts in the long-run demand for money function meant that the relationship between money growth and inflation in the longer term was likely to be unreliable, so that to control money growth became less important.

With some benefit of hindsight, it is fair to say that the pervasiveness of instability in long-run demand for money functions has been overstated. In some countries, for example the United States, Australia or New Zealand, the institutional change which underlay the instability in question seems to have stemmed from once and for all shifts in the regulatory environment; in others, for example the United Kingdom, it seemed to come as a response to a new policy regime; but in either case it was more of a one-off event, whose effects would in due course wear off, than a continuing source of trouble. Some countries, for example West Germany, were not afflicted with the problem at all. Others were, but without help from regulatory disturbances: about ten years ago the structure of the Canadian monetary system was markedly disturbed by the introduction of daily interest chequing accounts whose newly created feasibility seems to have been the product of advances in computer technology.[9] This last example is a particularly telling one, as far as monetarist policy doctrine is concerned, since it implies that the appropriateness of any pre-legislated constant money growth rate rule is vulnerable to exogenous and unpredictable institutional change. It implies that the authorities must retain the powers necessary to adapt their policy procedures to such change as and when it occurs.

IV. THE POLITICAL ELEMENT IN MONETARY POLICY

If it is agreed: that it is desirable to stabilize the price level; that the rate of growth of nominal money relative to that of the demand for real balances is the key to achieving this end; and that the demand for real balances function shifts around from time to time; then all that seems to be required is for the monetary authorities to monitor the latter function, to adapt nominal money growth to any shifts that occur, and to devise techniques for controlling money growth that do not rely on the stability of a short-run demand for money function. If it is also agreed that monetary policy should be directed to delivering price stability on average over a two or three year period, and not, say, on a quarter by quarter basis, and that it should not be given any subsidiary tasks involving attempts to stabilize real income and employment, can we not rely on the monetary authorities to deliver such an outcome?

If the fact of institutional change makes it impossible to reduce the future conduct of monetary policy to obedience to a legislatively predetermined money growth rule, that surely does not undermine a policy regime in which the authorities pursue money growth targets, but adjust them systematically in the light of new information as and when it arises. If the conduct of monetary policy was simply a matter of finding the appropriate technical means of achieving an agreed end, this conclusion would be defensible, and this chapter could be brought to an end with it.[10] The trouble is, though, that monetary policy is not just a technical matter. It is also a political matter. Moreover, just because there are good economic arguments for regarding the pursuit of price level stability as monetary policy's proper task does not mean that there are no others that it could conceivably be given. Nor does it mean that there are no political forces which attach value to pursuing other ends.

Earlier in this chapter I noted that the traditional analysis of the costs of inflation treated them 'as if' they were analogous to the welfare losses associated with an indirect tax. I argued that this treatment failed to get to the heart of the damage which inflation inflicts on a market economy; but this does not alter the fact that inflation is a source of revenue, and that the relevant authorities are, therefore, always open to the temptation to exploit it. Economic agents enjoy being the recipients of government expenditures, and dislike paying taxes. Deficit finance is always a temptation to governments seeking to maintain their popularity, and since private sector borrowers would just as soon not compete with the public sector in capital markets, so is the monetization of deficits. To say this is platitudinous, but the point is important nevertheless; and the same may be said of the observation that monetary policy is particularly vulnerable to time inconsistency problems. Even if the trade-off between inflation and output is, if anything, an inverse one in the long run, so that a low inflation steady state is always preferable to a high inflation alternative, it is nevertheless probable that, on the path leading from the former to the latter, there are gains to be had on the output front. Myopic policymakers who value such gains are all too likely to opt for them; and having moved the economy to an inferior steady state they are also likely to find the return journey an unattractive one. Time inconsistency, that is to say, tends to give an inflationary bias to monetary policy, with reinforces the temptation to use it as source of revenue.[11]

None of this is to say that inflation is, after all, inevitable. It is, however, to say that widespread agreement about the damage that it can do, combined with the technical knowledge of how it can be avoided, do not between them provide a set of sufficient conditions to ensure that inflation will not occur. The monetarist prescription that a money growth rule be legally imposed upon the authorities stemmed not just from a desire to ensure that anti-inflation policy was technically well conducted. It also sought to address the political question of how to constrain the authorities from using their technical expertise to pursue other goals whose attainment, though privately attractive, is not in the public interest. That is why a fairly extensive literature showing that such a simple rule provides a technically sub-optimal policy regime is quite irrelevant, and why the empirical fact of money demand instability raises more than simply technical questions. As Karl Brunner (1984) noted, the analysis of monetary policy requires us to consider not just the techniques employed in its conduct, but the regime – *the monetary order* – within which it is implemented. The monetarist money growth rule was more than just a technical device. The proposal that it be legislated involved the specification of a particular kind of monetary order, and the conclusion that a simple legislated rule is not after all desirable must lead us to consider alternative orders, not to return to discussing monetary policy as a merely technical issue.

V. MORE SOPHISTICATED RULES

To constrain by law the growth of a precisely defined monetary aggregate to a particular rate is a very specific monetary rule. If the problem with it is that institutional change might lead to the demand function for the aggregate in question, and hence its velocity of circulation, shifting over time, may it not be possible to design and legislate a more complex rule, linking the rate of money growth to the behaviour of velocity in such a way as to stabilize money income, and therefore the price level? This is the view of such analysts as Meltzer (1987) and McCallum (1988), each of whom has proposed a scheme of just this kind. One problem with feedback rules, of course, is that they may be de-stabilizing. In principle, this problem can always be overcome provided one knows enough about the dynamic properties of the system to be controlled; but apparently small errors can matter a great deal. This was the fundamental message of A.W. Phillips's (e.g. 1954) research agenda. Meltzer and McCallum are, of course well aware of this issue, and address it by proposing that the feedback relationships built into any variable money growth rule be slow moving. This would delay the system's response to institutional change, and hence tend to make policy less effective in stabilizing the price level, but it would at the same time reduce the chance of the policy rule becoming destabilizing.

Meltzer and McCallum are also aware that any rule of this kind would be subject, at least in principle, to problems which usually go under the heading 'Lucas Critique'. That is to say, the very dynamic structure of the system which they are seeking to control might change as agents seek to adapt their behaviour to the new policy regime. There is really nothing that can be said in general about this possibility. If we were sure that we had a coherent understanding of the economy's so called fundamentals – the tastes of its inhabitants, the technology available to them, not to mention the inventory of available resources – and if we could be sure that such fundamentals were invariant, we could predict such effects and incorporate them in the design of our feedback rule. But the moment one entertains doubts about the constancy of such factors, and about our capacity to foresee their future evolution, one must also start to entertain doubts about the durability of any analysis which treats them as given, however appropriate that might be at the time of its creation.

All this amounts to saying that the fact of unpredictable institutional change, whether policy induced or not, leads us into an infinite regress when we discuss legislated money growth rules. A constant money growth rule is inadequate, so we begin to look for a satisfactory second-level rule – a *meta-rule* as Brunner called it – whereby the first-level rule might be changed, but we cannot be sure about the durability of a meta-rule either. Surely the correct conclusion here is not that we should start looking for a meta-meta-rule, a rule for changing the rule governing the choice of money growth rule, but that it is in the nature of the monetary system that it cannot be locked into a particularly behaviour pattern for the indefinite future by a once and for all legislative measure enacted in the present. Though none of this is to deny that the conduct of monetary policy in many times and places might have been better if the prescriptions of Meltzer and McCallum had been followed, rather than the *ad hoc* measures that were in fact taken, it is to argue that their prescriptions seem to require room for someone somewhere to take discretionary actions to maintain their viability, as and when the unforeseen need arises, and that, therefore, it would be undesirable to lock them into place by legislation.

It is tempting to argue that, if perpetually binding quantity rules cannot be designed, then perhaps we should pay attention to price rules instead, not least because it is after all the price of money that we wish to stabilize. A large element of the traditional case for fixed exchange rates rests on just this premise, and it is, of course, true that an open economy which fixes the price of its domestic currency against another whose purchasing power is stable will itself tend to import price stability.[12] But the injunction to maintain a fixed exchange rate on a stable currency is an incomplete policy prescription. It does not tell us how the authorities in charge of the stable foreign currency are to be induced to create that stability, nor does it lay down any procedures to be followed by the domestic authorities for recognizing and reacting to any tendency for it to break down. Nor is a commodity based system – of which the gold standard is the archetype – proof against such problems. The purchasing power of money under such a regime is just as stable, and no more, than the relative price of the commodity upon which it is based, and as the monetary history of the late nineteenth century shows all too clearly, the matter is not made any simpler by the fact that the relative price in question is unlikely to be independent of the extent of monetary demands for the chosen commodity. Here as before, it is important to make the point that particular episodes in the past might have been better managed if fixed exchange rates, or a commodity standard had been in place, but it is also important to note that the adoption of an exchange rate or commodity convertibility rate does not obviate the desirability of the monetary authorities retaining discretionary authority to cope with unforeseen (and unforeseeable) eventualities.

In short, a monetary order which constrains the authorities to take only measures consistent with the pursuit of price stability has considerable attractions, but monetary institutions evolve over time, and monetary policy must be adapted as they do so. Because institutional evolution is unpredictable, the nature of that adaptation cannot be legislated in advance, and the monetary authorities must, after all, be granted discretion. To say that discretion can be misused, and has been misused, however, is not to say that it must be misused. If we cannot design a viable monetary order in which the authorities are constrained by rules to behave in an appropriate way, perhaps we can at least design one in which they are given sufficiently strong and appropriate incentives that they are likely voluntarily to deliver desirable policies. It is to consideration of this possibility that the next two sections of this chapter are devoted.

VI. FREE BANKING AS A MONETARY ORDER

Monetary policy is by no means the only activity which, if located in the public sector, is subject to political influences which might work counter to a broader public interest. For more than two centuries economists have suggested that, in such cases, location of the activity to the private sector might be the appropriate remedy. It is this preconception that underlies the so-called 'free banking' ideas to be found, for example, in Hayek's (1976) proposal for *Denationalising Money*, and there is a good deal to be said for them. The argument that, because the monetary system is a public good, its services must be supplied by government is, quite simply, invalid. The standard analysis of public goods suggests that if their provision is left entirely to the competitive market, a suboptimal amount will be forthcoming, but it leaves open a wide variety of possibilities for public sector intervention, other than direct government provision, in order to remedy the situation. No one would deny the utility of a framework of contract and taxation law, accounting conventions, and so forth, which define the economy's unit of account, and codify social conventions about what does and does not constitute a medium for the discharge of debts. But the advocates of private money are right when they argue that it is a far cry from this to suggesting that it is the inherent job of the state directly to involve itself in the provision of the economy's means of exchange and most liquid store of value.

Indeed, if money were no more than the economy's most liquid store of value, the role it plays in most macroeconomic models formulated in Walrasian general equilibrium terms – a range that covers just about everything from Hicks's IS-LM version of Keynes to Lucas's new-classical macroeconomics – the case for its private competitive provision would be compelling.[13] The case in question rests on two considerations. The first is that any competitive industry will price its output at marginal cost. Applied to the provision of the services of liquid assets, this would involve paying the competitive rate of return on real balances, which in turn would be equal to the market rate of interest on other illiquid stores of value minus the marginal cost of providing liquidity. By itself, this would simply guarantee that competitively supplied real balances would bear an appropriate real rate of return plus the expected rate of depreciation of the particular liability under analysis. However, the second consideration referred to above is that agents will wish to avoid the computational costs involved in holding assets whose real purchasing power is falling (even if their nominal rate of return is adjusted to compensate for the decline in question). This preference would ensure that only those issuers of money whose liabilities had stable purchasing power would survive.

In principle the above conclusion holds for privately issued notes as well as deposits, but like all conclusions yielded by competitive models, it rests on some rather extreme assumptions about agents' knowledge. In particular the conclusion requires that agents' costs of monitoring the soundness, and indeed the probity, of individual banks are negligible. If they are not, incentives exist for individual banks to exploit agents' ignorance by over-issuing liabilities. The answer which advocates of free banking offer to this problem is more convincing in the case of deposit liabilities than currency. They argue that an over-issuing bank will encounter an adverse clearing balance, and that the task of monitoring is therefore automatically transferred from non-bank agents to other banks. The mechanism here works essentially instantaneously for deposits, whose creation and utilization by agents automatically sets the clearing mechanism to work, but might work more slowly in the case of notes, which only generate clearing problems when they are redeposited with other banks. In the nineteenth century, arguments like this were important in persuading legislators to pay more attention to regulating note issue than deposit banking, but in modern circumstances, where currency plays a relatively minor role in the system, they seem to me to require only a very marginal retreat on the part of advocates of free banking.

The moment we invoke the clearing mechanism as a device for disciplining competitive banks, however, we give explicit recognition to the fact that their liabilities are not only liquid stores of value, but means of exchange too, and that the inter-bank transactions which this fact implies also require consideration. Just as non-bank agents find it convenient to adopt a common means of exchange, money, so do banks find it convenient to settle clearing balances in a common medium, high-powered money, and hold reserves of it. Also, and crucially, as Edgeworth (1888) and Wicksell (1898) showed long ago, economies of scale are inherent in the holding of reserves of high-powered money, and these create incentives for banks to merge, or if diseconomies inherent in other activities work against this, at least to pool their reserves and hold them with some institution which then begins to look like a central bank. That institution in turn is a natural monopoly, which, if privately owned and unregulated will have an incentive to manage its liabilities in such a way as to generate not price level stability, but a seignorage maximizing rate of inflation.

Although an unregulated and competitive banking system might well generate price level stability, then, an *unregulated banking system would be extremely unlikely to remain competitive*. Some centralized provision of high-powered money is needed to make an otherwise competitive system viable, and the question of how its quantity ought to be regulated in order to ensure that the economy remains inflation free cannot be avoided. Suggestions by free banking advocates that the currently existing quantity of high-powered money be frozen, once and for all, and the banking system otherwise be left unregulated, should be seen as attempts to come to grips with this issue by replacing a central bank with discretionary powers with a simple rule (zero growth) for the behaviour of high-powered money. Such a proposal has all the attractions of any money growth rule, but also its major drawback, already discussed, namely vulnerability to the unpredictable effects of institutional change. It does not seem possible to 'denationalize money' entirely, and the problem of designing monetary institutions to deliver price stability cannot be solved completely by this expedient.

VII. CENTRAL BANK INDEPENDENCE AS A MEANS TO PRICE STABILITY

The matter boils down to this: price stability will not just happen; it has to be engineered by some public body; and we must devise a framework which not only confers discretionary powers on that body, but also gives it the incentives to use them in a desirable fashion. When we put it this way, it becomes clear that we are discussing not some new issue, but an old one, namely the governance of the central bank.[14] The central bank, of course, is not an isolated institution, but part of the structure of government, even if, as sometimes happens, it is privately owned. Just as there is no uniquely ideal design for government which is suitable for all times and places, so too is there no optimal blueprint for a central bank that will fit all circumstances. A unitary state under parliamentary government might want to manage things in one way, a federal state where there are strong political conflicts among regions in another, and so on; but certain broad principles might nevertheless apply rather generally.

To begin with, on a purely technical level, if it is agreed that monetary policy is a matter of controlling the quantity of means of exchange available in the economy, then the central bank should have sufficient powers to do so. This in turn probably means that the economy's stock of high-powered money should consist of its liabilities, and that it should be endowed with whatever powers necessary to control their volume. Also, though I am prepared to believe that it is possible to design economic models of banking systems in which system-wide runs never take place, I am not prepared to believe that we shall ever be sure enough of their validity to dispense with a lender of last resort in any actual monetary system. The central bank should therefore have whatever powers are needed to fulfil this role too. Taken together, these prerequisites require that any central bank should have the authority to execute open market operations and provide rediscount facilities to commercial banks. Since all economies are open, moreover, the central bank must be able to deal in foreign exchange and foreign securities too.

At one time it was believed that incentives to use its authority in these matters in a socially desirable fashion could be provided simply by ensuring that the central bank was privately owned, and that its directors be drawn from those segments of the community whose interest in price level stability over-rode their narrow concern with the bank's profits.[15] Nowadays we understand that matters are more complicated. Regardless of whether the institution is privately or publicly owned, those running it need to be made accountable to the community at large for their activities, but the devices put in place to ensure such accountability must not simultaneously expose the central bank to the kind of political pressure which could lead it into myopic and ultimately destructive actions. As a first step, since it is hard to hold anyone accountable for their behaviour if its desired characteristics have not been clearly described before the event, this argues for giving the bank a clearly defined mandate to pursue and maintain price stability.

But a mandate alone is hardly sufficient if those who are expected to fulfil it are not insulated from pressures to set it aside.[16] Thus, we must not be misled into believing that central bank accountability to the public for its performance requires that it be under the day-by-day control of elected politicians. On the contrary, though the central bank must clearly consult regularly with those politicians about the interaction of monetary policy with other measures for which the latter are responsible, the legal framework within which such consultations take place should make it clear that the bank's obligation to fulfil its price stability mandate takes precedence over any requirement to co-operate in the execution of other measures. It is also desirable that the bank's officials be in a position to resist pressure to do otherwise, which means that they cannot be civil servants whose terms of service require their obedience to elected politicians on pain of dismissal; rather they must serve on 'good behaviour' terms, similar to those applied to the judiciary, which render their dismissal both difficult and potentially embarrassing to any politician seeking to over-ride them. Furthermore, it is important that their terms of office, and the timing of their appointments be carefully desynchronized from any electoral cycle.

If a central bank can operate independently of the day-to-day pressures which routinely fall upon politicians who must make public expenditure and taxation decisions, and who are subject to the control of a sometimes myopic electorate, it is hard to see why seignorage maximization should become one of its aims, or why it should indulge in the kind of time inconsistent inflation biased policies to which the exigencies of the electoral cycle otherwise give rise. If those running it are, moreover, ultimately accountable for fulfilling a price stability mandate, this absence of incentives to pursue inappropriate policies will be supplemented by positive incentives to behave wisely.

It is also important to understand that central bank independence does not imply that the institution's activities be shrouded in secrecy. Constant exposure to well informed and independent criticism may not be as binding as a legislated money growth rule, but it is nevertheless a potentially powerful constraint on the conduct of policy. Relevant data, then, should always be readily available, the minutes of meetings at which policy decisions are made should also be published in full and in a timely fashion, and where political institutions permit it, elected politicians should be given regular opportunities to receive reports from those in charge of monetary policy, and to question them in public about their conduct. No conceivable set of institutions will guarantee that those given discretionary power over monetary policy will always behave wisely, but a framework along the lines I have just sketched seem to offer good prospects of appropriate measures being followed.

VII. THE INTERNATIONAL DIMENSION

Economies are open, and the efficiency of international goods and capital markets is just as dependent on a smoothly functioning international monetary system as is the efficiency of domestic markets on the stability of a national system. This chapter needs to touch upon the international dimension, therefore, before it is complete. Its treatment of these matters can, nevertheless, be brief, given that the next chapter by Professor Rogoff, is fully devoted to international monetary questions.

In an ideal world, there might exist a supra-national government, one of whose institutions might be a world central bank charged with maintaining stability in the purchasing power of a single world money. That government might have powers to ensure world-wide labour mobility in order to help particular regions to adjust to various real shocks, and the authority to address such problems by way of fiscal transfer programmes as well. That is how existing federal states manage things, and how the EEC seems to be evolving too. But there is no prospect of anything remotely resembling this coming into being on a world-wide basis in the foreseeable future, and any blueprint for generating inflation-free growth in the world economy through the activities of national monetary institutions is bound to be incomplete. The best we can do is identify the gaps involved, speculate about their likely importance, and say something about which measures proposed to cope with them might help and which actually hinder, the achievement of the ultimate goal.

The first, and most obvious point to make here is that, if the central bank of an individual nation state is given a clear mandate to pursue domestic price stability, and sufficient independence of political pressures to enable it to fulfil that mandate, then it cannot simultaneously be required to stabilize its exchange rate. An international monetary order based on exchange rate flexibility between national currencies is not the result of applying any abstract optimizing analysis to the system's design. Indeed, the slogan 'one market, one money' would seem to point in a different direction altogether, and I shall comment on the question of optimal currency areas below. A flexible exchange rate regime is rather the natural corollary of a political order in which the highest level of reliable authority exists at the level of the nation state. At first sight, this does not seem to augur well for the future stability of the international monetary system.

Experience with flexible exchange rates during the last two decades has been far from reassuring.

However, things are not as bad as they seem. The problem which the last two decades have revealed with flexible exchange rates is not that they are themselves a source of instability, but that they amplify the effects of unstable monetary policies.[17] Price stability has emerged, or is emerging, as a domestic policy goal in a number of countries now, along with the recognition that it is the unique task of monetary policy to deliver it. This carries with it the promise that the major source of instability in the international monetary system is in the process of being removed. Nor is the emergence of this new concern with price stability merely fortuitous. Those same competitive forces which would drive an unregulated private banking system to emit stable valued liabilities also impinge upon central banks, particularly those of countries whose monies play an international role. They are subject to a market discipline imposed by the 'currency substituting' activities of agents engaged in international transactions.

Some governments have tried hard to avoid this discipline by bringing political pressure to bear on their competitors to indulge in inflationary policies (disguised as policies to support the exchange rates of currencies in which international markets were losing confidence), but their success so far has been limited. Some central banks, notably those enjoying a relatively high degree of political independence, insisted on maintaining the purchasing power of the monies for which they are responsible; and they therefore ensured that the international co-ordination of monetary policy about which we heard so much in the 1980s failed. Far from being a matter for regret, this failure was most welcome. It represented the defeat of an attempt to create an international seignorage maximizing cartel among central banks. Current moves towards making price stability the goal of domestic policy in a number of countries should be seen not as a new development, then, but as a continuation of a campaign against international inflationism which deserves widespread support.

A system of flexible exchange rates among the currencies of countries enjoying domestic price stability would itself tend to produce stable exchange rate behaviour, though not necessarily constancy: productivity growth differentials among sectors of domestic economies can produce terms of trade changes within and between countries which must be absorbed by exchange rate movements if domestic price levels are stabilized. But it ought not to be claimed on this basis that getting domestic monetary policy right in enough countries is in and of itself sufficient to produce a stable international monetary order too. I have just invoked the analysis of competitive monies to help explain why price stability is becoming a popular policy goal in a number of countries, but earlier in this chapter I pointed to the tendency to natural monopoly in the provision of high-powered money which seems inherent in the technology of banking. This tendency is surely as present in the international monetary system as in any national framework, where it will manifest itself in a movement towards the adoption of a single money for mediating international transactions, and a tendency for agents heavily involved in international transactions to demand stability of the exchange rate of their domestic currencies against the dominant international money – the key currency as it used to be called.

The argument here is, of course, not a new one. It is simply a variation on an analytic theme which used to bear the label, 'the theory of optimal currency areas'. It does not therefore necessarily point to the emergence of a single dominant world money. Indeed, if the world trading order evolves towards regional blocs, one dominant currency for each bloc seems the more likely outcome. But even this possibility raises issues about the design of domestic monetary institutions which we have not yet addressed, because the boundaries of currency areas are wider than those of individual nation states. Thus the injunction to give each national central bank a mandate to deliver price stability, and to create an institutional environment in which the incentives to take this mandate seriously are maximized, to which our earlier analysis pointed, is a bit too simple. For countries whose national money is not a key currency, it does not deal with the question of how to weigh the trade-off between stabilizing the domestic price level and stabilizing the exchange rate on the key currency; and for the key currency country it does not deal with the question of how to ensure the accountability of its monetary authority across its entire areas of dominance. The latter point is particularly important, because the provider of a key currency can extract seignorage from abroad. An arrangement which spreads inflation's costs across a currency area, but concentrates the revenue it can generate within the narrower jurisdiction which chooses the inflation rate, has a built in bias towards inflation.[18]

The formation of a monetary union, with a single currency for the whole area is one economically feasible approach to this problem. In this case a supra-national central bank, with a mandate to deliver price stability, accountable to an electorate drawn from the whole area, but insulated from those aspects of the political process which generate resort to the inflation tax and lead to electorally driven time inconsistent policies would seem to be in order. An alternative would be to maintain national currencies linked by market determined exchange rates, thus ensuring that the market for the services of a key currency remains contestable, and hence reducing the potential seignorage to be generated from its inflation. So long as at least one central bank in the group operated under a regime in which it had no interest in maximizing seignorage that would tend to discipline the rest. There are residual problems with either approach, however.

Monetary union involves a willingness to surrender a symbolically important trapping of national sovereignty, and rules out adjustment to real shocks by way of exchange rate changes. Since the possibility of international labour mobility and international fiscal transfers makes the latter loss less important, trading blocs which are also moving towards greater political integration – the EEC is the obvious example – are likely to find it relatively attractive. Where local political sensibilities argue against political integration – as in North America – a reliance on the mechanics of the contestable market would seem more appropriate. The danger here is the emergence of some intermediate arrangement involving pegged exchange rates. Such a system might leave the key currency country's monetary authority responsible only to its own electorate, make it difficult for other authorities to bring discipline to bear on it by revaluation in the face of inflation, and, most dangerous of all, might open up the possibility of elected politicians taking control of monetary policy by way of international agreements about its co-ordination within the currency area.

IX. CONCLUSIONS

I remarked earlier that, in matters of policy, it is more important to be right than original. Thus, I make no apologies for the unspectacular conclusions which emerge from this chapter. They amount to the following: price level stability is an economically desirable state of affairs, and monetary policy is the appropriate tool with which to aim for it; monetary policy has other effects on the economy too, and those in charge of it are always exposed to the temptation to misuse it; proposals to lock policy into an appropriate pattern once and for all by the enactment of some quasi-constitutional rule founder on the fact that the monetary system, like any other set of human institutions, is subject to inevitably unforeseeable change, while tendencies to natural monopoly inherent in its operation rule out a solution through the workings of a completely unregulated competitive market in the provision of money and its services; We are left, then, with relying on discretionary power in order to maintain price stability, and the best we can do to ensure that it is properly used is to protect those in whom it is vested from incentives to do otherwise; and, given the current state of the world political and economic order, independent central banks, insulated from day-to-day politics, and perhaps competing with one another in the provision of international monies, seem to offer the best chance of success here.

If the chance in question is far from a certain one, and if the matter of how to preserve and improve it must therefore attract continuous attention into the foreseeable future, perhaps that is the best we can expect. Perhaps, indeed, the quest for a once and for all guarantee of price stability inherent in one overarching monetary reform has, after all, been uncomfortably like those for perpetual motion or a squared circle.

Acknowledgements

I am grateful to Peter Howitt, Angelo Melino and Allan Meltzer for helpful discussion of an earlier draft.

Notes

1. See the preface to *Money and the Mechanism of Exchange* (1875).
2. My own first effort at criticizing the then orthodox analysis of inflation was prepared in 1975. See Laidler (1990, ch. 2) for a reprint of this paper. Our understanding of these matters has considerably deepened since then, and this section of this chapter owes a great deal to Peter Howitt's (1990) masterly discussion of these issues.
3. But they are not identical. Two agents separated in space can benefit from a telephone system. It takes three agents (and three goods too) before monetary exchange becomes useful.
4. Stanley Fischer (1986) remains the best single source of material on the theory – not to mention practice – of indexation against inflation.
5. A comprehensive two volume collection of essays dealing with these issues in the Canadian context, but in a manner that makes them worthy

of more than a national audience, is published in Richard Lipsey (ed.) (1990) and Robert York (ed.) (1990).

6. The *locus classicus* of the case for a money growth rule is Friedman (1960). Note that Brunner and Meltzer (1987) have explicitly abandoned the view that the dominant cyclical impulse is monetary in the light of the experience of the 1970s and 1980s.
7. Laidler (ed.) (1990) contains a representative selection of papers dealing with the current state of our knowledge of the demand for money function. This section of the current chapter draws heavily on my editor's introduction to this volume.
8. See Johannes and Rasche (1987) for a recent empirical study of the 'money multipliers', through which base control would operate, using US data. Their conclusion is that base control of money growth, at least on a quarter to quarter basis would indeed be feasible.
9. See Freedman (1983) for a detailed account of this episode.
10. And indeed an earlier essay by this author dealing with this topic did end on just such a note. See Laidler (1990, ch. 7).
11. The classic treatment of time inconsistency is, of course, Kydland and Prescott (1977). The matter is closely related to issues having to do with policy credibility. For a survey of the relevant literature see Blackburn and Christensen (1989).
12. I emphasize the word 'tend' here. Changes in the terms of trade between imports and exports can disturb the price level independently of monetary factors, and shifts in the domestic relative price structure between tradable and non-tradable goods can have similar effects; many modern applications of the purchasing power parity doctrine seem to me to pay insufficient attention to these important qualifications to its validity.
13. I am aware that it is hard indeed to give meaning to the word 'liquidity' without referring to money's function as a means of exchange. I take up this matter below.
14. Pioneering empirical work on the interaction of central bank laws and the outcome of monetary policy has been carried out by my colleagues Robin Bade and Michael Parkin. Their (1987) paper builds on work which they began in the late 1970s. The argument of this section of the present chapter has been much influenced by their finding that independent central banks seem, as a matter of fact, more prone to deliver stable prices than those whose conduct of monetary policy is subject to influence by politicians. Also, the discussion in the following few paragraphs about the interaction between central bank law and the incentives to which those institutions are subjected draws heavily on discussions with Peter Howitt. See also, Howitt (1991), particularly pp. 1–2.
15. These arguments were advanced by Walter Bagehot (1873) about the Bank of England, until 1945 a privately owned joint stock company governed by a board of directors whose members came from the business community, but could not be bankers. Bagehot was far from uncritical of the Bank's performance, however, but someone versed in the ideas of modern 'public choice' analysis must wonder whether he was right in ascribing the Bank's failings mainly to the directors' well meaning belief in erroneous economic doctrines.

16. Indeed Bade and Parkin (1987) find that a central bank's mandate *per se* has no discernible effect on its performance in the absence of political independence.
17. Note that, as long ago as (1953), Friedman made essentially the same point about the lessons of international monetary instability of the 1930s. If the argument advanced here differs at all from Friedman's it is in recognizing that exchange rate behaviour can do more than reflect domestic monetary instability, but can significantly amplify its effects. The key paper dealing with this matter is, of course, Dornbusch (1976). One caveat is in order here, however. If recent work casting doubt upon the efficiency of asset markets turns out to be relevant to the foreign exchange market, then the conclusion that the *only* problem with flexible rates is that they amplify the effects of disturbances originating elsewhere would have to be modified. See Fortune (1991) for a survey of the relevant literature as it applies to the stock market.
18. But experience in Western Europe gives grounds for optimism on this score. The Deutschmark is certainly the key currency of the European Monetary System, but the Bundesbank's degree of political independence within Germany has enabled it to bring a good deal of stability to the whole system. Against this example, however, we must set that of the United States' role in generating inflation throughout the Bretton Woods System during the Vietnam War. Perhaps the Federal Reserve System is not, after all, as politically independent as mere inspection of its formal governance would suggest. This was the view of Weintraub (1978).

References

Bade, R. and Parkin, M. (1987) 'Central Bank Laws and Monetary Policy.' University of Western Ontario. Mimeo.

Bagehot, W. (1873) *Lombard Street: a Description of the Money Market* (London).

Barnett, W. (1990) 'Developments in Monetary Aggregation Theory.' *Journal of Policy Modeling*, **12** (Summer): 205–58.

Bordo, M. and Jonung, L. (1990) 'The Long Run Behaviour of Velocity: The Institutional Approach Revisited.' *Journal of Policy Modeling*, **12** (Summer): 165–98.

Blackburn, K. and Christensen, M. (1989) 'Monetary Policy and Policy Credibility.' *Journal of Economic Literature*, **27** (Mar.): 1–45.

Brunner, K. (1984) 'Monetary Policy and the Monetary Order.' *Aussenwirtschaft*, **39**.

Brunner, K. and Meltzer, A.H. (1963). 'Predicting Velocity: Implications for Theory and Policy.' *Journal of Finance*, **18** (May): 319–54.

Brunner, K. and Meltzer, A.H. (1987) 'Money and the Economy: Issues in Monetary Analysis.' The 1987 Raffaele Mattioli Lectures, Carnegie Mellon Univ. Mimeo.

Dornbusch, R. (1976) 'Expectations and Exchange Rate Dynamics.' *Journal of Political Economy*, **84** (Dec.): 1161–76.

Edgeworth, F.Y. (1888) 'The Mathematical Theory of Banking.' *Journal of the Royal Statistical Society*, **51** (Mar.): 113–26.

Fischer, S. (1986) *Indexing, Inflation and Economic Policy* (Cambridge Mass: MIT Press).

Fortune, P. (1991) 'Stock Market Efficiency: An Autopsy?' *New England Economic Review* (Mar./Apr.): 17–40.

Freedman, C. (1983) 'Financial Innovation in Canada: Causes and Consequences.' *American Economic Review* **73** (May): 101–6.

Friedman, M. (1953) 'The Case for Flexible Exchange Rates.' In *Essays in Positive Economics* (Chicago: University of Chicago Press).

Friedman, M. (1960) *A Program for Monetary Stability*. (New York: Fordham University Press).

Friedman, M. (1969) *The Optimum Quantity of Money* (London: Macmillan).

Hayek, F.A. von (1976) *Denationalising Money* (London: IEA).

Howitt, P.W. (1990) 'Zero Inflation as a Long Term Target for Monetary Policy.' In R.G. Lipsey, (ed.) 1990.

Howitt, P.W. (1991) 'Canadian Monetary Policy.' Prepared for *Handbook of Monetary Policy* London, Ontario: U.W.O., Mimeo.

Jarrett P. and Selody, J. (1982) 'The Productivity-Inflation Nexus in Canada 1963–79.' *Review of Economics and Statistics*, **64** (Aug.): 361–67.

Jevons, W.S. (1875) *Money and the Mechanism of Exchange* (London).

Johannes, J. and Rasche, R. (1987) *Controlling the Growth of Monetary Aggregates* (Boston: Kluwer-Nijhoff).

Johnson, H.G. (1971) 'The Keynesian Revolution and the Monetarist Counter-Revolution.' *American Economic Review*, **61** (May): 91–106.

Kydland, F. and Prescott, E. (1977) 'Rules Rather than Discretion: The Inconsistency of Optimal Plans.' *Journal of Political Economy*, **85** (June): 473–91.

Laidler, D. (1990) *Taking Money Seriously* (Cambridge Mass: MIT Press).

Laidler, D. (ed.) (1990) *Understanding Velocity – Implications for Theory and Policy*. Special issue of *Journal of Policy Modeling*, **12** (Summer).

Lipsey, R.G. (ed.) (1990) *Zero Inflation: The Goal of Price Stability* (Toronto: C.D. Howe Institute).

McCallum, B.T. (1988) 'Robustness Properties of a Rule for Monetary Policy.' In Brunner K. and McCallum, B.T. (eds), *Money, Cycles and Exchange Rates: Essays in Honour of Allan H. Meltzer*. Carnegie Rochester Conference Series Vol. 29 (Amsterdam: North-Holland).

Meltzer, A.H. (1987) 'On Monetary Stability and Monetary Reform.' *Bank of Japan Monetary and Economic Studies*, **5** (Sept.): 13–34.

Phillips, A.W. (1954) 'Stabilisation in a Closed Economy.' *Economic Journal*, **64** (June): 290–323.

Weintraub, R. (1978) 'Congressional Supervision of Monetary Policy.' *Journal of Monetary Economics*, **4** (Apr.): 341–62.

Wicksell, K. (1898) *Interest and Prices*. tr. R.F. Kahn (1936) for the Royal Economic Society (London: Macmillan).

York, R.C. (ed.) (1990) *Taking Aim: The Debate on Zero Inflation* (Toronto: C.D. Howe Institute).

18 Monetarism – the unfinished business

Introduction

One of the curiosities of the 1980s and early 1990s has been the way in which the ideas that have made the running in academic macroeconomics – real business cycles, overlapping generations and cash in advance models of money, and so on – have had so little to say about current real-world problems. Thus, in the policy area, older and academically unfashionable analysis, Monetarist ideas included, have continued to be applied. The opportunity to give those ideas another airing in 1992, to an audience of academic, business and government economists, was too good to miss; so when the Cyprus Economics Society honoured me with an invitation to give their annual lecture, I took it.

I still have hopes that the continuity of monetary economics, which the New-classical revolution seemed for a while to break, will in due course be re-established (incorporating the best ideas of the New-classicals of course). I also have hopes that, as it is, what has recently been called 'Monetarism' but which as Chapter 16 has shown, is really a much older doctrine, will again occupy a central position in the area. That is the 'unfinished business' to which my title refers.

CYPRUS JOURNAL OF ECONOMICS, Vol. 5, No. 2, December 1992

MONETARISM - THE UNFINISHED BUSINESS

DAVID LAIDLER*

1. INTRODUCTION

When someone is described as a "monetarist" these days, it is seldom meant as a compliment. To the lay critic, monetarism is an amalgam of economic policy positions, associated with conservative governments, whose alleged legacy includes high unemployment and the decay of social programmes. To the academic, monetarism is a set of obsolete economic doctrines which, though they may have served a purpose in the past, have now been discredited by empirical evidence and overtaken by new theoretical developments. But we do not generally pin labels on our own lapels, and those of us who have been classified as "monetarists" for the last two decades have no alternative but to try to make that label mean what we, rather than our critics, would like it to mean. And that is what this lecture is about. In it, I shall first of all describe what traditional academic monetarism was, and defend it against charges of error and obsolecence. I shall also have something to say about its "guilt by association" with conservative politics.

But most important of all, I shall draw attention to elements in the monetarist literature which, to my mind, not only render it a "progressive research agenda" to use the currently fashionable Lakatosian phrase, but also suggest that it is in fact nothing more nor less than the latest manifestation of that same ongoing tradition in monetary economics to which Thornton, Ricardo, Marshall, Wicksell, and Keynes, among many others have contributed. The "unfinished business" of my title, indeed, is to draw attention to this interpretation of the doctrine, get it debated, and if it is correct, get it widely accepted too.[1]

2. MONETARISM AND IDEOLOGY

One cannot simultaneously characterise monetarism as a progressive research agenda, and then offer a definition of it which will fit at all times and

* University of Western Ontario. This was presented as the 1992 Cyprus Economic Society Annual Lecture. It was delivered at the Bank of Cyprus Cultural Foundation in Nicosia, on September 30, 1992.

places. A progressive agenda does make progress. It will nevertheless be helpful to begin by describing what the doctrine looked like a little over two decades ago when it was named, almost simultaneously, by Karl Brunner (1968) and Nicholas Kaldor (1970). Such a description may be organised in terms of the then popular IS-LM model of the macroeconomy's short-run (i.e. abstracting from growth) behaviour, and may be cast in terms of four propositions, three positive and one normative.

First and foremost among these was Friedman's (1956) contention that the demand for money function in the economy was a stable function of a few arguments. Second was the argument, most thoroughly developed by Brunner and Meltzer (eg. 1976) that the supply of money was controllable by the central bank. Third was the contention that the IS-LM model's inability to allocate aggregate fluctuations between real output and employment on the one land, and the general price level on the other, could be made good by supplementing it with an expectations augmented Phillips curve whose distinguishing characteristic was the absence of any long-run trade-off between these variables.[2] Finally came the normative proposition that, because the dynamics of the interaction of money and the macroeconomy were subject to long and variable time lags, and because the dominant shocks disturbing the economy's equilibrium were in any event monetary, it was desirable to govern the behaviour of the money supply by a constant growth rule, chosen in the light of the economy's real growth rate and the real income elasticity of demand for money so as to ensure negligibly low inflation.[3]

Now when we put it this way, monetarism appears to be a largely value neutral body of doctrine. Its positive elements were open to empirical test, and if they failed such a test, it is hard to see how even the most hardened ideologue could have persisted in defending its normative element. This is, and remains, my own position on the matter. Nevertheless, from the outset there was a strong ideological element about the monetarist controversy, and if one looks a little more closely at the positive content of monetarism, one can see why. An economy characterised by a controllable (and steadily growing) nominal money supply, along with an expectations augmented Phillips curve, will have its only equilibrium at the "natural" unemployment rate, and will, absent perverse dynamics, converge upon that equilibrium, in the wake of disturbances.

It is possible to mount a critique of market mechanisms based upon private property while conceding that they do not lead to economic chaos, but it is far easier to do so, and the critique is far more compelling, if it can be established that those mechanisms are inherently unstable; and the actual experience of the 1920s and 30s had persuaded many people that they were. What came to be called "Keynesian economics" provided both a non-marxist analysis of that instability and a set of policy doctrines designed to cope with it. To its adherents,

Kaldor (1970) is a prime example, monetarism, which attributed the experience of the interwar years to monetary mismanagement, looked like a throwback to the Austrian analysis of Hayek (1931) and Robbins (1934) who had argued for policy inaction as the best medicine for the Great Depression. Small wonder that anyone brought up on Keynesian economics and its diagnosis of the Depression found monetarism profoundly disturbing. And on the other side of the same coin, anyone prone to support market mechanisms for ideological reasons, could not fail to find attractive a doctrine which predicted that such mechanisms would in the past have produced full employment and low inflation, and were capable of doing so in the future as well, if governments would only deliver stable monetary policy and otherwise leave well alone.

Thus, deeply held and politically important beliefs, which had of course been matters of controversy long before the 1930s - consider the Ricardo-Malthus debates about Say's Law - were at stake in the monetarist controversy, and it is not surprising that market oriented politicians of the stripe of Mrs. Thatcher and Mr. Reagan should adopt, and sometimes ostentatiously so, variations on monetarist themes in their macroeconomic policies. But we must not over-simplify. It was the Callaghan, not the Thatcher government, that introduced money-growth targets to Britain, and before, not after an IMF visit; and Paul Volker was appointed by President Carter, not Reagan. Moreover, Mrs. Thatcher was still prime minister during the Lawson boom, while Reagan's macroeconimic policy seems to have had far more to do with "supply side" pop-economics than with the serious analysis of Friedman or Brunner and Meltzer. If monetarism's reputation has suffered from the policy experience of the 1980s, that is more the result of guilt by association than of the failure of any carefully executed policy experiment; and indeed, over that decade, where money growth was kept down, or reduced, so was inflation - a result quite in keeping with monetarist doctrine.

Monetarism, in short, could have survived its association with the policy experience of the 1980s rather easily had it not simultaneously lost much of its academic credibility. It is to this matter that I now turn.

3. STABILITY OF THE DEMAND FOR MONEY

Monetarism, I have argued, was at heart a body of positive economic doctrine, and as such it was a fair target for criticism with respect both to its empirical content and its logical coherence. These are the normal criteria employed in scientific debate, and it is no disgrace if a set of propositions fails to measure up to them. Indeed it would have been a miracle, never before seen in the history of economic thought, had the monetarism of 1970 vintage withstood all attempts to refute or modify it. Nor would it necessarily have been a welcome miracle. A research agenda is an agenda for creating new knowledge, and the discovery of flaws in existing doctrine is a necessary part of that process. Though current work on hysteresis phenomena in labour markets may yet undermine it, the monetarist hypothesis about the absence of a long run inflation-unemployment trade off proved remarkably durable, and became a central tenet of the New-Classical economics which succeeded monetarism in the 1980s and 1990s. Friedman's hypothesis about the simplicity and stability of the demand for money function proved less robust, and gave rise to much controversy, as we shall now see.

This hypothesis was surely the cornerstone of early monetarism. Even so, Friedman's (1959) suggestion that the demand for real money balances depended stably on real permanent income and nothing else did not long survive empirical scrutiny. By 1970 it was clearly apparent that some measure of the opportunity cost of holding money belonged in the relationship, thus reopening the possibility of IS curve shocks being a source of economic fluctuations, and of fiscal policy having a stabilisation role to play as well, and hence doing much to blur the distinction between monetarism and the macroeconomic orthodoxy it sought to replace. It was also by then apparent that the lag patterns in the data, which the permanent income hypothesis explained in terms of error learning, could equally well be explained by the presence of adjustment costs in an otherwise rather conventional "Keynesian" demand for money function. In short, this key component of monetarism had generated much fruitful work by 1970, so much so that it was ready to be absorbed into mainstream IS-LM macroeconomics, which it duly was in the next decade.[4] This was not to the ultimade benefit of monetarism, and for two reasons.

First, at the nands of mainstream macroeconomists, working with large scale econometric models largely designed with a view to generating forecasts useful to stabilisation policy, considerable emphasis came to the placed upon the short-run stability of the demand for money function. Friedman, on the other hand, had emphasised its long-run properties, and indeed had used cycle average data (he would later use cycle phase average data) to establish them. And this mattered, because a demand for money function stable on a quarter by quarter basis seemed to provide a sound basis for the design of an activist approach to monetary policy of which no monetarist could, or indeed did, approve.

Second, as Brunner and Meltzer frequently, and correctly, complained, the IS-LM model is inadequate as a device for analysing monetary policy.[5] It leads to the view that, if only the monetary authorites use some rerpesentative interest rate as their policy instrument, the quantity of money becomes not merely an endogenous variable, but a passively demand determined variable. The IS-LM framework appeared to suggest that, given a stable demand for money function, monetary policy was appropriately conducted by: setting a target for the quantity of money in circulation; estimating the current values of all arguments of the function, say real income and the price level (along with appropriately chosen lagged values too, to allow for adjustment phenomena); and then setting a current value for the rate of interest to ensure that the target value of the money supply would be demanded by the public. To put it charitably, policies so conducted did not work very well, leading mainstream macro-economists to reject the monetarist hypothesis of a stable aggregate demand for money function at least as quickly as they had adopted it. This was, in my view, a mistake; for as I shall suggest below, the problem in all likelihood arose from paying insufficient attention modelling the money supply generating mechanism, rather than from instability in the demand function - though there were some problems here, to be sure.

The results which recent econometric literature on the demand for money function has generated are relevant to this judgment. There, the application of co-integration techniques to time series data for a number of countries has permitted us to test hypotheses about the steady state properties of the function - the very properties which monetarist doctrine stressed from the outset - without simultaneously having to take a position about the mechanisms driving the short run dynamics of relevant variables about that state, and hence without their results being subject to distortion by errors in modelling those short run dynamics. Overwhelmingly, the application of these techniques confirms the stability of long-run demand for money functions, though it also reveals that they are, particularly those for narrowly defined aggregates, subject to occasional shifts stemming from institutional changes in the financial system, sometimes associated with regulatory changes and sometimes with technical developments, such as those associated with the adoption of computer technology.[6]

These results make it difficult to argue for rigid money growth rate rules, and hence provide the prime example of how monetarist doctrine of an earlier vintage has had to be modified in the light of subsequent debate. However they leave untouched, indeed they strengthen, the presumption that medium term money growth targets (open to revision as and when institutional developments require it) are a highly desirable basis for monetary policy. Moreover, and crucially in the current context, they tell us that the instability problems which created so much skepticism about the demand for money function in the 1980s, and did so much to prompt a premature abandonment of monetarist hypotheses among macroeconomists, stemmed in large measure from an inadequate handling of the adjustment dynamics of the short-run relationship.

Though I would like to argue that these results also imply beyond reasonable doubt that my earlier suggestion that the major source of difficulties with the demand for money function arose not from troubles with that relationship, but from neglect of the mechanisms determining the supply of money, I can not defend so strong a position. What I can do, however, is offer arguments in support of it which are firmly rooted in traditional monetary theory. I can also explain why this line of argument is disturbing both to adherents of new-classical economics and to orthodox Keynesians, and therefore why it is proving so difficult to get it taken seriously. As I shall now argue, getting attention paid to these matters constitutes an important part of the "unfinished business" of monetarism to which the title of this lecture refers.

4. THE MONEY SUPPLY PROCESS

To treat the quantity of money in circulation as measuring the quantity of money demanded, as the vast majority of studies of the demand for money do, is to assume that the economy is "on" its demand function for money. This assumption is probably adequate when dealing with long-run relationships but not in the short-run. That is why I believe that our inability to model the short run in a satisfactory fashion stems from our inadequate understanding of the mechanisms whereby the supply and demand for money are brought into equilibrium with one another in the wake of distrurbances. To say this is, of course, also to say that the conventional treatment of the supply of money as responding passively to changes in its demand, a treatment which seems so natural when IS-LM analysis is applied to a policy regime in which the authorities treat an interest rate as their policy instrument, is erroneous.

The issue at stake here is not simply a matter of the endogeneity or exogeneity of the quantity of money, much though this matter has been debated. It is true enough that a great deal of monetarist theorising has begun from the assumption of an exogenously given quantity of money, and I readily concede that such an assumption can be descriptively accurate only of an imaginary world. In the world we live in, money is created by a banking system, and its quantity does respond to impulses stemming from the economy, as well as to those imparted by the authorities. The quantity of money is, then, beyond doubt an endogenous variable. But an argument by analogy with a simple Marshallian partial equilibrium supply and demand apparatus will soon show that to concede this point settles next to nothing.

In a Marshallian market, taking it for granted that quantity demanded depends inversely on price, quantity supplied is only an exogenous variable if the supply curve is vertical. If it is not, then quantity supplied is certainly an endogenous variable; but an upward sloping supply function may still be subject to shifts which occur independently of factors affecting the demand curve, and reasonable predictions about the consequences of those shifts for market price might nevertheless be made while neglecting the upward slope of the supply curve and treading it "as if" vertical. The monetarist position, then, is not that the quantity of money is exogenous, but rather that its supply curve is an independent relationship which can be shifted by factors under the control of the authorities, and that the simplifying hypothesis that the quantity of money behaves "as if" an exogenous variable might be worth maintaining for some purposes and in some circumstances (but not when trying to estimate a short-run demand for money function, as my earlier remarks should make clear).

But suppose we carry the Marshallian market analogy a step further; suppose we picture the limiting case of such a market in which suppliers simply set the price and then supply any quantity demanded at that price. Then indeed quantity is not just an endogenous, but a completely passive, variable, and the only independent behaviour relationship in the market is the demand curve. This is surely the kind of thing that exponents of orthodox interpretations of the consequences of central banks treating the rate of interest as a policy instrument have in mind when they deny the existence of an independent supply of money function. To make use of Basil Moore's (1988) helpful labels, they are "horizontalists" just as monetarists are "verticalists" - the qualifier "as if" is understood to apply in each case. There are good reasons, however, for thinking that our analogy becomes misleading at just this point, because partial equilibrium analysis does not, when all is said and done, quite fit the case of money. There is another market involved here, which cannot be ignored, and consideration of which changes the picture. I refer, as readers of Brunner and Meltzer will have already guessed, to the market for debt, or as they call it, credit.[7]

The "horizontalist" view of the money supply process would have it that, by changing the price at which it stands ready to buy and sell debt, the banking system changes the value of the interest rate argument in the public's demand for money function, and the public exchange debt with the banks in order to restore their cash balances to equilibrium. It also has it that, to the extent that the changed interest rate has effects on other variables, such as output and prices, the changes in the demand for money induced by these will be satisfied by similar means. It also has it that, in the limiting case of a zero interest elasticity of demand for money, open market operations become quite impossible, so that traditional pre-Keynesian stories about the transmission of monetary policy, and some simplified monetarist stories too, told in terms of such a demand function, are seriously flawed. Such views can be found in the writings of many distinguished monetary economists - Hahn, Kaldor, Hicks, and indeed Keynes himself - so it is no light matter to disagree with them. But, as any monetarist must, disagree I do.

When the banking system changes the price at which it stands ready to buy and sell debt - raises it, say, for the sake of concreteness - it disturbs the margin between debt and physical capital (and indeed current consumption too) as well as that between money and debt. That is what Brunner and Meltzer mean when they say that such a step affects the the market for credit as well as the market for money. Specifically, the non-bank public may now want to hold more cash, and may be willing to offer debt to the banks in order to obtain it, but they will also want to acquire more goods in exchange for a further reduction in their holdings of debt. In a barter economy, in which "money" was nothing more than a pure non-interest-bearing store of value, there would, presumably, be a reshuffling of the balance sheets of firms and households to accomodate this change, but, in an economy characterised by monetary exchange, matters are radically different.

In order to acquire the money to buy the extra goods they now demand, agents must be net sellers of debt, and since the banking system is the residual buyer of debt this operation will involve the creation of money over and above that required to satisfy the increased demand for money. An excess supply of money is thus created, which, according to monetarist analysis will have its own impact on the demand for goods and services over and above the direct first round effects of the public's initial substitution of goods for debt. It is also worth pointing out explicitly that, in this view of the matter, the banking system's capacity to create money does not depend upon the existence of an interest elastic demand for money function. The latter phenomenon is simply a complicating factor in the mechanics of open market operations, not their *sine qua non*.

It should be emphasised that none of this is to deny that the initial substitution between debt and goods can have a significant impact upon aggregate demand. It is, however, to claim that these are first round effects, and to insist that the disequilibrium between the supply and demand for money that arises as the by-product of these first round transactions is also, and additionally important. It is not, however, claimed that the quantity of money created in these transactions must all remain in circulation ever afterwards. Some agents with excess cash holdings might well find it desirable to reduce indebtedness to the banks and thereby extinguish the money thus utilised. It is, however, reasonable to point out that, even for agents thus indebted, this is by no means the only option available for reducing excess cash holdings, while agents who are not indebted to banks are also likely to be among those finding themselves with excess cash.

Any attempt to adjust cash balances in other ways will of course affect the demand for goods and services, and will continue to do so until such variables as output and the price level have changed enough to lead to the money which remains in circulation being willingly held. Thus, I am claiming here that traditional cash balance mechanics, of a type implicit in the analysis of Thornton and Ricardo, and explicitly analysed in varying degrees of detail by Mill, Marshall and Irving Fisher, among others, still has a role to play in helping us understand the interaction of money and economic activity even in the presence of a banking system in which the rate of interest is the policy instrument.[9] Moreover, I would also claim that these second and subsequent round effects are of more empirical significance than those that arise from the first round substitution between debt and goods.

Let me draw explicit attention to the presence of the adjective "empirical" in the last sentence. *A priori* argument of the type presented here can establish at best the qualitative presence of effects, but not their quantitative significance. It could be that the propensity of the private sector to use excess cash to reduce indebtedness to the banks is always and everywhere so high that first round effects dominate the consequences of monetary policy, and that fluctuations in the observed quantity of money in circulation are indeed dominated by variations in the factors affecting the demand for money. If these things were so, though, we would have to explain how, during the 1980s in a number of countries, when it has been uncontroversial that tight monetary policy has precipitated two recessions, the behaviour of monetary aggregates, particularly narrow ones, has lead that of real economic activity and prices. Such timing is hard to reconcile with the idea that the quantity of money in circulation responds passively to arguments in its demand function.

And this brings us back to the empirical problem from which this section of my lecture began. If the dynamics driving the variations about their steady state in the relationships among money, interest rates, output and prices are the outcome of a complex transmission mechanism involving the interaction of the arguments of independent supply and demand for money functions, it is hardly surprising that attempts to model them as if they reflected only the properties of a demand function have led us nowhere. It is surely an important piece of unfinished business to investigate this question. But before we can expect much progress here, an important roadblock needs to be removed, namely the strongly held preferences of some of our discipline's most distinguished practitioners for a certain type of equilibrium modelling. The next and final substantive section of this lecture is devoted to exploring and explaining the relevance of this issue.

5. MONEY AND EQUILIBRIUM MODELLING

The word equilibrium has more than one meaning in economics, and that is why I referred above to a certain type of equilibrium modelling. The phrase "equilibrium behaviour" applied to the individual agent usually refers to the execution by that agent of plans drawn up in order to maximise some utility function subject to constraints imposed by endowments, available technology, not to mention market opportunities. I find it hard to see how economics can do without modelling equilibrium behaviour thus conceived. If individual agents cannot be treated as forming plans and then carrying them out, predictions about their behaviour cannot be made, and economics must forfeit any claim to positive content.

But agents do not usually act in isolation. The market opportunities of one agent are the result of, among other things, the attempts of others to execute their plans. The interdependence of agents must be of the essence in any social science, and the means whereby independently formed plans are co-ordinated is therefore an important element of economics' subject matter. At this point we meet another equilibrium concept: namely, market equilibrium, a state of affairs in which the plans of individual agents are compatible with one another. Defined sufficiently generally, there can be no objection to claims about the universal relevance of this concept either. Individual agents can hardly be expected to execute their own plans if those plans are not mutually compatible. But, as we all know, economics deals with some very particular co-ordination mechanisms involving prices, and has shown that a system of competitive markets with flexible prices is capable of producing a harmonous social outcome in which the maximising plans of individual agents are reconciled with one another.

It has also shown that one can feed informational asymmetries into such a system without destroying its capacity to equilibrate plans drawn up on the basis of information which *ex post* will be revealed to be false; though not surprisingly, in this case, agents might well be unhappy with the outcome of their market activities in a way in which they are not when those activities are the outcome of choices made in the light of correct information. And, into the bargain, there is a meaningful sense in which economic activities co-ordinated by such competitive markets maximise social welfare; while, even in the presence of mis-information, agents are doing the best they can in the circumstances. It follows that economic analysis based on such a framework leaves little room for policy. It implies that, if economic policy does not actually contribute to agents' errors, it is achieving all that can be expected from it.

Now, uncomfortable though it may make us, we should not reject competitive-general-equilibrium modelling on *a priori* grounds. It is logically coherent, and it has been shown to yield empirical predictions. In that sence, it is good science and ought to be treated with respect. This is, however, not to say that it is also correct science. That is a matter to be settled by reference to empirical evidence; and my concern about the current status of competitive-general-equilibrium theory is not that it is taken seriously, but that it is too often defended, not with reference to its compatibility with the facts, but rather as enbodying first principles which provide the only scientifically respectable way of approaching the subject.

But such an *a priori* defence is no more satisfactory than an attack would be. Because we cannot help but model individual agents as maximising subject to the constraints they face, it does not follow that we must also model their interaction in the context of a social framework that permits them to maximise all potential gains from trade among themselves. It is interesting to know that we can conceive of such a framework, but it is not hard to conceive of others in which such a happy state of affairs does not rule, even though agents' plans, being subjected to constraints that would not be encountered in a competitive market, are nevertheless co-ordinated once those constraints are allowed for. Such alternatives are equally worthy of serious consideration with respect to their empirical content.

Indeed, I would go further than this. Because the development of economic analysis is an historical phenomenon, it is not surprising that, at any particular moment, some hypotheses have been derived with greater logical coherence from individual maximising premises than others. The fact that a framework needs patching up with "free parameters" does not automatically render it empirically vacuous, and if it does not, then its predictions are worth testing. Should they turn out to have more empirical content than those of a more logically rigourous framework, then so much the worse for the latter. We certainly should be prepared to take seriously the hypothesis that the world behaves as if agents' plans were co-ordinated in continuously clearing competitive markets. Economists have been arguing about this matter in one guise or another for over two hundred years, and so should we. But we should not pretend that so fundamental a dispute can be settled by converting a controversial hypothesis into a non-debatable axiom.[10]

The relation of these considerations to the subject matter of this lecture is this: the traditional analysis of credit creation and cash balance mechanics, whose continued relevance I argued in its preceding section, distinguishes between the supply and demand for money and relies on the persistence over time of discrepancies between these two magnitudes; it is therefore incompatible with continuous Walrasian equilibrium, and an approach to monetary economics which insists on Walrasian foundations can have no room for such analysis. To insist on such foundations, therefore, is to deny the validity of monetarism. That is the nature of the "roadblock" to which I referred earlier, and that is why its removal is the crucial element in monetarism's unifinished business.

There has always been a non-Walrasian streak to monetarist analysis, even though it has seldom been at the centre of attention in debates about the approach, and has often been ignored or overlooked. I refer here to the idea that the institution of monetary exchange should be viewed as a means of coping with the information and co-ordination problems faced by a market economy which was first introduced into the monetarist literature by Brunner and Meltzer in (1963) and further developed by them in (1971). This way of looking at things treats money as an *alternative* to the Walrasian market and its mythical auctioneer, not as a supplement to these devices, and it has a long history in economics. It can be found in various guises and states of development in the *Wealth of Nations,* in the writings of Thornton, Mill, Jevons, Marshall, not to mention the *General Theory*; and the fact that it also underpins monetarism goes a long way to explaining why monetarists and economists working in the tradition of Clower (1984), Goodhart (1975) and Leijonhufvud (1981), not to mention such post-Keynesians as Chick (1992) and Davidson (1972) often seem to find it easier to talk to one another than to mainstream macroeconomists. Though these groups disagree about many things they all start from the position that the economy they are trying to understand is one to whose organisation money is essential.

There is, of course, nothing incompatible between this view of the world and the postulate of equilibrium behaviour at the level of the individual agent, nor does it deny the importance of taking account of the general interdependence of individual plans when dealing with market activity.[11] What it does do, however, is point to an alternative set of mechanisms to those of continuously clearing flexible price markets as a means of coping with the problems implicit in that interdependence. Specifically, as I have argued elsewhere, it leads one to postulate that precautionary balances of money are held by agents as a means of enabling themselves to carry through individual plans made on the basis of incomplete information and in response to price signals which may turn out to be, relative to those which would be given by a Walrasian auctioneer, "false". Moreover, precisely because money acts as a buffer against the consequences of mistakes that stem from these sources, its very existence reduces the incentives of agents to collect and process information and, in the case of price setters, to get the prices in question "right".

In particular, when information collection and processing is subject to rising marginal costs, the availability of buffer stocks of money will ensure that, contrary to the dogma of New-classical economics, agents will habitually use less than "all available" information, and where price changing is costly, it will also ensure that prices are habitually slow to move to the levels that would clear a Walrasian market in the wake of changed conditions. In such a world, excess demands and supplies for goods will occur not merely as notional entities during a tatonnnement process, but as observable market phenomena, with the incompatibilities between consumption and production plans implicit in them being abosrbed by changes in buffer stocks of money (and in inventories of other financial assets not to mention goods as well) pending the revision of those plans.[12]

To return to the topic of the preceding section of this lecture, the excess supply (or demand) for money that arises as a by-product of debt market transactions between banks and their customers, finds a natural role to play in the workings of such an economy. And a moment's reflection will also make it apparent why this line of analysis also leads to the view that monetary shocks are a serious matter: they have a potential for disrupting the economy's co-ordination mechanisms which is kept completely hidden from view by conventional Walrasian analysis.

6. CONCLUSIONS

I suggested earlier that it is an important piece of unfinished business for monetarism to get its analysis of the money supply process back onto the research agenda of monetary economics. It should now be clear that this is but one aspect of a more general piece of unfinished business, namely to get the central importance for the functioning of a market economy of the institutions of money and monetary exchange recognised. The currently dominant intellectual traditions in macro-economics have trivialised this issue, the "Keynesian" tradition by treating the quantity of money as an uninteresting passively adjusting variable, and the "New-classical" tradition by insisting on a type of micro foundation for macroeconomics which leaves no role for monetary exchange. I put quotation marks around both of these labels, because, as I hope is apparent from the foregoing arguments, I believe that this trivialisation of monetary economics is in the spirit neither of Classical economics, nor indeed of the economics of Keynes, and has been an aberration in the development of economics.

I have tried to show that monetarism has remained closer to the traditional concerns of monetary theory than other contemporaty and more popular "isms" in macroeconomics, and that, indeed, this closeness has been one of its strongly distinguishing features. If this is so, then when, as I hope will soon be the case, the unfinished business I have dealt with in this lecture is brought to completion, monetarism will lose its distinctive identity. But when monetary economists turn to deepening our understanding of those traditional concerns, that will not, I am confident, spell the end of debate. The very fact that I have cited such a diverse set of writers as Chick, Clower, Davidson, Goodhart and Leijonhuvfud, none of whom would ever be taken for a monetarist, as also addressing questions which arise out of those same traditional concerns, ensures that there will still be plenty to argue about. Though one might be able to foresee a time when monetarism's business is complete, therefore, that is unlikely to be the case for monetary economics. This, however, is hardly a matter for regret.

NOTES

1. Let it be clear that I claim no originality for interpreting monetarism's place in the history of economic thought along these lines. Brunner (1989) has also made this suggestion.
2. The expectations augmented Phillips curve, due to Firedman (1968) and Phelps (1967) was first formally incorporated in simple macro-models of the IS-LM variety (albeit with a vertical LM curve) by this author in a University of Manchester working paper of 1972 a version of which was finally published (1974).
3. They money growth rule was, of course, proposed by Friedman (1960).
4. My own 1969 book on the Demand for Money... surveyed much of the evidence referred to here.
5. See, for example, Brunner and Meltzer's two (1976) contributions to the Stein volume on Monetarism.
6. These matters are discussed in the latest (1992) edition of my Demand for Money...
7. On this matter, see again Brunner and Meltzer (1976).
8. I discussed this matter in greater detail in my paper on "The Buffer-stock Notion in Monetary Economics" which has been reprinted as Chapter 2 of Laidler (1990).
9. I have discussed the development of the analysis of each balance mechanics in the 1870-1914 period in Laidler (1991).
10. The arguments presented here have been developed further in an essay reprinted as Chapter 4 of Laidler (1990).
11. The extremely useful distinction between general economic equilibrium on the one hand, and interdependence on the other, seems to have first been made explicitly by Arthur Marget (1942).
12. The argument presented here is developed at greater length in the title essay, (Chapter 1), of Laidler (1990).

REFERENCES

Brunner, K. (1968) The Role of Money and Monetary Policy. Reprinted in *Federal Reserve Bank of St. Louis Review,* Vol. 71 (October), pp. 4-22.

——— (1989) The Disarray in Macroeconomics. In Capie, F. and Wood, G. (eds.) *Monetary Economics in the 1980s*, the Henry Thornton Lectures, London Macmillan.

MONETARISM - THE UNFINISHED BUSINESS

—— and Meltzer, A.H. (1963) "Predicting Velocity: Implications for Theory and Policy". *Journal of Finance*, Vol. 18 (May), pp. 319-354

—— (1971) "The Uses of Money: Money in the Theory of an Exchange Economy". *American Economic Review*, Vol. 61 (December), pp. 784-805

—— (1976) *An Aggregative Theory for a Closed Economy*, and Reply In Stein J (ed.) Monetarism, Amsterdam, North Holland.

Chick, V. (1992) *On Money, Method, and Keynes*. London, Mamillan

Clower, R.W. (1984) *Money and Markets* (ed. D. Walker). Cambridge. Cambridge University Press.

Davidson, P. (1972) *Money and the Real World*. London, Macmillan.

Friedman, M. (1956) The Quantity Theory of Money: A Restatement In *Studies in the Quantity Theory of Money*, Chicago, University of Chicago Press

—— (1959) "The Demand for Money, Some Theoretical and Empirical Results". *Journal of Political Economy*, vol. 67 (June), pp. 327-351.

—— (1960) *A Program for Monetary Stability* New York. Fordham University Press

—— (1968) The Role of Monetary Policy, *American Economic Review*. vol 58 (March), pp. 1-17

Goodhart, C.A.E (1975) *Money, Information and Uncertainty* London, Macmillan

Hayek, F von (1931) *Prices and Production* London, Routledge

Kaldor, N. (1970) The New Monetarism. *Lloyd's Bank Review*. July, pp 1-18

Laidler, D. (1969) *The Demand for Money - Theories and Evidence* (1st ed.). Scranton, Intext. (4th ed. New York, Harper Collins, 1992)

—— (1974) *A Monetarist Model of Simultaneous Fluctuations in Prices and Output*. In Frisch, H. (ed) Inflation in Small Countries, Berlin, Springer

—— (1990) *Taking Money Seriously* Hemel Hempstead, Philip Allan

—— (1991) *The Golden Age of the Quantity Theory*. Hemel Hempstead, Philip Allan.

Leijonhufvud, A. (1981) *Information and Co-ordination*. London, Oxford University Press.

Marget, A. (1942) *The Theory of Prices*. Vol. II, New York, Prentice Hall.

Moore, B.J. (1988) "The Endogenous Money Supply". *Journal of Post-Keynesian Economics*, vol. 10 (Spring), pp. 372-385

Phelps, E.S. (1967) "Phillips Curves, Expectations of Inflation and Optimal Unemployment over Time". *Economica*, NS 34 (August), pp. 254-281.

Robbins, L.C (1934) *The Great Depression*. London, Macmillan

Publications, 1966–95

A Books and Monographs

1. *The Demand for Money – Theories and Evidence*, Scranton, PA, International Textbook Company, 1969; 2nd edition, New York, NY, T.Y. Crowell, 1977. 3rd edition (*The Demand for Money, Theories, Evidence and Problems*) Harper Row, New York, 1985. 4th edition, New York, Harper-Collins, 1993. (Spanish translation, 1972, French translation, 1975, Italian translation, 1976, Spanish translation of 2nd edition, 1981, Japanese translation of 3rd edition, 1989, Chinese Translation of 3rd edition, Shanghai, 1990.)
2. *Introduction to Microeconomics*, Oxford, Philip Allan Publishers, Ltd., 1974; New York, Basic Books, 1975. 2nd edition, Oxford, Philip Allan Publishers, Ltd., New York, Halstead Press, 1981, 3rd edition (with Saul Estrin) Hemel Hempstead, Philip Allan Publishers, Ltd., 1989. 4th edition, with Saul Estrin, Hemel Hempstead, Harvester Wheatsheaf, 1994. (Spanish translation of 1st edition, 1979, Polish translation of 3rd edition, 1992, Italian translation of 3rd edition, 1992, Spanish translation of 3rd edition, 1992, Bulgarian translation of 3rd edition, 1992.)
3. *Essays on Money and Inflation*, Manchester, Manchester University Press, Chicago, University Chicago Press, 1975. Republished, Aldershot, Gregg Revivals, 1993.
4. *Monetarist Perspectives*, Oxford, Philip Allan Publishers, Ltd.; Cambridge, Harvard University Press, 1982. (Japanese translation, 1987.)
5. *Taking Money Seriously*, Hemel Hempstead, Philip Allan Publishers, Ltd.; Cambridge, MIT Press, 1990.
6. *The Golden Age of the Quantity Theory – The Development of Neoclassical Monetary Economics: 1870–1914*, Hemel Hempstead, Philip Allan Publishers, Ltd.; Princeton, NJ, Princeton University Press, 1991.
7. *How Shall We Govern the Governor? A Critique of the Governance of the Bank of Canada*, Toronto, C.D. Howe Institute, 1991.
8. *Two Nations One Money? Canada's Monetary System Following a Quebec Secession*, Toronto, C.D. Howe Institute, 1991 (with W.B.P. Robson, *et al.*).
9. *The Great Canadian Disinflation: The Economics and Politics of Monetary Policy in Canada 1988–1993*, Toronto, C.D. Howe Institute, 1993 (with W.B.P. Robson).

B Books, reports, etc. edited

1. *Readings in British Monetary Economics* (with H.G. Johnson *et al.*), London, Oxford University Press, 1972.
2. *Labour Markets and Inflation* (with David Purdy), Manchester, Manchester University Press; Toronto, University of Toronto Press, 1974.
3. *Report on the Role of Primary non-Labour Incomes in the Inflationary Process*

in the United Kingdom, Brussels, EEC Commission, 1976. (Dutch translation, 1978.)

4. *Approaches to Economic Well-Being* Vol. 26 of Research Studies prepared for the Royal Commission on the Economic Union and Development Prospects for Canada (The Macdonald Commission) Toronto, University of Toronto Press, 1985.
5. *Responses to Economic Change* Vol. 27 of Research Studies prepared for the Royal Commission on the Economic Union and Development Prospects for Canada (The Macdonald Commission) Toronto, University of Toronto Press, 1986.
6. *Understanding Velocity – New Approaches and Their Policy Relevance*, Special Issue of *Journal of Policy Modeling* **12**(2) Summer, 1990.

C Articles and notes in learned journals and their supplements

1. 'Some Evidence on the Demand for Money', *Journal of Political Economy*, February 1966, 55–68.
2. 'The Rate of Interest and the Demand for Money – Some Empirical Evidence', *Journal of Political Economy*, December 1966, 543–55.
3. 'The Phillips Relation: A Theoretical Explanation', *Economica*, May 1967, 189–97 (with B.A. Corry).
4. 'The Permanent Income Concept in a Macroeconomic Model', *Oxford Economic Papers*, March 1968, 11–23.
5. 'The Phillips Relation – A Reply', *Economica*, 1968, 184 (with B.A. Corry).
6. 'The Definition of Money – Theoretical and Empirical Problems', *Journal of Money, Credit and Banking*, August 1969, 508–25.
7. 'The Case for Raising the Price of Gold – A Comment', *Journal of Money, Credit and Banking*, August 1969, 675–8.
8. 'Money, Wealth and Time Preference in a Stationary Economy', *Canadian Journal of Economics*, November 1969, 526–35.
9. 'The Demand for Money in the U.K. 1956–1967, Preliminary Estimates', *The Manchester School*, September 1970 (with J.M. Parkin), 187–208.
10. 'The Demand for Money in the U.K. 1956–1967 – A Reply', *The Manchester School*, June 1971, 125–9 (with J.M. Parkin).
11. 'On Wicksell's Theory of Price Level Fluctuations', *The Manchester School*, June 1972, 125–43.
12. 'Expectations, Adjustment and the Dynamic Response of Income to Policy Changes', *Journal of Money, Credit and Banking*, February 1973, 157–72.
13. 'Simultaneous Fluctuations in Prices and Output – A Business Cycle Approach', *Economica*, February 1973, 60–72.
14. 'Monetarist Policy Prescriptions and their Background', *The Manchester School*, March 1973, 59–71.
15. 'Price and Output Fluctuations in an Open Economy – Abstract', *Nebraska Journal of Economics*, Autumn 1973.
16. 'The Influence of Money on Real Income and Inflation – A Simple Model with Some Empirical Tests for the United States 1953–1972', *The Manchester School*, December 1973, 367–95.

17. 'Information, Money and the Macroeconomics of Inflation', *The Swedish Journal of Economics* **76**, 1974, 26–42. (German translation by Klaus Hennings, Kieler Vortrage 81, J.C.B. Mohr, Tubingen, 1975.)
18. 'The 1974 Report of the President's Council of Economic Advisors: The Control of Inflation and the Future of the International Monetary System', *American Economic Review*, September 1974, 535–43.
19. 'Inflation – A Survey', *Economic Journal*, December 1975, 741–809 (with J.M. Parkin).
20. 'Expectations and the Phillips Trade-Off: A Commentary', *Scottish Journal of Political Economy*, February 1976, 55–72.
21. 'Mayer on Monetarism – Comments from a British Point of View', *Kredit und Kapital*, No. 1, 1976, 56–68.
22. 'Comment on Myhrman', *Scandinavian Journal of Economics*, 1976.
23. 'Inflation: Alternative Explanations and Policies – Tests on Data Drawn from Six Countries', in K. Brunner and A.H. Meltzer (eds), *Institutions, Policies and Economic Performance, Carnegie-Rochester Conference Series on Public Policy*, Vol. 4, North-Holland, 1976, 251–306.
24. 'Inflation in Britain – A Monetarist Perspective', *American Economic Review*, September 1976, 485–500.
25. 'Expectations and the Behaviour of Prices and Output Under Flexible Exchange Rates', *Economica*, November 1977, 327–36.
26. 'Inflation – Alternative Explanations and Policies – A Reply to Rasche', *Journal of Monetary Economics*, November 1977, 479–81.
27. 'Money and Money Income – An Essay on the Transmission Mechanism', *Journal of Monetary Economics*, April 1978, 151–91.
28. 'I Costi dell'Inflazione Anticipata', *Rivista Internazionale Di Scienze Sociale*, April–June 1978, 215–30. (Revised version of 'The Welfare Costs of Inflation in Neo-Classical Theory – Some Unsettled Questions', translated by M.F. Ambrosanio.)
29. 'Comment on Frenkel', in K. Brunner and A.H. Meltzer (eds), *Public Policies in Open Economies*, *Carnegie-Rochester Conference Series*, Vol. 9, Amsterdam, North-Holland, 1978, 141–4 (with R.S. Boyer).
30. 'Inflation in Britain – Reply to Fane', *American Economic Review*, September 1978, 726–9.
31. 'Recent Macroeconomic Policy Proposals of the Joint Economic Committee on the U.S. Congress: A Critique', *Journal of Monetary Economics*, July 1979, 397–412.
32. 'Concerning Currency Unions', *Zeitschrift für Wirtschafts-und Sozialwissenschaften* **99** (1/2) 1979, 147–62.
33. 'An Empirical Model of an Open Economy Under Fixed Exchange Rates – The United Kingdom 1954–1970', *Economica* NS 47, May 1980, 141–58 (with P. O'Shea).
34. 'Simmel's Philosophy of Money – A Review Article for Economists', *Journal of Economic Literature*, March 1980, 97–105 (with N. Rowe).
35. 'The Demand for Money in the United States Yet Again', in K. Brunner and A.H. Meltzer (eds), *The State of Macroeconomics, Carnegie-Rochester*

Conference Series on Public Policy, Vol. 12, Amsterdam, North-Holland, 1980, 219–72.

36. 'Monetarism – An Interpretation and an Assessment', *Economic Journal* **91**, March 1981, 1–21.
37. 'Inflation and Unemployment in an Open Economy – A Monetarist View', *Canadian Public Policy* **7**, April 1981, Supplement 179–88.
38. 'Has Monetarism Failed – Introduction', *Canadian Public Policy* **7**, April 1981, Supplement, 215–17.
39. 'Adam Smith as a Monetary Economist', *Canadian Journal of Economics* **14**, May 1981, 185–201.
40. 'Some Policy Implications of the Monetary Approach to Balance of Payments and Exchange Rate Analysis', *Oxford Economic Papers*, July 1981 (Special issue on 'The Money Supply and the Exchange Rate'), 70–84.
41. 'Friedman and Schwartz on Monetary Trends – A Review Article', *Journal of International Money and Finance* **1**, 1982, 293–305.
42. 'Jevons on Money', *The Manchester School*, December 1982, 326–53.
43. 'John Hicks' *Money, Interest and Wages: Collected Essays in Economic Theory* Vol. II – A Review Essay', *Journal of Money, Credit and Banking*, August 1983, 385–9.
44. 'A Small Macro Model of the Post-War United States', *The Manchester School*, December 1983, 317–40 (with Brian Bentley).
45. 'Misconceptions About the Real Bills Doctrine – A Comment on Sargent and Wallace', *Journal of Political Economy*, February 1984, 149–55.
46. 'The Buffer Stock Notion in Monetary Economics' (The 1983 Harry Johnson Lecture), *Conference Papers*, Supplement to the Economic Journal, 1984, 17–34.
47. 'Harry Johnson as a Macroeconomist', *Journal of Political Economy*, August 1984, 592–615.
48. 'Monetary Policy in Britain – Successes and Shortcomings', *Oxford Review of Economic Policy*, Spring 1985, 35–43.
49. 'Expectations and Adjustment in the Monetary Sector Revisited, A Comment', in K. Brunner and A.H. Meltzer (eds), *Understanding Monetary Regimes, Carnegie-Rochester Conference Series on Public Policy*, Vol. 22, Amsterdam, North-Holland, 1985, 243–54.
50. 'Comment on Money Demand Predictability', *Journal of Money, Credit and Banking* **17**, November 1985, Part 2, 647–54.
51. 'Money in Crisis – A Review Essay', *Journal of Monetary Economics* **17**, 1986, 305–13.
52. 'What Do We Really Know About Monetary Policy?' (The 40th Joseph Fisher Lecture in Commerce) *Australian Economic Papers*, June 1986, 1–16.
53. 'Wicksell and Fisher on the "Backing" of Money and the Quantity Theory: A Comment on the Debate between Smith and Michener', in K. Brunner and A.H. Meltzer (eds), *Empirical Studies of Velocity, Real Exchange Rates Unemployment and Productivity, Carnegie Rochester Conference Series on Public Policy*, Vol. 27, Amsterdam, North-Holland, 1987, 325–37.

54. 'Some Macroeconomic Consequences of Price Stickiness', *The Manchester School*, March 1988, 37–54.
55. 'British Monetary Orthodoxy in the 1870s', *Oxford Economic Papers*, March 1988, 74–109.
56. 'Are Perceptions of Inflation Rational? Some Evidence from Sweden' (with L. Jonung), *American Economic Review*, December 1988, 1080–87.
57. 'Presidential Address – Taking Money Seriously', *Canadian Journal of Economics*, November 1988, 687–713.
58. 'What Remains of the Case for Flexible Exchange Rates', *Pakistan Development Review* **24**, Winter 1988 (Papers and Proceedings), 1147–59.
59. 'Comment on "Development Policy in a Multiprovincial Economy"', *Pakistan Development Review* **24**, Winter 1988 (Papers and Proceedings), 419–20.
60. 'Dow and Saville's Critique of Monetary Policy – A Review Essay', *Journal of Economic Literature* **27**, September 1989, 1147–59.
61. 'Understanding Velocity: New Approaches and Their Policy Relevance – Introduction', in D. Laidler (ed.), *Understanding Velocity* ... Special Issue of *Journal of Policy Modeling* **12** (2), Summer 1990, 141–64.
62. 'Hicks and the Classics', *Journal of Monetary Economics* **25**, June 1990, 481–9.
63. 'Money as a Metaphorical Garment before the Great War – A Comment on Patinkin and Steiger', *Scandinavian Journal of Economics* **92** (4), 1990, 613–15.
64. 'What Was New About Liquidity Preference Theory?', *Greek Economic Review* **12**, Supplement, Autumn 1990, 9–37.
65. 'Karl Brunner's Monetary Economics – an Appreciation', *Journal of Money, Credit and Banking*, November 1991, 633–58.
66. 'The Quantity Theory is Always and Everywhere Controversial – Why?', *Economic Record*, December 1991, 289–306.
67. 'Monetarism – The Unfinished Business', *Cyprus Journal of Economics* **5**, December 1992, 60–74.
68. 'Hawtrey, Harvard, and the Origins of the Chicago Tradition', *Journal of Political Economy* **101**, December 1993, 1068–103.
69. 'Conference Summary and Wrap Up', in *Bell Canada Papers on Economic Policy 2 1994 Stabilization, Growth, and Distribution: Linkages to the Knowledge Era*, 411–32.
70. 'Robertson in the 1920s', *European Journal of the History of Economic Thought* **2**, Spring 1995, 151–74.
71. 'Monetarism circa 1970: A View from 1994', *Kredit und Kapital* **28**, 1995, 323–45.

D Articles and notes in edited volumes, bank reviews, other periodicals and pamphlets

1. 'Income Tax Incentives for Owner-Occupied Housing', in A.C. Harberger and M.J. Bailey (eds), *The Taxation of Income from Capital*, Washington, DC, The Brookings Institution, 1969.

2. 'Recent Developments in Monetary Theory – A Comment', in D.R. Croome and H.G. Johnson (eds), *Money in Britain 1959–1969*, Oxford University Press, 1970.
3. 'The Influence of Money on Economic Activity: A Survey of Some Current Problems', in G. Clayton, J.S. Gilbert and R. Sedgwick (eds), *Monetary Theory and Monetary Policy in the 1970s*, Oxford University Press, 1971.
4. 'The Phillips Curve, Expectations, and Incomes Policy', in H.G. Johnson and A.R. Nobay (eds), *The Current Inflation*, Macmillan, 1971.
5. 'Monetarism, Stabilisation Policy and the Exchange Rate', *The Bankers' Magazine*, September 1971.
6. *Memorial to the Prime Minister*, with 'The Economic Radicals' (H.G. Johnson, *et al.*), 1972.
7. 'Thomas Tooke on Monetary Reform', in M. Peston and B.A. Corry (eds), *Essays in Honour of Lord Robbins*, Weidenfeld & Nicholson, London, 1972.
8. *The Basis of Monetarism*, Audio Learning, London, 1973 (with J.M. Parkin).
9. 'The Current Inflation – Explanations and Policies', *National Westminster Bank Quarterly Review*, November 1972 and in J. Robinson (ed.), *After Keynes*, Blackwell, Oxford, 1973.
10. 'Income and the Demand for Housing: Some Evidence for Great Britain', in J.M. Parkin (ed.), *Essays in Modern Economics, Proceedings of 1972 AUTE Conference*, Longmans, 1973 (with I.C.R. Byatt and A. Holmans).
11. 'The Economy Mismanaged', *The Banker*, October 1973.
12. *Dear Prime Minister*, with 'The Economic Radicals' (H.G. Johnson, *et al.*), 1974.
13. 'A Policy for the New Government', *The Banker*, March 1974.
14. 'Money, Financial Markets and Economic Activity, Introduction', and 'Discussion Paper', in H.G. Johnson and A.R. Nobay (eds), *Issues in Monetary Economics*, Oxford University Press, 1974 (with J.M. Parkin).
15. 'Inflation and Its Control: A Monetarist Analysis', in B.M. Grant and G.K. Shaw (eds), *Issues in Economic Policy*, Oxford, Philip Allan Publishers, Ltd., 1975. Second edition, 1979.
16. 'The Crisis: When and Why Did it Start', in Lord Robbins *et al.*, *Inflation, Causes and Cures*, Institute of Economic Affairs, 1975.
17. 'Unemployment and Inflation, a British Commentary', in M. Friedman, *Unemployment and Inflation*, Institute of Economic Affairs, 1975.
18. 'Discussion of "A Dynamic Analysis of the Quantity Theory"', in J.M. Parkin and A.R. Nobay (eds), *Current Problems in Economics, Proceedings of the 1974 AUTE Conference*, Cambridge, Cambridge University Press, 1975.
19. 'Inflation, Excess Demand and Expectations in Fixed Exchange Rate Open Economies', in J.M. Parkin and G. Zis (eds), *Inflation in the World Economy*, Manchester, Manchester University Press, 1976 (with R.G. Cross).
20. 'International Aspects of Inflation: A Survey', in E. Claassen and P. Salin

(eds), *Proceedings of the 1974 Dauphine Conference*, Amsterdam, North-Holland, 1976 (with A.R. Nobay).

21. 'A Monetarist Analysis of Simultaneous Fluctuations in Prices and Output', in H. Frisch (ed.), *Inflation in Small Countries*, Proceedings of the 1974 Vienna Conference, Berlin, Springer Verlag, 1976.
22. 'Money Creation and the Revenue of the Monetary Authority', in M. Artis and A.R. Nobay (eds), *Essays in Economic Analysis, Proceedings of the 1975 AUTE Conference*, Cambridge, Cambridge University Press, 1976.
23. 'Comment on Boyer', in M. Artis and A.R. Nobay (eds), *Essays in Economic Analysis, Proceedings of the 1975 AUTE Conference*, Cambridge, Cambridge University Press, 1976.
24. 'Lord Kahn on Monetarism' (letter), *Lloyds Bank Review*, April 1976.
25. 'The Debate on Monetarism' (letter), *Lloyds Bank Review*, October 1976.
26. 'Comment on Sjaastad', in J.M. Parkin and G. Zis (eds), *Inflation in the World Economy*, Manchester, Manchester University Press, 1976.
27. 'Inflation and the Market for Owner-Occupied Housing', in D. Laidler (ed.), *Report on the Role of Primary non-Labour Incomes in the Inflationary Process in the United Kingdom*, EEC Commission, Brussels, 1976. (Dutch translation 1978.)
28. 'Anti-Inflation Policy: An Alternative to Wage and Price Controls', in J.L. Carr *et al.*, *The Illusion of Wage and Price Control*, Vancouver, British Columbia, The Fraser Institute, 1976.
29. 'Unwinding the Wage and Price Controls', in M. Walker (ed.), *Which Way Ahead?*, Vancouver, British Columbia, The Fraser Institute, 1977 (with J.M. Parkin).
30. 'Comments on RBA 76', in *Conference on Applied Economic Research*, Sydney, Reserve Bank of Australia, 1977.
31. 'The Welfare Costs of Inflation in Neoclassical Theory – Some Unsettled Questions', in E. Lundberg (ed.), *Inflation Theory and Anti-Inflation Policy*, London, Macmillan, 1978.
32. 'A Monetarist Viewpoint', in M. Posner (ed.), *Demand Management*, London, Heinemann, NIESR, 1978.
33. 'How to Maintain Stability – A Monetarist View', *The Banker*, April 1978.
34. 'Difficulties with European Monetary Union', in M. Fratianni and T. Peeters (eds), *One Money for Europe*, London, Macmillan, 1978.
35. 'Abba P. Lerner', in *International Encyclopedia of the Social Sciences*, Vol. 18 (Biographical Supplement), New York, Macmillan and the Free Press, 1979.
36. 'Recent Canadian Monetary Policy – A Critique', in R. Wirick and D. Purvis (eds), *Issues in Canadian Public Policy* (II), Kingston, Queen's University (with P.W. Howitt), 1979.
37. 'The Monetary Approach to Exchange Rate Analysis – A Discussion Paper', in L. Meyer (ed.), *Stabilization Policies: Lessons from the 1970s and Implications for the 1980s*, St. Louis, Federal Reserve Bank of St. Louis, Washington University, 1980.

38. 'Comments', in B. Griffiths and G.E. Wood (eds), *Monetary Targets*, London, Macmillan, 1981.
39. 'Comments', in D. Crane (ed.), *Beyond the Monetarists*, Ottawa, Canadian Institute for Public Policy, 1981.
40. 'Entrepreneurship and Labour Mobility', in *Growth and Entrepreneurship*, Paris, I.C.C., 1981.
41. 'Tips and Monetarism', *Canadian Taxation*, Summer 1981.
42. 'Botched Monetarism', *Journal of Economic Affairs*, January 1982.
43. 'Politica Monetaria e Rientro dall'Inflazione: Alcune Considerazione', in F. Spinelli and G. Tullio (eds), *Contributi al dibattito sull politica monetario e fiscale in Italia*, Milano, Angeli, 1982 (with and translated into Italian by F. Spinelli). English version: 'The Role of Money in Controlling Inflation – an Elementary Exposition', in F. Spinelli and G. Tullio (eds), *Monetary Policy, Fiscal Policy and Economic Activity*, Gower, 1983.
44. 'The Case for Flexible Exchange Rates in 1980', in M.T. Summer and G. Zis (eds), *European Monetary Union: Progress and Prospects*, London, Macmillan, 1982.
45. 'A Small Macro Model of an Open Economy – The Case of Canada', in E. Claassen and P. Salin (eds), *Recent Issues in the Theory of Flexible Exchange Rates*, Amsterdam, North-Holland, 1982 (with B. Bentley, D. Johnson and S.T. Johnson).
46. 'Roundtable: Comments', in *Interest Rate Deregulation and Monetary Policy*, Federal Reserve Bank of San Francisco, 1983.
47. 'Did Macroeconomics Need the Rational Expectations Revolution?', in G. Mason (ed.), *Macroeconomics: Theory, Policy and Evidence*, Winnipeg, Institute for Social and Economic Research, University of Manitoba, 1983.
48. 'What Could Reasonably Have Been Expected from Monetarism: An Overview' in *Challenging Complacency*, Focus No. 6, Vancouver, BC, The Fraser Institute, 1983.
49. 'Rapporteur's Remarks', in D.W. Conklin and T.J. Courchene (eds), 'Deficits: How Big and How Bad?', *Ontario Economic Council Conference Volume*, Toronto, Ontario, 1983.
50. 'Comments on G.H. Moore's Paper', in *Price Level Measurement, Statistics Canada Conference Proceedings*, Ottawa, Ontario, November 1983.
51. 'Comment on R. Gordon's Paper', in *Monetary Targeting and Velocity, Federal Reserve Bank of San Francisco Conference Proceedings*, San Francisco, California, December 1983.
52. 'Comments' (on Beckerman), in A.C. Harberger (ed.), *World Economic Growth*, San Francisco, Institute for Contemporary Studies, 1984.
53. 'Monetary Policy in an Open Economy', *The Economic Review*, March 1985.
54. 'The Monetary Approach and the International Monetary System', in *Champions of Freedom, The Ludwig von Mises Lecture Series*, Vol. 11: *The International Economic Order*, Hillsdale, Michigan, Hillsdale College Press, 1985.
55. 'Economic Ideas and Social Issues', in D. Laidler (ed.), *Approaches to*

Economic Well-Being Vol. 26 of Research Studies for the Royal Commission on the Economic Union and Development Prospects for Canada (The Macdonald Commission) Toronto, University of Toronto Press, 1985.

56. 'International Monetary Economics in Theory and Practice', in J. Sargent (ed.), *Post-war Macroeconomic Developments* Vol. 20 of Research Studies for the Royal Commission on the Economic Union and Development Prospects for Canada (The Macdonald Commission) Toronto, University of Toronto Press, 1986.
57. 'Summary Comments on the Symposium', in J. Sargent (ed.), *Foreign Macroeconomic Experience in a Symposium* Vol. 24 of Research Studies for the Royal Commission on the Economic Union and Development Prospects for Canada (The Macdonald Commission) Toronto, University of Toronto Press, 1986 (with D.D. Purvis).
58. 'The New Classical Contribution to Macroeconomics', *Banca Nazionale del Lavoro Quarterly Review* **156**, March 1986.
59. 'International Monetary Institutions and Deficits', in J. Buchanan, C.K. Rowley and R.D. Tollison (eds), *Deficits*, Oxford, Basil Blackwell, 1986.
60. 'The Political Control of Inflation', *Economic Affairs*, February/March 1987.
61. 'Buffer Stock Money and the Transmission Mechanism', *FRB of Atlanta Review*, March/April 1987. (Revised and extended version entitled 'Notes on the Idea of Buffer-Stock Money', in S. Honkapohja and A. Suvanto (eds), *Raha, Inflaatio, ja Talouspolitiikka*, Helsinki, 1988.
62. 'The Bullionist Controversy', in J. Eatwell, M. Milgate and P. Newman (eds), *The New Palgrave*, London, Macmillan, 1987 (reprinted in *The New Palgrave Money*, and in the *New Palgrave Dictionary of Money and Finance*, 1992).
63. 'Henry Thornton', in J. Eatwell, M. Milgate and P. Newman (eds), *The New Palgrave*, London, Macmillan, 1987.
64. 'Walter Boyd', in J. Eatwell, M. Milgate and P. Newman (eds), *The New Palgrave*, London, Macmillan, 1987.
65. 'Radcliffe, the Quantity Theory and Monetarism', in D. Cobham, R. Harrington and G. Zis (eds), *Money, Trade and Payments – Essays in Honour of Dennis Coppock*, Manchester, Manchester University Press, 1989.
66. 'The Context of S.C. Tsiang's Monetary Economics', in M. Kohn (ed.), *Finance Constraints and the Theory of Money*, Boston, Academic Press, 1989.
67. 'Rapporteur's Remarks', in D. Purvis (ed.), *The Medium Term Macroeconomic Outlook*, Kingston, Ontario, John Deutsch Centre, Queen's University, 1989.
68. 'Comment on Capie and Wood', in M. Bordo (ed.), *Essays in Honour of Anna J. Schwartz*, Chicago, University of Chicago Press, 1989.
69. 'Monetary Policy', in T. Kierans (ed.), *Getting it Right (1990 Policy Review)*, Toronto, C.D. Howe Institute, 1990.
70. 'The Zero Inflation Target – an Overview of the Economic Issues', in R.G. Lipsey (ed.), *Zero Inflation*, Toronto, C.D. Howe Institute, 1990.

71. *Mainly Money: The Cause of Canadian Inflation*, Toronto, C.D. Howe Institute, 1990 (with W.B.P. Robson), p. 15.
72. 'The Legacy of The Monetarist Controversy' (The 1990 Homer Jones Lecture), *FRB of St. Louis Quarterly Review* **72** (2), March/April (1990) 49–64.
73. 'Alfred Marshall and the Development of Monetary Economics', in J. Whitaker (ed.), *Centenary Essays on Alfred Marshall*, Cambridge, Cambridge University Press, for the Royal Economic Society, 1990.
74. *The Fix is Out: A Defense of the Floating Canadian Dollar*, Toronto, C.D. Howe Institute, 1990 (with W.B.P. Robson), p. 14.
75. *Money after Meech*, Toronto, C.D. Howe Institute, 1990, p. 12.
76. 'Rapporteur's Remarks', in R.C. York (ed.), *Taking Aim, the Debate on Zero Inflation*, Toronto, C.D. Howe Institute, 1991.
77. 'Comment', in R. Boadway, T.J. Courchene and D.D. Purvis (eds), *Economic Dimensions of Constitutional Change*, Kingston, Ontario, John Deutsch Institute, 1991.
78. 'Contributions to Discussion …', in R. Simeon and M. Janigan (eds), *Toolkits and Building Blocks: Constructing a New Canada*, Toronto, C.D. Howe Institute, 1991.
79. *Money Talks – so Let's Listen*, Toronto, C.D. Howe Institute, 1991, p. 16 (with W.B.P. Robson).
80. *One Market One Money?*, Toronto, C.D. Howe Institute, 1991, p. 8, also in *Policy Implications of Trade and Currency Zones*, Federal Reserve Bank of Kansas City, 1991.
81. *A Rough Re-entry*, Toronto, C.D. Howe Institute, 1991, p. 7 (with W.B.P. Robson).
82. 'The Austrians and the Stockholm School: Two Failures in the Development of Modern Macroeconomics?', 'Comments on Myhrman', 'Comments on Hansson', 'Contribution to Round Table Discussion on the Stockholm School', all in L. Jonung (ed.), *The Stockholm School of Economics Revisited*, Cambridge, Cambridge University Press, 1991.
83. 'Qualms About Inflation Targets', in M.F.J. Prachowny and D.D. Purvis (eds), *The February 1991 Federal Budget*, Kingston, Ontario, John Deutsch Institute, 1991.
84. *Wage and Price Stickiness in Macroeconomics – An Historical Perspective* (The 13th Henry Thornton Lecture) City University Business School, 20 November 1991.
85. 'Notes on the Case for Flexible Exchange Rates', in M. Thomas Paul (ed.), *International Monetary, Banking and Trade Systems and Economic Development*, Pune, National Institute of Bank Management, 1992.
86. 'Deflation', 'Fiat Money', 'Free Banking Theory', 'Overissue of Currency', and 'Unit of Account', all in J. Eatwell, M. Milgate and P. Newman (eds), *The New Palgrave Dictionary of Money and Finance*, London, Macmillan, 1992.
87. 'The Cycle Before New-Classical Economics', in M.T. Belongia and M.R.

Garfinkel (eds), *The Business Cycle: Theories and Evidence*, Boston, Kluwer Academic Publishers, 1992.

88. 'Issues in Contemporary Macroeconomics', in A. Vercelli and N. Dimitri (eds), *Macroeconomics: A Survey of Research Strategies*, Oxford, Clarendon Press, 1993.
89. 'Was Wicksell a Quantity Theorist?', in H. Barkai, S. Fischer and N. Liviatan (eds), *Monetary Theory and Thought, Essays in Honour of Don Patinkin*, London, Macmillan, 1993.
90. 'Price Stability and the Monetary Order', in K. Shigehara (ed.), *Price Stabilization in the 1990s*, London, Macmillan, 1993.
91. *Re-entry in Progress*, Toronto, C.D. Howe Institute, 1993, p. 14 (with W.B.P. Robson).
92. 'Commentary' (on Assessing Applied Econometric Research by Carl F. Christ), in M.T. Belongia (ed.), *Dimensions of Monetary Policy, Essays in Honor of Anatol B. Balbach, FRB of St. Louis Review*, March–April 1993.
93. 'Inflation in the 1990s', *The Global Asset Manager*, Summer 1993, 38–40.
94. 'Monetarism, Microfoundations and the Theory of Monetary Policy', in S.F. Frowen (ed.), *Monetary Theory and Monetary Policy: New Tracks for the 1990s*, New York, St. Martin's Press, 1993.
95. *The One to Three Percent Solution: Canadian Monetary Policy Under the New Regime*, Toronto, C.D. Howe Institute, 1994, p. 12 (with W.B.P. Robson).
96. *The Courage to Act: Fixing Canada's Budget and Social Policy Deficits*, Toronto, C.D. Howe Institute, 1994, p. 28 (with T.E. Kierans, W.B.P. Robson, *et al.*).
97. 'Hayek on Neutral Money and the Cycle', in M. Colonna and H. Hagemann (eds), *Money and Business Cycles – The Economics of F.A. Hayek, Vol. 1*, Aldershot, Edward Elgar, 1994.
98. 'Hicks' Later Monetary Thought', in H. Hagemann and O.E. Hamouda (eds), *The Legacy of Hicks: His Contributions to Economic Analysis*, London, Routledge, 1995.
99. 'Why do Agents Hold Money – and Why Does it Matter?', in Kevin Hoover and Steven M. Sheffrin (eds), *Monetarism and the Methodology of Economics, Essays in Honour of Thomas Mayer*, Aldershot, Edward Elgar, 1995.
100. 'Endogenous Buffer-stock Money', in *Credit and Interest Rate Spreads in the Transmission Mechanism*, Bank of Canada, Ottawa, 1995 (with W.B.P. Robson).
101. *Don't Break the Bank: The Role of Monetary Policy in Deficit Reduction*, Toronto, C.D. Howe Institute, 1995 p. 20 (with W.B.P. Robson).
102. *Too Much Noise: The Debate on Foreign Exchange Rate Variability and Policies to Control It*, Toronto, C.D. Howe Institute, 1995, p. 31 (with M. Chandler).

E Evidence to parliamentary and congressional committees

1. 'A Brief Note on Fiscal Policy, Inflation and the Balance of Payments', and Transcript of Oral Evidence in *Ninth Report from the Expenditure Committee, Public Expenditure, Inflation and the Balance of Payments*, London, HMSO, 1975.
2. 'The Finance of Government Expenditure and the Control of the Money Supply', and Transcript of Oral Evidence in *First Report from the Expenditure Committee, 1975–76: The Financing of Public Expenditure*, Vol. II, London, HMSO, 1975.
3. 'Statement', in *Recent Monetary Developments and Future Economic Performance, Hearing Before the Subcommittee on Domestic Monetary Policy of the Committee on Banking, Finance and Urban Affairs, House of Representatives 95th Congress*, Washington, DC, US Government Printing Office, 1977.
4. 'A Note on Recent Proposals for European Monetary Union', House of Commons Expenditure Committee, London, HMSO, 1979.
5. 'Notes on Monetary Policy, Inflation and the Behaviour of Interest Rates', and Transcript of Oral Evidence in *Minutes of Proceedings and Evidence of the Standing Committee on Finance, Trade and Economic Affairs, First Session of the Forty-First Parliament*, 27 November 1979, House of Commons, Ottawa.
6. 'Notes on Gradualism' and Transcript of Oral Evidence in *Third Report from the Treasury and Civil Service Committee Session 1980–81 Monetary Policy*, Vol. 2, London, HMSO, 24 February 1981.
7. 'Prepared Statement' and 'The Case for Gradualism', and Transcript of Oral Evidence in *Monetarism in the United States and the United Kingdom – Hearing Before the Joint Economic Committee of the United States Ninety-Seventh Congress*, Washington, DC, US Government Printing Office, 1982.
8. Transcript of Oral Evidence in *Minutes of Proceedings ... Thursday May 11, 1989 (Respecting ... Annual Report 1988 of the Bank of Canada)*, House of Commons, Standing Committee on Finance, Second Session of the 34th Parliament, Ottawa, Supply and Services, 1989.
9. Transcript of Oral Evidence in *Minutes of Proceedings of the Sub-committee on the Bank of Canada of the Standing Committee on Finance*, 9 December 1991, Third Session of the 34th Parliament, Ottawa, Supply and Services, 1991.
10. Transcript of Oral Evidence in *Journal des debats de la Commission d'étude des questions afférentes à l'accession du Québec à la Souveraineté* No. 26, 6 February 1992. Quebec National Assembly.
11. Transcript of Oral Evidence in *Minutes of Proceedings and Evidence of the Standing Committee on Finance*, Issue #59 (19 October 1994), (*Respecting ... Study on the Budgetary Policy*) First Session of the 35th Parliament, Ottawa, Public Works and Government Services Canada, 1994.
12. Transcript of Oral Evidence in *Minutes of Proceedings and Evidence of the Standing Committee on Finance* Issue #96 (5 December 1994) (*Respecting ... Study on the Budgetary Policy*) First Session of the 35th Parliament, Ottawa, Public Works and Government Services Canada, 1994.

Index

activist stabilisation policy 133, 150–51
adaptive expectations 221–2
adjustment costs 188–90, 209–12, 223–4
  real balance effect
    individual experiment 192–3
    market experiment 197–205
aggregate demand for money function 15–34, 270–74
Alchian, A.A. 259
allocation 116–31
amenity flow 51–9
Ando, A. 134, 212, 218
announcement effects 73–4, 79
anticipated inflation 329–31
anti-inflation policy 86–7, 99–100
Archibald, G.C. 35, 192, 195
Artis, M.J. 247
Australia 335
Austrian economists *see* neo-Austrian/new Classical economics
autonomous expenditure 42–6

Bagehot, W. 313
balance of payments 316–17
  endogenous nominal money 208–9
  monetary approach 133, 147–9
    monetarist model of inflation in open economy 108–13, 114, 129–30
  UK deficit 86, 96
Bank of Canada 154, 326
Bank Charter Act 1844 314, 320
bank deposits 314–15
Bank of England 312–13, 314, 320
Banking School 312, 314, 317
banking system
  credit market 206–8, 360–62
  deposit liability 52–4
  endogenous nominal money 206–8
  free banking 340–42
Barber, A. 223
Barnett, W. 334
Barro, R.J. 145–6, 161, 217, 218, 224, 248
  US new-classical model 163, 166, 169
    Laidler's model compared with 174–7
Baumol, W.J. 20–21, 24, 135, 191, 218
Begg, D. 216
behaviour relationships 218
Bergstrom, A.R. 212, 272
Blaug, M. 307
Bodin, J. 308
bonds/securities 206–8, 246–7
Bordo, M.D. 272, 334
Boschen, J.F. 224
Boyer, R.S. 290–92
Bretton Woods system 147, 149, 281, 299
brokerage fees 271
Bronfenbrenner, M. 29
Brown, A. 139
Brumberg, A. 218
Brunner, K. 132, 134, 137, 142, 259, 327, 337, 355, 365
  business cycle 258
  demand for money 26, 27, 28–9
  open market operations 206, 246–7
Bryant, J. 219
buffer stocks 115, 122, 233–51, 272–3, 365–6
  empirical questions 244–7
  market experiment, equilibrium and disequilibrium 237–9
  microeconomic background 235–7
  price stickiness and interest rate 239–44
business cycles 90–91, 224, 256–8
  equilibrium business cycle theory 238–9
  expectations augmented Phillips curve 143–6
  quantity theory of money and transmission mechanism 318–21

Cagan, P. 137, 142, 168, 225
Cairnes, J.E. 317
Callaghan, J. 356
Cambridge k 21
Cambridge version of quantity theory 310
Canada 154, 326, 335
Cannan, E. 317, 320
capital–output ratio 54–7
capital stock 52–7
Carr, J. 272
Carter, J. 356
cash in advance constraint 255–6
cash balance mechanics 361–2
causation
  correlation and 316–18
  reverse 139, 147–8, 312–13, 317–18, 319–20, 322

central banks 342
independence and price stability 342–4
and monetarist policies 154, 155
see also Bank of England; Bank of Canada
Chicago School 22
Chick, V. 115, 194, 205, 365
Chow, G. 165, 190
clearing markets 144–5, 216–17, 229–30
see also rational expectations
closed economy 89–91
monetarist model of inflation 103–8, 113
UK inflation and 90–91
Clower, R.W. 145, 218, 255, 365
Coats, W.L. 247
Coghlan, R. 248
co-integration techniques 358
competitive-general-equilibrium-modelling 363–6
competitive provision of money 296, 297, 340–41
consumption 35–48
'contracting out' of monetary policy 298–9
contraction, economic 128
convertibility 312–13
Cooley, T. 203
Cornet, B. 303
correlation 316–18
Corry, B. 60
cost of holding money 273–4
cost push inflation 313
credit
domestic expansion 108, 111–12, 113, 114
market 206–8, 360–62
Crow, J.W. 326
Currency School 314
currency substitution 290–92, 302, 305–6
Cuthbertson, K. 272

Darby, M. 272
Davidson, P. 365
De Prano, M. 15, 134
dealers 260–62
debt, market for 206–8, 360–62
demand, excess *see* excess demand
demand management policies 86–7, 97
demand for money 186–214, 235–7
aggregate function for US 15–34
endogenous nominal money 205–9, 210–11
individual experiment and the real balance effect 190–95
instability and money growth rule 332–5
interest elasticity of *see* interest elasticity of demand for money
interest rate and 1–14, 273–4
legal restrictions and 293–4
long-run 187–90
macro-model of post-war US 165–6
market experiment with exogenous nominal money 195–205, 210
monetarism: stability 135–7, 147, 356–9
permanent-income concept 36–48
precautionary *see* precautionary demand for money
predictions about 270–74
shifts in measured function 136–7, 155
short-run *see* short-run demand for money
depression 126, 128
devaluation 93, 112–13
UK 91, 93–4
see also exchange rates
Diewert, W.E. 271
disequilibrium inflation 125–6, 127–8
disequilibrium money *see* buffer stocks
distribution 98–9, 285–6
domestic credit expansion 108, 111–12, 113, 114
Dornbusch, R. 288, 306
Dow, C. 313
Dowd, K. 271
Dutton, D.S. 271

economic contraction 128
Edgeworth, F.Y. 297, 341
Eisner, R. 218
employment level
expectations augmented Phillips curve 139–47
information and inflation 123–6
monetarist model of inflation 104–8
see also labour market; unemployment
endogenous nominal money 205–9, 210–11
equation of exchange 309
equilibrium
buffer stock approach 237–9
inflation 125, 127
equilibrium modelling 238–9, 363–6
error learning hypothesis 89, 168, 216, 222
and macro-modelling 267–70
European Common Market 95
European Monetary System 282, 299
excess demand 141–2
inflation and 85–101
exchange rates
and British inflation 91–6
changes in monetarist model of inflation 112–13, 114
fixed 91–2, 147–8, 298

flexible *see* flexible exchange rates
monetary approach 133, 147–9
overshooting 288–9
price stability and monetary order 345–8
exogenous nominal money 195–205, 210
expectations
adaptive 221–2
and British inflation 87–9
information and inflation 121–6
lags 199–201
modelling expectations mechanisms 267–70, 272–3
rational *see* rational expectations
expectations augmented Phillips curve *see* Phillips curve
expenditure
autonomous 42–6
tax-expenditure systems 98–9, 285–6

feedback rules 337–40
Feige, E.L. 200, 274
fine-tuning 151–2
fiscal deficit 208
fiscal policy 17–20, 30–31
monetarism and 150–56
small macro-model of post-war US 169, 172, 178
Fisher, I. 20, 142
quantity theory 309, 310, 311, 315, 316–17, 319–20
fixed exchange rates 91–2, 147–8, 298
flexible exchange rates
and British inflation 95–6
case for 280–306
currency substitution 290–92, 302, 305–6
legal restrictions 292–5
money as a public good 295–9, 302–3, 306
traditional arguments 283–9
monetarism 148–9
price stability and monetary order 345–6
FMP model 212–13
France 223
free banking 340–42
frictional unemployment 63–4, 97–8
Fried, J. 271
Friedman, B. 201
Friedman, M. 15, 60, 132, 199, 211, 217, 218, 235, 245, 318
demand for money 22, 27, 188, 270, 355, 357
and interest rate 1, 2–3, 4, 10, 28
expectations augmented Phillips curve 140, 141–2
flexible exchange rates 280, 287, 302
inflation expectations 221–2
monetarism 134, 149, 327, 328
natural unemployment rate 255
permanent income 26, 30, 37
policy 150, 154, 227
quantity theory 133, 135, 137, 139, 310, 311, 315, 320
full information maximum likelihood estimation 171–4, 179–80
fully anticipated inflation 330–31

Galbraith, J.W. 264
Germany 93, 154, 281, 335
gold standard 299
Goldfeld, S. 200
Goodhart, C.A.E. 234, 248, 259, 365
Gordon, H.S. 228
Gordon, R.G. 15
Gordon, R.J. 272
government intervention 284–5, 292–5, 297–8
gradualism 154
Gramm, W.P. 271
Gray, M. 248
Grossman, H.I. 218, 224
Gurley, J. 243

Hahn, F.H. 147, 219, 255
Hahn Problem 302
Hall, R. 255, 293
Hamada, K. 306
Harberger, A.C. 135, 190
Harrod, R. 135
Hawtrey, R. 319
Hayek, F. von 144, 215, 296, 340, 356
Heller, H.R. 26, 27, 28–9
Hicks, J.K. 22
Hicks, J.R. 145, 219, 254, 259, 315
high-powered money 341–2
Holland, A.S. 266
'horizontalists' 360–61
Hostland, D. 315
Howitt, P.W. 248–9, 259, 260, 331
Hume, D. 308, 309–10, 314, 316, 318–19

ideology
monetarism and 354–6
and quantity theory 322–3
income
inflation rate and 104–8
measured 17–20, 29–31, 37–8, 44, 45–6
money growth and real income growth 256–8

permanent *see* permanent income
quantity theory and 138–9, 310
time path of 47–8
income velocity 310
incomes policy 96–7
monetarism 133, 152–3
Phillips curve, expectations and 60–84
increasing returns 303
individual experiment 190–95
inflation
anticipated 329–31
explanations and policies for Britain's 85–101
information, money and macroeconomics of 115–31
monetarism and 138–9
models 102–14
and money supply growth 125–9, 138–9, 256–8
Phillips curve *see* Phillips curve
price stability and the monetary order 326–52
quantity theory 308–9, 310, 311–12, 317–18
rational expectations 'revolution' 220–22, 223
small macro-model of post-war US 168–9, 176–7, 183–4
world inflation rate 93–4, 109, 112, 114
information 217, 222, 363
money and macroeconomics of inflation 115–31
precautionary demand for money 263–6, 273
inside money 243
institutional evolution 136–7, 337–40
interest bearing money 243–4
interest elasticity of demand for money 29, 31, 137–8
empirical estimates 2–3, 6–8, 10–13
interest elasticity of velocity of circulation 18–19
interest payments on money 52–8
interest rates 46, 88
aggregate demand function for money in US 26, 28–9
and demand for money 1–14, 273–4
discrepancy between money rate and natural rate 129
monetarism 154–5
price stickiness and role of 239–44
and quantity of money 205, 311, 318–19
small macro-model of post-war US 166–8, 170, 172, 173
international monetary system
flexible exchange rates 281–2, 294–5, 299, 306
price stability and monetary order 345–8
inventory fluctuations 248–9
IS–LM model 119–20, 218, 357–8
LM curve 13, 14, 17–19
monetarism 137–9
permanent-income concept 40–42

Jarrett, P. 331
Jevons, W.S. 317, 320, 327
Johnson, H.G. 16, 26, 135, 168, 228, 233, 234–5, 242, 249, 317, 327
Jones, R.A. 259
Jonson, P.D. 161, 172, 203, 212, 234, 248, 272
Jonung, L. 272, 334
Jorgenson, D.W. 218
Judd, J. 234, 247, 273

Kahn, R. 311
Kanniainen, V. 247
Kaldor, N. 311, 355, 356
Kantor, B. 157
Karekan, J. 219, 294
Karni, E. 271
Keynes, J.M. 20, 135, 191, 218, 219, 229, 254, 311, 327
price flexibility 266
quantity theory 310, 313
speculative demand for money 21, 23–4
Keynesian economics 150, 220–21, 254, 355–6
buffer stock approach and 238, 240–41, 244–5
money in 254–9
Khan, M. Ali 303
Knight, M. 248
Knoester, A. 234, 248
Kydland, F. 256, 320

labour income 52–7
labour market 219
efficiency 97–8
Phillips curve, expectations and incomes policy 60–84
see also employment level; unemployment
lagged dependent variables 187–90, 199–203, 211, 212–13, 223–4, 245–6
Laidler, D. 136, 137, 162, 172, 188, 211, 223, 245, 247, 263, 313, 315
aggregate demand function for money in US 26, 27, 28–9
lagged dependent variables 199, 200, 201

Latané, H.A. 26, 27
Laughlin, J.L. 293, 312, 313
Lawson, N. 356
legal restrictions 292–5
legal tender laws 296–7
Leijonhufvud, A. 218, 221, 242, 258, 259, 365
leisure 51–7, 58–9
Leroy, S. 203
Lewis, M. 212, 247
Lieberman, C. 137, 172
Lindahl–Hotelling equilibria 303
Lipsey, R.G. 35, 192, 195, 219
  Phillips curve 63–4, 65, 75–7, 139, 141, 221
liquidity preference 168, 241–2
liquidity trap 2–3, 8–10, 13, 14, 29
Liverpool econometric model 226
LM–IS model *see* IS–LM model
loanable funds 168, 241–2
long-run demand for money 187–90
Lucas, R.E. jr 115, 143, 157, 161, 219, 221, 248, 255, 259, 287, 319
  neo-Austrian approach 215, 216, 217
  policy 150, 227
Lucas Critique 338
Lundberg, E. 115

Malinvaud, E. 218
'Manchester monetarism' 85
market 157
  clearing markets 144–5, 216–17, 229–30
  information and macroeconomics of inflation 118–20
  Marshallian 359–60
  money and alternative market mechanisms 259–62
  theory and rational expectations revolution 218–20
market experiment
  buffer stock approach 237–9
  exogenous nominal money 195–205
Marshall, A. 21, 215, 311
Marshallian market 359–60
Marx, K. 320
Maskin, E. 303
Mason, W. 315
Mayer, T. 29, 134, 156
McCallum, B.T. 219, 337–8
McCraken Report 313
means of exchange 122, 254, 255–6, 315
  demand for money 20–21, 271–2
measured income 17–20, 29–31, 37–8, 44, 45–6
Meiselman, D. 134
Melitz, J. 259
Meltzer, A.H. 132, 137, 228, 259, 327, 355, 365
  business cycle 258
  demand for money 26, 27, 28–9, 211
  feedback rules 337–8
  open market operations 206, 246–7
Menger, C. 295
middlemen/dealers 260–62
Milbourne, R. 272
Mill, J.S. 314
Minford, P. 132, 226
Minsky, H. 115
Mises, L. von 144
Mishan, E.J. 194
Mock, E. 15
Modigliani, F. 134, 188, 212, 218, 318
monetarism 132–60, 353–68
  balance of payments and exchange rate analysis 147–9
  case for price stability 328–32
  expectations augmented Phillips curve 139–47
  guilt by association 356
  and ideology 354–6
  interpretation and assessment 132–60
  models of inflation 102–14
    closed economy 103–8, 113
    open economy 108–14
  money and equilibrium modelling 363–6
  money in 254–9
  money supply process 359–62
  policy issues 133, 150–56
  quantity theory 133, 135–9, 308–9, 310
  stability of demand for money 135–7, 147, 356–9
monetary order 326–52
  free banking 340–42
  international dimension 345–8
  money growth rule and demand for money instability 332–5
  more sophisticated rules 337–40
monetary policy
  aggregate demand function for money in US 17–20, 30–31
  monetarism and 133, 134, 150–56, 157
  political element 335–7
  transmission mechanism *see* transmission mechanism
monetary theory of balance of payments *see* balance of payments
monetary union 347–8
money growth rules 153–6
  and demand for money instability 332–5
  more sophisticated rules 337–40

money market hypothesis 206–7
money supply
  buffer stock approach 242–4
  changes and permanent income 41–6, 47
  endogenous nominal 205–9, 210–11
  exogenous nominal 195–205, 210
  growth and inflation 125–9, 138–9, 256–8
  monetarist models of inflation 103–8
  process 359–62
  rational expectations 'revolution' 223–6
  see also quantity theory
Moore, B.J. 360
Moses, E.R. 212, 272
Mundell, R. 317

natural rate of interest 129
neo-Austrian/new Classical economics 132, 265–6, 357
  alternative market mechanisms 259–62
  buffer stock approach 238–40
  and monetarism 144–5, 147
  money in 254–9
  rational expectations 'revolution' 215–32
new microeconomics 115, 116, 120–23
new monetary economics (NME) 255–6, 292–5
New Zealand 335
Niehans, J. 259

Ohlin, B. 315
open economy 91–2
  monetarist model of inflation 108–14
open market operations 206–8, 246–7
optimal currency areas 347–8
ordinary least squares estimation 174–5, 181, 182
ordinary shares 88–9
Ostroy, J.M. 259
output
  expectations augmented Phillips curve 139–47
  information and macroeconomics of inflation 123–6
  model of inflation in an open economy 108–13
  money, wealth and time-preference 54–7
  small macro-model of post-war US 163–4, 174–6, 178, 181–2
outside money 243
overshooting, exchange rate 288–9

Parkin, J.M. 65, 200, 248, 267–8, 307, 313
  Phillips curve 75–7
partial equilibrium analysis 359–60
Patinkin, D. 135, 138–9, 190, 195, 218, 221
  real balance effect 191, 194
Pearce, D.K. 274
pensions 98–9
permanent income 4–5, 27–8, 30–31
  in a macro-economic model 35–48
Pesek, B. 49, 243
Petty, Sir W. 311
Phelps, E.S. 60, 221–2, 259, 319
  expectations augmented Phillips curve 140, 141–2, 287
Phillips, A.W. 62, 71, 139, 337
Phillips curve 166, 221, 318–19
  expectations and incomes policy 60–84
  flexible exchange rates 286–7
  monetarism 133, 139–47
    models of inflation 104–6
Phlips, L. 271
Pigou, A.C. 21, 144, 215, 310
policy
  change and permanent income 41–6, 47
  monetarism
    guilt by association 356
    policy issues 133, 150–56
  rational expectations revolution 226–9
  see also fiscal policy; monetary policy
policy ineffectiveness proposition 226–7
politics
  element in monetary policy 335–7
  political process 228
Poloz, S. 315
Popper, K. 35, 270
portfolio adjustment *see* adjustment costs
portfolio choice theory 21–2
precautionary demand for money 271–3, 365–6
  and price stickiness 262–6
preference stocks 88–9
Prescott, E. 256, 320
price setting equation 166
price stability 326–52
  case for 328–32
  central bank independence 342–4
price stickiness 202–5
  buffer stock approach 239–44
  flexible exchange rates 287–8
  precautionary demand for money 262–6
prices
  expectations augmented Phillips curve 139–47
    and incomes policy 60–84
  information, allocation and 117–20
  modelling price formation mechanisms 267–70

money and alternative market mechanisms 260–62
rational expectations 'revolution' 223–6
reverse causation 312–13
see also inflation
prices and incomes policy 96–7, 133, 152–3
see also incomes policy
private money 296, 297, 340–41
public good 295–9, 302–3, 306
public sector borrowing 152
Purvis, D.D. 248

quantity theory of money 17–19, 104, 307–25
correlation and causation 316–18
criticisms 310–13
defining money 313–16
monetarism 133, 135–9, 308–9, 310
outline of 309–10
persistence of controversy 321–3
transmission mechanism and the cycle 318–21

Radcliffe Committee 311
Rapping, L.A. 216, 259
rational expectations
Phillips curve 143, 146–7
precautionary demand for money 263–4, 272–3
'revolution' 215–32
Reagan, R. 356
'real' adjustment model of the short-run demand for money 201–3
real balance effects 165–6, 172–3, 237, 243
individual experiment and 190–55
real bills doctrine 313
Reid, M. 135
reverse causation 139, 147–8, 312–13, 317–18, 319–20, 322
Richard, S.F. 228
Robbins, L. 307, 356
Robinson, J. 313, 322
Robson, B. 161
rules of thumb 267–70
Rymes, T.K. 219, 270

Samuelson, P.A. 219
Sargent, T.J. 150, 215, 217, 226, 248 270, 287, 293, 311–12
Saville, I. 313
Saving, T.R. 49, 243
Scadding, T. 234, 247, 273
Schwartz, A.J. 134, 137, 217, 245, 320
securities/bonds 206–8, 246–7
Selody, J. 331
Shaw, E. 154, 243
Shell, K. 302
shocks 287–8
short-run demand for money 187–90, 272
buffer stock approach 244–7
exogenous nominal money 201–5
short-term interest rate 2–3, 5–6, 7, 10–14
Sidrauski, M. 49
single currency 283, 347–8
Smith, Adam 285, 312
social utility function 227, 228
Solow, R.M. 144
speculative demand for money 21–2, 23–4, 254
Spinelli, F. 172
stabilisation policy, activist 133, 150–51
stagflation 223
state, role of 284–5, 292–5, 297–8
Stiglitz, J.E. 302
stop–go cycle 148
store of value 21–2, 254–5, 295–6
Storer, P. 315
Strotz, R. 218
structure of the economy 227, 267–70
structural unemployment 97–8
substitution effect 194
Sumner, M.T. 154, 287
Switzerland 154

Tarkka, J. 247
taxation
tax-expenditure systems 98–9, 285–6
Tobin's proposal 305–6
Taylor, M.P. 272
Teigen, R. 27
Thatcher, M.H. 356
Thornton, D. 272
Thornton, H. 307, 314, 319, 320
time preference 49–59
Tobin, J. 132, 135, 168, 191, 218, 219, 248, 313, 315
demand for money 20–22
tax proposal 305–6
Tooke, T. 85, 312, 314
trade union militancy 94–5
transactions costs 264–5
transactions demand for money 20–21, 23–4
transactions velocity of circulation 309, 310
transmission mechanism 134, 205, 246
and the cycle 318–21
Trevor, R.G. 212
Triffin, R. 281
trust 298–9

Tsiang, S.C. 255
Tucker, D. 35, 196–7, 199, 213

unanticipated money 166
uncertainty 121–2
unemployment
  Britain 86, 87
    minimizing 97–8
  frictional 63–4, 97–8
  Phillips curve *see* Phillips curve
  structural 97–8
  see also employment level; labour market
unit of account 122, 330
United Kingdom (UK) 154, 223, 335
  Bank of England 312–13, 314, 320
  inflation: explanations and policies 85–101
  monetarist analysis 147–9
  monetarist policy 356
  shifts in demand for money function 136–7
United States (US) 93, 94, 95, 147, 154, 266, 335
  Bretton Woods system 281, 295
  FMP model 212–13
  monetarist policy 356
  shifts in demand for money function 136–7
  small macro-model of post-war 161–85
    comparison with Barro's model 174–7
    data 169–71
    empirical results 171–4
    model 163–9

velocity of circulation 309, 310, 311–12
  interest elasticity of 18–19
Vohra, R. 303
Volker, P. 356

wage–price spiral 60–84
wage push inflation 313
wages
  downward rigidity 17
  flexible exchange rates 287–8
  incomes policy *see* incomes policy
  information and macroeconomics of inflation 124–6
  Phillips curve *see* Phillips curve
Wallace, N. 150, 219, 226, 287, 311–12
  legal restrictions 293–4
Walrasian economics 145
  auctioneer 260
  information and prices 118–19
  money 254–5, 260
Walters, A. 202
wealth: and time preference 49–59
White, L.H. 296
White, W.H. 199, 205, 245
Wicksell, K. 272, 315, 317, 319, 341
world inflation rate 93–4, 109, 112, 114
Wymer, C.R. 212, 248, 272

Economists of the Twentieth Century

Monetarism and Macroeconomic Policy
Thomas Mayer

Studies in Fiscal Federalism
Wallace E. Oates

The World Economy in Perspective
Essays in International Trade and European Integration
Herbert Giersch

Towards a New Economics
Critical Essays on Ecology, Distribution and Other Themes
Kenneth E. Boulding

Studies in Positive and Normative Economics
Martin J. Bailey

The Collected Essays of Richard E. Quandt (2 volumes)
Richard E. Quandt

International Trade Theory and Policy
Selected Essays of W. Max Corden
W. Max Corden

Organization and Technology in Capitalist Development
William Lazonick

Studies in Human Capital
Collected Essays of Jacob Mincer, Volume 1
Jacob Mincer

Studies in Labor Supply
Collected Essays of Jacob Mincer, Volume 2
Jacob Mincer

Macroeconomics and Economic Policy
The Selected Essays of Assar Lindbeck
Volume I
Assar Lindbeck

The Welfare State
The Selected Essays of Assar Lindbeck
Volume II
Assar Lindbeck

Classical Economics, Public Expenditure and Growth
Walter Eltis

Money, Interest Rates and Inflation
Frederic S. Mishkin

The Public Choice Approach to Politics
Dennis C. Mueller

The Liberal Economic Order
Volume I Essays on International Economics
Volume II Money, Cycles and Related Themes
Gottfried Haberler
Edited by Anthony Y.C. Koo

Economic Growth and Business Cycles
Prices and the Process of Cyclical Development
Paolo Sylos Labini

International Adjustment, Money and Trade
Theory and Measurement for Economic Policy
Volume I
Herbert G. Grubel

International Capital and Service Flows
Theory and Measurement for Economic Policy
Volume II
Herbert G. Grubel

Unintended Effects of Government Policies
Theory and Measurement for Economic Policy
Volume III
Herbert G. Grubel

The Economics of Competitive Enterprise
Selected Essays of P.W.S. Andrews
Edited by Frederic S. Lee and Peter E. Earl

The Repressed Economy
Causes, Consequences, Reform
Deepak Lal

Economic Theory and Market Socialism
Selected Essays of Oskar Lange
Edited by Tadeusz Kowalik

Trade, Development and Political Economy
Selected Essays of Ronald Findlay
Ronald Findlay

General Equilibrium Theory
The Collected Essays of Takashi Negishi
Volume I
Takashi Negishi

The History of Economics
The Collected Essays of Takashi Negishi
Volume II
Takashi Negishi

Studies in Econometric Theory
The Collected Essays of Takeshi Amemiya
Takeshi Amemiya

Exchange Rates and the Monetary System
Selected Essays of Peter B. Kenen
Peter B. Kenen

Econometric Methods and Applications
(2 volumes)
G.S. Maddala

National Accounting and Economic Theory
The Collected Papers of Dan Usher, Volume I
Dan Usher

Welfare Economics and Public Finance
The Collected Papers of Dan Usher, Volume II
Dan Usher

Economic Theory and Capitalist Society
The Selected Essays of Shigeto Tsuru, Volume I
Shigeto Tsuru

Methodology, Money and the Firm
The Collected Essays of D.P. O'Brien
(2 volumes)
D.P. O'Brien

Economic Theory and Financial Policy
The Selected Essays of Jacques J. Polak
(2 volumes)
Jacques J. Polak

Sturdy Econometrics
Edward E. Leamer

The Emergence of Economic Ideas
Essays in the History of Economics
Nathan Rosenberg

Productivity Change, Public Goods and Transaction Costs
Essays at the Boundaries of Microeconomics
Yoram Barzel

Reflections on Economic Development
The Selected Essays of Michael P. Todaro
Michael P. Todaro

The Economic Development of Modern Japan
The Selected Essays of Shigeto Tsuru
Volume II
Shigeto Tsuru

Money, Credit and Policy
Allan H. Meltzer

Macroeconomics and Monetary Theory
The Selected Essays of Meghnad Desai
Volume I
Meghnad Desai

Poverty, Famine and Economic Development
The Selected Essays of Meghnad Desai
Volume II
Meghnad Desai

Explaining the Economic Performance of Nations
Essays in Time and Space
Angus Maddison

Economic Doctrine and Method
Selected Papers of R.W. Clower
Robert W. Clower

Economic Theory and Reality
Selected Essays on their Disparities and Reconciliation
Tibor Scitovsky

Doing Economic Research
Essays on the Applied Methodology of Economics
Thomas Mayer

Institutions and Development Strategies
The Selected Essays of Irma Adelman
Volume I
Irma Adelman

Dynamics and Income Distribution
The Selected Essays of Irma Adelman
Volume II
Irma Adelman

The Economics of Growth and Development
Selected Essays of A.P. Thirlwall
A.P. Thirlwall

Theoretical and Applied Econometrics
The Selected Papers of Phoebus J. Dhrymes
Phoebus J. Dhrymes

Innovation, Technology and the Economy
The Selected Essays of Edwin Mansfield
(2 volumes)
Edwin Mansfield

Economic Theory and Policy in Context
The Selected Essays of R.D. Collison Black
R.D. Collison Black

Location Economics
Theoretical Underpinnings and Applications
Melvin L. Greenhut

Spatial Microeconomics
Theoretical Underpinnings and Applications
Melvin L. Greenhut

Capitalism, Socialism and Post-Keynesianism
Selected Essays of G.C. Harcourt
G.C. Harcourt

Time Series Analysis and Macroeconometric Modelling
The Collected Papers of Kenneth F. Wallis
Kenneth F. Wallis

Foundations of Modern Econometrics
The Selected Essays of Ragnar Frisch
(2 volumes)
Edited by Olav Bjerkholt

Growth, the Environment and the Distribution of Incomes
Essays by a Sceptical Optimist
Wilfred Beckerman

The Economics of Environmental Regulation
Wallace E. Oates

Econometrics, Macroeconomics and Economic Policy
Selected Papers of Carl F. Christ
Carl F. Christ

Strategic Approaches to the International Economy
Selected Essays of Koichi Hamada
Koichi Hamada

Economic Analysis and Political Ideology
The Selected Essays of Karl Brunner
Volume One
Edited by Thomas Lys

Growth Theory and Technical Change
The Selected Essays of Ryuzo Sato
Volume One
Ryuzo Sato

Industrialization, Inequality and Economic Growth
Jeffrey G. Williamson

Economic Theory and Public Decisions
Selected Essays of Robert Dorfman
Robert Dorfman

The Logic of Action One
Method, Money, and the Austrian School
Murray N. Rothbard

The Logic of Action Two
Applications and Criticism from the Austrian School
Murray N. Rothbard

Bayesian Analysis in Econometrics and Statistics
The Zellner View and Papers
Arnold Zellner

On the Foundations of Monopolistic Competition and Economic Geography
The Selected Essays of B. Curtis Eaton and Richard G. Lipsey
B. Curtis Eaton and Richard G. Lipsey

Microeconomics, Growth and Political Economy
The Selected Essays of Richard G. Lipsey
Volume One
Richard G. Lipsey

Macroeconomic Theory and Policy
The Selected Essays of Richard G. Lipsey
Volume Two
Richard G. Lipsey

Employment, Labor Unions and Wages
The Collected Essays of Orley Ashenfelter
Volume One
Edited by Kevin F. Hallock

Education, Training and Discrimination
The Collected Essays of Orley Ashenfelter
Volume Two
Edited by Kevin F. Hallock

Economic Institutions and the Demand and Supply of Labour
The Collected Essays of Orley Ashenfelter
Volume Three
Edited by Kevin F. Hallock

Monetary Theory and Monetary Policy
The Selected Essays of Karl Brunner
Volume Two
Edited by Thomas Lys

Macroeconomic Issues from a Keynesian Perspective
Selected Essays of A.P. Thirlwall
Volume Two
A.P. Thirlwall

Money and Macroeconomics
The Selected Essays of David Laidler
David Laidler

The Economics and Politics of Money
The Selected Essays of Alan Walters
Edited by Kent Matthews

Economics Against the Grain
Volume One
Microeconomics, Industrial Organization and Related Themes
Julian L. Simon

Economics Against the Grain
Volume Two
Population Economics, Natural Resources and Related Themes
Julian L. Simon